AMERICAN CLASSICIST

AMERICAN CLASSICIST

THE LIFE AND LOVES OF
✦ EDITH HAMILTON ✦

VICTORIA HOUSEMAN

PRINCETON UNIVERSITY PRESS
PRINCETON & OXFORD

Published by Princeton University Press
41 William Street, Princeton, New Jersey 08540
99 Banbury Road, Oxford OX2 6JX

press.princeton.edu

All Rights Reserved

Library of Congress Cataloging-in-Publication Data

Names: Houseman, Victoria, 1969– author.
Title: American classicist : the life and loves of Edith Hamilton /
    Victoria Houseman.
Description: Princeton : Princeton University Press, [2023] |
    Includes bibliographical references and index.
Identifiers: LCCN 2022040783 (print) | LCCN 2022040784 (ebook) |
    ISBN 9780691236186 (hardback ; acid-free paper) | ISBN 9780691236193 (ebook)
Subjects: LCSH: Hamilton, Edith, 1867–1963. | Women classicists—
    United States—Biography. | LCGFT: Biographies.
Classification: LCC PA85.H36 H68 2023 (print) | LCC PA85.H36 (ebook) |
    DDC 880.092 [B]—dc23/eng/20220826
LC record available at https://lccn.loc.gov/2022040783
LC ebook record available at https://lccn.loc.gov/2022040784

British Library Cataloging-in-Publication Data is available

Editorial: Rob Tempio & Chloe Coy
Production Editorial: Ali Parrington
Text and Jacket Design: Heather Hansen
Production: Erin Suydam
Publicity: Alyssa Sanford & Carmen Jimenez
Copyeditor: Leah Caldwell

Jacket image: Gjon Mili / The LIFE Picture Collection / Shutterstock

This book has been composed in Arno Pro with Gaultier

Printed on acid-free paper. ∞

Printed in the United States of America

10 9 8 7 6 5 4 3 2 1

For my parents, Gerald L. Houseman & Penelope Lyon Houseman

CONTENTS

ACKNOWLEDGMENTS

Many people contributed to the research and writing of this book. These include Alice Reid Abbott, granddaughter of Edith Hamilton, who met with me to discuss her grandmother and showed me many lovely photographs. Dr. Christina Marsden Gillis for discussing her memories of Elling Aannestad and his home on Gott's Island, Maine.

I would also like to thank the late president of the Michael Cacoyannis Foundation, Yannoulla Wakefield, for corresponding with me about her brother Michael Cacoyannis's admiration for the work of Edith Hamilton. Alexandra Georgopoulou, also at the foundation, also provided assistance. I would like to thank Kelsey Mesa, director of the 2017 Riot Grrrls of the Taffety Punk Theatre Company's production of *The Trojan Women*, which used Edith Hamilton's translation, for discussing with me the relevance of Hamilton's translation for theater today.

I would like to thank the Friends of Firestone Library, Princeton University, for the 2008 research grant that allowed me to conduct research in the library's Edith Hamilton Collection and the Van Dyke Family Papers. At Princeton, I would like to thank librarians AnnaLee Pauls, George Needham, and Linda Oliveira.

I owe thanks to the staffs of many libraries, including that of the Schlesinger Library at Radcliffe Institute. The library was especially generous in allowing me to read many of the microfilmed Hamilton family letters through interlibrary loan. The archives of Bryn Mawr College were similarly generous in lending the M. Carey Thomas Papers on microfilm.

There are many other librarians and curators to whom I am indebted. These include Gloria Gavin, longtime archivist of Miss Porter's School in Farmington, Connecticut; Heather G. Cole of the Houghton Library at Harvard University for facilitating my research in the Little, Brown Papers; Christopher M. Laico of the Butler Library at Columbia University for locating Howard P. Wilson's unpublished history of W. W. Norton; Laura Reiner of the Wellesley College Archives, who provided information about Edith Hamilton's 1950 visit to Wellesley College; Carol Leadenham and Ronald M. Bulatoff at the Hoover Institution at Stanford University, who aided my use of the General Albert Coady Wedemeyer Papers and the America First Collection; Sarah Hartwell of the Rauner Special Collections Library at Dartmouth, who facilitated my research in the Elling Aannestad and Henry B. Williams Papers. I would also like to thank the staff of the Lilly Library at Indiana University in Bloomington, where I conducted research in the Gilder Manuscripts, the Logan Pearsall Smith Papers, and the Pound Manuscripts, and the staff of the Herbert Hoover Presidential Library in West Branch, Iowa, for help in accessing the Felix M. Morley Papers.

At the Bryn Mawr School, the former archivist Elizabeth Nye Di-Cataldo, herself a historian of the school, was generous with her time and support for this project. The librarian Gail Batts also answered some of my queries and Jason George helped in establishing contact with the archives of the Bryn Mawr School.

Some colleagues and former colleagues at the University of Wisconsin-River Falls were supportive of this project, especially two emeriti faculty in the department of history and philosophy, Dr. Betty A. Bergland and Dr. Kurt Leichtle, who both read early drafts of the manuscript. Others at the University of Wisconsin-River Falls who deserve my thanks are Dr. Wes Chapin, associate vice-chancellor; Rebecca Raham, lecturer in German; and the interlibrary loan staff of the Chalmer Davee Library, Ann Welniak, now retired, and Anne Tuveson, for their patient help in accessing materials.

In Indiana, I would like to thank Dr. James H. Madison, emeritus professor of history at Indiana University Bloomington, who believed in this biography of Edith Hamilton from the beginning. I would also like to thank Dr. Callie Williamson, professor of ancient history, whom I met at Indiana University. On November 10, 2005, I had the pleasure of seeing Veraestau, the Aurora, Indiana, home of both Edith Hamilton's paternal grandmother, Emerine Holman Hamilton, and of her aunt Margaret Vance Hamilton. I am grateful to Veraestau's curator, Kent Abraham, and to the Indiana Landmarks Commission, which now administers Veraestau, for the tour of the property and for allowing me to read documents pertaining to the history of the home. In Fort Wayne, I would like to thank Mr. Craig Leonard for many good exchanges about Agnes Hamilton. I also wish to thank Shane and Amanda Pickett, John and Amy Beatty, and the late Dr. John L. Modic.

In Athens, Xenia Politou of the Benaki Museum was especially helpful, showing me the beautiful handwoven silk costumes designed by Eva Palmer Sikelianos for the productions of *Prometheus Bound* at Delphi and helping to determine which of these were used in the 1957 performance of the tragedy at the theater of Herodes Atticus, at which Edith Hamilton was honored. She also showed me the correspondence of Anna Antoniades and Angeliki Hatzimihali concerning the borrowing of the costumes from the museum. I was also greatly assisted by the staff of the Benaki Museum Historical Archives at Delta House in Kifissia, where I read Edith Hamilton's letters to Eva Palmer Sikelianos.

I also owe thanks to other scholars who have written about the Hamilton family or those associated with them. I have never personally met any of them, but their work inspired me to persist in my own work. These include Dr. Helen Lefkowitz Horowitz, Dr. Barbara Sicherman, Dr. Judith P. Hallett, Dr. Artemis Leontis, and Dr. Heather Sharkey.

For help with the photographs for this book, I would like to thank Mark Bearss on Mackinac Island for permission to use his photograph of the Hamilton Cottage. I would also like to thank Alison Mills of the Bryn Mawr College Archives, Claire Hruban of the archives of the Bryn Mawr School, Briana Cregle of the Special Collections of Princeton University Library, and the staff of the Schlesinger Library at Radcliffe Institute.

Most of all, I wish to thank my editor at Princeton University Press, Rob Tempio, for the unwavering interest he took in this biography of

Edith Hamilton from the moment he learned about the manuscript's existence. I am also grateful to editor Thomas Le Bien for his skillful work on the manuscript. He curbed many of my excesses and preserved the essential story of Edith Hamilton's life and accomplishments.

I also feel indebted to the personal support I received during the many years I worked on this book. Those who gave me this much-needed support include Peggy Fraver and Bob Cavanugh. My husband, Richard Horton, had read many of Edith Hamilton's books before we ever met. His admiration for her genius meant he scoured the internet looking for, and finding, Edith correspondence in many out-of-the-way locations and patiently accompanied me to many research libraries throughout the Midwest, New England, our nation's capital, and Athens. My sister Elisabeth Houseman patiently read drafts of the chapters as well as of the book proposal and offered keen and useful critical insights. My brother Christopher Houseman and his wonderful family of Linda, Rene, and Roland offered their support and encouragement throughout. Most of all, I want to thank my parents, Dr. Gerald L. Houseman and Penelope Lyon Houseman. Of all the people in my life, they taught me the most about the pursuit of truth. I was blessed to have parents of such great intellectual gifts and such inquisitive natures.

CHRONOLOGY

1840   Birth of Edith Hamilton's mother Gertrude Pond (April).

1843   Birth of Edith Hamilton's father Montgomery Hamilton (June 7).

1866   Marriage of Montgomery Hamilton and Gertrude Pond in Dresden, Germany (August 25).

1867   Birth of Edith Hamilton at Schweizermuehle, near Dresden (August 12).

1869   Birth of Alice Hamilton in New York City (February 27).

1871   Birth of Margaret Hamilton in Fort Wayne, Indiana (June 13).

1873   Birth of Norah Hamilton in Fort Wayne, Indiana (December 3).

1877   Edith Hamilton likely began the study of Latin under her father's tutelage; the study of Greek eventually followed.

1883   Edith Hamilton began study at Miss Porter's School in Farmington, Connecticut (October).

1886   Birth of Arthur Hamilton in Fort Wayne, Indiana, always called "Quint" (March 31).

1886   Edith Hamilton completed her studies at Miss Porter's School and returned to Fort Wayne.

1888   Completion of Hamilton family cottage on Mackinac Island.

1889   Edith Hamilton attended a performance of the *Electra* of Sophocles mounted by Franklin H. Sargent's American Academy of Dramatic Arts in New York City (March 20).

1891   Edith Hamilton successfully passed the entrance exams for Bryn Mawr College and began college (February).

1893   Edith Hamilton became a leader in student government at Bryn Mawr College when she was elected executive president of the student government board (February).

1894   Edith Hamilton granted both her bachelor's and master's degrees from Bryn Mawr College (spring).

1894–95   Edith Hamilton was fellow in Latin at Bryn Mawr College.

1895   Edith Hamilton was offered the position of headmistress of the Bryn Mawr School in Baltimore; she accepted.

1895   Edith Hamilton was offered the Mary E. Garrett European Fellowship, which would permit her to study in Germany for one year (spring).

1895   Birth of Edith Hamilton's future lifetime partner Doris Fielding Reid in Baltimore (September 4).

1895   Edith and Alice Hamilton sailed for Germany to begin their year of study there (October 5).

1895   Both Edith and Alice Hamilton studied at the University of Leipzig (autumn).

1896   Edith Hamilton became the first female student admitted to the University of Munich (May).

1896   Edith and Alice Hamilton returned to the United States (August–September).

1896   Edith Hamilton settled in Baltimore to begin her career as headmistress of the Bryn Mawr School (September).

1897–99   Edith Hamilton befriended Harry Fielding Reid, professor of geology at the Johns Hopkins University, and his wife Edith Gittings Reid.

1898–99 Edith Hamilton visited the Dewey School in Chicago and met John Dewey. She becomes interested in his concept of the school as a community that helps individuals achieve self-realization.

1899 Edith Hamilton's last mention in her correspondence of achieving a doctorate (June).

1899 Norah Hamilton suffered a nervous breakdown.

1899 Margaret Hamilton settled in Baltimore and began work at the Bryn Mawr School.

1900 Edith Hamilton recommended by her Bryn Mawr College friend Susan Walker to be the new dean of Barnard College, but due to illness in her family, Edith could not interview for the position.

1903 Visited Gertrude Stein in her atelier at 27, rue de Fleurus, Paris (fall).

1903 Doris Fielding Reid enrolled in the Bryn Mawr School (fall).

1906 The National American Woman Suffrage Association held its annual convention in Baltimore, including an evening devoted to women's education (February).

1907 Gilbert Murray visited Bryn Mawr College, giving Edith Hamilton a possible chance to meet him (May).

1909 Beginning of Edith Hamilton's suffrage activism with the Baltimore Equal Suffrage League.

1909 Doris Fielding Reid left the Bryn Mawr School to study at Peabody Conservatory in Baltimore.

1909 Death of Montgomery Hamilton (June 9).

1910 Edith Hamilton established the Bryn Mawr League in Baltimore, a social work organization in which the Bryn Mawr School students and graduates could participate.

1910 Edith Hamilton, accompanied by Lucy Martin Donnelly, visited Bernard Berenson's villa I Tatti outside of Florence (July).

1912   Edith Hamilton addressed the constitutional amendments committee of the Maryland state legislature on the subject of women's suffrage (February 12).

1912   Edith Hamilton visited Paris, saw the Salon d'Automne's exhibition of cubist paintings about which she would write in 1951 (fall).

1913   Doris Fielding Reid studied music in Europe.

1913   Edith Hamilton among the estimated five thousand to eight thousand women who marched for women's suffrage on the eve of President Woodrow Wilson's inauguration (March 3).

1913   Edith Hamilton diagnosed with breast cancer. Her struggle with the disease would continue until 1920 (December).

1914   Edith Hamilton had two more operations for breast cancer although the tumor later proved to be benign (December).

1915   Death of Mary Garrett, founder of the Bryn Mawr School (April 3).

1915   Edith Hamilton and Dr. Mary Sherwood among the sponsors of a production of *The Trojan Women* of Euripides in Baltimore intended to promote the pacifist cause (May).

1915   Arthur Hamilton married Mary Neal (June 15).

1915   Edith Hamilton and Lucy Martin Donnelly arrived in Yokohama, Japan (November).

1915–16 Edith Hamilton and Lucy Martin Donnelly spend the winter in Kyoto (December–March).

1916   Edith Hamilton visited China, accompanied by Lucy Martin Donnelly with whom she saw the cities of Shanghai, Nanjing, and Beijing (March–July).

1916   Purchase of house in Hadlyme, Connecticut, as a future home for all four of the Hamilton sisters (December).

1917   Edith Hamilton published her first article, "Interesting Schools," which defended the teaching of Latin at the Bryn

Mawr School. It appeared in the February 10, 1917, issue of the *New Republic*.

1917 Birth of Dorian Fielding Reid, who would eventually be adopted by Edith Hamilton (November 17).

1917 Death of Gertrude Pond Hamilton (December 10).

1918 Edith Hamilton forced to close the Bryn Mawr School completely during the worst period of the flu pandemic in Baltimore.

1918 Reappearance of breast cancer. Edith Hamilton underwent a fourth operation for the condition (spring).

1918 Edith Hamilton spent her first summer in Maine with the Reid family.

1919 Alice Hamilton became the first woman appointed to the faculty of Harvard University (March).

1919 Arthur Hamilton appointed professor of Romance languages at the University of Illinois.

1919 Edith Hamilton first submitted her resignation to the Bryn Mawr School's board of managers although she later withdrew it (October).

1920 Edith Hamilton first moved into the Reid family home on Cathedral Street in Baltimore.

1920 Edith Hamilton had fifth and final operation for the cancerous condition she had suffered since 1913 (summer).

1920 Edith Hamilton again submitted her resignation to the Bryn Mawr School's board of managers, stating that she wanted it to take effect in two years (October).

1921 Edith Hamilton spent time in Britain with Edith Gittings Reid and Doris Fielding Reid (June–November).

1922 Edith Hamilton submitted her resignation to the Bryn Mawr School board of managers for the third and final time, asking that the board either accept it or grant her medical leave. The board chose to accept the resignation (January).

1922   End of Edith Hamilton's career as headmistress of the Bryn Mawr School (June).

1922   Beginning of construction of summer house at Seawall Point on Mount Desert Island, Maine, with the Reid family (summer).

1923   Completion of the Seawall house (summer).

1923–24   Edith Hamilton and Doris Fielding Reid, together with Dorian, spend the winter at Seawall.

1924   Edith Hamilton began work on her translation of the *Prometheus Bound* of Aeschylus (July).

1925   Edith Hamilton's portrait painted by Lydia Field Emmet at the request of the Bryn Mawr School alumnae. The portrait now hangs in the school's library (spring).

1925   Edith Hamilton began to write "Tragedy," her first essay on a classical subject, with a plan to publish it in *Theatre Arts Monthly* magazine.

1925   Edith Hamilton read the translations of the poet H. D., or Hilda Doolittle (summer).

1926   "Tragedy" published in *Theatre Arts Monthly* (January).

1926   Edith Hamilton taught about ancient Greek tragedy at the American Laboratory Theatre with the future drama critic John Mason Brown, who became a lifelong friend.

1927   Edith Hamilton and Doris Fielding Reid moved into the Gilder family's apartment building at 24 Gramercy Park (early).

1927   Edith Hamilton likely saw the actress Margaret Anglin perform the *Electra* of Sophocles at the Metropolitan Opera House (May).

1927   *Theatre Arts Monthly* published Edith Hamilton's translation of the *Prometheus Bound* of Aeschylus (July).

1927 Edith Hamilton began to translate the *Agamemnon* of Aeschylus (summer).

1928 John Mason Brown took Edith Hamilton to the offices of the publisher W. W. Norton and introduced her to him.

1928 Edith Hamilton signed her first publishing contract with W. W. Norton for her translations, which will eventually be published in 1937 as *Three Greek Plays* (April).

1928 *Theatre Arts Monthly* published Edith Hamilton's article "W. S. Gilbert: A Mid-Victorian Aristophanes," which would become the longest chapter in *The Greek Way* (October).

1929 *Theatre Arts Monthly* published her essay on Sophocles (February).

1929 Edith Hamilton and Doris Fielding Reid, together with Dorian, embarked on their first trip to Greece (February).

1929 Edith Hamilton, Doris Fielding Reid, and Dorian spent ten days in Greece (March).

1929 *Theatre Arts Monthly* published her essay on Euripides (May). Together, with a chapter on Aeschylus, the chapter on Sophocles, and her earlier article on tragedy, the core of *The Greek Way* was completed.

1929 Doris Fielding Reid entered the firm of Shaw-Loomis-Sayles and began her long career as a stockbroker (October).

1930 First performance of Edith Hamilton's translation of the *Prometheus Bound* of Aeschylus, held at the Heckscher Theater in New York City as a fundraiser for the second Delphic Festival to be mounted at Delphi that summer (January).

1930 *The Greek Way* was published (spring).

1930 Edith Hamilton began to consider writing *The Roman Way* at the request of W. W. Norton, who was pleased with the success of *The Greek Way* (November).

1931 Edith Hamilton wrote the chapters on Cicero for eventual publication in *The Roman Way*.

1932 Publication of *The Roman Way* (November).

1933 Edith Hamilton began to develop the idea of a book on the Old Testament, moved by both the rise of Hitler and his persecution of German Jews and by the spiritual crisis she felt was brought on by the Great Depression (January).

1933 Edith Hamilton read *A History of the Jews* by Dr. Abram Leon Sachar, which also helped to inspire the book that will be published in 1936 as *The Prophets of Israel* (December).

1933 Margaret Hamilton became headmistress of the Bryn Mawr School.

1934 Dorian Fielding Reid graduated from the Gunnery School and entered Amherst College.

1935 Set designer Lee Simonson asked Edith Hamilton to translate *The Trojan Women* of Euripides for a possible production by the New York Theatre Guild.

1935 Edith Hamilton began to translate *The Trojan Women* and heard the actress Dame Sybil Thorndike read some of her lines of translation at the apartment of John Mason Brown (spring).

1935 Edith Hamilton learned that the New York Theatre Guild would not produce *The Trojan Women* (July).

1935 Margaret Hamilton retired from the Bryn Mawr School and settled permanently in Hadlyme with Clara Landsberg.

1936 Publication of *The Prophets of Israel* by W. W. Norton (spring).

1936 Severe flooding along the Connecticut River damaged the Hamilton house at Hadlyme (May).

1936 Edith Hamilton and Doris Fielding Reid moved to a larger apartment at 1165 Park Avenue as it became evident that two of the Reid daughters, Elizabeth and Mary, would reside permanently with them (September).

1937 Publication of *Three Greek Plays*, including Edith Hamilton's translations of the *Prometheus Bound* and *Agamemnon* of Aeschylus and her more recent translation of *The Trojan Women* of Euripides.

1938 First performance of Edith Hamilton's translation of *The Trojan Women* of Euripides held at the Master Institute Theater in New York City (January 24).

1938 Graduation of Dorian Fielding Reid from Amherst College. Elizabeth Reid graduated from the Brearley School in New York City and entered Wellesley College in the fall.

1938 More severe flooding on the Connecticut River caused further damage to the Hamilton house at Hadlyme (September).

1938 Proposal to write *Mythology* first brought to Edith Hamilton's attention by C. Raymond Everitt, an editor at Little, Brown publishers who wanted to create a more recent version of Thomas Bulfinch's work on mythology (October).

1938 Edith Hamilton signed a contract with Little, Brown for the publication of *Mythology* with an expected completion date of January 1, 1941 (November).

1940 Mussolini attempted to invade Greece from Albania, sparking the creation of the Greek War Relief Association by the American Friends of Greece. Edith Hamilton served on the National Citizens' Committee of the Greek War Relief Association (October 28).

1940–41 Doris Fielding Reid participated in the activities of the New York chapter of the America First Committee.

1941 Edith Hamilton completed the writing of *Mythology* (summer).

1941 Edith Hamilton began writing five additional chapters for *The Greek Way*, including three on the historians Herodotus, Thucydides, and Xenophon. The other two chapters were on the poet Pindar and "The Way of Greek Religion" (summer).

1941   Doris Fielding Reid coedited the volume *We Testify* with Nancy Schoonmaker as part of her activities on behalf of America First. The anthology of isolationist thought was published by Smith and Durrell (October).

1942   *Mythology* published by Little, Brown (spring).

1942   Dorian Fielding Reid married Gertrude Elizabeth Sharley, always known as Betty, in Pittsfield, Massachusetts (June 27).

1942   *The Great Age of Greek Literature*, the extended version of *The Greek Way*, published by W. W. Norton (autumn).

1943   Edith Hamilton gave a series of lectures on Christianity at the New York City home of Alida Milliken. These became the basis for Hamilton's book *Witness to the Truth: Christ and His Interpreters*, which would be published in 1948 (February–March).

1943   Alice Hamilton published her autobiography, *Exploring the Dangerous Trades*. Its first chapter, describing the Fort Wayne childhoods of the Hamilton sisters, was praised by Edith Hamilton and formed the basis for the first chapter of Doris Fielding Reid's 1967 book, *Edith Hamilton: An Intimate Portrait* (April).

1943   Edith Hamilton and Doris Fielding Reid decided to move to Washington, D.C., where Doris had been asked to start an office of Loomis-Sayles and serve as a vice president of the company (May).

1943   Edith Hamilton and Doris Fielding Reid moved to Washington, D.C., and settled into an apartment on Connecticut Avenue (June).

1943   Edith Hamilton and Doris Fielding Reid moved into a colonial-era house on P Street in Georgetown (autumn).

1944   Death of Doris Fielding Reid's father Dr. Harry Reid (June 18).

1944   Purchase of house at 2448 Massachusetts Avenue NW as home for Edith Hamilton, Doris Fielding Reid, and Edith Gittings Reid (autumn).

1944   Staging of Edith Hamilton's translation of *The Trojan Women* of Euripides at the Hearst Greek Theatre on the campus of the University of California-Berkeley under the direction of drama department chair Fred Orrin Harris.

1945   Death of Norah Hamilton at Hadlyme (February 9). She was buried at Hadlyme Cove Cemetery.

1945   Edith Hamilton proposed the concept for the book *Witness to the Truth: Christ and His Interpreters* to W. W. Norton editor Storer B. Lunt. The idea was rejected by Warder Norton (April).

1945   Staging of Edith Hamilton's translation of *The Trojan Women* of Euripides at the Hearst Greek Theatre on the campus of the University of California-Berkeley under the direction of drama department chair Fred Orrin Harris to honor delegates arriving in San Francisco for the opening of the United Nations (May).

1945   Edith Hamilton proposed the concept for the book *Witness to the Truth: Christ and His Interpreters* to Little, Brown editor C. Raymond Everitt, who accepted it for his firm (November).

1945   Death of Warder Norton (November 7).

1945   Reorganization of the firm of W. W. Norton by his widow Mary; Storer B. Lunt became president of the firm (December).

1946   Edith Hamilton met Huntington Cairns, secretary-treasurer of the National Gallery of Art. He would expand her social circle in Washington, D.C., and become her coeditor on the work *The Collected Dialogues of Plato*, eventually published in 1961.

1946   Marriage of Elizabeth Reid to Homer Fay Pfeiffer (May 7).

1947 Death of Little, Brown editor C. Raymond Everitt; all of Edith Hamilton's writing on the New Testament acquired by the firm of W. W. Norton to be published under the title *Witness to the Truth: Christ and His Interpreters* (May–August).

1947 Staging of Edith Hamilton's translation of the *Prometheus Bound* of Aeschylus at the Hearst Greek Theatre on the campus of the University of California-Berkeley under the direction of drama department chair Fred Orrin Harris (June).

1948 W. W. Norton published *Witness to the Truth: Christ and His Interpreters* (March).

1948 George Washington University drama department performed Edith Hamilton's translation of the *Agamemnon* of Aeschylus (March).

1948 Edith Hamilton proposed a revised edition of *The Prophets of Israel* to Storer B. Lunt. The new volume would be titled *Spokesmen for God: The Great Teachers of the Old Testament* (July).

1949 Publication of *Spokesmen for God: The Great Teachers of the Old Testament* by W. W. Norton (spring).

1949 Edith Hamilton introduced to Ezra Pound, who was incarcerated at St. Elizabeth's Hospital in Washington, D.C. She began work with Pound on the translation of the *Women of Trachis* of Sophocles (May).

1949 Marriage of Mary Reid to Boyd McKnight (June 25).

1949 Edith Hamilton received her first honorary doctorate, from the University of Rochester (June 20).

1949 Edith Hamilton began to write an essay on Plutarch as an introduction to an edition of the ancient author's *Lives and Essays*, selected and translated by Louise Ropes Loomis. The book would be published by the firm of Walter J. Black in 1951.

1950   Edith Hamilton received her first recognition from academic classical scholars when she delivered the Horton Lecture sponsored by the classics department at Wellesley College (March 20).

1950   Caricature sketch of Edith Hamilton by the artist Feliks Topolski placed her among the prominent figures in Washington, D.C., society and was published in *Vogue* magazine (August 1).

1950–51   Staging of Edith Hamilton's translation of the *Agamemnon* of Aeschylus on the Dartmouth College campus by drama professor Henry B. Williams (winter).

1951   Concept of the book that will become *The Echo of Greece* proposed to Edith Hamilton by Storer B. Lunt, who had discussed the idea with Doris Fielding Reid the previous month (January).

1953   Edith Hamilton received her second honorary doctorate, from the University of Pennsylvania (June 10).

1954   Death of Doris Fielding Reid's mother Edith Gittings Reid (April 5).

1954   Arthur Hamilton, having become dean of foreign students in 1946, retired from the University of Illinois and settled in Guadalajara, Mexico.

1954   Senator Ralph E. Flanders, a Republican from Vermont, initiated and led efforts to censure Joseph McCarthy, the Republican senator from Wisconsin, in the U.S. Senate, concluding with McCarthy's condemnation by the body. The efforts likely inspired Edith Hamilton's chapter on Demosthenes submitted to Storer B. Lunt in early 1955 (June–December).

1954   Edith Hamilton interviewed by Gertrude Stein biographer Elizabeth Sprigge (December).

1955   Edith Hamilton elected to the National Institute of Arts and Letters (January).

1955 First completed chapters of what will become *The Echo of Greece* submitted to Storer B. Lunt (February).

1956 Edith Hamilton and Doris Fielding Reid departed for a trip to Italy, beginning in Sicily, where they were joined by Francesca Gilder Palmer (February). Edith and Doris visited Rome, Siena, Perugia, Arezzo, and Florence. Due to unseasonably cold weather, they dropped plans to visit Spain.

1956 Edith Hamilton and Doris Fielding Reid return to Washington, D.C. (March).

1956 Edith Hamilton wrote the final chapters of *The Echo of Greece* on the Stoics and "The Greek and Roman Way" (summer).

1957 *The Echo of Greece* was published by the firm of W. W. Norton (January).

1957 *The Echo of Greece* was positively reviewed by academic classicists, including Richmond Lattimore, C.A. Robinson Jr., and Moses Hadas (January–March).

1957 Edith Hamilton made an honorary member of the Classical Association of the Atlantic States and invited to address their meeting at Columbia University (April).

1957 Official announcement of upcoming Delphic Festival to be held in Athens that summer made jointly by the Greek Ministry of Education and ANTA (the American National Theater and Academy), which would feature, in part, a production of Edith Hamilton's translation of the *Prometheus Bound* of Aeschylus. Edith Hamilton had learned of the plans and the proposal to bring her to Athens with the theater company a few months earlier (June).

1957 Edith Hamilton and Doris Fielding Reid, together with friends such as Elling Aannestad, Alida Milliken, and Sir George Paget Thomson, sailed from New York City aboard the *Queen Frederica*, bound for Athens (July 20).

1957   Edith Hamilton awarded the Gold Cross of the Legion of Benefaction by King Paul of Greece at a luncheon. She was made an honorary citizen of Athens that same evening before the performance of her translation of the *Prometheus Bound* of Aeschylus at the Roman-era theater of Herodes Atticus at the base of the Acropolis (August 8).

1957   The Book of the Month Club introduced a boxed set of *The Greek Way* and *The Echo of Greece* as a special offer for its members after Edith Hamilton's trip to Greece. In general, the trip increased the sales of Hamilton's books.

1957   Edith Hamilton turned ninety years old (August 12).

1957   Edith Hamilton proposed a book titled *Plato: An Interpretation* to Storer B. Lunt, who encouraged the project (October).

1957   Edith Hamilton elected to the American Academy of Arts and Letters (November).

1957   Huntington Cairns asked Edith Hamilton to help select the translations for his proposed complete volume of the dialogues of Plato (November).

1957   Edith Hamilton agreed to write introductions to all of the dialogues to be included in the volume (December).

1958   Edith Hamilton gave address at Washington's Institute of Contemporary Arts, of which a recording, "Echoes of Greece," was made (January 31).

1958   Edith Hamilton and Doris Fielding Reid traveled to Spain with Rosamond Gilder and Francesca Gilder Palmer (April–June).

1958   Edith Hamilton interviewed by Huntington Cairns at Seawall for an episode of the NBC television series *Wisdom* (July).

1959   Episode of the NBC series *Wisdom*, which featured Edith Hamilton, broadcast (February).

1959 Edith Hamilton had completed all but two of the introductions that she was writing for the Plato volume (February).

1959 Edith Hamilton received third honorary doctorate, from Yale University (June 8).

1959 Gen. Albert Coady Wedemeyer published his analysis of the American experience of the Second World War in his autobiography, *Wedemeyer Reports!* The book drew on the work of both Edith Hamilton and Doris Fielding Reid. The artist C. D. Batchelor, who drew a portrait of Wedemeyer for the book's frontispiece, also drew a portrait of Edith Hamilton at this time.

1960 George Washington University's drama department performed Edith Hamilton's translation of *The Trojan Women* of Euripides. Edith Hamilton attended the opening night performance with Greek Ambassador Alexis Liatis and his wife (January).

1960 Edith Hamilton named one of five most distinguished alumnae by Bryn Mawr College (March).

1960 Edith Hamilton again addressed the Classical Association of the Atlantic States when it held its meeting at George Washington University. Her lecture on Plato was largely drawn from the introductions to the dialogues that she had just finished writing (April).

1960 Edith Hamilton and Doris Fielding Reid traveled to France with Francesca Gilder Palmer and Dorna McCollester. It was Edith's last trip abroad (June).

1960 Edith Hamilton visited the Bryn Mawr School in Baltimore in honor of its seventy-fifth anniversary. The library at the school had been named in her honor (November).

1961 The Old Vic Theatre in London performed Edith Hamilton's translation of the *Agamemnon* of Aeschylus as part of its production of the *Oresteia*.

1961   Edith Hamilton invited to the inauguration of President John F. Kennedy. Due to the cold weather, however, she did not attend (January 20).

1961   Edith Hamilton spoke on *Voice of America* (summer).

1961   Edith Hamilton suffered a stroke but largely recovered by January 1962 (autumn).

1961   *The Collected Dialogues of Plato*, coedited by Edith Hamilton and Huntington Cairns, published (October).

1961   Edith Hamilton appeared in *Harper's Bazaar* magazine, photographed by Richard Avedon (December).

1962   Edith Hamilton interviewed by *Washington Star* editor and photographer Jim Birchfield, who compared John F. Kennedy's inaugural address to the opening chapters of *The Echo of Greece* (July).

1963   Death of Edith Hamilton (May 31).

1963   Edith Hamilton buried at Hadlyme Cove Cemetery next to her mother Gertrude (June 4).

1963–65   Greek-Cypriot director Michael Cacoyannis staged Edith Hamilton's translation of *The Trojan Women* at the Circle in the Square in New York City. Ultimately, it ran for six hundred performances (December 23, 1963–May 30, 1965).

1964   Edith Hamilton's collected essays published by the firm of W. W. Norton as *The Ever-Present Past* with a prologue by Doris Fielding Reid.

1966   Doris Fielding Reid began to collect Edith Hamilton's notebooks, her correspondence with John Mason Brown, and other records for a single comprehensive Edith Hamilton archive to be housed in the Firestone Library at Princeton University.

1966   Death of Clara Landsberg, lifetime partner of Margaret Hamilton (April 10). She was buried in Hadlyme Cove Cemetery, eventually lying next to Margaret.

1967   Doris Fielding Reid's biography of Edith Hamilton published by the firm of W. W. Norton as *Edith Hamilton: An Intimate Portrait*.

1967   Death of Arthur Hamilton (May 29). His wife, Mary Neal Hamilton, had died in 1965.

1969   An anthology of Edith Hamilton's writings selected by Doris Fielding Reid published by the firm of W. W. Norton as *A Treasury of Edith Hamilton*.

1969   Death of Margaret Hamilton at Hadlyme (July 6). She was buried in Hadlyme Cove Cemetery.

1970   Death of Alice Hamilton at Hadlyme (September 22). She was buried in Hadlyme Cove Cemetery.

1971   Film version of Edith Hamilton's translation of *The Trojan Women* of Euripides, directed by the Greek Cypriot director Michael Cacoyannis, released (September).

1973   Death of Doris Fielding Reid in New York City (January 15). She was buried next to Edith Hamilton in Hadlyme Cove Cemetery.

1977   Romanian director Andrei Serban staged Edith Hamilton's translation of the *Agamemnon* of Aeschylus at the Vivian Beaumont Theater in Lincoln Center (April–May) and then as part of the New York Shakespeare Festival at the Delacorte Theater in Central Park (August 2–28).

2008   Death of Dorian Fielding Reid in West Lafayette, Indiana (January 25). His wife, Betty, had died in 1995.

AMERICAN CLASSICIST

INTRODUCTION

On the afternoon of March 20, 1889, slender, brown-haired, twenty-one-year-old Edith Hamilton, visiting New York City from her hometown of Fort Wayne, Indiana, slipped into the Lyceum Theatre on Fourth Avenue and was transported back to ancient Athens—or so she told her cousin and confidant Jessie, almost three years her senior.[1] The vehicle for this remarkable experience was a production of the *Electra* of Sophocles conforming as closely as possible to the conventions of ancient Greek theater, complete with a brief ritual honoring Dionysus at an onstage altar before the play began. The entire performance was set before the exterior of the palace of Agamemnon, with its three doors. The only exceptions to the production's efforts to faithfully reproduce an ancient Greek tragedy were that the cast did not wear masks, the fifteen-member chorus was composed of women (not men), and the actors spoke English, but in verse form. Edith was enthralled, telling Jessie, "I enjoyed it all intensely, it was so entirely new."[2] For its producer, David Belasco, it was an experiment, one that was becoming increasingly common at the turn of the century, when devotees of the theater longed to see the stage freed from commercialism to pursue an artistic path.[3] Still, this production, mounted by Franklin H. Sargent's American Academy of Dramatic Arts, was the only ancient Greek tragedy seen on the New York stage between 1882 and 1908, making it an unusual event.[4] Edith was not alone in her enthusiasm; four additional performances had had to be added to the original schedule to accommodate the demand for tickets, and it was one of these that she attended.[5]

By that March afternoon, Edith Hamilton already aspired to a career as a writer and a classical scholar, two ambitions that she would eventually merge in her books. The 1889 performance of *Electra* was one of her first experiences of the movement to improve American theater through a deeper understanding of the historical roots of drama and the contexts in which genres such as ancient Greek tragedy had originally been performed. Such efforts would help to inspire Edith's first book, *The Greek Way*, still over forty years in her future.[6] At the age of twenty-one, however, she was already certain of her fascination with the ancient Greeks. To see a performance that so faithfully attempted to recreate one of their greatest artistic achievements thrilled her by making ancient Greece come to life. Her father, Montgomery Hamilton, had been her first classics teacher, beginning her instruction in Latin when she was ten years old. To this she had added her passionate study of the ancient Greeks, which had already developed to the point that she could discern to Jessie the few ways in which Belasco and Sargent had departed from the conventions of Greek drama in the presentation of *Electra*. Still, it brought the ancient Greeks near, prompting her to tell Jessie, "I have been in Ancient Greece to-day, I have been through one of the experiences of a Greek of the time of Pericles."[7] It was a significant moment for her, one demonstrating that, despite the span of centuries, the cultural achievements of the ancient Greeks endured. Moreover, this production of *Electra* showed that neither actors nor audience had to understand ancient Greek to appreciate tragedy. For Edith Hamilton, it was appropriate that her realization of the enduring nature of the ancient Greeks' achievement occurred in a popular setting, not a scholarly one. She would become the most prominent interpreter of the relevance of ancient Greek culture for the modern world, writing for an audience who had not studied ancient Greek but who sought knowledge of the roots of Western civilization.

More than fifty years after her death, Edith Hamilton's argument for the unique achievements of the ancient Greeks continues to attract readers. *The Greek Way* was first published in 1930, but it remains in print, as do all her other books. Her volume *Mythology*, which first appeared in 1942, has become the standard rendering of the ancient tales.[8]

Her distinctive writing style, with its remarkable lucidity, must account for part of this endurance. As an author, Edith Hamilton had a unique ability to explain to her readers the essence of an important idea.

Her inspiration was the ancient Greek language itself, a reflection, she felt, of the clarity of the ancient Greek mind.[9] The study of ancient languages, she believed, helped to produce clarity in writing, a notable aspect of her own style. Hamilton's essential ideas about the ancient Greeks began with the assertion that Athens in the fifth century BCE was the only society that had achieved balance between the individual's need for spiritual and intellectual development and society's need for ordered freedom. This freedom, political and spiritual, was a Greek discovery and could be maintained only if individuals practiced self-restraint.[10] The ancient Greeks were therefore relevant to the modern world, for which they had laid the groundwork by applying reason to solve problems. Seeking answers to intellectual, political, or spiritual questions from the ancient Greeks was possible both because of their essentially modern nature and the unchanging needs of humanity.[11] To Edith, the ancient Greeks had discovered the individual and permitted each member of society free inquiry to seek spiritual and intellectual truth.[12] In later life, she connected this more closely to early Christianity. She argued that the early church had been free of confining doctrines and formalism and had allowed individuals to follow, as best they could, the spiritual path set down by Jesus, to whom Socrates had been a worthy predecessor.[13] In her writings, Edith thus linked the two fundamental influences in her life: Christianity and ancient Greece.

Certain key phrases that appeared frequently in her texts reinforced her blend of classical and Christian inspiration. These included biblical phrases such as "clouds of witnesses" to describe the spread of the prophets' teaching.[14] She referred, often without quotation marks, to lines from English poetry that evoked classical themes, such as the close of John Keats's "Ode on a Grecian Urn": "Beauty is truth, truth beauty."[15] The phrase "sunlit heights," taken from the 1881 Oscar Wilde sonnet "Helas!," also appeared often in her texts. This last phrase Edith used in her later writing to describe humanity's quest for knowledge of the good.[16] Early in her writing career, however, she used it in the sense that

Wilde had intended, to convey the heights and corresponding depths of ancient tragedy. Appropriately, it opened Edith's January 1926 essay "Tragedy," which appeared in the magazine *Theatre Arts Monthly* and was the seed of *The Greek Way*.[17]

Such an individual approach to the ancient world was necessarily selective, and contemporary critics, as well as later ones, have questioned her claims to the unique qualities of the ancient Greeks. In the opening chapters of *The Greek Way*, Edith Hamilton asserted a stark dichotomy between East and West that was criticized by contemporary critics.[18] In the twenty-first century, her work has received more criticism. Classical scholar Dr. Bruce Thornton, one of her admirers, wrote in his volume *Greek Ways*, published in 2000, that Hamilton's assertion of the ancient Greeks as the founders of Western civilization has caused her to be viewed as among the "apologists for Western hegemony and oppression."[19] Her reputation among academic classical scholars has fallen due to the forces of multiculturalism—forces that question the assertions of superior qualities in Western culture as compared to other regions of the world. Her arguments for the relevance of the ancient Greeks to the modern world have been rejected.

This stands in contrast to her experiences later in life, as she reached her nineties, when academic classicists reviewed her book *The Echo of Greece* favorably and she was twice invited to address the Classical Association of the Mid-Atlantic States (in 1957 and 1960).[20] As the post–World War II world struggled with the spread of communism, the dissolution of old European empires, and the efforts to establish democracy in former colonies and in war-torn Europe, Edith Hamilton's *The Echo of Greece* was an exposition of how the United States should exercise its new political power cautiously and how its democracy, preserved by citizens, could serve as an example to other nations. It warned against the abuse of power in which Athens had engaged after leading the Greek city-states to victory in the Persian Wars. It showed Americans what the ancient Greek political experience could teach its twentieth-century practitioners and asserted the value of the continued study of the classical world. Academic classicists expressed their appreciation of Edith Hamilton's achievement in the wake of the book's publication. Of all

Hamilton's books, *The Echo of Greece* is the one that most fully reflects the historical and political context that produced it. However, a full understanding of Hamilton's arguments is impossible without consideration of the contexts in which she wrote them. Although her books separated East and West, her writing also showed her strong opposition to communism, anti-Semitism, fascism, and imperialism. She was a pacifist and, in her support of the League of Nations, she showed herself to be a supporter of equality among nations. She was an opponent of the use of the atomic bomb. These aspects of her thought show that she was far from a simple apologist for Western hegemony. To her, the development of the atom bomb was certainly proof that not all achievements of Western societies contributed to the knowledge of the good that Plato had sought. She also realized that if Cold War America was going to stand as a model of democracy, it had to extend justice to all its citizens. In August 1958, she was one of thousands who spoke out against the death sentence issued to Jimmy Wilson, an African American in Alabama who had been convicted by an all-white jury of the theft of $1.95. The case caused an outcry, both domestically and internationally, as many argued that the United States could not be the leader of the free world if some of its citizens were the victims of racism. Ultimately, Wilson received clemency.[21] Her letter to the editor of the *New York Times* on the Wilson case also revealed a broader opposition to the death penalty in general.

The examination of Edith Hamilton's personal life also brings to light the fact that she chose to live her life with another woman. Hamilton and her partner Doris Fielding Reid were together for over forty years and raised a family, composed of Doris's nephews and nieces. At first glance, this might seem to challenge the conception of Edith Hamilton as a conservative defender of Western values. In fact, it is rare to find anyone in their social circle, including their Republican friends in Washington, D.C., where Edith spent the last twenty years of her life, commenting on their relationship. They lived in the capital during the years of what historian David K. Johnson has termed the "Lavender Scare," which, from 1947 until 1955, linked homosexuality to adherence to communism and pushed thousands of homosexuals out of government jobs, particularly at the State Department.[22] Edith and Doris, both strong anticommunists, were not directly affected. Neither worked for the federal government, and lesbians were targeted in smaller numbers than gay men in the purges.[23] Still, Edith and Doris's life together was a challenge to some of the rhetoric in the capital during these years. They were well-known in the city's social and political circles, and the Washington press regularly reported on Edith's literary achievements. Although even her friend the drama critic John Mason Brown suggested that she often ignored the Greek attitude toward homosexuality, Edith was writing about how the political experience of the ancient Greeks was relevant to the twentieth-century world, just as Washington was referred to as "the Platonic and Socratic homosexual playground" of the nation by one of the promoters of the purges, the medical doctor Arthur Guy Matthew.[24]

The legacy of the ancient Greeks was a contested space that Edith entered into during these years, with the full approval of her politically conservative friends such as the journalist Felix Morley, the Republican senator from Ohio Robert A. Taft, and the U.S. Army general Albert Coady Wedemeyer. Although her personal life might place her on the political left in the twenty-first century world, her arguments in favor of continuing the study of the ancient classical roots of Western civilization were valued among her social circle in Washington, D.C. The few comments on their relationship that did survive expressed approval. Morley wrote privately in his diary about how well suited Edith and Doris were to each other. Another Republican senator, Ralph E. Flanders of Vermont, a longtime Washington friend, wrote Doris a letter of condolence after Edith's death in 1963, a tacit acknowledgment of his understanding of what the two women had meant to each other.[25] In her private life and in her published writing, Edith Hamilton was a strong advocate of individual freedom. This position was widely accepted by her friends, who worried that the spread of communism would make the individual citizen insignificant and powerless.

All of Edith Hamilton's books addressed contemporary problems, an aspect of her writing that became more pronounced as her career progressed. *The Greek Way*, while written amid a social circle dedicated to improving the artistic quality of the New York stage, argued for the status of the ancient Greeks as the first modern people, a characterization widely held to be true by writers after the First World War, who tried to understand how the Greeks had created such a culturally advanced civilization in the wake of their own conflagration, the Persian Wars. In the aftermath of the First World War and the establishment of the League of Nations, with its vision of equality among nations, *The Roman Way*, published as a companion volume in 1932, offered the Roman Empire as an example of the successes and pitfalls of international relations more closely bound. For Edith, the rise of fascism and the Second World War were crises that could only be answered by books that tried to address spiritual concerns. Horrified by Hitler's rise to power and his subsequent treatment of Germany's Jewish population, Edith wrote *The Prophets of Israel*, published in 1936, to emphasize the Jewish contribution to Western civilization and to describe what she felt was the prophets' idealist vision for society. Even her 1942 volume *Mythology*, devoted to the recounting of the great Greek tales, had an introduction filled with references to the unique place of Greece in Western civilization, a reflection of how the Nazi conquest of the nation the previous year had stifled its resistance to fascism. She characterized the titan Prometheus, chained to a rock by Zeus, as someone who "refused to submit to cruelty and tyranny," a portrayal that has struck some as unusual but which countered the Nazi claim to him as the progenitor of the Aryans, as asserted in Hitler's *Mein Kampf*.[26] That same year, her expanded version of *The Greek Way*, published as *The Great Age of Greek Literature*, included a chapter on Thucydides that offered a means of understanding the Second World War through the Peloponnesian War and the suffering it had engendered. Her second book on the bible, *Witness to the Truth: Christ and His Interpreters*, published in 1948, outlined an essential Christianity, free from dogma and miracles, which Edith thought would answer the great crisis of faith that many felt in the wake of the horrors of the Second World War. Her revised edition of *The Prophets of Israel*, published as *Spokesmen for God: The Great Teachers of the Old Testament*, published in 1949, made it clear that one of those horrors was the Holocaust. Finally, *The Echo of Greece*, published in 1957, was a Cold War–era attempt to ask citizens to exercise the responsibility that the maintenance of democracy demanded. All of Edith Hamilton's books tried to answer important questions raised by the times in which she lived. As the historical events that inspired her books have become more distant chronologically, it has been possible to see her legacy as only her arguments for the uniqueness of the ancient Greeks and the sharp division between East and West that was too pronounced even for some of her contemporary critics.

It is the goal of this biography to place Edith Hamilton's books in their proper historical context and to examine how her life experiences informed her works. Her written works, all published after she was sixty years old, encourage this. Snippets of autobiography, which appear in all of Hamilton's books, were meant as illustrations of how individual experience related to humanity. This book also remedies the fact that, in spite of Edith Hamilton's wide and enduring reading audience, no full-length biography of her has been written. The only such effort, *Edith Hamilton: An Intimate Portrait*, written by Doris, was published in 1967 and remains notable for the number of anecdotes she collected about Edith during the years of her writing career. But Reid left out much of Edith's life. After earning both bachelor's and master's degrees at Bryn Mawr College in 1894, Edith spent a year in Germany as a graduate student in classics at the universities of Leipzig and Munich. Upon her return to the United States, she began a twenty-six-year career (1896–1922) as headmistress of the Bryn Mawr School in Baltimore, a preparatory school then closely linked to the Pennsylvania college. During her years in Baltimore, Edith was active in the women's suffrage movement, formed a friendship with Gertrude Stein, and traveled extensively abroad, to Europe, Japan, and China with Lucy Martin Donnelly, an English professor at Bryn Mawr College with whom she tried, unsuccessfully, to have a romantic relationship. These formative events and experiences received short shrift from Doris, decades Edith's junior. For example, Doris left out Edith's participation in reform movements and her friendships with women reformers of the Progressive Era. Edith, a classic liberal in her political orientation, participated mainly in the

movement for women's suffrage, but also campaigned actively for compulsory school attendance laws in Baltimore and Maryland. Her later
writings indicate that she opposed some Progressive Era movements
such as temperance.[27] Nevertheless, Edith had been introduced to the
idea that women could play a role in reforming society, first in her childhood and later during her student years at Bryn Mawr College. In Baltimore, she fell naturally into a social circle of highly educated, activist
women; some, such as Dr. Mary Sherwood, were on the Bryn Mawr
School faculty and others, such as Elizabeth King Ellicott, had been
active in founding the school and later turned to suffrage activity. Doris,
decades younger than these women, felt uncomfortable around the independent, college-educated women who confidently set about the
tasks of municipal reform, increasing educational opportunities for
women, and securing the vote. Doris set herself and Edith apart from
them, referring, even in her biography of Edith, to the new women reformers as "old war horses."[28] Later in life, Edith downplayed her role in
the women's suffrage movement, yet doing so ignores how the movement helped to develop Edith's ideas of citizenship, which she would
discuss in *The Echo of Greece*, and it led eventually to her participation
in the Women's International League for Peace and Freedom, which led
to her support of the League of Nations.[29]

Doris's characterization of Edith as completely different from the
women campaigners of the Progressive Era, however, resulted in the
complete omission of many of the women who were important to Edith
before she began her writing career. Until she left the Bryn Mawr School
in 1922, she socialized almost exclusively with women of a similar age
and level of education as herself. These included Lucy Martin Donnelly,
probably the most notable omission Doris made from Edith's life. Lucy
was not only a woman who had, like Edith, embarked on a profession, she
was also a supporter of women's suffrage, and, more importantly, she was
Edith's aesthetic and intellectual guide. Doris certainly knew Lucy but
may have come to view her as a rival for Edith's affection.

Edith was a popular writer with some claim to a scholarly background, a condition that has given rise to questions about how to assess her
work. She herself valued creativity, and one of her editors understood

that she thought of herself as a writer more than a scholar.[30] Late in life, she embraced the identity of "popularizer."[31] It is appropriate and valuable to view her as her contemporaries did. Dudley Fitts, a poet whose translations of ancient Greek tragedy Edith respected, called her translation of *Prometheus Bound* "beautiful" and included it in a 1947 anthology of ancient Greek plays rendered in English.[32] Her friend the literary historian Van Wyck Brooks described her as a scholar, as did Huntington Cairns, the secretary-treasurer of the National Gallery of Art with whom she coedited an edition of Plato's dialogues.[33] Brooks may have recognized something of himself in Hamilton, since he too lacked a doctorate and wrote for a popular audience only to become a widely recognized authority on early American writers. To Cairns, who helped establish the Center for Hellenic Studies in Washington, D.C., Edith represented an ideal: an individual with the education of an academic classicist whose writing talents enabled her to spread the influence of classical thought in American society.[34]

The role Edith valued most was as an advocate for the continuing study of classics. As the Cold War developed, her stature as a public intellectual who stood for democracy and against communism increased. The greatest recognition she received was in 1957, when she was honored by the Greek government. She traveled to Athens to witness a performance of her translation of *Prometheus Bound* of Aeschylus, given in the ancient theater of Herodes Atticus at the foot of the Acropolis. It was a scholastic honor with contemporary relevance. The Delphic festival during which this took place was a Cold War event, meant to celebrate Greece's postwar emergence as a democracy in a region where communism had taken hold. Much to her delight, Edith was made an honorary citizen of Athens and given the Gold Cross of the Legion of Benefaction by King Paul of Greece.[35] This honor placed her in an elite circle of classicists, few of whom have received official recognition from the Greek government for their contributions to greater understanding of the nation's ancient history and culture.[36]

By the end of her life, Edith Hamilton was regarded as an authority on what twentieth-century America could learn from the ancient Greeks. After her death in 1963, at the age of ninety-five, her books continued to serve as a popular source of reference for the classical past. Her books have remained popular because of her ability to make the classical world accessible through her comparisons of ancient and modern authors. The classic liberal ideas expressed in her books, including her emphasis on the importance of the individual, continue to resonate with readers as well. Her own fascination with the ancient Greeks is also evident in her books, an interest that already was apparent as she watched the groundbreaking production of the *Electra* of Sophocles in 1889 and began to consider the enduring power of ancient Greek tragedy to affect audiences and to consider the relevance of the ancient Greeks to the modern world.

Chapter 1

SAXONY AND INDIANA

Appropriately, Edith Hamilton's birthplace was always given as Dresden, Germany, a city whose cultural riches had helped inspire the growth of modern Hellenism in the eighteenth century. Dresden was generally identified throughout Hamilton's life as her place of birth.[1] More likely, and more precisely, it was the nearby hamlet of Schweizermuehle, a spa where her father, Montgomery Hamilton, had spent the month between his engagement and wedding to her mother, Gertrude Pond, in 1866, the year before Edith was born.[2] It was twenty-eight miles from Dresden, the capital of Saxony and historically the home of the royal court, where, in the mid-eighteenth century, Johann Joachim Winckelmann, founder of German classicism and of the discipline of archaeology, had made a study of the classical sculpture collection of Saxony's then-ruler, Augustus II. In 1755 Winckelmann published his treatise *Thoughts on the Imitation of Greek Art in Painting and Sculpture*, and, in 1764, his major work, *History of Ancient Art*, was printed in Dresden. These books spurred intellectual and artistic interest in ancient Greece, idealizing its culture as one that at its apex in the fifth century had experienced political liberty maintained by individual self-restraint.[3] It was a portrayal of ancient Greece that would appear in Edith's writings.[4]

In 1864, a century after Winckelmann's manifesto, Edith's parents, the American expatriates Gertrude Pond and Montgomery Hamilton, met and fell in love in Dresden. Twenty-four at the time she met her future husband, Gertrude was the oldest daughter of a New York sugar importer. Montgomery, three years her junior, had just finished studying at the University of Jena. At home, their country was divided by a bitter war in which two of Gertrude's cousins, themselves brothers, were fighting on opposite sides.[5] She and her family, Southern sympathizers despite their Northern roots, were spending the years of the conflict in the safety of Dresden. Montgomery had spent a brief time at Princeton University before joining the Union Army, but his military service had barely begun before he was invalided home to Indiana, whereupon his family sent him to Germany to study for a year.

The sectional differences between him and Gertrude were not as great as their opposing loyalties might have suggested. Montgomery had joined the Union Army for adventure, not because he opposed the secession of the Southern states.[6] For her part, Gertrude was concerned about the safety of her cousin George W. Colles, who was a Union soldier.[7] Any political divide was therefore minimal and could be cast aside, since what drew Gertrude and Montgomery to each other was a shared social background and similar interests. Both were the children of successful merchants whose business networks had expanded as their families had intermarried with other members of the mercantile elite in their respective regions.

Neither Gertrude nor Montgomery, however, had much interest in increasing their families' wealth or social position. Both were drawn instead to cultural and intellectual pursuits. Gertrude loved Dresden, a city of baroque palaces and ornate gardens, crowned by the beehive dome of the Frauenkirche, or Church of Our Lady. Before studying at Jena, Montgomery had spent a period of time at the University of Goettingen, where he had encountered critical approaches to biblical texts, stimulating a lifelong interest in theology. His family in Indiana, however, expected him to follow in the footsteps of his older brother, Holman, who, after a short period of study at Goettingen, had entered Harvard Law School.[8] In 1864 Montgomery returned to America to do the same. Unable to forget Gertrude Pond, he went back to Dresden two years later and married her. There they would reside until just shortly after Edith's birth in 1867.

The daughter of Loyal Sylvester Pond, a Wall Street broker who imported Cuban sugar, and his wife, Harriet Taylor, Gertrude was the oldest girl in a family of eleven children—eight sons and three daughters whose Dutch ancestors had helped to settle New York. This large family lived on West 14th Street in New York City but also had a house in Tarrytown, New York, which Gertrude preferred.[9] From the age of eleven, she developed a friendship with her cousin George W. Colles, four years her senior and then a student at Mount Pleasant Military Academy in Ossining, New York.[10] When, to her delight, she became acquainted with Tarrytown's most famous resident, the writer Washington Irving, she invited George to accompany her on a visit to Sunnyside, Irving's seventeenth-century Dutch stone house on the banks of the Hudson River. A permanent resident of Tarrytown from 1846, when he returned from serving as U.S. ambassador to Spain, Irving befriended his neighbors, especially the younger citizens of the town.[11] Eighteen-year-old Gertrude promised George he would enjoy the company of the great writer, who liked playing host, and that of his nieces.[12] George was just about to embark on his own grand tour of Europe so it is not clear if he accepted his cousin's invitation. Irving himself passed away in November 1859, less than a year after Gertrude's letter of invitation. His funeral was held in Christ Episcopal Church in Tarrytown, the church that the Pond family attended. But perhaps it was from Irving that Gertrude first heard about the remarkable beauty of the city of Dresden, since he had spent several months there in the early 1820s.[13]

The outbreak of the Civil War disrupted Gertrude's life. Loyal and Harriet Pond had been dismayed by the election of Abraham Lincoln to the presidency and supported the Southern cause. Such sympathies were not unusual in their area of New York. Although much of the northern part of the state was Republican and supported Lincoln in 1860, the region including Tarrytown and extending farther south was Democratic.[14] The Colleses, the family of Edith's maternal grandmother, saw one son, John Henry, enlist in the Confederacy to defend New Orleans from the Union while their other son, George, joined the 22nd New York State Militia, which was eventually assigned to the Army of the Potomac. He would take part in the Union occupation of Baltimore.[15]

Like many of New York's elite families, the Ponds escaped the war by going to Europe.[16] As the war continued, the Ponds settled in Dresden, a city that in the nineteenth century was often compared to Florence for its artistic culture, which drew many expatriates.[17]

Born in 1843, Montgomery, the second son of Allen Hamilton and Emerine Holman Hamilton, was raised in Fort Wayne, a northeastern Indiana city that his father had helped to establish and develop.[18] Allen Hamilton, a Scots-Irish Presbyterian immigrant who had come to North America in 1817, had become wealthy from a succession of frontier enterprises, beginning with land speculation in Indiana. Hamilton's holdings and fortunes increased as he acquired land at the end of the portage route of the fur trade in what would become the town of Logansport on the Wabash River—and fur trading and land speculation were only the beginnings of a long and successful series of business ventures.[19]

Montgomery's mother, Emerine Holman Hamilton, was from the more settled region of southern Indiana, having been raised on an estate called Veraestau, located high on the bluffs above the Ohio River and the town of Aurora, Indiana, which her father, Jesse Holman, had laid out on the river bank. In 1814, two years before Indiana became a state, he was both elected to the territorial legislature and appointed a circuit court judge by Governor William Henry Harrison. Upon statehood, he became a judge of the Indiana Supreme Court, where he helped to establish that Indiana would not permit slavery.[20] A devout Baptist, he helped establish Franklin College in Indiana and promoted Sunday schools as well as missionary and Bible societies.[21] The Holmans played a large role in the settlement and development of southern Indiana, much of which was accomplished by migrants from Kentucky such as themselves.

On marrying Allen Hamilton, Emerine moved from the more settled southern Indiana to the northern reaches of the new state, still largely wilderness. As a newly married woman, she moved to a home within the confines of the old fort that gave the new city its name.[22] Of the eleven children born to Allen and Emerine Hamilton, only five survived to adulthood, including their sons Andrew Holman and Montgomery.[23]

Allen and Emerine raised their children on a ten-acre homestead in Fort Wayne, where in 1841 they completed the construction of an impressive three-story brick house.[24] Italianate in style, it had large, elegantly carved gables and a cupola crowning the roof that would become a beloved conversation spot for the Hamiltons of Edith's generation.[25] An imaginative local journalist once erroneously described the house as a copy of the Hamilton family estate in Ireland. In fact, its Italianate style was adopted by other prosperous Fort Wayne families, whose acreages were always referred to as "homesteads" and whose large houses were always certain to contain a library—the Hamiltons had fourteen-foot-high bookshelves reached by a walnut ladder attached to a rail.[26] Allen and Emerine became known as gracious hosts, on one occasion in 1850 entertaining 350 guests at a party that featured a wide array of refreshments.[27] As late as 1943, one Fort Wayne resident still remembered the home as it was in the late nineteenth century, with its expansive rooms abundantly decorated with large bowls of peonies.[28] The homestead had extensive gardens, surrounded by a high iron picket fence and beds of lilacs.[29] As their sons eventually built houses on the homestead for their own families, Allen and Emerine's became known as the "Old House."

After Allen Hamilton died in 1864 while on a visit to Saratoga Springs, New York, where he had gone in hopes of recovering his health, his older son, always called by his middle name Holman, turned his attention to managing the business empire his father had established.[30] A graduate of Wabash College in southern Indiana, he had subsequently studied at the University of Goettingen and later earned a law degree from Harvard.[31] He returned to Fort Wayne to practice law and to marry, sensibly, his father's ward, Phoebe Taber. The younger son, Montgomery, was in Germany at the time of his father's death, the same year he met his wife-to-be, Gertrude Pond. He had entered Princeton University before the age of nineteen but had then joined the Union Army. He served less than a year before he was discharged due to poor health. In 1863 his family had sent him to Germany to recuperate and to study at the universities of Goettingen and Jena. Montgomery spent a few months at each one, following a practice common among German students of frequently changing universities, acquiring some knowledge at each. In the nineteenth century, however, the University of Goettingen was the center of theological study, aided by philology, the study of language, a relatively new approach to ancient texts.[32] German scholars had developed new critical approaches to the study of biblical scripture, comparing the texts with the findings of archaeologists and employing literary and historical analyses in their scholarship. Although Holman had also studied at the university, Montgomery's time there made a great impact on his life, helping him to develop what his daughter Alice called a "passion for theology."[33] After his return to the United States, he often spoke of his wish to go back to Germany to see Gertrude, but in the spring of 1865, he entered Harvard Law School. He soon found it unfulfilling, confessing to his brother, "I don't allow my studies to have such a hold upon my mind."[34] He also wrote of his wish to travel to Germany and Switzerland with friends.

Instead, he returned to Fort Wayne and founded the wholesale grocery firm of Huestis and Hamilton with Alexander C. Huestis, a former professor of mathematics and natural philosophy at Fort Wayne Female College.[35] As early as May 1868, Holman invested a little over eight thousand dollars from his father's estate in the business and it evidently required subsequent infusions of cash.[36] The business may have suffered from Montgomery's neglect due to his lingering wish to return to Germany and see Gertrude Pond. When he finally journeyed there in the summer of 1866, he professed to be more surprised than anyone when Gertrude accepted his proposal of marriage. Montgomery told Holman, "This is Monday and on Friday last, I had as much hope of becoming Kaiser as of making Miss Pond think anything good of me. I intended to leave for home on Saturday—a word or two spoken and . . . I will be married in a month."[37] He spent the weeks between his proposal and his wedding in the spa town of Schweizermuehle, near Dresden.[38]

Initially his family greeted his impending marriage with ambivalence. Emerine had been traveling in Switzerland with her daughters, Mary, Ellen, and Margaret, when they received the news of Montgomery's engagement. Mary expressed dismay that her brother had chosen to marry without a profession or obvious means of supporting a wife. The firm of Huestis and Hamilton was only a year old and still largely dependent on capital from Allen Hamilton's estate. Mary thought her brother's habits were "very extravagant" and feared that "he will take all we have."[39] Her feelings about the marriage changed, however, once she and her mother and sisters traveled to Dresden for the wedding. Mary found Montgomery "so contented, and so much improved by happiness, that I have become perfectly satisfied with the present state of affairs." She told her sister-in-law Phoebe that "Gertrude is really a splendid girl, and will be just the right wife for Mont. I hope all of you will like her as much as I do, and that is not a little."[40] Montgomery echoed Mary's sentiments. He sought to reassure his brother that he would now be prepared to take his place in the family fold, writing, "I feel much more like submitting to your authority now than I used to." But he added that his marriage "has come upon me like a sudden shock & I think & hope it has changed me."[41] The wedding was quickly arranged and took place in Dresden's Episcopal Church on August 25, 1866.[42] The newly married couple traveled immediately to New York City where, in September, Montgomery met more of Gertrude's relatives and friends. They briefly went to Fort Wayne but soon returned to Germany, leaving Holman to explain Montgomery's continued absence to his business partner A. C. Huestis.[43]

They settled in the environs of Dresden, the city usually given as Edith's birthplace, but, at the age of ninety, in a letter to German journalist Eva Noack, Edith identified her birthplace more precisely as "Schweitzerhausen," near Dresden, though no place with this name exists.[44] Her birthplace was more likely Schweizermuehle, literally "Swiss mill." At the time, the town was only just turning into a cold-water spa, the first baths having opened the same year as Montgomery's first visit in 1865. Gertrude often suffered from rheumatism, and the couple likely went to the spa seeking treatment.[45] Here Edith was born at one o'clock in the morning on August 12, 1867.[46] Her later misidentification of her birthplace—"Swiss house" instead of "Swiss mill"—is understandable, given that she was only two months old when Montgomery and Gertrude returned to the United States. By early December the couple had

FIGURE 1. Montgomery Hamilton. Photograph courtesy of the Schlesinger Library, Harvard Radcliffe Institute.

settled in Fort Wayne.[47] Edith would not see Germany again until she was a graduate student.

Montgomery and Gertrude Hamilton took up residence in the Old House on the Hamilton homestead. On February 27, 1869, a second daughter, Alice, was born at the New York City home of Gertrude's parents.[48] A third daughter, Margaret, was born on June 13, 1871, followed by the youngest, Norah, born on December 3, 1873. The two younger daughters were both born in Fort Wayne.[49] As Alice's birthplace

FIGURE 2. Gertrude Pond Hamilton. Photograph
courtesy of the Schlesinger Library, Harvard
Radcliffe Institute.

suggests, Gertrude managed the adjustment to Indiana by frequent visits to her own family in New York and by hosting Pond family visits to
Fort Wayne. As children, Edith and her sisters sometimes spent part of
their summers at the seaside in Long Branch, New Jersey, as the Ponds
gradually abandoned New York City proper and settled in New Jersey's
cities.[50] Born within six years of each other, the Hamilton sisters were
close from birth and though they moved easily in their large circle of
Pond and Colles relatives, they grew up in close proximity, both physical and emotional, to their Hamilton cousins.[51] Both Holman and

Montgomery constructed houses on the Hamilton homestead for their families. Built side by side along a lengthy drive, the houses of the two sons sat perpendicular to the Old House.

Holman's red brick house was constructed in the 1860s soon after his marriage to Phoebe Taber. It had an elegant gaslit interior and a library and dining room paneled in solid walnut. It also had an extensive garden in back surrounded by a brick wall. An enthusiastic gardener, Holman ordered dozens of seeds from nurseries as far away as Boston and New York.[52] It was a house large enough for the five children born to the couple, and it was these cousins—Katherine, Jessie, Agnes, Allen, and Taber—who were the closest companions of the four Hamilton sisters. Edith, although nearer in age to Agnes, formed a close companionship with Jessie who, born in January 1865, was two and a half years her senior.[53] With Jessie, Edith shared a love of books and a deep commitment to Christianity that would endure even as both of their theological views shifted over the course of their lives. Edith always praised Jessie for her nonjudgmental attitudes. The two cousins were destined to enjoy a long and close friendship since Jessie, like Edith, lived to the age of ninety-five. She was, Edith felt, "fundamental in my life."[54] Alice, however, viewed Edith's friendship with Jessie as a reflection of Edith's greater maturity.[55] Alice, by contrast, formed a close relationship with Agnes, who was only two months her senior, having been born in November 1868.[56] Together, with their cousin Allen Williams, the son of their aunt Mary, they were known collectively to the Hamilton family as the "Three A's."[57] Edith, because she spent her time with the older cousins, missed some of the games that the Three A's, joined by Margaret, Norah, and Allen Williams's younger brother Creighton, played in the barn on the estate, which included reenactments of the legends of Robin Hood and the Trojan War.[58]

Montgomery Hamilton constructed a white frame house known as "The Hamilton White House."[59] It was, like the Old House on the homestead, Italianate in style, though instead of the cupola of the former, it had a large bay window jutting from the second floor above a broad front porch. Completed in 1871, it reflected Montgomery's social and political ambitions in the city that, soon after the house was built,

FIGURE 3. Edith Hamilton's childhood home, the White House on the Hamilton homestead in Fort Wayne, Indiana. The house looks darker than the surrounding snow. Photograph courtesy of Princeton University Library Special Collections.

were largely fulfilled. He was first elected to the city council in 1873, and the following year, when the new Hamilton Bank was incorporated, he was among the directors.[60] In her autobiography, Alice remembered a house that was built for entertaining with a wide central hall of black walnut leading to an equally impressive staircase, while the formal parlor and dining room were reached through triple doors.[61] Edith and her sisters, however, preferred the library, a room often animated by a coal fire with an armchair beside it. Edith knew exactly where to find each book on the shelves, and she liked to recall the home's intimate spaces, the side door frequently used by the family and the ink stain on the hall carpet that defied all attempts to remove it.[62]

During Edith's youth, Emerine continued to occupy the Old House and it was still the center of much of family life. Every Christmas, she decorated the house with a large tree, occasionally one cut down on the Hamilton homestead, and served Christmas dinner.[63] She was also largely responsible for carrying on some of the Hamilton family traditions that

Edith treasured. Since the homestead had luxuriant gardens, the women in the Hamilton family celebrated each other's birthdays with gifts of fresh flowers. For her birthday in March 1881, Edith's aunt Ellen Wagenhals received from her mother, sisters, and sisters-in-law roses, violets, and azalea blossoms and from Gertrude (but delivered by Alice) a calla lily already in bloom.[64] Edith would share her grandmother's fondness for flowers and animals (Emerine was known for her refusal to ever kill an insect).[65]

Emerine's participation in social causes also influenced Edith's generation of Hamiltons. She was a woman of great self-possession, apparently unflappable in the face of opposition to the controversial causes she espoused: abolition and women's suffrage. Her granddaughter Agnes remembered that Emerine greeted everyone with the phrase "I am very glad to see you," regardless of any difference of opinion she might have with them.[66] Although Emerine had inherited her abolitionism from her father, she modified his views. Far from believing, as he had, that former slaves should return to Africa, Emerine donated land for the first African American church in Fort Wayne, a gift still remembered by a plaque in one of the city's public parks.

The Civil War had concluded two years before Edith's birth, but she must have been aware that slave ownership had existed on both sides of her family. Decades later she frequently discussed the subject of slavery in the ancient world in her books, especially in her writing on the Roman poet Horace and on the Greek historian Herodotus, as well as on the fourth-century Athenian playwright Menander. And she was always drawn to the Stoic philosophers for their opposition to slavery, particularly to Seneca for his ability to view slaves as moral equals, even suggesting that slaves could be companions to their masters.[67]

At about the age of five, Edith was placed on the lap of the suffragist Susan B. Anthony, whom Emerine hosted on her three visits to Fort Wayne.[68] Emerine was an advocate of women's right to vote, feeling, as did Anthony, that both slaves and women endured oppression, a universal suffrage position adopted by women activists before the Civil War.[69] The first of Anthony's visits, likely the occasion of Edith's introduction to her, was the one sponsored by the local suffrage organization

founded in 1871, whose inaugural session had been held in a large building known as Hamilton Hall on Fort Wayne's Calhoun Street.[70] This
suffrage organization was dissolved after only three years in existence
despite the general robustness of Indiana's women's rights movement,
which had existed since the 1850s. Emerine's activism made an impression
on Edith and her sisters and cousins, all of whom became suffragists.
Anthony would visit Fort Wayne two more times during Emerine's lifetime, in 1878 and 1887.[71] As an adult Edith would enjoy repeating the
story of her placement on Anthony's lap to others, and she frequently
pointed out that the great suffragist had spent the last years of her life
studying ancient Greek.

By age seven, Edith was already an avid reader who often shared
her favorite books with Jessie. When, in 1874, Holman Hamilton was
elected to Congress as a Democrat, he moved his family to Washington,
where they remained for the two terms he served in the House of Rep-
resentatives. During this time, Edith and Jessie exchanged letters in
which they discussed their favorite books and magazines.[72] Both read
the English children's magazine *Little Wide-Awake,* and they read Louisa
May Alcott's *Eight Cousins* as it was serialized in the magazine *St. Nicholas.*[73] Sharing favorite reading with Jessie was a habit that continued as
both grew older. Apparently permitted to choose a book for her thirteenth birthday, Edith eagerly informed Jessie that she would be receiving the bound volume of *Wide Awake* for 1877.[74] As they grew older,
however, the two cousins found that the only author on whose merits
they always agreed was Sir Walter Scott. Edith ranked his novel *Rob Roy*
above *Lorna Doone.* For her, Scott's works created a desire to see the
Scottish Highlands, a wish she ultimately fulfilled.[75]

The Hamilton sisters read English poetry and other works of British
literature. Alice particularly remembered Edith reading the work of the
Hellenizing romantic poet John Keats, recalling that Edith could recite
the poet's entire "Eve of St. Agnes" by heart. It was an apt memory, as
Edith would come to see Keats as the English writer whose spare but
precise language was most like that of an ancient Greek poet. She called
his "Ode to Autumn" "a poem more like the Greek than any other in
English."[76] Keats's closing line from "Ode on a Grecian Urn"—"Beauty

is truth, truth beauty"—appears many times in Edith's work, including in the chapter titled "The Idea of Tragedy" in *The Greek Way*. She often used the line without quotation marks, what she termed "English fashion," which dictated that very well-known lines did not need the punctuation.[77]

By the age of twelve, Edith participated in an array of Hamilton family activities, including charitable work. In March 1881 the older Hamilton women gathered at the home of Ellen Wagenhals, wife of the minister of the English Lutheran Church, for a meeting of the Dorcas Society, which made clothing for the poor. Edith, Alice, and Agnes served the refreshments.[78] They often paid short visits to their uncle Thomas Hamilton's farm near Fort Wayne, where they would sometimes spend the night. Thomas, a brother of their grandfather Allen Hamilton, would die in 1887, but in the years that Edith and her sisters and cousins were growing up, his farm was an enjoyable place to visit, one where they could slide down a ridgepole, admire the newborn farm animals, or ride on horseback or in a wagon.[79] Christmas Eve was a time of anticipation and Christmas Day an occasion to visit St. Paul's, the German Lutheran Church near the Hamilton homestead, to witness its celebrations and to see the many Christmas trees illuminating the windows of Fort Wayne's German community.[80]

Montgomery and Gertrude Hamilton did not send their daughters to school. Alice asserted that this was because Fort Wayne had only public schools and their father disliked the curriculum, which he felt placed too much emphasis on mathematics and American history, and that their mother felt the school day was too long.[81] In fact, by the 1850s, Fort Wayne had developed a variety of schools, private, parochial, and, eventually, public.[82] Montgomery and Gertrude Hamilton chose to educate their daughters at home, thus exercising control over the subjects to which they were exposed but, more importantly, ensuring their daughters developed the skills to pursue intellectual inquiry on an individual basis.[83] The Hamiltons hired tutors to teach their daughters some subjects, such as German and math, with the German instructors coming from St. Paul's Lutheran Church and its school.[84] Gertrude belonged to a German club in Fort Wayne whose meetings she sometimes hosted, and she continued to speak the language, helping her daughters to learn it as well.[85] For the most part, however, education became a process of individual development. It was up to each daughter to teach herself what she wished to learn.[86] During her years at Miss Porter's School, Edith would encounter the classical idea of education as chiefly the development of individual character, but in the method of education in the Hamilton household, she first experienced the sense of the individual pursuing her own development.[87]

Edith credited Montgomery Hamilton with introducing her to the study of Latin. In her preface to *The Roman Way*, she recalled that this began at the age of seven, soon after the family moved into the Hamilton White House.[88] If she remembered her first Latin primer correctly, however, his tutelage was more likely to have begun when she was ten. Edith always identified her first Latin textbook as *Six Weeks Preparation for Caesar*, though its actual title was slightly longer: *Six Weeks Preparation for the Reading of Caesar*, published in 1877. Its author, James Morris Whiton, an instructor at Williston Seminary in East Hampton, Massachusetts, employed a method of teaching that was designed to spare the student too much drilling in Latin grammar, instead allowing him (as the student was presumed to be) to begin reading a work of Latin literature right away, in this case, Caesar's *Gallic War*.[89] Exercises in Latin grammar accompanied each selection from Caesar's work so that the student could learn the structure of the language by reading it. Whiton was undoubtedly responding to mid-nineteenth-century criticisms of Latin instruction, which emphasized grammar taught through drill at the expense of content. He felt his method encouraged the reading of Latin texts, a benefit to a future college student who would have to read directly from a Latin text in the presence of an examiner to gain admission to college.[90] Whether Montgomery believed that the primer's approach would be appealing to Edith, or whether he was swayed by it himself, the author's method was bound to be attractive to her. Although she would never object to the self-discipline required to study Latin, she would always be impatient with methods that emphasized drill over meaning. It would have been clear to Edith, however, that the Latin primer was intended for male students even if she agreed with the essence of Whiton's note at the beginning of the volume, which read, "The sooner a boy can draw his Latin from the living spring of a classic author, the better."[91] She may have formed, even in childhood, a sense that, outside of her own family, a classical education was largely the prerogative of boys, though she was fortunate to be born just at the time when it was beginning to become available to girls.[92]

Montgomery Hamilton ignored any such proscriptions, and he apparently also began to teach his daughters Greek. Regrettably, the extant record means it is not possible to determine when her instruction in Greek began. Edith, however, always stated that it was her father who started her on its study, always placing this chronologically at some point after he began her instruction in Latin.[93] Montgomery also wanted her to learn classical history and, in later life, during an appearance on NBC, Edith confessed that she had learned more from Gibbon's *Decline and Fall of the Roman Empire* than her father had intended. Gibbon had confined sexual episodes in Roman history to footnotes, passages that he left untranslated from Latin sources to limit the number of readers who could comprehend them. Edith, with her knowledge of Latin, learned not only Roman history but also what she termed "the facts of life" from Gibbon.[94]

The Hamiltons, like many of Scotch-Irish descent, were Presbyterians, and attendance at Fort Wayne's First Presbyterian Church, which they had helped establish, was a regular part of every Sunday. Edith would remember how her father called the family together when it was time for the walk to church, where for many years they listened to the sermons of Rev. David W. Moffat, a man who, as he once explained to Edith, had been either an agnostic or an atheist when he first entered college and had only later found his faith.[95] After the service, Edith and Jessie would walk home together, talking with each other until they heard the dinner bell ringing from the Red House. In the afternoon they attended Sunday school together, filling up the remaining hours before and after supper by reading together in Jessie's room. It was a routine that hardly varied as they grew older, except that they both became Sunday school teachers rather than students.

Edith and Alice were both required to memorize the Westminster Shorter Catechism, a task they disliked. Both sisters, however, committed it to memory so firmly that its opening lines appear in both Alice's autobiography published in 1943 and in Edith's work *The Echo of Greece* published in 1957, where she referred to the catechism as "a subject for reverential study in Presbyterian households for hundreds of years."[96] As an adult, Edith would reject formalism in religion and see the Westminster Shorter Catechism as an example of why she did so, feeling that it taught the existence of a cruel God who believed humans should suffer for their sins, a belief she felt had been used to justify humanity's cruelty to others. As she memorized the catechism in her youth, however, she may merely have shared Alice's objection to the tediousness of the task, which demanded only the work of memorization without awakening any spiritual sense. As Alice remembered, "We never bothered with the meaning."[97]

More significant to Edith was Montgomery's own interest in theology, which he shared with his daughters. It was likely from him that Edith learned to read the Bible critically, to understand that, as he had learned at Goettingen, the books of the Bible had been edited over centuries, with new verses added that sometimes obscured the original text. Alice recalled that she herself had once been assigned the task of seeking evidence for the trinity in the Gospels because Montgomery believed that this doctrine had been a later addition.[98] Edith retained this critical approach to the Bible throughout her life, and it appeared in her books on the subject.

Montgomery Hamilton played an important role in awakening Edith's awareness of literary style. This would have been reinforced by her own extensive reading, but when she was about thirteen, Montgomery gave her and Alice the task of reading the eighteenth-century English periodical the *Spectator*, edited by Joseph Addison and Richard Steele. The girls were then to write down as much of it as they could remember. In Edith's case, this was quite a lot, since one of the *Spectator*'s characters, Sir Roger de Coverley, would earn a passing mention in *The Greek Way*.[99] For Edith, the exercise helped awaken her interest in becoming a writer, and she joked that her writing style had become "quite Addisonian," telling Jessie, who was away at Miss Porter's School, "I hope you keep all my letters; some day, you know, they will be all treasured up as the works of 'Miss Hamilton, the American Addison, Scott & Shakespeare'!"[100] At home, Edith received a deeply individualized, if selective, education. As Alice recalled, "We learned what our parents thought important."[101]

This home schooling only reinforced the close bond that existed between Edith and Jessie as well as among the Hamilton cousins generally throughout their childhood. Edith and Jessie rejoiced when, on occasion, they were allowed to spend the night at each other's houses. Edith, her sisters, and her cousins spent hours in the children's room of the White House, reading and inventing games. The cousins could summon each other from the White House or the Red House just by standing outside and whistling.[102] Hamilton family society was almost self-sufficient and so exclusive that Agnes expressed surprise when in early 1884 Alice and Allen suggested that it would be enjoyable to have other friends. "I don't see why," Agnes wrote in her diary, adding, "I don't. I think the boys and girls in this town are very stupid and silly and I don't care to have anything to do with them."[103] Agnes, however, did attend a public school in Fort Wayne, in contrast to her cousins.[104]

In the autumn of 1883 Edith was sixteen years old and, according to Hamilton family tradition, it was time for her to enter Miss Porter's School in Farmington, Connecticut.[105] Leaving the close-knit society of her extended family was naturally difficult even though she would see her Pond relatives more frequently, spending her vacations between terms with them. Her childhood on the Hamilton homestead, where books were always plentiful, had already made her an avid reader. Her unique education ensured that as she entered school, she was well prepared in some subjects, such as Latin, but ill prepared for others, such as mathematics. Some aspects of her childhood would remain with Edith throughout her life, especially the closeness she felt to her sisters and cousins. Others, such as the family's adherence to old-school Presbyterianism, would be discarded. With her attendance at Miss Porter's School, Edith entered an environment that would draw her out of the exclusive society of her upbringing. She would learn how to form friendships with other young women of her social class, eventually becoming a popular and respected student among her peers.

Chapter 2

TO BE A CLASSICAL
SCHOLAR

Edith entered Miss Porter's School in October 1883. Her first glimpse of it was discouraging. She and Gertrude arrived by stagecoach from the town's train station on a cold and foggy evening marked by drizzling rain. The following day, however, the school's appearance improved markedly by sunlight. Still, after Gertrude had departed, she was too self-conscious to accept another student's offer to help her unpack, and when the supper bell rang she confessed to Jessie that it took all of her courage to enter a dining room full of girls whom she did not know.[1] During her three years at Miss Porter's School, Edith would emerge from her social shell and form lasting friendships with some of her fellow students. She would develop her ambitions to become a writer, and she would encounter her first classics teachers, including the classical scholar Nathan Perkins Seymour, the former chair of the classics department at Western Reserve College in Ohio. The classics instruction at the school was intended to help students cultivate their tastes by exposing them to the ancient cultures of Greece and Rome. Edith's education there would have a much greater impact, encouraging her to pursue her interest in the ancient languages long after she had departed from the school.

Attendance at Miss Porter's was a tradition in other families besides the Hamiltons, and its student body was partly made up of sisters, cousins, and daughters of previous students—"old girls," as they were customarily called. Edith's experience of following aunts and cousins to the school was not an unusual one, and on the night of her arrival Gertrude had been instantly mistaken for Aunt Phoebe leaving another daughter at the school. Edith's physical resemblance to her cousins was quickly noticed by the other students. Indeed, Edith's first friendships were with Katherine and Jessie's friends who remained at the school, including Susan and Lily Duryee. While initially the connection was through Edith's cousins, the sisters became genuine friends to Edith. After they left Farmington, she corresponded with them and visited them in New Jersey, a practice she would continue long after her departure from Miss Porter's School.[2] Eventually, Edith and Susan would live together for three years in Baltimore.

Gradually, Edith settled into the routines of the school. The day was defined by "divisions," class periods when students received instruction in different subjects. The day began with breakfast, followed by prayers, with a study hour filling part of each afternoon. Edith took French and German as well as singing and drawing.[3] The school provided only limited academic challenges for her, depending on the subject. Geometry proved difficult: "I don't think a more horrible study could be invented," she commented. More surprisingly, she revealed to Jessie that she did not enjoy the study of French, perhaps due to the manner in which it was taught: "I would not mind if the lessons were things to be learned, but yesterday I had to write a letter, and for Monday I have to tell a story (I haven't the slightest idea what it will be) and that is what I think is so difficult."[4] English literature, however, was easy, though she later remembered disliking having to memorize poems with martial themes such as "The Charge of the Light Brigade."[5] Latin, after years of Montgomery Hamilton's tutelage, was taught on such an elementary level that Edith felt that even Margaret, four years her junior, would not have encountered any difficulty.[6] Edith never studied Greek at Miss Porter's, perhaps because there was no qualified instructor in the subject during the years she was there.

Although she included academic subjects in her curriculum, Miss Porter still gave her institution some of the character of a finishing school.[7] The girls met in afternoon tea sets, the membership of which

Miss Porter required be regularly changed, a rule that initially filled Edith with dread but that would help her make friends with her fellow students. Students were expected to dress for dinner but were also permitted to practice ballroom dancing, including the waltz. The school was located near farm fields, country roads, and a natural landmark known as Sunset Rock. Friendships were often formed on long country walks, when they would exercise in pairs known as "walking girls."[8] Until girls became good friends, they did not address each other by their first names, a practice that Edith's friend Marion Hosmer found silly, preferring to address classmates more informally, a practice Agnes, during her time at Miss Porter's School, found much more natural.[9] There were no exams or grades given; nevertheless, Edith studied hard enough her first year that she began to have trouble with her eyes and was ordered to refrain from reading in the summer of 1884. She found this difficult but tolerable, especially when Alice read aloud to her.[10]

Despite Edith's initial lack of social self-confidence, she did, as her cousins had predicted, make friends of her own among the student body and, in her personality, there were already hints of the future student leader who would emerge at Bryn Mawr College. To her fellow students, Edith seemed to possess knowledge greater than her years. Agnes heard another student claim "that Edith Hamilton knew everything that there was to be known." One fellow student, Kitty Ludington, from New York City, identified Edith's strengths of character more precisely, telling Agnes that she "was the best talker and at the same time the best listener that she ever knew."[11]

During her years at Miss Porter's, Edith regularly spent school vacations with her Pond relatives, many of whom had settled in the New Jersey cities of Elizabeth and Plainfield, where her maternal grandfather Loyal Pond had been living at the time of his death in 1881. Her grandmother Harriet Pond continued to live in the area, and Edith saw her frequently. Two of Edith's Pond uncles, Charles, always called "Charley," and Frank and his wife Celia, as well as Edith's aunt Katherine, all lived in Elizabeth, from which Uncle Charley commuted to his New York City office.[12] Katherine, who lived with her husband Ned, was for some reason always referred to by the French word "tante" followed by her nickname Kitty. It was during such vacations that Edith had her introduction to the New York theater, the world in which she would begin her writing career.

Edith still spent summer vacations with her own family, but in 1885 this meant only a modest camping trip in the mountains of West Virginia, as the firm of Huestis and Hamilton had collapsed into bankruptcy and her family found itself in reduced circumstances.[13] Montgomery Hamilton and his business partner, Alexander C. Huestis, were much alike in their tastes; both were more intellectual than practical. After the failure of the business, Huestis would devote himself to the study of Shakespeare.[14] Montgomery, too, would eventually retreat to his private library and, more tragically, to alcoholism.

That winter, Montgomery and Gertrude had been forced to forgo a plan to take their family to Florida, but in 1885 they were faced with the outright bankruptcy of the grocery business. That February, money was so short that Gertrude, in New York City with Edith, had to forgo some much-longed-for sightseeing. During one of her visits to Pond relatives, Edith was dismayed to discover that she and her sisters were described in New York society as "the retired grocer's family."[15] Ultimately, the business failure gave Edith and her sisters the opportunity to pursue higher education, since it became clear that they would have to support themselves. Financial hardship, however, meant that tuition expenses had to be carefully monitored.

Although there are indications that she would miss one spring term at Miss Porter's School in early 1886, Edith was able to return to Farmington in October 1885 for what would be a momentous final school year, both personally and academically.[16] Once at school, Edith met Sarah Locke, whom she told Jessie she "liked very much indeed."[17] Sarah was from Buffalo, New York, the daughter of an attorney, Franklin D. Locke, and his wife, Frances Cooper.[18] Blonde, blue-eyed, and a little plump, Sarah, who had been born in May 1868, was less than a year younger than Edith, who described her to Jessie as "very pretty."[19] The pair began to go on walks together and, in November, Sarah and Kitty Ludington asked Edith to join a gathering held every Sunday evening for five or six girls who were, Edith told Jessie, "particular friends." Edith and Sarah began to spend much time together, writing letters in Sarah's room and staying with each other when roommates were away. Farmington Sundays followed a routine of church attendance in the morning, then Bible class followed by a long afternoon, which Edith and Sarah always spent together, before hymn singing in the evening.[20]

These romantic friendships were a normal part of school life and occasions for heartbreak. Happy in the relationship she had formed with Sarah, Edith was cynical about other intense friendships she observed. "I think of all silly creatures, schoolgirls are the very silliest," she told Jessie. She professed disdain for "girls who write notes pages and pages long with 'You kissed me good night so coldly. I am sure you are offended. What have I done to be treated so.' Or 'you did not smile at me to-day at dinner. Have I offended you?' etc." Edith, who wrote freely to Jessie about her feelings for Sarah, expressed sympathy for Miss Porter's assistant Mary Dow, writing, "It is a perfect mystery to me how Mrs. Dow advises and sympathizes, when I should not think she would be able to keep from laughing out right."[21]

Edith's last months at Miss Porter's School were notable for her studies in Latin with Dr. Nathan Perkins Seymour. His son, Thomas Day Seymour, was professor of Greek at Yale and a future head of the American School of Classical Studies at Athens. The older Seymour's influence on Edith may have been great since, according to Alice's description, his instruction consisted primarily of the ideas contained in the classical texts, not in philology, the textual analysis of ancient writings.[22] Seymour was the first classical scholar from whom Edith received instruction, and her fondness for him was evident when, in May 1891, after her first months as a student at Bryn Mawr College, she and Agnes, who had studied Shakespeare under the professor, paid a visit to him at Yale.[23]

Although Edith spent only three years at Miss Porter's School, the experience was a significant one in her life. For the first time she had made lasting friendships with young women outside her own extended family. She would remain friends with Sarah until the early 1900s, long after Sarah had married and had children.[24] When, in 1910, she happened to meet Marion Hosmer in the Academia in Venice, the two spent part of an afternoon together and Edith responded warmly to her friend, who, though battling tuberculosis, was still determined to pursue an active life.[25] During her years at Miss Porter's, Edith impressed others with her oratory, a skill she would use as a leader in student government at Bryn Mawr College, in her work as headmistress of the Bryn Mawr School, and among her friends during the years of her writing career in New York City and Washington, D.C.

Also influential on Edith was the character of the school's founding headmistress, Sarah Porter. During the years Edith attended the school, Miss Porter's powerful personality still set the tone of the school, although Mary Dow helped to manage it.[26] Sarah Porter did not encourage her students to attend college, nor did she seek college graduates as teachers at her school. She did believe, however, that the headmistress and teachers set the moral tone of the school, a lesson Edith would find valuable when she became a headmistress herself.

It was also during her years at Miss Porter's School that Edith confessed her own literary aspirations to Jessie, thoughts that were prompted by her love of novel-reading and by meeting a successful author for the first time. Dr. George Washington Hosmer, the father of her friend Marion, was a medical doctor and a Civil War veteran who had achieved literary success writing about his experiences in the conflict.[27] Edith admired Dr. Hosmer greatly, though she found him a little intimidating too, especially his habit of listening carefully to the opinions of his daughter and her friends. He offered Edith a glimpse, however, of the social life of a well-respected author, as he recounted to her stories about other writers he knew and events he had attended, including a reception where he had conversed with the poet and diplomat James Russell Lowell.[28] Such experiences fired Edith's ambitions. She was already an avid novel reader, and Anthony Trollope's *The Duke's Children* had quickly become one of her favorite books. It would remain so throughout her life—Jessie even joked that she had it memorized.[29]

Other favorites of Edith's included the work of another English author, Jean Ingelow. Although largely unknown today, Ingelow's poetry, which often evoked the natural beauty of her childhood home of Lincolnshire, was so popular in the United States at the end of the nineteenth century that when Alfred, Lord Tennyson, died in 1892 some Americans sent an unsuccessful petition to Queen Victoria asking that Ingelow succeed him as Britain's poet laureate.[30] Edith and her sisters also read the novels of the English writer Charlotte Mary Yonge, whose works sought to teach values prized by high church Anglicans such as respect and duty.[31] Edith's favorite among Yonge's many works was *The Dove in the Eagle's Nest*, probably because its German setting fed her natural curiosity about the land of her birth. Edith also began to read the novels of the British writer George Meredith, who was known for creating heroines with both emotional and physical strength. She never lost her appreciation of Meredith as a novelist who had drawn attention to the need for women's rights.[32] From such diverse influences, Edith reached the age of eighteen entertaining hopes of becoming a writer.

She returned to Fort Wayne in July 1886 to a family still experiencing financial strain. Her return meant her introduction to her brother Arthur, who had been born on March 31, as Gertrude neared her forty-sixth birthday.[33] Understandably, Montgomery and Gertrude had been expecting a daughter and had consequently selected the name Dorothy for the baby. The arrival of a son meant that they had to discuss a variety of names before settling on one.

Arthur's entrance into a largely female family caused some anxiety over how to relate to and identify with him, especially as he grew older. Initially, Alice was dismayed that his name was yet another beginning with "A," but Arthur was seldom called by his given name. By the time he was a year old, Arthur's status as the fifth child had been enshrined in the nickname Quint, for the Latin Quintus, that stayed with him all his life.[34]

Edith's return to Fort Wayne was the beginning of four and a half years at home, until her departure for Bryn Mawr College in late January 1891.[35] The Hamilton family finances prevented her from beginning her college education. Alice, Margaret, and Norah still had their years at Miss Porter's School ahead of them—Alice and Agnes were to enter the school that fall. In their reduced circumstances, the sisters took turns pursuing their education. Edith would stay at home while her sisters attended Miss Porter's. In her turn, Norah would have to miss a term at the school while Edith was studying at Bryn Mawr.[36]

Following the bankruptcy, Montgomery also suffered a loss of prestige. In 1887, he failed to become the president of the Hamilton National Bank, which his father had founded and which sat in a prominent location in Fort Wayne's downtown, across from the court house.[37] Instead, the board chose Charles McCulloch, a son of Allen Hamilton's business partner Hugh McCulloch, and a capable manager who would direct the bank successfully for over thirty years.[38] Eventually, the bankruptcy and the loss of leadership of his father's bank would contribute to Montgomery's almost complete withdrawal to his study and, eventually, to alcoholism. He would become a symbol of failure to Edith.

Despite the hardship, for Edith these years in Fort Wayne were busy. She taught Sunday school, read, and studied Greek. Once a week, Edith and Jessie discussed the planned Sunday school lesson. Edith also began to participate in Christian Endeavor, an evangelical organization that grew rapidly in the United States in the last two decades of the nineteenth century and that asked its members to promise to read the Bible every day.[39]

From at least 1880, the Hamiltons had begun to spend part of nearly every summer at Petoskey on Lake Michigan and later at Mackinac Island, Michigan, located in the straits of Huron, just below the state's Upper Peninsula.[40] During Edith's years at home, Mackinac Island grew as a resort, becoming a popular summer retreat for more Fort Wayne families, especially after the Grand Rapids and Indiana Railroad connected the city to the Straits of Mackinac.[41] The Hamilton family joined in the changes that were taking place on the island, as Montgomery decided to build a house on its East Bluff, on a site near a cottage they had rented. The small white frame Hamilton cottage was not as grand as many of the island's summer homes; its design came from a kit.[42] However, its wide wraparound porch, reached by a flight of stairs jutting out into the garden, commanded a view down the bluff to a small mission station on the island's shore. The Hamilton sisters' Mackinac summers were filled with outdoor activities, most especially a round of picnics that traditionally began at the cave known as Devil's Kitchen, the site of

FIGURE 4. The Hamilton family cottage on Mackinac Island, built in 1888.
Copyright © Mark Bearss. Reprinted by permission of the photographer.

a natural spring. Edith especially enjoyed walking in the island's birch
tree forests, the floors of which were carpeted with ferns. Occasionally,
when invited to use a neighbor's bathing house (a tent placed on the
beach), they swam in the lake's cool water, wearing gingham dresses as
bathing suits. Sometimes they were invited to join others on a moonlight sail. On one such night, when they did not return to their cottage
until one thirty in the morning, they were thrilled by the sight of a stag
swimming through the moonlit water toward another one of the
islands.[43]

It was during these years that Edith formed her goal of becoming a
classical scholar. As her experience with Dr. Seymour shows, she was
already drawn to the study of classics, but it was in the years after leaving
school that she began to focus on the study of Greek, which she sometimes pursued on her own, without the aid of a tutor. She developed a
fascination for ancient Greek and began to see the language as a reflection of the culture that had created it. Although she sometimes despaired
over the challenges of learning it, she revealed to Alice why she persisted,
writing in February 1887, "I am rather discouraged with my Greek. No

other words of the Greeks inspires me with half as much awe and respect as their verbs. A people who could invent those would be capable of anything else."[44] Learning ancient Greek was not incompatible with her wish to become a writer. Rather, to a nineteenth-century woman an understanding of ancient Greek was almost necessary to become an esteemed author.[45] Two years later, however, her continuing study of the language coalesced into the goal of earning a doctorate.

One event that also sharpened Edith's determination to pursue the study of classics was the performance of the *Electra* of Sophocles at the Lyceum Theatre in New York City, which she attended on March 20, 1889, and which further stirred her awakening passion for ancient Greek culture. Her enthusiastic response to the performance, relayed in a letter to Jessie, also revealed that she had studied the conventions of ancient Greek drama herself, noting that at the opening of the play, "an attendant came in and lit a fire on the altar, as it was always in honour of Bacchus that the play was given."[46] The production also had a chorus composed of fifteen women (in ancient Greece the members would have been men), giving Edith her first exposure to the question of the size of the chorus, one that she would endeavor to answer in her own studies of ancient Greek culture.[47]

By that summer, Edith had determined that she wanted to earn a doctorate, and she spent part of each day on Mackinac reading a portion of the *Odyssey*.[48] Her goal was determined in part by the recent opening of Bryn Mawr College, which offered women both undergraduate and graduate education. From at least April 1890, her cousin Katherine shared her ambitions. Born in September 1862, Katherine was five years older than Edith, but this did not deter her hope of attending college. Katherine was judged by her family, however, to have delicate health, one of the objections that evidently prevented her from fulfilling her ambition.[49] While Edith spent the summer on Mackinac, Katherine stayed in Fort Wayne and studied languages with a tutor. Bryn Mawr had rigorous entrance examinations, especially in Greek and Latin, areas where the admission requirements matched those of Harvard.[50]

Edith and her sisters all chose to pursue education beyond their years at Miss Porter's School. Edith and Margaret would both attend Bryn

Mawr College, while Alice entered medical school at the University of Michigan and Norah would study art in New York City and Paris. In her autobiography, Alice attributed their decisions to pursue professions to the reversal in their family's finances. Edith's initial calculation—that she could spend only a little more than two years at college due to the expense—supports Alice's statement.[51] More than this, however, determined the Hamilton sisters' high level of educational attainment.

They were encouraged in their pursuit of education, unlike their cousins Katherine, Jessie, and Agnes, all intelligent women who longed for the educational opportunities Edith and her sisters enjoyed. Their father, Holman, did not experience the financial troubles of his younger brother, and although he could have afforded higher education for his daughters more easily, he was evidently opposed to women pursuing professions. Agnes hoped to study architecture at Cornell, but Holman refused to send her to college. She was forced to give up her ambitions; though, after his death she worked for a time at a Fort Wayne architectural firm.[52] Jessie hoped to study art, preferably in Paris. She had received some encouragement of her drawing talent from the art instructor at Miss Porter's School.[53] But faced with family opposition, she was compelled, as she told Agnes in 1887, to place her dreams in the category of "what we want to do in life and what we know we can not do."[54] An opportunity to study art presented itself when their aunt Margaret Hamilton established an art school in the carriage house on the Hamilton homestead. Margaret hired William J. Forsyth, later an influential Indiana artist, to give instruction to the Hamilton sisters and cousins and others in the community. To Edith's delight, Forsyth spotted artistic talent in Alice.[55] Jessie, too, experienced greater freedom after her father's death and, in 1898, with Edith's encouragement, she moved to Philadelphia to study art under the portraitist Cecilia Beaux.[56] Money, either its presence or its absence, was not the sole determinant of women's opportunities for higher education in the Hamilton family.

Edith and her sisters enjoyed more freedom to pursue their educational ambitions thanks to Gertrude, who encouraged her daughters' autonomy. On her side of the family, the generation of Colles women born in the 1860s, like Edith, followed paths similar to their Hamilton

FIGURE 5. The Hamilton sisters, from left to right, Norah, Margaret, Alice, and Edith. Photograph courtesy of the Schlesinger Library, Harvard Radcliffe Institute.

cousins. George W. Colles's daughter Gertrude attended a girls' school in Northampton, Massachusetts, where she studied Latin during the years that Edith was at Farmington.[57] She eventually became an artist and a suffrage advocate. Harriet and Mary, the daughters of James Colles Jr. and the cousins of Edith, graduated from Teachers College at Columbia University and specialized in teaching kindergarten.[58] Like their Hamilton cousins, this generation of Colles women never married, choosing to pursue the more independent paths offered by higher education and careers.

The encouragement to pursue a college education and a profession may have contributed to Edith's self-confidence and poise, qualities Jessie found striking in her cousin. Always careful about her appearance, Edith looked elegant in a dark brown dress or a dark blue suit with a belt and a simple skirt—a style Jessie wanted to copy.[59] When she asked Edith, who was visiting Pond relatives in New Jersey, for advice on how to make a dress that would reflect the newest spring fashions, she received a lengthy letter in reply. While claiming to know little on the subject, Edith nevertheless provided Jessie with complete instructions on how to make a dress in the latest fashion of accordion pleats, down to the buttons and trimmings. Edith had already developed a sense that the individual should present themselves well, a conviction she never lost.[60]

Edith kept romance at a distance, due in part to her desire to pursue higher education and a profession, but also because it raised anxiety within her. This included the only occasion she ever recorded of a male suitor, one Mr. DeGoll, who had written art criticism and knew an impressive number of New York artists. After he asked her to accompany him to a meeting of the local dramatic club and to a supper and a dance afterward, she recorded, "It gave me a rather funny feeling to have such a thing proposed to me."[61] Regardless, her focus was elsewhere: Bryn Mawr College's entrance exams.

By November, Edith, Alice, and Agnes were all studying ancient Greek with Katherine's tutor Mr. Lane, who taught at the local high school. They began by reading the *Antigone* of Sophocles, which appeared on the Bryn Mawr entrance exam, a project that apparently occupied them until the following March, when they began the study of the *Prometheus Bound* of Aeschylus.[62] It was likely Edith's introduction to the tragedy, which she later translated. One sign of her tutelage under Mr. Lane was likely the reading of a book titled, simply, *Aeschylus*, by Reginald S. Copleston, a fellow and lecturer at St. John's College, Oxford. Agnes most certainly read the volume, to which she devoted several pages in her diary. Agnes was particularly impressed by Copleston's remark that the English word for school comes from the Greek word for leisure, a point Edith was to make in *The Greek Way*.[63]

Immediately upon her return from Mackinac in September 1890, Edith began to work under the tutelage of a Miss Sharp. The subjects she studied with her are unknown but might have included mathematics. Edith had studied algebra, geometry, and trigonometry at Miss Porter's School, but she still worried about the mathematics portion of the entrance exam, telling Jessie that when it came to such subjects there were "no words . . . strong enough to express my stupidity in that direction."[64] She had spent the summer of 1890 on Mackinac studying algebra.[65] But barriers still seemed to block Edith's path to college. Whether the questions were financial or whether Edith was convinced that she was not yet ready to take the challenging exams, some difficulty prompted Jessie to report to her brother Allen as late as September 23, 1890, that "Edith will not go to Bryn Mawr."[66]

In late January 1891, however, Montgomery, Alice, Margaret, Jessie, and Agnes accompanied Edith to Fort Wayne's train station to see her off to Bryn Mawr College to take its entrance exams. If she was successful, she would enter the college immediately, at the age of twenty-three, an age not unusual in the late nineteenth century, when many women had to wait for their opportunity to obtain higher education, often, as in Edith's case, due to family finances.[67] With an algebra text and a book on Roman history tucked under her arm, Edith, with obvious nervousness about passing the exams, boarded the train.[68] A few days later, on February 7, she telegraphed her family that she had successfully passed her entrance exams. Despite the challenge mathematics posed for her, Edith had been conditionally passed in only one subject, French grammar, of which she had previously felt confident of her knowledge. This meant that she could enter the college right away, with a year to retake the test in that subject. Moreover, she had had her first glimpse of the Bryn Mawr College campus, which was to play a central role in her life for over thirty years, until her retirement from the Bryn Mawr School in 1922. She wrote enthusiastically about the beauty of the college's gothic buildings and how the students always attended class wearing their academic robes, a habit she found "very becoming to pretty girls."[69] She also discovered that although the college's president was male, as she had expected, the secretary to whom she had been writing for over a year in letters addressed to "Dear Sir" was in fact a woman. Edith's college life had begun.

Chapter 3

ACADEMIC AMBITIONS

Bryn Mawr College, which opened its doors in the fall of 1885, had, under the guidance of its remarkable first professor of English and dean of faculty, M. Carey Thomas, established itself as the most academically rigorous women's college in America and the only institution where a woman could earn a doctorate. Thomas, who had received her doctorate in literature summa cum laude from the University of Zurich in 1882, was a widely known advocate for women's educational and political advancement, and she used her own academic accomplishments to open graduate education to American women.[1] While Thomas's reputation has been tarnished by her documented racism and anti-Semitism, leading Bryn Mawr College to remove her name from an award, two prizes, and a building, she played an important role in Edith's life for three decades.[2]

Edith first felt Thomas's influence as she studied for her Bryn Mawr entrance exams. Thomas was determined that the college would establish and maintain high academic standards and had insisted that it should have its own admissions tests. In the subjects of Greek and Latin, they were considered as rigorous as those of the most competitive all-male American universities.[3] Thomas ensured that Bryn Mawr was a college where a woman's scholarly ambitions would be respected and encouraged, and, in July 1892, after just a year and a half in the intellectual and cultural atmosphere that M. Carey Thomas had created, Edith reaffirmed to Jessie her goal of obtaining a doctorate.[4]

Thomas envisioned Bryn Mawr as largely dominated by the study of philology, a conception that ensured the study of classics would occupy an important place in the college's curriculum.[5] Classics was still sufficiently associated with the rigors of male higher education for Thomas to see it as a valuable means of demonstrating that women were as intellectually capable as men.[6] Thomas also convinced her friend, Baltimore heiress Mary E. Garrett, to endow a European fellowship named for Garrett, which would allow a graduate student from Bryn Mawr to pursue study in Europe for one year, an opportunity that stoked eager competition.

The academic caps and gowns that Bryn Mawr students wore routinely on campus and that had so impressed Edith when she took her entrance exams was only one sign of the seriousness with which academics were pursued at the college. From her first spring at Bryn Mawr, Edith was impressed by the model of scholarship and aestheticism that M. Carey Thomas presented to the students and that pervaded the campus atmosphere. Thomas resided in the Deanery, a white frame house she shared with her longtime companion Mamie Gwinn, who had accompanied her to Europe during their student years and who taught literature at Bryn Mawr. There they surrounded themselves with beautiful decor.[7] In her first recorded impression of Thomas, Edith described the dean in her domestic milieu, telling Jessie she had been shown "into a most charming room." She continued: "A great fireplace of terracotta colour was repeated in the tiles of the ceiling and the hangings at the windows, while everything else, walls, chairs, and rugs, were a clear deep blue. You have no idea how lovely the effect was."[8] Thomas herself, dressed in a gown embroidered with roses, seemed to match the arts and crafts decor. Thomas was barely older than many of the students, and the deep impression she made on Edith with her fashionable dress and her stately demeanor was one shared by many at Bryn Mawr in the early years of the college, when, despite Thomas's busy schedule, students were able to know her personally.[9]

Edith described Thomas and Paul Shorey, a Plato scholar of distinction, as "kindred spirits."[10] Shorey, who had joined the faculty at the college's opening in 1885, had been a contemporary of Thomas's at the University of Leipzig, although it was the University of Munich that granted him a doctorate in 1884. At the time Edith entered Bryn Mawr, Shorey was head of the Greek faculty and cut a familiar figure walking across the Bryn Mawr campus, always with a stack of books under his arm. He only taught Edith during her first year and a half at college since he departed for the University of Chicago in 1892. Edith's letters during this period, however, reflect both her admiration for Shorey and her struggles to meet his high expectations.[11]

Shorey's methods of instruction and his understanding of Greek literature were formative to Edith. During his years at Bryn Mawr, he experimented with a teaching method that consisted of identifying similarities between ancient and modern authors.[12] He tried to impress on his students that the great works of classical literature were the models for all great literature in the Western tradition. One acquaintance of Edith's, Emily James Putnam, who, as Emily James Smith was taught by Shorey as a freshman at Bryn Mawr in 1885, recalled: "We were not so much aware of reading dead, effete, negligible stuff as of dealing with the earliest examples of a continuous tradition."[13] Edith responded enthusiastically to his lectures, which seemed to confer an immediacy to ancient Greek authors. She wrote Jessie: "I am simply awed over Dr. Shorey. He is giving us a series of lectures on Attic Prose, and you cannot imagine anything more delightful than they are. I wish I could up every body else and only go to his classes."[14] To Alice, she wrote, "I have six lectures a week with Dr. Shorey, while four is considered a large number, as you have to work five times as hard for him, as for anyone else. But I am glad of it, for he is wonderfully fine. I come out of every lecture simply exhausted and wishing I had brains enough to take it all in."[15]

Shorey's influence on Edith is evident in *The Greek Way* and *The Roman Way*, since it was from Shorey that she first learned the technique of comparing authors across time periods. In her books, Edith followed Shorey's pattern of constructing parallels between ancient and modern authors, using as a basis of comparisons Plato's standard: "The excellency that is peculiar to each thing."[16]

During her first year at Bryn Mawr, however, Edith felt that she could not meet Shorey's intellectual expectations. In the spring of 1892, she told Jessie, "I wish Dr. Shorey would take a friendly interest in me, but alas, he views me with growing dislike, and the worst of it is that I cannot complain for I do so poorly in his classes."[17] Nevertheless, after his departure from Bryn Mawr, Edith felt that no one could take his place.[18] Shorey's indifference was compensated for only by the intellectual attentions of the Latin professor Dr. Gonzalez Lodge who, from Edith's first year at college, acted as her mentor. He was only four years her senior and had come to Bryn Mawr in 1889, having earned his doctorate at Johns Hopkins University under the guidance of Basil Lanneau Gildersleeve. Gildersleeve was a significant figure in establishing the field of classics in the United States, and Edith would come to know him during her early years in Baltimore.[19] Although not the first American to bring German philological methods to the United States, Gildersleeve had organized the profession of classical scholars by serving as founding editor of the *American Journal of Philology*, thereby encouraging the growth of serious classical scholarship in America.[20]

When Lodge and Edith met, Lodge had just published a translation of Plato's *Gorgias*, which Edith would later identify as her favorite among the dialogues.[21] He would become better known, however, for his Latin scholarship. During Edith's years at Bryn Mawr he was editing the third edition of Gildersleeve's *Latin Grammar*, still known today as the Gildersleeve-Lodge *Latin Grammar*. Eventually, during the longer phase of his career at Teachers College, Columbia University, he became known for his study of the Roman playwright Plautus. Lodge was an accomplished philologist, but more important for his influence on Edith was his wider interest in the relevance of the ancient Greeks and Romans to the modern world, particularly where the role of the individual in maintaining democracy was concerned.[22]

Lodge's mentorship began during Edith's first term when, as she was reading in the college library before dinner, he sat down beside her and politely asked if he could "disturb" her. He then admitted that he had been observing her from the time she first entered college, impressed by how well she was progressing despite having begun her classics course in the middle of the academic year. Moreover, the students majoring in Greek and Latin were, he told her, the "most brilliant class in college," a condition that only made it harder for Edith to catch up. During their conversation, Lodge was, Edith told Jessie, "just as nice as he could be." She could not help comparing his sympathy to Shorey's distance, writing Jessie, "You don't know how pleased I was, for it was quite cheering to find some one taking a friendly interest in me, in contrast to the entire want of any, I have usually found. He talked to me for nearly an hour, and really grew quite charming, confiding his views on Latin literature."[23] Although in later life Edith would refer to herself as Shorey's student, it was Lodge who first spotted her potential as a classicist.[24] His interest in her intellectual development explains why she took Latin as her major subject for her master's degree, wrote her thesis on a subject in Latin literature, and, although she would become known to the world for her writings on ancient Greece, was Bryn Mawr's fellow in Latin for 1894–95 but never the college's fellow in Greek.

During her first two years at college, Edith found that she had to study very hard to meet the challenges posed by Shorey's teaching. She told Alice that the Bryn Mawr students studied an average of ten hours per day but that twelve was not uncommon. The long hours initially made it difficult for her to form friendships.[25] The college's graduation requirements demanded that a student pair two subjects or, essentially, double major. By pairing Greek and Latin, Edith was creating a demanding curriculum for herself and one that she was trying to complete in a short period of time.[26] The constraints of the Hamilton family's finances and the necessity of educating Margaret and Norah when the time came meant that Edith originally planned to study at Bryn Mawr for only two years.[27] She rose to the challenge and excelled academically while still participating in student government and other social activities.

A year after entering Bryn Mawr, Edith distinguished herself academically in another subject important to her: English composition. In January 1892, her writing instructor singled out her essay on Jane Austen—always one of Edith's favorite authors—for the coveted honor of "high credit." Not only did Edith repeat this phrase to herself for most of the day on which she learned of it but it also brought her to the attention of her fellow students. Bryn Mawr students respected academic achievement, and graded essays were posted in the English classroom for one week, where others were free to read them. For Edith, the distinction of a "high credit" was a heady moment in the early academic career of a budding writer. January, however, included exam week for the fall term, and as Edith studied for her upcoming tests she had to push her recent honor to the back of her mind. She slept little, never for more than six hours at a time, as she studied for tests on Plato and Lucretius and the philosophies of Heraclitus and Empedocles. In the end, the entire student body of Bryn Mawr was so exhausted by the final exams for fall term 1891 that the administration extended the winter vacation by two days.[28]

Despite the long hours of studying, Edith did begin to form friendships with her fellow students. One of her first was with Olivia Susan Clemens, the daughter of Mark Twain.[29] Bryn Mawr in its earliest years had a tradition of staging Gilbert and Sullivan operettas, and Olivia, or Susie as she was known to her friends, performed in the college's production of *Iolanthe* in the spring of 1891, which Edith enthusiastically described to Alice as a "very remarkable performance for college girls."[30] Susie's mother, also Olivia Clemens, helped to prepare the costumes for the production, and it was likely during her visit to the college that Edith met the wife of the famous author.[31] Edith's acquaintance with the Clemens family, however, was to be short-lived. Illness and homesickness prevented Susie from returning to Bryn Mawr the following year.[32]

Another early friendship formed at Bryn Mawr was due to a connection she had made at Miss Porter's School. During her first year at college, her next-door neighbor in her dormitory Denbigh Hall was Emma Bailey, an acquaintance of Sarah Locke. Emma, who was five years younger than Edith, was the daughter of a wealthy iron manufacturer in Harrisburg, Pennsylvania.[33] The two became good friends, and in January 1892 Edith spent part of the college winter break at Ingleside, the Baileys' country home in Thorndale, Pennsylvania. Emma hosted eight college friends for a house party, during which they spent their evenings sitting near the fire talking about the role of college-educated women in urban social reform movements. They also read the Bible together and said a blessing at each meal.[34] Emma's friends included Margaret Shearman, from Wilmington, Delaware, whose religious background was, like Bryn Mawr itself, Quaker.[35] Margaret was to become Edith's lifelong friend and, along with Emma, someone with whom she could discuss the social reform movements to which Bryn Mawr students were exposed.

Early in 1892, Emma, who was already interested in the formation of working girls' societies, invited Robert E. Speer, a prominent Presbyterian layman and a leader in the Student Volunteer Movement, to speak at Bryn Mawr. M. Carey Thomas herself invited Speer to return in March. The Student Volunteer Movement, founded in 1889, recruited college students to serve as missionaries in China and other parts of the world.[36] Edith was impressed by Speer and praised his enthusiasm for foreign missions. At least for a time, Edith, together with her Farmington friends Susan and Lily Duryee, and Emma, considered the possibility of becoming a missionary.

In 1890, the Duryees' father, William Rankin Duryee, had accepted a position as professor of ethics at Rutgers College, and the family had settled in New Brunswick, New Jersey.[37] The sisters soon invited Edith to visit them, but her studies delayed her accepting their invitation until November 1892.[38] It was a visit followed by many others during Edith's time at Bryn Mawr. The Duryee house on New Brunswick's Union Street became a second home to her, a place where she went to rest when exhausted by the demands of class work and student government.[39] Lily, who was intent on becoming a missionary, extended Edith's consideration of her doing the same. During one visit to the Duryees, Edith told Jessie: "Sometimes when one listens to Rob Speer for instance—it seems the only thing in the world worth giving up one's life, time, talents, energies to."[40]

In 1892, Emma decided not to return to Bryn Mawr but to marry Robert E. Speer instead.[41] Her departure from college was a source of regret for Edith, although she expressed happiness and admiration for Emma as she embarked on a new life with the possibility of overseas mission work.[42] Both Susan and Lily would have long careers as missionaries in China, but Edith's interests lay elsewhere. During the course of 1892, as Edith learned that her family could finance two more years of study at Bryn Mawr, and as she made friends with some of the most intellectually gifted among her fellow students, her initial determination to pursue an academic career returned.[43]

By then Edith had met tall, dark-haired Lucy Martin Donnelly. Lucy, with whom Edith would have, almost fifteen years after graduation, a fitful, sporadic, and unfulfilling romantic relationship, made an enduring impact on Edith's intellectual and aesthetic tastes, introducing her to the works of such British thinkers as the philosopher Edward Caird and the classical scholar Gilbert Murray. Three years younger than Edith, Lucy was the daughter of a New York City attorney, Henry Donnelly, a Union Civil War veteran who had been decorated for bravery after his side had been routed at Chancellorsville, and to whom she would always remain close.[44] He was also a Unitarian who held a wide range of progressive views and who encouraged his daughter to pursue her education, sending her to Brooklyn's Adelphi Academy for her final three years of schooling, from 1886 until 1889. The school had been coeducational almost from its founding during the Civil War; it was the first in New York City to admit girls to its college preparatory curriculum, which meant that Lucy had the opportunity to study both Greek and Latin.[45] She had entered Bryn Mawr in September 1889, a year and a half before Edith, and was majoring in Greek and English.[46]

While the study of Greek would always draw Lucy and Edith together, their friendship was based on their mutual appreciation of the aesthetic and scholarly atmosphere the college offered women. Edith was impressed by Lucy's keen critical insight and described her as "a poem, so dainty and so original."[47] Lucy, Edith told Jessie, "never looks at anything or expresses anything in quite the way other people do."[48] Lucy paid her first of many summer visits to Mackinac Island in 1893 and, when absent, corresponded with Edith. Lucy's letters, however, made Edith feel she could never match Lucy's literary talents.[49] That Lucy's literary talent was superior to Edith's would remain an axiom of their relationship for as long as it endured, though ultimately Edith would prove to be as talented a writer as Lucy, and more prolific.

During their college years, Lucy's particular friend was Helen Thomas, the youngest sister of M. Carey Thomas. Lucy and Helen had entered Bryn Mawr at the same time, and their relationship grew to have a romantic element, an aspect common to friendships on the Bryn Mawr campus during Edith's years there. As had been true at Farmington, romantic friendships involved a deep emotional bond between two women, who expressed their feelings for one another in terms of affection and endearment. A physical element could be, but was not necessarily, present in the romantic friendships at Bryn Mawr. These romantic relationships gave women the support they needed to pursue their educational and professional goals at a time when marriage to a man meant forgoing a career.[50] Lucy and Helen roomed next door to each other and were, Edith commented, "so intimate that you say 'Helen and Lucy', as naturally as you speak of a cup and a saucer."[51] The pair were a striking couple: Lucy, tall and willowy, wore her hair pulled straight back into a bun at the nape of her neck. In photographs taken during her years as a college student, Lucy gazed at the camera with steady confidence through a pair of horn-rimmed glasses. Helen, by contrast, was small, with a mass of curly red hair. She shared Lucy's passion for literature, and their romantic friendship continued through their time as students and into the early years of their careers as writing instructors at Bryn Mawr.

Edith also added to her social circle another friend of Lucy's, Laurette Potts, who was studying English and Latin and whom Edith described as "brilliant, clever."[52] Through this circle Edith also met Louise Brownell, an economics student who was a close friend of Susie Clemens and who roomed next door to Lucy and Helen. Among these women, Edith found both intellectual companionship and intellectual challenge. To Edith, their company was both stimulating and intimidating. As she told Jessie, "I have a feeling when I am with Lucy, or with Helen Thomas, or Louise Brownell, that I have never had before, that I am with someone whose mind is of a higher order than my own, and I am afraid I will say something to jar upon them, or else not fully take in what they say." Although the women often discussed heady topics together, on occasion they could act "in a most school-girl fashion."[53] On a snowy Sunday morning in early 1893, Edith, Lucy, and Louise, having overslept breakfast because of an especially late night of conversation, made "scrambled eggs, buttered toast, and chocolate" in Louise's room with nothing but "a coal fire and a chafing dish." Edith's friendship with these women, especially with Lucy and Helen, stimulated her ambitions and intellect, increasing her determination to pursue graduate study abroad and helping to direct her reading.

Socially, Edith had two distinct experiences at Bryn Mawr College, the first was the feeling that she should become a missionary, prompted by her friendships with Emma Bailey Speer and the Duryee sisters. The second, and much more enduring, was her dedication to the life of a scholar and writer once her friendship with Lucy Martin Donnelly and other intellectual women solidified.

At Bryn Mawr, Edith encountered Victorian Hellenism as she and other students were introduced to nineteenth-century English authors who saw the ancient world as a source of aesthetic inspiration. This experience was largely due to the English lectures given by M. Carey Thomas and Mamie Gwinn, who taught the works of Walter Pater and Algernon Swinburne, among others, in a two-year course that all students were required to take.[54] As a result, admiration for British arts and letters flourished on the campus; one student, who entered the college in 1896, remembered that there was "a sort of cult for the English language" at Bryn Mawr in which Lucy played a large role.[55] Mamie Gwinn in particular was an expert on the work of Swinburne, and under her instruction Edith developed an appreciation for the poet, whose work was often inspired by ancient Greek literature, including the tragedies of Aeschylus.[56] Swinburne's verse play, *Atalanta in Calydon*, portrayed the Great Calydonian Boar Hunt, an episode in the story of the mythical huntress Atalanta that was given particular attention by Edith in *Mythology*.[57] By the time Edith began to write about the Greeks, however, Swinburne's verse had declined in popularity, and ultimately she would find much of his poetry too sentimental to reflect the Greek quality of restraint that she admired.[58]

The 1885 novel *Marius the Epicurean*, written by Walter Pater, a fellow in classics at Brasenose College, Oxford, was also widely circulated among the students. Pater was a scholar of Greek mythology and sculpture as well as of ancient texts, but it was his novel that brought the ancient world to life, as it traced its eponymous character's search for religious fulfillment. Pater drew upon his understanding of the classical world, derived from his studies at Oxford, but combined it with the aesthetic pursuit of appreciation for artistic beauty. Edith was especially thrilled with Pater's vivid portrayal of the ancient Roman world, which was based on his own archaeological knowledge.[59] Pater also dealt with themes Edith would engage in her writing, including the rejection of religious formalism. His central character, Marius, rejects the "severe and archaic religion" of old Roman tradition and begins a spiritual journey, seeking education to help him understand beauty.[60] Pater's novel taught that beauty had a moral effect, helping to increase an individual's religious understanding. As Marius learns to appreciate beauty, he is moved closer to Christian belief by the end of the novel.

At Bryn Mawr, student pageants frequently made use of classical themes, making the ancient world come alive as Pater did in his novel. Helen Thomas participated in a freshman pageant in which the students placed lanterns symbolizing the light of learning around an altar to Pallas Athena, the goddess of wisdom. The students wore Greek drapery, performed a Greek dance, and mounted "a series of tableaux from the *Iliad* and the *Odyssey*."[61] They also sang a hymn to Athena in ancient Greek created by two members of the class of 1893, which asked that the goddess of wisdom aid them in their pursuit of knowledge. Lantern night, as it was called, became an annual tradition at the college.[62]

The aesthetic of Victorian Hellenism was manifested by an appreciation for the British Pre-Raphaelite school of art. Bryn Mawr students in the early 1890s decorated their studies with copies of the paintings of Dante Gabriel Rossetti and Edward Burne-Jones, whose many portraits of women in gently draping gowns were inspired by ancient Greek art.[63] Lucy and Louise even wrote complementary poems inspired by Burne-Jones—with Louise describing his portrayal of "Day" and Lucy of "Night"—that they published in Bryn Mawr's literary magazine, *The Lantern*.[64] At Bryn Mawr College, the serious study of classical texts was mixed with a romantic and aesthetic sensibility typical of late nineteenth-century Hellenism, when admiration for the ancient Greeks was also frequently associated with progressive ideas.[65] The imagery of ancient Greece was invoked to argue that educated women, who had partaken of Western civilization's store of knowledge, could be active citizens, taking a role in social reform.

At Bryn Mawr, Edith read the works of the nineteenth-century English social commentators John Ruskin and Matthew Arnold, both of whom had an enduring effect on her thought.[66] Ruskin's 1865 book *Sesame and Lilies* argued for free libraries and galleries so that the poor could access morally uplifting works of literature and art. The volume also promoted education for women to better prepare them for a role in social reform. More influential on Edith, however, was Ruskin's belief that a nation's art reflected its moral state, an idea he had advanced in his multivolume mid-nineteenth-century work, *The Seven Lamps of Architecture*, and returned to in the first volume of *The Stones of Venice*, initially published in 1851.[67]

Edith also read some of the writings of Matthew Arnold, the mid-nineteenth-century professor of poetry at Oxford. At Bryn Mawr, Arnold, like Pater, was considered one of the "college gods."[68] In the 1860s Arnold had turned from writing poetry, often on classical themes, to social criticism. He was widely read among American intellectuals after his successful lecture tours of the United States a few years before his death in 1888.[69] His impact on Edith's thought was evident as early as 1895, when she told Jessie she was writing an essay on ancient authors' opinions of Thucydides and avowing that someday she would write an article titled "The Function of Criticism in Ancient Days," inspired by Matthew Arnold's 1865 essay "The Function of Criticism at the Present Time," with which she was obviously familiar.[70]

In the fourth chapter of his well-known work *Culture and Anarchy*, first published in book form in 1869, Arnold had argued that the two main roots of Western civilization were "Hebraic" and "Hellenic." Both cultures, he argued, shared the aim of helping humanity to achieve spiritual perfection, though they differed in their methods. While Hebraism stressed ethical conduct, Hellenism emphasized the need for humanity to perceive reality clearly in order to address societal problems. Throughout history, the forces of Hellenism and Hebraism had often been seen as antagonistic to one another, and some societies had emphasized one over the other. Ideally, according to Arnold, society would accord equal voice to both forces. To demonstrate their mutually reinforcing goals, he compared Christian and ancient Greek writers, suggesting that both St. Paul, in his letter to the Corinthians, and Plato, in the *Phaedo*, had dealt with the idea of human immortality.[71] Arnold's interests were not merely academic, but, rather, contemporary. Writing at a time when the British Parliament was debating another extension of the franchise, Arnold argued that Hellenism gave the British people the ability to perceive the social problems requiring reform while Hebraism gave them the sense of ethical responsibility to carry it out.[72]

Edith's writing testifies to the impact of Arnold's conceptions of "Hebraism" and "Hellenism" on her thought. She took these two roots of Western civilization as a given, often positioning them side by side in her writing; she felt, as Arnold had argued, that the language of these two forces was similar. There were other aspects of Arnold's Hellenism that Edith found appealing. Arnold argued for the relevance of the ancient Greek experience for nineteenth-century society, a common view among classicists and other intellectuals of the time.[73] Edith would make the same argument for the twentieth century, long after ancient Greece had ceased to be the assumed basis of comparison for political and societal questions as it had been in the Victorian era. Arnold's ideal Greece had been limited to fifth-century Athens, an emphasis that would become common among Hellenists who followed him, including Edith. Likewise, she would echo Arnold's themes that presented the Greeks as essentially modern, an achievement made possible in great part because ancient Greek society had given individuals freedom of thought.[74] Arnold's definition of culture, which he stated in *Culture and Anarchy*, would also form a persistent theme in Edith's work. Arnold believed that culture was "the best that has been thought and known in the world," and Edith gave as a reason to become acquainted with the Greeks that their cultural achievements have "never been surpassed and very rarely equaled."[75]

It is likely that Edith also read Arnold's 1873 essay "Literature and Dogma," since, during her years at Bryn Mawr College, her religious views changed as she moved away from the doctrinal Presbyterianism of her youth. Arnold's essay argued in favor of a critical reading of the

Bible, a position that Edith, who had grown up in a home that accepted biblical criticism, would have understood. The Old Testament, according to Arnold, defined ethical conduct, but the gospels showed Jesus trying to teach his followers the method of achieving it. Arnold believed that he was living in an age less likely to accept the idea that Jesus had performed miracles, but he told his readers that Christian faith did not depend on belief in miracles, and that faith, in fact, was likely to emerge stronger if belief in miracles diminished.[76] During her years at Bryn Mawr College, Edith's reading of Arnold helped spark her lifelong opposition to dogmatic Christianity, but other social and intellectual forces she encountered at college likely contributed to this theological shift as well. At Bryn Mawr, Edith found her Sundays less structured than at home in Fort Wayne and, exposed to a wider range of theological beliefs—the student body was more religiously diverse than any society she had previously encountered—she began to grow away from the dogmas with which she had been raised. Moreover, she discovered the British school of philosophic idealism, a blend of Christianity and Platonism that satisfied her firm belief in the individual's need to aspire to their higher self.

It was likely during her years at Bryn Mawr College that Edith encountered the writings of the Scottish philosopher Edward Caird, whose thought would suffuse her books and her life, particularly shaping her own views of Christianity. His idealist philosophy would become so important to her that she would eventually refer to him as "my beloved Caird."[77] Caird created a system of thought that incorporated his views on religion, philosophy, and art, although even his admirers expressed doubt as to whether to consider him a philosopher or primarily the disseminator of others' ideas. To read his two-volume work *The Evolution of Religion* is to encounter almost every major philosophical and theological idea in Edith's writing.[78] Caird was the longtime professor of moral philosophy at the University of Glasgow, though he became the master of Balliol College, Oxford, in the autumn of 1893, just as Lucy began her studies in Greek there.[79]

Lucy went to Balliol at a critical time, when its longtime master Benjamin Jowett, the translator of Plato, had just died and Caird, his former student, had been elected to succeed him. Caird was a longtime supporter of women's access to higher education. His leadership in the struggle to get women admitted to the University of Glasgow had lasted all but two of the twenty-seven years he had spent there. As master of Balliol, he became known for his informal Sunday morning breakfast parties, at which male and female students could take part in intellectual conversation. He supported the campaign to confer Oxford degrees to women, and he was a friend to the cause of women's suffrage. Caird reached out to Lucy, one of the first American women to study at Oxford.[80] When she found herself the only female student in one of her classes, he asked her and another student to pursue special work with him in his Balliol study.[81] It was likely due to Lucy that Edith began to read Caird, one of several instances in which Lucy introduced her to the British literature and thought that would exercise such a powerful influence on her.

Caird was an adherent of the British Idealist school of philosophy that developed at Oxford in the late nineteenth century. Platonic and ultimately Hegelian in its inspiration, idealism tried to account for the roles of religion and aesthetics in human life. The idealists were also concerned to absorb Darwinian natural selection and therefore used the term evolution, arguing that it was just one manifestation of God that humans perceived as their consciousness grew.[82] Idealists argued that God was present in the natural world through the concept of divine immanence and that individuals were aided in their efforts to perceive God by spiritual and artistic forces. In his major work *The Evolution of Religion*, Caird sought to "explain man as a spiritual being" with a "moral and religious consciousness."[83]

According to Caird, humanity had undergone a process of development, gradually evolving from an objective religious sense to a higher, subjective one. Objective religion, taught Caird, had been composed of experience and feeling, as humans had perceived a divine force present in nature. Subjective religion had appeared when humanity perceived divinity as having a moral basis, whereby religious experience became reflective and God was perceived as present in the individual conscience.[84] Caird's work noted key points in humanity's religious development. He placed special emphasis on the Greeks as the first people to anthropo-morphize their gods, which he considered an essential step in the evolu-tion of religion, making the gods closer to humanity than to nature. He therefore classified ancient Greek religion as between objective and sub-jective, crediting the Greeks with beginning essential change in human religious experience.[85] Roman civilization and Judaism had prepared the way for Christianity.[86] To Caird, Stoicism represented an essential stage in the development of religion. He characterized it as a subjective reli-gion, one that demanded much individual reflection, through which the believer grew in their understanding of the unity of the divine. It lacked, however, an understanding of the essential unity of all things that was characteristic of Christianity.[87] Finally, Caird argued that as the nine-teenth century came to a close a "new Christianity" was developing, one that emphasized spiritual principle free of the "extraneous support" of dogma, miracle, or formalism.[88]

Caird's effect on Edith is most noticeable whenever she wrote about religion. His influence is clear in the early chapters of *The Greek Way*, which draw a sharp dichotomy between the Greeks and Eastern peoples, as illustrated by images of their divinities. She emphasized the theme of the Greeks' anthropomorphizing their gods in the introduction to *My-thology* as well as in a chapter she later added to *The Greek Way*, "The Way of Greek Religion."[89] Her two books on the Bible also reflect Caird's teaching, especially *Witness to the Truth*, which, while following Matthew Arnold's methods, also offered Caird's new Christianity as an antidote to the loss of faith that she felt had been one of the effects of the Second World War.[90]

Caird also gave her a sense, often invoked in her books, that the an-cient Greeks had not been very different from later peoples, including her contemporaries. Caird thought that all humanity was united by the principle of development. Peoples of the past differed from those of the present only by being in an inferior state of development. To Caird, knowledge of the highest good was potentially open to all, though peoples of the past were hindered in their pursuit of the good by their more primitive state.[91] In the opening of *The Greek Way*, Edith wrote that although the study of ancient Greece might be reserved for specialists, "the outside of life changes much, the inside changes little, and the lesson-book we cannot graduate from is human experience."[92]

Caird influenced Edith personally as well, helping to shape her views on social reform, women's suffrage, and aesthetics. To Caird, religion was defined as consciousness of a divine presence and manifested itself as an individual's attitude toward their place in the universe. Once individuals experienced a religious awakening, they began to reflect on their own role in society and were prompted to embark on efforts to solve the problems of humanity, including engaging in social reform. To Caird, the divine presence in each individual was manifested through reason. It was the duty of individuals to make the most of their reason and fully realize their potential through social service, making the practice of religion, according to Caird, "the highest form of citizenship."[93] Artists and writers could play a considerable role in helping an individual's religious development, stimulating their spiritual awakening through their portrayal of beauty and helping to ascribe meaning to life.[94] Caird's conviction that citizenship should be open to women was influential in Edith's decision to become a suffrage activist. Her belief that the works of great artists and writers, created in the course of their own search for spiritual truth, could aid others on their own such journey often led her in later life to criticize modern artists whose works seemed to obscure truth rather than help reveal it.[95]

During Edith's college years, her reading of Arnold and Caird and her acquaintance with students of other faiths, particularly Unitarians, permanently altered her spiritual life. After college, Edith rarely attended church services, a contrast to her youth when church attendance and Sunday school had been part of every week.[96] Christianity remained an important aspect of her life, but it was an essential belief, free of the dogmas and doctrines that had been part of the Presbyterianism of her youth. This willingness to challenge Calvinism was not unusual among college women of Edith's generation, who sought a more active role in intellectual and public life than this doctrine accorded women.[97] At college chapel services, which Edith attended regularly, religious belief was often mixed with calls for student participation in social reform efforts.

Bryn Mawr's Sunday meeting frequently highlighted women's ability to exercise a positive influence on society. Faculty, but occasionally other speakers, used the occasion to raise awareness of social issues, particularly those concerning women. During her second year at Bryn Mawr, Edith deeply regretted the purchase of a ticket to see the great actor E. H. Sothern perform since it prevented her from hearing Lady Henry Somerset, the British temperance advocate, speak at the Sunday meeting.[98] Lady Henry was to address the subject of women's suffrage, which, if it was introduced in Britain, would, it was believed, help to enact temperance laws.[99] Edith had no interest in temperance but was deeply interested in the question of women's suffrage.

Some of the presentations Edith heard in chapel prompted her to reflect on her responsibilities as a citizen. One such occasion was a speech on the sweating system given by one of Bryn Mawr's English instructors, Abby Kirk, in the spring of 1895. Kirk, Edith told Jessie, "spoke on our relation to the working classes." Kirk urged Bryn Mawr students not to purchase ready-made clothing because she had "satisfied herself that there was no way in which ready made clothes could honestly be bought." The presentation provoked Edith to reflect on her own purchases. She and her sisters bought few ready-made clothes, preferring to select styles and fabrics themselves. But she was prompted to seek the advice of Alice and Agnes on the question of "what I shall do about my jackets."[100] Bryn Mawr students took calls to participate in social reform seriously. One of Edith's contemporaries, Edith Wyatt, who like Lucy was studying Greek and English, left the college to devote herself entirely to protesting against methods of slaughtering animals in the Chicago stockyards, demonstrating a commitment to the cause Edith Hamilton still remembered with admiration as late as 1958.[101] Kirk's presentation had made a clear call to Bryn Mawr students, and Edith's own family background, coupled with her reading of idealist philosophy, informed her feeling that educated women could make a positive impact on society, especially if given the right to vote.

Edith found an outlet for such feelings through participation in student government, an activity in which she participated with her friend Laurette Potts. Student government at Bryn Mawr began during Edith's years at the college. In 1891, Susan Walker, a student from Boston, had initiated the request for self-government, which M. Carey Thomas and the college's trustees approved.[102] As Edith was aware, Bryn Mawr College was the only institution of higher education in the United States to have student self-government, giving it a unique status among colleges.[103] The government structure consisted of four students sitting on an executive board, one of whom was president. The president of the executive board was, according to Edith, the "first and most responsible position in college."[104] In January 1893, Edith was approached by two of the graduate students in classics, Susan Franklin and Nan Emery, who suggested that she run for the executive board.[105] The possibility filled her with a mixture of elation and panic. She realized that to even be talked of for such a position was a measure of what her fellow students thought of her character. According to Helen Thomas, a student elected to student government was considered to have "unusually strong character and principles."[106]

Though Edith may have felt somewhat intimidated by the intellectual brilliance of some of her Bryn Mawr friends, she nevertheless possessed her own oratorical skill. Jessie felt that Edith was especially good at constructing persuasive arguments that would convince others to follow her lead.[107] After at first demurring on the grounds that she might not be able to exercise the moral leadership expected of a member of the executive board, Edith agreed to become a candidate. In February 1893, she was elected president of the executive board, with Laurette Potts as vice president.[108]

Edith was glad to be serving in student government with Laurette, whom she described as "very fine looking, a girl born to always lead."[109] During the time they served in student government together, Laurette was Edith's "chief defender in all self-government matters."[110] But Laurette suffered a nervous breakdown in the months after the election and was not fully rested when she returned to campus the following autumn. She soon became ill again and had to leave college completely.[111] By late 1893, Edith was already completing some graduate work at Bryn Mawr. She had to prepare lectures in both her graduate Greek and Latin classes. Laurette's illness placed an added burden on

Edith, who had to take on extra duties in student government and fell ill herself as a result.[112]

As Edith found opportunities to exercise influence through leadership, she began to reflect on her decision to pursue higher education and to become a scholar rather than to marry. It was during her years at Bryn Mawr that Edith recognized that she had no plans to marry, in part since it would prevent her from pursuing an academic career. In November 1893, while listening to Dr. James Rhoads, the first president of Bryn Mawr, lecture in ethics class on the subject of marriage, Edith decided to write Jessie a letter, having determined that "I do not find it applicable, personally."[113] Such reflections were also prompted by the marriages of her friends Emma Bailey and Sarah Locke. After leaving Farmington, Sarah had made such a successful social debut that Edith was surprised when she became engaged to the Reverend Charles Alexander Richmond, a graduate of Princeton Theological Seminary who had been ordained by the presbytery in Buffalo. Edith felt that Sarah was "the last girl in the world to marry a country clergyman."[114] Sarah visited Edith at Bryn Mawr a few months before her wedding, and Edith told Alice that, although the visit had been a happy one, they had done "little but sit and talk of Mr. Richmond" because Sarah was "fathoms deep in love."[115] She was planning to marry on June 4, 1891, the very day Edith was to take her final exams, a coincidence that only seemed to emphasize the growing distance between them and the different lives they had chosen.[116] Edith often stated her decision not to marry in a matter-of-fact tone to Jessie, expressing no regret that she must choose between a career and marriage. At Bryn Mawr she enjoyed what M. Carey Thomas had created: an environment where women could pursue challenging academic study, certain that her goals would be treated seriously.

Edith's lack of interest in marriage, however, was likely due to more than just her pursuit of a career. None of her sisters or her Hamilton cousins ever married either, a circumstance that raises the question of why this generation of Hamilton women displayed so little interest in conventional marriage. Only Edith and Margaret would find permanent lifetime partners. As Edith observed shortly before she entered Bryn

Mawr, the youthful closeness and self-sufficiency of the Hamilton sisters and their cousins, as well as their intellectual qualities, posed barriers to marriage. The Hamilton sisters had suitors but, as Edith saw during her summer on Mackinac in 1890, after watching Alice being courted by a Mr. Rowland and Norah by a man identified only as Dave: "I wonder why it is that the men to whom we are attractive should all belong more or less, like Dave, to the genus bore." Clearly Edith felt that neither of these men could match her sisters' intellectual capacities. She told Jessie: "I don't believe there is anyone in the world, outside of my own family, whom I want every day in the week."[117] This comment reveals much about not only Edith's but all of her generation of Hamiltons' attitudes toward marriage. Brought up so closely in each other's company, the cousins struggled to develop intimate relationships outside their own family. It was a quality Edith recognized in herself. In the 1920s, she revealed to her friend the drama critic Rosamond Gilder: "I have always been told that I had to know people twenty years before I felt intimate with them."[118] Rosamond would prove one of the few exceptions.

During her years at Bryn Mawr, Edith was aware of her feelings for women. She would, on one occasion, declare herself to be in love with another student, and she reflected on her relationship with Sarah even as her romantic feelings for her faded as their lives took different paths. By the end of her years at Bryn Mawr, Edith had identified another potential risk in marriage: the danger of falling out of love. It was prompted by a postgraduation visit to Charles and Sarah Richmond, one that provided Edith with some much-needed rest. The Richmonds were pleasant company, but Edith had lost her attraction for Sarah. As Edith told Alice, "I came nearer to being in love with her than I have with anyone. I used to love to watch her, and every movement and gesture had a charm for me. She is the only person I have ever felt this with, and I hoped I could have again this time."[119] For Edith, the experience of falling out of love became one more drawback to marriage though she realized that this had not been the fate of the Richmonds. Their marriage was dedicated to church work, in which Sarah took an active part.[120] Although Edith acknowledged the Richmonds' dedication to their calling, she recognized that it was Charles Richmond's career that defined the scope of Sarah's activity.

Edith sought more equality in a romantic relationship and became a close observer of some of the romantic friendships that existed among women at Bryn Mawr. The closeness of Lucy and Helen's friendship sometimes made Edith feel excluded from their company. In January 1893, Edith told Jessie, "Instead of being glad over the girls who are fond of me, I am sorry because Lucy and Helen Thomas do not like me as much as I like them. It is always so."[121] Lucy and Helen's closeness emphasized the exclusiveness that often went with romantic friendship. As Edith realized, such feelings often required a painful readjustment if one or the other friend decided to marry. She observed how Margaret Shearman continued to struggle with her feelings for Emma Bailey Speer, as before Emma's marriage she and Margaret had "been each other's most intimate friends."[122] In the examples of romantic friendship she witnessed at Bryn Mawr, Edith saw both risk and reward.

She herself hardly had time to pursue any romantic relationships during her years at college. During her first term at Bryn Mawr she rejected the attentions of Helen Bartlett, a student from England who would later earn her doctorate at the college. This rebuff, however, may have been because Bartlett's attentions coincided with the only time during her college years that Edith professed to have fallen in love. The object of her attraction was Edith Child, who had graduated from Bryn Mawr in 1890 and subsequently worked for a time as Mary Garrett's secretary.[123] She only stayed on campus for a few months after graduation, and Edith's description of her feelings for the other Edith indicates that the two women were most likely never close. Indeed, in her letter to Jessie describing her feelings, Edith got the name of the object of her affection entirely wrong, calling her "Ethel Childs," but nevertheless writing, "I am in love! Hopelessly! Desperately!" But she added: "And I have never even spoken to her!"[124] The fascination with Child, however, was evidently brief. The extravagant language Edith used soon disappeared, and she returned to focusing on her education. The same letter in which she described her feelings for Child devoted almost as much space to her developing intellectual rapport with Dr. Gonzalez Lodge.

Edith's path to achieving a doctorate had crystallized by the summer of 1892. In July, on a visit to Mackinac, she wrote a letter to Jessie outlining her plans for the completion of her education. Montgomery Hamilton had promised Edith two more years at Bryn Mawr, by which time she intended to have both her bachelor's and master's degrees, essential steps to her ultimate goal of earning a doctorate. She confided to Jessie, "I shall never be content until I have my Ph.D."[125] The heady intellectual atmosphere of Bryn Mawr had stimulated her ambition to become a classical scholar, a goal bolstered by the sense of confidence she felt after two years at the college. In the spring of 1892, as she helped to plan a breakfast for the senior class, she felt a "positive happiness" that she had earned "a recognized position in the college," both socially and academically.[126] The Hamilton family's financial resources, however, remained limited, especially since by that summer Edith had also convinced Margaret to study at Bryn Mawr.[127] Bryn Mawr, as Edith told Jessie, required three years' of residence after the bachelor's degree in order to award a doctorate. The year in which Edith studied for her master's would count as one of the years of residence, but she realized that after that she would have to compete successfully for at least one of Bryn Mawr's fellowships in order to pursue her doctorate. The college offered fellowships in both Latin and Greek. It was possible, Edith thought, to win the fellowship in Greek for the first year and the fellowship in Latin the following in order to complete three more years of residence at the college.

Though Edith's academic career would not proceed exactly according to the plan she laid out to Jessie that summer, she would continue to find academic success at Bryn Mawr. During her first two years at the college Edith had been introduced to two approaches to classical studies: the German and the British. The former aimed at philological precision, viewing this as the core of the work of a classical scholar. Its mastery was necessary for obtaining a doctorate in the field. The British aesthetic approach, which emphasized ancient Greece as the source of Western civilization and was the particular interest of Shorey, was popular with Bryn Mawr College students.[128] Its focus on the enduring spirit and ideals of ancient Greece would ultimately prove more attractive to Edith and would help her to form the key themes of her writing on the classical world. Ultimately Edith would find that philology did not interest her and she did not want to complete the philological work required for a doctorate in classics. That summer, however, as Edith aspired to eventually gain one of Bryn Mawr's graduate fellowships, she was still intent on obtaining a doctorate.

Chapter 4

AMONG THE
PHILOLOGICAL GODS

Edith realized that completion of her doctorate meant obtaining at least one, if not two, of Bryn Mawr's fellowships. Following the summer of 1892, she returned to the college determined to compete for one. According to Edith, the fellowships paid all of a student's college expenses as well as a stipend of two hundred dollars.[1] They were an indication of how seriously M. Carey Thomas took the college's commitment to providing graduate education for women. Edith was chiefly focused on achieving the college's highest honor: the Mary E. Garrett European Fellowship, which allowed a student to pursue graduate work abroad for one year.

Her plan to win the European fellowship as she was just beginning her graduate work was an overly ambitious one. Bryn Mawr College students did not receive grades—Edith had at one point hoped to earn a "high credit" in a course on Plato—but the winner of the European fellowship was determined on a points system, where the candidates for the award were ranked numerically.[2] By completing her bachelor's degree in only two and a half years, Edith had made herself unlikely to compete successfully for the fellowship, which generally went to students who had been at the college longer.[3] She wrote Jessie that she felt ungrateful because, in spite of the opportunities she had found in her Bryn Mawr education, she wanted more; in short, she wanted the European fellowship.

Edith welcomed Margaret's arrival on the Bryn Mawr campus in the fall of 1893, and the two sisters roomed near each other in Merion Hall.[4] Margaret took courses taught by the college's eminent geneticist Thomas Hunt Morgan and quickly settled on biology as her major, pairing it with chemistry, and expressing to Agnes a desire to make it her life's work.[5] Margaret's presence, however, was another reminder to Edith of the Hamilton family's mounting tuition expenses, reinforcing her determination to earn a fellowship.

Determined to receive both her bachelor's and her master's degrees in the spring of 1894, as indeed she did, Edith told Jessie that her studies kept her busier than ever. That February she had to pass her senior orals in foreign language, which meant reading and translating by sight portions of French and German in front of six faculty members. Margaret, who walked over to Taylor Hall, the main building on campus, to bring Edith back to their rooms after the exam, was pleased to find her "quiet and collected." Still, Edith spent the afternoon relaxing, drinking chocolate, talking to Margaret Shearman, and reading Mrs. Henry Wood's *East Lynne*, "the trashiest novel she could find."[6] It was a temporary respite, however, since she had to prepare for her master's exams to be held that spring.[7]

In addition to preparing for her senior orals and master's exams, Edith was taking the entire Greek and Latin graduate program as well as undergraduate philosophy. She was concentrating on Latin for her doctorate but was still deeply drawn to the study of Greek, in which she hoped to minor, telling Jessie, "If ever I shall do anything hereafter I sometimes fancy I shall do it in Greek."[8] In spite of her attraction to Greek, the mentorship of Dr. Gonzalez Lodge caused her to take Latin as her major subject for graduate work. In early March, Lodge offered Edith the Fellowship in Latin for the academic year 1894–95.[9] The award would allow her to continue her graduate work at Bryn Mawr free from financial worry. But initially her reaction was disappointment, since he had discussed the possibility of the European fellowship with her the previous week. She understood Lodge's offer of the Latin fellowship as an indication that she would not receive the European one.

FIGURE 6. Edith Hamilton upon her graduation from
Bryn Mawr College in 1894. Photograph courtesy of the
Schlesinger Library, Harvard Radcliffe Institute.

The news of the Latin fellowship did, however, prompt Edith to con-
fide in Lodge her hopes for her future and her commitment to her education. To Lodge's inquiry about her plans, she replied: "I told him that
I meant to teach, and that I could not be more serious than I was in fully
intending to give my life up to that." In response, Lodge repeated a

rumor that she was "a society girl, 'a fashionable young lady', so to speak, who are purposing to take your degree merely from a whim." Such a characterization of Edith may seem patently inaccurate, but throughout her life she wore her scholarship lightly and always retained her sense of humor—aspects of her personality that must have been apparent to her Bryn Mawr contemporaries. Lodge's allegation may also have been a test to see how much she wanted the Latin fellowship.

She responded by telling him "exactly how things were." As she told Jessie, "When I had finished he looked at me very kindly and said, 'Miss Hamilton, I think you will have the Latin Fellowship next year.' So I said 'I know what you mean, Dr. Lodge, and I thank you for telling me', and went away." Shortly after receiving his assurance about her Latin studies, she spent an evening in Taylor Hall, awaiting the announcement of the European fellowship winner. Lodge called down to her from the top of the stairs that it was Mary Breed, a member of the class of 1894, who had majored in biology and chemistry.[10] Lodge was imparting confidential news to Edith, as the winner would not be publicly announced until the next day, further evidence of the bond they shared as mentor and student.

During the year of Edith's Latin fellowship, she and Lodge grew closer, in part because he relied on her as a teaching assistant. On one occasion, she had to administer a Latin exam.[11] At other times, however, she and Lodge socialized with the Bryn Mawr College history professor Charles McLean Andrews and his fiancée Evangeline Walker, a student and friend of Edith's. As Edith knew from her first semester at college, romances between professors and students were forbidden.[12] As a women's college, however, Bryn Mawr could often attract only male professors who were just beginning their careers and who were sometimes still unmarried. Dr. Andrews was, according to Edith, "very young and very good-looking," an estimation shared by other students who referred to him as "the babe."[13] Andrews and Walker married during Edith's year as Latin fellow and moved into a rented house near the campus while they built a house of their own. Edith described to Jessie and Margaret a visit with Lodge, Andrews, and his bride on one beautiful evening in the spring of 1895. The foursome had cake and tea in the afternoon, and, eventually, dinner. When Lodge and Edith returned to campus, Edith had intended to spend the evening studying Greek rhetoricians, but Lodge wanted to continue their conversation. They did so.[14]

Such interaction with Lodge could suggest the beginnings of a romantic relationship, yet there is little sign that Lodge awakened any romantic impulse within Edith. She was grateful for the intellectual interest he showed her. She evidently found that he was prone to enthusiasm on topics, an aspect of his character she initially welcomed, but by the year of her Latin fellowship she merely stated that she "did not specially object" to Lodge's efforts at conversation.[15] Regardless, Edith had already decided that she would not marry, and her focus on her career must have been evident to him.

During her Latin fellowship, Edith began a thesis on Seneca the Younger and his use of the genitive case in his writings.[16] Although she did not find the subject an "inspiring" one, it was certainly not an unusual choice for a graduate student in classics at Bryn Mawr.[17] A demonstration of philological knowledge was necessary for earning a doctorate in the field. Edith's friend Nan Emery, for example, was granted hers in 1896 on the basis of a work titled *The Historical Present in Early Latin*.[18] Even if she eventually wearied of the philological study of Seneca's works, Edith would always remain drawn to the Stoic philosopher, the tutor and friend of the Emperor Nero, who had nevertheless ordered his suicide.[19] She may have been drawn to Seneca because Edward Caird had particularly valued Stoicism as representing an advance in the spiritual growth of humanity through one of its paradoxes: Stoicism's emphasis on individual reflection prompted greater realization of the common bond of all humanity.

Moreover, the Stoics had believed that every individual, free or enslaved, was capable of envisioning the highest good.[20] Edith would mention Seneca in three of her books, most notably in *The Roman Way* as "the best exposition there is in Latin of the Stoic doctrine."[21] Although the philological study of Seneca may not have been intellectually stimulating, it produced an abiding admiration for the philosopher. Of more immediate importance, her year as a Latin fellow allowed her to compete once again for the European fellowship, this time successfully.

Edith was awarded the Mary E. Garrett Fellowship for the year 1895–96.[22] As was customary at Bryn Mawr, she was given the news the night before the winner was announced publicly. The faculty always met on a Monday evening near the end of March to decide the winner. The night before the fellowship was to be announced, curious Bryn Mawr students watched the doors of the likely candidates' rooms to catch sight of the messenger bringing word to the recipient. Edith believed that the award was likely to go to one of two other fellows, Frances Hardcastle in mathematics or Helen Shute in Teutonic philology. Edith, who savored the dramatic aspects of the ritual by which Bryn Mawr conferred its highest academic honor, shared the joyous news with Margaret Shearman, who then became "so afraid she would let people know that she assumed a terribly melancholy look, and made everyone suspect something. It was rather terrible in chapel next morning, as you can imagine. But on the whole yesterday was a beautiful day to remember."[23]

That final spring at Bryn Mawr, Edith filled her letters from college with references to the beauty of campus, although the news from home marred her happiness. Uncle Andrew Holman had died suddenly on May 9, 1895. Additionally, Edith was also beginning to feel unwell. The long hours of study needed to complete both a bachelor's and a master's in four years had taken their toll, and she began to experience pain in her side. Upon consulting a doctor, she was informed that the pains were "neuralgic"—nervous—and that she could continue working at her studies without endangering her health.[24] Ultimately it was discovered that a large but benign growth, initially feared to be an ovarian tumor, was developing. It would have to be surgically removed that summer once she had left Bryn Mawr as a student for the last time, having graduated with both her bachelor's and master's degrees the year before.[25]

Edith had initially hoped to study in Paris, a further indication of her literary rather than philological interests.[26] Winners of the European fellowship, however, had to have their plans of study approved by the Bryn Mawr faculty, who considered Germany, not France, the center for the study of classical philology. Edith's initial attraction to France was due to the experiences of Lucy and Helen, who had spent time at Leipzig during the summer of 1894 but found the experience unsatisfying intellectually.[27] But the influence of M. Carey Thomas and Paul Shorey, who had both attended the University of Leipzig, pointed Edith toward that institution, in spite of its reputation for a precise philological approach that Edith's college friends had rejected.

Alice's decision to join her in her year of study abroad also dictated the choice of Leipzig. Alice had graduated from the University of Michigan's medical school in 1893.[28] After two internships, as well as a period of laboratory work again at the University of Michigan, she had decided to accompany Edith to Germany to study pathology. The sisters spent the spring of 1895 searching for a university that would accept them both. German universities in the 1890s still did not allow women to matriculate. An American woman who wished to study at a German university had to correspond with individual professors, asking for permission to attend lectures. While some professors were inclined to accept female students, others were not, and the climate of German universities could be overtly hostile to women. In November 1895, one month after Edith and Alice arrived in Germany, Heinrich von Treitschke, the well-known historian at the University of Berlin, angrily ordered some women students to leave his lecture hall. Although he later apologized publicly, it was not for expelling the students, but for using profane language in doing so.[29] The incident inspired a public debate in Germany on the question of women's admission to the universities. Nevertheless, German women remained excluded from their own institutions of higher learning until 1900.[30] American women, however, were permitted to enter universities as auditors. Although finding an institution that would grant her a degree could be difficult, she could, as an auditor, have access to the same quality of education as men.[31]

Edith was admitted to lectures at Berlin, but Alice was not, and the two sisters settled on Leipzig, where they could both study.[32] The university was home to such "philological gods" (as Edith referred to them) as professors Otto Ribbeck, an expert on Roman poetry, and Karl Brugmann, a comparative philologist.[33] Even before embarking for Germany, Edith was already showing an inclination to move away from philological scholarship and toward the intellectual and moral qualities of classical texts. A paper that she wrote in the spring of 1895 on the topic of the "opinions of ancient writers on Thucydides" gave her pleasure even though she described it to Jessie as "something rather trivial and dilettante & unphilological, and altogether adapted to a non-scholarly mind."[34]

Before she would commence her overseas studies, Edith underwent an operation in Ann Arbor, during which it was discovered that the benign growth inside her had fortunately not affected any of her internal organs.[35] In the close-knit Hamilton family, the June operation was an occasion for great anxiety. Reflecting on the impending operation, Agnes wrote, "We don't realize it at all. We think of other things. It only hangs over us like a great weight, indefinite and obscure."[36] Ten days later, however, she recorded the arrival of a telegram stating that the operation was over and had been successful. After a summer spent recuperating on Mackinac, Edith and Alice sailed for Germany on October 5, 1895.[37]

Edith's months at Leipzig that autumn were filled first with elation at attending the lectures of well-known philologists and then gradual disillusionment, similar to that felt by Lucy and Helen, at German interest in linguistic precision, not in classical thought, as the foundation of Western civilization. During her first months at the university, Edith pursued the unique opportunity she had been given with enthusiasm, telling Jessie that she would "get up at seven, dress and swallow with speed a roll and a cup of coffee" in order to arrive at the campus by eight.[38] By December, however, she informed Jessie that her "reverence for German learning does not increase with familiarity." The largely aesthetic ambience of Bryn Mawr had not completely prepared her for German scholarly interest in determining precise answers to such questions as "if the Spartans took part in the Olympic games first in 776 or 734." Such questions, she continued, "have their place, but that place is, I hold, a big folio in a library and not a lecture room. My lectures are so dull! I did think in Bryn Mawr days that it was bad to have a lecture on the correct way of spelling Aeschylus's brother's name, when Aeschylus never had a brother, but that is very mild compared to what must be endured here."[39] Despite this disillusionment, Edith continued to work on a thesis even as she once more considered attending lectures at the

University of Berlin. It was not unusual for American women studying at German universities to begin a thesis at one institution and then search for a university that would grant a degree based on the work. Nor was it unusual for students in Germany to move frequently from one university to another, as Montgomery Hamilton had done thirty years earlier.[40]

Edith's dissatisfaction with the teaching offered by Leipzig's philologists, coupled with Alice's discovery in December that, as a woman, she would not be permitted to participate in postmortem work, caused the sisters to decide to leave the university. That month, they planned to spend a week in Dresden, which Edith was naturally curious to see.[41] She ranked her day in the city's art museum, the Dresden Gallery, as one of her "pleasantest experiences in Germany." She still hoped to go to the University of Berlin and the sisters spent two days there in January 1896, interviewing with professors in the hopes that both could gain admission to lectures. They were unsuccessful, however, and returned to Leipzig by January 18, in time to witness the celebrations of the twenty-fifth anniversary of German unification and the establishment of the German Empire under the first Kaiser Wilhelm.[42]

Through January 1896, Edith devoted her time "chiefly to thesis and general cramming."[43] She still hoped to find a university that would accept her work. But in March 1896, the sisters went to Frankfurt am Main, where Alice had been given the opportunity to work in the laboratory of the neurologist Dr. Ludwig Edinger. Alice found the work satisfying, but Edith was not attending lectures in Frankfurt, and when she was successful in obtaining entrance to the University of Munich the sisters decided to spend the late spring and summer there.[44]

It was Edith's request to study classics that led her to become known as the first woman to be admitted to the university when she finally entered it that May.[45] It is true that she was, in fact, the first woman to be formally admitted to the University of Munich, meaning that she was not simply an auditor and that, had she continued her studies there, she could have been granted the doctorate. It was an achievement that would be discussed periodically over Edith's long life but one in which the distinction between attending the university and actually being granted formal admission was lost. There was a history of women auditing classes at the University of Munich, as Edith and others had done at Leipzig. In fact, Edith's former Denbigh Hall neighbor, the Norwegian-born historian Agnes Wergeland, had studied history as an auditor at the University of Munich ten years before Edith's admission.[46] Certainly her formal admission was an achievement that Edith valued and for which she received warm approval at the time. As a student at Bryn Mawr, she had been part of a culture that celebrated women's intellectual achievements and women's "firsts." M. Carey Thomas, upon hearing of Edith's admission, responded, "I was very much interested in your account of your reception at Munich and congratulate you very sincerely on triumphing over all the lions in your path."[47] Edith's accomplishment was well known enough on the Bryn Mawr campus that another classics student from the college, Winifred Warren, also a winner of the European fellowship, quickly followed her there later in 1896.[48] Ultimately, Edith's admission had a larger impact, since the University of Munich became one of the most popular of the German universities among American women studying in the country.[49]

Edith's status as the first woman admitted to the University of Munich was only one story about her German experience that circulated widely on the Bryn Mawr campus during her time abroad, when she continued to correspond with college friends such as Helen Thomas and Dr. Gonzalez Lodge. Another was that during her classes Edith had to sit in a chair on the lecturer's platform so that she would not come into any contact with the theology students. This condition of her class attendance seems to have prevailed early in her time at the university, though she was later permitted to sit with the other American students in the class and to share manuscripts with them.[50]

Edith found the University of Munich's approach to the study of classics more congenial than that of Leipzig. The institution had a unique relationship to modern Greece. It had been Otho, son of Bavaria's King Ludwig I, who had assumed the Greek throne when Greece had emerged as an independent state at the conclusion of its nineteenth-century revolution. Although Otho had been overthrown in 1862, scholars at the University of Munich had been firm supporters of Greek freedom and

FIGURE 7. An undated photograph of Edith Hamilton.
Photograph courtesy of the Schlesinger Library, Harvard
Radcliffe Institute.

architects of the developing Greek state, helping to design its education
and legal systems. Scholarship at Munich had demonstrated that the
struggles and achievements of Greece's classical past were relevant to
the nineteenth century, as Greece developed into a stable constitutional
monarchy under the Danish-born prince, who accepted the title King

of the Hellenes when he became King George I in 1863.[51] This concentration on the endurance of ancient Greek ideas accounts for Alice's assertion that "Edith found the Munich professors of the classics more interesting than those in Leipzig."[52] Still, the classics faculty was committed to philological study, organized on the basis of seminars, the nineteenth-century term for academic departments.[53]

Edith also found a more congenial social atmosphere as her presence on the campus gradually became less of a novelty. As at Leipzig, fraternities, each with its own coat of arms, played a prominent role in student social life.[54] Edith even received an invitation from a fraternity to what would be one of her most memorable experiences at Munich, a chance to attend a Salamander Reiben, the festival to celebrate the new spring beer. Initially, Edith felt she must refuse, but a faculty member's wife encouraged her to accept, promising that her husband and father would accompany her. Edith's letters from Germany indicate that she and Alice enjoyed witnessing the celebrations of the university students even though these tended to reinforce the inequality and separation of the sexes in German society. In Leipzig, Edith and Alice were allowed to observe the celebration of the twenty-fifth anniversary of German unification but only from the galleries of the university's great hall.

Student celebrations were only one means by which Edith and Alice gauged the social status of German women. Both made observations about the difficulties endured by German women, especially those who could not marry because they lacked a dowry. Such women could rarely obtain an education that would allow them to support themselves. In Munich, Edith learned that German women had recently protested against a new law that had tightened a father or husband's control over a dependent woman's earnings. "The protest," Edith told Jessie, "states that Turkish women have more property rights than men."[55] Alice recalled that during their year in Germany they were sometimes forced to step off the sidewalk and into the street if they encountered a group of students, who generally walked in groups with their arms locked.[56] Beginning with her year in Germany, Edith became a keen observer of the status of women in the various countries she visited, including Japan, China, and Greece.

The beauty of the city of Munich, and the progress that Edith felt she had made in her studies there, made her reluctant to contemplate the return to the United States. There were many enjoyable moments during her time in Munich, including hours spent in the university's classical philology library, with its tall arched windows that nearly reached the ceiling and a circular stairway leading to a gallery with bookshelves that ran the length of the other three sides of the room.[57] She took a walking tour of the scenic Isenthal Schaftlarn region of Switzerland with a fellow student, Bella Hummel.[58] But chief among the causes of her happiness during these months was the news that her professors believed that with another year of study she would be able to take a doctoral degree with honors at Munich.[59] Such a degree would still have been a rare achievement for a woman at a German university, though 1897—when Edith would have earned hers—was the year in which the Universities of Heidelberg and Goettingen granted the first doctorates in philology to women—both Americans.[60] Though Edith entertained doubts about her interest in philological methods, financial considerations also loomed large as a barrier to finishing her degree.

Edith did not have the funds to remain in Germany another year and therefore, especially during her months in Munich, she considered a professional opportunity that she had accepted before her departure for Germany. In early 1895, several months before learning that she had won the European fellowship, Edith had been offered the position of headmistress of the Bryn Mawr School for Girls in Baltimore.[61] During her time in Germany, Edith considered whether to follow through with this commitment and under what terms. She felt considerable doubt about pursuing it, due to her interest in research and scholarship instead of secondary education and due to the public perception, common at Bryn Mawr College, that the school was not successful. In addition, Edith was reluctant to fulfill her commitment because of the necessity, imposed by those who had offered her the position, of binding herself to it for a period of five years.

Thomas, who led the board of managers of the Bryn Mawr School, wanted to appoint a student who had excelled in classics since the inclusion of this subject in the curriculum of the Bryn Mawr School was a sign of its serious intent in preparing girls for a college education equal to that of men. Laurette and Edith, the two students to whom Thomas first offered the appointment, had majored in at least one of the classical languages and had pursued graduate study in Europe. Both had also served in student government at Bryn Mawr.

In the winter of 1894–95, after Laurette had rejected the position, Thomas, Gwinn, and Garrett offered Edith the appointment of headmistress of the Bryn Mawr School after a short evening interview—Edith estimated it lasted fifteen minutes—at the Deanery.[62] The exact content of the conversation would, in the spring of 1896, become the subject of much disagreement between Edith and the three women who comprised the board of managers of the Bryn Mawr School. It is clear, however, that some of the terms of the offer were discussed with some specificity, including the proposed salary of fourteen hundred dollars a year, to be raised to two thousand dollars if the school continued to grow its enrollment.[63] Thomas later argued that she stated at the interview that the new headmistress was to stay for at least five years; Edith, for her part, would insist that Thomas had spoken only of the need for a permanent head of the school. The position was also described to Edith in a manner indicating that acceptance did not preclude achieving a doctorate. Mamie Gwinn considered it important that Edith have a competent assistant at the school so that she would have the ability "to teach & write & study."[64] Edith's response that winter evening at the Deanery was to ask for a brief period of time to consider the matter.

This would allow her to consult her family, friends, and the classics faculty at Bryn Mawr College. Her inquiries quickly made her aware of the common perception that the school was a failure. Both Dr. Herbert Weir Smyth, who taught Greek, and Dr. Lodge, who graded Latin exams for the school, expressed reservations. Smyth advised her that a teaching position at a western college would be more advantageous.[65] Two of Edith's college friends who were teachers at the school, Bertha Putnam, who taught Latin, and Jane Louise Brownell, the mathematics teacher and aunt of Edith's friend Louise Brownell, warned her that the school had been unsuccessful in attracting students. Nevertheless, seeing few job prospects for herself, Edith returned to the Deanery the following morning where, finding only Thomas and Garrett, she informed them of her decision to accept.[66] She asked, however, that the appointment remain a secret. Edith's decision was based on financial considerations. As early as 1892, when she had first voiced her ambition to obtain a doctorate, she had realized that "teaching in between" the completion of her master's degree and her doctorate might be necessary to fund her education.[67] Edith remained ambivalent and only confided the news to Alice, who expressed her enthusiasm. In asking Alice to temper her delight, Edith explained that the school's future was "still trembling in the balance. And there is a general feeling of insecurity about it."[68] In addition to the reservations expressed by those familiar with the school, Edith also continued to hope for the completion of a doctorate and the attainment of a position as a college professor.

Yet, Edith realized, there might be few prospects awaiting her upon her return from Germany, even with the successful completion of her doctorate. With doubts about the school's future and, more importantly, doubts about her own interest in the position of headmistress, Edith desired to keep the offer a secret, a decision supported by M. Carey Thomas, who advised her to be cautious about informing others. During her time in Germany, Edith wavered. She apparently communicated her hesitation to both Helen Thomas and Dr. Lodge in letters she sent to Bryn Mawr. An alarmed M. Carey Thomas wrote Edith in Germany, asking that she either confirm or deny her reluctance about fulfilling her commitment.[69] In her response to Thomas, Edith spoke frankly: "I remember when I first saw you about the matter telling you that I had always hoped for a college position and looked forward to doing scholarly—not executive—work."[70] Edith's hesitations were several but included her own personal lack of familiarity with secondary education, having only attended Miss Porter's School for a brief time. As she would remind Thomas in their correspondence, she "had been educated at home."[71] Most of all, as she told Thomas in March 1896, she could not imagine committing herself to five years as headmistress.

Her hesitation prompted Thomas and Gwinn in late May to lessen the required commitment from five years to three, but they remained firm in their need for Edith to commit herself definitely to the Bryn

Mawr School for that length of time.[72] Edith hesitated, until she finally cabled back, declaring that she could not commit herself to the school for more than two years.[73] In the meantime, in late April or early May, she had received a more attractive job offer from the Packer Collegiate Institute, an elite girls' school in Brooklyn Heights, New York, whose graduates largely attended Vassar.[74] Yet, feeling bound by her promise to Thomas, Edith refused the position.[75]

Thomas, however, interpreted Edith's acceptance of the position for only two years as tantamount to a refusal and she once again offered it to Laurette Potts.[76] Laurette, however, loyally cabled Edith in Munich to ask if she had indeed decided not to accept the position at the Bryn Mawr School. Laurette confessed to Thomas that as Edith's friend she had already heard of her reluctance to occupy the post, but she assured Thomas that she found it regrettable, "believing as I do that Miss Hamilton was in every way fitted for the management of the School."[77] Laurette determined, however, that she could not accept unless Edith herself told her that she had definitely given it up.

Thomas's renewed offer to Laurette left Edith anxious. She had realized that she needed the position financially. Due to Montgomery Hamilton's alcoholism, the Hamilton sisters were convinced that they could not leave Gertrude alone in Fort Wayne.[78] Edith's solution was to have her parents settle with her in Baltimore, an arrangement dependent on the position at the Bryn Mawr School.[79] Additionally, she saw a path by which the following year she might complete the work for a doctorate. Thomas assured Edith that although the work of administering the school would occupy much of her time in the autumn of 1896, by spring she would have the time to write.[80] At the end of July, Edith wrote a lengthy letter to Thomas, insisting that she had considered herself committed to the Bryn Mawr School all along and on July 21, 1896, she received a telegram from Thomas informing her that she was formally engaged for three years and to plan on arriving in Baltimore by September to begin her work. [81]

Edith had accomplished much during her five years of study at Bryn Mawr College and her year abroad. Bryn Mawr had introduced her to the study of classical literature in the context of a Western tradition and to some of the great British thinkers of the late nineteenth century—John Ruskin, Matthew Arnold, and Edward Caird, among others—whose ideas would suffuse her own writing. Her years as a student, including her studies at Leipzig, had shown her how to conduct philological research, the primary activity of a nineteenth-century classical scholar. As much as she had enjoyed her experience at Munich, where she could have obtained a doctorate, one of her discoveries during her year in Germany was that philological study completely failed to interest her.

Edith's student years ultimately determined that she would be a classicist in the sense of her interest in the spirit of classical thought. Her two years as a graduate student were not sufficient to earn a doctorate. During her first year at the school she continued to work on a thesis and as late as 1899 she asserted that she would earn a doctoral degree the following year, but the cherished goal of earning her PhD was ultimately unfulfilled.[82] Initially committed to the Bryn Mawr School for only three years, she would in fact remain headmistress of the institution for twenty-six. The position that she had been hesitant to accept would offer her an opportunity to consider and enact her own ideas on the intellectual, spiritual, and moral development of the individual, themes apparent in her writing.

Chapter 5

MISS GARRETT'S SCHOOL
FOR GIRLS

The Bryn Mawr School occupied an impressive six-story brick building on a triangular lot at Cathedral and Preston Streets in Baltimore. Both aesthetically and practically, the structure reflected the vision of its founder, Mary Garrett. In 1888, Garrett had commissioned the New York architect Henry Rutgers Marshall to design a building that would reflect the serious purpose of the school: the preparation of its students for college.[1] She had also chosen the site for the new school. As it was constructed, its slender chimneys and terra-cotta roof had risen above a part of the city still largely devoted to coal and lumber yards. The area was noisy and dirty yet still sufficiently close to some of Baltimore's fashionable neighborhoods, from which, it was hoped, the school could draw its students. These included Mount Vernon Place, Baltimore's most exclusive address, and the more modest Bolton Hill, where Edith would live in her second decade as headmistress.[2] The exterior of the new school was striking: sandstone at its base, the highly polished bricks of its upper stories reflected a yellow hue. It had opened in 1890 with a library, a laboratory, and, in its basement, a gymnasium with an indoor swimming pool. Outside, a wide set of six steps led up to the door, with the school's name rendered in mosaic above. Inside, Tiffany lamps lighted the school's wide central stairway, leading up to a large study hall. A set of plaster casts of classical statuary, purchased by

Mary Garrett, adorned the school. On the main stairway, a replica of the Venus de Milo, one of her favorite examples of classical statuary, stood across the landing from a model of a caryatid from the Acropolis's Erechtheum.[3] A plaster copy of the Parthenon frieze occupied all four walls of the school's study hall.

In her first years as headmistress, Edith would have to define the scope of her authority over the school that was still commonly referred to among Baltimoreans as "Miss Garrett's School for Girls." She would have to learn to manage teachers who had been at the school longer than her and address the concerns of parents nervous about giving their daughters a college preparatory education. Most of all, Edith would have to define her educational philosophy in order to provide what the school had lacked: firm guidance by a headmistress who had both practical and moral authority. During her first four years at the school, she had to balance these new responsibilities with her own continuing goal of finishing her thesis and earning her doctorate. These ambitions would remain unfulfilled, however, as the administration of the school consumed her time and as she gradually became drawn into reform movements in Baltimore.[4]

The school, the collective effort of Garrett, Julia Rogers, Elizabeth King, M. Carey Thomas, and Mamie Gwinn, had opened on September 21, 1885, in rented rooms near the Johns Hopkins campus, only days before Bryn Mawr College welcomed its first students.[5] From the beginning, a close relationship existed between the two institutions. The college, especially in the early years of the school's existence, provided qualified teachers for the school, so much so that recruitment of teachers for the Bryn Mawr School was a chief reason for the rise in the number of college-educated women in turn-of-the-century Baltimore.[6] Bryn Mawr College's entrance exam was established as a requirement for graduation from the school, and each year students from the school paid a daylong visit to the Bryn Mawr College campus, often lead by a teacher who had graduated from the college.[7] A scholarship, endowed by and named for Mary Garrett, was to be awarded to a Bryn Mawr School graduate who planned to attend Bryn Mawr College.[8] Most of

FIGURE 8. The Bryn Mawr School about 1896. Photograph courtesy of the archives of the Bryn Mawr School.

all, there was the shared leadership of the two institutions: Thomas was dean and then president of Bryn Mawr College as well as an active member of the school's board of managers.

As Edith had known from the time she was offered the position of headmistress, the school was not successful in its early years.[9] As Mary Garrett had recognized, socially prominent Baltimore families did not see any reason to prepare their daughters for college.[10] The school also suffered from lack of administrative attention, having been under the daily supervision of a secretary with little authority. Four women had occupied this post between 1885 until 1895, when Thomas, having taken on new responsibilities when she succeeded to the presidency of Bryn Mawr College, had finally decided to appoint a headmistress.[11] Edith was made a member of the board of managers, though the extent of her powers still needed to be defined.

Romantic friendships among the five founders had contributed to dissent among the board of managers.[12] Initially, close relationships had existed between Mary Garrett and Julia Rogers and between M. Carey Thomas and Mamie Gwinn. But as Garrett and Thomas grew closer to each other, Julia Rogers dissociated from the school. Rogers and King had both left the board of managers in 1891, five years before Edith's arrival.[13] Mamie Gwinn would leave during the early years of Edith's tenure. When Edith started as headmistress, however, the board of managers resolved to place new emphasis on presenting a united front to students, teachers, and parents in an effort to overcome the divisions that had dogged the school during its early years.[14]

By the time Edith began as headmistress, the school was showing signs that it would prosper after all. Mary Garrett's new building had impressed Baltimore parents, and the primary school, which had started two years before Edith's arrival, was establishing itself.[15] The Johns Hopkins's faculty members supported the girls' preparatory school from the beginning, and in return the school offered reductions in tuition to daughters of the Hopkins faculty.[16] This helped to recruit desirable students while reflecting the close relationship between the school's founders, whose fathers sat on the Hopkins board, and the university. Edith took over a school of one hundred and eleven students, sixty-one of whom (over half) were in the primary department, justifying Thomas's belief that its establishment had helped the school to grow.[17] Still, during her first year as headmistress, Edith found herself combating what she termed "that vague thing called 'a general impression'" that the school was not a success.[18]

Edith's adjustment to Baltimore was aided by Alice, who had decided to study at the Johns Hopkins Medical School. After a search of almost forty boarding houses, the better establishments having already been secured by Hopkins students, they settled into one managed by the Miss Tysons at 1114 McCulloh Street.[19]

Edith's first task, as it would become every year following, was to meet with parents and enroll students. As she quickly learned, potential students were closely examined before admission. Her challenge was to find students who met the many demands of the board of managers. Ideally,

Bryn Mawr School students were supposed to possess the intellectual ability to complete the rigorous curriculum and the moral character that would make them a positive influence on the other students. Preference was given to students from socially prominent families in an effort to make the school more acceptable in Baltimore and because the board of managers wanted to minimize the risk of the school failing financially through inability to collect tuition.[20] Parents had to apply to send their daughters to the school, a process that required an interview.

Mary Garrett's close supervision of her school, coupled with Edith's newness to Baltimore, meant that during her first years as headmistress Edith had to secure Garrett's approval for the admission of new students. She regularly sent applications or lists of names for Garrett to examine.[21] Garrett would often telegraph her reply to Edith, noting those she approved and, on occasion, those whom she wished to be excluded.[22]

In the admission of students, as in almost every other aspect of her role as headmistress, Edith first had to learn the extent of the power Garrett and Thomas were willing to cede to her and then to develop her own admission standards, the enforcement of which helped to build up her own influence over the school. That first September, however, Edith was surprised, given Garrett's scrutiny of the school, that she was entrusted to exercise some of her own judgment.[23]

September 23, 1896, was the first day of school over which Edith presided as headmistress. She could tell Mary Garrett that "it was very pleasant to me personally to see the children and find them so generally attractive in appearance and manner."[24] It also began Edith's relationship with the teachers, one area where her experience as a student government leader was helpful. Some of the teachers who had been at the school much longer than her were accustomed to their own routines. Clara Oldham, who taught Latin and history, and Olga Schroeder, who taught Greek and German, did not feel that the presence of the more senior teachers should be required on the first day of school. Wisely, Edith decided not to press the matter.

Edith's ability to assert her authority over the faculty was inhibited by an old practice of the board of managers, which had apparently been in the habit of promising concessions to favored teachers. The English teacher Mary Hoyt, as well as Schroeder and Oldham, all insisted that they had been excused from the duty of monitoring the school's large study hall.[25] Five months into her tenure as headmistress, Edith felt compelled to explain to Schroeder that she had to take her part in recess duty and was relieved by Schroeder's reasonable response.[26] Gradually, Edith's relations with the older teachers improved.[27] Her recognition of the teachers' individual talents won her their respect and their support in dealing with the other members of the board of managers on their behalf.

Edith was sensitive to the needs of teachers as well. The Bryn Mawr School's teachers worked long hours for salaries that were raised only in cautious increments. Edith tried to ensure that the teachers would feel that their hard work and dedication was acknowledged and re-warded. In her first spring Edith tried—unsuccessfully—to secure raises for two of the teachers, arguing that it "would make them feel that their faithful work this year had been appreciated, and would give them a stimulus for their work next year."[28] Edith also tried to limit the num-ber of classes a teacher taught each week and argued that variations in teaching loads disrupted the harmony of the school and prevented all the teachers from working effectively together.[29] And while the board of managers tended to value certain instructors above others, Edith carefully observed the work of all the teachers, one of her efforts that increased the faculty's trust in her leadership.

There would be only one lingering misunderstanding between Edith and the board of managers concerning the admission of students and the hiring of teachers: the status of Jews at the Bryn Mawr School. Edith encountered a lingering impression among Baltimore's Jewish families that the Bryn Mawr School was at best reluctant to accept their daughters, a legacy of an article in a Baltimore Jewish newspaper in 1890 charging that the school had a quota system. The admission of Jewish students was a delicate subject between Edith and her employers in the early years of her tenure. It was also a subject that divided the board of managers, with Thomas believing that sharp limits should be imposed while Garrett was more willing to admit Jews.[30] As Edith asserted herself in the matter of admissions, she sought—but never received—a clear response from the board of managers on whether Jewish students were permitted to enter the school.

Edith was anxious to please her employers and would therefore follow their policies whenever these were clearly stated. There is evidence, however, that she did not share their reservations about Jewish students since she did not share the board's objections to hiring Jewish teachers, a question that would prove to be a greater source of contention between Edith and the rest of the board.[31] Since the much larger, and more openly stated, barrier to hiring Jewish teachers was eventually overcome, at least by the end of Edith's tenure at the school, it seems likely that the prejudice against admitting Jewish students was overcome as well, probably at an earlier date.

It is clear that Edith did not share the board's prejudices against the hiring of Jewish teachers, and the explanation for her tolerance lay, once again, in the philosophy of Edward Caird. Caird emphasized the essential unity of humanity while arguing that humans underwent a process of development in which their religious ideas evolved.[32] While Christianity was the apex of this evolution, Caird's idealism acknowledged the value of the religious beliefs that had preceded it. Edith therefore did not distinguish Jews from the rest of humanity and saw the essential connection between their religion and her own. "Jews and Christians have the same foundation—not a creed, but conduct, and the Lord our God, the Lord is one," she would later write to a Jewish friend, Edith J. R. Isaacs, the editor of *Theatre Arts Monthly* magazine.[33] Edith Hamilton could not share the prejudices of her employers even if, as a practical matter, she had to defer to their wishes.

Gradually, however, Edith established her own procedures for hiring teachers. After less than a year as headmistress, she determined that she could not hire any teacher without a personal interview.[34] She also tried, whenever possible, to observe a teacher in the classroom before offering them a job. She established a policy of consulting Frances Karr before making any new appointments, a recognition of Karr's responsibilities as head of the primary department and her expertise in the field of childhood education.[35] While teachers without a college degree could be hired for the primary department, this was not the case for the main school, where a college degree was considered essential. The only exceptions were for instructors in German and French, subjects in which there was a perceived advantage in hiring native speakers. Edith often studied lists of recent Bryn Mawr College graduates, looking for potential teachers. Many of the graduates she remembered from her own years at Bryn Mawr, giving her additional insight into their potential as teachers. She wanted bright, dependable women whose personalities would be attractive to students.[36]

Edith's hiring standards meant that, on occasion, she had to oppose candidates M. Carey Thomas particularly wanted. When, in the spring of 1899, Thomas pressed the candidacy of a Bryn Mawr College student whom she particularly liked, Edith found a tactful way to express her reservations and then frankly asked the board to determine who had the responsibility of hiring teachers: herself or the board of managers as a whole.[37] A policy emerged gradually, one that gave Edith control over the hiring of teachers.

For Edith, the Bryn Mawr School faculty provided some of her first friendships in the city. One of the longest was with the school's doctor, Mary Sherwood, who had directed its gymnasium since 1894. Mary Garrett was particularly eager to refute criticisms that education damaged a daughter's health, and the school had employed a doctor from the time it was founded.[38] During Edith's first year at the school, she discovered that many Baltimoreans were still convinced that studying was bad for their daughter's health. As Edith pondered how to challenge this assumption, she welcomed Sherwood's wise counsel. Edith's relationships with the members of the board were more varied. During her first years at the school, Edith continued to enjoy frequent trips to Bryn Mawr College, where she sometimes had lunch at the Deanery.[39] The main sources of tension between Edith and Thomas were Edith's lack of knowledge of financial matters and Thomas's occasional reluctance to relinquish control over the school. Thomas did realize, however, that for Edith to be successful in establishing her leadership over the school, open communication between the headmistress and the board of managers was necessary. For her part, Edith continued to see Thomas as a highly effective leader of Bryn Mawr College, especially as the campus expanded in 1902, with the construction of a new dormitory, Rockefeller Hall, built with gifts from that family, and a new library, eventually to be named after Thomas.[40]

In Edith's early years as headmistress, Mary Garrett was still intimately involved in the school she had founded. Edith consulted Garrett about supplies and decor, and Garrett even visited the school to see to the positioning of a new cabinet two teachers needed.[41] Garrett still had a considerable amount of money invested in the school, and she watched its bills carefully, on one occasion expressing alarm about the amount of the water bill, to which Edith responded by promising to watch the water use more carefully.[42] With Garrett, who still lived in her large house on Monument Street, only blocks from the Bryn Mawr School, Edith enjoyed a warmer, more personal relationship than with Thomas. She occasionally went for drives in Garrett's carriage, and she eventually joined the Arundell Good Government Club, of which Garrett, along with Sherwood and her partner Dr. Lilian Welsh, was a member.[43]

In her supervision of students, Edith also moved quickly to establish her authority over the school. In its early years, the students had simply petitioned the board of managers for redress of any concerns, a practice Edith was determined to stop. A petition she received in December 1896 caused her to remark to Mary Garrett, "It seems to me rather a pity that the children should be so intimately acquainted with the workings of the school."[44] The board was happy to allow Edith to put a stop to the practice.[45] Thus Edith established herself as head of the school, the mediator between the students and the board, and an authority who had to be consulted first before any resolution could be adopted.

Edith gradually accustomed herself to the routines of the school. She soon found that on a typical day her duties included making sure that all the rooms in the school were at the same temperature, showing a student how to plan her hours of study, inspecting the kitchen to make sure it was being properly cleaned, and listening to the sixth class's geometry lesson.[46] During her first term, she told Jessie that "most of the time it seems the perfectly natural thing to be interviewing teachers, and having corrective talks with the girls, and consulting with parents."[47]

The only part of the school's schedule she disliked was the teachers' meeting, which always took up most of the afternoon of the last Friday of the month. During the meetings, she told Jessie in December 1896, "nearly every girl in the school is brought up and discussed and it lasts hours, and one is half dead at the end of it."[48]

That monthly meeting notwithstanding, Edith's success as headmistress was evident even before her first school year ended. In February 1897, M. Carey Thomas told Edith's friend Nan Emery that the "school is in a far better condition than ever before, Miss Hamilton having done for it just what those of us who knew her felt sure she would."[49] Despite her success and the demands of the position, Edith still hoped to complete her doctorate and teach at a college. She still moved firmly in the Bryn Mawr College orbit, frequently taking the train up to the campus for board meetings, which Thomas often preferred to hold on Sunday afternoons. She also became chair of the Academic Committee of the Bryn Mawr Alumnae that helped to choose the fellows for the following academic year, and she still socialized with Lucy and Helen, both of whom had become instructors in English composition at the college.[50] She also saw Dr. Gonzalez Lodge on his visits to the school. These activities reminded Edith of her own scholarly aspirations, to which leading the Bryn Mawr School sometimes paled in comparison intellectually. In her first term as headmistress, she described her position to Jessie by writing, "It is pleasant work and has ceased now to be appalling." She cited her concern, however, that her position "does tire the mind without giving it any food, and that is the sad part of it." She confided to Jessie that "I doubt if I am fit for anything better, if I ever could have made anything approaching a scholar, but I should like to have tried."[51]

Edith hoped to write a thesis during the summer of 1897, which she spent on Mackinac Island. After commencement she went directly to Bryn Mawr College for a board of managers meeting and to help Margaret, who was graduating, pack up her room. She then journeyed to Fort Wayne, where she found Montgomery Hamilton seriously ill, a condition that delayed her departure for Mackinac by a week. By the end of June, however, she and Quint had opened the Mackinac house for the family; as Edith wrote Jessie, "we are all settled now and the summer looks cozy and quiet and pleasant. I am going to try and write a thesis, but I feel more than doubtful as to succeeding."[52] The summer passed pleasantly, if not productively. There were the usual excursions to Arch Rock for sketching or letter-writing, but there was no progress on her thesis. Edith told Jessie that she found herself more exhausted by the school year than she had expected. Over the course of the summer, she had "given up all work." She told Jessie: "I do not think of doctor's degrees, and I am utterly and absolutely lazy."[53]

Somehow, during Edith's early years at the Bryn Mawr School, the resolution to obtain a doctorate slipped away. The workload of administering the school undoubtedly played a large part in her losing sight of her original goal: upon her arrival on Mackinac in June she had found sixty-three letters concerning the school awaiting her reply. With dismay she told Jessie, "I had never thought of being busy at the school work during the summer."[54] Her tasks included answering many requests for the school's catalogue and distributing the list of summer reading to the students.[55] Gradually she realized that the work of administering the school and the life of a scholar were as incompatible as she had feared they might be during her time in Germany. A larger barrier to Edith's completion of a doctorate, however, was subject matter. A dissertation in classics at Bryn Mawr College was an exercise in philological study, an aspect of classical scholarship Edith had never found intellectually satisfying.

Another barrier to finishing her doctorate arose as Edith assumed the responsibility of caring for Margaret and Norah, who both suffered periods of ill health during her first years in Baltimore. Margaret's decision in 1899 to settle in the city, where she soon started work at the Bryn Mawr School, kept Edith there as well.[56] Having failed to complete a doctorate and having devoted herself to family responsibilities, Edith signed a new one-year contract with the board of managers in 1899, renewable annually, and in 1902 she committed herself to two more years.[57] In the 1890s the slow ebbing away of the desired goal must have been a source of frustration: the intellectual life of a university scholar had been Edith's stated aim since before she had entered college. It was a life to which both she and her family felt she would have been well suited. Nevertheless, only Alice and Quint would spend any part of their careers as professors. It was a loss, as Norah commented, "I think Edith and several of us, would have liked university life—it seems to fit into the ways of our youth."[58]

In the autumn of 1897, with no progress made on the thesis, Edith returned to Baltimore alone. Alice had accepted a position teaching pathology at the Women's Medical School of Northwestern University in Chicago and had secured living quarters at Jane Addams's Hull House.[59] Edith did not return to the Miss Tysons after M. Carey Thomas and Mary Garrett told her that she ought to live "on a more fashionable street" than McCulloh.[60] She did not welcome having to move, but the board of managers had given her an extra stipend of four hundred dollars so she could rent quarters that would include a sitting room where she could receive visitors. In return, this meant that she would have to secure the acceptance of the board to any living arrangements she made for herself. Ultimately, Edith was happy to settle into a boarding house run by a Miss DuBois that was conveniently located at the corner of Centre and Cathedral Streets, from which she could walk to the Bryn Mawr School.[61] With Alice gone, Edith was surprised to discover that she felt "desperately forlornly lonely," having always believed, she told Jessie, that she was very independent.[62]

Edith began an ever more deliberative search for an overarching philosophy and system of discipline for the school. Her own education had been on an individual basis, a mix of Montgomery Hamilton's tutoring supplemented by some instruction from others in foreign languages. Miss Porter's School had produced lasting friendships, but in educational terms its value as a model for Edith was limited. The Bryn Mawr School, with its exams and team sports, provided a much more competitive environment than Miss Porter's School had allowed. What she lacked was a well-defined educational philosophy.

Edith realized a headmistress must impose her personality on a school. Through this, she could articulate a clear educational philosophy and communicate expectations about behavior and academic achievement. The Bryn Mawr School was still in its experimental stage, and it was one of Edith's duties to visit other schools to learn about potentially useful practices and to share the Bryn Mawr model. She did not always find the task fulfilling.[63] In late 1898 or early 1899, however, Edith was inspired after a visit to Chicago's Dewey School and a meeting with its founder, the philosopher John Dewey.

The opportunity came on a visit to Alice, when Edith also met Jane Addams and observed life at Hull House. Edith met Dewey at what was officially called the Laboratory School of the University of Chicago, which was better (and more appropriately) known as the Dewey School. The philosopher, who was head of the university's Department of Philosophy, Psychology, and Education, had made the establishment of the experimental school a condition of taking an appointment at the University of Chicago.[64] The school, only in existence from 1896 until 1903, served as a testing ground for his educational theories. By the time of Edith's visit, Dewey had had enough opportunity to observe the results of his work that he had begun the revision of some of his ideas; he would publish his work *The School and Society* the following summer. His school was intended to be a model of progressive education. It had regular visiting hours, as it routinely welcomed administrators and teachers from other schools.[65] Edith found herself "somewhat fired," by her visit to the school and "a long talk with Professor Dewey."[66] She even recommended to the members of the Bryn Mawr School's board of managers that Frances Karr, head of the primary department, visit the Dewey School as well.[67]

Edith never expressly stated what educational ideas she gleaned from Dewey, despite the evidence of her enthusiasm for him. Some of Edith's changes to the Bryn Mawr School, however, suggest what she adopted from him. The philosopher envisioned a school as a community, one that helped students to develop character as they interacted with others, especially as they worked at problem-solving with their fellow students.[68] The key was to balance the need for individual development with the sense of community. While Edith's favorite philosopher Edward Caird believed that as individuals strived for self-consciousness they grew in their understanding of God's unity, Dewey believed in individual self-realization, and he hoped that his school provided the appropriate conditions for the individual to achieve it.[69]

The similarities in the two men's ideas were not coincidental, as the two men were acquainted with each other.[70] Caird's self-consciousness was more rooted in religious experience than Dewey's self-realization, but both men stressed the development of the individual as they learned to interact with society. Indeed, the balance between the individual and humanity would become an essential component of her sense of "mind and spirit," the balance she believed that only the ancient Greeks had successfully achieved but for which all societies since had unsuccessfully strived.[71]

Edith found much to admire in Dewey's concept of self-realization, which shifted the emphasis of education away from teachers and pedagogical practice and toward the development of the individual student. To Dewey, self-realization was the fulfillment of an individual's capacities, helping them to find satisfaction and happiness in life. In growing toward self-realization the individual developed morally and intellectually as they learned to assume responsibilities by making choices. Growth was a lifelong process as the individual encountered new experiences, making their surrounding environment the key to self-realization. To Dewey, the environment could constitute the natural world or aesthetic or intellectual experience, but all helped to form the individual. School, as one community that the individual encountered early in life, could aid in its students' development toward self-realization. Dewey therefore envisioned a school as a community where, through interaction with others, the individual both developed and aided in the development of others. At school, the student would encounter a community's values and would go on to reaffirm and share those values with the community.[72] Due to her meeting with Dewey, Edith wanted to establish at Bryn Mawr a system of discipline with few rules and few penalties, meant to encourage individual character development, as a student learned to govern herself.[73]

In fact, Edith readily adapted Dewey's vision of the school as a community developing individuals to her ideal of ancient Athens. She believed that when it came to education, the Greeks had focused on the individual. Ancient Athens had provided the context for the indivdual's pursuit of intellectual inquiry, a process that also allowed for their moral growth, as demonstrated in Plato's dialogues in which Socrates was the chief speaker. Character development was an essential component of classical conceptions of education.[74] Dewey had demonstrated how it might be applied in practical terms.

To Edith, the Bryn Mawr School became comparable to the fifth-century Athens of Pericles where, according to Thucydides, a society of individuals was bound together not only by their patriotism but by the shared goal of pursuing the common good and by their willingness to serve their society.[75] Even in the conclusion of *The Greek Way*, Edith argued that modern American society was struggling to balance the claims of the individual versus those of the community, a balance that the ancient Greeks had accomplished.[76] Dewey gave her a conception of school that fit her own predispositions toward individuality and helped her to balance the seemingly rival claims of individual development and classroom education, of which she herself had had so little experience.

Even before her visit to the Dewey School, Edith had begun crafting her system of discipline at the Bryn Mawr School. It not only relied on students learning to govern themselves but also on the teachers' ability to exercise a strong presence in the classroom. Edith found that not all were able to do so. She determined a teacher's ability to control her class by careful observation. In December 1898 she told Garrett that a new science teacher, a Bryn Mawr College graduate, held promise as an instructor but had trouble maintaining discipline in her classes. Edith showed her power of perception, however, writing Garrett that the teacher's difficulties were due to "her extreme self distrust. But as she feels herself succeeding in her teaching this diminishes, and she holds her classes better."[77] The school as a community could help teachers as well as students to achieve self-realization.

It was an interplay of mutual benefits with which she was familiar. Edith's interactions with students came not only in her role as headmistress but as a teacher as well. Her contracts specified that she was head of the school's classics department and would teach Latin as well as lead the school.[78] Edith took the senior Latin class, which focused on reading the *Aeneid* of Vergil. Teaching the most advanced students in the school meant that Edith could partly avoid teaching grammar and drill, both of which were taught in the lower levels of Latin.[79] Edith did teach some grammar—early in her career at the school she complained to Jessie of needing "a holiday from moods and tenses."[80] But she must have preferred teaching the senior Latin class, where the students were encouraged to read and understand Latin literature for its beauty and meaning. Edith would later call Vergil "Rome's greatest poet" and "one of the world's greatest romanticists."[81] Those in senior Latin class would always have the opportunity to get to know their headmistress personally, since Edith's classes were small, especially in her early years as headmistress, when the school's graduating classes were made up of only a few students. Ethel Browne, later Harvey, of the class of 1902, remembered her enjoyment of being one of four senior Latin students who met in the intimate setting of Edith's first-floor office for class.[82] Though a rigorous class, Edith's students found she brought Vergil to life.[83]

They also remembered Edith's spiritual influence. From 1901, Edith established the practice of inviting older students to her home one afternoon a week. A portion of these afternoons was clearly devoted to reading the Bible, as Emilie Packard of the class of 1904 referred to them as "Bible afternoons," when, from Edith, she learned "an entirely new conception of the Bible."[84] Likely Edith introduced some of her Bryn Mawr School students to the biblical criticism she had learned in her youth. Within ten years of assuming the leadership of the Bryn Mawr School, Edith was already leaving a strong impression on the graduating classes of the early 1900s.

The wider world of education took notice. During Edith's first years as headmistress, she received offers to lead other schools. As Norah and Margaret entered periods of ill health at the turn of the century, Edith became conscious of how much more she could earn if she could be paid in part from some of the school's profits. Northeastern boarding schools were especially profitable and northern schools in general paid higher salaries than those offered in Baltimore. The first offer from another school came in January 1899. Edith used the offer as a bargaining chip, one that allowed her to argue for both a higher salary and a more secure future, since it prompted her to ask the board to make an early decision about the renewal of her contract.[85] In truth, she was reluctant to leave Baltimore, telling Garrett that she planned to look for an apartment—rather than a boarding house—to live in for the following year, therefore indicating that her plans were to make her life in the city more comfortable and permanent. Edith's decision to stay was reinforced by Margaret, who later that year settled permanently in Baltimore and almost immediately began teaching at the Bryn Mawr School.[86]

A more significant opportunity seemed to present itself in 1900, when Edith learned that she was under consideration for the deanship of Barnard College, a position for which her friend Susan Walker, the founder of student government at Bryn Mawr College, who had become an administrator at Barnard, had apparently recommended her.[87] Barnard had just begun to transform from a women's annex into one of the colleges of Columbia University under the leadership of its first dean, Emily James Smith Putnam, an acquaintance of Edith's. Upon Putnam's resignation, Columbia President Seth Low had to search for a new dean of Barnard.[88] Sadly, the offer of an interview coincided with the illness of Norah, which demanded much of Edith's attention. Norah's condition prevented Edith from making the journey from Fort Wayne to New York City.

By 1901 the Bryn Mawr School was close to capacity. In five years, Edith had learned how to manage teachers. She had also established a warm but firm relationship with the school's students, creating a community that encouraged their individual talents while providing the structure and guidance that the school had lacked. Devotional exercises, team sports, the annual drawing reception, and the school's newly established literary magazine all gave individual students a chance to pursue personal development while establishing shared traditions for the school. Edith, having considered her educational philosophy in her first years as headmistress, was fully implementing it by the early 1900s. Doris proudly recalled that by the time she entered in 1903 "it was the school for girls in the city."[89] During these first years at the Bryn Mawr School, Edith's old ambition to become a classical scholar slowly ebbed, to be replaced by a newfound conception of herself as an administrator.

It was a role to which she had never aspired, but one in which she excelled. It was not just her aspirations to become a scholar, however, that were delayed. Even as she became an active participant in Baltimore's civic causes and emerged as a local leader in the women's suffrage movement, Edith pushed aside her dreams of becoming a writer.

Chapter 6

"A RAZOR TO SHARPEN A LEAD PENCIL"

As Edith settled into her role as headmistress of the Bryn Mawr School, she began to form friendships with the single, educated women of Baltimore. These included the school's faculty as well as students at the Johns Hopkins Medical School, including Gertrude Stein. She continued to witness the romantic relationships between women that she had seen as a college student, when she had sometimes considered entering such a relationship herself. Her romantic interest, however, had centered on Lucy Martin Donnelly, whose partnership with Helen Thomas seemed inviolable. During Edith's early years in Baltimore, however, the relationship between Lucy and Helen unraveled, seemingly offering Edith an opportunity to assume the role of Lucy's partner. Lucy, however, would prove unresponsive to Edith's romantic overtures. Still, to Edith, it must have become clear during these years that her romantic interests were focused on women, a common feeling among those with whom she socialized. In Edith's social circle there was only one woman who was not a single, college-educated professional: the society hostess Edith Gittings Reid. Four years older than Edith Hamilton, she was the wife of the Johns Hopkins geology professor Dr. Harry Fielding Reid. Edith's friendship with the Reid family would have a lifelong impact, as their daughter Doris, twenty-eight years younger than Edith Hamilton, was to become Edith Hamilton's romantic partner. Throughout the early 1900s Edith's friendships with women made her consider the challenges of finding professional fulfillment in a society that offered women limited employment opportunities. She often reflected on the potential limits of personal freedom and how to balance independence with family responsibilities.

During Edith's first year in Baltimore, she and Alice enjoyed a brief friendship with an English boarder on McCulloh Street, Bonte Amos, who was spending six weeks studying physiology at the Johns Hopkins Medical School.[1] She had come to America with a family friend, the English philosopher Bertrand Russell, and his wife, Alys Pearsall Smith, the cousin of Helen Thomas.[2] At age twenty-two, Bonte was seven years younger than Edith, and although her friendship with the Hamilton sisters was brief, her intelligence, her free thinking, and her ability to travel widely made a deep impression on Edith.[3] Moreover, through her own connections to Bryn Mawr College, Edith soon became acquainted with some of the ideas of the Russells, including their espousal of sexual freedom, or "free love" as it was often termed.

During Bertrand and Alys Russells' 1896 visit to America, Alys spoke at Bryn Mawr College on temperance and suffrage. In a discussion with students after her lecture, however, she suggested that it might be appropriate for a college girl to deceive her mother. Later, Alys also apparently presented a defense of free love. M. Carey Thomas had to act quickly to stop rumors from circulating and to reassure parents that the college did not support any of the more controversial views Alys had voiced.[4]

Edith, as well as Alice and Norah, rejected free love, but Edith, who envied Bonte Amos's freedom of movement and thought, pondered the beliefs of the Russells, especially equality in marriage. Edith questioned the commitment that marriage demanded of women, owing to the plight of her mother, Gertrude, who had stayed with an alcoholic husband. As she told Jessie, some of the ideas of the Russells were immoral, such as "it is permissible under some circumstances to act deceitfully." Yet as an independent career woman, she told Jessie, "On the whole I think they are the swing of the pendulum away from the morbid apotheosis of self-sacrifice, and from the sentimentality that will not face facts."[5] Her encounter with Amos and the Russells sparked one of her few frank discussions of the questions of sexual freedom and equality in marriage.

At this time, the word "morbid" appears in her writing alongside the term "self-sacrifice." Soon after the Russell visit, Dr. William Duryee, the father of her friends Lily and Susan, died, and Susan decided to remain for a time in the house in New Brunswick with her stepmother, even though they were not close.[6] Edith described Susan's decision as "no morbid idea of self-sacrifice." Instead she was "quite the most admirably reasonable person I know."[7] In rejecting the idea of empty self-sacrifice, Edith was drawing on the teaching of Edward Caird, who believed that self-sacrifice was worthwhile if it brought an individual closer to self-realization, a state in which the individual's consciousness was brought closer to God. But he opposed self-sacrifice for purely ascetic motives. Edith was voicing the arguments of new women generally, who believed that women should be free to pursue self-actualization, free of sentimental demands that suggested that part of a woman's role was to sacrifice herself for the benefit of others.[8]

As Edith pondered whether a woman could marry without engaging in self-sacrifice, she became fascinated by the idea of a marriage between equals, which Bertrand and Alys advocated and tried to enact. Her brief acquaintance with the Russells occurred at a time when she was considering how she could both pursue a career as a headmistress or scholar and find a fulfilling romantic relationship.

The Russells made her aware that relationships between men and women could follow less conventional paths. This willingness to at least explore the ideas of the Russells differentiated Edith from her sisters and her cousins, Katherine, Jessie, and Agnes.

When Edith first moved to Baltimore, she encouraged her cousins, particularly Jessie and Agnes, to pursue independence and find fulfillment in occupations of their own choosing. Jessie, however, had taken to her bed after the death of her father in 1895, and during Edith's first two years in Baltimore she continued to suffer from an illness diagnosed only as nervousness.[9] Edith urged her to leave Fort Wayne, where she had been under the care of the same doctor for over a year, and come to Baltimore to consult the gynecologist and surgeon Dr. Howard Atwood

Kelly, whom Edith herself would trust for her own care during her years in Baltimore. Edith described him to Jessie as the best women's doctor in the United States. Edith even urged Jessie to sell one of the lots she had inherited from among the Hamilton properties if it was necessary to raise money for the trip, telling her, "I want so much for you. I see all you are, or at least a very great deal of what you are, and I can't bear to have it this way."[10] Edith also sounded out the art teacher at the Bryn Mawr School, Gabrielle Clements, about the possibility of Jessie studying with the portraitist Cecilia Beaux in Philadelphia.[11] Finally, in September 1898, Jessie did go to Philadelphia, and the following year she began to study under Beaux as she had longed to do.[12] In the winter of 1898, Agnes visited Alice at Hull House and decided to commit herself to settlement house work, a decision warmly approved by Edith.[13] After a brief time studying art with Jessie in Philadelphia, Agnes joined a settlement there called the Lighthouse, which had been founded by Esther Kelly Bradford, the sister of Dr. Howard Kelly.[14]

In Marian Walker, the fiancée of her cousin Allen Williams, Edith met another woman, slightly younger than herself, who was trying to pursue a profession, though in this instance also balancing it with the competing demands of romantic love. Though supported by Allen, Marian's goal of becoming a doctor met with disapproval from her widowed mother, who considered it an inappropriate profession for a lady, especially one from a prominent Cincinnati family. Marian therefore welcomed the friendship of an educated professional woman such as Edith, who was sympathetic to her goals. Allen welcomed the model of Bertrand and Alys Russell as a sign that marriage between equals, demanding no self-sacrifice of the woman, was possible. The couple, envisioning a future in which they both would be practicing physicians, would marry in 1901.[15]

In Marian's friend Gertrude Stein, her classmate at both Radcliffe and the Johns Hopkins Medical School, Edith met a woman trying to balance personal and artistic freedom with the pursuit of a medical degree. Edith found Gertrude's company stimulating and was impressed by her intelligence.[16] Both women enjoyed attending the melodramas that were sometimes performed on the Baltimore stage.[17] They also shared a love of language and sometimes discussed writing techniques.[18] At the time, Edith was still considering writing a thesis and earning a doctorate.

Gertrude would also begin writing during her last years in Baltimore. As a student at Radcliffe, she had conducted experiments in automatic writing, a phenomenon then believed to tap into a subject's subconscious thoughts, an experience that has often been linked with the writing style she later developed.[19] Edith in turn told Gertrude that words sometimes drifted randomly through her mind just before she slept, comparing this to Gertrude's experiments.[20] Although some of Gertrude's fellow medical students found her conceited, Edith did not.[21] More socially awkward than many of the Bryn Mawr alumnae in the city, Gertrude lacked the social self-confidence of the other women, and she enjoyed an easier relationship with Edith, seven years her senior.[22]

In 1901, Gertrude failed to take her medical degree, an event she subsequently dismissed casually but that, at the time, Edith felt caused her much distress.[23] Ultimately, Gertrude left Baltimore and settled permanently in Europe. Her friendship with Edith, however, continued beyond her years in Baltimore. Edith would visit her in the autumn of 1903, just after she had moved into her brother Leo's apartment on Paris's rue de Fleurus. As late as 1910 the two women would meet at the art connoisseur Bernard Berenson's villa I Tatti just outside Florence.[24]

Edith's public statements about her friendship with Gertrude, nearly all made after Gertrude's death in 1946, belied the enjoyable intellectual exchange in their turn-of-the-century fellowship, when both women moved in the small social circle of Baltimore's college-educated women.[25] During the Cold War, Edith became a spokesperson for art as a means of effectively communicating an individual vision, and it was in this period that she mentioned Gertrude's work as an example of the modernist spirit that she deplored. To Edith, Gertrude had been guilty of deliberate obfuscation in many of her literary works, though not *The Autobiography of Alice B. Toklas*, in which Edith had found Gertrude's accounts of French soldiers in the First World War moving.[26]

Gertrude, like Bonte Amos, enjoyed freedom of thought and movement, including the ability to abandon her pursuit of a medical degree outright. Gertrude permitted herself to indulge her aspirations and could leave her medical studies behind for an uncertain literary career. Edith was more self-disciplined and, while giving up her pursuit of a doctorate, remained in her position at the Bryn Mawr School to be better able to take care of her family.

During her years of friendship with Gertrude, Edith was forced to distinguish between false and genuine self-sacrifice, the latter of which could, according to Caird, help bring an individual greater consciousness of God. She willingly assumed responsibility for the care of those she loved when both Margaret and Norah suffered severe health problems, conditions that would require her attention for most of 1900.

Margaret had graduated in 1897 from Bryn Mawr College, where she had studied chemistry and biology.[27] During her student years she had met the woman who would become her lifelong partner, Clara Landsberg. The two women were exact contemporaries at Bryn Mawr, from which Clara graduated with a degree in Greek and Latin.[28] But, in May 1894, while Edith was still at Bryn Mawr, Margaret had suffered a serious hip injury in a carriage accident.[29] It would take her several years to fully recover. Yet, in spite of her injury, she persevered in her studies and, in March 1897, just before her graduation, she won the European fellowship, an opportunity she planned to use to study embryology at the Sorbonne.[30] But a full recovery from the accident proved difficult; at times she had to cope with a large steel and leather brace that forced her to keep her spine straight.[31] Other times, she had to walk with crutches. In February 1898, Margaret was dismayed when doctors recommended their use for six more months at a high altitude if she wanted to walk again without any visible limp.[32] She therefore prolonged her departure for Europe until that autumn, spending the spring of that year at Saranac Lake, New York, resting in preparation for her time abroad.[33]

Norah was an aspiring artist who had studied at the Art Students' League in New York City until at least 1895.[34] Edith hoped that she too would have the opportunity to study in Paris. In the autumn of 1898, Margaret, Norah, and Clara sailed to Europe together and settled in Paris. Margaret studied embryology and Clara studied Latin, while Norah enrolled at the Académie Carmen, an art school recently established by the American-born painter James Abbott McNeill Whistler.[35] The artist was then in the last years of his life, and his school, to which he paid brief visits to offer criticism to students, would only survive for three more years. Yet Norah believed that from Whistler she learned "more than from anyone I ever worked under."[36] She trusted his judgment and as an artist she would excel in etching, one of Whistler's favorite artistic media. Margaret and Clara later went to study in Munich while Norah went to Florence.[37]

By late 1899, Margaret had returned to the United States and settled in Baltimore, where she began work at the Bryn Mawr School.[38] Norah went to Switzerland, where that autumn she suffered a nervous breakdown.[39] There were hints, however, that Norah's mental illness might have begun sooner. As early as January 1897, Edith had described Norah's letters as "vague and incoherent."[40] Their mother, Gertrude, went to Europe, where she put Norah in a sanatorium. Edith anxiously awaited her reports on Norah's condition and sometimes visited Jessie in Philadelphia, for moral support. By December, however, it was painfully clear to the family that Norah's illness was, in Margaret's words, "assuming a very serious form."[41] In the spring she had to return for a time to a European sanatorium and was unable to come back to the United States until the summer.[42]

As the summer of 1900 drew to a close, decisions concerning future living arrangements for Margaret and Norah had to be made. Norah was of special concern since her ill health continued and her doctors had suggested that she not return to painting for two years. The Hamiltons, however, faced financial and practical constraints; the expense of a nurse could no longer be borne. Travel to a southern climate— recommended as the best treatment for Norah's condition—proved to be unaffordable. Montgomery Hamilton's alcoholism, however, made the idea of Margaret and Norah living in Fort Wayne unacceptable to Edith and Alice. Ultimately, Alice decided to take Norah with her to Hull House, to help in the kindergarten.[43] It was an arrangement designed to deal with Norah's need for some kind of distracting work and Edith and Alice's need to return to their own positions at the end of the summer.

At times, Norah evidently felt guilty at the sacrifice Edith made to take care of her, though Edith reassured her that there was no need for her to feel this way.[44] Although opposed to pressuring individuals into self-sacrifice, as she felt the institution of marriage demanded of wives, Edith recognized that she had chosen to help care for Norah in her illness. As Edith saw, an individual could make such a decision, but without the obvious constraint of marriage, society did not recognize the sacrifice women made in assuming the responsibilities of family life. Edith would always remain sensitive to the criticism that the "single woman selfishly escapes domestic cares."[45]

In the face of Norah and Margaret's health problems, one of the few bright spots in Edith's life in late 1899 was her move with Margaret into the St. Paul, a newly constructed apartment house on Mount Royal Avenue. Edith had long admired some of the elegant apartment houses in Baltimore, such as the Arundel on North Charles Street, where doctors Mary Sherwood and Lilian Welsh lived together.[46] An apartment was an attractive but expensive alternative to a boarding house, a change desired and carefully budgeted for by Edith.[47] It was possible in part because Margaret had settled in Baltimore. That autumn, she taught history and performed secretarial work at the Bryn Mawr School when one of the teachers had taken an extended absence.[48] It was a modest beginning to Margaret's successful thirty-five-year career at the school, of which she too would eventually become headmistress. In the meantime, she earned less than Edith, who would only allow her to contribute nineteen dollars a week—what she would have paid at a good boarding house—to the household expenses. The rest of the cost was made up by Susan Duryee, who soon joined their household, in part to leave the home of her now widowed stepmother.[49]

With Susan, Edith returned, at least occasionally, to church attendance, which she had largely abandoned during her first years in Baltimore.[50] Together the women went to hear the sermons of Rev. John Timothy Stone at Brown Memorial Park Avenue Presbyterian Church, a large and impressive structure at the corner of Park and Lafayette Avenues frequently attended by members of the Johns Hopkins faculty and renowned for its music. Stone, who had only assumed the pulpit of

Brown in 1900, was known for his support of missionary work. His sermons may even have influenced Susan's eventual choice to follow her sister Lily to China.[51]

Even as she cared for and supported Norah, Edith, too, suffered from ill health during her years in the St. Paul when, beginning in March 1901, she endured several attacks of appendicitis.[52] On this occasion, she was advised against having surgery. The following spring, however, Edith did have an operation, performed in Chicago by Dr. Rachel Yarros, a Hull House acquaintance of Alice's.[53] Her mother and Alice took turns nursing Edith back to health and, when she had recovered sufficiently, they took her to Mackinac for full recovery over the summer.[54] The operation was apparently not an appendectomy, however, since the following March, Edith again suffered an appendicitis attack. In this instance, Edith soothed the pain with ice, relieved, she told Jessie, not to have to endure another surgery. In at least one other respect, however, Edith was happy that spring, since she learned that Margaret would be kept on at the school. At a meeting of the board of managers, Thomas announced that the board was pleased with Margaret's work and they offered her a position at the school paying nine hundred dollars for the 1903–4 academic year and a thousand dollars for the year following. As Edith told Jessie, "I have never known them to do a thing like this before. They never give an increase until it is insisted upon, and never make a promise for more than one year. It has pleased us greatly."[55] It was one sign that the school's managers valued Edith's work; and, as she recovered, her room gradually filled with spring flowers, some from members of the board of managers, including a bowl of lilies of the valley sent by Mamie Gwinn.

The household in the St. Paul, however, was breaking up. By April 1902, Susan had settled on her life's work, resolving to join Lily as a missionary in China. Her younger sister Alice, who had been recruited by the Student Volunteer Movement while at Smith, would accompany her.[56] The sisters would sail for China in the autumn of 1903.[57]

Meanwhile, Edith, accompanied by her sister Alice, as well as by Margaret Shearman and her mother, traveled that summer through Italy and France.[58] By September, the women were enjoying Paris, where

Edith called on Leo and Gertrude Stein.[59] Gertrude had only just arrived in the city and had moved into the Left Bank studio Leo had rented at 27, rue de Fleurus. Edith, arriving in the autumn of 1903, was one of the first visitors Gertrude received, and their studio, with its distinctive entrance through a glass pavilion facing a courtyard, was not yet decorated with modernist art, nor was it yet the famous salon for artists and writers.

Edith returned to Baltimore to find that the two romantic relationships of the Thomas sisters—M. Carey and Helen—that had been evident to her as a college student were coming to an end. In the fall of 1895, Lucy and Helen were appointed instructors in writing at Bryn Mawr College. Both women wanted to be writers—Helen a novelist and Lucy an essayist—and although both possessed literary talent, their productivity was limited by a tendency toward perfectionism. In 1898 the pair had settled into an apartment on campus.

Lucy and Helen's life together was based on their shared literary aspirations, their guidance of Bryn Mawr students through the freshman essay course, and an aestheticism reflected in a deep appreciation for English literature. They also took turns examining the Bryn Mawr School in English punctuation and composition, making it necessary to send exam papers and their results to Edith.[60] Edith frequently had reason to visit the Bryn Mawr campus for meetings of the board of managers or in her continuing capacity as chair of the academic committee.[61] On such occasions, she stayed with Helen and Lucy, making it possible for her to observe the relationship.[62] Edith was present as it began to unravel.

In December 1900, Lucy, always prone to nervous collapse, decided she needed rest and found the prospect of socializing with Helen's extensive family in Baltimore overwhelming. Edith, who had herself spent the summer taking care of Norah on Mackinac, took Lucy to Annapolis to rest.[63] It was during that December, however, that Helen decided she wanted to have children and began to extricate herself from her relationship with Lucy. Helen had been introduced to Dr. Simon Flexner, a graduate of the Johns Hopkins Medical School, who, in 1901, became the director of the Rockefeller Institute of Medical Research in New

York City.[64] As Helen was drawn to Flexner, the division between herself and Lucy grew. From the end of 1900 it must also have been evident to Edith. Helen and Simon became engaged at the end of 1902. Lucy was devastated, and the couple had a series of quarrels, at least one of which, in May 1903, became violent when Lucy hurt Helen's arm. Helen and Simon were married at the Deanery on September 17, 1903.[65]

During her early years in Baltimore, Edith had not ceased to admire Lucy. At the end of the winter vacation of 1896–97, she had spent two days with her at Bryn Mawr College, time that she described as "charming," telling Jessie: "I feel my own coarseness of fibre when I am with her. There is something very specially delicate and high and spiritual about her. I don't know if she will ever make anything great and fine in her own way, whether she ever gets at herself or not." Edith continued: "But she is simply charming. I can't give you any idea of it, but one feels in another world, as if we had been off on the moon or Mars, when one has been with her."[66] In the summer of 1897, Edith had written to Jessie of Lucy: "You know I care very much for her."[67] Now that she faced the prospect of Lucy free of Helen—a condition she had never known—she only wanted Lucy if and when she had truly recovered from her loss.

In the spring of 1904, as Edith contemplated the possibility of a relationship with Lucy, Mamie Gwinn announced her intentions to resign from the Bryn Mawr faculty, to give up her life at the Deanery with M. Carey Thomas, and to marry the writer Alfred Hodder, who had been a professor of English at the college from 1895–98.[68] During his years at Bryn Mawr, he and Mamie had fallen in love, though Hodder had initially told his colleagues he was married and had introduced the mother of his two children to them as his wife. Thomas had forbidden Mamie from pursuing her love for Hodder, both because it violated the exclusivity of their relationship and to protect the college from scandal. When Gwinn announced her intention to marry Hodder, all contact between Thomas and Mamie Gwinn came to an end.[69]

Against the tumult of these fractured relationships, Edith had a sense of permanency through the continuation of the most significant relationship she had established in Baltimore: her friendship with the Reid family. Edith met Dr. Harry Fielding Reid, a Johns Hopkins geology professor, and his wife, Edith Gittings Reid, during her years living at the boarding house of Miss DuBois. The boarding house at 517 Cathedral Street had been less than a block from the Reid family home at 608 Cathedral Street, a three-story townhouse with sandstone facing, distinguishable from those around it only by the carved rope pattern that framed its windows. Not only did Edith live close to the Reids during these years, she socialized frequently with members of the Johns Hopkins faculty. She was invited to the home of the university's founding president, Daniel Coit Gilman, and met one of his daughters, Elisabeth, who was active in a variety of social reform causes.[70] As the head of Mary Garrett's school, Edith was invited to the medical school reception every autumn, as it had been Garrett's fortune that had endowed it.[71] She also came to know Basil Lanneau Gildersleeve, who had served as an outside examiner in Greek and Latin at the Bryn Mawr School for the first seven years of its existence.

Edith Gittings Reid developed a reputation as an outstanding hostess. During the early years of her marriage, her and Harry's friends among the graduate students at Johns Hopkins included Woodrow Wilson and, later, his first wife Ellen Axson, who approved of her husband's friendship with Edith Reid.[72] Eleanor, the Wilsons' youngest daughter, would remember that she saw her father "in a new light" in the Reids' Baltimore drawing room, as the conversations between her father and Edith Reid roamed over a broader range of topics than she had realized her father liked to discuss.[73] Edith Reid was also an acute observer of character, a talent that informed her later career as a writer. From early in Edith Hamilton's years at the Bryn Mawr School, Edith Reid was intrigued by the intellect and personality of her new friend. Reid recorded the description of one of Edith's early Baltimore friends on her position as headmistress as "using a razor to sharpen a lead pencil," indicating that Edith's abilities far outweighed her responsibilities at the Bryn Mawr School.[74]

If the friendship between Edith and the Reid family began as early as the spring of 1897, which a letter to the Baltimore artist Grace Turnbull seems to indicate, then Edith was almost thirty when she met her future lifetime partner.[75] The Reids raised two children: a son, Francis Fielding

Reid, born in Baltimore on April 15, 1892, and their daughter, Doris Fielding Reid, also born in Baltimore, on September 4, 1895.[76] Doris, less than two years old at the time, would not have been able to remember a life in which Edith was not present. Many of Doris's first memories of Edith would also have been as headmistress. She was eight years old when, in 1903, she was enrolled at the Bryn Mawr School.

Edith's sense of permanency in Baltimore, reinforced by her success at the Bryn Mawr School and her friendship with the Reid family, was especially valuable to her in late 1904, when she apparently approached Lucy and was rebuffed.[77] Lucy, who had fallen in love with Bertrand Russell during her visit to London shortly after Helen's wedding, confided to him that Edith had suggested a romantic relationship, which Russell discouraged.[78] Lucy had still not recovered from the loss of Helen. Almost a year later, in November 1905, Russell had to console her over the pain she still felt upon seeing Helen, newly settled into her married life in New York City.[79] Moreover, Lucy sensed that Edith cared more for her than she did for Edith, an imbalance that Russell felt was certain to cause unhappiness. Lucy only considered a romantic relationship with Edith because of the strain Edith was under in caring for her sisters, especially Norah.

Russell, however, told Lucy that she could not solve the problems in Edith's life, advising her not to allow Edith's persistent loyalty to weaken her desire to keep Edith at a distance.[80] He further warned that Edith might in time become jealous of Helen, an emotion that Edith had probably already experienced. In short, Russell's advice to Lucy was to see as little of Edith as possible. Lucy's rejection must have caused Edith much pain. Clearly, she had not waited a sufficient amount of time for Lucy to fully heal from the loss of Helen. Edith and Lucy would not spend exclusive time together until 1909, and even then Lucy would never fully commit herself to Edith. In the meantime, Edith felt once again that she needed the rest that a summer in Europe would provide.

In June 1905 she traveled to Britain with Gertrude and Alice.[81] They sailed to Glasgow, from where they soon set off for the seaside resort of Oban. Edith, a reader of Sir Walter Scott's novels, had long hoped to see the Scottish Highlands. She was impressed by their beauty and the

Scottish air, which she found "misty and blue and silvery."[82] The family visited the Isle of Iona and saw Loch Lomond and Edinburgh before going south to London and Oxford. In several respects the 1905 trip to England prepared Edith for her future. At last she saw Oxford, where Lucy had done graduate work that had reinforced her love for British literature. In the near future, Edith would further experience the trans-Atlantic exchange of ideas and culture that she had seen in her first years in Baltimore through her friendships with Bonte Amos and Gertrude Stein, a world that Lucy would open to her more widely.

Chapter 7

SUFFRAGIST

✦ Edith returned home to evidence of preparations for the annual
convention of the National American Woman Suffrage Association, to be held in Baltimore in February 1906.[1] Edith would become
a prominent local activist, especially in the years between 1909 and
1913, when her interest in the cause was spurred by the founding of the
Baltimore branch of the Equal Suffrage League.[2] Her position as headmistress of the Bryn Mawr School gave her a high profile in Baltimore,
and although she had to avoid offending her students' parents, not all
of whom supported the women's franchise, she eventually found herself
in demand as a suffrage speaker. In 1910, as women staged parades to
draw attention to their cause, she joined in, marching in her first
women's suffrage parade.[3]

Edith's sisters and cousins also supported the cause. Jessie had "Votes
for Women" engraved on her stationery. Agnes, drawn into reform work
at the Lighthouse, became a supporter of women's suffrage. Katherine
would also join the Equal Suffrage League and became the president of
the Fort Wayne branch, which was organized in 1912.[4] Alice linked suffrage work to peace activism, a path Edith would eventually follow.

In the early twentieth century, college-educated women such as
Edith held the conviction that the vote would enhance women's power
in a variety of social reform efforts, especially concerns directly affecting
women. Edith's name for the cause was "the great movement for the
betterment of women."[5] Edith was characteristic of some in her generation in her belief that the right to vote should be limited only to educated

or property-owning women.[6] Edith therefore joined the Equal Suffrage League, which argued that women should be granted the vote on the same basis as men.

Equal Suffrage Leagues—there was an active one in nearby Virginia as well—stressed that women were taxpayers who were denied the full rights of citizenship. They often emphasized women's educational achievements—or at least their capacity for them—as reasons to give women the right to vote.[7] Equal suffragists accepted some limits to the right to vote, including literacy qualifications, in part because the leagues existed in states that also wanted to avoid federal pressure to extend the right to vote to African Americans, among others.[8] Equal suffrage advocates argued that women voters had a positive effect on society since they tended to support social and political reform. Equal suffragists used examples of how women in states that allowed them to vote—Colorado was frequently cited—had used their right to elect public officials who avoided corruption.[9] Equal Suffrage League literature tended to predict that the positive results of women having the right to vote would lead to the extension of suffrage to more states and more countries in the future.[10]

Edith's embrace of the Equal Suffrage League placed her in the moderate wing of the movement for women's right to vote. As Thaddeus Thomas, a professor of sociology and economics at Baltimore's Goucher College and a supporter of the cause, pointed out, equal suffrage was not for "those ultra-enthusiastic suffragists who expect it to bring in the millennium."[11] Edith was drawn to equal suffrage because it stressed women's role as citizens affecting positive change and took an optimistic view of the future, suggesting that more women would soon have the right to vote. She quickly became a regular at the Equal Suffrage League's rooms at 817 North Charles Street, attending its Thursday afternoon meetings, where tea was served while a suffrage speech—which she sometimes delivered herself—was heard.[12]

In her support for women's suffrage, Edith owed yet another intellectual debt to Edward Caird, whose idealist philosophy argued that all individuals could, by striving to achieve their higher selves, become better citizens.[13] Caird shaped Edith's views on all social reform movements, ensuring that she focused on causes that were likely to help the individual achieve their potential. It dulled her interest in socialism. During her visits to Alice at Hull House, Edith confessed to her cousins that the conditions she witnessed in the tenements of Chicago might have made her a socialist too. But she worried that socialism obscured the individual and felt that her "natural bias" was "on the other side."[14] Edith saw a role for government in efforts to eliminate prostitution and child labor (the focus of Agnes's reform activity) but she remained firmly within the bounds of classic liberalism. Edith focused on two causes she saw as likely to aid the individual—promoting compulsory school attendance and women's right to vote—believing that it would empower women's reform efforts.

During her early years in Baltimore, Edith participated in the Arundell Good Government Club, an offshoot of the Arundell Club, originally founded in 1894 as a literary and artistic society for women. Created in 1896, the Good Government Club's focus was on addressing Baltimore's civic problems.[15] Edith was active in both the artistic and reform efforts of the club, which included serving on a committee to investigate school attendance in Maryland. In December 1901, the club proposed a law that demanded attendance for children between the ages of eight and fourteen while banning them from paid labor.[16] By 1905, such a law had been passed for the city of Baltimore, though the state dragged its feet. Edith also served on the Good Government Club's executive board, and in 1907 she was elected a vice president of the original club, helping to plan its series of cultural events.[17] The Arundell Good Government Club was one of many Progressive-Era women's organizations whose efforts at reform illustrated how giving women the vote would enhance their abilities to act as responsible citizens.[18]

Edith shared her commitment to suffrage with Lucy, also a supporter of the cause. During her years as a suffrage activist, Edith drew closer to Lucy, and they eventually took three extensive trips abroad together. Although Edith would always hope that Lucy would commit herself fully to a relationship, Lucy always refused. Devastated by Helen's decision to marry in 1903, Lucy had taken a year off to recover, traveling to England where she visited Bertrand and Alys Russell and a

FIGURE 9. Lucy Martin Donnelly as an
instructor in English at Bryn Mawr College. Photograph courtesy of the Bryn
Mawr College Special Collections.

sympathetic Logan Pearsall Smith, a first cousin of Helen's and a writer
whom Lucy respected. He encouraged her to rebuild her relationship
with Helen on a new basis.[19] But during her visit to the Russells at their
home on Cheyne Walk in London's Chelsea, Lucy fell in love with
Bertrand Russell, whose marriage to Helen's cousin Alys was already
troubled.[20] Russell did not return her affections yet the two formed a
close friendship, a condition that undoubtedly helped prevent her from
committing herself to Edith.[21]

Lucy returned to the United States in June 1904 and to Bryn Mawr
College that autumn.[22] She had wondered if she ought to come back
to the college at all, feeling uncertain of her future on the faculty since

she was no longer Helen's partner and did not have a doctorate. The campus was also a constant reminder of their former relationship. The lack of any other prospects, however, dictated her return.[23] Through 1905 she struggled to feel secure in her position at Bryn Mawr, and though expressing jealousy and regret that her and Helen's lives had taken such different paths as late as 1911, she gradually developed a new relationship with Helen, becoming an aunt to the Flexners' two sons, William and James.[24]

By 1908, as Lucy was finding her footing both personally and professionally, she began to grow closer to Edith. And while no correspondence exists between them, it is clear that Lucy also enjoyed the company of the Hamilton family, whom she found "full of so many liberal interests despite some remnants of Presbyterianism left among them."[25] She was privy to the painful story of Norah's breakdown and Edith's sadness after the death of Montgomery Hamilton in June 1909, just as Edith was aware of tensions in the Donnelly family.[26] The most obvious evidence of the closeness between Edith and Lucy, however, was Edith's reaction when it ended between the years 1919–23.[27] As the relationship deteriorated in 1921, Margaret felt that Edith was "still very upset about Lucy."[28]

Although Lucy would never commit herself exclusively to Edith, the two women cared for one another in illness, studied art, and traveled together. Edith regarded taking trips abroad with Lucy, instead of with her family, to be a significant change in her life, marking the first time a potential romantic partner took priority over her family and a prelude to the life she would share with Doris.[29] In their partnership, however, the two played different roles. Lucy's was that of the creative artist and arbiter of aesthetic taste, Edith's that of practical leadership. Though their final separation would reveal that the relationship between Edith and Lucy had an emotional intensity, it was likely not physically intimate. Both women had matured in the nineteenth century, when the ideal of Platonic love between friends had shaped romantic relationships between women. Edith's letters to Jessie reveal that on their travels the two women slept in separate bedrooms.[30]

Lucy, however, played a central role in Edith's intellectual life during her years of suffrage activism. Lucy, too, had studied Greek as an undergraduate at Bryn Mawr, and the two women shared a love of the subject that may have resulted in Lucy introducing Edith to the classicist Gilbert Murray, who visited Bryn Mawr College in May 1907.[31] Lucy, who had first met Murray during her visit to the Russells in the winter of 1903, held a dinner for him during his visit to Bryn Mawr.[32] Murray, whose wife was a cousin of Bertrand Russell, had enjoyed a long friendship with the philosopher.[33] At the time of his visit to Bryn Mawr College, Murray had just finished giving a series of lectures at Harvard. He had been professor of Greek at the University of Glasgow from 1889 until 1899. There, he had been a friend of Edward Caird and produced a new critical text of Euripides, published in three volumes by Oxford University Press between 1901 and 1909.[34] The work was largely responsible for creating twentieth-century interest in the tragic playwright.

At the time of his visit to Bryn Mawr College, Murray was already a celebrity. In Britain, he was widely known to the reading and theater-going public, a reputation established through his translations of Euripides's tragedies into English verse. His translations of *Hippolytus*, *The Trojan Women*, and *Electra* were successfully produced on the London stage between 1904 and 1906; his *Medea* would follow in 1908.[35] Murray shared literary and political interests with his friend George Bernard Shaw, who satirized him and his wife, Lady Mary, a daughter of the ninth Earl of Carlisle, in his play *Major Barbara*, produced in London in 1905.[36]

After Edith began her writing career, she was frequently compared to Murray, including by her Washington friend Huntington Cairns, among others.[37] Central to Murray's thought, as to Edith's, was how classical study helped one understand the Hellenic spirit. His 1907 Harvard lectures, published under the title *The Rise of the Greek Epic*, were widely read by American classicists.[38] The first chapter of *The Rise of the Greek Epic* was particularly influential on Edith since it posited that the Greeks were the first to question slavery and to contemplate women's rights, two arguments she would make in her own books.[39] Both Murray and Edith looked to the ancient world for an understanding of contemporary political events, hoping their readers would see the same parallels. An outspoken opponent of the South African War of 1899–1902, the

Australian-born Murray was wary of how Britain wielded the political power it drew from its enormous empire, using the example of Athens's decay after her victory in the Persian Wars to warn the British to exercise their power wisely.[40] Edith's *The Echo of Greece* would largely address the same theme, though directed at the American public as the United States became a Cold War superpower.

During his 1907 visit to Bryn Mawr College, Murray gave two lectures, one on Homer and the other on Greek tragedy. All of the students in Greek classes were invited to the latter. As Murray and his wife, Lady Mary, were both supporters of women's suffrage, Lady Mary delivered a lecture on the subject.[41] Edith, with her close relationship to Lucy and her frequent visits to the college, could well have heard Gilbert Murray speak. Ultimately, Murray's visit to the campus inspired Bryn Mawr College's production of *Medea* the following year.[42]

During her years at the Bryn Mawr School Edith remained abreast of intellectual currents in the study of classics. Helen Evans, later Lewis, of the class of 1909, recalled one Greek class in February 1909 in which Edith taught the students on the "subject of Greek religion [sic] development from Homer's time to Plato's philosophy."[43] This discussion of gradual change in the theology of the Greeks may indicate that Edith was reading and absorbing the works of the scholars known as the Cambridge school. This group included Murray, though intellectually it was led by the Cambridge classicist Jane Ellen Harrison.

Harrison's introductory works describing Greek archaeological sites and interpreting vase painting appealed to a wide audience, including female readers hungry for knowledge about the ancient world. Mary Garrett, for example, purchased Harrison's early works for the library of the Bryn Mawr School.[44] The group, which also sought to apply the work of anthropologists and archaeologists to the study of ancient texts, focused on the study of Greek religion and was especially active in the years just after Murray's 1907 visit to Bryn Mawr.[45]

While Lucy felt some sense of fulfillment through introducing students to Murray's work, the years after her return to Bryn Mawr were still stressful. Edith would often find herself taking care of Lucy during her breakdowns, but early on in their relationship Lucy also took care of

Edith. It was during her years with Lucy that Edith began to experience the hearing loss that would eventually lead to deafness. The condition began in the early 1900s, with the loss noticeably greater in one ear than the other.[46] Edith consulted a number of doctors about her condition, receiving a variety of opinions that she often discussed with Alice. But Edith also considered Lucy's views of the various doctors from whom she sought treatment. Both liked a soft-spoken (but long-winded) one in Boston who advised against surgery and prescribed a listening exercise instead. This trip, probably in early 1910, was one of the first Edith and Lucy took together, and it gave them the opportunity to visit the newly constructed Museum of Fine Arts. Edith and Lucy enjoyed going on excursions to appreciate art together. During this museum visit, however, Edith began to feel faint as a result of some tests the doctor had performed earlier in the day. Lucy helped guide her to a tram and then to a taxi to return to their hotel, leaving Edith to feel that "poor Lucy had a poor holiday with me."[47] The Boston trip was a brief prelude to the three longer trips abroad that Edith and Lucy would take together and, like their subsequent trips, was devoted to a mix of art appreciation and physical reenergizing.

On January 28, 1909, visiting English suffragist Ethel Arnold gave a speech on behalf of the Equal Suffrage League—the league's first large event in Baltimore—at McCoy Hall on the Johns Hopkins University campus.[48] Edith brought a contingent of Bryn Mawr School students to hear Arnold speak. She shared the platform, introducing Dr. William Sydney Thayer of the Johns Hopkins Medical School, who in turn introduced Arnold.[49]

Arnold was the niece of Matthew Arnold and the sister of the novelist Mrs. Humphry Ward, who, the previous year, had founded the Women's National Anti-Suffrage League in Britain.[50] Arnold's Baltimore speech occurred on the first of two tours of the United States that she made for the women's suffrage cause in the years between 1908 and 1912, engagements that point to the high level of interaction between British and American suffragists in the years just before the outbreak of the First World War.[51] Her position on women's suffrage fit closely with that of the Equal Suffrage League. Although some British suffragists had adopted universal suffrage, along with militant tactics in the early 1900s, Arnold rejected these, preferring the classic liberal arguments that favored women's right to vote as a measure of equality.[52]

Acquainted with the literary and social criticism of Matthew Arnold from her time as a student at Bryn Mawr, Edith was well aware of Ethel Arnold's connections to a great literary family.[53] It is not clear if Edith had read Ethel Arnold's only published novel, *Platonics*, which celebrated the romantic bond between two women. But Arnold clearly influenced Edith's own suffrage speeches. The only surviving fragment from one of Edith's suffrage speeches—given in November 1912—shows that she echoed Arnold's words.[54]

In early 1910, Edith became involved with the Equal Suffrage League's efforts to secure women the right to vote in Baltimore's municipal elections.[55] Elizabeth King Ellicott, one of the founders of the Bryn Mawr School, began the campaign by inviting a series of well-known local activists to give lectures at homes of supporters. The list of speakers included Ellicott herself, as well as Edith, Dr. Mary Sherwood, Dr. Lilian Welsh, and Dr. Howard Kelly, president of the Men's League for Women's Suffrage.[56] Edith's talk, delivered on January 11 at a home on Mount Royal Terrace, stressed a common theme among equal suffragists, that women's disinterested influence on municipal government would counter the commercial interests frequently expressed by men.[57] She was persuasive: the *Baltimore Sun* reporter who covered the meeting noted that a number of women joined the Equal Suffrage League. Others signed a petition to the Maryland legislature that asked to amend the charter of the city of Baltimore to allow for women's suffrage, an effort that ultimately proved unsuccessful.

For Lucy, however, the winter of 1909–10 had been a difficult one, marked by illness both physical and mental.[58] Family problems also weighed on her and, though she longed to go abroad, she decided to remain closer to her family and to accompany Edith to Mackinac Island.[59] Once on Mackinac, Edith soon convinced Lucy that the pair should travel to Europe, where they would be joined later by some of the Hamiltons. Edith and Lucy began their European travels in southern Italy, staying in Ravello on the Amalfi coast and likely visiting Pompeii as well.[60] In July, they moved north to Rome and Vatican City and spent four days in Siena. By the middle of that month they were in Florence, visiting its art galleries in the mornings—the Uffizi, the Accademia, and the Pitti Palace—and spending the afternoons visiting churches.[61] Edith was adopting a role that had formerly been filled by Helen Thomas: accompanying Lucy abroad during the long periods that she needed for rest and recuperation.

Edith was relieved that Italy had a positive effect on Lucy's health almost immediately. For her part, Lucy found Edith a perfect traveling companion, describing her as "always in good spirits & always interested in external things."[62] This was high praise from Lucy, who was particular about her traveling companions. She closely guarded entrance into her intimate circle, telling her former student Mildred Minturn that there were only two or three people with whom she felt she could take long journeys. Mildred and Edith were among the few.[63]

Although it was Edith's second trip to the country and she had once helped sponsor a series of lectures on Italian art given at the Arundell Club, Edith willingly submitted to Lucy's aesthetic sensibilities. Edith at this point did not claim to be a writer, whereas Lucy was a successful author, with several essays published in a national magazine. To Jessie, Edith related an incident in the Uffizi that reflected both her efforts to follow Lucy's guidance and her own sense of humor, as they toured the museum without the benefit of a guidebook known as a Baedeker, which used a system of stars to identify cultural attractions:

> Yesterday in the Uffizi Lucy, who had informed me beforehand that one of the recumbent Venuses in the Tribuna was good & to be admired & the other not, & that she would see whether I could tell which, when to her disappointment I liked best the one she thought I shouldn't, as she was talking to me very eagerly & saying didn't I see that it was hard & the background uninteresting, a young man near us suddenly turned around & glared at her. 'I suppose you are not aware', he said superbly, 'that Baedecker [sic] double stars the picture

you are talking of.' Then he walked on, despising us too much even to wait for us to say anything.[64]

In fact, it was Edith and Lucy who felt superior, capable of judging pictures without the aid of a popular travel guide. Edith tried to see Italy's great works of art through Lucy's eyes. Through her she also had entrée into the extensive Anglo-American community in both Florence and nearby Fiesole, whose hills were dotted with villas inhabited by expatriate artists and writers.

Lucy's friends included Edith Petit Borie, a Bryn Mawr College classmate who, with her husband, the impressionist artist Adolph Borie, was living at Il Palmerino, the hillside farmhouse of the writer Vernon Lee, near the village of Maiano. Although there are no indications that Lucy and Edith met Lee herself, the writer, born Violet Paget and English by nationality, was a well-known author on aesthetics and Italian history and culture.[65] From Il Palmerino, Edith and Lucy were taken for a visit to the nearby medieval castle Poggio Gherardo, where, Edith told Jessie, they were shown "the pool where the ladies of the Decameron used to bathe."[66] The castle was the home of the indomitable Janet Ross, author of several books on Tuscan life, an Englishwoman who, in her youth, had been a friend of George Meredith. Then nearing seventy years old, Ross had lived at the castle, thought to be one of the settings of Boccaccio's work, for over twenty years and received visitors at afternoon receptions every Sunday.[67] Through Helen, Lucy also had an introduction to I Tatti, the home of the art connoisseur Bernard Berenson, whose wife, Mary, was a first cousin of Helen's and the sister of Alys Russell. Lucy had previously visited the sixteenth-century villa at Settignano, where, amid their collections of Renaissance and classical art, the Berensons offered gracious hospitality.[68] Edith would long remember her visit to one of the great expatriate homes in Italy, in part because at I Tatti she once again met Gertrude Stein, also staying at Fiesole that summer.[69]

As Lucy's traveling companion, Edith briefly felt part of Tuscany's artistic expatriate community, an experience that helped awaken her own desire to pursue the life of an artist, a role that would always be occupied by Lucy in their years together.

Edith and Lucy continued on to Venice, where they visited the Accademia, and to Cortina, before crossing the Alps into Switzerland. In Zermatt, they stayed at a small inn where their window was decorated with a box of pink geraniums framing their view of the Matterhorn. They then entered southern Germany. Edith spent her birthday in Munich, seeing it for the first time since she had studied there in the spring and summer of 1896.[70] Lucy hoped to read in the University of Munich's library, but she suffered a relapse, enduring painful headaches and making Edith anxious that her health was not improving enough for her to return to Bryn Mawr College in the fall.[71] She gradually recovered, however, and Edith was pleased to show her Munich, where they enjoyed cakes and coffee in a cafe overlooking one of the city's many open squares. Edith still found the city and its people charming.

While in Germany, Edith met up with her mother and sister Alice. In the early years of the twentieth century, Alice had found what would become her lifelong subject of research: industrial toxicology. In 1910 she had embarked on a study of lead poisoning, and she traveled to Europe that summer for an international conference on industrial disease in Brussels.[72] Edith met them in Oberammergau, where they attended a performance of the Passion Play. She then continued to travel with Alice and Gertrude through Germany, visiting Ulm and Strasbourg before arriving in Belgium. Ulm was the setting of Charlotte Mary Yonge's *The Dove in the Eagle's Nest*, a novel of which Edith had always been fond. She loved the city, calling it "as charming a little town as, I believe, can be found outside of Italy."[73] They visited the cathedrals in both Ulm and Strasbourg, the latter of which deeply impressed Edith. In Antwerp—which Edith found disappointing—she separated from Alice and Gertrude. They stayed in Brussels while she sailed for England to join Lucy, who, eager to see Bertrand Russell, had traveled there ahead of her.

Edith and Lucy were entertained at one of the Russells' teas at their home at Bagley Wood, near Oxford.[74] Edith was enthralled by Lucy's descriptions of the large luncheon parties for which the Russells were known, where "the talk is always brilliant and delightful." As a guest at the tea, Edith described the conversation to Jessie: "I have never heard in my life such talk as I heard there that Sunday afternoon, no argument, playing with a subject matter and yet in such a way that it was illumined by it. I felt all stirred up by it and as if my own mind was working more quickly."[75] Edith was intimidated by the cleverness of Bertrand and Alys Russell and their friends. Bertrand, Edith told Jessie, was "a determined radical, really something of a socialist." Russell was heir to an earldom, but Edith felt that "he works as hard as any man who must earn his own living." She was impressed with Alys, who was committed to the cause of women's suffrage and to charitable work, including hunger relief among impoverished English children. Altogether, Edith admired the Russells because they "absolutely live up to their principles." She told Jessie, "They live with the most extreme simplicity; they keep only one servant." It was Bertrand's custom to wait on his guests himself. The visit to the Russells concluded with a short journey along the River Thames to Iffley, where they visited Alys's brother and Lucy's literary mentor, the author Logan Pearsall Smith. His fifteenth-century home, Court Place, had a small garden that bordered a churchyard, the sight of which made Edith feel that "life seemed full of interest and beauty there."[76]

On her European trip, Edith experienced the thrill of travel with Lucy, whose wide acquaintance had opened the doors of the great expatriate villas near Florence and of Britain's intelligentsia. It was rarefied company, made more attractive for Edith by Lucy's aesthetic appreciation and, of course, her almost continual presence. Once back in the United States, Edith wanted to remain close to Lucy. Circumstances made it impossible for the two women to live together, but, in order to be closer to Lucy, Edith considered opening a boarding school of her own near Bryn Mawr College.[77]

As Edith knew, it was a financially risky proposition. Not only had she seen the Bryn Mawr School struggle, her friend Abby Kirk's school, known as the Miss Kirks' School and located in Rosemont, not far from Bryn Mawr College, had also met with financial difficulties.[78] To Lucy, Edith explained that her growing deafness made it more practical for her to have a school of her own, since she was afraid that total deafness would result in the board of managers dismissing her from the Bryn Mawr School. With Margaret's help, Edith felt that she could give fifteen years of her life to the project of starting a new school. Lucy was uncertain as to whether or not to encourage Edith. She wished to avoid commit-ting herself to Edith entirely, feelings she confided to Bertrand Russell.[79] In the end, Edith of course remained at the Bryn Mawr School. Finan-cial considerations may have prevented the establishment of her own school, and Lucy's unwillingness to devote herself exclusively to Edith made the proposition less attractive. Instead, the year 1910 further solidi-fied Edith's commitment to the Bryn Mawr School, as it saw Margaret's appointment as head of the primary division.[80]

Throughout 1912 Edith maintained a busy schedule as a suffrage speaker, sometimes in meetings held in private homes but also in public venues. That year, the Maryland legislature debated a proposed consti-tutional amendment that would have granted suffrage to women taxpayers in the state.[81] Edith, as well as Dr. Mary Sherwood and Julia Rogers, another former founder of the Bryn Mawr School, were among the six hundred suffrage advocates from Baltimore who journeyed to Annapolis to listen to the debates of the committee on constitutional amendments.[82] On February 13, 1912, Edith was again among those who—numbering eight hundred this time—gathered in the state capital to ask the legis-lature to pass the bill that would enable Maryland voters to decide whether or not to amend the constitution. On this occasion, Dr. Mary Sherwood presented the petition of 88,000 signatures in favor of the bill, and Edith was among those who addressed the constitutional amendments committee.[83] The following day, she spoke at the weekly meeting at the Equal Suffrage League's headquarters on women's right to vote "from an educational point of view."[84] In March, she lectured in a private home, where another speaker and tea followed her own presentation.[85]

On November 5, 1912, Edith gave a speech at the casino at Mount Washington, near Baltimore, which was quoted in the *Maryland Suffrage News*: "To those who are not at present interested in the subject, woman suffrage is coming today—it will be here tomorrow. It will come without your help, but if you do join us, you will have the knowledge that you were part of the great movement for the betterment of women. Tomor-row it will be too late."[86] These three sentences are the only surviving fragments of Edith's suffrage speeches. Yet they conveyed her sense that the vote was only a part of a larger effort to enlarge the scope of women's activities and opportunities in society. Her words also reflected the optimism of the Equal Suffrage League that women in all fifty states would soon have the right to vote.

Edith was one of between five thousand and eight thousand women who marched in the great suffrage parade in Washington, D.C., held on March 3, 1913, on the eve of Woodrow Wilson's inauguration.[87] She was a prominent member of the Maryland delegation that marched to Baltimore's railroad station to board the trains for the U.S. capital. A procession of women workers and of men active in the women's suffrage cause preceded the leaders of the movement in Maryland, but all marchers were accompanied by bands and banners. Edith, asked to represent the College Equal Suffrage League, marched with Elizabeth King Ellicott, leading the delegation from the state Equal Suffrage League. As the parade reached the station it joined with marchers from neighboring counties.[88]

Once in Washington, the marchers followed a route down Pennsylvania Avenue, from the Capitol building to the Treasury Department, to the accompaniment of ten women's marching bands. The entire procession was led by New York City lawyer Inez Milholland, dressed as Joan of Arc astride a white horse.[89] The Baltimore participants' experience in the parade was similar to that of other marchers: they quickly learned that the Washington police were ill prepared to prevent assaults on the female demonstrators, a condition that meant the parade moved very slowly.[90] The Maryland delegation scattered in the face of the violence only moments before the U.S. Cavalry from Fort Myer intervened, allowing the parade to continue. Edith felt nervous when a man prepared to shake his fist at her. Almost fifty years later she recalled:

> A big man lifted a big arm as I went by. Undoubtedly, he was only going to shake his fist at me, but I wasn't very cool at the time and I keep in grateful remembrance a very small boy-scout who rushed to my defense and drew down the laughter of the crowd.[91]

The great range and amount of Edith's activism in the years 1912 to 1913 justified M. Carey Thomas's description of her to LeBaron Russell Briggs, the president of Radcliffe College, as "one of the leaders of suffrage work in Baltimore."[92] Uncertain as to how Briggs felt about women's suffrage, Thomas wanted to warn him before he gave the Bryn Mawr School's 1914 commencement address that all of the members of the board of managers were active in the cause. It is not surprising that Edith, given her heritage of suffrage activism, her education, and her choice of profession, became a well-known suffrage advocate in Baltimore. In later life, however, she sometimes gave the impression that she had been uninterested in the movement, once telling her friend John White, a journalist in Washington, D.C., that she marched in a 1910 suffrage parade only to please Alice.[93] It may have taken Alice's convincing to persuade Edith, who stood on the more conservative end of the suffrage spectrum, to march. Once she did so, however, she continued to march until 1913.

Her subsequent reminiscences about her participation in the women's suffrage movement were few and, as with all subjects, she looked at it through the lens of classical antiquity. In later life, when she spoke of Susan B. Anthony, she noted that the great activist had decided at the age of eighty to embark on the study of ancient Greek, thus linking the cause of women's suffrage to the culture that had developed democratic ideas.[94]

Edith was not the only women's suffrage advocate to see the classical world as an inspiration for greater political freedom for women. Among the most criticized marchers in the 1913 Washington parade were women who appeared barefoot wearing draped gowns in a style reminiscent of ancient Greece.[95] The Washington marchers in ancient Greek dress discarded the confining clothes considered proper for women along with the political attitudes that denied women the vote.

The 1913 Washington march marked the peak of Edith's suffrage activism. In the months that followed, her own health declined, and, in May 1914, Elizabeth King Ellicott, the Equal Suffrage League's first president, died.[96] The organization she had founded and led subsequently turned many of its efforts to war work. Edith had no objections to humanitarian efforts during the war, but peace activism took priority for her as for some other suffragists.[97] Edith would soon become a supporter of the Woman's Peace Party, which was founded by Alice's mentor Jane Addams in 1915 to work for the complete abolition of war, though it also argued for women's suffrage.[98] Soon after Alice and Jane Addams helped establish the Women's International League for Peace and Freedom in 1919, Edith would, along with Edith Reid and others, organize a chapter in Baltimore.[99]

Pacifism would prove to be a much longer commitment in Edith's life, in part, of course, because women eventually obtained the right to vote. Once Edith began her writing career, however, she seldom reflected on the years she had spent among the women reformers of the Progressive Era. The social circles in which she moved as a successful writer were not the almost exclusively female ones that marked her time in Baltimore, and she left women-identified politics behind.

Chapter 8

HEADMISTRESS AND STUDENT

Between 1909 and 1914, Edith was at the height of her powers at the Bryn Mawr School. The battle for girls' college preparatory education had been won. In fact, criticism of the school would no longer come from conservatives but from progressives, who saw the school as a bastion of the elite.[1] Edith took steps to counter the economic and social advantages enjoyed by some of her students, most visibly by introducing a uniform. She also helped spark a Baltimore-wide movement to prioritize study over social activities for the city's young elite, and she founded the Bryn Mawr League, a chapter of the Y.W.C.A., to give social work opportunities to graduates of the school, thereby bringing them into contact with the underprivileged.

As Edith exercised her authority at the Bryn Mawr School, she also continued to support the causes of women's suffrage and compulsory school attendance legislation. In Baltimore, progressives supported efforts to improve the lives of workers by shortening working hours and introducing minimum wage legislation. Edith would have been aware of these issues in Baltimore, especially as Alice was involved in the same reform efforts in Chicago.[2] Baltimore, which grew rapidly in the decades in which Edith led the Bryn Mawr School, had an African American community and small groups of immigrants from Russia, Poland, and Germany. Between 1910 and 1913, the city sought to impose segregation by law on some of its neighborhoods, and after American entry into the

First World War, anti-German feeling would manifest itself.[3] Edith's feelings about the city's proposed segregation ordinances are unknown, although, as a classic liberal, she may have felt that choice of residence should not be dictated by law, as segregation in Baltimore had historically been a matter of custom. She may have known little about the city's African American community, though she had once attended a funeral service held in one of the city's African American churches.[4] While some progressives spoke out against legislating segregation, many Baltimore reformers did not. She would be more outspoken about anti-German sentiment. Such views challenged those of Edith and her sisters, whose experiences of German culture included respect for its intellectual achievements. Eventually, as the United States grew closer to entering the war, the main focus of Edith's political activity would turn from suffrage activism to pacifism.

The varying intensity of Edith and Lucy's relationship accounted for some of the changes Edith made at the school. Also significant was that in 1912, Mary Garrett was diagnosed with leukemia, which would result in her death three years later.[5] Garrett's weakening condition contributed to Edith's growing power at the school. But as Edith reached the peak of her influence, the seeds of her eventual departure from the school were being sown. After Garrett's death, Thomas, critical of Edith's management of the school, began a series of quarrels that would ultimately lead to Edith's resignation. These were also the years directly after Doris Fielding Reid's departure from the school. She went to Europe to study music, but she and Edith corresponded, even as Edith's relationship with Lucy slowly winded down.[6]

In June 1912, Lucy and Edith went to Europe again, a journey in which they were joined by Gertrude and the Hamilton sisters. Crossing the Atlantic in the months just after the *Titanic* disaster, the women had a longer than usual voyage since the shorter, northerly route of the ill-fated ship was being avoided. They landed in Dover in late June and immediately separated, Edith going to France with Gertrude and Margaret, while Lucy remained in England to see Bertrand Russell. Unlike their previous trip, most of Edith's time on the continent in 1912 would be spent with her mother and sisters.[7]

This trip to France left several vivid images in Edith's memory. One day, while walking across the Breton countryside, she encountered an abandoned church. Though its entry was obscured by overgrowth, she found her way inside and discovered a little round glass window that, despite the neglect, had remained intact. She always regretted not making an effort to preserve it.[8] She was also moved by her visit, accompanied by her mother and sisters, to the Provence fortress hill town of Les Baux, whose lonely beauty attracted her. She was particularly impressed by its church, where the phrase "After darkness light" was carved into the door. She was so drawn to the site that she revisited it on her last trip abroad, in 1960.[9]

The Hamiltons lingered in France until the fall, when, in Paris, Edith saw one of the first exhibitions of cubism.[10] The year 1912 was an important one in the Parisian art world, marked by two major cubist exhibitions held that fall, including the Cubist House at the Salon d'Automne, where the works of the cubist painters filled two large galleries with an array of European artists painting in the style.[11] Edith found herself in what she later described as a "room where the walls were covered with canvases full of brown and tan planes."[12] She was unimpressed, finding that cubism represented a reality too personal to the artist to communicate his or her vision effectively. In later life, as she became a spokesperson for the continuing study of the ancient Greek and Roman world, she would use cubism as an example of a great turning inward that she saw as a sign of societal decay.

To an extent, the European trip was a working vacation for Edith. It is likely on this occasion that she went to England, where she visited Cheltenham Ladies' College. Situated in the Gloucestershire town of Cheltenham, the institution had been founded in 1854, making it one of the oldest day schools for girls in Great Britain. It had been shaped largely by its longtime lady principal, Dorothea Beale. Beale had built the school into a college preparatory institution, even establishing St. Hilda's College, Oxford, to help aspiring teachers acquire more formal education.[13]

The chief result of Edith's visit to Cheltenham was the introduction of a uniform to the Bryn Mawr School. Edith, who valued individual expression, had long debated the use of a uniform, but finally chose to introduce one in 1913.[14] She found the decision a difficult one, as it had been for Dorothea Beale, who had also felt that uniforms obscured the individual.[15] Edith finally chose to emphasize that the pursuit of knowledge did not recognize social advantages. The Bryn Mawr School's uniform, which was meant to counter the disparity in the wardrobes of wealthy and poorer students, was modeled on Cheltenham's and consisted of a blue serge tunic and skirt in the winter and blue linen in the warmer months.

Edith remained attentive to the students as individuals. Although in the 1910s there were over three hundred students in the school, she always went over the grade reports with each one individually, sitting with them on a shared step of the school's back staircase. Such meetings had their reward, especially for students who had to be convinced that the long hours of study necessary to pass the Bryn Mawr entrance examination would result in eventual success. One student remembered (four years after Edith's death), "I didn't have a bit of self-confidence and she gave it to me."[16]

As headmistress, she paid as much attention to students who did not intend to pursue a college education as to those who did, as evident in her establishment of the Bryn Mawr League in 1910.[17] The league, essentially a Bryn Mawr School chapter of the Y.W.C.A., was intended to provide opportunities for volunteer social work for the school's graduates, especially those who did not plan to continue their formal education. It functioned as a settlement house, with its own headquarters on Light Street, eventually offering classes in English and French as well as skills such as dressmaking.[18] By the end of its first year, 197 working girls had attended the league's activities, which included public lectures. It was another example of Edith's belief in the positive influence of women in society, creating a community that gave both its workers and its participants a sense of purpose and an opportunity to develop themselves as citizens.

Edith also encouraged her students to take an interest in the cause of women's suffrage, as when she took them to hear Ethel Arnold speak.[19] As Edith herself was drawn into the cause, the students were as well, only one sign of her influence at the school. In March 1911, students established the Bryn Mawr School Suffrage Club.[20] It proceeded cautiously on the issue, a reflection of the atmosphere of the school, where not all students came from families that supported the cause. As Dorothy Sippel, the club's vice president recalled, the members began by acquainting themselves with the arguments in support of, or in opposition to, the cause and welcomed those against women's suffrage to attend meetings. They also listened to speakers representing both sides.[21] From its modest beginnings, the Suffrage Club joined the larger State Equal Suffrage League as the Junior Suffrage League of the Bryn Mawr School, with its emphasis on equal suffrage, again a sign of Edith's direction of her students in the cause.[22]

As always, Edith's perspective on social reform remained firmly focused on the development of the individual. This was the purpose of the Bryn Mawr League and the school's suffrage activity, which made individuals consider the role of the citizen in society and helped them to articulate it in debates on the subject held at the school. Edith believed that citizens working together could effect change, but her goals in the social reform movements of the Progressive Era remained modest, a position that suited her role as headmistress. In Baltimore, some social reform efforts sprang from St. Paul's Episcopal Church, a center of the social gospel, an early twentieth-century movement that posited that the teachings of Jesus could provide the answers to social problems. Edith would have been aware of this, as the minister of St. Paul's, Rev. Arthur B. Kinsolving, sent his daughters to the Bryn Mawr School. Although a few advocates of the social gospel, such as Edith's acquaintance Elisabeth Gilman, a well-known Baltimore social reformer, became socialists, many found fulfillment in remaining firmly in the fold of Christian-inspired social work, as at the Bryn Mawr League.[23]

For several students during this period, Edith's devotional exercises were a highlight of the day. What she had begun on a small and cautious scale in the 1890s had turned into the primary means by which she established and maintained her moral influence on her students, something she considered as important as their intellectual development. To Anne Kirk, later Cooke, the gathering in the big study hall at the beginning of each school day was an "exciting" time, marked with the singing of hymns, a practice Edith had established in her first year at the school.[24] Helen Evans felt that Edith could "unintentionally preach as good a sermon as any minister."[25]

Millicent Carey, later McIntosh, a niece of M. Carey Thomas who attended the school from 1905 until 1916, remembered Edith standing before the Parthenon frieze that lined the great study hall, ostensibly reading from the Bible but in reality reciting its verses from memory.[26] It was a fitting image of Edith, linking her work at the Bryn Mawr School with her later role as exponent of ancient Greece for a wide readership, and an image remembered by many of the students. Ruth Taneyhill, later Shafer, of the class of 1909, recalled that Edith "would often look away and beyond the Bible she was holding, reciting the verses surely & calmly."[27] Edith's presence every morning in study hall obviously made a deep impression, even if she was merely sitting at the desk, with the frieze surrounding her.[28]

Edith still welcomed senior girls to her home for Bible study, her final opportunity to offer moral guidance to the students as they prepared to leave school. She encouraged her students to use their intellect in discerning moral standards. Helen Evans remembered one class in February 1909 where the discussion centered on "whether greatness and goodness went hand in hand or whether a man could be great without being good." Helen and the other students argued that a man could be great without being good, but Edith took the opposite view. The debate, Helen recorded, "waxed warm."[29] Helen was an apt pupil who recorded her admiration for her headmistress in her diary, revealing that Edith's influence on her students was due to her interest in each one as an individual. Students respected her firm moral sense and appreciated her enduring ability to see humor in situations as they arose.[30]

Away from the Bryn Mawr School, Edith and Lucy did spend time together, including a summer on Mackinac Island in 1913. And that winter, Edith and Lucy were brought together again when Edith faced a serious health crisis. Just before Christmas 1913, Edith took Margaret to a doctor only to find out that she herself was gravely ill, potentially with cancer. An operation was performed immediately.[31] Between 1913 and

1920, she would have four operations to remove growths on her breast. Apparently only one of these—removed in a later operation—proved to be malignant. Others, including a cyst, were removed by her surgeon, Dr. Howard Kelly, as a precaution. At the time of Edith's diagnosis in 1913, Gertrude was recovering from pneumonia, and it was Lucy who came to Baltimore to nurse Edith back to health. As soon as she could leave the hospital, Lucy took Edith to her flat on the Bryn Mawr College campus, where she remained until February. But, as Lucy told Bertrand Russell, Edith was very "brave spirited."[32] She was soon taking on new challenges, organizing a campaign in Baltimore to limit the social activities of the city's preparatory school students, challenging M. Carey Thomas on the question of Bryn Mawr School graduation requirements, and helping Lucy to plan Bertrand Russell's visit to Baltimore and Bryn Mawr College.

On March 30, Edith opened a meeting held at McCoy Hall on the Johns Hopkins campus by telling an audience of parents, clergy, businessmen, professionals, and heads of other schools that many teachers struggled trying to instruct students who were too tired to learn after participating in social activities late into the previous night.[33] Those who attended the meeting agreed. The meeting determined that a committee would be formed to create a list of theatrical productions and films—the students were beginning to attend movies—whose content was considered inappropriate for adolescents. Balls, it was determined, would be thrown less frequently and would begin and end at earlier hours. It was an ambitious movement for Edith to initiate while still recovering from surgery but one that sheds light on some of the challenges she faced leading the Bryn Mawr School. There was always a balance that needed to be found between attracting the prominent families of Baltimore to the school and satisfying their social expectations.

As Baltimore's population continued to grow, mainly through migration into the city from rural areas, the Bryn Mawr School's position as an elite institution became more pronounced. The school had been innovative at its founding and had initially struggled to attract students. Edith's emphasis on education as a force for molding character had reassured many parents and had contributed to the growth of the institution.

Progressives, however, would soon argue for a more practical education that would reach a wider population, seeking to eliminate Greek and Latin from school curricula on the grounds that these subjects were only for the leisured class who had the time to study them. The first such attack on the Bryn Mawr School would come in 1917. In the meantime, Edith felt that cultivating the self-discipline necessary to acquire a college preparatory education was well worth an individual's efforts, even if the student did not intend to go on to college. Such an education would help Bryn Mawr School graduates become responsible, engaged citizens.

The school had become a Baltimore institution and, eventually, Edith would recognize that the school's relationship to Bryn Mawr College was becoming more distant. Yet she still prized the closeness of the two institutions. When, that spring, the college held one of its May Day celebrations, she resolved to bring some of the students to the campus for the festivities. The fete copied Elizabethan models, and most of the college students participated, with many of them wearing Elizabethan dress. Thomas approved Edith's plan to bring some students, acknowledging her influence as headmistress, writing, "It seems to me your going will make a great difference in the enthusiasm and interest of the children in attending May Day and that it will also make a difference in the willingness of the parents to have the children come."[34]

Even as Edith made changes to the school, the stage was being set for the series of confrontations with M. Carey Thomas that would contribute to Edith's decision to resign as headmistress in 1922. The alumnae were becoming more active and also, through their seats on the board of managers, more powerful at the school. They became a source of support for Edith, as Thomas and Garrett became increasingly absorbed with Garrett's declining health. Garrett had largely left Baltimore after the women's suffrage convention in 1906. Preferring to live at the Deanery at Bryn Mawr College with Thomas, she had closed her house on Monument Street. Though sometimes hospitalized in Baltimore, her increasing ill health made it difficult for her to take part in the administration of the Bryn Mawr School.

In the spring of 1914, in the last year of Garrett's life, an issue that would become an enduring source of conflict between Edith and

Thomas came to the fore: the requirement that a student pass the Bryn Mawr College entrance examination to graduate from the Bryn Mawr School. It had been the requirement for graduation from the school's inception.[35] Edith believed that any student who was determined to pass the exam could do so, even if it meant studying long hours. She was always convinced during both her years as a student and as a headmistress that mastering intellectually rigorous material was its own reward. But, as Edith learned in dealing with Baltimore's socially prominent families, failure to graduate could mean postponing a daughter's social debut.[36] Some parents simply removed their daughters from the Bryn Mawr School before their senior year, rather than risk their failure on the examination.[37]

As the school grew larger, Edith accepted the reality that not all of her students wished to attend college and, of those who did, not all wanted to go to Bryn Mawr. By 1914, she was questioning the assumed link between the school and the college, as she felt that girls who attended the Bryn Mawr School but did not graduate still benefited from their years at the institution. Edith believed that the school experience molded character, a function as important, if not more so, than the formal education it offered. (Edith would not fully articulate her ideas until 1917, when she argued for the continued teaching of Latin in girls' schools. She expected girls to become members of a democratic society and therefore they needed to acquire the self-discipline necessary for citizenship.[38]) She also hoped that their years at the Bryn Mawr School stimulated their curiosity and their enjoyment of learning.[39]

Edith began to doubt the appropriateness of the school's graduation requirement in 1914. That May, M. Carey Thomas's sister Margaret Carey, who had married the businessman Anthony Morris Carey and who was a member of the board of managers, reported resistance to the exams. She repeated a rumor, current at the time, that the ones for that year were more challenging than those from previous years. Thomas's reply reflected the level of influence she felt Edith exerted at the school: "The examinations are not a particle more difficult but Miss Hamilton thinks so and of course if Miss Hamilton thinks so and says so other

FIGURE 10. Edith Hamilton as headmistress of the Bryn Mawr
School circa 1916. Photograph courtesy of the archives of the Bryn
Mawr School.

people will say so because she does. I have repeatedly asked Miss Hamilton to show me any instances of an increase of difficulty in the examinations but she has failed to do so."[40] Edith, however, raised another
issue: increasingly, material on the exams did not reflect what was taught
at the school, another sign of the growing distance between the school
and the college.[41]

By August, Thomas appeared to offer a compromise: a preliminary
entrance examination. Writing to Edith, who was spending the summer

on Mackinac, Thomas mentioned that Vassar was among the colleges using a preliminary entrance exam, a proposal she was prepared to make to the faculty of Bryn Mawr College. Such an examination would, as Thomas informed Edith, "make sure the children were on the right road" and "reduce the strain" of studying for the final examination before graduation, though ultimately no change was made.[42] The debate was the first instance of what would become a serious source of contention between Edith and Thomas, one that would be revived in 1919, ultimately beginning Edith's long process of resignation from the Bryn Mawr School.

In the spring of 1914, Lucy also found herself in conflict with Thomas over the proposed visit of Bertrand Russell to Bryn Mawr College. That March, Thomas wrote Lucy at least three times to voice her opposition to Russell giving a lecture on the campus due to the previous Russell visit—in 1896—in which Russell's then-wife Alys, a cousin of M. Carey Thomas, had spoken to the students about free love.[43] Russell was now separated from Alys and felt that Thomas opposed his visit out of consideration for her feelings.[44] Edith helped Lucy plan Russell's visit to Baltimore, arranging for him to stay with the Reids and helping to set an April date for a lecture in the city.[45] The positivist philosopher was critical of the British School of Idealism that had influenced Edith, but she was enthusiastic about his Baltimore lecture.[46] As war clouds gathered in Europe, Russell would become a more controversial figure for his advocacy of a neutral stance in the conflict, a view initially shared by the Cambridge physicist J. J. Thomson, a friend of the Reid family. Russell then traveled to Bryn Mawr College to see Lucy, where, despite Thomas's prohibition, he gave a lecture to a small group of students in her apartment on the campus. Lucy felt deep satisfaction with Russell's visit, urging him to return to Baltimore soon so the Reids could introduce him to President Woodrow Wilson.[47] Edith and Lucy then spent much of the summer together on Mackinac Island.[48]

Margaret could not help Edith in her conflict with M. Carey Thomas since, in the spring of 1914, enjoying a period of good health, she had gone to the University of Munich to do laboratory research, accompanied by Clara Landsberg. By July her work was completed and, despite the increasing tensions in Europe, the pair traveled to Switzerland and Germany. That month Margaret and Clara spent time in Bad Harzburg, hiking in the mountains and preparing to join Clara's father, Dr. Landsberg, for more sightseeing in Germany.[49] Margaret was particularly eager to see Dresden, one of Gertrude's favorite cities. It was in Dresden, however, on August 1, that Margaret, Clara, and the people of Germany learned that the country would soon be at war: martial law had been declared and troops were mobilizing.[50] They managed to board one of the last passenger trains out of Germany and arrived safely in Amsterdam on August 4, 1914, just one day after war was declared between Germany and France.[51] Three days later, as Margaret was about to board a boat bound for England with Clara and Clara's father, she saw Doris Fielding Reid among the crowd. Doris was waiting by the gangway, hoping that Margaret's party would be among the many hastening aboard.[52]

In the summer of 1914, Doris Fielding Reid was eighteen and soon to pose a challenge to Edith's affection for Lucy. In fact, she and Edith were already corresponding.[53] Doris had spent only six years at the Bryn Mawr School, leaving, along with her cousin Gladys, in 1909, thus avoiding the rigors of studying for the Bryn Mawr College entrance exam but also forgoing graduation from the school.[54] Doris's own memories of her school years consisted chiefly of basketball games, both among the school's intramural teams or the annual extramural game between the Bryn Mawr School and St. Timothy's School.[55] Although Edith and Doris once apparently told a Washington friend, the journalist Felix Morley, that from the time Doris entered the Bryn Mawr School they were "never spiritually divided," there is no record of such a relationship dating from Doris's years at the school.[56]

In her final year at the school, as Edith became involved in the Equal Suffrage League, Doris's class held a debate on the women's vote. Doris was assigned to argue the opposition's side as her classmates already considered her to exhibit the "conservative turn of mind." They found her skilled in debate—a trait they attributed to the influence of her father—and she forcefully countered one of the arguments often put forward by the Equal Suffrage League: that the women's vote was useful in reforming social ills. To the suggestion that women acted against the

detrimental influence of alcohol in society, Doris replied that temperance was a "thing of the past."[57] Her willingness to argue against women's
suffrage may have been due in part to her dislike of the new women,
often suffrage advocates—"Those old war horses"—as she described
them in her memoir, who "simply despised the southern people, who,
in turn, could not abide them."[58]

Her remark emphasized one aspect of Doris's identity: southerner.[59]
In fact, Doris supported women's right to vote, and she would become
politically active as an adult. Yet by 1909 it was also clear that she did not
identify with women's reformist causes as Edith sometimes did. Instead,
Doris as a teenager had already arrived at the individualistic views that
would eventually lead her to adopt politically conservative stances
throughout her life, a reputation she had firmly established among her
classmates, one of whom invoked the words of her uncle the poet Henry
van Dyke in rebuttal.[60]

Doris had left the school to concentrate on her piano studies at Baltimore's Peabody Conservatory; she was serious about her artistic
pursuits but not, necessarily, her scholarly ones.[61] Like Edith, she had
acquired a deep opposition to war in her childhood, and as she entered
adolescence she had developed a taste for the poetry of Emily Dickinson.[62] She carried a well-worn volume of Dickinson's poems in her
pocket and could still, as late as 1954, copy some lines of her poetry from
memory into a letter.[63] After leaving the Bryn Mawr School, Doris spent
a year in London studying piano.[64] In the summer of 1913 she traveled
to Italy with Mary B. Harris, who had been her Latin teacher at the Bryn
Mawr School. Harris had taught Latin at the school from 1906 until 1911.
A former Hull House volunteer who had earned a doctorate in Sanskrit
at the University of Chicago, Harris became a lifelong friend of both
Edith and Doris.[65] Although Doris spent time with her parents after
their arrival in Europe, she and Harris lived for much of the winter of
1913–14 in Berlin, where Doris studied piano and vocal music and Harris
studied numismatics.[66]

The life that she shared with her former teacher made a profound
impression on Doris, who, twenty years into her relationship with
Edith, wrote in a description of Harris, "It is rare that in any one person

are combined the qualities and attitude of the artist and at the same time those of a scholar." Doris continued: "When she was listening to music or playing it, or looking at paintings, or reading poetry, or sitting on the Palatine contemplating the scene, I thought she was first and foremost the artist."[67] The portrait might almost be one of Edith—even in its reference to the enjoyment of listening to music, which, as late as 1922, her deafness still did not entirely prevent.[68]

The year with Harris created an ideal for Doris: a relationship with an older, intellectual woman who also possessed artistic yearnings, a foretaste of the life she would share with Edith. It also established an idea that would be key to the relationship between Edith and Doris: Edith could be both scholar and artist. She could be a writer, drawing on her knowledge of the classical world. She would no longer have to yield to Lucy's superior writing talent.

In the summer of 1914, Harry and Edith Reid had traveled to Europe, where both of their children were studying. The Reids visited Ellen and Henry van Dyke, Harry's sister and brother-in-law, in the Netherlands. Originally sent to Europe by President Woodrow Wilson in 1913 to promote a plan for European peace, Henry van Dyke had quickly been appointed U.S. ambassador to the Netherlands.[69] The outbreak of the war was a source of fresh concern for the Reids, since their son Francis, who had recently graduated from Cambridge University, immediately expressed a wish to join the German army.[70] Accordingly, he left his parents for a time, creating anxiety until early August, when he was successfully located by Henry van Dyke, who asked the U.S. ambassador to Germany to look after him. Ultimately, Francis would join the U.S. Army and see service in the First World War. After her struggle to get out of Germany, Margaret was delighted to meet up with the Reids in the Netherlands. They invited her and Clara to sleep in their shipboard cabin while Clara's father and Harry slept on the deck. Once in England, both parties settled into a hotel in London's Bloomsbury Square for the long wait to secure passage back to the United States. Although Britain was, by August 7, at war, the home front was not yet dominated by the desperate search for supplies Margaret had witnessed in Dresden.

Stranded in England from August 7 until September 9, Margaret had many opportunities to observe the Reid family, whom she largely found high-strung, making their company tiring. The Hamilton sisters, as Doris would come to learn, were devoted to each other but did not express their feelings as openly as the Reids did. The time spent in London was the beginning of Margaret's antipathy for the Reid family, which would reach its peak in the years when Edith began the process of resigning from the Bryn Mawr School.[71] Still, Margaret managed to enjoy one excursion to Cambridge with the family to visit their friends, the physicist J. J. Thomson and his family. Their son, the future physicist George Paget Thomson, soon became an admirer of Doris, though Margaret noticed that Doris studiously avoided him during the visit.[72]

Edith and Doris had corresponded during Doris's time in London, but Margaret confided to Gertrude that "Edith must take what Doris writes with a grain of salt—she is morbid and has a chip on her shoulder all the time, as regards her mother."[73] Doris felt that Francis was her mother's favorite child. Edith would often observe that Edith Reid was indulgent with her son. When Rosamond Gilder, a New York friend of Doris's who had studied psychoanalysis, declared that Edith Reid had a "mother-and-son complex," Edith Hamilton agreed.[74] From the winter of 1913–14, Doris sought the companionship of an older woman, first Mary B. Harris, and, eventually, Edith Hamilton, both women of her mother's generation. It is tempting to see both of Doris's companions as giving her the maternal love she may have felt she lacked. Both women, however, also gave Doris the freedom to pursue her artistic goals.

For Doris, a sense of personal freedom was essential. During these years she often found it in the automobile. Though Doris did not necessarily identify with the new woman's search for liberation, she was of the generation of new women for whom the automobile was a symbol of autonomy and the practical means of achieving it. The pursuit of a career was another means by which Doris secured freedom for herself. While the life of a concert pianist would have allowed for individual artistic expression, Doris found freedom in her ultimate career as a stockbroker, which permitted her to focus her energies on the business world instead of on trying to resolve Reid family troubles.[75] Through-out her life, Doris believed in the necessity of personal freedom for the individual, a value that determined her political views. The individual's need to pursue self-actualization was the greatest bond Edith and Doris shared.

For the Hamilton sisters, the United States' war with Germany cre-ated conflicting feelings about a culture they esteemed. As Alice would write in her autobiography, the family had warm memories of German Lutheran Christmas celebrations during their childhood in Fort Wayne, and Montgomery, Edith, Alice, and Margaret had all studied at German universities.[76] Two years before the outbreak of the war, Edith had writ-ten a letter to the editor of the *Baltimore Sun* in favor of a compulsory school attendance law for the state of Maryland. Comparing the United States to Germany, which did have such a law, Edith argued that as a result Germany had the fewest illiterate citizens in the world and a rec-ord of great intellectual achievements.[77] The United States, as a democ-racy that welcomed immigrants, had, in Edith's opinion, even more need of compulsory education to train future citizens than the German Empire. After the United States entered the war, the conflict would raise more specific questions about the connection between the study of clas-sics and their role in creating responsible citizens, resulting in Edith's first published article, which would appear in the *New Republic* maga-zine. But at the outbreak of the war the Hamilton family had to balance their respect for German culture and intellectual life with Edith and Alice's experiences during their year of study in Germany, when they had often felt there was a militaristic aspect to the culture.[78]

Respect for German intellectual achievement was also great among the Johns Hopkins faculty with whom Edith frequently associated. As she would discover, she would face no general opposition to continuing instruction in the German language at the Bryn Mawr School, where some of the students were the daughters of Hopkins faculty.[79] Edith's friend Dr. Howard Kelly was married to a German, Laetitia Bredow, the daughter of a Danzig (Gdansk) medical doctor.[80] Edith had befriended the Kellys from her first years in Baltimore, and she had joined them for a camping trip along the Mississauga River in 1906.[81] One of their daughters, Olga, had graduated from the Bryn Mawr School in 1909 and had subsequently involved herself in Bryn Mawr League work. Eventually, she would graduate from Bryn Mawr College.[82] From 1913, another bond had developed between Edith and Dr. Kelly, as he had become her surgeon. As she had during her first years in Baltimore, when she had urged Jessie to consult Dr. Kelly, Edith placed her trust in the Johns Hopkins gynecologist who, through early detection and the series of operations that followed, saved her life.

For Edith, the war would create challenges in administering the Bryn Mawr School, especially after American entry into the conflict. These compounded the difficulties of her position at the school that began with the death of Mary Garrett at the Deanery on April 3, 1915.[83] Edith took part in a memorial service for her held at McCoy Hall, at which Dr. Lilian Welsh also spoke.[84] Garrett's death was recognized by the students, the alumnae, and by Edith herself as a turning point for the school.[85] To Edith, Garrett had been a strong advocate of women's suffrage who had allowed her to promote her vision of citizenship at the school. Garrett's death, however, would create more tension between Edith and M. Carey Thomas. In her will, Garrett left the Bryn Mawr School its building and an endowment. This was necessary since, at the time of her death, the school had not yet met its own expenses and would not until 1917.[86] Her death, however, also increased M. Carey Thomas's power at the school since the will made her the executor of Garrett's estate, a responsibility that included ensuring that the institution remained exclusively a college preparatory school for girls.[87] The impact of Thomas's enhanced position—she became both president and treasurer—would not become apparent until after the First World War. The disagreements between Edith and Thomas would also contribute to the deterioration of Edith and Lucy's relationship.

At the same time, Edith was preoccupied with Alice's safety and her own health. In April, Alice accompanied Jane Addams as she attended the International Congress of Women held at The Hague to try to work for a European peace settlement.[88] Edith supported Alice's efforts, realizing that she was potentially risking her life for the cause. The sinking of the *Lusitania* in the month after her departure, however, caused Edith to feel that the war put the lives of all civilians at risk. One of Alice's Farmington friends, the architect Theodate Pope, was among the passengers aboard the *Lusitania*, and Alice was relieved to find her listed among the survivors.[89] Edith, writing to Jessie soon after the disaster, told her, "It seems now that anything may happen and that nobody's rights count at all."[90] Alice cabled her mother and sisters to assure them of her safety, but her messages arrived long after the events she reported in them had already been published in newspapers.

In the meantime, Edith may have drawn comfort from the school's commencement address, given by former President William Howard Taft, who spoke on "The Permanent Basis of International Peace."[91] It was a speech that, in its general arguments, Taft gave often that spring, including at the June commencement of Bryn Mawr College, where his daughter Helen was among the graduates.[92] Taft assured his audience that President Wilson would not bring the United States into the war and spoke about his own efforts to create a lasting peace through the establishment of an international body to adjudicate disputes. He soon became president of the League to Enforce Peace, an organization that eventually supported U.S. membership in the League of Nations.[93]

Edith also became active in the Woman's Peace Party, led by Jane Addams, which supported the cause of women's suffrage but gave priority to pacifism. Edith had first met Addams in late 1898, on a visit to Alice at Hull House, the same occasion on which she had met John Dewey. Addams impressed Edith, who had told her Hamilton cousins, "I wonder just what makes her so wonderful, so unlike everyone else in the world."[94] The party would later become the Women's International League for Peace and Freedom in which Alice would participate. Edith, along with Edith Reid, would establish the league's Baltimore chapter in 1922.[95]

Edith claimed that she had opposed war from childhood, when she hated having to memorize poems that celebrated conflict. Though she never thought of the ancient Greeks as pacifists, she would always see them as the first people to fully understand the horrors of war and to portray its harsh realities.[96] This interpretation of the ancient Greeks was evident in one of the first projects of the Woman's Peace Party in which Edith took part. That May, she and Dr. Mary Sherwood were among the sponsors of a Baltimore performance of *The Trojan Women* of Euripides, given by the touring Chicago Little Theatre Company.[97] The production, which used Gilbert Murray's translation, was one of many given in the United States by the Chicago troupe as the war developed in Europe, helping the tragedy to become known as an antiwar play.[98] It would be in a similar context, just before the Second World War, that Edith would produce her own translation of the work.

Edith also defended the free speech rights of pacifists. She was especially sympathetic to the sentiments of her friend Margaret Shearman, who had been brought up in the Society of Friends.[99] The public hostility that pacifists such as Jane Addams endured during the war was still a source of outrage to Edith in 1927, when she published an essay on Aristophanes in the magazine *Theatre Arts Monthly* arguing that the citizens of fifth-century Athens enjoyed a freedom of speech surpassing that of Americans during the First World War.[100] In explaining the Athenians' commitment to the principle of free speech, Edith wrote, "If an American had produced a play, after we entered the war, which represented General Pershing and Admiral Sims as wanting to desert; which denounced the war, praised the Germans, glorified the peace party, ridiculed Uncle Sam, that play would have had a short life."[101] In comparison, the fifth-century Athenians had displayed much more tolerance of opposing opinions, attending the plays of Aristophanes whether they agreed with his sentiments or not. The article largely became the chapter on Aristophanes in *The Greek Way*, but the passages referring to pacifism during the war were moved to the second chapter, retaining their function as an illustration of the level of free expression the Athenians enjoyed.[102] Edith's advocacy of pacifism and civil liberties were a natural development from her position as a suffragist and anticipated the noninterventionist positions she adopted in later life.

The outbreak of war posed a challenge to some key aspects of Edith and Lucy's relationship: the enjoyment of travel in Europe and the appreciation of its cultural heritage. The war began the dismantling of much of the expatriate community around Florence to which Lucy had introduced Edith and which had thrived on aesthetic pursuits.[103] But Edith and Lucy's years together were not quite over; as Edith tried to recover her health, she and Lucy would find the opportunity to spend almost an entire year together in Japan and China.

Chapter 9

"THE WHOLE WONDER OF THE EAST"

In the spring of 1915, Edith decided that she needed a lengthy vacation from the Bryn Mawr School. Her recent brush with cancer left her determined and, after a summer spent on Mackinac, where in July Alice was finally able to join her, Edith requested and received a yearlong leave of absence at half salary. Margaret was appointed acting headmistress in her place.[1] The leave and the pay enabled Edith to join Lucy on a nine-month trip to Japan and China. While the outbreak of war in Europe made travel there impossible, since their years as students at Bryn Mawr College, Lucy and Edith had had an interest in visiting Asia. They now found the opportunity to fulfill their wishes.

Edith's exposure to Japanese culture had come in forms that encouraged her to think of Japan as a nation making progress in Westernization. During her first two years at college, both she and Lucy had befriended a Japanese student, Ume Tsuda, who as a child had been educated in the United States as part of a Meiji government experiment in the education of women. Edith and Lucy would visit her in Tokyo during their time abroad. Edith and Lucy held the assumptions common among Westerners of the time who saw Japan as striving for modernity while China's development lagged. Japan was, as Lucy would write in her reminiscences of their trip, "borrowing modern technique from us."[2] Just as Edith adopted generally held attitudes toward Japan, she would also adopt perspectives on China informed by missionaries, in part a reflection of her continuing correspondence with Susan and Lily Duryee.

Edith had promised the board of managers that she would open the school and preside over the first weeks of the new academic year.[3] Her departure was also delayed by an illness Margaret suffered. For a time it looked as if she would be unable to act as headmistress in Edith's absence, but Margaret thought Edith needed rest and urged her to take the trip.[4] Although Lucy lingered at Seal Harbor, Maine, until late September, she ultimately departed without Edith, who therefore traveled west alone by train to meet Lucy in San Francisco, where they were to board a ship.[5] Edith had never traveled beyond the Mississippi and was thrilled by the beauty of the American West. Particularly enthralling were the sights of the New Mexico desert and the Grand Canyon, which she would describe decades later in *The Echo of Greece* as "stupendous."[6] She was amazed to find that in California flowers were still in bloom in late October. In San Diego she stayed in the rambling but elegant Hotel del Coronado located right on the shore of the Pacific Ocean.[7] She then traveled north along the coast from San Diego to San Francisco, admiring the beauty of Santa Barbara, whose shoreline reminded her of the Bay of Salerno.

Edith attended the world's fairs that were held in both San Diego and San Francisco to celebrate the recent opening of the Panama Canal. The Japanese Empire had numerous exhibits at San Francisco's Panama Pacific International Exposition, many of which were housed in a replica of the Golden Pavilion in Kyoto and set in a Japanese garden. Much of what she would see would fuel her anticipation of Japan: in the exposition's amusement area, known as the Zone, a 120-foot-tall golden Buddha, a full-scale replica of the one she would soon see at Kamakura, sat at the entrance to an exhibit called Japan Beautiful. There were other attractions to draw Edith's attention: the Congressional Union for Women's Suffrage was soliciting signatures for a federal women's suffrage law since women in California had already been granted the right to vote. Some of the exposition's buildings had been constructed based on classical models: the Oregon Building was a Parthenon, constructed entirely of Douglas firs, and the Machinery Palace took its design from the Baths of Caracalla in Rome.[8] Like many attending the Pan-Pacific, Edith was impressed by the fair's beautiful architecture and wished that the buildings could remain standing forever, telling Jessie, "I can't bear to think that they are not permanent & that everyone will not be able to see them."[9] She wished that her family, especially Gertrude, could see the beauty of California.

After a rough sea-crossing, brightened only by their brief stop in Honolulu, Edith and Lucy landed at Yokohama in early November and settled just south of the port city in the village of Kamakura.[10] The beauty of Japan soon compensated for the unpleasantness of the voyage. One of their first sightseeing ventures was to Nikko, famed for its temples set in high mountains and reached by crossing a sacred bridge. Edith was struck by how the brightly painted temples contrasted with the dull colors of the setting. The temples, she told Jessie, "are of red lacquer, which is the most beautiful Indian red, and their roofs of shining black lacquer bound with bright brass and they stand on terraces deep in the hillside, surrounded by great grey stone walls all lichen grown, and by cedars, the tallest, straightest, most solemn trees I have ever seen."[11] At Nikko, Edith developed a fascination with Japanese pilgrims, whom she would later admire in the temples of Kyoto.[12] She was still new to the customs and manners of Japan, however, and inadvertently offended a pilgrim who offered her a photograph of a well-known Buddhist priest as a gift. When Edith mistakenly tried to pay him for it instead of accepting it outright, the pilgrim responded with a look of pain. In the months that followed, she grew to better understand and appreciate the Japanese, who seemed to her entirely capable of balancing ancient tradition with modernization.

Edith enjoyed walking through the streets of Kamakura, where their stay was slightly lengthened by an illness Lucy suffered. Edith, who frequently went out to buy food and other supplies, was fascinated by the small houses she passed. During her winter-long stay in Japan, however, Edith would always ponder how the Japanese managed to stay warm with only small coal braziers to heat their homes. The seeming Japanese indifference to cold meant that Edith and Lucy were always careful to stay at hotels that catered to Europeans.[13] From the streets of Kamakura, Edith could occasionally enjoy views of Mount Fuji.

When Lucy recovered, they visited Tokyo, where they spent a week with Helen and Simon Flexner, who were about to embark on their return voyage to the United States after visiting China.[14] They were also able to renew their friendship with Ume Tsuda. Ume, who had been born to a samurai and who had formerly taught at a school attended by aristocratic women, moved in court circles and took Edith and Lucy to a coronation ball.[15] Edith professed to be disappointed by the experience, not only because the Mikado himself was not present but also, in spite of her sense that Japan was modern, because the Japanese men wore Western suits. The women, by contrast, wore Japanese dress, except for the princesses. Always a close observer of the status of women, Edith noted that the women barely socialized at the ball. She explained to Jessie that the women had "no idea of social life. You see women have never been admitted to it, men gave entertainments to each other with geisha to entertain them. So the women don't know anything about it." She continued: "These were the aristocratic women of Tokyo, but they huddled together, a gentle, shrinking, speechless body, while the men stood by themselves and talked."[16] She admired the kimonos of the women, however, especially the brightly colored silk sashes they wore. In addition to the coronation ball, they also attended a performance of a historical drama at Tokyo's Imperial Theater.[17]

Edith and Lucy decided to spend the winter in Kyoto. The city's location in a river basin made its winters cold, meaning that it would be off-season there and the two could stay cheaply in the European-style Hotel Miyako, where they planned to remain for a total of eight weeks.[18] Edith spent her time touring Kyoto's temples, admiring the distinctive roof of the Nishi O'Tami, made of "thick cedar wood bark, many, many layers, & it is bound with copper that has turned in hundreds of years a greenish blue."[19] She also visited the Golden Pavilion, a replica of which she had seen in San Francisco. The pavilion, called the Kinkaku-ji, had been built in the fourteenth century by the Shogun Ashikaga Yoshimitsu and stood three stories tall, each story in a different style of architecture.[20] It was not leafed in gold as its builder had intended but, Edith continued, it was "considered the most perfect building in Japan."[21] She described it as "truly Japanese, utterly simple, of unadorned brown wood. But people here think its line and proportions absolutely perfect."[22] She also observed the practice of Buddhism, and a reference to the Amida School, the distinctive form of the religion evident in the city, would appear in *The Greek Way*.[23]

The wide streets of Kyōto, lined with shop houses of a distinctive architecture, which Edith described as "not Japanese & not European," would have been delightful but for their unfamiliar smells. Still, Edith was enthusiastic about an evening walk along one of Kyōto's canals, which was "crossed by such nice tiny stone bridges."[24] All around them Lucy and Edith witnessed a scene with elements of both the familiar and the exotic, as Edith told Agnes: "On either side supper was going on. Often the paper walls were closed, but the light shone through in big pale-yellow oblongs. Sometimes we could look into the dim interior where the family were sitting near a brazier. All along on both sides hung paper lanterns of white and red. Queer strumming sounds of a kind of mournful guitar came sometimes, and often a wailing song. And the whole wonder of the east and my being in it rushed over me."[25]

Japanese Christianity may not have been widespread—Ume Tsuda was one of the few Japanese Christians they met—but those who had adopted the religion impressed Edith by their devotion. During her winter in Kyōto, she attended church services regularly—as she did not in Baltimore—finding that she enjoyed the simple and sincere worship of the Japanese Christians. In a non-Christian culture, she told Agnes, "One gets a different feeling about being a Christian, a sense of loyalty—I never had it before—a passionate sense of Christ not having what is His."[26] During her weeks in Kyōto she attended an Episcopal church where both of the Japanese clergymen conducted the service entirely in their own language except for a brief sermon. The service struck her as deeply genuine, making her "feel in the air that everyone there is there because of a deep personal belief."[27] In contrast to their experience in China, Edith and Lucy had little contact with missionaries in Japan. The American woman who headed the women's Doshisha, or Christian school, in Kyōto was one of the few missionaries with whom they socialized. Edith found that she preferred the Japanese Episcopal services to the more stilted Congregational service in English that was held in the Doshisha's chapel.[28] The experience of attending Japanese Episcopal services convinced her that the culture was open to the adoption of Christianity as part of the nation's modernization process. Missionaries seemed unnecessary and the services at the Doshisha artificial.

For Edith, only Greece would ever compare to the beauty of Mount Fuji and its environs.[29] She hoped, however, to visit Lily, who lived in Amoy (Xiamen), and Susan, who lived farther inland at Changchow (Zhangzhou). In December 1915, Edith feared that she and Lucy might not be able to go on to China at all, due to what she dimly referred to as "disturbances," which seemed to suggest the possibility of a revolution.[30] By March the danger appeared to have subsided, and Edith and Lucy separated for two weeks. Lucy went directly to Shanghai, where, despite her genuine fascination with the city, she continued to feel some anxiety about a possible revolt.[31] Edith sailed for Foochow (Fuzhou), where she boarded a steamer that would take her to Amoy.[32] Her first glimpse of China made her feel "farther away than ever in my life before," an impression created by the dramatic appearance of the bay at Foochow, which was lined on each side by steep, rocky cliffs.[33] She barely had time to enjoy its beauty, however, before she boarded another boat to continue her journey to Amoy. Lily met her boat in the harbor, distinguished by the island of Kulangsu, which gave the appearance of a large pile of rocks where brightly colored stucco houses with verandas perched.[34] Although Edith may not have realized it immediately upon her arrival, the island, a self-governing international settlement, was the center of activity for the Dutch Reformed Church's Amoy mission. Among the institutions that the mission had located there was the Charlotte Duryee School for Girls, named for Lily and Susan's mother.[35]

In spite of the colorful buildings on Kulangsu, Edith was struck by the starkness of the house that Lily shared with two other missionaries, Katherine and Mary Talmage. The sisters were well established in the Amoy missionary community, since their father had served the mission for forty-five years before his death.[36] Lily, Edith felt, was devoted to Mary Talmage, who was familiarly known as Molly. Edith was sympathetic to the household, composed of three single women. "Ladies' houses" such as theirs were a common living arrangement for single female missionaries in China and one that allowed them to enjoy a semblance of family life.[37] The missionaries seemed to live in deprivation, but there was no discussion of the hardships. Instead the atmosphere of the house, Edith told Jessie, was one in which there was "no show of religion, practically no talk of it, and yet you feel their true saintliness and you see every hour the steady, unremitting hard work they are doing for nothing but the Kingdom of God."[38] To Edith, the simple one-story house with a large veranda and high ceilings was too cold for the March weather, but she understood that it was built to remain cool during the summer. The two Talmage sisters devoted their time to increasing literacy among Chinese women, an effort intended to encourage evangelization. Lily, who had lived in Amoy since 1911, taught at the girls' school, assisting Mary Talmage.[39]

Edith's approval of missionaries' activities in China was due in part to the attention they paid to the status of women. She was right about the combination of unceasing toil and little reward that missionaries in China endured. The workers in the Amoy mission had seen only slow increases in church membership, and their converts numbered just over two thousand in 1915, seven hundred having been made since the Boxer Rebellion.[40] Edith felt no return of the earlier interest that she had felt as a student at Bryn Mawr for missionary work, but she did express admiration for some of the missionaries' efforts, especially those on behalf of women and the sick. The missionaries opposed the practice of foot binding, especially after Chinese movements to stop the practice had begun in the late nineteenth century.[41] Missionaries condemned it not only because it was potentially hazardous to women's health but also because it inhibited Chinese women from walking to church services or mission schools. Edith noticed the practice, writing to Norah in May on a postcard that apparently showed an image of a Chinese woman gathering fuel: "This poor old thing has her feet bound as almost all the old women have."[42] During Edith's visit to Amoy, Lily was engaged in helping a twelve-year-old servant girl who had been badly burned by her mistress. The girl had been hospitalized for two months, during which time Lily had learned that the only means to avoid returning the girl to her former employer was to purchase her.[43] Missionaries in China did sometimes purchase potential converts. The story Edith told Jessie of Lily's work with the unfortunate girl was the kind of tale that frequently found its way into the correspondence of American missionaries in China, illustrating to those at home the positive good the missionaries accomplished.[44] Edith's recitation of the story was therefore another indication of her approval of their work.

Lily took Edith to visit Susan at Changchow, where her husband administered a hospital. In May 1905, less than two years after arriving in China, Susan had married Dr. Ahmed Fahmy. A widower with three children, Fahmy was an Egyptian-born convert to Christianity who had been sent to China by the London Missionary Society.[45] Edith and Lily traveled by riverboat to see them, an experience that allowed Edith to observe the great variety of boat traffic along the river. As Edith knew, the Fahmys had endured great losses in the years just before her visit. Lily and Susan's brother George had died of tuberculosis in June 1912.[46] Alice, the youngest of the Duryee sisters, who had accompanied Susan to China in 1903, had suffered from depression and died by suicide after throwing herself overboard off the coast of Nagasaki, Japan, while on a journey back to the United States in January 1911.[47] Edith felt that by 1916 Susan had still not fully recovered from Alice's death. Moreover, in December 1915, as she stayed in Kyoto, Edith learned that one of Dr. Fahmy's sons from his first marriage, Eric, had been killed on the Western Front.[48]

Susan, who had given birth to a daughter, Alice, in 1908, threw herself into missionary work.[49] On a visit to the Duryee home in New Brunswick in November 1897, Edith had told Jessie: "Susan does one more good than anyone in all the world. She lifts me up. Life is always simpler, truth surer, when I have seen her."[50] Susan brought such qualities to her missionary work—preferring not to stress doctrine but to provide an example of the Christian life, an approach that Edith, with her own dislike of dogma, approved. Early in her career as a missionary, Susan made a deep impression on the future writer and philosopher Lin Yutang, who, from 1935, would live in the United States and write a series of novels and philosophical works explaining Chinese culture to Americans. From the age of ten, Lin had been educated at a boys' school in Amoy, where he met Susan, whom he still remembered over fifty years later as a missionary filled "with the Christian spirit of regard and care for others." According to Lin, Susan possessed "the presence of the true spirit of Christianity," an example of how "Christians breed Christians, but Christian theology does not." Edith would not hear Lin speak until 1936, when she and Susan would attend a speech he gave in New York City, but he exemplified the link between Christianity and Chinese Nationalism that both Edith and Lucy noticed in China. Edith would read his books approvingly.[51]

The Fahmys' house at Changchow was set in a wide valley of rice fields visible from the French windows that opened onto a latticed veranda. But its isolation, coupled with the multiple losses of family members, meant that Susan had eagerly awaited Edith's visit.[52] Edith met seven-year-old Alice, whom she described as a "lovely winning child, very intelligent and of a great sweetness" and for whom Edith developed an enduring fondness.[53] She also visited Dr. Fahmy's hospital, which consisted of a row of low buildings and a courtyard. Patients would arrive early in the morning, hoping for a chance to see the doctor. Edith watched Dr. Fahmy at work for several hours, fascinated by how, in the midst of so much suffering, he remained "calm, strong, sure, ordering everything."[54] But Edith's visit to Susan lasted only a week, too brief for Susan's comfort, and she found Edith's departure difficult.[55] Susan's own years in China, however, were drawing to a close. Dr. Fahmy would retire from active work at the end of the First World War.[56]

Edith reunited with Lucy by traveling north to Shanghai, disembarking at its enormous bund, or wharves.[57] From Shanghai they ventured into the interior, to Nanking, where they visited the examination halls of the university. Both Edith and Lucy were impressed by their tour guide, who argued in favor of traditional Chinese learning and against the science courses taught at the government school in the city.[58] They were so struck by one of his comments that they would both include it in accounts of their trip to China. Lucy would remember the young guide's triumphant assertion that his "grandfather had passed three examinations of the old schools, the last in extreme age, and could write a letter that only two or three men in China could understand!"[59] Edith, remembering their trip in 1951, wrote that in response to her question of whether he preferred Eastern or Western learning better, the guide had replied, "My father knows a man, a very great writer, who can write in a way only one other man in China can understand."[60] Edith and Lucy left behind little documentary evidence of the bonds of their relationship and this, their shared response to an incident during their travels in China, is a small but important indication of the closeness of the viewpoint they once had.

From Nanking, they proceeded north to Tsingtao, taking the German-built Tsingtao-Tsinanfu railway through the province of Shantung. South of Tsinanfu, near Chufu (Qufu), they visited the temple built on the site where Confucius had preached. Lucy compared it favorably to a gothic cathedral, of which she and Edith had seen many together during their travels in Europe. Instead of gargoyles, the temple had pillars carved with dragons and small animals, the symbolism of which she could not discern.[61] By contrast, they were touched by the simplicity of Confucius's grave nearby—a mound partially shaded by trees, marked only by a small altar.[62]

From Nanking and Tsinanfu they proceeded north. By late May they were walking along the Great Wall and exploring Peking (Beijing). Although the weather was hot and dry at that time of year, and Lucy claimed that she kept dreaming of strawberries, the two explored the Ming tombs, surrounded by gates and temples that Edith found more impressive than the tombs themselves.[63] She was, however, enthusiastic about the beauty of Peking, describing its architecture to Gertrude: "The tiled roofs are just the colour of lapis lazuli; The painted bands are deep blue & green & gold."[64] Excitedly, she wrote about a Chinese dinner of forty different dishes, beginning with a bowl of sweet syrup made from lily root and ending with another bowl, this one of a brown mutton soup. Their host was Roger Green, who was accompanied by a Chinese man "in such a lovely robe of white silk, a kind of silk we never see at home, with the high lights all silver."[65]

Their time in China, however, was drawing to a close. The women had previously considered returning to the United States via the Trans-Siberian Railway, a route that would have landed them in war-torn Europe but one that would have allowed Lucy to see Bertrand Russell.[66] In the end, this route seemed too impractical, and, on July 4, 1916, Edith and Lucy sailed for Vancouver.[67] They then boarded the Canadian Pacific Railway to Fort William (now Thunder Bay, Ontario), returning to the United States by sailing across Lake Superior to Mackinac Island, where Gertrude had been spending the summer. Edith and Lucy stayed with her before Edith brought Gertrude to Baltimore.

Upon her return from Asia, Edith tried to settle into life with Margaret and Gertrude at 1312 Park, newly decorated with souvenirs of her travels: some Chinese carved tabletops and a pair of matching porcelain vases, blue with pink roses.[68] The winter of 1916–17, however, provided one significant change. In November 1915, during Edith's absence, Alice and Norah had dismantled the Fort Wayne house, assuming that Gertrude would reside with Edith and Margaret in Baltimore.[69] Alice, however, wanted the family to have a permanent home, especially one where the sisters could eventually retire. Fond of the Connecticut countryside since her days at Miss Porter's School, Alice found and purchased an eleven-room federal-style house along the Connecticut River near Hadlyme in December.[70] The house had formerly belonged to a family of sea captains, and there was a small ship chandlery on the property. Some of the surrounding landscape was reminiscent of Mackinac Island; near the house was a westward-facing cliff that towered over a wide point in the river.[71]

From the beginning, there was a conscious effort on the part of the sisters to make Hadlyme feel as if it was a permanent home all four of them could share. That March, the sisters made a point of staying at the house at the same time. As Margaret explained to Katherine, "We wanted our first time here to be all together with no one else—to make it seem home."[72] The Hamilton cousins—Katherine, Jessie, and Agnes—would also eventually purchase a home nearby at Deep River, Connecticut, making it seem for a time as if the close-knit circle of Hamilton cousins would reconstitute their Fort Wayne life along the banks of the Connecticut River.[73] The Hadlyme house, however, would become home mainly to Alice and Margaret, as well as Clara Landsberg. Edith would first spend time in Maine in the summer of 1918, and by 1922 she would make a summer home there with the Reid family. Norah, Margaret felt, never really settled at Hadlyme, though the shop on the property was intended as a studio for her work.[74]

The first visit to the Hadlyme house, however, was quickly followed by U.S. entry into the war. Allen and Taber Hamilton—the brothers of Katherine, Jessie, and Agnes—were soon in military service. Quint looked for a job working for the war effort, but his sisters frequently worried that he would be drafted for military service. He was thirty-one at the time the United States entered the war. After finishing his doctorate in French at Johns Hopkins in 1914, he had taught at two universities. On June 21, 1915, he had become the only one of his siblings to marry, wedding a musician and Wellesley graduate, Mary Neal. His mother and sisters attended the wedding in the bride's hometown of Newark, Ohio.[75] Ultimately Quint volunteered for Red Cross work and was sent to Europe in the summer of 1918. He would spend fourteen months in France, investigating the uses of humanitarian aid.[76]

Edith minimized the ways in which the war affected the Bryn Mawr School. All Baltimore schools were required to close on Mondays because of fuel rationing.[77] Edith, however, felt that since the school's furnaces had been supplied earlier in the week, the school building was warm enough to continue to hold classes on Saturdays to compensate for the lost school day, a decision that caused consternation among the members of Baltimore's ration board. Moreover, the war created other challenges for Edith, such as teachers departing for war relief work. At its headquarters on Light Street, the Bryn Mawr League also turned its attention to the war effort. Finally, during the worst weeks of the flu pandemic in 1918, Dr. Mary Sherwood would close the school entirely.[78]

Despite the war, Edith saw no reason to discontinue instruction in the German language, a decision that met with protest only from one student,

Isabel Blogg. Isabel's parents, however, did not share their daughter's opposition, which suggests that Edith did not experience any further pressure during the war to curb the teaching of German. The large numbers of Johns Hopkins faculty whose daughters attended the school may account for the continuing acceptance of German instruction. Though Isabel's parents still regarded Germany as a center of learning, Edith arranged for Isabel to study Greek instead, since in her protest she had expressed interest in the roots of Western democracy apparent in the American political system. Decades later, Isabel recalled Edith's wisdom in dealing with her opposition, allowing her to make her own choices as to what language to study, gently pointing out the value of each.[79]

As Edith responded to Isabel's challenge, she began to express in print the ideas for which she would become famous: the continuing need for the study of classical antiquity, a subject she and academic classicists began to consider as the U.S. entry into the war prompted discussions of the meaning of civilization.[80] Her first published work, which appeared in the progressive magazine the *New Republic*, was a response to the ideas of the education reformer Abraham Flexner. Flexner, the older brother of Dr. Simon Flexner, was preparing to open the Lincoln School of Teachers College in New York City that spring. It was in fact Lucy's responsibility to take Simon and Helen's sons, William and James, to school on their first day, a task that may have helped to draw Edith's attention to the new institution and the educational ideas for which it stood.[81]

Abraham Flexner, who considered himself a proponent of the educational philosophy of John Dewey, had described the theory behind the Lincoln School in his pamphlet *A Modern School*. He argued that the school should only teach subjects that would prepare students for life in the contemporary world—which meant that it would not teach Greek or Latin, or algebra or geometry.[82] The inclusion of such subjects in school curricula, he wrote, was due only to tradition. Moreover, he believed that these subjects were studied largely through rote, preventing students from learning through critical thought. He rejected any idea that the subjects had value because their study disciplined the mind.[83] Although Edith, in her response to Flexner, would address the question of education in the classics for girls specifically, Flexner insisted that he made no distinction between what was appropriate for either sex to study, though he added that "the *Modern School*, with its strongly realistic emphasis will undoubtedly not overlook women's domestic role and family function."[84] Edith interpreted this as instruction in domestic skills.

Flexner's pamphlet prompted Edith to write a response titled "Interesting Schools," which was published in the February 10, 1917, issue of the *New Republic*. She was particularly upset about a plan to establish a school open to girls where the students would be taught practical domestic skills but not academic subjects such as Latin and mathematics.[85] As Edith pointed out, late-nineteenth-century women had waged an intense battle to create schools that would teach them these as opposed to the finishing schools of the nineteenth century. Edith, of course, had been part of this struggle. She had had to study hard for her Bryn Mawr College entrance exam to make up for the deficiencies in her own education. She had then devoted her career to ensuring the high academic standards of the Bryn Mawr School. She was, therefore, deeply opposed to the idea that finishing school subjects might return to girls' education, not under the guise of accomplishments but due to the demands of "practicality."[86]

Edith also argued for the continuation of Latin in education even if the subject, at least at its early stages, was often learned by rote. She made a connection between self-discipline and citizenship, which demanded of an individual a sense of responsibility and self-restraint. As late as 1957, in *The Echo of Greece*, she wrote of the fourth-century BCE Athenian orator and teacher Isocrates that he understood the "the moderation and gentleness and self-control without which there is no civilization."[87] In "Interesting Schools," Edith stated her belief that even a woman who devoted her life to the care of her home and family needed to be self-disciplined to be a good citizen.[88]

Central to Edith's public debate with Flexner were the questions of what sort of education prepared students to participate in a democratic society and what was the correct interpretation of John Dewey's educational philosophy. To her opponents, Edith simply looked elitist. The

Bryn Mawr School, once a radical institution boldly preparing girls for a college education, had become a conservative institution in the eyes of its opponents. This was partly due to Edith's success at convincing the Baltimore elite to send their daughters to the Bryn Mawr School.[89]

The *New Republic*, in a "Reply" authored by the radical journalist Randolph Bourne, also accused Edith of being unfamiliar with the educational theories of John Dewey, though Edith of course had been influenced by the philosopher after she had visited his school.[90] Bourne largely concurred with Flexner's program, expressing his support for the Lincoln School. In an essay titled "Class and School," Bourne criticized institutions such as the Bryn Mawr School as the "last stronghold of educational conservatism" and for adhering to "obsolete educational theory of formal discipline and salvation through drudgery."[91] This educational philosophy, Bourne argued, was antidemocratic since it perpetuated the idea that a wealthy, leisured class had time to devote to learning subjects without obvious usefulness such as classics and advanced mathematics. In the early twentieth century, radicals such as Bourne often favored spreading knowledge of the classics to those who had traditionally been denied such education, seeing this as a progressive act. Bourne, an admirer of Gilbert Murray, believed that students could become acquainted with classical thought through translations.[92] To Bourne, a functioning democracy needed men and women who had been educated to understand the modern world, ideally through Dewey's method of having students first gain familiarity with an object, stimulating them to learn about its context: where, when, and how it was produced.[93] Edith, however, had valued a different aspect of Dewey's educational philosophy: how it balanced the individual and the community, creating the conditions for an individual to achieve self-realization.

The question of what form of education best equipped students for their future role as citizens was one that Edith would return to in her writing many times, especially during the Cold War. It was in 1917, however, that she first entered the debate concerning the role of classics in education, and she found support for her position in academia. At Princeton University, the classicist Andrew Fleming West was arguing for the continuing study of the classical languages on the grounds that an understanding and use of their structures helped individuals to express themselves more clearly and to have a deeper understanding of English, a position with which Lucy concurred. West did not feel that most translations fully conveyed the meaning of ancient authors, whose works were the foundation of Western civilization. West expressed approval of Paul Shorey and his work *The Assault on Humanism*, which originally appeared in the *Atlantic Monthly* but was later published separately as a monograph. It was highly critical of the theories of Flexner and Bourne.[94] At the University of Chicago, Shorey had become an adherent of the literary movement known as New Humanism, which placed a high value on individual self-realization but also stressed that this could only be achieved through an individual's recognition of their responsibility and their willingness to exercise self-discipline.[95] As the New Humanists engaged in debates about education, Shorey came to Edith's defense. In his response to Bourne's *Education and Living*, published in *The Nation* in September 1917, Shorey criticized the condescension with which he had treated Edith Hamilton.[96] In the following decade, Edith would herself become an advocate of the study of classics in translation as she formed friendships in New York theatrical circles with those eager to become better acquainted with ancient Greek drama. In the meantime, she came to the defense of the study of Greek and Latin.

In the spring of 1917, Edith enjoyed good health with no signs that her cancer would return.[97] It was Gertrude's decline that worried the family. She periodically suffered difficulty with her heart, but she wanted to spend at least part of the summer of 1917 on Mackinac Island. It was the last summer that would include any time spent there by the family. As Norah noted, the cottage would be closed up after Gertrude's visit.[98] Although Gertrude withstood her return journey from Mackinac to Baltimore and initially seemed in good health upon her arrival, she frequently used a wheelchair and that October she had a stroke.[99] She would continue to live until December.

Her final hours made a deep impression on Edith. In her last days, before she became unconscious, Gertrude told Edith that she had feared death until she became certain that Montgomery, who had died in 1909, "had been with her and told her it was nothing to be afraid of and he would be with her through it." To Edith, such emotions seemed "very strange," given that "for years and years she had never thought of him as a help or one to stand by her."[100] Gertrude's sense of reassurance in her final hours gave her the strength to face death. She died on December 10, 1917.[101] In another indication of their commitment to their new home at Hadlyme, the sisters chose to bury their mother nearby, in Cove Cemetery, a small burying ground on a bluff overlooking a backwater of the Connecticut River, only yards up the road from their house. Eventually, it would become the burial site of all of the Hamilton sisters and their partners.

Montgomery Hamilton's death eight years earlier had ultimately left Edith with a sense of freedom to try new experiences, such as traveling abroad with Lucy instead of with her family. Gertrude's death, however, gave Edith new responsibilities while creating a deep sense of loss and emptiness, since Gertrude had always encouraged her daughters to pursue their own interests. When the news reached Susan Fahmy in China in January, she aptly described the effect of Gertrude's death as leaving a circle of devoted sisters with the "centre removed."[102] The loss, both Jessie and Norah agreed, seemed to fall most heavily on Edith.[103]

In the months after Gertrude's death, Edith began to consider what she might still accomplish with her life. In doing so, she had to reflect on her own recent brush with cancer, her interest in writing, the slow deterioration of her relationship with Lucy, and her attraction to Doris Reid.

From the time of Gertrude's decline and death, the relationship between Edith and Doris began to take shape. In her memoir, it was during the last year of Gertrude's life that Doris began to inject a personal note, writing accurately that Gertrude's death was "a great blow, as Edith was deeply devoted to her."[104] Doris spent the winter of 1916–17 in Baltimore, but by the spring she had settled in New York City to pursue her career as a pianist. That May, Edith went to New York to see her, and the two women took a motoring trip together.[105] It was the first of dozens of such trips Edith and Doris would take throughout their lives together.

Edith never learned how to drive, but together Edith and Doris would make many annual trips to Maine by car and would explore Greece, France, and Spain by automobile.

In the spring of 1917, Doris looked at the new freedoms the war was according to women with a mix of seriousness and exhilaration. She had made friends among the large artistic community of New York City. These included two sisters, Francesca and Rosamond Gilder, whose father, the poet Richard Watson Gilder, had been the longtime editor of *The Century* magazine. The sisters lived at 24 Gramercy Park, an apartment building in which their father had been one of the original investors.[106] After the United States entered the war, Doris hoped to find volunteer work. Twenty-eight years younger than Edith and born in the 1890s, Doris belonged to a generation that was even more directly affected by the war. Her brother Francis had entered the U.S. Army in 1916 and would see action in France.[107] In England, her former suitor George Thomson had joined the Royal Flying Corps, though, due to his knowledge of physics, he would spend much of the conflict helping to design aircraft.[108] One of her Baltimore friends, the artist Grace Turnbull, became a nurse at a military hospital in Koblenz.[109] Another female friend had become a driver in France after learning how to disassemble and reassemble an entire car. Edith sympathized with Doris's interest. "Doris," Edith told Jessie, "has none of the excitement & adventure about going that young people so often have, but she feels the duty."[110]

Other factors besides Doris's increasing presence in Edith's life led to a deterioration in the relationship between Edith and Lucy. During their travels—whether in Europe or Asia—Edith had often found herself, like Helen Thomas before her, nursing Lucy. In the spring of 1918, however, Edith had her own serious health problem to confront since the tumor on her breast reappeared. Edith expressed fear that she would have to undergo a mastectomy, though in the end it proved possible for Kelly to remove the tumor alone.[111] The surgery was performed just after the Bryn Mawr School commencement, since upon examination Dr. Kelly had recommended its immediate removal. To Jessie, Edith described Kelly's response to the tumor, writing, "I showed it to him and he said it must come out at once, & I said when can you do it, and he looked at his watch & said well, its three twenty-five. Can you be ready by four?" Edith readily assented, and the operation was performed that afternoon, with Kelly later commenting, "When you are the patient & I the doctor, we don't waste time in preliminaries."[112] Edith would have a third and final surgery for the cancer in 1920, after which there is no mention of its return. The frequent checkups with Dr. Kelly and his quick response to any sign of the tumor's return were undoubtedly significant factors in her ultimate survival.[113] Faced with her own health problems, Edith turned from a romantic relationship with Lucy that sometimes demanded she act as nurse. Instead, she sought the company of Doris.

Edith and Doris's romantic relationship began to flourish that summer, when she rented a house with the Reids on Mount Desert Island, Maine. It was called "World's End Cottage" since it was located on a hill by itself, surrounded only by a thick wood.[114] That summer, Edith read Plato while Edith Reid worked steadily at her writing. Doris practiced her music, "working," Edith told Jessie, "better than ever in her life before she says, and she is gay, as I love to see her. It is a summer of pure happiness for her."[115] The days passed peacefully, with each of the three women working at their chosen interest. After the difficulties of the previous winter and spring, Edith enjoyed the rest she found with her companions in the hidden cottage near the sea. Occasionally, she and Doris ventured into the cold water for a swim but found they could not stay in for more than a few minutes. Afterward, Doris would build a fire and toast sandwiches. Many of the influences that would bring Edith to leave the Bryn Mawr School were present that summer of 1918: Edith was reading Greek and would soon begin to consider a means of returning to the study of the language as her main occupation. Moreover, the attractive aspects of life with Doris and the Reids was becoming apparent to Edith.

Chapter 10

"I SHALL TAKE UP MY GREEK AGAIN"

By the end of the First World War, Edith was beginning to tire of the Bryn Mawr School. The days spent in Seal Harbor in the summer of 1918 had exposed her to the cultural life enjoyed by the Reids and the Van Dykes. The prolonged dispute with M. Carey Thomas, the failure of her relationship with Lucy, coupled with ill health and a growing attraction to Doris, all meant that between 1919 and 1924 Edith made a series of decisions that fundamentally altered the course of her life and allowed her to become a successful writer on the ancient world. In the next five years, Edith ended her relationship with Lucy, retired from the Bryn Mawr School, built a home on Mount Desert Island, adopted a son, divested herself of Hamilton family property in Fort Wayne, and ultimately settled with Doris in New York City's Gramercy Park, a neighborhood known for its literary and theatrical associations. Such great changes did not come easily: Edith would always remember her years directly after leaving the Bryn Mawr School as some of the most difficult of her life.[1]

That summer of 1919, as soon as the school closed, Edith went to Hadlyme and from there joined Doris on a motoring trip through upstate New York and Canada before driving down through Maine to Seal Harbor.[2] There, she stayed a week with the Reids and Van Dykes before joining Lucy on a visit to Helen and Simon Flexner at Chocorua, New Hampshire. Edith and Lucy then went to Hadlyme, where Edith spent much of the summer with Norah and Margaret, as well as Quint and Mary. They had decided to settle in Champaign-Urbana, Illinois, where he had been appointed to the department of romance languages at the University of Illinois.

Edith continued to sustain her old relationships that derived from her years at Farmington and Bryn Mawr College, as she spent time first with Lucy and Helen and then the Duryee sisters, Lily and Susan, who visited Hadlyme. As Dr. Fahmy had retired from his hospital, he and Susan were spending time in the United States before their eventual retirement in Edinburgh.[3] There were also signs, however, of Edith's growing relationship with Doris. The trip together through the Adirondacks and Canada had provided Edith with a much-needed rest and the chance to share once again Doris's sense of freedom through the medium of the automobile. In addition, Doris, who was to return to New York City that autumn, promised to keep an eye on Norah, who had settled in the city to pursue her work as an artist. Later that summer, Edith and Lucy took their last recorded trip together—driving through the Berkshires to Seal Harbor—accompanied by Edith Reid.[4]

By the fall it was clear to Edith that her relationship with Lucy was deteriorating. Lucy had been unable to help Edith in her struggle with Thomas over the poor performances on the entrance exams. In fact, she had little ability to deal with the pressures of college political disputes. Her physician Simon Flexner even recommended on medical grounds that she not be exposed to heated discussions of campus matters.[5] There were additional signs of Edith and Lucy's separation. At the beginning of October, Lucy's sketch of her trip with Edith to China, "The Sage of Shantung," was published in the New Republic.[6] The essay discussed the visit to the tomb of Confucius, which they had made together, but there was no mention of Edith as her traveling companion.[7] For Edith, the failure of her relationship with Lucy was simultaneous with her decision to leave the school. When the board of managers met later that month, Edith submitted her resignation.[8] Though she apparently later withdrew this first resignation, that winter she would move into the Reids' house on Cathedral Street.[9] While Thomas tried to invoke Lucy's opinion on the quality of instruction at the school, the Reids would be Edith's most outspoken supporters in Baltimore during the escalating conflict with Thomas, and they would encourage Edith to leave the Bryn Mawr School.

In the autumn of 1919, as Edith offered her resignation for the first time, she also complained once again of poor health. Her students, especially the seniors, noticed her frequent absences from Latin class.[10] Edith would later use her poor health as a reason to move in with the Reids, as she began to seriously consider a life with Doris, who still spent the winter months in Baltimore. Their relationship had been slowly developing since Doris had returned from Europe, but from early 1920 Edith began to sleep at the Reids' house on Cathedral Street.[11] Jessie, visiting Baltimore at the time, felt that Edith took pains to conceal this from her, and she regretted seeing Edith "go out into the dark night." But Susan, who stayed at the apartment later that spring, assured Jessie that Edith's departures were voluntary.[12]

Susan, who had known Edith during her years as a student leader and as a highly capable headmistress, was also unpleasantly surprised by the extent of Doris's control in the relationship. That February, Susan told Jessie, "Edith is completely absorbed by that Doris."[13] That winter, Edith rarely took meals at her apartment and when, in February, Doris became ill, she immediately took her to the Adirondacks to recover.[14] They returned to Baltimore by the end of the month, but Edith again stayed mostly at the house on Cathedral Street.[15] By March 1920, Susan was emphasizing to Agnes that "Edith lives altogether at the Reids."[16] Since the Fahmys had to leave for Scotland that spring, Susan arranged for Jessie to come to Baltimore and live with Margaret until the end of the school year in June.[17]

A small crisis developed in April when the owner of their Park Street apartment informed Margaret that he wished to move into it himself, although he gave the women until the middle of May to find new lodging. Margaret dreaded informing Edith of this development, correctly predicting that Edith's response would be to urge her to move in with the Reids as well. It was a course of action Margaret adamantly refused to take and she was grateful that Jessie's presence in Baltimore provided a plausible reason to avoid it. Margaret, remembering her experience with the Reids in London in 1914, was loath to move in with them, though Edith Reid, evidently in agreement with Edith, tried hard to convince her to do so.[18] Jessie loyally agreed to remain in Baltimore as Margaret's excuse for avoiding the Reid house. Eventually, a solution to the housing problem was found when Margaret was offered Mary Garrett's country home Montebello for the summer.[19] By December 1920, Edith had apparently moved back in with the Reids.[20]

Clearly, in the spring of 1920 Edith Reid was glad to have Edith living under her roof and, recognizing Edith's closeness to her sisters and the length of time Edith and Margaret had lived together, was willing to have Margaret reside there as well. The reason given for this was always Edith's health. As Edith prepared to enter another conflict with M. Carey Thomas—this time over the composition of the board of managers— Edith Reid wanted to offer her friend her support. She had observed Woodrow Wilson's battle with M. Carey Thomas and his ultimate resignation from the Bryn Mawr College faculty and was therefore inclined to take Edith's side in any confrontation with the college president. She recognized Thomas's intelligence and the challenges that Thomas faced as a female college administrator, but she also saw her as capable of ruthlessly crushing a sensitive spirit.[21] Moreover, Edith Reid may have felt that with Edith under her own roof she would be able to encourage her to write, an activity in which she herself was engaged during these years.[22]

It was also clear that Edith faced opposition, primarily from Alice and Margaret, not only to her desire to leave the Bryn Mawr School but also to establish a life with Doris. These goals mystified Lucy as well. Lucy, due to her age, education, and political convictions, had always socialized easily with the Hamilton family. She especially admired Alice and sometimes hosted her when she gave special lectures on industrial toxicology at Bryn Mawr College. Doris, by contrast, had—as Margaret must have been aware—left the Bryn Mawr School before graduating. Her subsequent musical training in Europe made up for some of this lack in formal education, but Doris's highly individualistic views revealed her skepticism about the women's social reform movements so important to the Hamilton family.[23] While Doris shared the Hamiltons' pacifism, she eventually linked this view to isolationist conservatism rather than to progressivism. The twenty-eight-year age difference between Edith and Doris may have also puzzled Alice and Margaret, even though there are signs that Doris's youth and vigor were just what drew Edith to her. Most of all, however, Margaret was not ready to give up her teaching career at the Bryn Mawr School, and she resented the Reid family's approval of Edith's decision to resign.

Shortly after the school year ended, Edith had another surgery, the last for the cancerous condition with which she had intermittently struggled. She spent the summer with the Reids at Seal Harbor. Feeling depressed, she blamed the ether that was used during the surgery for causing it, although she must have been aware that in June Lucy was to travel to Italy, to join M. Carey Thomas at Genoa.[24] Lucy had tried to persuade Edith to accompany her, but Edith had refused, perhaps preferring the atmosphere of Seal Harbor for her recuperation.

As Edith contemplated returning to the Bryn Mawr School for the autumn term, she read an essay titled "Just Because I Want to Play" by the publisher and philanthropist Edward Bok in the September 1920 issue of the *Atlantic Monthly*.[25] The son of Dutch immigrant parents, Bok had made a fortune in publishing, but he had relinquished control of his firm to devote all of his time to philanthropy. He stated his case for constructive retirement on grounds that resonated with Edith: idealism.[26] Retirement permitted individuals to give full scope to their dreams and allowed for meaningful social and intellectual activity. Bok's words struck a chord with Edith as she searched for a way to leave the Bryn Mawr School. Increasingly, all that kept her at the school was Margaret's love of the work.[27] After her quarrels with M. Carey Thomas, Edith feared that her retirement could jeopardize Margaret's position at the school. She therefore moved cautiously, hoping that a gradual retirement would give both Margaret and the school time to adjust to her departure.

That October, Edith returned to Baltimore and once again offered her resignation to the board of managers, asking that it take effect in two years.[28] The board allowed the resignation to be recorded in the meeting's minutes but expressed regret that she wished to leave. To Edith, however, even the prospect of two more years as headmistress seemed daunting. She wrote Jessie: "I never want to see the Bryn Mawr School again and I don't think I can make myself keep on at it for more than two years' more."[29] She nevertheless committed herself, to avoid upsetting Margaret. That autumn, she was rarely at the school in the morning hours. Doris began to take an even more active role in her life, helping her to answer some of her Bryn Mawr School correspondence and convincing her to seek medical advice from the New York physician Dr. Walter Walker Palmer—always called Bill—who would marry Doris's friend Francesca Gilder in 1922.[30] Edith's consultation with Palmer, who apparently diagnosed her with heart trouble, was another sign of Doris's growing influence on Edith's life, since he took the place of Dr. Howard Kelly, on whom she had long relied.

As soon as the school year ended, Edith sailed for Britain with Doris and Edith Reid, intending to stay only for the summer.[31] The trip marked another step in the dissolution of Edith and Lucy's relationship, as Lucy was to spend the summer in Europe with M. Carey Thomas. Both Edith and Lucy found the separation painful. Earlier that year, Lucy had made suggestions to Bryn Mawr College's entrance examinations standards committee that M. Carey Thomas supported, work that had implications for the Bryn Mawr School.[32] Edith had been unable to see Lucy before leaving with the Reids and apparently wrote a departing letter that left Lucy visibly shaken and deeply dismayed. But Lucy also felt that although Edith professed she was deeply hurt by her actions, she recovered quickly enough in the company of the Reids. Lucy vowed to never again believe Edith's protestations.[33]

Edith and the Reids first took a motoring trip through Scotland, stopping in Edinburgh to see Susan, who would always be kind to Doris, even though she saw a distinct change in Edith's behavior from the time that Doris began to play such a large role in her friend's life. She was delighted to see Edith again so soon, although she told Jessie that she thought her friend "looked badly" and was suffering from "nervous exhaustion."[34] Susan hoped that the three women would find a more permanent place to stay, and they did settle for much of the summer in Colwyn Bay, Wales. There, Edith celebrated her fifty-fourth birthday, and the Reids presented her with a green and blue silk dress that they had made for her.[35] Doris, who had made a modest concert debut at Baltimore's Little Lyric Theatre the previous April, found a place in the village where she could practice piano, an activity to which she devoted most mornings and afternoons.[36] Edith Reid shopped, worked at her writing, and corresponded with friends.

Edith herself, however, did little. According to Doris's reports to an anxious Margaret, Edith went to bed very late and consequently slept late in the mornings. Yet she experienced less pain, and her heart, which Dr. Palmer had judged to beat too loudly the previous spring, had quieted.[37] Nevertheless she read little and had almost no energy; her only frequent activity was motor rides. Doris believed, however, that Edith's mental health had improved, which must have reassured Margaret, who had felt at the beginning of the summer that Edith was "still very upset about Lucy."[38]

Although their original plans had been to sail for the United States on October 1, the three women spent that month living on Half Moon Street in London.[39] Edith Reid was searching for a producer for her play about Florence Nightingale, and she succeeded in briefly sparking the interest of the actress Irene Vanbrugh.[40] Rosamond Gilder, who had spent the summer in France with the artist Cecilia Beaux, briefly joined the trio in London but returned to New York later that month. Edith, Doris, and Edith Reid lingered in England, with Edith and Doris taking frequent trips through the countryside, including one to Canterbury Cathedral in November.[41] Doris gave Edith's continuing poor health as the reason for lengthening their stay, telling Rosamond in New York that Edith recovered her strength "with amazing slowness."[42] For the first time in her tenure as headmistress, Edith would not be in Baltimore when the Bryn Mawr School opened for the year.[43]

Upon her return to Baltimore in November, Edith once again moved in with the Reids, claiming that due to her health she needed attention that Margaret with her work at the school could not provide.[44] She no longer maintained the appearance of residing with Margaret as she had previously. Instead, the Bryn Mawr School catalogue gave her address as the Reid house at 608 Cathedral Street. It was clear that Edith had taken up residence in the home of a former student, a condition she knew would attract the ire of M. Carey Thomas and the censure of some in the broader school community. In February 1921, during Edith's earlier period of residence at the Reid house, Thomas had written that she felt "it highly desirable that you as principal of the school should have an independent residence and should not live in some one else's house where you cannot be as influential and independent as if you had a flat of your own."[45] Thomas had been willing to grant her a housing allowance, as she had done in Edith's early years at the school, to help her maintain a separate residence. Thomas's implication was clear, however: Edith must not reside with the Reids. Edith saw clearly the stark choice that must be made between continuing her position as headmistress or building a life with Doris.

It was Doris's status as a former student at the school that made the relationship between the two of them unacceptable to Thomas. Both Edith and Thomas had grown up in the nineteenth century, when elite women were encouraged to have close emotional relationships with other women, a pattern that continued in adulthood for some while others formed romantic attachments to men. In Edith's early years at the Bryn Mawr School, some of the teachers had had female partners, a condition that still existed at the time of her resignation. Dr. Mary Sherwood was still living with her partner, Dr. Lilian Welsh, a circumstance that would continue well after Edith's departure, since Sherwood remained the school's doctor until her death in 1935.[46] Moreover, just as Edith prepared to submit her resignation for the last time, Clara Landsberg was hired to teach German at the school.[47] At last it became possible for Margaret and Clara to establish a permanent life together, one in which both partners taught at the school. The existence of such relationships between faculty members, the old relationship between Edith and Lucy, and Thomas's own history of sharing her life with female partners, make it unlikely that Edith's choice of a female partner alone forced her departure from the school. Rather it was Doris's status as a former student that provoked Thomas's criticism.

Early in 1922 Edith finally made her decision about her future clear to the board of managers. At its meeting on January 27, she asked the board to accept her resignation as headmistress or grant her another medical leave, stating that the months in England had not, in the end, provided a sufficient rest cure. She believed she would be able to carry out her duties as headmistress until the end of the school year but was uncertain if she would be well enough to return for the following one. After some deliberation, the board chose to accept her resignation.[48] At a meeting held on February 21, the board of managers, at Edith's request, first discussed a possible successor and voted on a salary for Edith for the next three years with the understanding that she would remain on the board and advise the school. They also paid tribute to "the force of her unusual personality and intellectual enthusiasm."[49] Edith made no public mention of her intention to resign until March 8, when she announced it to a gathering of two hundred alumnae.[50] The result was an outpouring from the faculty, the alumnae, and the parents' association expressing regret over her departure.[51]

Edith had never expected her departure from the Bryn Mawr School to be an abrupt one, as shown in her resignation of 1920, which had stipulated two more years at the school. Her plans for a gradual departure had been made out of consideration of Margaret's feelings and her own uncertainty about her future.

However, that March a prolonged quarrel broke out between Edith and M. Carey Thomas, who was herself retiring as president of Bryn Mawr College.[52] The sources of the quarrel were deep, lying in Thomas's close management of the school and her increasing reliance on Lucy as both a traveling companion and in the work of administering Bryn Mawr College, coupled with her objections to Edith's residency with the Reids. As Edith's retirement from the Bryn Mawr School drew closer, the differences with Thomas manifested themselves in the decision over Edith's successor and the share in the school's profits that she had been promised. Edith hoped that Mary B. Harris, the former Latin teacher with whom Doris had lived in Berlin before the First World War, would succeed her as headmistress, but Thomas wanted the position for her niece, Millicent Carey.[53] In the end, neither was chosen.

After a meeting with M. Carey Thomas in March Edith resigned from the board entirely.[54] From that point on, it was clear that she wanted a clean break with the school, one that would allow her to completely alter her future life. On March 23, three days after her resignation from the board, she wrote to its members declining the three years' salary she had been offered, giving as her reason her inability to work with M. Carey Thomas.[55]

Further exacerbating the tensions between Edith and Thomas had been the question of Edith's share of the profits of the Bryn Mawr School, which she had been promised in her contracts since 1902. Eventually, a committee composed of fathers of alumnae who had expressed their support for Edith collected subscriptions and raised a fund to benefit her, to be presented with a resolution thanking her for her service.[56] This compensated Edith for the three years' salary that she had declined and for any share of the profits to which she might have been entitled.

For Edith, the worst aspect of her confrontation with Thomas was that it made Margaret submit her resignation to the board on March 23, days after rumors emerged of Thomas threatening to close the school and just as Edith rejected the three years' salary she had been offered.[57] The board of managers refused to accept it. When she learned of Margaret's proffered resignation, Edith wrote Agnes that she was "going through some of the very hardest weeks of my life."[58] She continued: "The day she came & told me she had sent in her resignation was one of the most bitter of my whole life." By contrast, the board's determination to keep Margaret was for Edith "almost like a physical balm poured into me and healing me."[59] Margaret continued as head of the primary school and she would eventually, in 1933, succeed Edith as headmistress of the Bryn Mawr School.[60] But in the meantime, Edith's resignation from the board came as a heavy blow and, much to Edith's distress, Margaret talked about their "partnership being ended."[61]

A final casualty of Edith's departure from the Bryn Mawr School was her relationship with Lucy. In the bitter weeks of argument with M. Carey Thomas, Edith had felt that Lucy was taking Thomas's side, defending Thomas in the face of Edith Reid's accusations that Thomas had started the gossip surrounding Edith's residence at the Reids. Lucy, like Edith's sisters and Susan Fahmy, seemed to believe that Edith was "under the spell" of the Reids.[62] But, as Lucy told M. Carey Thomas, she felt a sense of betrayal over the loss of Edith's companionship in travel abroad. Therefore, in April 1922, as the argument between Edith and Thomas calmed, Lucy, though professing to still be "devoted" to Edith, nevertheless painted a picture of her friend as isolated and angry. Edith was blaming Margaret, the teachers, and the board of the Bryn Mawr School for abandoning her. It was not a picture Lucy could easily reconcile with the Edith she had known so well, as shown in her conclusion of her letter to Thomas, "This is terrible for a person as proud as she & quite breaks my heart."[63]

In May 1923, Lucy's father Henry Donnelly died.[64] Edith sent a letter of condolence, the tone of which indicated to Lucy that Edith still did not resemble the woman she had known since college. Lucy was always very loyal to her friends, and she had even managed to rebuild her relationship with Helen on different terms after what had seemed to her Helen's devastating desertion. But Lucy could not find any way to rebuild her relationship with Edith after her departure from the Bryn Mawr School. Edith's letter of condolence was the last recorded contact between them for twenty-five years, until just a few months before Lucy's death.[65]

After almost three years of struggle, Edith had extricated herself from the Bryn Mawr School. She had paid a high price for her new freedom, damaging her relationship with her sisters and with old friends. To leave the Bryn Mawr School was to leave the circle of educated, progressive women in which she had moved since her years as a college student and to finally sever her long connection to Bryn Mawr College itself. In the tentative plans Edith began to make for her future, she revealed what lay at the heart of her decision to leave the school and start a new life. In her retirement, she had determined, "I shall take up my Greek again very hard."[66]

Edith had spent almost half her life in Baltimore, where she had been active in municipal reform movements and built an extensive network of friends. In March she had told the committee of fathers of Bryn Mawr School alumnae and students, "I feel myself a Baltimorean."[67] Before leaving the city, Edith gave Dr. Howard Kelly a photograph of herself. She was now fifty-five, and she wore her brown hair, graying at the roots, swept neatly back. Wrapped in a coat with a fur collar, she gazed directly at the camera, ready to continue life, even in the face of uncertainty. It was a fitting gift for Kelly, whose early intervention in her cancer had saved her life.[68] Edith would not find a new home until her move to New York City in 1924. Until that time, she continued to keep her bank account in Baltimore.[69]

Edith wanted to ensure that every record was in order for the new incoming headmistress, Amy Kelly, an effort that left her exhausted. Ordered by a doctor to spend a month in bed, she immediately went to the Reids in Seal Harbor. They erected a tent for her to rest; it faced the ocean on one side and, on the other, a forest of northern trees—spruce and white birch. In spite of having no clear future plans, Edith looked forward, not back, and later that summer she found a new project on which to focus her energies.

That summer, Edith and the Reids' began to build a new vacation home in Maine. It was another sign of Edith's commitment to a life with Doris. Previously, Hadlyme had been assumed to be as much Edith's summer home as that of Alice and Margaret. By now, summers in Maine had become Edith's habit, and she took an active part in selecting the location for the house. The remote spot she and the Reids chose on Mount Desert Island's Seawall Point did not have a house, but one was for sale on the island's main road and was purchased and moved a third of a mile out to the point that faced south to the Atlantic Ocean and east to the Western Way. Throughout the autumn of 1922, work continued on the house, but much of it had to wait until the following summer.[70] With no obvious home to return to, and no employment, Edith and Doris decided to remain at Seal Harbor very late in the season, lingering until the middle of November.[71]

Leaving the Bryn Mawr School and building a summer home on Mount Desert Island were two of the major decisions Edith made in 1922. By the end of the year she was considering another: the adoption of Dorian Fielding Reid, the oldest of Harry and Edith Reid's five grandchildren through their son Francis.[72] Francis had joined the U.S. Army in 1916 and had married the Norwegian-born Marie Magdalene Swenson in February 1917. Their son Dorian was born nine months later, on November 13, 1917, in Mount Ida, Virginia, located next to Alexandria, probably while his father was stationed at nearby Camp A. A. Humphreys (now Fort Belvoir).[73] Soon after, his regiment was sent to France. He returned from the war unsettled. The army had been his initial career choice, but after the conclusion of the war, he tried to become a lyricist for musical comedies and, like his mother, he sought advice from the successful writer in the family, Henry van Dyke.[74] His career as a musical comedy writer was complicated by the premature birth of twins, Elizabeth (always called Betsey) and Ernest, on February 10, 1920.[75] The births of two more daughters followed: Edith Madeline in May 1921 and Ellen Mary in April 1922.[76] Both were always called by their middle names.

Harry and Edith Reid were concerned about Francis's mental health and his seeming inability to find a successful career path. Francis eventually earned a medical degree, but Doris felt her brother was indulged and resented being told by her parents "that he is not to be judged by or treated according to normal standards."[77] As Doris's new partner, Edith fully sympathized with her, as she largely had since 1914.[78] Harry and Edith Reid evidently worried about the possible ill effects of their son's behavior on their young grandson Dorian.[79] Looking for a means by which to separate Dorian from his father they evidently settled on the decision to have him live with Edith and Doris, an arrangement that would eventually lead to Edith's decision to formally adopt him.[80]

A date of March 1922 has been cited for Dorian's adoption, but this was right in the middle of Edith's final conflict with M. Carey Thomas.[81] Though Edith was living in the Reid house at the time, as Dorian likely was as well, it seems unlikely, at such an uncertain moment, that she would have committed herself to raising a son. Edith sometimes misidentified the exact time when Dorian had become her responsibility, an indication that he was probably spending much of his time with his grandparents, his aunt Doris, and Edith well before the legal adoption took place. In the summer of 1923, when Dorian was five years old, Edith recounted to Agnes that "he has been with me, now nearly two years," which would have placed his adoption in 1921, much of which she spent in England, not returning to Baltimore until late in the year, also an unlikely time to take such a significant step.[82] As a four-day camping trip around the Maine islands suggests, Dorian was already a part of Edith's life as early as the autumn of 1922. This may have been when she first began to develop a real bond of affection with him, but his formal adoption may have occurred as late as 1925.

The question remains as to why, now in her fifties, Edith chose to adopt a child. She did not think of herself as particularly fond of children, telling Jessie in 1925, "I am not a child lover. I think they are far nicer after fifteen than before, and still nicer after twenty." It was a description of herself that she repeated the following year: "I wish I were a child-lover, but I never shall be."[83] At periods when all five of the Reid grandchildren were at Seawall, and decades later, when grandchildren had arrived, Edith expected a nursemaid to take care of them.[84] Among educated professional women of the late nineteenth and early twentieth centuries, however, the adoption of children was not unknown. While society demanded that women choose between a career and marriage and motherhood, some women professionals did not want to forgo the latter. As one recent American historian has argued, it was among Progressive-Era women that adoption as a solution for a child in difficult circumstances first took root.[85] Edith's education, career, and belief in self-realization meant that she shared similar characteristics with other single women who adopted children. She was also sympathetic to children who lived with uncertainty.

Edith confided to Rosamond Gilder, already a close friend of Doris, her belief that the Reid grandchildren suffered from neglect and, possibly, abuse. In her early years of friendship with the Gilder sisters, Edith often referred to them as primarily friends of Doris. She realized that Rosamond was already familiar with the Reid family's private difficulties.[86] She therefore wrote openly to her in letters, revealing her ability to enter into a child's world where a parent's kiss good-night was a loving reassurance—and one that on at least one occasion was denied to four-year-old Betsey, much to Edith's horror.[87] To Doris, there was little doubt that Edith loved children. As the Reid children spent more time at Seawall, particularly in the summers of 1924 and 1925, Edith devoted time to educating them, giving special care to Ernest, whom she regarded as fragile in health. In the summer of 1925, Doris told Rosamond,

"If we get off without adopting two at least I'll be surprised. Edith needs a keeper."[88] Indeed, Edith's love for Dorian must be considered her primary reason for adopting him. It is evident in the letters she sent to Jessie and Agnes, despite her claims of not being particularly fond of children, and evident in her letter to Dorothy Bruce, a 1920 graduate of the Bryn Mawr School, where she described him as "a delightful child, very, very intelligent and very warm hearted."[89] At the time she expressed such sentiments, she may still have been facing opposition to her hope of formally adopting him.

Marie, quite understandably, objected to the adoption of her oldest son. For her part, Edith was deeply critical of Marie's parenting, complaining that she sat in an armchair all day and smoked, refusing to administer cod liver oil to her younger son Ernest, though a doctor had recommended it. Even worse, Ernest was put down for a nap next to an open window and contracted a cold as a result. Edith was most critical, however, of what she regarded as Marie's attempt to manipulate Dorian's affections, telling Rosamond, "It is all incredible. But of course for Dorian to be worked on like that is just impossible."[90] Marie felt pain at the loss of her son, but in the Reid household, her wishes were overruled. Marie was not of the same social class as her in-laws, on whom she was financially dependent as her husband searched for a career path. She may have felt powerless to prevent Dorian's adoption, an event in which Edith Reid played a significant role and which probably took place in 1925, when she also prohibited Ernest's adoption by Edith.[91]

The summer of 1923 was the first Edith spent entirely with Harry, Edith Reid, Doris, and Dorian at Seawall in the house that had been named Long Ledge on account of its location. During August, as Edith observed her fifty-sixth birthday, she considered her future. Her health was still deemed to be uncertain, however, and Dr. Palmer urged her to spend the summer on a rest cure. She often wrote letters in bed as she looked through the house's sleeping porch to the sea and listened to the sound of waves crashing against the rocky point on which the little house sat. With delight, she described to both Jessie and Rosamond how her bed was situated so that on one side she had a sea view and on another a large, crackling fire. She tried, however, "to look chiefly forward" and to identify some work that she could do.[92] She was certain that she did not want to follow the example of Montgomery Hamilton, who had retired to his study to read after the failure of his business. As the summer drew to an end, Edith and Doris began to consider their plans for the winter. They discovered that their financial resources would not allow them to go to New York City as they had hoped. They considered Europe instead, where Doris could continue her musical studies and where the cost of living was less. As the end of the summer neared, however, the couple decided on what Edith told Rosamond was "a wild plan of staying up here."[93] A grand piano was moved into the sitting room at Long Ledge. Harry and Edith Reid departed in mid-September, leaving Edith, Doris, and Dorian to spend the winter together in the new house.

The Maine winter sometimes cut off their contact with others. Supplies for the cottage had to be left where the entrance to their long driveway met the road to the village. Edith was often the one who would make the journey to collect them, taking Dorian's sled.[94] On one occasion, Edith reported to Rosamond that they were marooned in the house since no supplies were able to reach them.[95] That January, temperatures were below zero every night and did not climb above ten degrees during the day. Often, there was a strong and persistent north wind.[96] For Edith, however, the natural beauty of the Maine winter compensated for the challenges that it posed. She relished waking up on cold clear winter mornings to find icicles hanging from the eaves and the house surrounded with snow. On such mornings the sea and the sky were blue, and there was bright sunshine. Outside, Doris would play with the Newfoundland puppy they had acquired that winter. He had quickly been named Don Quixote on account of being "so melancholy looking and such a gentleman."[97]

Pets—dogs and cats—became a permanent part of Edith's life after she left the Bryn Mawr School. From her retirement on she was never without them. Early on in their life at Seawall, Don Quixote and the cat White Emperor were the first of a long line of animals. Cats adjusted more comfortably to the New York apartments in which she would soon find herself living, so that while Don Quixote had to be boarded, Edith could write Jessie from their Gramercy Park apartment with a cat "purring companionably beside me."[98]

Edith hoped to spend the winter writing, plans she confided only to Doris.[99] In addition, Edith also began educating Dorian, who turned six in November 1923 but was, to Edith's shock, still unable to read. Doris ordered primers for him, and Edith taught him to read in twenty-minute lessons.[100] She also continued his literary education, reading to him, as Dorian told Rosamond, the poetry of Wordsworth, Tennyson, and Browning, as well as Kipling's *Just So Stories*.[101] Edith delighted in his growing list of accomplishments as she began Dorian's religious instruction. When he heard adults discussing the recent forest fires in the area, he asked Edith, whom at this stage he called "Eda," "Why don't the people pray to God for rain?" Doris told Rosamond: "Edith beamed with pleasure at the first signs of promise from her little religious pupil." Edith responded by assuring Dorian that the locals were doing so.[102]

The happiness with which Doris recalled the winter of 1923–24, spent in a house that offered little protection from the cold, is evident in her memoir, in which she devoted an entire chapter to their winter at Seawall. As Doris constructed her interpretation of their life together, these months became a critical point, the time when their relationship, including the commitment to raising Dorian, became permanent. There would be more summers at Seawall followed by winters spent at various apartments in the neighborhood of Gramercy Park. But there would only be one winter at Seawall, which ended in the middle of March 1924.[103]

Edith spent much of the spring in Baltimore, working out the division of some Hamilton family property left by the death of her aunt Mary Hamilton Williams in 1922.[104] Both Edith and her cousin Creighton Williams were executors. At this point, Edith decided to sell her interests in Hamilton property in Indiana to other family members, yet another sign of the large role Doris had come to play in her life.[105] Doris was already investing in the stock market, activity that would eventually lead to her career as a stockbroker.[106] She evidently convinced Edith to give up the Hamilton family penchant for real estate and purchase stocks instead. The division of property added more stress to the already strained relationship Edith had with her sisters. Alice and Margaret especially were still struggling to comprehend her decision to leave the Bryn Mawr School and build a life with Doris.

In the summer of 1924, Alice and Margaret paid their first visit to Seawall, though their presence did not automatically mean reconciliation. On this occasion the Hamilton sisters avoided conflict as, in Doris's mind, they often did by not discussing any subjects on which they disagreed. As Doris was learning, the Hamilton family handled conflict in a far more restrained manner than the Reids.[107] For Alice and Margaret, the changes in Edith's life must have been difficult to absorb. Edith had become dependent on Doris for medical and financial advice, and she had now built a house and was raising a son with her new partner. Susan Duryee Fahmy expressed the changes evident in Edith's life and character best when she distinguished between Edith before Doris and Edith after, calling the former "the Edith of before-I-went-to-live-with-her days."[108] Alice and Margaret may also have felt some skepticism about Edith's plans to write, goals she had not yet accomplished.

That fall, Edith, Doris, and Dorian moved into the Hotel Irving, 26 Gramercy Park.[109] They intended to spend only the winter in New York City, but by the spring of 1926 they had settled at 47 Gramercy Park, a gray stone building that would be their home until 1927.[110] The neighborhood had been known for its associations with literary and theatrical figures since 1888, when the actor Edwin Booth had founded the Players' Club in his house on the square.[111] A statue of Booth, who had impressed Edith when she saw him perform during her years at Miss Porter's School, stood in the square's private park.[112] Doris recalled that their first year in New York passed uneventfully. She taught piano, and Edith kept house. In fact, the move to New York City was accomplished after a flurry of communication with Rosamond that had resulted, to Doris's disappointment, in a conclusion that Edith and Doris would be unable to move into the Gilder family apartment building at 24 Gramercy Park. It also clarified a necessary readjustment in the relationship between Rosamond and Doris.

Rosamond had expressed an unwillingness to live with both Edith and Doris, apparently recognizing the quality of the relationship that the two had established. By the end of 1923, Edith felt she had been accepted by Rosamond, Francesca, and her husband Bill Palmer, and indeed she had.[113] Rosamond clearly enjoyed corresponding with Edith and sent small gifts to Dorian. She would also be critical in helping Edith to start her writing career. But there is evidence that Rosamond and Doris had once enjoyed a romantic relationship of their own, one that was effectively ended—at least in Rosamond's mind—by Edith's new place in Doris's life.

The relationship between Doris and Rosamond remains obscure, but there were hints of physical intimacy that point to the generational differences between Edith and Doris. Edith, raised in the nineteenth century, with its conception of Platonic love, may have been aware that that idea sometimes concealed a physical intimacy, but there is little proof that she experienced this herself with either Sarah Locke Richmond or Lucy Martin Donnelly, with whom she never had the exclusive relationship that she sought. Edith must have been aware of the intensity of the relationship between Lucy and Helen Thomas Flexner, as she saw Lucy's pain when it ended. Edith remained reluctant to refer to physical and emotional intimacy, and there is nothing in her surviving correspondence to compare to Doris's open expressions of her feelings for Rosamond. Doris and Rosamond, both born in the 1890s, experienced the more sexually permissive atmosphere of the 1920s while still in their thirties. At this time, love between women acquired the more open sexual connotation that had been absent from the women's world in which Edith had moved when she had first experienced romantic feelings. Part of the difference was due to the dissemination of Freudian ideas, of which Rosamond, who was interested in psychoanalysis, would have been aware.[114] Edith, however, was critical of Freud, suggesting that she was not entirely comfortable with the popularization of his ideas.[115]

Doris certainly took advantage of the new opportunities open to women in the twenties. Her sense of independence was expressed by her short hair, her adoption of men's clothing as she worked on the Seawall house, her love of the automobile, and her smoking. She apparently embraced the decade's willingness to allow sexual experimentation too. The more physically intimate relationship Doris and Rosamond shared carried over into the romantic relationship between Doris and Edith, though there are few traces of it. Even the emotional intimacy between Doris and Edith is most often simply implied in their letters. One reads with surprise Edith's reference to "my Doris" in a letter written two years before her death.[116] The women kept separate bedrooms, and their natural reserve shielded their intimacy from others. Yet there are signs that Edith and Doris's relationship had a physical element that may have been previously absent from Edith's life. One of its few indications was in their delighted thanks to Jessie for the gift of a horsehair mattress on which they had both slept.[117] It is clear that Doris continued her expressions of affection for Rosamond for at least several years after she had established her relationship with Edith. But Rosamond eventually adjusted to Doris's new partner.

In the spring of 1924, Rosamond joined the staff of the magazine *Theatre Arts Monthly*. Doris immediately purchased a subscription so she could read Rosamond's first signed article, which appeared in the July issue, a review of several books published under the collective title "The Season in Print."[118] Rosamond soon prodded Edith to write for *Theatre Arts*, but she resisted, fearing that she would be unable to produce an article of the quality that Rosamond and others contributed to the magazine. She generously praised Rosamond's writing, calling it "accomplished." In the same letter, however, Edith informed Rosamond that she had found a project to which she wanted to devote her intellectual energies: the translation of ancient Greek tragedies into English. As she told Rosamond that July, "I am really working at last on Aeschylus."[119]

Chapter 11

THE GREEK WAY

◆ In the spring of 1925, Edith had one last duty to discharge for the Bryn Mawr School. A group of alumnae had commissioned her portrait to be painted by the artist Lydia Field Emmet, who had a studio in New York City.[1] She sat for Emmet dressed in an academic robe and clutching a book in one hand, gazing directly at the viewer while the artist, who was known for her portraits of upper-class women and children, painted with her usual attention to detail. That it was ever completed is a testament to the artist's skill rather than Edith's patience. By that spring, Edith's life had progressed from hours of rest cure to one filled with the pursuit of a writing career and the raising of Dorian. Edith devoted so little time to sitting for the portrait that Emmet resorted to placing an academic robe on a mannequin to complete it. When Edith arrived for Emmet to paint her head and facial features, she entered the studio so hurriedly that she reminded Emmet's maid of someone who was being pursued.[2] The completed painting was sent to the Bryn Mawr School, where it remains today.

Edith had at last embarked on her career of writing on the classical world, beginning with an essay about ancient Greek tragedy for publication in *Theatre Arts Monthly*. Between 1926 and 1932, six of the chapters of her first book *The Greek Way* and one of *The Roman Way* would first appear as articles in the magazine, which would also publish one of her translations.[3] Through Rosamond Gilder, Edith had been drawn into the theatrical and literary society of Gramercy Park and into the nexus of *Theatre Arts Monthly*. Its staff had close associations with the experimental

FIGURE 11. Formal portrait of Edith Hamilton by Lydia
Field Emmet commissioned by the alumnae of the
Bryn Mawr School in 1925. Photography courtesy of
the Bryn Mawr School.

American Laboratory Theatre and with the new publishing firm of
W. W. Norton. This social circle helped Edith establish her new career,
as she taught classes at the theater and began to publish with W. W.
Norton, a company with which she was to have a close relationship for
the rest of her life.

After the First World War, the study of ancient Greece and the performance of ancient Greek tragedy were means of expressing hopes for peace
and democracy. In literature and drama, nineteenth-century sensibilities

about translation were discarded as writers and other creative artists tried to produce more authentic renditions of ancient Greek plays.[4] As evident in *The Greek Way*, Edith became aware of the revival of interest in ancient Greece and of the postwar understanding of the Greeks as the originators of the modern spirit through the wide circle of literary and theatrical society in which she and Doris now moved. Doris, together with Rosamond and *Theatre Arts Monthly* editor Edith J. R. Isaacs, encouraged Edith to pursue a new career as a translator of ancient Greek tragedies and eventually as a writer on the ancient world.

Rosamond had met Edith J. R. Isaacs as a Gramercy Park neighbor before she had begun to work for the magazine.[5] Isaacs, born Edith Juliet Rich, was a Milwaukee native, twenty years younger than Edith Hamilton. In 1904 she had married New York City attorney Lewis Montefiore Isaacs, who had composed the music for a libretto she had written. The couple settled in New York City with their three children.[6] Since 1919, Edith J. R. Isaacs had been serving as an editor of the magazine *Theatre Arts*, which was devoted to encouraging experimentation in the theater, challenging its commercialism through an emphasis on the new stagecraft, the European movement for greater realism, an aim often expressed in set design as well as acting.[7] Isaacs was known for her ability to encourage aspiring writers: the magazine helped to launch the careers of many associated with the theater. Some, like Thornton Wilder, wrote dramatic criticism for *Theatre Arts* for only one month, while others, including set designers, found the magazine receptive to publishing drawings of their innovative work.[8] Many authors appreciated Isaacs's interest in their writing even when her criticism was sharp. The writer Lewis Mumford, responding to Isaacs's evaluation of his play, told her she had "bulldog teeth," though he admitted that her comments correctly identified his work's weak points.[9] Isaacs also commanded loyalty. The young staff was underpaid and worked hard. Though all had assigned roles at the magazine, they in fact took on any task necessary to complete the next issue, sharing their editor's dedication to the encouragement of the new stagecraft. They were rewarded by the intellectually stimulating atmosphere that pervaded the magazine's offices and by the opportunity to develop their writing skills.[10]

Edith always felt that she owed her writing career to Edith J. R. Isaacs and the staff of *Theatre Arts Monthly*. Isaacs's support came at a critical time, when Edith was just beginning to return to classical studies after two years of rest cure, when she still felt some uncertainties about her health. As she told Isaacs in 1940, "You know I always feel that you are the reason I am writing—and how great a benefit that is to me no one can know but myself."[11] Rosamond was especially helpful to Edith's early writing career, suggesting the topic of Greek tragedy for her first article, and, as Edith was considering methods of translation, presenting her with a new model by sending her a book of poems by the American poet H. D. (Hilda Doolittle).[12]

Edith continued to aspire to the role of translator. While she argued for the continuation of the study of Latin, she began to realize that the decline in the study of ancient languages was irreversible. But despite ever fewer Americans being able to read the ancient languages, the First World War had sparked interest in the classical roots of Western civilization, creating a demand for translations. Encouraged by her growing acquaintance with the staff of *Theatre Arts Monthly*, Edith, from at least 1924, turned her attention to the intellectual challenges of translating.

The Collected Poems of H. D., which contained the poet's translations of choruses from such Euripidean tragedies as *Iphigenia in Aulis* and *Hippolytus*, proved a catalyst. Edith was deeply impressed by H. D.'s work, especially the spare style of the choruses. She told Rosamond:

> There is beautiful translating, if you please. It is sheer genius to be able to keep the clear simple directness of those Euripides choruses as she does. If only you could know what an achievement the one from Iphigenia in Aulis is. I have been in despair over it—and here she does it so simply and lucidly and it comes out beautiful poetry. It is really an inspiration to me.[13]

H. D.'s work stimulated Edith's own thinking about the question of accuracy as it pertained to the text. She pondered the responsibility of the translator: Was it to offer a precise rendering of the text or to be faithful to the ideas it contained? Ultimately, she determined that she wanted to aim for precision while realizing that creativity could not be completely avoided. She did not want readers to be turned away from Greek tragedy because the plays had been rendered in an uninteresting manner.[14] Edith kept the original Greek meter in her translation of the choruses in the *Agamemnon* and in some of her translations of Aristophanes. But in general, she did not feel that a translator was obligated to do so.[15]

Key to Edith's understanding of the process of translation was her belief that translations dated quickly, and each generation had to produce its own as it rediscovered the ancient Greeks. And, although she never lost interest in the intellectual challenges of translating ancient Greek, she eventually concluded that poets were the best translators, as they had the creative imagination to convey the essence of what the ancient tragedians meant. By the 1930s she could write confidently that the "ideal translator of Greek tragedy would be a great poet and Greek scholar combined."[16]

In reading the work of H. D., Edith was drawn into the classical revival that occurred as a result of the First World War. The conflict had created interest in ancient Greece, the birthplace of democracy, as its survivors tried to come to terms with the scale of the destruction and build a more equal world in its wake. It was a result of a longing for a return to order, found in the ancient Greek sense of harmony in structure and proportion. It would manifest itself in postwar art and architecture, in the work of Pablo Picasso and Le Corbusier, among others.[17] Edith would encounter it in both literature and drama, and she was discernibly influenced by the works of W. Macneile Dixon, a literature professor at the University of Glasgow, with whom she later corresponded.[18] Dixon was the author of *Hellas Revisited*, an account of his 1928 trip to Greece in which he emphasized how the Greeks had established the roots of Western culture against a background of war.

After the First World War, the culture of ancient Greece also became linked in the minds of some to efforts to promote greater international political understanding that would help to avoid future military conflicts. Dixon, despite acknowledging that war had been a frequent occurrence in ancient Greece, also pointed out that the Greeks had established the Olympics, during which the city-states had expressed their competitiveness through the games while a state of truce prevailed. Edith would reiterate this point in *The Greek Way*.[19] In the postwar environment, the experience of the ancient Greeks, whose societies had struggled to achieve peace, often unsuccessfully, was being invoked in a new vision of internationalism in which all nations were equal. Gilbert Murray turned his attention to promoting the League of Nations. Eva Palmer Sikelianos, whom Edith had known as one of Lucy's students at Bryn Mawr College, would try to usher in a world of greater international understanding by mounting festivals in 1927 and 1930 at the ancient religious center of Delphi, which had been a meeting place of nations for athletic games and peace negotiations.[20]

One of the reasons that H. D. had been drawn to ancient tragedies was the view that ancient Greece was the birthplace of the "modern spirit," a claim made by Dixon in *Hellas Revisited* and by Edith in *The Greek Way*.[21] Edith would write in the opening chapter of *The Greek Way*, "the spirit of the West, the modern spirit is a Greek discovery and the place of the Greeks is in the modern world."[22] She would argue that some of the value of studying the ancient Greeks was to learn how to defeat irrational forces and construct a rational world in their wake. Writing that "we have seen an old world swept away in the space of a decade or two," a return to the study of ancient Greece would help to resolve the "confusions and bewilderments of the present."[23] To Edith, the Greeks had triumphed not so much over war as over the power of despots supported by an almost equally tyrannical clergy. She compared ancient Greece primarily to Egypt, where the pharaoh's divine status was actually dependent on the support of a powerful priestly class who claimed a monopoly on human knowledge, a claim that ultimately led to their intellectual decline as the priests began to assume that there was no new knowledge to acquire. This ancient tyranny subsumed the individual, causing a great turning inward, an overemphasis on the spirit. It was Greece, Edith argued, that had learned how to balance the claims of the spirit with intellectual pursuit, thus making the Greeks the first modern civilization.[24]

The postwar world had found a new use for classicism as it rebuilt itself, and it had rejected nineteenth-century styles of translation. The time was right not only for experimentation with translations but also for clear and coherent exposition of what the ancient Greek experience could teach the twentieth-century world. The relevance of the Greeks was not always clear. As T. S. Eliot had pointed out in his essay "Euripides and Professor Murray," the Cambridge school of classics, whose influence had reached its height at the start of the First World War, had drawn from the disciplines of archaeology and anthropology, ultimately emphasizing how different the ancient Greeks were from twentieth-century peoples, an allusion Edith would also make in the opening chapter of *The Greek Way*. Eliot still argued, however, for the relevance of classicism, respecting Murray as a Hellenist, if not as a poet. Hellenism called attention to the ways in which the ancient Greeks had faced and dealt with problems similar to those that plagued the postwar world.[25]

As Edith reflected on Aeschylus that summer at Seawall, she had just completed her first article for *Theatre Arts Monthly*, the essay "Tragedy," which would appear in the January 1926 issue of the magazine. She was nervous as she wrote what would be her first published work on the subject of ancient Greece. Its writing provided Doris with one of her first opportunities to demonstrate her support for Edith's new career, and she gave Rosamond a detailed description of Edith's mental state as she composed the essay: "She writes in it somewhere 'one must feel either tragically or joyously; one cannot feel tamely'. Well that describes identically her state of mind while she was writing the thing! Such ups and downs! Mex.[ican] Pet.[roluem] on the stock exchange was inactive in comparison." She prided herself on keeping the article "out of the scrap basket for several months."[26]

Finally, Doris reported to Rosamond that "the article is finished! If it is never printed it won't be because it has not been sweated over! Whether it is too condensed or not I am no longer capable of judging— she could make a young book out of what she has left out. To my mind she has material for a series of articles, to hers she could not put everything she has said that is worth saying into two sentences—so there you are."[27] Doris considered Edith entirely capable of writing a book. But the amount of editing Edith did for her first article suggested that Edith was still finding her writing style. She still felt uncertain about her ability to explain Greek tragedy clearly and concisely to the magazine's readers.

Once she had submitted the article, she asked Rosamond to read it even though the task of editing the piece would fall to Dorna McCollester, who became Edith's first editor.[28]

Under McCollester's direction the essay was condensed: a mere five pages long, but taking as its theme the definition of tragedy, determining what was essential to the art. It approached this central question by calling attention to the philosophical problem of tragic pleasure: Why does an audience enjoy watching an individual suffer through trials ending in death? This response to tragedy was described in the metaphor "tragic heights," conveying an elevation of the soul, an effect that mere sadness could not produce.[29] Her essay concluded that the effect of tragedy on its audience was due to the nature of the central character in the play: "Tragedy's one essential is a soul that can feel greatly."[30] This was what defined tragedy as opposed to mere pathos.

The argument was Edith's own, though her essay could be understood as a response to the work of W. Macneile Dixon, who had published his book *Tragedy* in 1924 and whom Edith quoted in her essay. He contributed some of the core concepts of Edith's article, including the emphasis on Periclean Athens and Elizabethan England as the two eras of national confidence that had produced the world's great tragedies and the identification of four great tragic playwrights, three of whom were Greek.[31] Dixon had raised questions that Edith tried to answer in her own work, such as whether or not realism was a necessary part of tragedy or a barrier to the audience experiencing it. Edith concluded that realism and tragedy had little to do with one another, since the truly tragic figure was an unusual character more than a realistic one. Dixon had argued that the essence of tragedy lay in the individual of strong morality and unusual talents, but he had not, as Edith had, defined the art as dependent on the tragic character's depth and capacity for suffering.[32]

The essay was finished at Seawall in 1925, before the arrival of Francis and Marie Reid's children, who were to spend the summer with Edith, Doris, and Dorian. Although Edith had feared that the children's presence might prove a distraction from her work, the summer passed peacefully. Doris constructed an outdoor play area for the children consisting of a sand box, a seesaw, and a swing, and she made over a room in the house, formerly used for storing wood, into a nursery, complete with a small table for meals. A local girl was hired to act as nurse.[33]

Edith continued to find delight in Dorian, and Doris received a boat, eventually named *The Goblin*, as an early birthday present and sailed it out by herself.[34] As the summer wore on, however, a new problem arose: the children resisted any mention of returning to Baltimore, expressing instead a desire to live with Edith and Doris in New York City. Edith developed a particular attachment to Ernest and Betsey, who had turned five the previous February. It was especially difficult for Edith to resist Ernest's pleas to live with his aunt and her partner. He would, according to Edith, wrap his arms around her neck, put his cheek next to hers, and whisper, "You'll let me go to New York, won't you?" This, Edith told Rosamond, "goes to my heart. I would give anything to take him. I think I could make him live—even perhaps grow stronger. I know I could make him happy."[35] By the end of the summer, however, the question of adopting any more of the Reid children was resolved. Doris was obviously reluctant, but Edith Reid, decisively, refused to consider allowing Ernest to be adopted. In the face of such opposition, Edith resigned herself to not adopting any more of the Reid children.[36]

After their return to New York, Edith began to lecture at the American Laboratory Theatre, which had just moved to new quarters on MacDougal Street in Greenwich Village. It was an experimental institution closely modeled on the Moscow Art Theatre, functioning as both a drama school and a theater, mounting productions in which the students took part. Its principal drama teachers were the Polish-born actor and director Richard Boleslavsky and the Russian actress Maria Ouspenskaya, both of whom had been trained at the Moscow Art Theatre.[37] The Laboratory Theatre, which had been founded in 1923, had a close relationship to *Theatre Arts Monthly*. Besides Boleslavsky, its founders included four prominent New York art patrons, among them Isabel E. Levy, a close friend of Edith J. R. Isaacs.[38] Boleslavsky publicized the Laboratory's school in the pages of *Theatre Arts Monthly*. Such figures as the aspiring playwright Thornton Wilder moved frequently between the magazine's offices and the school, and his first full-length play, *The Trumpet Shall*

Sound, was performed by the American Laboratory Theatre in 1926.[39] Edith met Wilder during these years, though her more lasting friendship was with his novelist sister Isabel.[40] Beginning in 1926, Edith's friend John Mason Brown taught a course on the history of drama at the Laboratory Theatre that began with the ancient Greeks, and to which Edith contributed. The experience consolidated her friendship with Brown, an associate editor of *Theatre Arts Monthly*.[41]

When Edith met Brown, he and set designer Donald Oenslager shared an apartment in Greenwich Village.[42] They frequently socialized with others on the magazine's staff and with Edith, widening the social circle to which Rosamond had introduced her. These included Brown's eventual wife, Catherine Meredith, an aspiring actress he first met at the Laboratory Theatre and whom he married in 1933.[43] Edith and Doris befriended Oenslager, who, along with John, visited Seawall. When Oenslager eventually married a young socialite, Mary Polak, always called "Zorka," Edith embraced her as well.[44] Through John and Don, Edith met the set designer Lee Simonson, who also published his work in the magazine.[45] He would later encourage Edith to translate *The Trojan Women* of Euripides.[46] She also met Norris Houghton, another set designer and author of the 1936 volume *Moscow Rehearsals*.

Others besides set designers began to appear in Edith and Doris's social circle. John sometimes took Edith to see the performances of Dorothy Sands, with whom he had acted in student productions at Harvard and who had since made her New York stage debut.[47] Other Gramercy Park neighbors included Brooks Atkinson, who sometimes wrote for *Theatre Arts Monthly* but who was drama critic for the *New York Times* from 1925, and his wife, the writer Oriana Atkinson.[48] Sands, as well as the Atkinsons, became lifelong friends of Edith.

Edith's lectures on the Greek tragedians at the Laboratory Theater only increased her interest in publishing her translations. Her students, mostly aspiring actors, had not studied ancient Greek and, as she told Dorothy Bruce, she had found that "one essential was to give my class translations."[49] Edith began to actively seek publication of her translations of Greek tragedies, convinced there was a reading audience in need of them. But to her dismay she met with little encouragement.

Edith was disappointed by a meeting with an editor from Macmillan who told her that since few college students studied Greek, there was little interest in publishing translations. She felt frustrated because this seemed to her the best argument for publication.

The community of academic classicists was opposed to translations on the grounds that they undermined the study of Greek and Latin. "And," Edith explained to Dorothy Bruce, "they despise them too." She persisted in pursuing the publication of *Prometheus Bound*, however, because, as she told Dorothy, "even from my own limited experience, I feel convinced that there is a wide field for translations that give, in some faint degree, an idea of that almost unsurpassed beauty and truth which so few to-day can know anything about."[50]

It was *Theatre Arts Monthly* that first published her *Prometheus Bound*, devoting much of its July 1927 issue to the translation. That May the tragedy had attracted worldwide attention as a production of it—not using Edith's translation—was mounted at Delphi. The magazine issue was illustrated with a photograph of the ancient theater at Delphi and a drawing of one of the masks used in the production.[51] The performance was part of the effort to promote the Delphic Idea, the dream of Eva Palmer Sikelianos and her husband the Greek poet Angelos Sikelianos.[52]

In the wake of the First World War, Eva and Angelos hoped to restore ancient Delphi's reputation as a meeting place of nations for peace negotiations. In their commitment to their ideal, the couple mounted two Delphic festivals in 1927 and 1930, both featuring performances of the *Prometheus Bound* of Aeschylus.

Edith did not attend either of the Delphic festivals; she would travel to Greece in 1929. But she could not help being interested in Eva's staging of ancient Greek drama and she studied photographs of the productions.[53] She spied in the festivals reasons to hope, despite the reactions she had received from Macmillan. It was a hopefulness she would work to sustain. After the magazine publication of her *Prometheus Bound* translation, Edith evidently sent copies of the issue to classicists, historians, and English professors in the hope of drawing attention to it.[54] The only response she received, however, was from the literature professor W. Macneile Dixon at the University of Glasgow. He was encouraging, calling her translation of the tragedy "simple and intelligible," an evaluation that must have pleased her.[55] He also praised her essay "Comedy," which had appeared alongside her translation in the same issue of *Theatre Arts Monthly*.[56] To her dismay, however, no classical scholars seemed interested in her translation, and she saw little hope of publishing in book form the work she had already completed and the translations she intended to produce in the future. She would never again attempt to consult an academic classicist about her work.

Edith continued to translate Aeschylus, beginning on the *Agamemnon* at Seawall in the summer of 1927.[57] In her translation, she wanted to do justice to the playwright. He was, she felt, the greatest tragedian after Shakespeare, to whom she would compare him in *The Greek Way*.[58] In the years after the First World War the *Agamemnon*, the story of the soldier returning from war, was seen by those widening the audience for classical literature and thought as a work that particularly illustrated ancient Greece's relevance to the modern world.[59] This understanding of the tragedy was likely one reason she chose it as the second translation she would complete.

Edith and Doris returned to New York City, where Edith continued to work at translating Greek, spending two or three hours a day writing, a life she still considered less busy than her days as a headmistress.[60] During these years she often read in the New York Public Library. Dorian went to school during the day, where he stayed until after five in the evening, playing sports with the other students on the school's athletic field. At ten years old, he was, Edith told Jessie, "absolutely independent about amusing himself when he is at home: he never wants to be amused, so that except for a kind of supervision of his homework, I have almost nothing to do for him."[61]

That October, her essay "W. S. Gilbert: A Mid-Victorian Aristophanes" was published in *Theatre Arts Monthly*. The magazine printed the article with some of Gilbert's own illustrations from his early humorous poems, *The Bab Ballads*, and the article featured lengthy translations from Aristophane's plays, on which Edith had worked for two years.[62] Edith had first seen Gilbert and Sullivan operettas performed in New York during her vacations from Miss Porter's School, and her essay

revealed her considerable familiarity with the canon.[63] For Edith, it was
a demonstration of how ancient works had provided the models for all
later Western literature. Comparing the two comic playwrights, Aristophanes and W. S. Gilbert, Edith wrote that both felt free to make fun
of contemporary politics and politicians, military generals, superficial
intellectuals, and women's dissatisfaction with their social status. Both
were, she wrote, "topical writers . . . given over to the matters of the
moment."[64] Their differences were ones of manners, derived from the
need, especially on Gilbert's part, not to offend his audiences. Edith
acknowledged that Gilbert differed from Aristophanes due to the era
in which he had lived; Gilbert could poke fun at, but ultimately had to
reaffirm, the standards of Victorian society. Aristophanes, Edith wrote,
had a greater freedom to mock the sacred institutions of the Athenians.
Gilbert had to add a touch of pathos to his librettos to please a more
sentimental Victorian audience; Aristophanes had been free to be
downright bawdy.[65]

"W. S. Gilbert: A Mid-Victorian Aristophanes," which eventually became the sixth chapter of *The Greek Way*, was Edith's first in which she
relied so strongly on drawing parallels between ancient and modern writers to convey to her readers a sense of the content and spirit of Greek
literature. She had first encountered this technique as one of Paul Shorey's teaching methods at Bryn Mawr College, where he had invited his
students to make such comparisons.[66] The ability to draw such parallels
was part of the enormous power of *The Greek Way* to explain Edith's view
of Greek literature to its readers and reflected the lasting influence of
Shorey, one of whose translations of Pindar appeared in the book.[67]

Edith also, however, drew on the work of the British classical scholar
R. W. Livingstone, who spent much of his career at Corpus Christi College, Oxford. An educational reformer, he was eventually knighted for
these efforts in 1931.[68] Edith identified his 1912 volume *The Greek Genius
and Its Meaning to Us* as one of the principal influences on *The Greek
Way*, and she would cite his work as late as 1957.[69] Livingstone wrote for
a broad audience, hoping to explain to his readers what he saw of enduring value in ancient Greek culture. In *The Greek Genius*, Livingstone
compared ancient and modern authors, seeing both Homer and Sir

Walter Scott as epic storytellers. He also identified the essential characteristics of the Greeks as "beauty, freedom, directness, and humanism," all qualities Edith would discuss in the opening chapters of *The Greek Way*. In his discussion of beauty, for example, Livingstone argued that the ancient writer would describe the scene, but the modern writer, not content to do only this, would also instruct his reader on how they should feel when contemplating beauty.[70]

Soon after "W. S. Gilbert: A Mid-Victorian Aristophanes" was published, John Mason Brown took Edith to the offices of W. W. Norton.[71] The firm was new to the New York publishing world, having been founded in December 1923 by William Warder Norton and his wife Mary.[72] Known initially as the People's Institute Publishing Company, Warder wanted the firm to encourage adult education. But the publishing house had advanced steadily, and in 1925 it had begun to expand the number of fields in which it published. That year, Warder had met Edith's former acquaintance, the philosopher Bertrand Russell, and had subsequently become Russell's American publisher.[73] In May 1926, to indicate the new and broader scope of its publishing interests, the firm became officially known as W. W. Norton and Company.[74] A close relationship existed between the publishing house and *Theatre Arts Monthly*. Additionally, Edith's work fit easily into the firm's early mission of encouraging adult education. She had had academic training in classics, enough to be an expert in her field, but she could also write for a broad audience on the meaning of the ancient world for the modern one. The firm was also especially open to publishing new authors.[75]

On April 6, 1928, Edith signed a contract with W. W. Norton for her translations, a book that would eventually be published in 1937 as *Three Greek Plays*.[76] Initially, Edith planned to bring out a book much sooner—Margaret was under the impression that she would publish one soon after the contract was signed.[77] Edith, however, did not feel she had all of the necessary material for a book. She had only completed two translations, *Prometheus Bound* and the *Agamemnon*. In fact, her first book would be *The Greek Way*, comprised largely of the articles she had written for *Theatre Arts Monthly*, only three of which had so far appeared, though a fourth would be published in May.[78]

Edith still had much writing to do before she would complete a book. But, as a result of the visit to W. W. Norton, she would always feel that John Mason Brown was, along with Edith J. R. Isaacs, one of those largely responsible for her success as a writer.[79] She also formed an enduring friendship with Warder Norton's editorial assistant Elling Aannestad.

Elling was among the closest friends whom Edith would make during her writing career.[80] Elling had been the first employee hired when W. W. Norton needed additional staff in 1927, a sign of the firm's growing success. He started as Warder's assistant. Later promoted to associate editor, he traveled to England in 1929 to secure more titles for the firm, evidently meeting with Bertrand Russell in the process.[81] Elling would later settle in Maine, having seen the state for the first time when he brought Edith's contract for *The Greek Way* to Seawall.[82] Elling's personal writings clearly indicate that he was homosexual, but he took care to hide this, fearing the harm it could cause to his career and the possibility of blackmail.[83] This aspect of his life may explain his attraction to Edith and Doris, a same-sex couple whose warmth toward him he remembered with gratitude. Deeply sensitive, and harboring his own ambitions to become a writer, Elling would become a lifelong friend of Edith's. She would dedicate *Witness to the Truth* to Elling, a genuine mark of her closeness to him, since her first three books were all dedicated to Doris.

Friendships with men over thirty years younger than her, such as John Mason Brown, who had been born in 1900, and Elling Aannestad, who had been born in 1904, marked a new departure for Edith, one of the changes in her life that came with her writing career.[84] Formerly, Edith's friends had largely been among women committed to social reform. In the past, her only male friends had been Dr. Harry Reid and Dr. Howard Kelly, both men of her own generation. As she began her writing career, Edith befriended men who were slightly younger than Doris. It was this generation of men, born at the turn of the twentieth century—one could later add the college president Alan Valentine and the secretary-treasurer of the National Gallery of Art Huntington Cairns—who would encourage Edith's writing career and regard her as an accomplished classicist gifted with a unique ability to clearly communicate her interpretation of the ancient world to others.

Throughout 1928, Edith worked on the studies of the three tragic playwrights, Aeschylus, Sophocles, and Euripides, that would appear in *Theatre Arts Monthly* in the early months of 1929 and subsequently as chapters in *The Greek Way*. Her admiration for Aeschylus was already evident in her decision to translate his plays, but in her chapter on the playwright she argued for the significance of Aeschylus as "the first tragedian" and she identified what she felt were autobiographical passages in his plays.[85] Tragedy was not only the experience of suffering that resulted in elation for the audience, it was also, in the plays of Aeschylus, the experience of individual suffering that revealed, she wrote, "the awful truth of human anguish."[86]

Aeschylus was, to Edith, the tragic playwright who most embodied what Edith referred to as "mind and spirit," a concept to which she devoted one of the opening chapters of *The Greek Way*. She argued that the greatest artists, Aeschylus among them, were able to balance "mind and spirit," the individual experience and the universal human one, in their work.[87] Writers, she felt, could include autobiographical references in their writing if these could embody "mind and spirit," the balance between the particular and the universal. Edith never hesitated to reference her own experiences in her writing, and the early chapters of *The Greek Way* included several autobiographical references to illustrate larger points, an aspect of the tragedies of Aeschylus that she admired.

She identified with Aeschylus, too, as both a deeply religious man and a radical. His realistic portrayals of war, which predated those of Euripides, appealed to her pacifism, as she recognized his resistance to glorify even the Greek victory at Marathon, a battle in which he had fought.[88] Like Edith, who had found in her reading of Edward Caird the ability to cast aside religious dogmas for an essential "New Christianity," Aeschylus had "pushed aside the outside trappings of religion to search into the thing itself."[89] He had questioned the ancient Greek belief that hubris was punished by the gods and had pondered if it was just that the children could receive divine punishment for the sins of their parents, an assertion that earned him a comparison with the prophet Ezekiel.[90]

Aeschylus, Edith believed, was reaching toward monotheism. Edith's chapter on the playwright reflected her close identification with him, implicitly suggesting to her readers that the ancient Greeks were not distant from twentieth-century readers; their personal experiences could still be identified and understood.

Her chapters on Sophocles and Euripides, published in the February and May 1929 issues of *Theatre Arts Monthly*, did not show the same depth of passion as her study of Aeschylus. Following the argument of the Victorian critic Matthew Arnold, she compared Sophocles to John Milton, who had himself been inspired by ancient Greek tragedy.[91] In her chapter on Euripides, she recalled the great revival of interest in the tragic playwright created by Gilbert Murray's translations in the early twentieth century. Euripides was the "modern mind," calling attention to the injustices of the world and therefore speaking to the concerns of twentieth-century audiences, who had in many cases abandoned many of the late-nineteenth-century writers held in high regard during Edith's years as a college student.[92]

As Edith assembled what would become the chapters of *The Greek Way*, the work often proceeded slowly. Sometimes she wrote only a few lines a day, going to bed with a feeling that she had accomplished nothing.[93] The original volume published in 1930 was composed of the articles she had published in *Theatre Arts Monthly* in modified form. An essay she published in the magazine in May 1928 as "Greek and the English Genius" became chapter four of *The Greek Way*, "The Greek Way of Writing," but also provided the opening sentences of her book.[94] Edith edited the work she had already published, taking material from some of her articles and using it as the basis for new chapters, mainly the introductory and concluding ones. These included the book's first chapter, "East and West," as well as the second and third, "Mind and Spirit" and "The Way of the East and the West in Art." Although Edith may have begun writing these in 1928, the descriptions of Greece and Egypt suggest that she completed them after she visited these countries in the spring of 1929.

It is possible to read these chapters autobiographically. In explaining the value Edith felt Western society placed on human life, she wrote in

"East and West," "Nothing so cheap as human life in Egypt and in Nineveh, as nothing more cheap in India and China to-day."[95] This sentence reflects in part Edith's continuing contact with Lily Duryee, who, despite worsening conditions, including growing Chinese opposition to missionaries and increased regulation of their schools, was only driven home by the Japanese bombing of Amoy in 1937.[96] In "The Way of the East and the West in Art," Edith drew on her experiences traveling abroad, referring to the Amida Buddhism she had seen practiced in Kyoto.[97] In her discussion of how the Renaissance had rediscovered classical models, she used as an example the painter Luca Signorelli, whose works she had encountered during her 1910 visit to I Tatti. Her travels with Lucy in Italy, especially their time in Venice, were also invoked in the fourth chapter, "The Greek Way of Writing," in which she asked her reader to compare the Venetian St. Mark's Cathedral to the Parthenon, and a Titian painting to the Venus de Milo, a plaster cast of which had occupied a prominent position at the Bryn Mawr School.[98]

It was the book's second chapter, "Mind and Spirit," that was the most autobiographical of all. It established what she thought was the essential achievement of the ancient Greeks, their ability to balance the mind and spirit, which she had, in turn, adopted as her philosophy of life. "Mind and Spirit" argued that one of the accomplishments of the ancient Greeks was to find joy in life, an impossible accomplishment for other ancient peoples who had lived under oppressive rule. As she wrote:

> To rejoice in life, to find the world beautiful and delightful to live in, was a mark of the Greek spirit which distinguished it from all that had gone before. It is a vital distinction. The joy of life is written upon everything the Greeks left behind and they who leave it out of account fail to reckon with something that is of first importance in understanding how the Greek achievement came to pass in the world of antiquity. It is not a fact that jumps to the eye for the reason that their literature is marked as strongly by sorrow.[99]

As she would write many times in the book, a civilization capable of knowing great joy is the same one that is capable of producing tragedy.

Edith's concept of "mind and spirit" had its intellectual origins in her reading of Matthew Arnold and Edward Caird. Though the phrase became associated with her, its origin was the opening pages of Matthew Arnold's 1869 essay *Culture and Anarchy*, where Arnold had argued that "an inward condition" of "mind and spirit" was necessary for a society to produce cultural expressions.[100] From her reading of Caird, Edith absorbed the idea that great art and poetry balanced the particular with the universal, presenting an individual vision that spoke to humanity as a whole.[101] That the ancient Greeks had been unique in their ability to balance "mind and spirit" and that such a balance was ideal for a society to maintain were themes to which Edith returned throughout her life.

By early 1929, Edith had written much of *The Greek Way*, with only the descriptions of Greece and Egypt in the book's opening chapters left to complete. The book would be published one year later, in the spring of 1930, to largely positive reviews. In four years, Edith had left behind the hours of rest cure that had filled her time after leaving the Bryn Mawr School. Among her new Gramercy Park social circle, she had found the encouragement to commit her most cherished conceptions about the ancient Greeks to paper. Starting as a translator, she had hesitantly moved on to writing about ancient Greek culture for an audience of adherents of the new stagecraft. She had introduced the conception of the Greeks as the first modern people her readers, an audience increasingly interested in the significance of the Greeks for the twentieth-century world but less likely to have studied the ancient languages. In February 1929, when *Theatre Arts Monthly* published her essay "Sophocles: Quintessence of the Greek," Edith prepared for her first trip to Greece.[102]

Chapter 12

THE ROMAN WAY

By late 1927, Edith and Doris were finally able to move into the Gilders' apartment building at 24 Gramercy Park.[1] It was the New York address where they lived the longest and where they were residing when both *The Greek Way* and *The Roman Way* were published. They evidently occupied an apartment on its ninth floor, but the following year, when a larger apartment became vacant, they moved into it, making it into what they assumed would be a longtime residence. The new apartment had two floors, a fireplace, and plenty of windows. They took care in its decoration. Edith chose the wallpapers, with Donald Oenslager advising on the color schemes. He offered other decorating advice as well, especially concerning the construction of numerous built-in bookcases.[2] Finally, when the Steinway Company moved Doris's piano into the new apartment, it was ready for occupancy. Creating a home that reflected their shared artistic aspirations was one step toward permanency in their relationship, and they settled into the new flat with such a sense of relief that Doris told Rosamond, "Here we will stay until they pull the apartment house down."[3]

As Edith pursued her new career, she also began to write literary criticism and book reviews. From 1926, she occasionally reviewed books for *Theatre Arts Monthly*, and in June 1928 she published her first review of a book in the field of classics, *Dithyramb, Tragedy, and Comedy* by the Oxford-educated classical scholar A. W. Pickard-Cambridge.[4]

As its title suggested, the book explored the origins of the dithyramb, a form of poetry honoring Dionysus, many examples of which told the story of the god's birth. Pickard-Cambridge was highly critical of the methods of the Cambridge school of classical studies, and he preferred to draw largely on ancient texts for evidence relating to the origins of the poetry form and its association with Greek drama festivals dedicated to Dionysus and other deities.[5] Edith's favorable review reflected her knowledge of intellectual currents in the field of classics, including the first shifts away from the Cambridge school of classical studies, about whose methods she shared Pickard-Cambridge's reservations. The Cambridge school, whose work Edith had encountered when it had been at the height of its influence before the First World War, had sought to apply the work of anthropologists and archaeologists to the study of the classical past in addition to a traditional textual analysis.[6] Edith was open to the Cambridge school's interest in Greek religion but often felt the group of scholars relied too heavily on intuition. Her argument in favor of Pickard-Cambridge's book was that she felt his conclusions about the dithyramb as a form connected to Dionysus were based on critically examined textual evidence, or "brass tacks" as she termed it in her review.[7]

Edith never became a prolific book reviewer. In the early years of her writing career, when *Theatre Arts Monthly* was the main outlet for her work, her ventures into criticism were few. From 1935, she occasionally reviewed books for the *Saturday Review of Literature*, beginning with Gilbert Murray's translation of the *Seven against Thebes* of Aeschylus.[8] The number of reviews she published grew accordingly with her stature as a writer and as a classicist, though occasionally she reviewed books outside her field. Already fond of detective fiction, which she would read with regularity for the rest of her life, she published a favorable review of Dorothy L. Sayers's *Gaudy Night*. The book's characters evidenced familiarity with classical literature, quoting Aristotle with ease, and, untranslated lines from Vergil, as Edith pointed out, were actually a significant clue to solving the crime.[9]

Edith also began to write literary criticism, publishing in the *Atlantic Monthly* for the only time in May 1929. She had completed the essay titled "These Sad Young Men" by February and could not resist telling Agnes that it would soon be published in the *Atlantic*.[10] It was a criticism of the postwar literary emphasis on pessimism and advanced an argument for classical education as a panacea. Edith focused on the early works of Ernest Hemingway and Aldous Huxley, such as the latter's *Point Counter Point*, which was published in 1928. The novel, a portrait of bohemian social circles in postwar England, reflected the disillusionment of the generation most affected by the First World War.[11]

Edith, however, was critical of what she felt was an inability to probe deeply into the challenges of life after wartime and saw nothing attractive about a dismissive attitude toward human emotions such as love. She argued that the value of a classical education was that it enabled an individual to see the enduring qualities of the human condition. One of the attractions of Euripides had been that readers found him modern. The popularizing of this dramatist essentially demonstrated that Euripides could address twentieth-century concerns when it came to subjects such as the suffering engendered by warfare or questions concerning the status of women. In her essay Edith distinguished between what she termed "the modern spirit," which had "its roots in pain; it suffers for mankind," and the "Byronic" spirit she saw in Huxley and other postwar writers in which "despair is not the result of suffering, but the source of gratification."[12]

"These Sad Young Men," in its rejection of contemporary literary tropes and its prescription of a classical education as a cure for the postwar generation, anticipated much of Edith's later writing. A series of magazine articles she would write in the 1950s, for example, criticized William Faulkner on much the same grounds and deplored what she saw as the deliberate obfuscations in the poetry of Dylan Thomas and Gertrude Stein.

The publication of "These Sad Young Men" in May 1929 occurred simultaneously with Edith's essay "Euripides: The Modern Mind" in *Theatre Arts Monthly*, the last chapter of *The Greek Way* to appear in the magazine before the book itself was published. There was still introductory and concluding material to write. The articles Edith had already produced for the magazine fueled her desire to go to Greece, though she still needed some encouragement from Doris to make the journey.[13]

In late February 1929, Edith, Doris, and Dorian embarked to Europe aboard the *Adriatic*, which eventually sailed into the Mediterranean, calling at Madeira and Algiers, among other ports. At such points, the three could take a guided tour or hire a car and see the area themselves. Finally, the ship entered the Bay of Naples, a familiar sight to Doris, who had visited Italy when she studied music in Europe. Mount Vesuvius, towering above the city, had had a minor eruption three years earlier, and Doris could see how the mountaintop's shape had changed (it would have a larger eruption in June 1929, shortly after their return to New York).[14] But the women looked forward to the *Adriatic*'s five o'clock evening departure from Naples. They were growing steadily more excited at the prospect of Greece, hoping they would have the opportunity to see the Acropolis by moonlight, a common goal of travelers to Athens, since on such occasions the Parthenon's marble columns were known to reflect the night sky.[15]

Finally, after a total of nineteen days of travel, the *Adriatic* sailed around the Peloponnese and into the Bay of Phalerum, finally docking at the port of Piraeus, where they entered Greece. Upon passing through customs, Edith and Doris found that their visas allowed them to stay for only a few hours instead of the ten days they had planned, a misunderstanding that was resolved but not before, according to Doris, it had "caused the most excited comment in Greek and lost us twenty dollars." In addition, Marian Isaacs, the daughter of Edith J. R. Isaacs, had given them a pair of silk stockings to deliver to a Greek friend which, Doris told Rosamond, "I thought would land us in jail. Edith got off some conversation in Clytemnestra's best rhetoric and finally, after weighing the stockings on an enormous pair of scales, they let us go!"[16] Greece in 1929 was a republic, its monarchy having been sent into exile five years earlier. The country was being governed by a series of parliamentary governments that came and went in rapid succession. Economically, the nation was already beginning to experience deflation, making it difficult for merchants to afford to restock their stores; luxuries such as silk stockings were difficult to obtain.[17]

It was the remains of ancient Greece, however, that the women, with Dorian in tow, had come to see. Doris had set an ambitious schedule of sightseeing, which included not only Athens and nearby Sounion but Marathon and Delphi, as well as several sites on the Peloponnese:

Corinth, Mycenae, Epidaurus, Argos, Tiryns, and Nafplio, a port city that both Edith and Doris identified by its older name Nauplia. That first afternoon in Athens, after Edith had rested at their hotel, the Grande-Bretagne-Lampsa, all three went to the Acropolis, where Doris and Dorian left Edith alone for a time. Doris fully realized what the experience of reaching Athens meant to Edith, telling Rosamond simply, "Edith has waited so long to see Greece."[18] Edith would share some of her reflections atop the Acropolis with Jessie, telling her that the Greeks, "in the most beautiful setting of sea and mountain," had said, "We will build here a temple that will draw men's eyes away from all else. And they did it. The mountains around Athens are indescribably beautiful, of rock that forever changes colour, soft gray, mauve, violet, and at their base the bluest sea there ever was—but the Parthenon dominates all. It is greater than they. I had always thought of it as lovely, but it is far more—it is strength and majesty."[19]

Such sentiments would find expression in *The Greek Way* as well, where the descriptions of the Parthenon and the Doric temple at Sounion have the ring of writing by one who had not only seen them, but for whom they had made the Greeks come alive. In *The Greek Way* she described the views from these sites as she had experienced them, writing: "The Greeks flung a challenge to nature in the fullness of their joyous strength. They set their temples on the summit of a hill overlooking the wide sea, outlined against the circle of the sky." The exhilaration she felt in seeing the traces of ancient Greece was evident in her comment in the book's third chapter: "It matters not at all if the temple is large or small; one never thinks of the size. It matters not—really—how much it is in ruins." Her appreciation of the landscape was clear in her confident statement: "A few white columns dominate the lofty height at Sounion as securely as the great mass of the Parthenon dominates all the sweep of sea and land around Athens."[20]

The rest of their tour of Greece, however, was slightly delayed by a fever eleven-year-old Dorian had contracted by the end of their first day there. He was confined to bed while Doris revised their schedule. The women rented a car, and Doris realized that if they took all of the trips from Athens that they had planned in quick succession, not allowing, as they had hoped, for a day or two of rest in between, they would still be able to see all of the ancient sites they had planned on visiting. Dorian soon recovered and proved to be an otherwise hardy traveler. For the next nine days, they followed a hectic schedule that Edith managed with aplomb. As Doris told Rosamond, "Edith is in great shape, up to any sightseeing."[21] Edith was particulary impressed by Delphi, where, even in spring, snow still covered the nearby mountaintops.[22] At Epidaurus, she saw the large fourth-century amphitheater of which she would write about four years later, when considering the problem of the size of the Greek chorus. The amphitheater could seat fourteen thousand spectators, and she would remember standing, "looking up to the endless tiers of seats and down to the enormous circle of the dancing floor." The theater's size would make her feel as if the Greeks must have used a chorus larger than fifteen, otherwise it would be an insignificant factor in the performance of a tragedy.[23]

When their ten days in Greece were over, the three boarded a White Star Liner that sailed first to Constantinople (as Edith referred to it) and then to Egypt, where they spent seven days in Cairo. There Edith began to tire of sightseeing, but the three still rode on camels to see the Pyramids and took a boat down the Nile as far as Sakkara.[24] Edith was pleased that Dorian proved eager to learn all he could about the ancient sites they visited. She told Jessie that he "enjoyed it all keenly," adding that "he never got tired of tracing out the ruins, and the most loquacious guide could not tell him enough. And he read all the books on Greece he could lay his hands on."[25]

After Egypt, they spent some time cruising the Mediterranean, traveling down the coast of Italy, past Sardinia and Rome, of which they could just glimpse the dome of St. Peter's with the aid of binoculars. They stopped briefly at Monte Carlo. There they evidently saw and parted from Rosamond Gilder, who was on a visit to France. The experience of leaving Rosamond, Doris claimed, was such a painful one that neither she nor Edith had much appetite for sightseeing. They therefore did not venture into the casino, though something of Monte Carlo's atmosphere as a seaside resort would stay with Edith. In her next book, *The Roman Way*, it would bear comparison to the ancient Italian resort of Baiae.[26]

They finished their trip with a stop in England, where Edith saw Susan Fahmy, now settled with her husband in the Golders Green area of London. Susan was relieved that Edith seemed much happier than she had during her visit to Edinburgh eight years earlier. Although disappointed that she was only able to see her alone for two hours, Susan told Jessie that "I had never returned as near to the Edith of before-I-went-to-live-with-her days as this time." Susan protested that she had always considered Doris to be "sweet" and that she found her so on this visit as well. But she had little to say about Dorian, only commenting that "Edith with a son still strikes hard on my sense of the ludicrous. But one would not dare to laugh—I have no one I could laugh with over it." Susan summarized the visit by writing, "As Edith and I had drifted apart for many years past it was a great pleasure to find her so much the old self."[27] Susan realized that Edith had recovered some of the sense of purpose that she had felt during her middle years at the Bryn Mawr School.

One of the reasons for Edith's restored happiness was her newly established writing career, enhanced by the publication of *The Greek Way* in the spring of 1930. It was a step that came with Edith's usual ambivalence. She wanted to be a writer, but as soon as she had submitted her manuscript to W. W. Norton, she no longer wanted to see it. She saw, she told Jessie, "its faults and failings," just as she had once ruminated on what she could have done better each year when she had closed the Bryn Mawr School for the summer. This reluctance became a lifelong habit: Edith made it her practice to throw her manuscript away once it was typed.[28] Moreover, Edith was bemused by the volume's success. She had longed to be a writer since her years at Miss Porter's School. But she greeted the positive reception of *The Greek Way* almost with disbelief.

In fact, only Edith's stark contrast between East and West drew criticisms from reviewers who otherwise praised her book. Hetty Goldman, the Bryn Mawr College-educated archaeologist who reviewed the book for the *Saturday Review of Literature*, praised Edith's approach of drawing parallels between ancient Greek literature and modern poets, and she offered only one serious criticism. Goldman drew on her own understandings of the relationship between ancient Greece and the civilizations of Egypt, Crete, and Asia Minor in faulting Edith's portrayal of Crete as an Eastern civilization whose population suffered under tyrannical rule. Goldman counseled caution in making such judgments, even about Egypt and Asia, but argued there was no evidence at all to support such an assertion about Crete.[29] Percy Hutchison, who reviewed the book for the *New York Times*, also questioned Edith's dichotomy between East and West, suggesting, as Goldman had, that there had been more exchange between Greece and Asia Minor than Edith had indicated. But Hutchison praised the balance Edith had struck between appreciation for the nineteenth-century romantic tradition of Hellenism and current understandings of the Greeks as the first modern people. He concluded that *The Greek Way* was "too distinguished and secure a study lightly to be gainsaid. Altogether it is a notable book."[30]

Jessie was delighted with the modest manner that she felt Edith assumed at any mention of the book's success. At lunch at Jessie and Agnes's home in Deep River, Edith's cautious acceptance of her success was evident. Jessie told Agnes that Edith "seems to me to take it as a game as if she were saying—as she says she is—can this be I?"[31]

It was the English edition of *The Greek Way* that created feelings of uncertainty in Edith. When the book was published in England a few months after its appearance in the United States, Elling brought a copy of the English edition to 24 Gramercy Park. Doris welcomed its plain green cover, which she thought would appeal to Edith as "dignified and quiet."[32] However, the book received some negative reviews in England, including one by the writer Vita Sackville-West, who, Edith long remembered, called her "childishly naïve."[33] Sackville-West had no training as a classicist but by 1930 she was a highly successful writer, having published a best-selling novel a few months before *The Greek Way* appeared in Britain.[34] As late as 1952, when Edith discussed the review with her friend the historian Vail Motter, who was upset about a poor review of one of his books, she recalled that Sackville-West had argued that she "was skimming the surface of a great subject because I had not the scholarly equipment to penetrate the depths." As she told Motter, "It was a serious matter for me. I was unknown; my publisher, like all the rest, believed in advertising only a successful book." She added: "I suffered so much over that review. I was sixty-two years old, and I felt the folly of ever trying again to write."[35] She told Motter, however, that she had never doubted the correctness of the editors in printing the review since they had asked Sackville-West to write it.

In general, English critics were less enthusiastic in their response than American ones. This might have been in part because, as the reviewer in the *Times Literary Supplement* pointed out, *The Greek Way* was only one of many recent books on the relevance of ancient Greece to the modern world to be published, a part of the revival of interest in classics that had followed the war. Edith's book had therefore entered a crowded field in which it was difficult to distinguish oneself. The British writer Naomi Mitchison, who reviewed the English edition of *The Greek Way* for *Theatre Arts Monthly*, wrote one of the kinder reviews, praising Edith's translations of Aristophanes though doubting that W. S. Gilbert could reach the ancient comic playwright's heights as a poet. She did not feel that Edith had provided enough historical context in analyzing the tragic playwrights, and she was somewhat critical that by "Greece" Edith really meant "Athens."[36] In general Edith's books would never sell as well in Britain, where the academic tradition of classics remained strong.[37] But as Edith began work on *The Roman Way*, Sackville-West's negative review may have weighed on her mind. It certainly contributed to the anxiety she felt in November 1932 as she awaited the reviews of her second book.[38]

For the firm of W. W. Norton, however, *The Greek Way* had been an unqualified success, a volume that had added to the growing prestige of the company. So, too, it contributed to the enduring Norton backlist of books that continued to sell long after their initial publication. The idea to write the companion volume *The Roman Way* clearly came from Warder himself and evidently quite quickly, as by November 1930 Edith was writing Jessie: "I am leading a very pleasant, very lazy life—trying to see if I can write a Roman Way as the publishers want me to. But no ideas yet."[39] In keeping with the firm of W. W. Norton's commitment to adult education, Warder may have initially envisioned an entire series of books exploring the roots of various cultures, all using "the way" in their title. Such a project never came to fruition, instead becoming a joke between

Edith and Warder, with her promising to write a "Portuguese Way" if he could produce a "Chinese Way."[40] Over the course of her writing career, Warder would put forward a number of potential book projects to Edith, including a study of how dramatic tragedy differed in various cultures and a study of the founders of various religions, but *The Roman Way* was the only book that he suggested that she ever completed.

At first, work on the new volume was slow. "I am trying feebly to write the book on Rome," she told her cousins.[41] However, she ultimately progressed quickly, and the book was written in the two years after the publication of *The Greek Way*. In fact, Edith wrote it more quickly than any of her other books, a testament to her self-discipline, but it left her exhausted. By the spring of 1931 she was so tired that she checked into New York's Presbyterian Hospital only to be told nothing was wrong with her, that she simply needed more rest.[42]

The Romans simply did not inspire Edith as the Greeks did. Edith, Bryn Mawr College's former fellow in Latin, who had aspired to write her dissertation on the Stoic philosopher Seneca, now found she had to prod herself to write on the Romans. John Mason Brown would later write that, in *The Roman Way*, "she could not hide her dislike of Imperial Rome," though he added that the book's chapters on Horace reflected her fondness for the poet.[43] It was a fair appraisal since there were no chapters in *The Roman Way* to compare to *The Greek Way*'s "Mind and Spirit." As Edith would write on the final page of *The Roman Way*, the Romans had completely failed to find the balance between the two, which had so characterized the Greeks. Had they done so, they might have retained their empire much longer, she argued.[44] In the Romans, Edith saw none of the passionate embrace of life that inspired her thinking on the Greeks. Her greatest praise of the Romans was that the empire they had built allowed a Greek conception of "universal community" to flourish through the granting of Roman citizenship to all free male inhabitants.[45]

Some of her feelings about ancient Rome had been evident in the first chapter of *The Greek Way*, where she had argued that the Greeks were the originators of the modern spirit. By contrast, in the Roman Empire "the ancient and oriental state had a true revival." She had added: "Athens and Rome had little in common." While the Greeks had known how to find pleasure in sports and other amusements, "Roman games were bloody and brutal."[46] As she asserted in *The Roman Way*, Homer's heroes had wanted to live, regarding death as "the worst of ills," but the Roman writers had celebrated the sacrifice of one's life for one's country.[47] The Athenian gentlemen of Plato's *Symposium* had seen a dinner party as primarily an occasion for brilliant conversation, stimulating their intellects and thereby leaving to posterity a sense of the lively social life of ancient Athens. By contrast, the banquets attended by the first-century Roman poet Horace were chiefly occasions of "spectacular display and extraordinarily elaborate and overwhelmingly abundant food."[48] Instead of being aspiring Christians as, to Edith, the Greeks had been, the Romans were persecutors of them.[49]

To Edith, Roman literature was derivative. As she wrote in *The Roman Way*'s first chapter, "No other great national literature goes back to an origin borrowed in all respects." And, she added in a later chapter, "All Roman culture came from Greece."[50] An essentially derivative literature lacked the artistic vision of the Greeks. It also meant that the writers to whom she devoted the most study in *The Roman Way* were those who owed the most inspiration to ancient Greece. Three chapters were devoted to the comedy of Plautus and Terence, three to Cicero, two to Horace, and two to Seneca.

In general, *The Roman Way* became a study of contrasts, not just between the Greeks and the Romans but also among the Romans themselves. Edith distinguished between the comic spirit of Plautus and that of Terence. The immoral world of imperial Rome in the first century, as seen through the eyes of the satirist Juvenal and the stern historian Tacitus, existed alongside the steadier one of the Stoic philosophers, Seneca, Epictetus, and Marcus Aurelius. Edith's writing was often at its strongest and most appealing when she was drawing contrasts, since such writing often inspired the clear definitions that were an essential component of her lucid style. This was especially evident in the eleventh chapter of *The Roman Way*, in which she compared the classic and romantic visions in literature. The fifth-century Greeks had embodied the classic vision: "To the classicist the nature of things is the truth and he desires only to see clearly what it is." Vergil, whom she termed "Rome's greatest poet," was, by contrast, the "romanticist," the "adventurer drawn on by the new and the strange where to him truth is to be found."[51] The contrast between the classicist and the romanticist, her notes for her manuscript indicate, was partly drawn from the work of Henry Nettleship, Corpus professor of Latin at Oxford from 1878, whose work was largely devoted to Vergil.[52] Nettleship's definitions of romanticism and classicism dealt with the differing views of God that each held, the classical viewing God intellectually, the romantic emphasizing spiritual experience. Edith's definitions focused on what these concepts meant in terms of literary style. It was her ability to define such ideas clearly that drew readers to *The Roman Way* and to her other books.

Throughout the book she dwelled at length on the status of Roman women. Cicero's letters to Atticus, concerned as they were with Cicero's daily life, had revealed his love for his daughter Tullia and the deep despair he had felt after her death. His first wife, Terentia, had been a "submissive lady," and the marriage had ended in divorce.[53] The comic playwrights had provided a few clues as to the standards of public morality to which Roman women were held compared to the extent of their personal influence in domestic life. As she noted in the comedies of Plautus, a Roman husband and father might be "hen-pecked" but he could not be deceived. During the Roman Republic, which celebrated the virtuous Mother of the Gracchi, a "Roman Pater Familias, weightily endowed though he was by law and edict and tradition, might meet his match in the determined virtues of the Roman matron."[54] To Edith, who argued in the book's opening chapters that the comedies of Plautus and Terence were reflections of the culture that produced them, the distinctions between what was and was not permissible in Roman comedy reflected the moral standards of the Roman Republic. Roman audiences found a powerful wife humorous but not an unfaithful one.

To Edith, the result was that Roman comedy produced the first clear manifestation of different standards of morality for men and women. It was, she thought, one of Rome's most enduring legacies to the Western world. In Greek tragedy, women had been the equals of men in their capacity to achieve moral insight and to suffer as a result. Antigone and

Iphigenia were as capable of courage as men. But Roman literature, and Western literature after the Roman period, had praised women primarily, and often only, for their adherence to strict standards of sexual conduct. As Edith admitted, this enduring theme often left modern readers identifying more clearly with Roman literature than Greek.[55]

To Edith, how a society regarded the individual, male or female, was a mark of how advanced it was. During the period of the empire, royal women could exercise some influence. They did not exercise any real political power, though within the domestic circle they were much to be feared. Agrippina, Nero's mother, who had murdered her husband the Emperor Claudius, did not truly challenge Roman mores until she walked into the same room where her son was receiving Armenian ambassadors. Women of the imperial family, however, only reflected the decline in Roman morals generally. Among the Romans, Edith found that only the Stoic philosophers, to whom she felt drawn, had any real conception of the idea of equality between men and women, an example of what she termed their "astonishing modernity."[56]

Where Edith's criticism of the Romans was most noticeable was in her discussion of the role of war in the creation of the Roman Empire. The book's tenth chapter, simply titled "The Roman Way," argued that the Romans, in constructing their empire, had learned how to indulge in excess. They were "unlimited" in "desires, in ambitions, in appetites, as well as in power and extent of empire."[57] The Roman soldier was not trained to cultivate self-discipline, only to adhere to a system.[58] He therefore lacked the idealism that had made a Greek soldier confront the Persians, despite the seeming likelihood of defeat. The Roman Empire's origins in war made brutality such a part of Roman life that the Romans became prone to the excesses of violence and cruelty as witnessed in the gladiatorial games. Such excesses, Edith assured her readers, were not permitted in Greece, where the violence of the games was rejected. Athens tried to ban gladiatorial games altogether and twice succeeded in preventing them. On another occasion, the Athenians destroyed the altar of pity before the games were held. Among the Romans, Edith identified the Stoic philosophers as unique, the only ones with the moral sense to condemn the gladiatorial games.[59] In her research notes for *The Roman Way* she commented that the best Roman emperors were drawn to Greek games stressing athleticism, not mortal combat. The Emperor Marcus Aurelius, a Stoic, allowed gladiators in his presence only if they engaged in athletic competitions in which their lives were not at risk.[60]

The writing of *The Roman Way*, however, was also an opportunity to return to the study of the Roman authors she did admire, including Horace and Seneca, both of whom she had read at Bryn Mawr College. After the publication of *The Roman Way*, Edith was pleased when Jessie told her that she liked the portion on Horace the best. Edith felt it was a reflection on her own feelings about Horace, telling Jessie, "I have always liked him best of all the Latin writers."[61]

Edith made it clear that she admired Seneca, the friend and tutor of the Emperor Nero, as a Stoic philosopher more than as a playwright, though she admitted he was probably better known for the latter. Seneca the Stoic, however, was one example of how during its first two centuries the Roman Empire had produced great literature and great spiritual reflection. Edith was drawn to the Stoics, though, in the conclusion of *The Greek Way*, she had argued that Stoicism represented a turning away from the visible world to the "kingdom of the spirit," abandoning the Greek emphasis on realism.[62] In religion, more than in any other area of life, she drew a sharp contrast between ancient Greece and ancient Rome, a theme that was to recur throughout her writing, most notably in *Witness to the Truth* and *The Echo of Greece*, in both of which she returned to the subjects of Seneca and Stoicism. The Greeks, she would always argue, were particularly prone to question dogma as they engaged in a relentless search for truth, but the more practical Romans embraced Stoicism, seeing in it a means of discerning moral principles to guide them in life. In her own ability to embrace life, she felt closer to the Greeks than to the Stoics.

In many of her arguments about Stoicism, Edith was especially indebted to the classical scholar Edward Vernon Arnold, whose volume *Roman Stoicism*, published in 1911, she cited.[63] Arnold, who had been educated at Cambridge, was, from 1888, the professor of Latin at the University College of North Wales at Bangor, and his work on Stoic philosophy was widely read, in part because it eschewed the philological approach that Edith had once considered using in the study of Seneca, in favor of exploring the origins and content of Stoic philosophy.[64] Arnold's work would also have appealed to Edith because he believed that contemporary Western society was greatly influenced by Rome and that the Romans had dealt with political problems much like those that still faced modern peoples. From Arnold, Edith derived her argument that although Stoicism had developed in Greece, it had quickly become a religion only in Rome. Arnold had argued that the serious moral tone of the Stoics had made little impact on the people of Athens but had found a much greater response in Rome.[65] In Greece, Edith wrote, "pleasure and morality" were not seen as in conflict with one another, but the Romans regarded them as such. Some Romans had quickly adopted Stoicism because of what she termed its "dogmatic theology" and because, in Stoicism, some Romans found the strength of will to govern themselves, allowing them to carefully avoid both excess of feeling and of luxury in imperial Rome.[66]

In understanding Stoicism, however, she also relied on Edward Caird, who had regarded Stoicism as a "subjective" philosophy, too focused on the individual yet still representing a significant step in the spiritual growth of humanity.[67] For her, Caird had elucidated one of the Stoic paradoxes.[68] The Stoics, troubled by a world that seemed irrational and immoral, withdrew from it and cultivated an inner light of reason, the small portion of divinity that existed in every human being. Though the divine light was unique to each person, its cultivation led the individual to an understanding of their connection to the rest of humanity and to the universe, itself an expression of the divine reason.[69] As Edith wrote in her notes under "Caird," "The deepest & most individual experiences are the most universal."[70] Seneca, she argued in *The Roman Way*, felt that "a holy spirit dwells within us," and the Roman Emperor Marcus Aurelius had spoken of a God within each individual.[71] In *The Roman Way* she would describe how Zeno, the fourth-century BCE Greek philosopher who had founded Stoicism, had spoken of "a God not to be worshipped in temples but to be found within, uniting all into one great commonwealth."[72]

The Stoics therefore tried to achieve a balance between the individual and the universal, an idea they owed to the Greeks who, to Edith, were particularly prone to ideas of equilibrium and how to achieve it. One sign of the continuing influence of the Greeks on their thought was the interplay between the real and ideal that was fundamental to Caird. The Stoics recognized that "the power there is in an ideal to bring about its own reality was exemplified many a time in those last days of Rome. In the city where Tacitus and Juvenal saw public exhibitions of unnamable vice, the Stoics lived lives of austere purity."[73] Since the Stoics believed that all shared the divine inner light, they believed in equality as others in the ancient world did not. The Stoics, as Edith noted, demanded the same moral standards of men as of women, slave and free. Seneca had even argued that slaves were "comrades."[74] The Stoic attitude toward slavery was one she would invoke again in the many discussions of slavery that filled her books, including *Witness to the Truth*, which she published in 1948.[75]

Writing a little over a decade after the First World War, Edith argued in the opening chapter of *The Roman Way* that the world was living in an "age of internationalism."[76] Edith, always drawn to pacifism, realized that she was writing *The Roman Way* at a time when the international peace movement was particularly active. She recognized this not only from Eva Palmer Sikelianos's work at Delphi but also from Dorothy Detzer, who had grown up on the Hamilton homestead in Fort Wayne and who had become the secretary for the Women's International League for Peace and Freedom. In February 1932, as Edith continued work on *The Roman Way*, an international disarmament conference got underway at Geneva, reported on by Detzer among others.[77] Writing when the League of Nations was attempting to operate on the basis of equality among nations, Edith felt that twentieth-century society could learn from the Roman decision, made in the third century, to grant every free person in the empire Roman citizenship.

Although Edith argued that the Romans were "violent by nature," they had accomplished much by the creation of a legal system that extended throughout their empire.[78] The Romans, though not philosophical, were practical and saw the value of establishing an authority that could be recognized by all. This system ensured a certain equality for all free-born citizens of the empire, including St. Paul who, arrested for preaching, invoked his Roman citizenship and his right, therefore, to be sent to Rome for trial.[79]

In trying to determine the legacy of Rome, she argued for the legal acumen of the Romans combined with their ability to recognize the great Greek idea of a single human society of equals. The Romans, Edith argued, had developed an idea of a "universal community, over-riding narrow national bounds, and of a world-peace, the ideal men have always yearned for, seemed on the point of accomplishment."[80] The Romans had been able to establish this as a result of years of conquest and warfare. But, she believed, the idea of the universal community of equals was Greek, not Roman, in origin. The Romans, however, had managed to implement this conception whereas the Greeks, even during the period of Alexander the Great's empire, had not. The Greeks were the originators of ideas; the Romans, recognizing their brilliance, sometimes brought Greek ideas to fruition.[81]

As one of the reviews of *The Roman Way* pointed out, Edith did not attempt to give any cause for the Roman Empire's ultimate decline, though she described it as essentially a spiritual one, evident in some Roman writers' longing for a return to the early Republican virtues.[82] Edith did, however, suggest that the modern day could learn from Rome's failure to govern its empire prudently. The Romans, for all their practical accomplishments, could not fundamentally transform their world into one that elevated the conditions of life for humanity. Looking at the postwar world, Edith wrote, "To overcome nature or nations calls for one set of qualities; to use the victory as a basis for a better state in human affairs calls for another."[83] Though establishing equality through Roman law, they had remained indifferent to their empire's spiritual state.

In two years, Edith had produced a companion book to *The Greek Way*. The effort had sometimes been a tiring one, with personal circumstances not helping. Before *The Roman Way* was published that fall, both Katherine Hamilton and her mother, Edith's Aunt Phoebe, had died, losses that affected Jessie and Agnes in particular, but Edith as well. Katherine, the oldest of Edith's generation of Hamilton cousins, who had hoped to attend Bryn Mawr College with her, had been diagnosed with breast cancer in 1925 and had apparently undergone an operation, most likely at the Mayo Clinic in Rochester, Minnesota.[84] Her illness returned, however, and she died on February 5, 1932.[85] The loss of Katherine was quickly followed that summer by the death of Phoebe Taber Hamilton, who had turned ninety the previous year. For Jessie and Agnes, it was a miserable time, during which Edith tried to offer comfort. She sat with Jessie along the river bank at her Deep River, Connecticut, home while Jessie mused, "Nothing to come will ever be as hard."[86]

By that November, Edith was anxiously awaiting the critics' verdict on *The Roman Way*. "This is a horrid time," she told Jessie, "waiting to see how the critics will either jump upon me or ignore me."[87] But Norah, reading the book that same month, remarked to Jessie, "It is terribly good, isn't it?"[88] Many of the critics agreed with her assessment. Reviewers, including novelist Elmer Davis, who had trained to be a classicist, praised Edith's lucid style and found her interpretations of Roman authors unique but well-argued. In his notice in the *Saturday Review of Literature*, he wrote, "You may quarrel with some of Miss Hamilton's opinions, but they are grounded on a thorough scholarship and on a sensitive understanding of what national character and national ideals really mean."[89] The anonymous reviewer for the *New York Herald Tribune* concurred, noting that it was a book of interpretations rather than a textbook about Roman life. Yet the reviewer asserted that she had "sufficiently competent mastery of the material," adding that "one may hope it will find the wide circle of readers that it deserves." Despite John Mason Brown's suggestion that Edith could not hide her dislike of the ancient Romans, the *New York Herald Tribune* reviewer praised the "enthusiasm" with which the book had been written.[90] Only a few reviews remarked on Edith's attempts to show the relevance of the Romans to contemporary international relations.[91] W. W. Norton had, once again, reason to be satisfied, as, like *The Greek Way* before it, *The Roman Way* made the American Library Association's list of books for libraries, which was not only a mark of achievement but also guaranteed the sale of several hundred copies.[92]

By the end of 1932, Edith's writing career was well established as she had produced two successful books. During the years she was becoming a noted writer, Doris, too, had decided to embark on a new career, choosing, at the inauspicious time of October 1929, to give up her career as a pianist and enter the investment firm of Shaw, Loomis, and Sayles as a stockbroker.[93] Her decision was due in part to a persistent injury that she had developed by 1923, a weeping sinew in her wrist. Unable to practice often enough to pursue a career as a concert pianist, she faced a lifetime of teaching, a prospect that did not interest her.[94] Her correspondence with Rosamond occasionally went into some detail about her financial transactions. In June 1928 she reassured Rosamond that although she had at one time purchased stocks on margin she had been gradually selling the investments in her marginal account—a wise choice in the year before the crash.[95]

Doris's decision to sell her riskier investments may have been due to the influence of A. Vere Shaw, whom she met in 1928. He was the president of the firm of Shaw, Loomis, and Sayles, which had been founded in Boston two years earlier.[96] It was Shaw who got Doris a job in the firm's New York office, beginning her long and successful career as a stockbroker. It was still an unusual career choice for a woman, though not entirely without precedent. There were at least two female stockbrokers in 1920s New York, one of whom worked with an exclusively female clientele. In fact, the Great Depression opened opportunities for women in the financial services industry as men sought careers in fields that seemed more promising.[97]

The firm Doris joined operated on an innovative model of charging fees for investment counsel rather than relying on commissions earned by the sale of stock. This business plan may explain how it survived the financial failure that hit only weeks after Doris began her new position, on October 1, 1929.[98] In spite of the crash, the firm continued to advise clients on how to invest their sometimes greatly reduced capital. Although Doris knew little about advising others on investments, Shaw had felt she would learn quickly. He was correct, for Doris was a quick study. She would remain with the firm long after his own departure in 1930, whereupon it became known simply as Loomis-Sayles.[99] Doris found an exhilarating freedom in her work. She was undaunted by the occasionally discriminatory but more often perplexed attitudes of her male colleagues, a factor that helped her to become, in less than fifteen years, a vice president of the company.[100]

Just after *The Roman Way* was published, Dorian, who had attended a day school during their early years in New York City, entered Avon Old Farms School in Avon, Connecticut. Edith and Doris quickly became disillusioned with it, particularly since the school allowed him to charge any items he wanted, such as cartridges or tennis balls, to an account. They were dismayed to receive a bill of over fifty dollars for only one month.[101] He was finally enrolled at the Gunnery School in Washington, Connecticut, where Hamilton Gibson, the husband of Doris's cousin Brooke van Dyke, was head, and from which he would graduate in 1934 at the age of sixteen.[102]

Through these changes in their personal lives, Gramercy Park remained a constant for Edith and Doris. As they recognized, it was still a neighborhood that retained its associations with the theater. The onset of the Great Depression created some vacancies in the Gilder family's building, sometimes making it difficult for the family to maintain. But two longtime occupants of number 24, still living there during the first years of Edith and Doris's tenancy, were the actor Francis Wilson, who had starred in light-hearted operettas in the late nineteenth century, and the artist Jules Guerin, one of the original investors in the building. Both were longtime members of a Gramercy Park institution, the Players' Club.[103] Wilson and Guerin's residency helped preserve the old ambience of Gramercy Park as a neighborhood of artists, and Edith grew fond of the area, which seemed like a village surrounded by a large city. She enjoyed shopping in the small shops on Third Avenue, where the butcher asked her opinion of Prohibition and the baker told her about the most recent church social.[104]

As pleasant as their life in Gramercy Park had become, the world's troubles encroached. The deepening economic depression turned Edith's thoughts toward the spiritual crisis she felt arose in the wake of the financial one. She discarded the idea of a second book on Rome and turned her attention instead to writing about the Old Testament prophets who, in their efforts to address the problems of everyday life, had answered a deep spiritual need.

Chapter 13

JERUSALEM AND TROY

By 1933, Edith was considering writing a book on the Bible, an idea sparked by the twin crises of the continuing Depression and the rise of Adolf Hitler, who became chancellor of Germany that January.[1] As close observers of conditions in Germany, Edith and her sisters responded to Hitler's ascendency with alarm. They also felt firsthand some of the uncertainties of the worldwide contracting economy. Although Edith had allowed herself to be bought out of Hamilton family properties in Fort Wayne, the failure of the former Hamilton bank in early February 1933 badly affected the finances of Margaret as well as those of Jessie and Agnes, who were still recovering from the deaths of Katherine and Phoebe the previous year.[2] In the months that followed the bank failure Jessie and Agnes waited anxiously for their financial affairs to stabilize, uncertain of the depth of their losses.[3] Fortunately for the sisters their financial affairs did stabilize, and by 1936 their finances had recovered sufficiently to allow them to take an extensive trip through Europe.[4] As Edith considered the economic crisis, she told Agnes: "Truly I do not much mind it for myself—but for you and Jessie and Margaret and Edith and Harry Reid—I don't know how to bear it."[5]

By 1933 it was also becoming clear that Doris would have to help raise Francis's other children in addition to providing financially for Dorian. In spite of Doris's success in her new career, Edith feared that this left her with a large emotional and financial burden.[6] Edith confessed to Jessie that she felt "sheltered from all the suffering around, but even upon me it presses. It is a fearfully hard time."[7] The Depression had taken what Edith termed "outer security."[8] As she observed its effects on her family, she explained her reaction in religious terms to Agnes, quoting the Japanese Christian Toyohiko Kagawa, "It is impossible to love and not to suffer."[9]

The presence of Kagawa's thoughts in her mind was an indication of Edith's interest in the religious movement known as the Oxford Group, to which Jessie and Agnes had introduced her in 1930.[10] Known from 1938 as Moral Re-Armament, the religious movement was an evangelical lay organization founded in New England by Rev. Frank N. D. Buchman, an ordained Lutheran minister. It took the name the Oxford Group in 1928.[11] Today, the Group, as it was often simply called, is mainly remembered for its development of Alcoholics Anonymous.[12] The Oxford Group's roots were in Protestant evangelicalism, but it was officially without a theological orientation. Its purpose was to convert individuals to a morally and spiritually enriched life through confession of their past sins and resolution to follow its four moral absolutes: "perfect honesty, purity, unselfishness, and love."[13] Robert E. Speer, the husband of Edith's Bryn Mawr College friend Emma Bailey Speer, had drawn these tenets from the Sermon on the Mount, which had been the subject of his 1902 work *The Principles of Jesus*.[14] Buchman subsequently adopted them as the guiding theology of the Oxford Group.

Through the early 1920s, the Group called itself A First Century Christian Fellowship. Among the general public, however, its theology was often referred to as "Buchmanism," a term that Edith also used when she first encountered it.[15] The fellowship initially sought conversions among college students. Recruitment to the Group came through a combination of campus evangelical associations and invitations to its "house parties," weekends at country hotels where prospective members were persuaded to contemplate their past sins and consciously adopt what the Group termed "the changed life."[16] The Group distinguished itself from other evangelical organizations in its use of such informal settings, distinctive terminology, and lack of dogma. Its methods, especially confession between individuals, drew criticism that eventually resulted in a much-publicized investigation of its activities on the Princeton University campus in 1926.[17] The Group was eventually cleared of wrongdoing, but thereafter the focus of its activity moved to Christ Church College, Oxford. In 1928, the organization officially adopted the name Oxford Group and held a large house party in the city.[18]

After the Oxford house party, the Group movement began to grow in the United States again. By 1930, both Jessie and Agnes were Group adherents, attending its house parties and reading its publications, some of which they sent to Edith.[19] Edith encouraged Jessie to write about Group activities in her letters, though she often excused herself from participating due to her hearing loss.[20] Still, she encouraged Agnes's participation and, on occasion, she observed the Group herself.[21]

In Gramercy Park, Edith lived close to the center of Oxford Group activity in the United States, which from 1932 was the brownstone gothic Calvary Episcopal Church at the corner of Fourth Avenue and Twenty-First Street.[22] That same year Edith began to walk the short distance to the church to attend the Thursday noon communion service, her curiosity aroused by the British journalist Arthur James Russell's book on the Oxford Group, *For Sinners Only*, which described Calvary's services.[23] Its minister, Samuel Shoemaker, was an early follower of Buchman. Shoemaker had become the rector of Calvary in 1925 and had subsequently attended the Oxford House Party of 1928.[24] Under his leadership, Calvary Episcopal transformed itself from a dying parish church to a center of Group activity, where, following Group traditions, laymen were allowed to conduct part of the services. Shoemaker added the noonday services, including the midweek communion, to reach out to those living and working in the neighborhood. He placed a large white lighted cross over the door of the church and began the evening services in Madison Square.[25]

Edith's interest in the Oxford Group coincided with the restoration of the circle of friends she had developed at Miss Porter's School and Bryn Mawr College, women who had devoted much of their lives to Christian mission at home and abroad. After making friendships in New York publishing and theatrical circles, Edith reconnected with her older nexus of friends whose lives had been shaped by their religious commitment and who exerted influence on the writing of *The Prophets of Israel*. Her neighbors at 24 Gramercy Park included Robert and Emma Bailey

Speer, with whom Edith renewed her friendship.[26] Margaret Shearman, who had remained good friends with all of the Hamiltons, was also drawn into Oxford Group activity.[27] Susan Duryee Fahmy, hesitant about the Oxford Group at first, became a supporter as well. She returned to the United States from England permanently in 1936, three years after the death of her husband.[28] She, too, visited Calvary Episcopal Church, and she and Edith once again spent time together, on one occasion hearing Susan's old friend the novelist and philosopher Lin Yutang speak at New York's Cosmopolitan Club.[29]

Edith had encountered evangelistic organizations throughout her life: Christian Endeavour in her adolescence and the Student Volunteer Movement during her college years. In both instances she had been a keen observer and, in the case of Christian Endeavour, an occasional participant. For Edith, however, the appeal of the Oxford Group was far stronger. The Group drew from the idealist philosophy that she had absorbed as a college student, separating faith from dogma and focusing on individuals as agents of change through its conception of the apostle, which was at the core of the Group's activities. The Group viewed itself as a contemporary version of the early bands of apostles who had traveled the Roman Empire, sharing their faith. The process of sharing was based on the work of St. Paul, who persuaded people to convert to Christianity by telling the story of his own conversion.[30] Those who chose to attend Group meetings for the first time experienced the Group custom of sharing: listening to stories of changed lives told by those who had already been influenced by the Group. These "life-changers," as the Group termed them, engaged in both confession and witness as they told how their lives had been altered by their resolution to strive for the four moral absolutes.

Importantly for Edith, these modern apostles were idealists: illustrating how human beings could strive to achieve their higher selves. Edith would read and quote its literature, observe Group religious services, and finally write a book that largely incorporated the Group's conception of the Old Testament prophets, leaders who had urged their society to develop a spiritual basis that would sustain it through crisis. To Jessie

she wrote: "I love the way the Groups live and do not defend themselves. That is a new thing in religious history."[31]

She was, however, aware of the criticisms that continued to be
launched at the Group. Buchman was often seen as interested primarily
in recruiting the wealthy or influential. He did not deny this, instead
referring to such figures as "key men," leaders who could set an example
that others would wish to follow.[32] He openly sought famous people to
endorse his movement, even securing a fruitless interview with Mussolini in the spring of 1927.[33] Edith herself was critical of the ways in
which Oxford Group literature permitted religion to be associated with
financial profit.[34] She read Group literature extensively, however, and
she was fond of repeating stories of the changed lives experienced by
those who came into contact with it.[35] In January 1934 she told Agnes:
"I think often of what I found in one of the Groups' papers: 'God cannot
use people with merely an interest in His will, but only those for whom
it is the very core of living.'"[36]

To Edith, the success of the Oxford Group in the years of the Depression seemed to confirm that the poor economic conditions had
created a religious revival.[37] Indeed, the Oxford Group tended to view
the Depression as a primarily spiritual problem, minimizing the economic
factors that had caused it.[38] Edith, while well aware of the economic
effects of the Depression on those closest to her, also viewed the economic crisis as a spiritual one. By early January 1933, Edith was contemplating a book on the Bible, although she often doubted her ability to
write one sufficient to the perceived spiritual needs of the Depression.
In late 1933 in the face of the twin crises of the rise of Hitler and the
Depression, Edith abandoned the book on ancient Rome on which she
had begun work, telling Agnes, "This world in the state it is in—and I
writing essays on ancient Rome!"[39] By that December she was reading
the sources that would contribute to her next book, *The Prophets of
Israel*. She was studying the Old Testament and, she told Jessie, finding it
"intensely interesting." She had also finished reading "an enormous history of the Jews," writing Jessie that it "leaves me feeling them the most
extraordinary and incomprehensible people."[40] The volume to which

she referred was *A History of the Jews*, by the historian Dr. Abram Leon Sachar, eventually the founding president of Brandeis University. The volume, published in 1930, provided Edith with several translations for the book on the Bible. Its sixth chapter, devoted to the prophets, would also provide several of the interpretations of them that she would offer in her book.[41]

Doris had initially responded to the Depression by joining a technocracy committee.[42] The one in which she participated was one of many that formed in response to the original Committee on Technocracy established by Columbia University engineering professor Walter Rautenstrauch and engineer Howard Scott in the autumn of 1932. The technocrats believed that improvements in factory machinery were so great that the need for human labor had entered a precipitous decline. The solution to the crisis was a planned economy that would restore the balance between production and consumption. Doris's conservative instincts might have balked at the idea of a planned economy; regardless, her enthusiasm for technocracy—as well as the public's—proved to be short-lived.[43] For her part, Edith found technocracy dull and off point.[44] To Edith, science, technology, and economic theory could not offer hope to those who were suffering and who needed religious belief, both powerful and practical, she would argue in *The Prophets of Israel*.[45]

Technocracy, however, marked the beginning of Doris's political activity. It was in the early 1930s that she moved further away from the Southern Democratic views with which she had been raised. Through her work in the financial sector, Doris was counseling wealthy clients and making new friends who would push her political views to the right. These included Alida Milliken, a socialite and philanthropist who lived in a large brownstone on Madison Avenue with her husband, the surgeon Dr. Seth Milliken, and their five children. Their wealth, which derived from the Deering-Milliken textile firm started by the doctor's father, was devoted to a mix of artistic and conservative causes.[46] Doris would eventually be caught in the upsurge of isolationist thinking in the late 1930s. By the 1950s she and Alida would work together in conservative political causes.[47]

Doris's career was progressing in spite of the inauspicious time in which she had become a stockbroker. Her work was demanding, requiring her presence at the office not only on weekdays but for a half day on Saturdays as well. Despite obstacles, however, in 1932 Doris became the first woman to become an executive vice president of the Loomis-Sayles Mutual Fund.[48] She felt that investment counseling was a "gentler art," and in the early years of her new career she had learned how to interview potential clients and establish new accounts. She also managed to successfully navigate a male-dominated profession at a firm composed mostly of "Boston bluebloods"—as Doris, with justification, called them—among whom her gender, southern origins, and status as a Baltimorean made her an outsider.[49] But through her skill counseling clients, she became indispensable to the New York office. In the summer of 1933 the head of the New York office, Mr. Robinson, became ill, and in July Doris was promoted to co-head of the New York office.[50] The news took her by surprise, in spite of her obvious capabilities. While the number of women entering the financial services field was increasing, a female office head was a rarity. As an office head, she was subsequently elected to the Loomis-Sayles board of directors but was told that as a board member she must always identify herself as "D. F. Reid so that," as she told John Mason Brown, "the public at large will not know the hideous truth—that I am indeed a woman!"[51]

Edith supported Doris's career, which sometimes meant a far shorter stay at Seawall so Doris could remain close to New York City, and, in January 1933, when the couple entertained Ralph T. Sayles, the vice president of the firm, she found a surprising level of agreement on the solution to the Depression.[52] Sayles was firmly of the opinion that the Depression was good for business because it had essentially abolished the poor business practices that had caused the economic failure. But he surprised Edith by the seriousness of his tone when he told her: "Miss Hamilton, I am not a religious man—I am certainly not a Christian, but we shall get things right only when we go back to the principles of Jesus Christ." Edith told Jessie, "Really, it was like a bomb exploding— as unexpected."[53] For Edith, however, the remark provided more evidence of the increasing interest in religion that she felt the Depression had generated, creating both a need and a potential market for a work of biblical interpretation.

The rise of Hitler also contributed to Edith's decision to write about the Old Testament prophets. The book would focus on the Jewish contribution to Western civilization, which the Nazis sought to obscure. The Oxford Group gave the prophets an added currency, since, in addition to the apostles, the Group modeled itself on the Hebrew prophets, religious messengers who remained laymen.[54] The prophets were realists who could give practical advice, even if their message proved to be unpopular.[55] As Edith wrote in the foreword of *The Prophets of Israel*, "Their eyes were keen to see into basic problems of life. It would have been inconceivable to them all that religion was not directly concerned with everything that bore in any way on life; the whole life belonged to religion."[56] The Oxford Group viewed the prophets as the necessary groundwork for Christianity: the discussion of how to live a moral life prepared human beings for Jesus's arrival by making clear to individuals the need to acknowledge their sins.[57]

Moreover, during the years in which Edith was writing *The Prophets of Israel*, she frequently read the works of a man widely hailed as a modern prophet: Toyohiko Kagawa. His conversion to Christianity, his renunciation of wealth, his pacifism, and his desire to live among the poor whom he served earned him a reputation in the United States and elsewhere as a prophet, one who sought to make Japanese society more ethical. A popular figure among the Oxford Group, Kagawa met Frank N. D. Buchman during Buchman's travels in China, and his ecumenical approach to Christianity was similar.[58]

Edith, who had been impressed by Japanese Christianity during her winter in Kyoto, was reading Kagawa's works by January 1933, telling Agnes, "I have never found anyone who speaks to me as directly as Kagawa—all the others seem to me to put safety first—at least to do that often—and he never does. He says Live dangerously in the true sense. Love and love and through love open your heart to the pain of the world. He helps me so."[59] Moreover, in his *Meditations*, Kagawa suggested that Socrates could be the model for Jesus, an idea Edith would later employ in *Witness to the Truth*.[60] Kagawa's influence was also apparent in *The Prophets of Israel*.[61]

Edith would begin *The Prophets of Israel* with a chapter titled "Fear and Form in Religion," which argued that religion had evolved in stages. This concept would have been familiar to her through her reading of the British idealist Edward Caird but also through the work of the scholars known as the Cambridge school, who, in the years before the outbreak of the First World War, had sought to apply the work of anthropologists and archaeologists to the analysis of Greek religion.[62] This group of scholars had formed around Jane Ellen Harrison, scholar of Newnham College, Cambridge, and the author of *Prolegomena to the Study of Greek Religion* (1903) and *Themis: A Study of the Social Origins of Greek Religion* (1912). Edith found Harrison's discussion of the social origins of Greek religion in *Themis* useful, arguing in her opening chapter, as did Harrison, that there was a social purpose to religion and to ritual, which provided a systematic means of keeping the individual soul responsive to others and open to the possibility of understanding the purpose of human existence.[63]

Edith's notes for *The Prophets of Israel* also show that she read Gilbert Murray's contribution to the thought of the Cambridge school, *The Four Stages of Greek Religion*, which had been published in 1912 and which he subsequently altered to *The Five Stages of Greek Religion* in 1925.[64] What interested her about Murray's work was his essential argument that religion progressed in definable stages.[65] Worship had begun, wrote Edith, out of primitive humanity's fear of the gods. The ancient Greeks had offered examples of this in their mythology, including Agamemnon's sacrifice of his daughter Iphigenia, as told in the tragedy of Aeschylus.[66] From these attempts to appease the gods, ancient religion among the Hebrews and the Greeks had gradually come to emphasize the accuracy with which a sacrificial rite was performed.[67] Once the demand for accuracy was satisfied, aesthetic concerns, the need to make the ritual beautiful, became the chief object of worship, a development that made the practice of religion spiritually unsatisfying. Ritual had become an end in itself, separated from the moral conflicts individuals faced in daily life, problems to which religion, concerned with representation, not spirituality, could not provide answers.[68] In her first chapter, Edith made her objections to formalism in religion clear, and she saw the arrival of the first prophet, Amos, as the final stage of religious development, in which human spiritual needs properly became its focus.[69]

In the prophets, Edith saw the effort to make the ideal a reality in human society. The prophets, she wrote, were practical men, concerned with how to apply religious teaching to all aspects of life. They were apt to see moral failings but also the ability of individuals to improve; as she wrote in her notes, Isaiah "preached the depravity of men, but never apart from their possibilities."[70] They were also, as she would call them in her third chapter, realists, who saw that humans struggled with the problem of how to live a good life during times of crisis, such as the Great Depression. Edith wrote in her foreword that the prophets "did not think at all about fitting men for heaven, but only about fitting men to make the world a good place to live in."[71] How people dealt with the moral questions of life seemed to be changing during the Great Depression, but, in reality, as Edith saw it, people ultimately settled on age-old solutions, confirming that the moral exhortations of the prophets were still relevant.

Some of Edith's examples of moral confusion involved Doris, providing a picture of their relationship during the early 1930s. Doris's work schedule, her growing interest in politics, and her continued socializing meant that although the two women lived together, Edith often found herself home alone in the evenings writing letters or reading. There was, as yet, no definite understanding between them that their relationship was exclusive and lifelong. Edith knew that in her round of social activities Doris acquired admirers, a circumstance she accepted. Edith had seen several women in romantic friendships ultimately choose marriage to a man. A letter she wrote to Jessie in late 1932 showed that she still had not ruled out this possibility for Doris, even as Doris approached her late thirties.[72] She described a marriage proposal that Doris had received—and rejected—from a man who had previously advocated the practice of trial marriages. Edith was skeptical, however. "Well—he fell in love with Doris—and all that sort of thing became as nothing.

The one thing he wanted was to marry her—and have a little house—and some children—just as men really in love always will. He would have rejected the idea of a trial marriage with indignation."[73] Still, Edith assured Jessie that she hoped for a happy marriage for Doris, indicating that in late 1932 Edith still had no sense of the relationship between her and Doris as permanent.

Edith saw debates such as those over trial marriages and even matters of fashion as highly relevant to her study of the prophets and their legacy, since the prophets had considered all aspects of life. Questions of fashion, Edith would write in the *Prophets*, were not too minor to deserve the consideration of these realists. Isaiah, Edith wrote, described in detail the jewelry and other finery worn by individual women in Jerusalem through eight verses, his "wrath increasing at each item."[74] Isaiah's criticisms of women's dress gave him an immediacy to contemporary readers of the Old Testament, but he was, according to Edith, a committed social reformer and diplomat: "Outside Jerusalem he was a statesman; inside he was a prophet."[75]

The prophets were clearly concerned with economic exploitation and wealth accumulation, issues raised by the Great Depression. Edith identified Amos as "the ancestor of all labor agitators," adding that, "in his book is the first recorded attack of labor upon capital."[76] Amos was familiar with the luxurious lives of the wealthy yet, Edith wrote, "he knew the poor, too; He had not to go far afield to learn their ways. He saw them 'crushed and oppressed', 'swallowed up', by the rich."[77] The prophets were able to address the concerns of Depression-era readers, such as economic inequality and labor-management relations.

Edith's work on *The Prophets of Israel* was interrupted by the Theatre Guild's proposal to stage a production of a tragedy of Euripides as well as by Ernest and Betsey Reid's stay at Gramercy Park in the winter of 1934–35. Their visit was prompted by the poor behavior of Francis, though exactly what Francis had done remained obscure in Edith's correspondence.[78] Dorian had graduated from the Gunnery School in the spring of 1934 and entered Amherst College the following autumn.[79] Of the twins, who would turn fifteen in February 1935, Betsey was also showing signs of being an apt student. But Ernest, who suffered from a short attention span, appeared unable to compete with his more intellectually gifted siblings, though Edith considered him to have an artistic temperament. Just before his visit to Gramercy Park, Ernest was expelled from his school for poor behavior. Doris assumed the responsibility of finding both a new school for him and a psychiatrist, Dr. Florence Powdermaker at Columbia University, who could treat his behavioral problems. Ernest's inability to concentrate, Dr. Powdermaker told them, was prompted by the almost constant state of fear in which he had been compelled to live due to the behavior of both Francis and Marie.[80]

A new school was eventually found for Ernest, but in the meantime his behavior caused concern for his future. Edith wrote: "I simply cannot conceive of his growing up into a reasonable, responsible person. The longer he stayed here, the more frightened I was about the future for him. He is suspicious, utterly, of every body. He will not believe either Doris or me."[81] She respected Dr. Powdermaker, hoping that the psychiatrist would be able to influence Ernest's behavior.[82] Sympathetic as Edith was, Ernest's visit stopped work on *The Prophets of Israel*.

In the spring of 1935, as Edith returned to the writing of *The Prophets of Israel*, Lee Simonson decided that the Theatre Guild might be able to mount a production of *The Trojan Women* of Euripides.[83] He remembered Edith's lectures at the American Laboratory Theater. He had also read her unpublished translation of the *Agamemnon*, which he convinced the Theatre Guild's board to read, although its members remained firm in their wish to stage a work of Euripides.[84] Simonson believed it possible that *The Trojan Women* could be produced as early as the fall of 1935. The Guild's main concern was finding actresses capable of performing the three main roles.[85] Simonson therefore asked Edith if she would consider translating *The Trojan Women*, the tragedy recounting the experiences of Hecuba, the widow of King Priam of Troy; Andromache, widow of the slain Hector; and the priestess Cassandra, Hecuba's daughter. Set just outside the gates of Troy as the women wait to be taken into slavery by the victorious Greeks, the play depicted the callous effects of war on civilians.

To Edith, Euripides was not far removed from the study of the Old Testament prophets. Gilbert Murray had argued that *The Trojan Women* had been written shortly after the Athenian conquest of the island of Melos, which had hoped to remain neutral in the conflict between Athens and Sparta. The Athenians had refused to allow this, and in the course of their victory had killed all of the adult men on the island while enslaving the women and children. Murray had called Euripides a "prophet" for daring to write a play during wartime that interpreted a Greek victory in a cruel light.[86] Edith, too, not only compared Euripides to Isaiah but remarked on how the Greek victory over Troy, so often celebrated in the Homeric poetry as a great military achievement, had been used by Euripides to show the harsh reality of war and its devastating effects on individuals.[87] She would call *The Trojan Women* the "greatest piece of anti-war literature" ever written.[88]

The guild's insistence on a work of Euripides was due to the perceived ability of the tragic playwright to confront the challenges of the twentieth century. As Europe's fascist leaders consolidated their hold on political power, the Theatre Guild judged that the antiwar message of *The Trojan Women* would find a ready audience. Gilbert Murray's verse translation of the tragedy, with which Edith had been familiar since at least 1907, reinforced the play's reputation as an antiwar polemic. Murray, a pacifist before his support for the British cause during the First World War, was an ardent supporter of the League of Nations.[89]

In considering whether to attempt her own translation of the tragedy, Edith professed to be hesitant in part because of the brilliancy of Murray's version. As Edith was well aware, to translate Euripides was to invite comparison to Gilbert Murray, whose name in the thirties was still associated with the translation and interpretation of the great tragic playwright. Edith's willingness to produce her own version of *The Trojan Women* was an indication of the strength of her belief in free verse translations of Greek plays. It also signaled the need to abandon the poetic approach favored by Murray, whom she described that June as "born under a rhyming planet."[90]

That spring, despite her anxiety about translating the tragedy, Edith agreed to allow John Mason Brown to arrange a lunch with Dame Sybil Thorndike, who was in New York to appear in a Broadway production.[91] Edith took her translation to the meeting, where Dame Sybil read the part of Hecuba. The actress, a friend of Gilbert Murray who had played the role in London, tended to prefer translations in verse, feeling that poetry offered the performer more scope. But Edith was impressed with Dame Sybil's reading of her translation, telling Margaret that she read Hecuba's lines "grandly, magnificently."[92] She was also pleased that Dame Sybil had read *The Greek Way*. In the end, the Theatre Guild never produced *The Trojan Women*, and Edith returned to *Prophets*. By May 1935, she had "three prophets" ready to send to Warder Norton.[93] She continued to write and revise what W. W. Norton editor Storer Lunt was already calling *The Prophets of Israel*, a title Edith approved.[94]

In 1936, just as *The Prophets of Israel* was published, the Connecticut River flooded, damaging Alice and Margaret's house at Hadlyme, which sat directly on its bank. Although the Hamilton sisters' greatest cause for alarm—that the Holyoke Dam would break—did not occur, houses nearby were carried down the river and cattle were drowned while still in their barns.[95] The flood waters apparently caused the Hamilton house to resettle on its foundations, cracking 130 glass window panes.[96] More-over, the river washed across the yard, stranding boats in nearby trees. Edith, visiting Hadlyme in May, told Agnes, "Where you expect to see grass along the river banks you are surprised by a dull grayness—sand, inches deep with a topping of slimy mud."[97] Despite the damage Had-lyme sustained, by early summer of that year, the house was in good enough repair for Edith to bring Betsey to stay for a month.[98]

Edith spent the rest of the summer at Seawall. She read Oxford Group literature and the reviews of *The Prophets of Israel*, which was well re-ceived. Its initial printing of two thousand copies had sold out by mid-May, and W. W. Norton had received a large order from England for the book.[99] Alice reported that a prominent Boston rabbi had recommended the work to his congregation.[100] The reviews were also generally favor-able, including one written for the *New York Herald Tribune* by Dr. Abram Leon Sachar, who praised *The Prophets of Israel* as equal in quality to *The Greek Way* and *The Roman Way*. He recognized that Edith had drawn some of her portrayals of the prophets from his own work, but he saw her largely as an interpreter of the works of others. Sachar also saw the contemporary appeal of the prophets at a time when the United States and Europe were facing the twin crises of the Great Depression and the consolidation of the Nazi state and its anti-Semitic policies. The prophets had sought to remind early Jewish society of the primary importance of ethical conduct even in a time of national crisis.[101]

That September Edith and Doris moved from Gramercy Park to a larger apartment at 1165 Park Avenue.[102] It was now understood that Ernest and Betsey, as well as their younger sister Mary, would live permanently with Edith and Doris, but the apartment at 24 Gramercy Park was too small to accommodate all of them. The new Park Avenue apartment had five bedrooms and two sitting rooms as well as a dining room and kitchen.[103] Dorian, though away at college, still had a bedroom reserved for his use. From early in 1937 Ernest's behavior showed signs of improvement.[104] Although he did not cease to cause worry—in early 1938 Edith mentioned family troubles to John Mason Brown—a new boarding school was found for him from which he graduated later that year.[105] He subsequently pursued a career in the Navy.[106] The Reid daughters, who had attended the Bryn Mawr School in Baltimore, were now enrolled in the Brearley School in New York City, where Edith's former student, Millicent Carey McIntosh, was headmistress. One year before graduation, Betsey's class performed *The Trojan Women*, possibly using Edith's translation.[107]

Edith's theatrical friends, especially Lee Simonson, still urged her to publish her translations, though she had become reluctant to do so. In the twenties Edith had actively sought the publication of her translations and had ultimately in April 1928 been given her first W. W. Norton contract for these works.[108] By the thirties, she was more hesitant, having achieved success as an author with the publication of *The Greek Way* and remembering the cool reception to her translations that she had encountered among academic classicists in the twenties. Moreover, she had finally read recent translations of Euripides that she truly admired. This growing body of work, created by academics and poets, may have made her reluctant to publish her own translations, just at the time that W. W. Norton became more interested in publishing them. She finally agreed to their appearance in print even though in April 1937 she informed Warder "I am not very keen to have them published."[109]

The critical response to the translations, published as *Three Greek Plays*, was much as Edith expected: praise from theatrical circles but more severe commentary from scholars. Among the former, Rosamond published a favorable review in *Theatre Arts Monthly* and, as if to confirm Rosamond's assertion, the American Actors Company almost immediately began to prepare a production of *The Trojan Women* using Edith's translation. It was staged in a small venue, the Master Institute Theater, on the evening of January 24, 1938. Both Brooks Atkinson and John Mason Brown reviewed the production favorably.[110] As war began in Europe, the relevance of *The Trojan Women* increased. Another production was given in New York City in April 1941 by the Experimental Theater using Gilbert Murray's translation. The antiwar message of the play was clear: the Greek soldiers who came to take the infant Astyanax away from Andromache wore Nazi uniforms. Although Atkinson reviewed the production favorably in the *New York Times*, he complained about Murray's translation, commenting, "It is a play of words; and to modern ears, Edith Hamilton's words are much sharper and crisper."[111]

As Edith was aware, the increasing power of fascism in Europe changed the Oxford Group as well. In 1936, after being criticized for his appearance at the Berlin Olympics, Frank N. D. Buchman announced the creation of Moral Re-Armament, a broader movement that opposed fascism and communism, taking its name from Hitler's rearmament. He formally introduced the new movement in 1938.[112]

Initially, Edith read about it with interest while on vacation in Bermuda, where she had taken Doris in the hope that she would get an opportunity to rest.[113] In the creation of Moral Re-Armament, however, the practices of the Group that had made it attractive to Edith, and to some of Buchman's followers, diminished. Some of his critics, including Rev. Samuel Shoemaker of Calvary Episcopal Church, formally broke with Moral Re-Armament, believing that the hallmarks of the Group— its emphasis on the individual adoption of the changed life and the informal leadership structure—had been lost.[114] As Edith had observed during the years she was writing *The Prophets of Israel*, religion had "advanced enormously. It is freeing itself from the old shackles."[115] With the arrival of Moral Re-Armament and the end of Calvary Episcopal as a

center for the Group, Gramercy Park, from which Edith had moved
away in 1936, ceased to have the religious activity she had noticed in the
early years of the Depression. Jessie and Agnes remained followers of
Buchman, and Edith would continue to sympathize with the pacifism
and anticommunism of Moral Re-Armament.[116]

In revealing Edith's objections to formalism in religion, *The Prophets
of Israel* expressed her unconventional theological perspective. To Edith
it had been unsurprising that a time of economic crisis had produced a
noticeable rise in spiritual need, one that the Group had attempted to
fulfill. Moved by the various effects of the Great Depression on individuals and alarmed at the rise of Nazi Germany, Edith had produced a
volume that emphasized the Jewish contribution to Western civilization
and tried to help spiritual seekers to better understand the Old Testament. In 1944, she would tell C. Raymond Everitt, her editor at Little,
Brown, that *The Prophets of Israel* was "the book of those I have written
which I care so much the most for."[117] It was a remarkable statement,
given that by then she had experienced success with an expanded version of *The Greek Way*, titled *The Great Age of Greek Literature*, and *Mythology*, arguably her greatest achievement and most enduring work. *The
Prophets of Israel*, however, had been her first to emphasize the direct
relevance of the ancient world to twentieth-century America. Soon, the
Nazis would engulf Europe in war, giving Edith a chance to demonstrate
that ancient Greek struggles against tyranny could inform a world in
the grip of violent conflict.

Chapter 14

"THE MIRACLE OF GREEK MYTHOLOGY"

After the publication of *Three Greek Plays*, Edith planned to write a book on tragedy, an idea she had suggested to Warder when, in April 1937, he had encouraged her to publish her translations. He had responded favorably to her proposal, initially hoping for a volume that would include her translations along with chapters on tragic forms of literary expression in different cultures.[1] The book was never completed. This was due in part to an increasingly tense relationship with Warder but, more importantly, to the appearance of another, more enticing, project that came her way in the autumn of 1938, the suggestion that she write a modern version of Thomas Bulfinch's *The Age of Fable*, a work often better known as *Bulfinch's Mythology*.

It was the idea of C. Raymond Everitt, an editor at Little, Brown publishers, a friend of John Mason Brown, and, as he saw himself, "an old admirer of Bullfinch [sic] and his work."[2] In the summer of 1938, Everitt had described the project over a cup of coffee with John, who had immediately suggested that he contact Edith, not necessarily as the potential author of the book, but as an advisor for a revised edition of Bulfinch.[3] Intrigued, Everitt wrote Edith, who invited him to tea at the Park Avenue apartment that October.[4]

From the time that the proposal for a new mythology book was brought to her attention, Edith was interested in being its author, not merely an advisor. She quickly grasped the literary possibilities of the new volume and the significant place of mythology in stirring readers' curiosity about ancient Greece. Edith and Everitt quickly established a rapport. While Warder viewed Edith primarily as a scholar, Everitt understood the value she placed on creativity. Based on Everitt's enthusiasm for Edith, Little, Brown decided to proceed with the project.[5] By the end of November a contract had been signed, and the project had acquired the working title of *Classic Myths* with a tentative completion date of January 1, 1941.[6]

Edith set out to create an entirely new version only of Thomas Bulfinch's first mythology book, *The Age of Fable*, which had contained Greek, Roman, and Norse myths. Bulfinch, who had received his education in classics at the Boston Latin School and at Harvard, had died in 1867, the year Edith was born. He had been a Boston bank clerk when he had published *The Age of Fable*, which was subsequently revised many times; the title *Bulfinch's Mythology* was generally used for later editions of the work, which included not only the myths of the first volume but also Bulfinch's later works *The Age of Chivalry* and *Legends of Charlemagne*, initially published in 1858 and 1863, respectively.[7] Edith's model was confined to *The Age of Fable* since she originally intended to include only the Greek and Roman myths, with the brief section on Norse mythology a slightly later addition.[8]

Edith was enthusiastic about mythology even though she later confessed that when she had first taken on the project she had known little about the subject. In fact, she was so eager to start work on the volume that her proposed completion date far outpaced Everitt's expectations. She initially predicted that she could finish it in two years or even sooner. Everitt, while setting the manuscript's delivery date for January 1941, informed her that she should feel no sense of urgency in completing the work.[9]

The project's attraction lay in its subject's wide appeal: mythology was an aspect of ancient Greek culture with which a potentially large reading audience hoped to become more familiar. As Bulfinch's biographer Marie Sally Cleary has pointed out, one reason for the success of *The Age of Fable* was the existence of a public eager to better understand mythological references in Western art and literature.[10] By writing a new mythology book, Edith could tap into the primary means by which readers became curious about ancient Greece. Bulfinch had aided his readers' quest for greater appreciation of art and literature by including quotations from poems that alluded to a myth before his telling of each story, something that Edith also originally intended to do in her volume.[11] Instead, she commented on the sources for each story, identifying the ancient authors from whom she had drawn the tale, a change that indicated the ultimate limits of Bulfinch as her model. As she began work on the book it quickly became apparent that in terms of content she would vary considerably from the earlier author.

Edith found Bulfinch's work readable but felt that the large number of quotations from poetry actually defeated the purpose of making the subject of mythology accessible to readers. Edith's approach was therefore the opposite of Bulfinch's. Rather than providing excerpts from the poems inspired by a particular tale, she imagined the reader encountering a reference to a myth in either art or literature and subsequently wishing to read only the story, not other allusions to it. Nevertheless, she was conscious of which mythological tales a potential reader might encounter, causing her to include at least one story that Bulfinch had left out: the tale of Amphitryon, whose wife Alcmena bore a son, the hero Hercules, by Zeus. Finding Bulfinch occasionally old-fashioned, she felt he had omitted the tale, along with the Roman story of Lucretia, because both narratives revolved around tests of a woman's virtue. Edith, however, initially planned to include both tales, as she felt there were many allusions to both characters in English poetry, though only the story of Amphitryon actually appeared in *Mythology*.[12]

She also wanted to arrange the stories differently than Bulfinch, paying more attention to chronology, beginning with what could be identified by authorship as the oldest tales, the ones drawn from the Homeric Hymns and from Hesiod. She also wanted to add more context before each story, explaining "the way the myths may have originated and the way they have developed." By late 1938, she already envisioned, she told Everitt, "a book a little more grown-up than Bulfinch, but only a little."[13]

Only in two respects was Bulfinch's work a definite model. Edith, like Bulfinch, wrote a lengthy section at the beginning of the book describing the attributes of the gods and goddesses and the other lesser divinities. Also, from its inception Everitt felt that *Mythology* should have illustrations.[14] Ultimately, the publisher commissioned Steele Savage, who had illustrated Sally Benson's mythology book three years earlier, to create the artwork for Edith's volume.

Bulfinch's influence on the content and the length of Edith's work was limited. For the latter, she turned to Charles Mills Gayley's *Classic Myths* as a guide. It was a work with which she was familiar, having told its stories to Dorian and the other Reid children.[15] Gayley, an American who had largely been raised in Ireland, had received a British education in classics before becoming head of the English department at the University of California in 1889. He had written and published *Classic Myths* early in his thirty-four-year tenure at Berkeley. There were several aspects of Gayley's work that mirrored Edith's. Like her *Mythology*, Gayley's work was commissioned by a Boston publisher, Ginn and Company, as a modern version of Bulfinch.[16] In length, Edith tried to match Gayley closely, eventually producing a book that was, including the genealogical trees of famous families of mythology at the end, only slightly longer.[17]

In terms of content, the writer on mythology who most influenced Edith was the English clergyman Charles Kingsley, the author of *The Heroes*, originally published in 1855.[18] Edith had long been familiar with Kingsley's works. His mythology book, *The Heroes*, which was limited to the stories of Perseus, the Argonauts, and Theseus, had been frequently used at the Bryn Mawr School as the text that determined the reading ability of a girl applying for admission, helping to establish in which class a new student would be placed.[19] Though Kingsley's work was far more limited in scope than Edith's, there were key similarities in their prefaces. Kingsley, like Edith in her introduction to *Mythology*, identified the ancient Greeks as the founders of Western civilization, in his case by giving examples of how their achievements had influenced Victorian British society.[20] Kingsley also used a contemporary, idiomatic

English style of writing in his retelling of the stories, hoping to make them easily understandable.

Like *Bulfinch's Mythology*, Kingsley's *Heroes* was reprinted in many editions and proved an enduring work. Kingsley, however, had chosen a half-metrical poetic form in which to recount the stories, and he intended children to be his audience.[21] Edith's *Mythology* would differ sharply from Kingsley. She rejected any idea of retelling the stories in metric verse, and she deliberately wrote for a less precisely defined audience. Both, however, tried to explain the connection between mythology and religion. Yet Kingsley, seeing pantheism as devolving from monotheism, saw the ancient Greeks as following a downward spiral morally, though, at the time of the mythological stories, still retaining some sense of right and wrong.[22] Edith, writing at a much later date and having absorbed the ideas of the Cambridge school, saw just the opposite path: the Olympic gods had evolved out of the earliest Greek deities, such as the Furies, but the Greeks had gradually tried to make their gods fulfill human needs for protection and affirmation of moral standards.[23]

As Edith researched *Mythology*, she compiled lists of the stories she wanted to include. In the first pages of her notebook she listed forty-four stories under the heading "Done," including the fifteen tales comprising Jason's quest for the Golden Fleece.[24] She also made notes of stories she had yet to write, organized into "Important," "Fairly Important," and "Unimportant."[25] Included under the heading "Important" were such myths as Hercules, Perseus, Phaeton, and the legend of Theseus.[26] These were all included in the final volume, but some of the tales that she listed as "Unimportant," such as the story of King Midas or those of Callisto or Antiope, nevertheless found their way into *Mythology* in the sections titled "The Less Important Myths" and "Brief Myths."[27] She found other ways to include stories that she had labeled "Fairly Important" in the book. As Edith organized her material, she found that the stories of Ceyx and Alcyone, and Pygmalion and Galatea, rounded out the section titled "Eight Brief Tales of Lovers." This section also included myths she had listed as "important," including Pyramis and Thisbe and the story of Orpheus and Eurydice.[28] She also made lists of characters or mythological creatures she wanted to research, such as Orion, Astraea, and the Cranes of Ibycus.[29] When she finished writing a story, she crossed it off her list. Concern about the length of the mythology book, however, meant that some myths had to be excluded. Edith was always cautious about the length of *Mythology*, feeling too large a volume would defeat the purpose of making the subject accessible.[30]

For a long cycle of stories, such as those associated with the Trojan War, her notes comprised a lengthy list of characters she planned to introduce to her readers. Edith's surviving notes, however, do not mention every story she ultimately included. In her list of figures associated with the House of Atreus, from which Agamemnon came, there is no mention of his ill-fated daughter Iphigenia, though the story of her father offering her as a sacrifice to the gods at Aulis was included among the myths of the Trojan War.[31]

Edith found the Norse portion of the volume the most challenging to write. Initially, she had not planned to include it at all.[32] Norse mythology was not a subject with which she felt familiar, having gained her knowledge of it largely through listening to Wagnerian opera. She had, however, likely read the *Germania* of the Roman historian Tacitus, which described the rituals used in worshipping the Norse gods.[33] Both Bulfinch and Gayley had included Norse mythology in their own books, one reason why Edith may have at last added it to hers. The time period in which she wrote *Mythology* suggests another. Interest in Norse mythology revived with the rise of Nazism in Germany, making it a potentially contentious subject on which to write.[34] A section on Norse mythology, however, would help readers to at least understand some of the Third Reich's symbolism.

Edith, in her introduction to the section on Norse mythology, drew a sharp dichotomy between the culture that had produced these tales and Christianity. She painted a picture of the early Christians as almost completely successful in their efforts to stamp out the literature of the pre-Christian Norse on the European continent. The result of this struggle, Edith argued, was that Christians drew no inspiration from Norse culture. The Nazis might use it for their symbolism, but they were drawing on a cultural tradition completely different from Christianity.

Edith did considerable research in order to write the section on Norse mythology. She composed a glossary of terms for herself.[35] She read articles in the journal *Scandinavian Studies* and books on runic inscriptions to understand the subject.[36] She frequently reflected on its differences with Greek mythology, ruminations that would find their way into the book, writing in her notes "Gk. mythology an epic—Norse a tragedy."[37] The result of her work was a brief survey of Norse mythology that reflected the tense political atmosphere of the time in which it was created. Other parts of *Mythology*, particularly her retelling of the story of Prometheus, would also reflect the political context in which the book was written. Yet only her introduction to the Norse section would attract criticism from a reviewer.[38]

As the Second World War got underway, circumstances dictated that the book's introduction would be devoted entirely to the Greeks. As Edith would argue, Greek mythology reflected the value the ancient Greeks placed on humanity. Echoing the opening chapters of *The Greek Way*, Edith's introduction compared ancient Greece and Egypt and argued that the Greeks had been the first people to place humanity at the center of the universe. "The miracle of Greek mythology," as Edith wrote in her introduction, was that Greeks had imagined deities in human form.[39] It was an idea she derived from the philosopher Edward Caird, who, in the late nineteenth century, had argued that the Greeks had been the first people to link deities more to humanity than to the natural world and to endow the forces of nature with such completely human personalities.

The classical scholar R. W. Livingstone, whose book *The Greek Genius and Its Meaning to Us* greatly influenced Edith, had reinforced Caird's point. If Edith minimized the violence of the myths, as she has sometimes been accused of doing, it was also likely due to Caird, who had argued that the "poetic imagination" of the Greeks had tamed the brutality of the early legends.[40] Edith, for example, included the story of Daphne in her "Eight Brief Tales of Lovers" section of *Mythology*, although in the tale the huntress had to accept being turned into a laurel tree as the only means of avoiding an unwanted sexual encounter with the god Apollo.[41] As Edith realized, it was not a story of romantic love but of unwanted pursuit. She prefaced Daphne's story with a discussion of how the nymphs of mythology generally tried to avoid romantic encounters with the gods, fully aware of the terrible consequences that often ensued. Edith was therefore aware of the violence against women in Greek mythology, as she sought to put Daphne's story in a broader context. However, her inclusion of Daphne's story in "Eight Brief Tales of Lovers" suggests that she was capable of minimizing the violence of the myths.

Overall, however, Edith felt that by compiling a book of Greek mythology she was highlighting their literary achievements; as she told her readers, "The myths as we have them are the creation of great poets." Her introduction concentrated on the special claims of Greece on the world's attention at a time of widespread crisis. Since the ancient Greeks were the creators of Western civilization, Edith asserted, "nothing we learn about them is alien to ourselves."[42]

As Edith worked on *Mythology*, war broke out in Europe and eventually spread to Greece. On October 28, 1940, fascist Italian forces attempted to invade the country after the Greek government rejected an ultimatum issued by Mussolini. To the surprise of the world, the Greek army, with civilian help, held the potential invaders at the Albanian border, preventing the fascists from entering the nation.[43] Almost immediately, an organization called the American Friends of Greece established the Greek War Relief Association to provide humanitarian aid. The association collected funds, with committees in major Greek cities distributing the aid, but it had only a limited window of a few months to operate. In the spring of 1941, the Nazis helped the fascist Italians by launching their own invasion of Greece and defeating the British troops who had landed there.

In her greatest period of activism since her years as a suffragist, Edith participated in the relief efforts, sitting on the National Citizens' Committee of the Greek War Relief Association, along with Edith J. R. Isaacs, Brooks Atkinson, and Eva Palmer Sikelianos. Other members of the National Citizens' Committee included the first lady, Eleanor Roosevelt, a former first lady, Grace Coolidge, and a number of Hollywood producers including Louis B. Mayer, Samuel Goldwyn, and David O. Selznick.[44] Although Greek war relief had a brief life, its rhetoric influenced Edith's writing, particularly the introduction to *Mythology*. The cause prompted her to consider more directly the relevance of the ancient Greek political experience to the twentieth-century world.

Edith's dismay at the fascist takeover of Greece was accompanied by deep regret and puzzlement over German adherence to Nazism. In her reflections on the Nazi state she always found the decline of German intellectual achievement that had occurred in her lifetime, and the willingness of the German people to submit to Nazism, some of the most difficult aspects of the German experience to understand. After the United States entered the war, she would tell John Mason Brown that she was reading about the romantic relationship between Robert and Clara Schumann "to carry me back to the Germany of great achievement." Providing him with a list of the great German writers and composers of the nineteenth century, including Heine, Beethoven, Schubert, Schumann, Mendelssohn, Wagner, Liszt, and Brahms, she concluded, "Such a galaxy. Elsewhere in Europe nothing comparable. It is very sorrowful."[45]

In late 1940 and 1941, in the months after the successful Nazi blitzkrieg through northern Europe, Edith, while still writing *Mythology*, turned to the study of Goethe, whom she called "the greatest German of them all."[46] The result of her reading of Goethe's autobiography and published letters was an essay, "Goethe and Faust," published in *Theatre Arts Monthly* in June 1941. It was an attempt to explain the central problem of Goethe's play: Faust's abandonment of Gretchen at the end of the first act.[47] Edith argued that the solution to Faust's indifference to Gretchen's fate at the hands of the executioner could be found in Goethe's own life story, in which he frequently abandoned women he had professed to love. There was no explicit political message in "Goethe and Faust." It was a tribute to Goethe, whom Caird had termed "the modern Greek" for his revival of Hellenism, an opportunity for Edith to reflect on Germany's golden age as the Nazis expanded in Europe.[48]

By the summer of 1941, much of *Mythology* had been completed, suggesting that Edith had finished her project fairly quickly but not by

Everitt's original January deadline.[49] Portions of the book—retellings of the stories about the god Dionysus, to whom drama festivals were dedicated, and of Oedipus and the royal house of Thebes, the basis for the trilogy of Sophocles—were published in *Theatre Arts Monthly* in 1940. She then began to work on five additional chapters for a new edition of *The Greek Way*.[50]

As at least one critic had pointed out, the great poets of Greece had been omitted along with another accomplishment of the time, the beginnings of historical writing.[51] The latter omission seemed even more apparent in light of the modern nation's struggle against fascism. The rhetoric of Greek war relief had suggested that the writings of the ancient Greek historians could be used to demonstrate the relevance of the Greek experience to the conflict of the Second World War.

Three of the new chapters were to be studies of the first historians: Herodotus, Thucydides, and Xenophon. The others were a chapter on the sixth-century poet Pindar and "The Way of Greek Religion," largely drawn from her reading of the works of the Cambridge school. Greek religion was a subject she also considered as she wrote about its relation to mythology. Pindar's odes she had ranked on equal terms with Hesiod's *Theogony* as sources of Greek myths in her introduction to *Mythology*.[52] She had also drawn on Pindar's works as she wrote the stories of the "Quest for the Golden Fleece" and "Pegasus and Bellerophon." Yet she explained to her readers in her new chapter on Pindar that he was the most challenging Greek writer to translate.[53]

It is unclear whether the idea for the new chapters of *The Greek Way* originated with Edith or with Warder. Yet her own ideas for the new edition, to be called *The Great Age of Greek Literature*, suggested that the conflict in Europe made her anxious to demonstrate how the ancient Greek experience of war was relevant to the twentieth-century world. Edith and Doris felt that a new jacket would help to attract interest, with Edith telling Warder that she wanted for the cover "a photograph of some beautiful valley or hill in Greece." She added: "Not a temple or a statue, but something which has not changed from Greek days to this," an indication of how she hoped that the new volume would show the immediacy of the ancient Greeks to readers.[54]

The Great Age of Greek Literature was scheduled for publication in the autumn of 1942.[55] As Edith was writing the new chapters, the Japanese Empire attacked Pearl Harbor, drawing the United States into the war. Warder, writing to her only four days later, reassured her: "We don't believe the events of the last few days should effect the publication of this book next autumn. Indeed we believe there is all the more reason for having the spirit of the Greeks with us."[56] Edith expressed similar sentiments in her preface to *The Great Age of Greek Literature*, "I have felt while writing these new chapters a fresh realization of the refuge and strength the past can be to us in the troubled present."[57] In the additional chapters, Edith celebrated the ancient Greek achievement of democracy, again constructing an argument for the special claims Greece could make on the world's attention as it endured fascist occupation.

It was Edith's first statement of the relevance of the ancient Greek political experience to the twentieth century, laying the groundwork for her Cold War–era arguments for the continuing study of the classics. As such, the chapters should be analyzed alone since their particular context was lost when they were subsumed under the title *The Greek Way* in 1947.[58]

Edith used the chapter on Herodotus, the historian of the Persian Wars, to illustrate the extent of freedom the fifth-century Greeks had established. It began with a long discussion of the Greeks as the first to question slavery, a practice not examined even by the Old Testament prophets, about whom she had recently written, or by St. Paul. She credited Euripides as the first author to express antislavery sentiment, using lines from his tragedy *Hecuba* to support her argument. In her narrative, Edith connected the celebration of the Greeks as the first to question slavery only somewhat tenuously to her study of Herodotus. His histories had rejoiced in the Greek victory over the Persians as the triumph of freedom over tyranny without noting the existence of slavery within Greece itself.

Despite overlooking slavery, the work of Herodotus showed the extent of the liberty the Greeks enjoyed. He had been able to freely question ancient geography, particularly the idea of a large river called Ocean girding the circumference of the earth, even though there were religious implications to such doubts. He had even been free to criticize the most sacred of Greek customs: the consultation of the Delphic Oracle. He argued that this practice had been subject to corruption in the past, a claim he made after a thorough investigation. In its portrayal of the Greek struggle and victory against Persia, Herodotus's history showed the power of free men in facing a daunting and oppressive tyrant.[59] It was therefore a bitter irony that Greece, the culture that had given the idea of political freedom to the world, now suffered under fascist occupation.

In Thucydides, the historian of the Peloponnesian War, Edith found a more direct parallel with the Second World War, where, as she wrote in her chapter's opening sentence: "The greatest sea power in Europe and the greatest land power faced each other in war." Athens (or Britain) was trying to retain her imperial position, Sparta (or Germany) was trying to build one, but both sides "were uneasily conscious that an important and even decisive factor might be an Asiatic nation."[60] The value of Thucydides as a historian, however, was in his cyclical view of history; his book warned that a destructive war could happen again. She presented a humanist conception of Thucydides as a man bent on shaping character, arguing that "Thucydides wrote his book because he believed that men would profit from a knowledge of what brought about the ruinous struggle precisely as they profit from a statement of what causes a deadly disease."[61] As the Second World War progressed, Edith would find additional reasons to compare the conflict to the ancient one Thucydides had analyzed. Much of what Edith argued about the ancient historian was shaped by the war in Europe and her own and Doris's response to it.[62]

It was in her chapter on Xenophon, however, that Edith first voiced what would become the themes of her books when, during the Cold War, she returned to writing about ancient Greece. The chapter explored the meaning of citizenship in a democratic society. Xenophon, born toward the end of the fifth century, was the author of a history of Greece after the Peloponnesian War and a portrait of Socrates, the *Memorabilia*. But the main work for which he was known was the *Anabasis*, which told the story of the retreat of ten thousand Greek soldiers from

Asia Minor.[63] Xenophon had been a mercenary fighting for Cyrus, who was unsuccessfully attempting to replace his brother Artaxerxes as Persian emperor, when the army with which he served endured defeat at the battle of Cunaxa in 401 BCE.[64] The *Anabasis* was Xenophon's account of how he had helped lead the survivors back to Greece, with the soldiers voting on strategic decisions and electing their leadership along the way. Edith called this book "an unsurpassed picture of what the democratic idea can accomplish."[65] These soldiers' ability to engage in an orderly retreat after experiencing defeat was, she felt, due to the freedom in which the Greeks believed. Instead of merely following orders, each soldier was permitted to consider what the best course of action might be and vote accordingly. To Eva Palmer Sikelianos, she argued that this work of Xenophon's was "really the locus classicus for the individual acting on his own," a view she conveyed in her published chapter on the historian.[66] Edith viewed the *Anabasis* as a political work, meant to promote Greek ideals of self-government, with the ten thousand soldiers functioning essentially as a city-state during their dangerous journey, an understanding of the work that has been offered by others.[67]

Edith's arguments from Xenophon stressed not only the individual's right to freedoms but also the responsibilities of a citizen in helping to govern society. The Greek citizen did not want the opposite: the government imposing too much on him. Showing the firm commitment to classic liberalism that she shared with Doris, Edith wrote that an Athenian did not expect the government to "limit the amount of liquor he could buy, or compel him to save for his old age. Everything like that a citizen of Athens had to decide for himself and take full responsibility for."[68] Xenophon, despite being a nobleman and eventually living much of his life in Sparta, illustrated the ideal citizen of democratic Athens, a polymath whose knowledge covered a wide variety of subjects and who could take on a variety of tasks, including serving in the military at a time of need. A citizen such as Xenophon had to be able to consider a wide number of opinions and ideas before arriving at common-sense solutions to political or societal difficulties.[69] In Edith's idealized vision of fifth-century Athens, its citizenry had been particularly well suited to face their responsibilities, composing poetry and dramas and also tak-ing up arms and defending their state.[70] Even if Edith found Eva's dream of reviving the Delphic spirit impractical, her chapter on Xenophon in *The Great Age of Greek Literature* called attention to the ancient historian's suggestion of "making Delphi a meeting place for the nations, where they can talk out their differences."[71]

In her study of Xenophon, Edith once again confronted the reality that ancient Athens had not been truly democratic. Women had been entirely left out of political processes. Edith's writing from this time pe-riod contains her two most comprehensive statements on the status of women in ancient Athens. One of these was a story she recounted in *Mythology* about the founding of the city and how an angry Poseidon's deluge had caused Athenian men to deprive women of their right to vote.[72] In her chapter on Xenophon, Edith lingered over one of the his-torian's accounts of domestic life drawn from his treaty on estate man-agement, the *Oeconomicus*, because it contained, as she wrote, "a glimpse of that person so elusive in all periods, the woman of ancient Greece." Xenophon's narrative described a newly married man giving instruc-tions to his wife on how to manage their household. As Edith analyzed the story, the new wife was a "blank page," a person of "no consequence" herself, to whom her husband could give specific directions.[73] Though her husband liked outdoor exercise, she was not to leave the house. The only opinion the wife in the story was permitted to express was that she might enjoy the duty of caring for the ill.[74] Xenophon's story of the newly married couple revealed an ancient Greece where women's lives were strictly circumscribed, a story at which Edith, in her retelling, gently poked fun, describing the couple as "the dutiful young wife and the happily important husband."[75] The only feminist statement Edith al-lowed herself was to point out that Xenophon also recorded Socrates as stating that "a woman's talent is not at all inferior to a man's."[76] Despite her subtle humor, it was her most complete statement on the daily lives of women in ancient Greece.

Edith had two books published in 1942: *Mythology* in the spring and *The Great Age of Greek Literature* that fall. *Mythology* had a striking cover, with Steele Savage's art deco rendering of Bellerophon riding Pegasus against a black background. The volume earned especially good reviews due to the quality of the narrative storytelling. The writing of *Mythology*, unlike her other books, had been a test of Edith's skill in this area. The drafts of some of the tales survive, indicating how she added details to the stories to bring them to life.[77] John Cournos, writing in the *New York Times* praised her "orderly and lucid mind" and her "warm sympathy for her material."[78] The *New Yorker* magazine responded positively to the sense of immediacy in Edith's narratives and remarked on the high level of knowledge she brought to the work in her discussions of the ancient authors as sources for the tales. Its only criticism was that the section on Norse mythology was brief in comparison to the treatment of Greek and Roman myths.[79]

Brevity, however, was not the only criticism offered of the section of Norse myths. Padraic Colum, the folklorist and poet of the nationalist Irish Renaissance, who taught comparative literature at Columbia University, was more critical of it in his review published in an August issue of the *Saturday Review of Literature*.[80] Colum had had no formal training in the classics but was nevertheless drawn to the ancient world. He had published several books of Greek myths for a juvenile audience and a book of Norse mythology, *The Children of Odin*, which had appeared in 1920.[81] Colum had considerable success as a children's writer, and Edith was certainly aware of his work, which she referred to in her own notes for *Mythology*.[82]

Colum was critical of Edith's introduction to the section of Norse mythology, calling it "wrong-headed in a way surprising to find in the work of a scholar such as Miss Hamilton."[83] He was dismayed that Edith had described the English as a primarily Teutonic people, a claim he disputed, along with Edith's use of Norse and Teutonic as virtual synonyms. In Edith's conception of "Teutonic," Colum saw, correctly, the influence of Charles Kingsley, who had briefly referred to both the eddas and the sagas as well as to *Beowulf* in his introduction to *The Heroes*, without distinguishing among the cultures that produced them.[84] Colum, probably also reacting to the rise of the Nazis and their racial theories, opposed Kingsley's conception of "muscular Christianity": firm belief in both Protestantism and the physical and mental superiority of the Teutonic peoples.[85] Moreover, he strongly disagreed with Edith's assertion that early Christians had seen Christianity in conflict with Norse mythology to such an extent that clergy had expended much effort in stamping out the Norse tales. Colum used Ireland as an example of where Christian theology and Norse mythology had coexisted, with the clergy actually preserving Norse literature. Edith, however, had been mainly interested in separating Christianity and Norse mythology in Germany itself, where the Nazis were using the Norse literature to create a mythology of their own.

Colum understood the fundamental purpose of Edith's book: to provide a reference for readers seeking to understand mythological allusions in other works of literature. He praised the volume as a thorough survey of Greek and Roman mythology, singling out especially Edith's rendition of the story of the maiden Marpessa who, urged by Zeus to choose between her two suitors, Apollo and a mortal named Idas, one of the Argonauts, chose the latter. It was a myth that Edith had labeled "unimportant" in her own notes for the manuscript, and it appeared in "Brief Myths Arranged Alphabetically" at the end of the book.[86] Similarly, Colum welcomed Edith's clarification of another myth that involved violence against women, the story of Procne and Philomela, daughters of King Erechtheus of Athens, who were both transformed into birds to escape the vengeance of Procne's husband, Tereus. In his anger, Tereus had cut out Philomela's tongue, but she had been nevertheless described by Roman and later English poets as the nightingale. In the Greek story, the gods had turned Philomela into a swallow, a bird that cannot sing, while Procne had become the nightingale.[87]

Mythology proved to be Edith's most enduring book despite the contemporary references in some of the stories. Edith's opposition to fascism was particularly noticeable in her telling of the tale of Prometheus, chained to a mountainside in the Caucasus for giving humans the gift of fire and for refusing to reveal the name of the mother who would bear a son who would challenge Zeus. For these, Prometheus was viewed as the friend of humanity and a symbol of free thought as opposed to tyranny.[88] This had been evident to her when she had translated the *Prometheus Bound* of Aeschylus but was more pronounced in

Mythology, since the Nazis made use of Prometheus as an "Aryan," helping to bring forth Western civilization.[89] Edith therefore constructed a Prometheus who stood for spiritual freedom, one who "has stood through all the centuries, from Greek days to our own, as that of the great rebel against injustice and the authority of power."[90] She would echo similar sentiments in her speech in Athens in 1957 as she received her honorary citizenship to the city before a performance of her translation of *Prometheus Bound.*[91]

As Edith gave her support to Greek war relief and wrote about the role of the citizen in democratic societies, Doris advocated nonintervention in the European war, joining the New York chapter of the America First Committee.[92] During the two years of its existence, from 1940 until 1941, America First was the largest group opposing U.S. entry into the war. It had been formed in September 1940 by some Yale students, including one studying law, Robert Douglas Stuart Jr., who tried to recruit prominent citizens of various political views to support American nonintervention.[93] Until its dissolution after Pearl Harbor, the America First Committee argued that the European conflict posed no security threat to the United States and that the war represented yet another European power struggle, not a conflict solely against fascism.[94]

Doris's interest in politics had started to develop during her brief participation in the technocracy movement and had been further influenced by her career as a stockbroker, which helped to mold her opposition to government regulation of the financial services industry, particularly through the Securities and Exchange Commission.[95] She had become a classic liberal in her political philosophy, albeit on the conservative side, believing in individual rights and a limited role for government. She also had a deep opposition to war, and, while America First was not a pacifist organization, some members of the New York chapter were, and the chair of the New York chapter, John T. Flynn, believed that the organization should reach out to pacifist groups.[96]

The peak of Doris's activity occurred when the organization was already in decline due to its failures to prevent the enactments of conscription and lend-lease.[97] Her main work for the committee became the compilation of an anthology of readings advocating nonintervention, to be published in September 1941 as *We Testify*.[98] Her coeditor was Nancy Schoonmaker, a well-known speaker on international affairs and a former (unsuccessful) Democratic congressional candidate for a New York district.

Together, Doris and Schoonmaker compiled an impressive list of eighteen contributors, which included a former president, Herbert Hoover, and two sitting U.S. senators, both of whom supported America First, Democrat Burton K. Wheeler of Montana, who led campaigns in the Senate against the reinstatement of conscription and lend-lease, and Republican Robert A. Taft of Ohio. In their efforts to solicit opinions from the political left, the women collected contributions from journalists Carleton Beals and Frances Gunther as well as socialist leader Norman Thomas. The women also secured the participation of the most famous voice for nonintervention, aviator Charles Lindbergh, as well as his wife Anne Morrow Lindbergh and helicopter designer Igor Sikorsky, with whom Lindbergh worked closely in the years before the Second World War.

Published in September 1941 by the New York firm of Smith and Durrell, *We Testify* made no impact.[99] The book received no critical attention. That same month, Charles Lindbergh gave a speech in Des Moines, Iowa, in which he blamed America's Jewish population, the British, and President Roosevelt for driving the United States toward war.[100] His words drew immediate criticism. Although the national committee of America First did not censure him, John T. Flynn, though not entirely disagreeing with Lindbergh, denounced the speech, feeling that charges of anti-Semitism damaged the noninterventionist cause. Norman Thomas and Vassar President Henry Noble MacCracken, who had also contributed to Doris's anthology, refused to appear at America First events.[101] Regardless, time was running out; with the Japanese attack on Pearl Harbor, Flynn and other America First leaders decided to dissolve the committee, and Flynn disbanded the New York chapter.[102]

Both Edith and Doris saw themselves as working for the pacifist cause as the Second World War got underway in Europe and the direct involvement of the United States appeared imminent. Doris's efforts on *We Testify* were not wasted since it introduced her to the political philosophy of Senator Robert A. Taft, whom she would support in his unsuccessful bids for the Republican nomination for president, the second of which occurred in 1940.[103] Moreover, the book had a second life, circulating among her Taft Republican friends in Washington in the 1950s. Gen. Albert Coady Wedemeyer, an American commander in the Southeast Asia theater during the war, and a friend of both Edith and Doris in the years after the conflict, cited the volume as one that had been formative to his own critique of the war.[104]

In early 1943, Edith began to write a series of lectures on Christianity that she gave at the home of Alida Milliken. Doris's friendship with Alida had continued, and the two women had found common cause in America First, to which Alida became a large donor.[105] Edith was hesitant to agree to Alida's plan for the series of lectures. Initially, she felt she had little to say on the subject despite her years of instruction on the Bible when she was headmistress of the Bryn Mawr School and the experience of writing *The Prophets of Israel*. Finally, however, Edith agreed to write and give the lectures, afraid, she told John Mason Brown, that "I was shirking & being a coward."[106] The lectures proved to be successful, drawing an audience of about eighty people to Alida's brownstone each time.[107]

From these lectures, Edith developed the idea of writing a book about the New Testament, one that she would develop into her volume *Witness to the Truth: Christ and His Interpreters*. Warder, however, was cool to Edith's proposal. Instead, he envisioned what Edith described as a "comprehensive book which will include all the great religious leaders, Buddha, Confucius, Mahomet, et. al." causing Edith to complain to John: "It is so like him. Imagine me writing about Confucius."[108] The comment was a sign of the growing rift between Warder and Edith. Doris, who was naturally sympathetic to Edith's desire to write about the New Testament alone, argued with Warder on the subject. In fact, *Witness to the Truth* would mark the beginning of Doris's deeper involvement in Edith's writing career, sparked in great part because of Warder's continuing refusal to publish it. After Warder's death, Storer B. Lunt, his successor as president of W. W. Norton, would, however, bring it into print.[109]

Throughout the years in which Edith wrote *Mythology* and *The Great Age of Greek Literature*, she and Doris saw their family obligations decreasing. Ernest had joined the Navy and would see service in the Second World War.[110] In 1938, the year that Edith began work on *Mythology*, Dorian graduated from Amherst College and Betsey from the Brearley School.[111] While Madeline apparently went to reside in Florida, where her father lived, Mary returned to New York and for a time pursued an unsuccessful career as an actress, an effort apparently encouraged by Edith. Eventually she settled into work in the sales department of a publishing house.[112]

Early in 1943, after almost ten years as the co-head of the New York branch of Loomis-Sayles, Doris was offered the opportunity to establish and lead the firm's new office in Washington, D.C. The firm had decided that the new office was necessary since the war had caused the population of the capital to grow rapidly. The promotion presented a test of the permanency of Edith and Doris's relationship. In the early thirties, Doris had frequently socialized among her New York friends without Edith. She had even, with Edith's apparent approval, had the occasional romantic relationship with a man. Edith had considered it possible, perhaps even desirable, that Doris would marry.

By the spring of 1943, however, Edith and Doris had built a life together. Doris, who would turn forty-eight in September of that year, had evidently decided to forgo conventional marriage. Instead, she and Edith had raised a family together through the decade of the thirties. The quality of Edith and Doris's relationship is evident in Edith's decision to move with Doris to Washington, D.C. It was a sacrifice for her, since she had developed her successful writing career among her circle of friends in New York City. To Isabel Wilder, she described the upcoming move as "sad" news, while making it clear that she was proud of Doris's progress in her career.[113] She even allowed that the decision to move to the capital was a harder one for Doris than her. Doris's New York friends were the closest she had—many, including the Gilders, dating from her years as an aspiring pianist. Edith, by contrast, counted her close New York friends as only three: John Mason Brown and Catherine as well as Elling. And when John insensitively suggested that Doris was moving

Edith to Washington merely to make more money, Edith was quick to come to Doris's defense. Edith was proud that Doris's hard work had been recognized and, raised among a generation who measured women's progress in part through the achievements of individual "firsts," it was significant that Doris was the only woman executive in all of Loomis-Sayles, certainly the first woman to head a new office, one of the company's most important new ventures. Edith correctly assessed that Doris's new position was a mark of the high esteem in which Loomis-Sayles regarded her.[114]

Edith's response to the conflict between Doris and John says much about the quality of Edith and Doris's relationship in the spring of 1943: Edith's concern for Doris's hurt feelings, her ability to see beyond Doris's steadfast reserve, Doris's guilt over Edith's sacrifice, their mutual desire to maintain their life together—even if it meant frequent commuting for Doris—and, most of all, a sense that the life they shared together must continue. By the end of May, John had written Doris a letter that resulted in a full reconciliation.[115]

The argument, however, had touched a nerve with Doris; she was sensitive about the sacrifice she was asking of Edith, and the argument seemed to challenge her ability to take care of her partner. She alluded to it in her memoir, without mentioning John by name.[116] Edith, however, was delighted by John's apology and comforted him with the thought that she could not "help feeling we'll come back to New York."[117] But it was only Doris who would return to New York City to live after Edith's death. Edith would spend the last twenty years of her life in Washington.

Chapter 15

WITNESS TO THE TRUTH

Edith and Doris moved to Washington, D.C., in June 1943. They first settled into an apartment at 2101 Connecticut Avenue, an area of high-rises near Rock Creek Park from which Doris could walk across the long span of the Taft Bridge to her new office in the Shoreham Building. They felt fortunate to have found housing since it was difficult to obtain in the capital during the war. Washington was undergoing rapid growth during the Second World War. Its population had begun to climb with the staffing of the government agencies created by the New Deal but had grown even more with the influx of war workers. By 1942, it was the fastest-growing city in the United States.[1]

During her first years in Washington, Edith frequently expressed her sense of isolation from New York and the social circle among whom she had considered writing a book about the New Testament.[2] Her sense of the brutality of the war further encouraged her conviction that a greater understanding of Christianity was needed if belief in its teachings was to survive the conflict. As Edith tried to write what became *Witness to the Truth*, she corresponded frequently with John Mason Brown, as he too was struggling to produce books that would speak to the horrors of the war. During his August 1943 visit, Brown gave Edith a copy of his introduction for *To All Hands*, the book he had written on the Allied invasion of Sicily in which he had participated the previous month. Edith was impressed. Brown, due to his wartime service, began to consider, as Edith also would, the meaning and future of democracy as it confronted fascism. During the invasion of Sicily, he had served under Rear Admiral Alan G. Kirk as a bridge announcer, responsible for relaying information to the sailors aboard ships. It was a duty that prompted him to reflect on how democracy relied on an informed populace. A democratic government was not afraid to share information about the progress of the war with its citizens—at least to an extent that would not compromise security.[3] Brown therefore titled his introduction "This Is a Democratic War" and filled his work with allusions to ancient history.[4]

Brown's wartime experiences also linked the survival of Christianity with the fragile state of Western civilization. In February 1944 he was briefly in Italy, where, he told Edith, the destruction caused by the war was evident as he traveled north from Naples, especially as he visited the battlefield of Monte Cassino, which lay on the Allied path to Rome. The sixth-century Benedictine monastery that had sat high on a promontory overlooking the town of Monte Cassino had been destroyed by Allied aerial bombing on February 15, 1944. To many, its destruction was a metaphor for the fate of Western civilization in the face of a brutal war.[5] Such thoughts reinforced Edith's own thinking about the war, which, she increasingly feared, would destroy the Christian belief that underlay Western civilization.

During her first year in Washington, Edith tried to write, but personal distractions, including a move to a house in Georgetown just a few months after settling in the capital, made the task difficult. The rented house at 3023 P Street was a typical one for the neighborhood, with a plain brick front relieved by long shutters on the windows and two dormers breaking the roofline. It was nearly two hundred years old and, inside, the floorboards were uneven, a condition Edith felt was compensated for by the large number of fireplaces.[6] In fact, Edith preferred both the house and the neighborhood to the area of high-rise apartments in which they had previously lived. Georgetown evoked the same atmosphere as Gramercy Park, reminding her of a "village street, quiet and friendly" with "not a suggestion of the city only ten minutes' walk away." But the new surroundings did not necessarily facilitate her writing, as she told John in January 1944, "I am struggling to write, but so far have succeeded only in making an ill-connected mess."[7]

Compared to John, however, Edith felt that she and Doris were "sheltered and hidden" from the conflict.[8] Their challenges were domestic ones. The spring of 1944 was marked by Edith falling and breaking a hip and by the deteriorating health of Harry Reid. Edith was dismayed that her fall had no obvious cause; it had happened on a smooth sidewalk. Her fracture was such, however, that it would mend, and her doctor assured her that she would be able to walk again. In the meantime, she had to spend two months lying still in a cast.[9] She made little progress on the book she was writing, however, a situation that did not improve as Harry Reid weakened. He died in Baltimore on June 18, 1944, at the age of eighty-five.[10]

Edith Reid accepted her husband's death with a stoicism Edith respected. His death, however, meant the closure of the Cathedral Street house and its eventual sale.[11] The widowed Edith joined the household in Washington, feeling that she must live with Doris, for whom the commute from Baltimore to her Washington office would have been far too long, even if wartime gas rationing had not made it an outright impossibility. She found the adjustment to Washington life difficult. Eventually, however, Edith Reid grew to enjoy the lively society that Edith and Doris attracted to them in the years after settling into their final Washington home.

Harry Reid's death, followed by Edith Reid's decision to reside with Edith and Doris, led to their purchase in late 1944 of a three-story, ten-room brick row house at 2448 Massachusetts Avenue NW. This was to be both Edith Hamilton's and Edith Reid's home for the rest of their lives. It was in the neighborhood just west of Dupont Circle that had already become the location of numerous foreign embassies.[12] The house stood at the end of a terrace, and a flight of steps led up to its front door, over the garage. The front door led first into a vestibule, which, later, visitors would find painted black, with a classical frieze lining the top of the walls. The kitchen and dining room occupied the first floor. The second-floor living room, where Edith Hamilton would write and receive visitors, was lined with bookshelves and had French windows that looked out on the broad tree-lined Massachusetts Avenue. She felt, sitting near the windows, that she "might be in the deep country."[13]

FIGURE 12. Edith Hamilton's Washington, D.C., house on Massachusetts Avenue NW, her home from 1944 until her death in 1963. Photograph by Victoria Houseman.

Behind the house was a tiered garden overlooked by a small balcony and surrounded by a brick wall that backed up to Rock Creek Park. The house also had something of a novelty in 1940s Washington; it was "air cooled"—as Edith termed it—making the summer months before they could go to Seawall comfortable.[14]

Then, on February 9, 1945, the death of Norah at the age of seventy-one came as a severe loss to Edith and her surviving sisters.[15] Norah had spent the last years of her life living on Perry Street in Greenwich Village. But, apparently struggling with illness, her final days were spent at Hadlyme.[16] She was buried next to Gertrude at Cove Cemetery.

Despite these losses, Edith and Doris saw their family grow during their early years in Washington. Dorian and his wife Betty had settled in Beaver Falls, New York, and had a son, Harry Fielding Reid II, born in 1945, and a daughter, Alice, born in June 1947.[17] Betsey, who had graduated from Wellesley with a degree in architecture, married a naval architect, Homer Fay Pfeiffer, on May 7, 1946. Her son George, often called Jay, born in February 1948, was Edith and Doris's third grandchild.[18] That same year Homer was posted to Japan, and that September Betsey went to reside there with him, becoming an English teacher to Japanese doctors. Edith was pleased that Betsey liked Japan, a country of which she herself had many pleasant memories.[19] Finally, Mary, the youngest of the Reid daughters, was married to the engineer Boyd McKnight on June 25, 1949, in the garden of the house on Massachusetts Avenue. Mary, who for a time had worked in sales for a publishing firm, had been living in New York City. Edith Reid hosted the wedding, and Francis gave Mary away. The couple would spend their honeymoon at Seawall, as both Dorian and Betsey had with their spouses before them.[20] Edith and Doris, though sadly affected by losses and by the distance from their New York friends, were now becoming grandparents.

From their early years in Washington, their relationship found a new stability based in part on the stronger supporting role Doris began to play in Edith's writing career. In New York, Edith had enjoyed a close relationship with her publisher and the couple's wide social circle, advantages she had given up to continue her life with Doris. Although Edith missed such stimulating company, she did not believe in self-sacrifice.

Her statements to Isabel Wilder and John Mason Brown indicate how consciously she had made the choice to move to Washington with Doris. Eventually, the two women would make friends in the capital, and the house on Massachusetts Avenue would become known to some in the city as simply "2448."[21] But during her first years in Washington, Edith missed her New York friends. Although settled comfortably in the house on Massachusetts Avenue, she told John in October 1944 that "ungratefully I long for New York."[22] Edith and Doris, however, were drawn closer together as they faced the challenges of starting their Washington life.

Doris took on an active role in Edith's career due to the difficult processes of writing and publishing *Witness to the Truth*. Edith's decision to write *Mythology* for Little, Brown, her frustration with Warder's conception of suitable subjects on which she could write, combined with Elling's departure from W. W. Norton, all contributed to the deterioration of her relationship with Warder and the firm, which initially rejected *Witness to the Truth*. It was the first time Edith had faced outright rejection of a proposed book subject. Doris and Elling, however, encouraged Edith to persist, with Doris assuming a practical supporting role that she was to maintain for the rest of Edith's life.

The dropping of the atomic bombs that August only reinforced Edith's conviction that if Christian belief was to survive the war, its essence needed to be explained to a wide reading audience. Edith was a frequent reader of the *Saturday Review of Literature*, then under the editorship of Norman Cousins. Its August 18, 1945, issue published Cousins' editorial condemning the dropping of the atomic bombs on Japan.[23] Edith shared this view, perhaps thinking of Toyohiko Kagawa, the Japanese Christian and committed pacifist whose works she had read in the 1930s. Kagawa had opposed Japan's invasion of China and had spoken out against the American firebombing of Tokyo in March 1945, and he subsequently protested the dropping of the atomic bombs.[24] Edith rarely referred directly to political events in her letters, but to Storer she expressed her horror at the dropping of the atomic bombs, asserting, "It will be a black mark on our name always."[25] She worried that, for many, the horrors of the war would destroy what little faith in Christianity they might still possess. She believed that only an understanding of Christ and his message could overcome a world of despair. In *Witness to the Truth* she explicitly linked the power of Christ to the new realities of the atomic age, writing, "Christ looked into the impenetrable blackness of the mystery of Power which calls the stars into being and moves in the atom and through it he saw the light of God."[26]

Despite Warder's rejection, Edith began to write *Witness to the Truth*. In the autumn of 1945, she sent drafts of her chapters on Christ and St. Paul to John and Catherine Brown, soliciting their criticisms.[27] Although praising the chapters, John offered a rare critique of her literary style. After reading the draft of her opening chapter on Christ, John suggested that she shorten her paragraphs, advice to which Edith responded favorably.[28] She also decided to approach C. Raymond Everitt at Little, Brown, who, after receiving the chapters on Christ and St. Paul, responded with enthusiasm—and many suggestions.[29] Doris felt it was one more instance of John aiding them from afar, since he had brought Edith and Everitt together to create *Mythology*. Now Everitt's interest in the book encouraged Edith to continue.[30]

As she worked on the manuscript, she often read drafts to Elling and Doris, who in turn offered criticisms.[31] As a result of these exchanges, Edith paid tribute to Elling in her text by including a brief reference to his favorite artist, El Greco, whom she would come to admire on her 1958 trip to Spain. Although she had dedicated her first three books to Doris, *Witness to the Truth* was dedicated to Elling, with an inscription from Shakespeare's *Julius Caesar*, "A friend should bear his friend's infirmities."[32] It was with Elling and Doris in mind that Edith wanted to write a book that would assure readers that they could still believe in Christianity, even if they could not accept miracles or dogmas or the formalism in religion that she had long ago rejected.

She proceeded with the writing on the assumption that Little, Brown would publish the volume, a condition that changed when, on November 7, 1945, Warder Norton died unexpectedly at the age of fifty-four.[33] Edith deeply regretted his death: "I have lost a true and valued friend," she wrote Storer Lunt.[34] Within a month, Warder's widow, Polly Norton, had reorganized the firm into an employee-owned company with

Storer as president.[35] Edith promptly congratulated Storer on his new position, writing that she was certain he would find "that the additional responsibility would be a stimulus, not a weight." She encouraged him to trust his own judgment in guiding the company, writing, "Your way will not be Warder's way and should not be."[36]

Storer, a native of Maine, was a few years younger than Doris. He had joined W. W. Norton in 1929, after graduating from Yale and completing some postgraduate work at Cambridge.[37] Edith had known him since at least 1933, but she and Storer became especially close from 1945, when he assumed the presidency of W. W. Norton.[38] He immediately expressed interest in publishing the book on the New Testament, and his determination to obtain the manuscript of *Witness to the Truth* for the firm solidified their working relationship. For the rest of her writing career, Edith would enjoy a privileged place among the authors the company frequently published.[39]

By January 1946, Edith was deeply engrossed in the book and had conferred with C. Raymond Everitt, who had offered criticisms and suggestions that she had accepted.[40] She felt unable to withdraw from her obligation to Little, Brown, and until the following year she envisioned what became *Witness to the Truth* as two separate books. Little, Brown was to have the chapters on Christ and the Gospels, which were to be published as *Witness to the Truth*. Storer was to have the chapters on St. Paul and the other material to publish for W. W. Norton under the title *A Cloud of Witnesses*, a favorite biblical phrase of Edith's that would appear in both *Witness to the Truth* and her next book, *Spokesmen for God*.[41] But untimely death once again altered the fate of *Witness to the Truth*. In May 1947, Everitt died suddenly from a heart attack at the age of forty-five. In the aftermath of his death, Storer arranged for all of Edith's writing on the New Testament to be published by W. W. Norton under one title.[42]

The writing of *Witness*, however, proceeded more slowly than Edith had hoped. The initial division of the work into two separate books may have hindered its progress and, in the fall of 1946, Edith was naturally concerned when Doris became ill with viral pneumonia. The illness began in October, and on November 23 Doris departed for Arizona to recuperate in the warmer climate, where Edith eventually joined her. Doris's condition was severe enough that Edith inscribed both the date of Doris's diagnosis and her subsequent departure on her list of important dates.[43] She was still worried about Doris's health the following August at Seawall, feeling that the pneumonia might have had a lingering effect. Adding to their difficulties was the health of Edith Reid, who had broken her hip in early July, necessitating surgery that meant she had to avoid putting weight on her leg for several months. The operation took place not long before the annual journey to Seawall, but Edith and Doris still managed to take Edith Reid with them to Maine, where they hired a nurse to look after her.[44]

On August 12, 1947, Edith celebrated her eightieth birthday, a milestone she noted to Jessie and Agnes, themselves now eighty-two and seventy-eight, respectively. She confessed that she moved at a much slower pace than previously when walking on the rocky shoreline in Maine but added that "I should like to be able to walk fast and far, but I am very content without." Indeed, she felt that old age was of "no consequence."[45] It was not going to hinder progress on the manuscript.[46]

In writing *Witness to the Truth*, especially the chapters on the Gospels, Edith relied heavily on her own familiarity with the Bible, which dated back to her childhood. Throughout her life, Edith continued to read the Bible frequently and wrote comments in the margins. In *Witness to the Truth*, her early training in biblical criticism was evident when she argued that what was essential about the Gospels was not that they portrayed inconsistencies, but that Jesus "himself is always consistent."[47] Her familiarity with the Bible was clear when she pointed out that St. Paul never invoked Jesus's name in any of his moral admonitions and that he never quoted him directly, except for once in the epistles.[48]

Much of the book reflected Edith's reading during her years as a student at Bryn Mawr College, when she had broken with the Presbyterianism of her youth. Her argument in *Witness to the Truth*, that Jesus's method for achieving righteousness could be discerned by a close reading of the gospels, drew on Matthew Arnold's essay "Literature and Dogma." But *Witness to the Truth* owed its greatest intellectual debt to the idealist philosophy of Edward Caird, particularly to the second volume of his 1891–92 Gifford Lectures, *The Evolution of Religion*, given at the University of St. Andrews, Scotland. Both Caird and Arnold had emphasized that belief in the supernatural actually hindered adherence to Christianity rather than encouraged it. And Caird felt that adherence to dogmas or creeds only set false limits on Christian belief. Edith, writing in what she considered a time of crisis in faith, turned readily to Caird as her inspiration for *Witness to the Truth*, portraying the life of Christ as the battle of idealism against realism, as Caird had done over fifty years earlier.

Edith's book assured war-weary readers that to embark upon the discovery of Christ was not to venture into the world of acrimonious theological dispute, writing, "Extraordinarily, the bitter differences that divided Christians, the excommunications, the persecutions, the religious wars, were never due to different opinions about Christ himself. There people have always agreed. Christians fought each other to the death not on what he was, but on how he was to be explained."[49] She believed that a careful reading of the Gospels would demonstrate that Christ himself was always consistent in his teachings, though he had never written them down himself. The life and work of Jesus, much like that of Socrates, had to be pieced together from a variety of different and sometimes conflicting accounts.

Edith therefore chose to begin her study of the character of Christ in the Gospels with a chapter on Socrates. She had first suggested that Socrates had searched for God in her study of Greek religion in *The Great Age of Greek Literature*, where she had written of Socrates: "Nothing to him was important except finding the truth, the reality in all that is, which in another aspect is God. He spent his life in the search for it, but he never tried to put what he had seen into hard and fast statements."[50] The portrayal of Socrates as a Christ-like figure was centuries old—Erasmus, as Edith pointed out, had made the comparison.[51] She could have been familiar with comparisons between Jesus and Socrates from Montgomery Hamilton's extensive theological study. It was an idea that had found some favor in Germany, where, during the nineteenth century, parallels were drawn between Socrates and Jesus. Some nineteenth-century English writers had also made the comparison. Kagawa, in his *Meditations on the Cross*, published in 1935, had also compared Socrates to Jesus.[52] More importantly for Edith, Edward Caird had compared the moral impacts of the deaths of Socrates and Jesus.

Edith saw Socrates and Jesus as sharing the same method of teaching through the example of their own lives. Neither told individuals what to believe but instead urged others to seek the truth as they did. Both sought to help individuals do so, not by retiring from society but by being active in its daily life. Socrates flourished in fifth century BCE Athens, whose citizens were eager to engage in philosophical discussion with him, even as war began between Athens and Sparta. Edith was quick to point out that, in times of war, philosophical discussion, with its exchange of ideas, was even more vital than in times of peace.[53]

Initially, war had not stopped the circulation of ideas on which the Athenians thrived. The staggering length of the Peloponnesian War, which lasted twenty-seven years, and its conclusion in the defeat of Athens, however, produced a sea change in the city's values, the kind of societal moral shift to which Edith was always sensitive. The Athenians sentenced Socrates to death five years after the war's conclusion. To Edith, the reason for this sentence, corrupting the young through the introduction of new gods, only supported her argument that Socrates's method had helped lay the groundwork for Christianity. The Olympic gods, she had argued in her introduction to *Mythology*, had ultimately been unable to fulfill human longing for a divinity who protected humanity and who both stood for and demanded ethical behavior.[54] Socrates, by urging the young of Athens to search for the good, had discarded the official religion of Athens, as belief in "Homer's jovial, amoral Olympians [was] impossible for any thinking person to take seriously."[55]

In defeat, however, Athenians treated Socrates with suspicion. He had no fixed dogmas or creeds to substitute for the gods he had discarded. Instead, he offered only a method of questioning, of searching for the good. As Edith explained to Storer a few months before *Witness to the Truth* was published, "Socrates by temperament and his basic point of view was closer to Christ than anyone else. I believe he is a help to understanding Christ, a stepping-stone to an apprehension of that greatest of all figures."[56]

Throughout *Witness to the Truth*, Edith offered her readers various solutions to the challenges of maintaining Christian faith. In the book's third chapter, "How the Gospels Were Written," she explained how to approach reading the Gospels, to which various additions had been made over time, including recitations of miracles and messianic predictions. She identified the list of miracles at the end of the Gospel of Mark as one of these later additions, arguing that the "entire passage is on a level immeasurably below the rest of the Gospel" and that as early as the fourth century it was recognized as being a substitute for the original ending of Mark, which had been lost.[57] The persecutions that Mark and other Christians experienced in the first century of the Roman Empire accounted for the Gospel's messianic statements. But Jesus, Edith argued, was independent of concern for time and place. "If Christ is here for the modern world, it is because he is independent of changes of time and stages of knowledge. Today it is impossible to find a refuge from the evils of the world in an expectation that presently God will intervene to destroy the wicked and exalt the good."[58] Belief in Jesus's message, she argued, should not be dependent on the supernatural.

The book also explored the question of when and how the Gospels came to be understood as the word of God and therefore unalterable. Edith posed a contrast between Papias, the second-century bishop of Hierapolis in Phrygia, Asia Minor, who had not seen the number of gospels as definitively determined, and Bishop Irenaeus of Lyon, France. Irenaeus had been born during Papias's lifetime and had outlived him by thirty-seven years, dying in 200 CE, but he had argued for a "sacred limit" of only four.[59] In doing so, Edith made clear her sympathies for Papias and the early Christian church. Papias, frequently described by the later church historian Eusebius, had lived at the crucial period when the New Testament canon was coming into existence. He was one of the first church officials to collect records from the disciples of Jesus of Nazareth. His five-volume work *Interpretations of the Lord's Sayings* was largely lost, though some extracts of the work did survive.[60] Edith may have had a long acquaintance with Papias, since his writings were read by Jessie and Agnes.[61] His evocation of the early church, devoid of a fixed dogma, appealed to Edith, as was evident in her description of early Christian communities drawn from the Book of Acts.[62]

In her lengthy chapter on Christ, Edith had pieced together a narrative of his life through the Gospels, thus demonstrating her argument that, through the various Gospels, some vision of the character of Christ—who he had been—could be established. She acknowledged some limits to knowledge about Jesus's life, especially concerning his childhood, ultimately determining that only about three years of his life were recorded in any detail.[63] Nevertheless, she used the stories from the four Gospels to construct his biography, one that demonstrated his essential humanity and his rejection of rituals, creeds, and dogmas in favor of the adoption of a way of life.[64]

The chapter on St. Paul was also a lengthy one, divided into two parts, a reflection that it had once formed the core of another book. Clearly, Edith regarded Paul as a figure who had much relevance to the postwar world, an opinion shared by theologians who saw Paul's efforts to cope with the problem of evil as relevant to a world trying to recover from the horrors of the Second World War.[65] To Edith, Paul's life was an example of the power of Christ's love to confront evil, illustrating the success of Christ's method. In his early life, Saul, as Paul had been known, had been a persecutor of Christians. Edith described the striking scene at the start of the Book of Acts where Stephen became the first Christian martyr, suffering a cruel death at Saul's hands before Saul's departure for Damascus and the journey that transformed him into the Christian Paul. Though modern scholars believe that Paul was not present at Stephen's death, to Edith the incident illustrated a harsh turning point in the history of the Western world. While the ancient world had largely tolerated a variety of religious opinions, Stephen's death for his religious beliefs showed "a new spirit stirring in the world, one of the worst that has ever moved mankind." Saul, she wrote, "was destined to have a long line of successors."[66] In fact, it was possible to see Paul before his conversion as just as capable of evil as the Nazis. "It does not take much imagination to see back of him, waiting to follow after him, a great host of men, all those who in the name of the true religious faith or the true political faith, have killed and imprisoned and tortured hundreds and hundreds of thousands, very many of whom died rather than give up what they believed. Foremost in the vanguard of that dreadful army St. Paul once stood."[67] Yet Paul had been transformed by his vision of Jesus on the road to Damascus.

To Edith, other aspects of Paul's life and thought made him a relevant figure to the postwar world. Paul was not interested in miracles and never referred to any that Christ was believed to have performed, only to the resurrection. As the earliest Christian writer, writing before the creation of the Gospels, he had little need to argue for a Christ who performed them.[68] In her interpretation of Paul, Edith, often sensitive to the status of women, paid little heed to Paul's attitudes toward them, including his dismissal of marriage and his opposition to women teaching. Edith wrote that there had been some women Paul had respected but that "some experience in Paul's early life had coloured all his thought of women."[69]

One of the book's final chapters, "The Failure of the Church," introduced themes in Edith's writing that she would return to in her final book, *The Echo of Greece*, and in other later writings: the early church's need to create a formal structure built on a defined theology to which individuals must adhere. In *Witness to the Truth* she made clear her own preference for the simple Christianity portrayed in the opening of the Book of Acts, devoid of formalism and endeavoring to follow the message of Christ's life.[70] To Edith, this period of Christianity had been all too brief. The spiritual demands on individual adherents were lowered, and Christianity was reduced to observance of outward ritual and formalized into dogmas and creeds of which the mere recitation constituted the practice of Christianity. The church, argued Edith, had chosen quantity of members over quality and through the number of adherents had made the church safe from persecution. Like Caird, however, Edith argued that such formalism only hindered spiritual life and stifled Christianity. "The life of the spirit," Edith wrote, "could not be ensured by outside means."[71]

In the summer of 1947, Edith was devoting much attention to the completion of the book. By its end she had finished all but the last chapter. Writing from Seawall, she thanked Storer for his support of the project and asked him to find a biblical scholar to read the manuscript to guard against any inaccuracies in her research on Papias or others. She was, however, very specific in asking him not to allow a theologian to read the manuscript, warning Storer that the book was likely too unconventional to please theologians. On the other hand, she felt it was too traditional to appeal to intellectuals or younger readers, though she hoped her book would be a guide for them.[72] There remained only the title to determine. After reading the manuscript, Storer was not convinced that the title Edith had chosen, *Witness to the Truth*, was appropriate. Elling had suggested *The Christian Way* or *The Way of Christ* as titles that would link the book to Edith's previous successes. But Edith, as was to become her habit with her last three books, remained firm.[73]

In March 1948, Doris held a party in their Washington home in honor of the publication of *Witness to the Truth*.[74] That same month, John Mason Brown celebrated its arrival by devoting his *Saturday Review of Literature* column "Seeing Things" to a tribute to Edith. Brown, who had joined the magazine as an associate editor as his wartime service drew to a close, had become a frequent traveler on the literary circuit.[75] In his column, John wrote that he met a small but select number of readers of Edith's books nearly everywhere he went. The column contained some of the phrases that would often be repeated about Edith as her fame grew in her later years, such as, "In any period Edith Hamilton would be exceptional; in ours she is unique." He also praised Edith's literary style, aptly describing it as "Doric in its simplicity, its strength, its beauty." He termed her a "popularizer," a mantle she would eventually accept.[76]

Edith immediately wrote John to thank him. John's *Saturday Review* column had ostensibly been a review of *Witness to the Truth*, but in it he had disclaimed any knowledge of theology and put himself forward only as a Christian who had found his faith strengthened by reading the book. Edith, however, had fully expected that her book would be rejected by more orthodox Christians, as it soon was.

In early May, the book received a negative review, written by George R. Stephenson, in the *New York Times*.[77] He objected to Edith's dismissal of theology and her overemphasis on the simplicity of the early church's message. He also claimed that Edith had overestimated the influence of Greek thought on Paul. Although Stephenson praised Edith's account of the writing of the Gospels, he felt that she had slipped into the error of making herself an interpreter even as she sought only to describe the contributions of others.[78] While the review did not surprise Edith, it caused Doris to spring into action. Later that month she went to New York City, in part to meet with Storer concerning publicity for the book. For five hours she discussed possible advertising for the volume, growing slowly more frustrated with W. W. Norton's small publicity budget.[79]

Doris seized on a positive review by journalist Felix Morley, who had served as president of Haverford College during the war, regretting only that his newspaper *Human Events*, where it had appeared, did not have a larger circulation. She envisioned a large advertisement for *Witness to the Truth* appearing in the *New York Times* with quotes from positive reviews to make up for the negative one the newspaper had published. Doris had formed a working relationship with Storer, who understood that Doris was often the more effective of the two women when it came to discussions of the business side of publishing. And he appreciated Doris's suggestions of who might be likely to help publicize Edith's books, making them probable recipients of a free copy.[80] Their only real disagreement was over *Witness to the Truth*, which Doris felt Storer did not do enough to publicize. Doris ultimately convinced Storer to invest in the advertisement she envisioned, and it appeared in the *New York Times Book Review* on August 1, 1948, complete with quotations from Thomas Sugrue (who had reviewed it in the *New York Herald Tribune*), Rufus Jones, John Mason Brown, and Felix Morley.[81]

Edith, however, remained dissatisfied with the book's reception, both as measured in sales figures, on which she always kept a careful eye, but, more importantly, in her effectiveness in conveying the book's essential message.[82] In March 1948, two months before most reviews of *Witness to the Truth* were published, Edith confided to a visiting *Washington Post* reporter that she was already planning another book.[83] By July 1948, she had suggested the idea of a companion volume to

Storer. The result would be *Spokesmen for God: The Great Teachers of the Old Testament*, a revised version of *The Prophets of Israel*, which would be published in 1949.

Some of Edith's changes to *The Prophets of Israel* were merely organizational. Other changes were more substantive. While still focusing largely on the prophets, the new volume discussed the Old Testament in its entirety. Two entirely new chapters were added to the beginning of *Spokesmen for God*, "Many Men of Many Minds" and "The Pentateuch," both of which she felt dealt with parts of the Old Testament that were particularly difficult to read.[84] And while *The Prophets of Israel* had been Edith's response to both the economic difficulties of the Great Depression and to the rise of the Nazi regime, in the wake of the genocide that had been inflicted on Europe's Jews, elucidation of the Jewish contribution to Western civilization became more urgent. Edith therefore argued in the book's second chapter, "The Pentateuch," that the Old Testament was "a history of the Hebrew nation from the creation of the world to about 450 B.C." It was an "account of a people's progress in the knowledge of God." As she explained to Storer once the manuscript was finished, "My aim has been to show how the men of the Old Testament slowly rose from the idea of the very human and irresponsible deity who is found in Genesis to the idea of God in the Psalms and the Prophets, an idea so lofty that it has never been surpassed even in the New Testament."[85]

In her two concluding chapters, Edith posited the unchanging nature of human experience, which included both suffering and striving to achieve a better world. The prophets, through their growing understanding of a loving God, had set out a vision of an ethical society, "where no individual was sacrificed for an end," which she believed humanity had to continue to try to achieve despite the catastrophe of the Second World War.[86] As usual, Edith saw no value in doctrines, dogmas, or ceremonies but only in what she felt was the clear message of the prophets that humans should behave with justice and mercy toward each other.[87] The book's conclusion, "The Sunlit Heights," summed up in less than eight pages Edith's conviction that the entirety of human experience was its effort to achieve knowledge of the good, an essentially Platonic struggle that unified all humanity across time. The horrors of the Second World War had not ended humanity's desire for greater understanding of the good. If anything, she concluded, these experiences strengthened it.[88]

Edith spent her first six years in Washington, D.C., writing two books on the Bible. These books were always to be both a source of pride and of frustration. Neither achieved the commercial success of her books on Greece and Rome, but the works did help her establish new friends in Washington. For Edith this was probably the greatest result of *Witness to the Truth*. The book was praised by her friends, such as the drama critic Brooks Atkinson, as well as by those who would soon join her Washington social circle, including the Republican senator from Vermont Ralph E. Flanders, who regarded it as a "neglected book."[89] For these men and others, the volume enhanced her status as an authority on the ancient world and the roots of Western civilization.

Chapter 16

ATTIC NIGHTS

✦ The years spent writing *Witness to the Truth* had led to the construction of a circle of Washington friends who would steer
Edith's interests to questions concerning the relevance of the ancient
Greek political experience to postwar America. In New York, Edith and
Doris had socialized largely among the theatrical community. In Washington, however, the couple would build friendships with civil servants,
journalists, diplomats, and, eventually, members of the U.S. Senate.

The capital's social life, muted during the war itself, blossomed once
the conflict was over. No longer hindered by blackouts, Sunday socializing moved from afternoon garden teas to evening dinners. Edith and
Doris quickly found their way into Washington's lively postwar social
scene. By October 1945, two years after their move to Washington, the
pair were attending a birthday party for His Imperial Majesty Moham-
med Reza Shah Pahlavi, to be held at the home of the Iranian ambassador.[1] Cocktail parties became more common, and salons, each with its
own political alignment, flourished. In Edith and Doris's old neighborhood of Georgetown, social life became centered on the supper parties
hosted by journalist Joseph Alsop. The "Georgetown Set," as this group
became known, was interventionist, in contrast to those who gathered
at Edith and Doris's house, who were more skeptical of the United States'
ability to intervene beneficially in the postwar world.[2]

The neighborhood into which Edith and Doris had settled contained the homes of two women well-known in Washington society,
both of whom they would befriend. Only a few blocks away, at 2009

Massachusetts Avenue, was the home of the prominent political hostess Alice Roosevelt Longworth.[3] Closer to them, at 2346 Massachusetts Avenue, was the home of Elizabeth Cabot Lodge, to whom they were introduced during their first years in Washington. She was the widow of the poet George Cabot Lodge, who, during his brief life, had published several volumes, some of which, including the verse drama *Herakles*, had been inspired by classical themes. Widowed only nine years after her marriage, Elizabeth Cabot Lodge watched her son Henry Cabot Lodge Jr. become a Republican senator from Massachusetts. A devout Christian, she was an intelligent and well-read woman who befriended Edith and Doris, eventually giving Edith the elegant gold-lamé cloak she would wear on the night she became an honorary citizen of Athens.[4]

Edith and Doris's circle of Washington friends grew more rapidly from the spring of 1946, when they met Huntington Cairns, the secretary-treasurer and general counsel for the National Gallery of Art. Their introduction came when Huntington approached Edith concerning his anthology *The Limits of Art*, on which he had begun work two years earlier.[5] The volume, which he researched in the Library of Congress, was an attempt to identify the best of what Western literature had produced, and it served as his own affirmation of the value of Western culture.[6] Although originally confined to fifty examples, it had gradually grown to include many more, among them Edith's brief description of Thucydides's rendition of the failed invasion of Sicily during the Peloponnesian War and the deaths of the Athenians in the quarries of Syracuse from *The Great Age of Greek Literature*.[7]

Edith's correspondence with Huntington, who also served as a press advisor and board member of the Bollingen Foundation, began in 1946 with the formal salutation "Dear Mr. Cairns."[8] This was later replaced by "My dear boy" and, when writing to both Huntington and his wife, Florence, "Dear People"—the salutation she used with her own family, especially in her letters to Jessie and Agnes. Eventually, Huntington would become her only coauthor, when they edited *The Collected Dialogues of Plato* together, a project they began in 1957.[9] As Edith acknowledged,

Huntington, through his own expansive Washington social circle, helped to establish her as an authority on how the modern world could learn from the past.

During their nearly twenty years of friendship, Huntington would introduce Edith to a number of writers whose work was published by Bollingen, including the Zen Buddhist D. T. Suzuki, whom she met in 1956, and a year later Mircea Eliade, the Romanian-born professor of philosophy at the University of Chicago and an expert on Hindu mythology.[10] Huntington sent her copies of Bollingen Press books. Accordingly, Edith read some of Carl Jung's works as well as volumes such as the *Hieroglyphics of Horapollo* by the Johns Hopkins philosophy professor George Boas. More influential, however, were the individuals she was introduced to.[11]

In Washington, Huntington and his wife, Florence Faison Butler, whom he had married in 1930, enjoyed a wide social circle.[12] Edith grew fond of Florence, who had a deep interest in literature and was capable of writing verses that Edith declared were "Gilbertian."[13] The Cairnses lived in apartment 23 at 2219 California Street NW, a five-story Italianate building only blocks from Edith and Doris. Among those whom the Cairns entertained were members of the capital's diplomatic community, including Chinese Ambassador Hu Shih. Huntington also counted Charles Malik, the minister of the Legation of Lebanon, a philosophy professor, and "the most interesting man in Washington," a friend.[14]

By 1939 Huntington had formed a conviction that ancient Greek thought was the core of Western social and political ideas and that there had not been substantial progress since the Greeks.[15] This belief may have stemmed from his reading of Ralph Waldo Emerson's 1850 essay on Plato that argued, "Out of Plato come all things that are still written and debated among men of thought." The opening line of the essay's second paragraph—"Plato is philosophy and philosophy Plato"—would stay with Huntington for decades.[16] By 1939 he had visited Athens and determined to devote as much of his time as possible to the study of Plato. One result of his resolution had been the study of the works of Edith's former Bryn Mawr professor, the Plato scholar Paul Shorey, who had died in 1934.[17] On learning that Edith had been his student, Huntington occasionally sought her help in understanding some of Shorey's work.[18]

In addition to his studies of Shorey's works, Huntington had other intellectual interests he shared with Edith, including British Idealist philosophy. He was also familiar with writers who had influenced her, including Matthew Arnold, on whom he published an essay.[19] H. L. Mencken, however, had been an important mentor for Huntington, who had grown up in Baltimore, and he shared Mencken's concern for the functioning of democracy, telling a friend that "the clarification of the democratic process is one of the necessities of the age."[20] Like Mencken, Huntington believed that democracy relied on competent leadership, sharing Mencken's commitment to the free circulation of ideas, conditions that were necessary for culture to flourish.[21]

Soon, Huntington and Florence were spending practically every Sunday evening, Washington's traditional time for socializing, with Edith and Doris.[22] Huntington always found intellectual discussions stimulating and often referred to these conversations as "sessions."[23] He used this term with Edith as well, but in August 1946, only months after they met, Edith, Doris, Huntington, and Florence shared an evening discussing Greek thought. To Huntington, who felt that there was too little prized philosophic conversation in Washington society, the evening with Edith was a revelation, prompting him to write her that it was "an Attic night, and I shall long remember it." He added: "It is always such fun and so profitable to talk to you. Your learning and your wisdom set a standard that no one else I know equals. I hope that this coming winter we will have many evenings together."[24] Edith had already written: "A party to which you and Mrs. Cairns come is never dull" and later, to John Mason Brown, she described Huntington as a man "who seems to me the most brilliant of any I have met in these last years."[25] At the root of Edith and Huntington's friendship was a mutual intellectual respect and a conviction that the political and cultural achievements of the ancient Greeks were directly relevant to the modern world.

Both Huntington and Florence readily accepted Edith as an authority on ancient Greece, and her letters to them sometimes resembled her published works. In June 1948, in an answer to a question posed by Florence about the Sirens, Edith responded:

> You see the Sirens were bent upon charming Greeks, so they did not say, "Come hither to the most beautiful of women, we are waiting for you in all our loveliness. Here are soft couches and red wine and the fairest maidens upon the earth." No—To the Greeks they sang, "We know all, both the past and the future and we will give you knowledge." What Greek could withstand that, unless his ears were stopped or he was fast bound to the mast?[26]

Among her friends in Washington, Edith soon became an authority on how ancient Greek thought and experience related to the problems of the twentieth-century world.

Conversations on this subject could sometimes be light-hearted. By 1946, the year he met Edith, Huntington had begun to throw an annual birthday dinner for Plato. He had learned that the philosopher was born on the seventh in the Greek lunar month of Thargelion, in the first year of the eighty-eighth Olympiad, or May 21, 427 BCE, as Shorey had identified it in his brief biography of the philosopher in *What Plato Said*. On these occasions, Huntington would assume the role of Agathon, the host of the dinner party in the *Symposium*.[27] For Edith, it was a return to the Greek-inspired celebrations she had known in her days as a student at Bryn Mawr College.

Journalist Felix Morley first visited 2448 Massachusetts Avenue in May 1948, brought by Huntington and his own admiration for *Witness to the Truth*.[28] He and his wife, Isabel, lived on Westmoreland Circle in a terrace house called Millstone. Felix in particular would become one of Edith and Doris's closest friends in Washington. Felix's social and intellectual connection to Edith and Doris really began during the post-war years in Washington, but he was slightly known to them before due to his childhood in Baltimore. There, his father, Dr. Frank Morley, had been professor of mathematics at Johns Hopkins and friends with Harry and Edith Reid. Edith, during her years as headmistress of the Bryn Mawr School, had had at least a passing acquaintance with Dr. Morley, who lived with his wife and family on Baltimore's Park Avenue, as did Edith during some of her years in the city.[29] Felix Morley had been a Rhodes Scholar before pursuing a career in journalism, eventually joining the staff of the *Washington Post*, where, in 1936, his editorial writing earned him a Pulitzer Prize, the newspaper's first.[30] Four years later, however, Morley's pacifism and anti-interventionism lost him his job as the *Post*'s editor.[31]

When he first became a regular visitor to Massachusetts Avenue, Morley was in the process of writing his book, *The Power in the People*, which argued that American federalism had been damaged by the New Deal and the Second World War and urged postwar Americans to revive their federal republic, the best guarantor of individual freedom. To Morley, liberty was essentially a spiritual quality. It was up to citizens to maintain their liberty by taking an active interest in political life and by exercising self-restraint, respecting the opinions of others. Morley thought that Christian belief was the basis of liberty since in Christianity the individual found the moral basis for self-restraint and the will to follow sometimes exacting standards of conduct. Christianity, Morley felt, always stood in opposition to totalitarianism by urging the individual to comply with a higher, divine law. The future of the American republic was, therefore, dependent on continued belief in Christianity, and Edith, by demonstrating how Christian faith could survive the horrors of the Second World War, had contributed to an essential component of maintaining liberty. His "selected bibliography" at the end of the book recommended *Witness to the Truth* as further reading.[32]

The exchange of ideas apparent in *Witness to the Truth* and *The Power in the People*, published just one year apart, marked the beginning of a close intellectual relationship between Edith and Felix.[33] Edith's positive review of Morley's book in a September 1949 issue of the *Saturday Review of Literature* reflected how deeply she shared Morley's classic liberalism.[34] Edith had expressed her own doubts about the growth of the federal government on several occasions before Morley became a frequent visitor to her Washington home. In her chapter on Xenophon in *The Great Age of Greek Literature*, she had signaled her opposition to government intrusion on individual choice in areas of education, alcohol consumption, and retirement savings, instead arguing that these were personal decisions and responsibilities. To friends, she had expressed other reservations about Roosevelt, including criticism of the president's "Four Freedoms," feeling that a government could do little to remove freedom from fear.[35] Even in her work as a Progressive-Era reformer, Edith had confined herself to causes that focused on individual rights and opportunity, women's suffrage, and the passage of mandatory school attendance laws. In Morley, she found an articulate defender of classic liberalism, and her last book, *The Echo of Greece*, would largely be inspired by Morley's *The Power in the People*.

Her relationship with Morley, however, was not merely intellectual. As Felix became close friends with Edith and Doris, he also became a keen observer of the two women's relationship. From his visits to Massachusetts Avenue and later to Seawall, Felix described the two as a couple whose talents and skills complemented one another. Edith, when drawn into conversation, was capable of quickly identifying the intellectual question at the heart of any topic. Doris, more outgoing, did not wait for an entrée into conversation but went speedily to current political questions.[36] They were, he confided to his journal, "a wonderful combination."[37] He seemed to largely assume that the two women's relationship was not physical. After Edith's death he privately pondered whether Doris might choose to marry her widowed former suitor Sir George Paget Thomson. He quickly dismissed the idea, however, on the grounds of Doris's age, not on his understanding of her sexual orientation.[38]

Comments on Edith and Doris's relationship during this period were rare. Most visitors to their house seemed to take the women's partnership as a given, but Felix had a journalist's eye, and his observations were some of the few made about the couple. When, in 1967, he published a review of Doris's biography of Edith he described their relationship as the "perfect friendship" of two women widely divided in age. Felix was one of the few reviewers of Doris's book to find that it deserved its subtitle "An Intimate Portrait," although as he wrote his assessment he drew on his own knowledge of their relationship. His review included some observations not drawn from Doris's narrative, such as Edith and Doris's feeling, which probably originated later in their relationship, that they had been close from the time that Doris had attended the Bryn Mawr School. In his review, Felix wrote that "from that time on they were never spiritually divided." He also realized that in their early life together in New York City, Edith and Doris had seen themselves as artists supporting one another in their creative endeavors. Ultimately, his review compared Edith and Doris to Johnson and Boswell, suggesting that he saw Edith as the intellectual and Doris as the observant amanuensis.[39]

It was most likely Morley who brought Gen. Albert C. Wedemeyer to Massachusetts Avenue. Wedemeyer had spent the last two years of the war as commander of U.S. forces in the Southeast Asian theater, where he had replaced Gen. Joseph Stilwell and served as chief of staff for Gen. Chiang Kai-Shek.[40] Wedemeyer had spent the first half of the conflict, however, in the War Plans Division of the War Department General Staff, helping to plan for a decisive strike against Nazi-occupied Europe.[41] Ultimately, he would express disappointment in a war that he felt should have been a struggle between fascism and communism but that ultimately strengthened the global influence of the latter.

Wedemeyer's leadership of the Southeast Asian theater, however, earned much praise, and he emerged from the Second World War with a reputation as an effective commander. His friendly relationship with Chiang Kai-Shek ultimately led to his appointment by Secretary of State George C. Marshall as leader of a 1947 diplomatic mission to China to convince the Nationalist government to engage in reforms that would allow the United States to continue to aid its struggle against the Communists. During what became known as the Wedemeyer Mission, the general met with Chiang Kai-Shek and members of his government. He was openly critical of the corruption he saw in the Nationalists' ranks and called for economic reforms. However, in the report he wrote for the State Department upon completion of his mission, he recommended continued U.S. support for the Nationalist cause. A convinced anticommunist, Wedemeyer was fearful that unless the Nationalists received crucial U.S. aid, they would collapse.[42]

In 1948, when he was introduced to Edith and Doris, Wedemeyer was facing deep disappointment over the State Department's refusal to publish his report, on the grounds that some of its recommendations regarding Manchuria necessitated keeping the document secret. The aftermath of the mission, when he met Edith and Doris, was to be the most challenging time of Wedemeyer's life.[43] Among those who met at Edith and Doris's house he found a sympathetic circle.

Doris especially welcomed Wedemeyer. As a soldier assigned to the War Plans Division, he had been unable to openly express his opposition to U.S. entry into the Second World War, but he had privately sympathized with America First.[44] The refusal of the State Department to publish the report of his mission stirred another source of anxiety in Wedemeyer: lack of transparency in government. Doris shared his feelings.[45] Indeed, transparency in government—or lack of it—was to become a recurring subject of discussion for those who gathered on Massachusetts Avenue.

Edith and Doris's neighbor, Alice Roosevelt Longworth, Washington's most prominent political hostess, also became one of their visitors. The daughter of President Theodore Roosevelt, and the widow of Ohio Congressman Nicholas Longworth, she had befriended Huntington and discovered that she enjoyed exchanging books with Edith.[46] She and Doris shared many similar political views: Mrs. Longworth had been active in America First, and she had supported Ohio Republican Senator Robert Taft's presidential candidacy for as long as Doris had—from about 1939—and she would support him again in 1948 and 1952.[47] Edith never grew as close to her as she did to her other Massachusetts Avenue neighbor Elizabeth Cabot Lodge. Edith apparently found the self-confident Mrs. Longworth intimidating—"formidable" was the word Elling, a frequent visitor to Washington, used to describe her.[48] On at least one occasion Edith used Florence Cairns as an intermediary to communicate with her.[49]

There were other famous visitors and frequent guests as well. The labor leader John L. Lewis, introduced to Edith either by Felix Morley or Alice Roosevelt Longworth, was among them.[50] By the time he met Edith, Lewis, by then the president of the United Mine Workers of America for nearly three decades, was a widower who lived in a colonial-era house in Alexandria. Although deeply opposed to the antiunion Taft-Hartley Act of 1947, named in part for its Senate sponsor Robert Taft,

Lewis shared other concerns common to Edith and Doris's social circle.[51] He had also been an isolationist, believing that wartime regulation of industry would remove some of the gains workers had made during the Roosevelt presidency. He feared the growth of the federal government that would accompany the war, believing it would lead to repression of democratic freedoms. Enhanced American power after the war, he thought, would lead to the creation of an American empire that oppressed other societies around the world. Along with his familiarity with classical literature, Lewis was a lively conversationalist able to make Edith laugh by constructing sentences in his self-taught Latin.[52]

Not all who came to Edith and Doris's were socially prominent. John Clendenin, who taught writing, met Edith in 1948 and came to tea in November of the following year. He was delighted to find himself, together with his wife and two children, invited back soon after and subsequently paid a number of visits to Seawall.[53] Poets were also among those who came to Massachusetts Avenue. Edith's friendship with the poet Marcella Miller du Pont began in 1950, and four years later Edith was offering Marcella critiques of her work.[54]

By 1948, the year *Witness to the Truth* was published, a group of friends had been established who would direct Edith's intellectual interests toward consideration of the United States' position in the postwar world. Many of their new visitors espoused Doris's openly stated political views, with which Edith sympathized. Morley, Wedemeyer, Lewis, and Mrs. Longworth had all either been sympathetic to, or active in, America First.[55] They were also strong anticommunists, a position common among former adherents to America First, who were troubled by the U.S. alliance with the Soviet Union during the war.[56] They were, like Doris, isolationist Republicans who favored the presidential candidacy of Robert A. Taft, whom Morley had personally urged to run and whom Edith and Doris would befriend during their years in Washington.[57] During this time, Doris became increasingly active in politics, making her political views more easily identifiable than Edith's. There are, however, indications that Edith shared much of Doris's political outlook.

Doris's earliest political activities in Washington were election-night parties, including a dinner she hosted in November 1948. Senator Taft had lost the Republican nomination to New York Governor Thomas Dewey, but Doris, hoping to see President Truman defeated, invited Huntington and Florence Cairns, Felix and Isabel Morley, Albert Wedemeyer and his wife, Dade, as well as her New York friends Seth and Alida Milliken as guests for her election-night dinner party, with everyone invited to stay and listen to the returns.[58] Of course, the presidential contest between Truman and Dewey was not resolved until the next day, and the result was unsatisfactory to Doris and her guests.

Nevertheless, the parties held on Massachusetts Avenue were some of Doris's fondest memories of her life with Edith in Washington. She often served as hostess to take some of the pressure of entertaining off of Edith, who sometimes found she had to rest for a few days before a scheduled party.[59] Along with recurring philosophical and historical themes, a subject discussed was the fate of Nationalist China. From the end of the Second World War until the Chinese Communist victory in 1949, political debate about U.S. foreign policy toward China, particularly concerning the extent of aid the United States should give the Nationalists, flourished in Washington.[60]

Besides Edith, Gen. Wedemeyer, Felix Morley, and Alice Roosevelt Longworth all had had some first-hand experience with China, Longworth having visited the country as part of a diplomatic delegation sent during her father's presidency.[61] Edith's new friendships with Morley and Wedemeyer kept the question of China's future before her. But Edith's sympathy for the Nationalist cause was due in part to the large role missionaries had played in developing her understanding of China. Many missionaries, including her friend Lily Duryee, had returned to the United States during the Japanese invasion of China in the 1930s. Firmly anticommunist, returning missionaries had become active in American groups supporting both humanitarian relief for the Chinese people and the Nationalist cause.[62]

Those who gathered at Edith and Doris's discussed the roots and survival of democracy in part through the writings of the nineteenth-century historian Lord Acton. The English baronet, who had died in 1902, had spent the last years of his life as Regius Professor of modern history at Cambridge. A liberal Roman Catholic, he had challenged both the doctrine of Papal Infallibility promulgated by the Vatican Council of 1870 and the force of extreme Ultramontanism. Acton's reputation as a scholar grew in the postwar world as readers discovered that his works addressed relevant themes, such as upholding the rights of the individual against a state (or a church) that sought absolute authority over its populace. A champion of liberty—political, intellectual, and spiritual—Acton had predicted that the extreme nationalism of the German Empire would ultimately threaten political freedom and would result in the denial of rights to minorities. Such prescience led to a postwar revival of interest in Acton, and some of his works, including *The History of Freedom and Other Essays*, originally published in 1907, were reprinted.[63]

Huntington and Felix in particular were drawn to the study of Lord Acton. Huntington even sent Felix a copy of the historian's list of the ninety-eight greatest books ever written, which Acton had originally sent to his friend Mary Gladstone, daughter of Prime Minister William E. Gladstone, in 1884. Though the list included Plato's *Laws* and Aristotle's *Politics*, it contained few ancient Greek authors.[64] More importantly for Felix, Acton was both a classic liberal and a proponent of federalism as a guarantor of liberty and, having visited the United States in 1853, of the American federal system in particular.[65] Felix found Acton's belief that each generation must vigilantly maintain democracy and that a federal system helped preserve individual liberty relevant to postwar America, and he cited the historian in his book *The Power in the People*.[66]

Edith, too, began to read Acton.[67] In her essay on Plutarch, published in 1951, she was partly influenced by Canadian classicist H. J. Rose but also likely by Acton when she argued that the early Christian church ultimately "took the Roman way," meaning the path of formalism she deplored. Echoing Lord Acton's opposition to a church that sought to stifle individual reflection, Edith wrote that the Romans "were great organizers and an organization is not a place where individuals are encouraged to seek or to be free."[68] Lord Acton's influence would be more noticeable in her next book, *The Echo of Greece*, the opening chapters of which stressed the need of individuals to preserve liberty by exercising responsible citizenship. She twice paraphrased the historian's famous maxim—"All power tends to corrupt and absolute power corrupts absolutely"—which Acton had written to the Anglican Bishop of London Mandell Creighton in 1887, concerning the political might of Renaissance popes and monarchs. The phrase had recently been published and appeared in chapters four and ten in her book, where Edith felt she knew the source of Acton's words, writing, "All power tends to corrupt, Lord Acton said as Plato had said before him."[69]

It was around this time that, through Huntington, Edith was introduced to Ezra Pound, who was incarcerated in St. Elizabeth's Hospital in Washington.[70] The poet had been indicted for treason in July 1943 for making radio broadcasts in Italy on behalf of Mussolini. He had been arrested in Rapallo in May 1945 and had been brought back to the United States the following November. By pleading insanity, he avoided a trial on the charges and a possible death sentence.[71]

Pound would remain a controversial presence, particularly when he was awarded the Bollingen Prize for Poetry. Critics decried that such a committed fascist as Pound could receive an award for his poetic contribution to American culture when fascists opposed freedom of literary expression.[72] Edith gave few indications of how she coped with Pound's politics and prejudices—he was a known anti-Semite. But their correspondence, especially on classical texts, make clear that on a personal level she took pleasure in the company of Pound and his wife, Dorothy.

While paper shortages had hindered the reprinting of some of Edith's books during and just after the war, Storer had seen to it that *Three Greek Plays*, which had gone out of print, became available again in early 1946.[73] She was pleased by its reappearance with a newly designed book jacket. In the years that followed she saw her translations used more frequently in college productions, especially the *Agamemnon*, which, as the story of the soldier returning from war, spoke most immediately to college performers and audiences. There were at least two college productions of this translation during these years, one given in March 1948 by students at George Washington University, which was reported on by the Washington press, and one in the winter of 1950–51 at Dartmouth College, under the direction of its professor of drama

Dr. Henry B. Williams. The Dartmouth performance drew the praise of writer Vincent Sheean. Edith was delighted by the photographs of the production that Williams sent her.[74] Edith was experiencing the satisfaction of seeing her translations used in actual productions.

Edith would never lose interest in the intellectual challenges of translating Greek tragedies. The list of translators she praised grew to include Witter Bynner, Robert Fitzgerald, Dudley Fitts, Herbert Schaumann, and, soon, Ezra Pound. Pound published his translations with the subtitle "a version" to indicate that style and meaning took precedence over word-for-word accuracy. In the spring and summer of 1949, Edith joined Pound and Rudd Fleming, a literature professor at the University of Maryland, in translating the *Women of Trachis (Trachiniae)* of Sophocles, which Pound apparently planned to stage as a Noh drama, possibly in Japan.[75]

Noh's similarities to ancient Greek tragedy had long been noted by Pound and careful observers of the Japanese form, which combined music, movement, and speech on stage using a chorus and masked performers. Like ancient Greek tragedy, its origins were in religious rite, and it frequently portrayed interaction between humans and deities, incorporating themes such as revenge. Eventually, Greek tragedies would be staged in the Noh form in the United States.[76] As Pound biographer Michael Reck argued, when he considered staging a Greek tragedy as a Noh drama in Japan, Pound may have imagined bringing the cultures of East and West together, an idea that Edith, with her concern for the future of China, might have found appealing.[77]

Edith found the process of working with Pound stimulating, telling him in June 1949, "Please, please boil over again about Sophocles when next I see you," adding: "I shall try to think up some remarks to stimulate the boiling."[78] In April 1950, as she began work on an essay on Plutarch, she wrote: "But no weather, however wintry, would keep me from delightful company, dear Mr. Pound, and no soft spring airs add to its attraction."[79] Edith clearly enjoyed the company of both Ezra and his wife, Dorothy, to whom she never failed to offer her "warm regards" in her notes to the poet. She found Pound's mischievous sense of humor appealing and enjoyed working out the meaning of notes he wrote to her in his own idiosyncratic style.[80] Two of his letters to her, with his unique spellings and punctuation, dating from near the end of his time at St. Elizabeth's, have survived in Edith's papers, probably preserved by Doris.[81]

When Pound's *Women of Trachis* first appeared in print in the *Hudson Review* in 1954, Edith eagerly read it and encouraged Pound to continue his work of translating tragedy, expressing hope that he would turn next to the *Oresteia*.[82] Reading the translation again in December 1956, when it had been published in book form, she told the poet that she still felt "its freshness and strength." She added: "It is laughable to put it on the shelf beside other translations," and again urged him to continue his work.[83] Pound's *Women of Trachis*, however, was rarely produced, with one performance given on BBC radio and one in Darmstadt, Germany, in 1959. It was also produced in New York City in June 1960, but the performance received a negative review from Edith's friend Brooks Atkinson.[84]

In the context of Edith's intellectual interests after the Second World War, the friendship between her and Pound has been viewed as an exceptional moment in her life, even by Doris, who recalled that Edith was unappreciative of Pound's literary style.[85] Doris chose to emphasize the artistic differences between Pound and Edith, who, in the years just after she met the poet, was to write essays critical of the works of twentieth-century writers and artists due to what she felt was their deliberate obfuscation of their own individual visions. Increasingly, Edith would be seen as arguing against modernism, in spite of her friendship with Pound, which continued until the poet's release from St. Elizabeth's in 1958 and his return to Italy, where he lived until his death and from where he invited Edith to visit him.[86] However, Pound's view of classical antiquity as a source of cultural authority appealed to Edith. In the context of her interest in translation and her willingness to embrace new styles of this work, her friendship with Pound is understandable.[87]

The postwar interest in the roots of democracy helped prompt Edith's decision to once again write about the ancient Greeks and eventually resulted in her first recognition from academic classicists. In 1949, Edith was asked by the Classics Club to write an essay on Plutarch to be used as an introduction to a collection of his *Lives and Essays*, translated by Louise Ropes Loomis, a historian at Wells College.[88] The Classics Club's publications were intended to reach a wide reading audience, and its board's selection of Edith to provide the introduction was a measure of how she had come to be regarded as an authority on ancient Greece as well as a popular writer. For Edith, the study of Plutarch became her main work as a classicist during the immediate postwar years. Her studies of Plutarch provided her first interaction with academic classicists, when, on March 20, 1950, she delivered the annual Horton Lecture sponsored by the classics department at Wellesley College. She spoke on "The Age of Plutarch: The Greco-Roman Background of the Early Christian Church."[89]

Her study of Plutarch was her first reflection on Greece when it was long past its height of power in the fifth century BCE. Plutarch lived seven hundred years later, after the Roman conquest of Greece, and his ability to exercise citizenship was necessarily limited in scope. There was, Edith wrote, much less emphasis on public life than in Periclean Athens. But, writing for a postwar audience, she added, "the mighty Greek spirit which had suffered so much had not lost its power to learn and to perceive new forms of excellence."[90] Plutarch showed the Athenians that what few government tasks for them remained should still be done to a high standard, and he wrote his *Lives* to provide models of past achievement. In Plutarch, Edith saw an example for the postwar world of how the leaders of victorious nations should treat those whom they had defeated, a question much on her mind as she contemplated the fate of postwar Germany.

Plutarch, though open about the faults of past military leaders, nevertheless provided examples of their acts of greatness, thus providing, according to Edith, a model for Victorian renderings of great military engagements, including Tennyson's *The Charge of the Light Brigade*. Plutarch and Tennyson understood the principle of the victors, treating those they had conquered with generosity, but Edith saw little of this in the postwar world.[91] Edith had been prompted to draw this lesson after reading *The High Cost of Vengeance*, which had been published as she wrote her essay.[92]

The book was the work of the English-born journalist Freda Utley, an anticommunist and former supporter of America First, who had spent the last months of 1948 as a correspondent for *Reader's Digest* in Germany.[93] Utley's investigative reporting from Germany under Allied occupation was highly critical of the victors' economic and political policies as well as some Allied actions during the war, including the firebombing of Dresden in February 1945.[94] Most importantly for Edith, Utley reminded her readers throughout her text that nothing less than the future of Western civilization was at stake as West Germany hoped to avoid becoming part of Stalin's empire.[95]

Edith followed the debate about American actions in postwar Germany closely. Among the critical reviews of Utley's book was one published in the *New York Times*. But a few months later, in November 1949, the newspaper published an editorial that Edith praised. In the wake of the Berlin Airlift, the newspaper stressed the need for Americans and Western Europeans to allow West Germany to develop economically and encourage its nascent democracy. Unless many of the former Allies reached out to West Germany, there was a great danger that it would grow closer to the Soviet Union.[96]

Edith believed that Plutarch's *Lives* had lessons for the postwar world and that Plutarch himself was a witness to moral change, which, she argued, he saw coming over Greek society in the first century CE as the region was reduced to a province of the Roman Empire. Just as Edith was seeing contemporary American society move away from conventional Christianity in a postwar crisis of faith, she saw Plutarch trying to exhort Greeks to aspire to high ethical standards through the examples he had provided in his *Lives*. Though Plutarch did not have contact with Christianity, he was, to Edith, an example of how the Greeks anticipated the rise of the new religion through their growing awareness of ethical standards. She saw him as a Platonic idealist, struggling for greater knowledge of the good—"typically Greek," she told her readers.[97] It was this aspect of Plutarch's life that she emphasized to her Wellesley audience when she spoke at the college in March 1950. It was her first presentation in front of academic classicists, as she spoke to faculty and to students in the college's classical club in an annual lecture that honored Mary E. Horton, Wellesley's first professor of Greek.[98]

Edith's essay on Plutarch explicitly linked ancient Greece to the twentieth-century world. In her willingness to befriend Ezra Pound and in her espousal of Freda Utley's *The High Cost of Vengeance*, her studies of the ancient Greeks had sprung from very contemporary controversies. Political concerns had never been entirely absent from Edith's writing. In her earlier books, the Greeks and the Romans had both tried but failed to construct a peaceful world order in the wake of war. *The Prophets of Israel* and her translation of *The Trojan Women* of Euripides had both been inspired by fear of fascism and its ability to create another conflict. In the wake of the Second World War, with fascism defeated, Edith turned her attention more fully to questions raised by the United States' victory and its new status as a superpower facing a newly strengthened Soviet Union. The wide social circle to which Huntington had introduced her would only grow in the future. Her Washington friends would prompt her to consider even further questions such as the future of Western civilization and what the United States in the Cold War era could learn from the experiences of the ancient Greeks.

Chapter 17

AN AGE OF EXTERNAL
GREATNESS

✦ Edith's role as an advocate for the continuing study of the classical world in the Cold War era grew during her second decade in
Washington, D.C. At home her circle of friends grew to incorporate
more of the city's prominent residents. Elling, a frequent visitor during
these years, recognized that Edith had created a Washington salon, with
senators, generals, and ambassadors among the regular attendees. Huntington photographed many of her famous guests, creating a record that
supported one *Washington Star* reporter's description of Edith as "the
grand old lady of the Washington literary scene."[1] She had become such
a well-known figure in the capital that when the Polish artist Feliks
Topolski visited the city in 1950 he sketched a portrait of her as part of
his series of caricatures of Washington notables for publication in an
August issue of *Vogue* magazine. Others portrayed included Robert A.
Taft, the Republican senator from Ohio.[2]

Edith's final completed book, *The Echo of Greece*, published in 1957,
reflected the contemporary political climate of the capital as experienced
by her social circle, composed mainly of the Cold War noninterventionists who gathered around Senator Taft. Edith was particularly well suited
to give voice to the concerns of the Taft Republicans, for whom the
political experience of ancient Greece had become a symbol of humanity's continual struggle for liberty.[3] From the beginning, *The Echo of
Greece* was a Cold War exposition on what the twentieth-century United

States could learn from the experience of Athens's decline. Its opening chapters reflected the ideals of Taft Republicanism, emphasizing that a nation's strength lay in the character of its citizens, not in the size of its military or the breadth of its foreign policy commitments. Those latter commitments would lead only to an "age of external greatness," as Edith termed it in her notes to her manuscript.[4]

The book's genesis was a conversation between Storer and Doris in late 1950 in which they both envisioned the work that Edith could write on the individual responsibilities of citizenship in a democratic society. Shortly after, Storer wrote Edith that he and Doris wanted "the book that you could write around the subject of 'The Democratic Way of Mind', bringing to such a piece of writing your wisdom, your reflections, and your skills of writing." He hoped that the book would be "a reaffirmation of the best in democratic thinking."[5] Feeling that the subject was an important one, he ambitiously set the possible publication date for the fall of 1952. In fact, he would not see any of the manuscript until February 1955.[6]

Since at least the years before the United States had entered the Second World War, Edith and Doris had shared similar political views. Both were pacifists and noninterventionists who had hoped that the United States could avoid direct involvement in the conflict. In the wake of the war, however, noninterventionists, or isolationists as they were often called, faced new challenges as the United States took on greater foreign commitments to try to ensure a lasting peace. The founding of the United Nations, the Truman Doctrine (inspired by Greece's postwar struggle against communism), the Marshall Plan, and, finally, NATO, all required greater degrees of American involvement overseas, a challenge to the noninterventionists who still looked to Senator Robert A. Taft as their leader in Congress.

The son of President and Supreme Court Justice William Howard Taft, Senator Robert Taft ran for the presidency four times. He never succeeded in obtaining the Republican nomination, campaigning for it for the last time in 1952. During Edith and Doris's years in Washington, he became known as "Mr. Republican," or sometimes "Mr. Conservative," for his enduring opposition to much of the New Deal. Though leader of the noninterventionists in Congress, Taft cautiously endorsed many of the United States' new foreign commitments. He continued to believe, however, that government should not interfere with individual liberty. The role of government was to create equality of opportunity so that individuals were free to achieve their potential through hard work and self-discipline. Taft also argued that rather than use the United States' growing political power to determine outcomes to international questions, the United States should strengthen itself internally, ensuring that it retained its commitment to individual liberty, thereby serving as an example of democratic freedoms to the rest of the world.[7]

Edith and Doris befriended Taft, who lived in Georgetown with his wife, Martha, and who had several connections to Edith and Doris's social circle.[8] The Tafts were frequent guests of Alice Roosevelt Longworth, a staunch Taft supporter. Felix Morley also knew Taft and was an enthusiastic advocate of a Taft presidency, encouraging the senator to seek the Republican nomination in 1948, and again in 1952.[9]

It is unclear when Edith first met Robert Taft, but Ralph E. Flanders, the Republican senator from Vermont whom she befriended during her Washington years, would long remember a conversation between Edith and Taft over tea in the small brick-walled garden of the Flanders' home on Georgetown's O Street. During her last years as headmistress of the Bryn Mawr School, Edith had known Taft's sister, the historian Helen Taft Manning, who had then been a dean at Bryn Mawr College. After Taft's death, Edith expressed her admiration for the senator to Gen. Wedemeyer, praising his courage when defeated for the nomination.[10]

Undoubtedly, one of the reasons, besides pacifism, that Edith was drawn to Taft Republicanism was the close link between noninterventionism and individual liberty, of which she had always been a strong proponent. Noninterventionists feared the growth of the federal government, believing that it limited the scope of the individual. As Edith began work on her book on fourth century BCE Athens, she described it to Agnes as a study of "individuality and freedom."[11] Storer referred to it as a study of "the plight and triumph of the individual."[12] In keeping with Taft Republicanism, the extent to which American society supported individual opportunity had become a central concern of Edith's Washington social circle.

Although Edith tentatively began work on *The Echo of Greece* in early 1951, she would not be ready to show any of her manuscript to Storer until four years later. In the meantime, she wrote a series of three articles for the popular magazines *Vogue* and the *Saturday Review of Literature*, which in 1952 became simply the *Saturday Review*. These articles can be read almost as a trilogy, though they were not intended as such. They addressed a common theme: what Edith saw as the diminishing ability of artists and writers to communicate their vision effectively to a wide audience. As an adherent of Edward Caird's philosophy, she believed that the purpose of the creative act was to help reveal knowledge of the good. She asserted that every artist should strive to achieve the balance between the particular and the general, a feat achieved by ancient Greek writers.[13] Her three essays made the argument for the preservation of culture as a means of maintaining strength in the face of the growing power of communism. They were also, in effect, her only published pieces of autobiographical writing. In the first, titled "Private Idiom," published in *Vogue* in September 1951, she recalled her visit to one of the cubist exhibitions in Paris in 1912 and discussed her friendship with Gertrude Stein, the only time she did so in print.[14] In her essay on William Faulkner she revealed her acquaintance with the poetry of Swinburne that she had acquired at Bryn Mawr College. And, in the last of these articles, titled "Words, Words, Words," she recalled her childhood fondness for the poetry of Jean Ingelow.[15]

"Private Idiom" was Edith's first Cold War–era protest against the world she felt had been created by Sigmund Freud and Albert Einstein. Her arguments were not new; she had presented them in the conclusion to *The Greek Way* over twenty years earlier. Then she had written more positively about twentieth-century science, acknowledging that scientific advances had helped humanity, even if she felt that the Greek scientists, unlike their modern counterparts, had paid the appropriate amount of attention to the care of the spirit.[16] Still, Alice's work in the field of industrial toxicology had demonstrated to Edith how science could help humanity, unlike the invention of the atomic bomb, the use of which she had opposed and which illustrated the horrific possibilities of scientific achievement. In "Private Idiom," she protested the pursuit of science in the absence of clear indications of what the possible outcomes could be. To continue the study of nuclear energy was to venture into an unknown world with only dubious benefits to humanity.

Whereas in *The Greek Way* Edith had protested against "over-individualization," she now argued against Freud, who she felt had helped to create a world where the artist or writer's individual feelings were paramount yet not to be communicated clearly to others.[17] The artist influenced by Freudian thought did not perceive that their own personal experiences were connected to the larger experience of humanity as a whole. She used such terms as "self-engrossed" and "self-absorption" in her criticisms of writers such as Thomas Wolfe. She regarded the cubist style of Gertrude Stein as an authorial choice, pointing out that, by contrast, Stein's *The Autobiography of Alice B. Toklas* was written in a clear and appealing style.[18] Edith had always been attuned to society's shifting moral standards. Declining artistic expression was an indication of national moral decay, more worrisome to Edith than fading military or political strength because it reflected the failures of individuals to balance the freedom of expression with the responsibilities of citizenship.

Edith's essay "Faulkner: Sorcerer or Slave?" appeared in the July 12, 1952, issue of the *Saturday Review*, which was largely devoted to critical discussions of Faulkner. Her concern about the popularity of his work had been aroused during the winter of 1951–52, when she had suffered ill health and had felt herself unproductive. She spent part of her time reading Faulkner, seeing in his work many of the same flaws she had criticized in "Private Idiom," this time attributing the twentieth-century trend toward obfuscation in abstract art to Picasso.[19] Both articles dealt with a similar theme: the conscious turning away from the knowledge of the good that was, in Edith's opinion, a deplorable feature of twentieth-century art. Faulkner, she argued, may have felt that he was writing realistically about complex human dilemmas, but his characters were far too individualized for ready identification by a reader. In this exaggeration he became, unintentionally, a romantic yet puritanical writer.

The last of her essays criticizing twentieth-century artists focused on the work of the Welsh-born poet Dylan Thomas and was published in the *Saturday Review* in November 1955, two years after his death in New York City at the age of thirty-nine. In the last years of his life, soon after his *Collected Poems* had been published, Thomas had given readings of his poetry in the United States, attracting large audiences.[20] Edith, however, found his poems too laden with obscure metaphor to clearly communicate meaning. She also argued that there was nothing essentially new about Thomas's work, comparing it critically against Jean Ingelow's work. Only the effect of Ingelow's and Thomas's poetry differed: the earlier poet's works charmed and delighted with their cleverness. Thomas's poems, however, did not reveal beauty as Edith felt the creative act should do, only gloominess and despair.[21]

These three essays, written as Edith began *The Echo of Greece*, helped her to reach a potentially wide audience with her argument that the deteriorating quality of individual artistic expression was a sign of the need to preserve Western civilization in a world where it was threatened and perhaps already in a state of decline.

In *The Echo of Greece* cultural decay would also be identified as a sign of political decline. As she worked on the new book, Edith reached back to the Victorian British social critics she had read as a student at Bryn Mawr College and to the work of the classicists of that period, writers who had mined the ancient Greek authors for insights into their own society. Chief among these were Matthew Arnold and John Ruskin, who believed that what defined a nation was its culture and that the state of culture was a reflection of a society's moral strength or weakness. In the book, she made an argument drawn from Ruskin: "Greek art at its best and most characteristic is kept within the limits of the real world."[22] This contrasted favorably to the art of the Assyrians, which reflected imagination gone rampant. The qualities of Greek art at its height were visible in the Parthenon frieze, a copy of which Edith had seen every day during her years at the Bryn Mawr School. Over thirty years later, she still felt that the classical figures represented the balance between the ideal and the real. As she wrote, "The young men of the Parthenon frieze were not copies of real men the artist knew; they were not portraits of individuals, but they were not purely imaginary creations. They had more than natural human beauty; nevertheless they were natural human beings."[23]

The fourth century, however, had seen a marked decline in the Greek ability to produce or appreciate works of beauty. Under the heading "Age," she wrote in her notes, "An age of external greatness attended by signs of mental decay. No sense of beauty. No great characters, no great writers trying to invent, a new shudder instead of bringing to birth healthy living creatures."[24] In *The Echo of Greece* she wrote that the Acropolis had not been damaged by the Peloponnesian War. Athens "was as beautiful as ever. The change was in the people."[25]

Edith's notes for *The Echo of Greece* also indicated that she consulted the work of the Irish classicist J. P. Mahaffy, who had been a scholar at Trinity College, Dublin, until his death in 1919. Mahaffy was one of the few nineteenth-century classical scholars who chose to write about the Hellenistic period, making him a useful source for Edith, who consulted his *Greek Life and Thought*, first published in 1887.[26] The Hellenistic age had largely been seen by nineteenth-century classical scholars as a period of decline. Mahaffy argued that internal decay was a prerequisite for a society's defeat.[27] His *Greek Life and Thought* drew many historical parallels between the late nineteenth century and the Hellenistic age— too many some of his critics thought. For Edith, as she began to write *The Echo of Greece*, Mahaffy must have provided a model for illustrating the similarities between the Hellenistic age and the modern era.

The challenges of writing *The Echo of Greece* stemmed from her lack of familiarity with fourth-century Greece and with American history, a subject Montgomery Hamilton had thought unimportant. Both made it difficult for her to create the parallels she wanted her readers to see between ancient Greece and twentieth-century America. Sometimes she stretched her comparisons to the bounds of credibility. In *The Echo of Greece* she would mention the "Founding Fathers" of a "new republic" debating in "some Athenian Independence Hall" and an effort to create a United Greece. The schoolteacher Isocrates became a pamphleteer.[28]

As she wrote, she therefore turned to more recent sources of thought. Much of the book drew on the political influences surrounding her in

Washington. Her attempts to absorb these and relate them to the ancient Greek experience may have been one of the reasons for the delay in completing the book, which took her five years to write. Ultimately, *The Echo of Greece* fell into four sections. The two opening chapters were an allegory reflecting Taft Republicans' qualms about imperialism. These were intended to show how Athens's abuse of power after its victory in the Persian Wars ultimately led to the Peloponnesian War in which Athens was defeated and entered a period of decline. This section was followed by two chapters on the schools of Athens and its schoolteachers. The third portion of the book consisted of studies of seminal figures of the fourth century: Demosthenes, Alexander the Great, and Menander. The book concluded with her chapters on the Hellenistic period: the Stoics, Plutarch, and a discussion of early Christianity.

Edith, unschooled in American history, was reliant on Felix Morley as she tried to construct parallels between the experience of the ancient Greeks and Cold War America. She appreciated Morley's argument that the founders, among them Madison and Washington, had been inspired by the example of Athenian democracy to put their faith in ordinary men and to understand that liberty for everyone was guaranteed only by individual restraint. The book's opening chapter, "Freedom," sought to draw parallels between Athenian democracy and the founding of the United States. Many isolationists, fond of reflecting on the early republic, often compared it to Rome, but Edith used Athens, stressing the influence of Solon, who had created a society where every citizen was free to participate.[29] Morley fully believed that the founding fathers had valued the contributions that each individual could make to effective government, as James Madison had shown when he referred to the "capacity of mankind for self-government" in *The Federalist* No. 39, which Morley quoted in *The Power in the People*. The same quote appeared in the first chapter of *The Echo of Greece*, where Edith wrote, "'The capacity of mankind for self-government', a statesman, Athenian in spirit, phrased it around the year 1776 A.D. No doubt James Madison had never an idea that he was speaking Greek. Athens and Solon were not in even the farthest background of his mind, but, as Aristotle said, the excellent becomes the permanent."[30] In fact, Madison had seriously studied classics both under a private tutor and as a student at the College of New Jersey (the future Princeton University).[31]

Edith's uncertainty when it came to American history and government meant that work on *The Echo of Greece* often proceeded slowly. Edith's writing was halted altogether by the death of Edith Reid, at the age of ninety-two, on April 5, 1954.[32] Edith had been expecting Edith Reid's death for at least a week before it occurred, but she did not share her forebodings with Doris, who was deeply shocked, feeling it had been sudden. Edith and Doris's different understandings of the gravity of Edith Reid's illness revealed that the twenty-eight-year difference in their ages was still relevant, even as Doris entered her fifties and approached retirement. Edith, soon to turn eighty-seven, had quickly realized that her friend was nearing death.

Almost immediately after Edith Reid's death, however, Doris, already in grief, learned that her brother Francis, who had settled in Fort Lauderdale, Florida, with his second wife, Frances, had been charged with murder. Tertius van Dyke agreed to accompany Doris to Florida for the trial. Edith was relieved that he would help as she felt that her own presence would be a hindrance rather than a support, since Doris always looked after her.[33] Instead, she decided to visit Hadlyme while Doris was away. By the end of April, Francis had been acquitted and Edith and Doris were reunited in Washington on May 1.[34] By the end of that month Edith felt it was possible to tell John Mason Brown, "Doris and I are slowly pulling up."[35] After such a difficult spring, the women naturally looked forward to the annual trip to Seawall. There, Edith and Doris received a welcome visit from Betsey's three children, George, Dorrit, and Elizabeth, who, as their mother had done during her childhood, quickly befriended Elling.[36]

Through 1955, Edith continued to make progress on the manuscript, although the structure of the volume was still unclear in her mind. Its first two chapters were obviously connected and, Edith hoped, would provide an introduction to her study of the fourth century. She realized, however, that any discussion of the time period had to include studies of Plato and Aristotle, although she had not initially intended to write about either. She confessed to Storer that her knowledge about the philosophers was "scrappy and amateurish," a surprising admission for someone who had written about Plato in *The Greek Way* and who had discussed Plato many times on Attic nights with Huntington.[37] After the completion of *The Echo of Greece*, she would devote all of her time to the study of Plato, but, in the meantime, she worried about being able to write enough about the fourth century to produce a full-length book.

Edith had kept abreast of certain developments in twentieth-century classical scholarship and was well aware of the great study of fourth-century Greece written by the German classicist Werner Jaeger. Jaeger's three-volume study, *Paideia: The Ideals of Greek Culture*, had been published in the thirties and forties, the first volume appearing in Germany in 1933. The first two volumes were later published in the United States in 1944, translated into English by the classical scholar Gilbert Highet and reviewed favorably by Edith that January in the *New York Times*.[38] Indeed, Edith credited Jaeger with the possession of wisdom, a deep understanding of human beings. She argued that although Jaeger was writing about ancient Greece, his concerns about the development of individual character were easily applicable to the world that would need reshaping once the conflict of the Second World War was resolved.[39]

Edith's research for her chapter on the fourth-century orator Demosthenes included the careful reading of another work by Jaeger, a series of lectures on the orator he had delivered at Berkeley soon after his arrival in the United States.[40]

Ultimately, however, much of her interpretation of Demosthenes was inspired by her friendship with the Republican senator from Vermont, Ralph E. Flanders, and his wife, Helen. Flanders, who until the age of sixty-six had never held an elected office, had won his Senate seat in 1946.[41] Among the senators known to have visited Massachusetts Avenue, Edith was closest to Flanders. It is not certain when she first met the senator, but it was before Taft's death in 1953.[42] Both he and Edith valued the principle of avoidance of war, and he had chaired the Vermont branch of the League to Enforce Peace just before American entry into the First World War.[43] In *Letter to a Generation*, which he published in 1956, Flanders proposed "universal controlled disarmament" as an ultimate solution to the threat of nuclear war.[44] He feared that victory in war would bring moral failure and saw Athens's decline after the Persian

FIGURE 13. Ralph E. Flanders, the Republican senator
from Vermont whose confrontation with Senator Joseph
McCarthy inspired Edith Hamilton's characterization of
Demosthenes. Photograph courtesy of the Senate Historical Office.

War as a powerful lesson, evidence of Edith's influence on him.[45] She
wrote a generous comment of praise for *Letter to a Generation*, suggesting it should be required reading for college students, which was printed
on the book's jacket when it was published in the summer of 1956, a few
months before *The Echo of Greece*.[46] Flanders sometimes embraced
Taft's isolationist positions although he sometimes rebelled against
Taft's leadership of the Senate Republicans. Flanders described Taft as
"a man of simplicity and directness." Explaining how his positions sometimes differed from Taft's, he called the senator from Ohio the "patron
saint of the ultra-conservative."[47]

As Edith was writing *The Echo of Greece*, Flanders was entering the most challenging period of his senatorial career, leading the movement to censure his fellow Republican, Senator Joseph McCarthy of Wisconsin. The two had entered the Senate at the same time and had clashed almost immediately, especially over the reputation of Flanders's friend, the Republican senator from Connecticut Raymond Baldwin.[48] Baldwin, who had also been elected in 1946, befriended Edith and Doris as well.[49] In what became his last months in the Senate, Baldwin became the focus of McCarthy's ire and would be subsequently identified as the "first victim of McCarthyism."[50] Flanders was alarmed by McCarthy's treatment of Baldwin, but it was not until March 1954 that he made his first speech cautioning him, suggesting that the Wisconsin Republican was ignoring "the larger scene and the present danger."[51]

To Flanders, McCarthy's emphasis on domestic communism distracted from the larger international threat that communism posed.[52] In June 1954, Flanders introduced Senate Resolution 261, which accused McCarthy of unbecoming conduct and suggested that he be removed from his Senate committee chair. The following month he modified this to Senate Resolution 301, which called for censure of the Wisconsin senator.[53] It was not the first attempt by members of the Senate to curb McCarthy, but Flanders, now in his second term, had decided not to run for reelection and he judged that the political moment to challenge McCarthy had arrived. That December, the Senate voted to censure McCarthy, though the resolution was modified to condemnation of his behavior.[54] Flanders's willingness to challenge members of his own party earned him a long-lasting reputation for rare political courage.[55]

Flanders's experience, however, also provided the inspiration for the chapter on Demosthenes in *The Echo of Greece*, in which the ancient orator was portrayed as Joseph McCarthy. As Edith wrote, fourth-century Athens had faced two possible threats of invasion: the Persian Empire and Macedon, then under the rule of Philip, just to the north of Greece. While the more distant Persian Empire might have been the obvious foe, Demosthenes insisted that Philip of Macedon was the greater threat.[56] Edith drew a parallel between Demosthenes's portrayal of Macedon and Senator McCarthy's focus on domestic communism.

McCarthy was therefore a twentieth-century Demosthenes, ignoring the larger threat from afar.[57]

Edith cautioned that Demosthenes had united the Greek states with a deceptively simple analysis of the challenge faced by Greece as it confronted Macedon: "He fired that soft, irresponsible, apathetic mass of city folk to take up arms and fight to the death. He won over Greek states that had been bitter enemies of Athens to join her."[58] The result of this effort, however, had been disastrous for the Greek states, which were decisively defeated in a military confrontation with Philip at the Battle of Chaeronea in 338 BCE.[59] Athens fell under Macedonian rule. The chapter on Demosthenes therefore drew much of its inspiration from contemporary events. Yet it ended with the Victorian classical scholar George Grote's analysis of the importance of Demosthenes, that his suicide after Chaeronea spelled the end of Athenian democracy.[60] The implications of following McCarthy beyond the Army-McCarthy hearings of 1954 were evident: doing so would endanger American democracy by weakening it internally.

In her notes, Edith did make one positive argument about Demosthenes, one that further hints at her view of Senator Joseph McCarthy. Her notes on the ancient orator include the phrase "only his patriotism redeems him—the apparent sincerity of his despairing cry for freedom."[61] From Demosthenes came one of Edith's favorite quotes that came to define, for her, the value of studying the ancient world: "the time for extracting a lesson from history is ever at hand for them who are wise." Edith first used it in the introduction to the Swedish edition of *The Echo of Greece*, published in August 1958, and then as the conclusion to an essay she published in the *Saturday Evening Post* the following month.[62]

Too much focus on an internal enemy had contributed to Greece's fall and allowed for the emergence of Philip's son Alexander, who, through military conquest, subsumed Greece and other parts of the world into his vast empire. Thus, Edith compared the empire constructed by Alexander the Great to the Soviet Union after the Second World War, both in the pace of its creation—eleven years in the case of Alexander's—and in their attempts to impose a system of rule.

Alexander, she wrote, envisioned an empire as "One World to be brought into union by himself."[63] Alexander had also studied biology under his tutor Aristotle, absorbing his teacher's argument that there were no essential physical differences among human beings but failing to appreciate Aristotle's assertion that there were differences of character: "peoples who sought for freedom and those who acquiesced in slavery."[64] Thus Edith responded to the growing pressure for equal rights experienced by American society after the Second World War. Differences among human beings were only differences in character without any biological basis. Alexander's empire-building, however, had illustrated the folly of ignoring differences among nations in the character of its peoples.

In her interpretation of Alexander, Edith hoped readers would see parallels with the creation of the Soviet empire and reject the uniformity both had intended to impose at the expense of individual expression. She also deeply opposed the use of force to impose a system, such as the one she saw created by the Soviets in the postwar world. She sympathized with the Hungarians in their 1956 Revolution and betrayed one of her noninterventionist positions by describing the United Nations as ineffective in the crisis.[65]

Edith's anticommunism was also evident in her approval of the Moral Re-Armament publications Agnes continued to send her during these years. Moral Re-Armament, the movement founded by the Reverend Frank N. D. Buchman to replace the Oxford Group, had first opposed fascism but turned decidedly anticommunist after the Second World War.[66] From 1946, it was headquartered at Mountain House in Caux, Switzerland, where it held its annual assemblies promoting its message of world peace, to be achieved through adherence to Christian principles and democratic processes.[67] Buchman was still criticized for his expensive lifestyle and his tight hold on the movement, but the latter attracted some of the leading political figures of postwar Europe, and Jessie and Agnes had remained adherents.[68] Edith read some of the movement's publications such as its monthly magazine, the *New World News*.[69] She saw the strength of Buchman's movement as reaffirmation of her own belief that "Communism could never defeat Christianity."[70]

Edith's comments on the need to preserve culture in the communist world were mainly focused on China. Concern about the fate of China, and the cause of the Nationalist collapse, had been avidly debated by noninterventionists even before the Chinese Communist victory in 1949. With such friends as Morley and Wedemeyer, who had both spent time in China, Edith would have listened to debates about its future even before the subject became a frequent concern of isolationists.[71] In the fifties Edith began to frequently discuss her own travels in China, even stretching the four months she had spent in the country to a year when she spoke to *Christian Science Monitor* journalist Frances Willard Kerr in 1958.[72] As she followed debates among her Washington friends about the "loss of China," it was the country's ancient culture that she felt was disappearing as the Communists took control.

Along with chapters on Demosthenes and Alexander, the chapter on Menander was part of the segment in *The Echo of Greece* discussing the outstanding figures of fourth century Greece. In her chapter on the fourth-century Greek playwright, she argued that Menander's elegant domestic comedies, though highly esteemed in the ancient world, were a reflection of the decline of Athenian political life. Athens had been conquered by Macedonia, and its political freedom had come to an end. It was not a Nazi occupation, as Edith wrote, and "secret police and concentration camps were unknown." But Athens's elite had retreated from public life, forgetting the "unpleasantness of the political situation" as they were safe in "the comforts of domesticity."[73] This meant an end to the satire of Aristophanes, who had felt free to poke fun at Athens's political leadership. Menander's works instead found their humor in the sudden uprooting of luxurious and well-established domestic arrangements and the efforts of the characters to restore normalcy. Though fourth-century Athens had produced such great figures as Plato and Aristotle, Menander's comedies, in which his characters were absorbed in their own domestic cares rather than affairs of state, were proof that the great days of Athenian freedom were at an end.[74]

As Edith made progress on her book, Doris decided, in 1955, to retire from Loomis-Sayles. In the years after Taft's death in 1953, she had continued to be active in Republican politics, attending with her friend Marcella Miller du Pont such events as a Republican Party dinner at the Sheraton-Park ballroom held that May.[75] She also studied under the guidance of a trained motivational speaker at the Capitol Hill Club in order to participate in the upcoming presidential campaign. She excelled and was voted the best of the ten speakers in her class after making a presentation titled "The Sad Life of a Conservative" to the National Capital Speakers Bureau in December. Her topic signaled that Doris felt increasingly out of sympathy with the more interventionist Eisenhower administration at a time when conservatives were relegated to the fringes of political life.[76]

Doris's plan to retire met with objections from Loomis-Sayles. She was only sixty, five years younger than Loomis-Sayles's retirement age, and the board expressed reluctance to see her depart. Ultimately, the firm offered her three-quarters of her salary to remain at her job half-time and readily agreed to grant her a seven-week vacation, since Edith had already planned a trip to Italy and Spain for them.[77] Its original purpose had been to help Doris adjust to her new life of retirement, but it turned into a long working vacation, with Edith taking her manuscript with her. It was the couple's first trip abroad since their 1929 journey to Greece. At eighty-eight, Edith was as healthy as Doris and as able to travel, though to Jessie and Agnes she at least acknowledged that her age had been a consideration in their decision to go to Europe.[78]

In February 1956, Edith and Doris sailed aboard the *Italia* bound for Palermo. They had a surprisingly large sending-off party: fourteen guests arrived, though they had only been expecting Elling, Alida, and Dorian and his family. To Jessie and Agnes, Edith compared her time aboard the ship to the much simpler conditions that had prevailed on her crossing to Italy in 1903. By comparison, this voyage was luxurious, as the two women had booked a stateroom. Doris, however, was anxious about Edith's balance. She carefully watched every step Edith took, even though Edith insisted she was developing her sea legs.[79] They landed in Sicily, where Francesca Gilder Palmer, who had been widowed five years earlier, joined them as a traveling companion.[80]

At sea the weather had been warm and pleasant. But Edith and Doris arrived to find much of Europe in a deep freeze, which would make their sightseeing difficult. They drove from Sicily to Rome, a city they had visited before and where one warm sunny day allowed them to visit the Forum and the Coliseum.[81] The cold weather persisted. Though Edith found the scenery beautiful as she and Doris drove to Siena, Perugia, Arezzo, and Florence, the car had to make its way through high banks of snow. In Siena, they awoke one morning to find that a fresh layer had blanketed the city. In Florence, their hotel was warm, but museum galleries were frigid. Outdoor sightseeing was very limited, consisting of stepping out of the car for only a few minutes at a time. Due to the cold, the women canceled their plans to visit Spain, which was experiencing similar weather. They had arranged to return home by plane from Portugal, however, so they therefore returned to Rome to catch a train to Lisbon.[82]

Edith returned home with her still unfinished manuscript.[83] She had promised to have the manuscript completed by June 15, leaving her little time to concentrate fully on the last portion of the book, which was to focus on the Hellenistic period, with chapters on the Stoics and Plutarch and a conclusion on the development of Christianity.[84] That summer, spent at Seawall, Edith tried to complete her book, even amid the company of Mary, who fell ill, and her four children. By summer's end, however, the manuscript was almost complete except for a chapter on Stoicism.[85]

Edith had written on Stoicism in *The Roman Way* and *Witness to the Truth*. In the former, she had called Stoicism a "second-rate Greek philosophy" that had "developed into a first-rate Roman religion."[86] In *The Echo of Greece* she still emphasized that Stoicism had flourished in Rome and therefore properly belonged to a discussion of the lasting influence of Greek culture. In fact, she modified her earlier argument about Stoicism, arguing that it "never became really Romanized in spite of the great Romans who adopted it."[87] She also tried to discern the Greek roots of Stoicism, acknowledging the importance of Socrates as a model for the Stoics. The Stoics admired Socrates for his self-control and for his willingness to fulfill his public responsibilities while still pursuing a philosophic search for knowledge of the good.[88] Moreover, as Edith pointed out, Socrates had died for his beliefs, illustrating to the Stoics that the soul was independent of the problems of this world. Edith saw a great difference

FIGURE 14. Edith Hamilton with three of Mary Reid
McKnight's children in July 1958. Photograph by Gjon Mili
for *Life* magazine. Shutterstock.

between the Stoics, and their efforts to remove themselves from the pain
of life, and Socrates, who she felt embraced all of life, according to the
Greek ideal. Greek self-mastery and Greek moderation, in keeping with
the themes of *The Echo of Greece*, also remained key aspects of Stoicism
long after it had made the journey to Rome.[89]

Storer had arranged for Edith's earlier essay on Plutarch, written as an
introduction to a volume of his *Lives*, to be reprinted as a chapter in the

new book. All that remained, therefore, was for her to complete a conclusion to *The Echo of Greece*. The result was a chapter titled "The Greek and Roman Way," which traced the differences between the contributions to Christianity by the two respective cultures. The ancient Greeks, Edith argued, had learned through defeat and annexation to the powerful Roman Empire that only "mind and spirit" endured.[90] The early church had taken what she termed the "Greek way," focusing solely on the individual pursuit of spiritual truth. By contrast, the Romans, who had figured out how to govern an empire, inspired the early Christian church to organize and codify its beliefs. The result was the development of the church as an institution, reduced to telling its followers to put their faith in creeds. To Edith, who followed the undogmatic new Christianity of Edward Caird, such formalism was deplorable as it discouraged the individual from seeking spiritual truth.[91]

Edith's delineation between "The Greek and Roman Way" in the early Christian church had grown much sharper in the years since she had written *Witness to the Truth*. This was due to her reading of the works of the Christian existentialist Nicolas Berdyaev, whose book, *The Realm of Spirit and the Realm of Caesar*, she had read in April 1953.[92] Berdyaev was a Russian nobleman who was exiled from the Soviet Union in 1922.[93] In Berdyaev's work Edith found reaffirmation that dogma was a hindrance to the pursuit of spiritual truth and that only spiritual solutions would solve the problems of a world that had recently fought two great wars and seemed to be preparing for a third.[94] In the final chapter of *The Echo of Greece*, she asserted more strongly that the early church had taken the Roman way, the "realm of Caesar," because of its fragile presence in the ancient world. In doing so, the church had discarded the spiritual freedom to pursue Christian truth that had been a marked characteristic of its early existence. As Edith had always believed, an imbalance in society, either of mind and spirit, or of the realm of Caesar and that of spirit, stifled cultural expression, another manifestation of spirit. Like Berdyaev, Edith believed imperialism led to a societal imbalance that destroyed culture. Berdyaev had pointed out that the great culture of fifth-century Athens was the product of a small city-state.[95]

There remained only the title to consider. Since at least early 1956, the forthcoming book had been referred to as *The Echo of Greece*. It is unclear why Edith's working title *This Constant World* was discarded.[96] It may have been considered too indistinct or lacking in any reference to Greece, Edith's area of expertise in which she had an established reading audience. In the summer of 1956, when the manuscript was largely completed, Storer revisited the question of the title. Since Edith was essentially trying to tell the story of how the Athenians had lost their freedom, Storer considered the use of words such as "fall" or "decline" in the title, though he worried that readers would hesitate to purchase a book whose title conveyed negative connotations.[97] Ultimately Storer, as he had with Edith's two books on the Bible, agreed to the title she had selected: *The Echo of Greece*. Shortly after the book was published, he wrote her, "I like to think that *The Echo of Greece* is *The Echo of the Greek Way*, and may they reverberate down through the ages!"[98]

Chapter 18

A CITIZEN OF ATHENS

The Echo of Greece was published in early 1957, its arrival announced by the appearance of its first chapter in the January 12 issue of the *Saturday Review*.[1] The book would bring Edith unprecedented success. It immediately became a Book of the Month Club selection and received more critical attention from academic classicists than any of her previous books.[2] In April, she was made an honorary member of the Classical Association of the Atlantic States, only her second experience of recognition by academic classicists.[3] But the new book brought her international fame as well. In the summer of 1957, she would travel to Greece as a guest of its government to take part in a Delphic festival during which her translation of *Prometheus Bound* would be performed in the ancient theater of Herodes Atticus in Athens. She would be made an honorary citizen of Athens and receive the Gold Cross of the Legion of Benefaction from King Paul. For Edith, it would be a year of triumph mixed with some regret, a feeling she often experienced after the completion of a book.

It was also a year that began quietly, in bed, as ten days before Christmas Edith had slipped on one of her daily walks, and, as she explained to her New York friend Elinore Blaisdell, hit a metal bar that hung over the sidewalk. The result was a broken pelvis. To Elinore she confided her irritation that everyone subsequently told her how lucky she had been, that the accident could have been worse.[4] She was cheered, however, by John Mason Brown's playful admonition to "leave that pelvis stuff to Elvis."[5] To combat the danger of pneumonia, she was encouraged to move about in a wheel chair, and she was able to enjoy the winter sunshine coming into the sitting room, decorated with plants and flowers sent by well-wishers. But she was warned that at her age it might take some time for the bone to knit. By the end of January, she was still largely bedridden, though she told Vail Motter, "By now I am almost mended and expect to be walking in two or three weeks. And I have had a very pleasant convalescence."[6] Huntington, visiting her in early January, was delighted to find her cheerful and vibrant despite the wheelchair, and by the end of the month he brought philosophy professor Mircea Eliade for a brief visit to 2448. When Huntington introduced her to the British poet Cecil Day-Lewis in March, Edith was in fine intellectual form, conversing eagerly with her visitor.[7] By April, she was well enough to receive guests at a small party Doris held just before they traveled to New York City.[8]

Storer was pleased with the sales of the book, which was heavily advertised in the *Saturday Review,* whose subscribers, he felt, were one of Edith's primary audiences. By February, the initial printing of four thousand copies had sold out. He had to order a second printing of two thousand copies and was hopeful that he would soon have to order a third.[9]

One key difference in the critical reception of *The Echo of Greece* from Edith's earlier books was the relatively large number of academic classicists who reviewed the volume in popular publications, generally praising it. Acceptance from classical scholars had begun with her invitation to Wellesley in March 1950, but now Richmond Lattimore, professor of Greek at Bryn Mawr College, suggested in his review in the *New York Times* that classical scholars could benefit from reading her book. Impressed by Edith's writing style, Lattimore wrote, "Time and again difficult thoughts come through with this lucid force. She writes for a general public, but experts can learn from her too."[10] He could fault only Edith's ignoring of some of the cruel acts, such as mass executions, which could be attributed to the ancient Greeks, a criticism also made by the Brown University classical scholar C. A. Robinson Jr., who reviewed it for the *Saturday Review.* Robinson, though writing that the book was "no unadulterated eulogy of Greece," felt that in the conclusion

her distinction between the Greek and Roman ways of execution (poisoning versus crucifixion) served only to downplay the cruelty of the
Greeks at the expense of the Romans. Still, Robinson recognized the
contemporary message of the book: the need for individuals to preserve
freedom by fully exercising citizenship. Like Lattimore, he also connected her to the world of academic classicists by pointing to her formal
education in the field, calling her "a jewel in the crown of Bryn Mawr
College, her alma mater."[11] While Edith felt that too many critics ignored the parallels she had tried to construct between the ancient Greek
political experience and that of twentieth-century America, classical
scholars such as Robinson and Moses Hadas, the Columbia University
professor who reviewed the book in the *New York Herald Tribune*, did
not.[12] Soon to publish his own book on the Hellenistic period, Hadas
praised *The Echo of Greece* as "edifying and informing" and devoted
much of his review to the opening chapters about the Greeks' loss of
freedom. Hadas, for whom teaching soldiers returning from the Second
World War had been a formative experience, was receptive to Edith's
discussion of how highly the "Greeks regarded freedom and the civic
responsibility which is its concomitant."[13]

Published reviews by academic classicists were both more plentiful
for *The Echo of Greece* and more favorable than for any of her previous
books, because in the postwar world classical scholars now understood
that their discipline's future would have to include students who could
not read Greek or Latin but who were nevertheless curious about the
ancient world and its significance for the modern one. In the mid-1950s,
American classical scholars found a new role in universities, teaching
classical civilization courses rather than languages. Such courses were
dependent on the many fine translations of classical works, such as
those by classical scholars Robert Fitzgerald and Richmond Lattimore,
which had become available and which were now finding acceptance
among classical scholars. Their popularity contrasted to Edith's experience in the 1920s, when she had encountered resistance to the idea of
translation from academic classicists. By the fifties, translations formed
the basis for many classical civilization courses that encouraged students to compare the experiences of ancient Greek and Roman societies

with their own. Edith contributed to the classical civilization curriculum through her books and translations. One classical scholar, W. Robert Connor, has even argued that the 1950s witnessed a "modest classical renaissance" in which classicists began to play a role in the "public realm," factors that contributed to the attention Edith began to receive from academic classical scholars.[14]

In the wake of the publication of *The Echo of Greece*, Edith received a complimentary letter from Werner Jaeger. He, too, acknowledged Edith's academic training but also her "deep and genuine love of the classical world of Greece and Rome," which, he felt, "has inspired thousands of grateful readers with sympathy and admiration for the great ancients which you are presenting to our contemporaries with so much eloquence and human warmth." Remembering the review Edith had published of his *Paideia* in the *New York Times*, he told her that he felt she understood his work and that he, too, saw the fourth century "as a highly problematic age resembling our own situation in more than one respect."[15] With her study of how the Athenians had lost their democratic freedoms, Edith had demonstrated the relevance of the ancient Greek experience to the Cold War world, making an argument for the continuing study of classics that academics recognized as one that could be useful in attracting students to their field.

It was an argument that resulted in another sign of acceptance from academic classicists. That April she was made an honorary member of the Classical Association of the Atlantic States and invited to deliver an address at their meeting at Columbia University.[16] Before departing for New York, Edith read her paper to a gathering of eighteen to twenty friends, what Doris termed "a little group of serious thinkers," whom she had invited to 2448, including Huntington and Florence as well as Senator Flanders and his wife Helen.[17] They formed an attentive audience as Edith read an address, simply titled "The Classics," which was intended to fit the theme of the convention, "Classics and the Related Disciplines in American Education." Doris noted that Edith, testing the speech for length, spoke without notes, having completely memorized it, as she would with her speech in Athens later that year. Indeed, a journalist who interviewed her in New York City for the *New Yorker* used

Edith's careful timing of her speech as the title of the article that followed: "Nineteen and a Half Minutes."[18]

The talk drew from *The Echo of Greece*, continuing the theme of the importance of classical education in a democracy. Addressing an audience of classicists, she recalled her Baltimore friendship with Basil Lanneau Gildersleeve and paid tribute to Sir Richard Livingstone, the Oxford scholar whose influence had been apparent in *The Greek Way*.[19] The talk introduced themes that would become common in Edith's public lectures and writing in the last years of her life. She told a story about Gildersleeve, relating that the classicist had claimed that the greatest compliment he ever received was from a student who said that he gained so much enjoyment from the use of his mind. Edith repeated it a number of times as she spoke to Washington's Institute for Contemporary Arts in January 1958 and in an essay she wrote for the *Saturday Evening Post*.[20] The frequency with which Edith told this story during these years was due to the new emphasis she placed on the subject of education. It was one she had addressed at length in *The Echo of Greece* with its chapters on "The Schools of Athens" and "The School Teachers: Isocrates, Plato, and Aristotle."

The aims and purpose of education would become more frequent subjects in Edith's writings and lectures after the Soviet launch of *Sputnik*, when she would become a vocal opponent of education as a means of defeating the Russians militarily. In her address to the Classical Association of the Atlantic States, however, she was already arguing for the continuing study of Greek and Latin in the atomic age. Only the study of the ancient languages, she told her audience, produced the clarity of mind needed to meet the challenges of the Cold War world, including the maintenance of political freedom. The citation for her honorary membership invoked *The Greek Way*'s use of Matthew Arnold's phrase "mind and spirit" as it praised the clarity of her writing and her impact in creating interest in the classical world as the basis of Western civilization. It did not identify Edith as a classical scholar but called her "creative and artistic," words that were likely to please her.[21] Still, she was all too aware of what she identified as the faults of her recent book.

To Edith, *The Echo of Greece* was, she told Huntington, "so far and away my poorest book." Almost immediately after its publication, she was filled with regret, especially after discovering a sentence in which she had erroneously written that Plato never mentioned Aristotle.[22] It appeared in chapter four, in which she discussed the relationship between the two philosophers who had been teacher and student at Plato's Academy. While Aristotle had written appreciatively about his former teacher after his death, Edith wrote, "What Plato thought about him is far from clear. He never in any of his writings mentioned his name."[23] Her discovery of the sentence prompted her to tell Huntington privately that it had been "hubris" to "write a book at my age."[24] She felt the need to confess to him, but, otherwise, in the face of the work's enormous success, she largely kept her mistake a secret, especially from Doris, who felt deep pride in her accomplishments. Besides Huntington, she told only Werner Jaeger, to whom she apologized.

In the letter he had written to Edith praising *The Echo of Greece*, Jaeger had indicated his approval of the discussion—concerning Aristotle's intellectual influence on Plato—that followed the errant sentence. If Jaeger had noticed the mistake, he did not dwell on it. He instead agreed with Edith that in fact the student had influenced the teacher, though it was difficult to discern exactly how and to what extent, given that many other students had also participated in the intellectual discussions at the Academy.[25] The error did not damage the book's reputation even with academic classicists nor did it lessen Huntington's assessment of her as an accurate scholar.[26] Edith also felt that she might have been mistaken in including the book's final chapter, "The Greek and Roman Way," which had received additional editing. Brooks Atkinson reassured her by telling her that the "idea that the church followed the Roman Way instead of the Greek way is an essential link in spiritual history." He added: "You have fortified my distaste for organized religion by distinguishing between the church and the Christian ideal."[27]

The book was warmly received in her Washington social circle, where comparisons between the political experiences of ancient Greece and twentieth-century America had long been made. Marcella Miller du Pont told Edith that she would doubtless reread the book many times in the future and wrote effusively: "The lucidity of your style and the grandeur of your subject-matter (which you know how to bring home to each of us, however small we may feel) take the book to you, again and again for sustenance."[28] Farther afield, Edith's Maine acquaintance, the poet Hortense Flexner King, also wrote to praise the volume. A niece of Dr. Simon Flexner, Hortense had attended Bryn Mawr College and subsequently published several volumes of poetry, often evoking the beauty of Sutton Island, where she spent her summers, just across the Western Way from Mount Desert.[29] Edith especially prized her critique of *The Echo of Greece*, feeling that the poet had understood the essential aim of the book, to explore the similarities of Greece's position after its victory in the Persian Wars to the United States' emergence as a superpower after the Second World War.[30] Otherwise, Edith professed some puzzlement over the critical reception of the book, telling Vail Motter that while she was pleased by the book's positive reception she did not understand her critics' basis for awarding praise or blame.[31]

The book's meditation on the need to maintain vigilantly democratic freedoms also held significance for the modern state of Greece. The emergence of a fragile democracy in the nation in the 1950s ultimately resulted in Edith receiving the greatest honor of her life: Greek recognition of her achievements. Early in 1957, Edith received a telephone call from the Broadway producer James E. Elliott, inviting her to join him and a company of actors who were to perform her translation of *Prometheus Bound* at a Delphic festival, which, despite its name, was to be held in the city of Athens that summer. This was quickly followed by a formal invitation from the Greek actor George Bourlos, who had participated in the Delphic festivals produced by Eva Palmer Sikelianos and her husband Angelos Sikelianos thirty years previously.[32] The planned festival was intended to celebrate the reestablishment of Greek democracy after a long period of warfare. It was to be sponsored by the government of Constantine Karamanlis, a center-right politician who had become prime minister in 1956. He enjoyed the support of President Eisenhower, whose administration viewed him as a reformer.[33]

Both the Truman and Eisenhower administrations had watched events in postwar Greece closely as, with U.S. aid, it became the only

Balkan nation to escape Communist rule following the Second World War. During the fifties it was emerging from decades of turmoil, including Nazi occupation and a civil war that had ended with the defeat of the Communists in 1949.[34] In its wake, President Truman had initiated American efforts to preserve the fragile peace in the nation. Greece became dependent on the United States for military aid, help that had been supported by the Republican senator from Massachusetts, Henry Cabot Lodge Jr., among others.[35] In early 1952, Greece adopted a new constitution that, mindful of the recent civil war, allowed for oppressive measures to be taken in the event of a national emergency but still ensured many civil liberties.[36] That same year, Karamanlis, who had already served in several cabinets, was invited to spend three months in the United States.

After his return to Greece, the U.S. ambassador to the country, John Peurifoy, continued to view him in a positive light. In 1955, the United States expressed support for a Karamanlis government. But it was not until early the following year that he and his newly formed political party, the National Radical Union, were able to win a plurality of the popular vote and form a government. It was the first Greek government to include a woman, Lina Tsaldari, who became minister of social welfare, an appointment that contributed to Karamanlis's reputation as a supporter of women's political rights. The new prime minister was also sometimes described as a political leader "deeply conscious of history," recognizing the symbolic importance of Greece as the birthplace of Western democracy. His wife, Amalia, was interested in arts and culture and was credited with introducing her husband to theater.[37] In 1957, the Karamanlis government decided to sponsor a Delphic festival that would highlight Greece's contributions to world culture.

The close connection between the U.S. and Greek governments was evident as the festival was planned. James E. Elliott, who had built his reputation on staging the plays of his friend Tennessee Williams, had hatched the plan to bring an American company to Athens to perform a Greek tragedy at the festival. He had convinced the State Department and the American National Theater and Academy (ANTA), which had received a congressional charter in 1935, to sponsor the effort, along with

the Greek Ministry of Education. After reading a number of translations, Elliott had settled on Edith's *Prometheus Bound* to perform in Athens.[38] The Delphic Festival of 1957 would thus link American democracy
to its ancient Greek roots, just as it would celebrate Greece's reestablishment of democracy after years of warfare.

In June, the upcoming festival was officially announced when the
Greek Ministry of Education and ANTA publicized their plans to produce Edith's translation of *Prometheus Bound* on the stage of the second-
century Roman-built theater of Herodes Atticus, at the base of the
Acropolis in Athens. At the same time, the Greek government announced that it would recognize Edith for creating interest in ancient
Greek culture by making her an honorary citizen of Athens. Edith and
Doris were to sail aboard the *Queen Frederica* with the cast and crew of
the production in July 1957, initially on the eleventh but, when the festival's dates were altered, on the twenty-first.[39]

As the day of departure drew near, Edith's anticipation grew. "God
bless you for making this chance possible for me" were her words of
greeting to James E. Elliott and George Bourlos when they called at
Massachusetts Avenue soon after the official announcement had been
made.[40] They took her to tea at the Greek Embassy, where she was introduced to the ambassador, George Melas. After these preliminaries,
there was just enough time, Edith and Doris felt, to spend two weeks at
Seawall before their original sailing date, a journey made more desirable
by the breakdown of the air conditioning in the Washington house in
the middle of the month.[41]

As Edith and Doris prepared to depart for Greece, their friends
helped to celebrate Edith's achievement. Some would even join them
on their trip abroad. Before their departure, Elizabeth Cabot Lodge,
their Massachusetts Avenue neighbor, presented Edith with the gold
lamé cloak she would wear on stage the night *Prometheus Bound* was
performed.[42] Her son was no longer in the Senate, but the Lodge family
took a personal interest in the Delphic Festival's celebration of the
establishment of Greek democracy. Edith had worried about what to
wear on the night of the performance and friends such as Lucia Valentine, wife of the college president Alan Valentine, had offered her advice,

suggesting that she wear a simple black dress with something more elaborate over it, such as a black scarf with silver embroidery, an idea Edith adopted upon receiving the gold lamé cloak from Mrs. Lodge.[43] Storer planned a bon voyage party for Edith aboard the *Queen Frederica* on the night of its departure, July 20, 1957. Dorian and his family came to see Edith and Doris off, and the party attracted many guests.[44] Several of their friends sailed with them, including Elling, Alida Milliken, and Sir George Paget Thomson. Other friends, Rosamond, Francesca, and Storer, would meet them in Athens.[45]

As an ANTA production, the cast of *Prometheus Bound* included actors who had long been involved in theatrical politics, among them the president of the organization, actor Clarence Derwent, who was also to serve as artistic director for the production, and the actress Blanche Yurka, an organizer and leader of Actors' Equity Association. The English-born Derwent had begun his career on the stage in 1902.[46] In 1927, he had appeared in two of Margaret Anglin's productions of the *Electra* of Sophocles. He praised Anglin's abilities as a director and credited her with creating interest in ancient Greek drama.[47] Just a few months before his departure for Athens, he had been elected president of Actors' Equity, a role in which he had become an enthusiastic supporter of cultural exchange. That May, he testified before a U.S. Senate subcommittee, arguing for more federal funding for the arts.[48] He was also likely partly responsible for the choice of actress Margaret Phillips for the cast of *Prometheus Bound*, since, ten years earlier, she had been the recipient of a Derwent Award, an acting honor he had created and endowed for the New York stage.[49]

During the voyage, Edith befriended the cast and crew, especially Blanche Yurka, who was to play the role of Io.[50] Twenty years younger than Edith, Yurka had achieved critical acclaim for her interpretations of Ibsen heroines on the New York stage in the 1920s. In the following decade she had played the title roles in the *Lysistrata* of Aristophanes and the *Electra* of Sophocles.[51] The former production had been praised by New York critics, in part for its strikingly simple sets designed by Norman Bel Geddes. Yurka's interpretation of the role of Electra in 1932, however, had been treated harshly by many critics, including

Edith's friends Brooks Atkinson and John Mason Brown. Yurka had introduced more realism into her portrayal of Electra, a style that New York critics of the thirties felt was inappropriate to ancient Greek tragedy.[52] Yurka's characterization of Electra anticipated later twentieth-century performances of the tragedy. She believed in the use of classical drama as a means of understanding contemporary events. Of Czech descent herself, she had played Hecuba in an NBC radio production of *The Trojan Women* broadcast just after Hitler had annexed Sudetenland in 1938.[53]

Edith and Yurka formed a lasting friendship. As the two women conversed during the voyage, they discovered that they had many friends in common in the New York theatrical community. Yurka knew Norris Houghton and had appeared under Lee Simonson's direction. She amused Edith by recounting some of her experiences in the theater. The women also shared a love of Maine, where Yurka sometimes spent her summers. In her autobiography, Yurka referred to her performance as Io in *Prometheus Bound* as "playing a heifer" (the word Edith had used for Io in *Mythology*) but she ultimately settled on an interpretation of the role that pleased Edith. To Yurka, Io was the "Eternal Artist," burdened with "genius which gives no rest, no lasting peace of mind to its possessor."[54] Doris recalled that it was Yurka who was given the seemingly delicate task of approaching Edith concerning some necessary cuts in the play but found that Edith, to her surprise, agreed to them with alacrity.[55]

Edith and Yurka had also both been friends with Eva Palmer Sikelianos, who had died in Athens in 1952 while another festival, at which *Prometheus Bound* was performed, was being held at Delphi.[56] She had been given a state funeral and had been buried, appropriately, at Delphi. Edith and Eva had sometimes crossed paths in the years after their mutual work for Greek war relief. In 1944, Eva had sought and received Edith's permission to use her translation in a proposed production of *Prometheus Bound*. After Eva's death, Edith had counted herself and the weaver Mary Crovatt Hambidge as among the "sincerest mourners" for Eva. She had asked Hambidge to send her any accounts she had heard of Eva's last days.[57] During Edith's time in Athens in 1957, she tactfully told Eva's Greek friends that she had come to Greece to honor Eva's memory.[58]

Even though it was Edith's translation of *Prometheus Bound* that was being performed, and Edith who was being honored by the Greek government, Eva's groundbreaking work in the revival of Greek tragedy was evident in the 1957 production. When the Greek actor George Bourlos had first invited Edith to come to Athens for the performance he had described it as being held in honor of the thirtieth anniversary of the first modern Delphic Festival.[59] Bourlos, who would play Prometheus in the 1957 performance, had been discovered and trained for the role by Eva for the earlier productions.[60] The music that would accompany the performance would be Byzantine in style, another debt to Eva, who had argued that Byzantine music was the closest to that of ancient Greece.[61] Some of the costumes that would be worn in the 1957 performance had been handwoven by Eva and her assistants for the previous festivals. They were retrieved for the occasion from Athens's Benaki Museum, where they had been deposited after Eva's death.[62] Eva's legacy was therefore evident in the performance that honored Edith, a circumstance Edith recognized and readily accepted.

Upon their arrival in Greece, Edith and Doris met Rosamond and Francesca and embarked on a six-day motor trip around the country to revisit many of the places Edith and Doris had seen in 1929.[63] Their itinerary included Olympia and, for the others, the great amphitheater at Epidaurus, though Edith was tired and stayed at the hotel during the latter.[64] After visiting Delphi, the party lingered for several days at a home owned by friends of Rosamond's that overlooked the Aegean, a view that inspired Edith to begin writing the speech she would have to give before the performance of *Prometheus Bound*.[65] Their final visit was to Nauplia, from which they drove back to Athens, stopping at Mycenae, where more ancient tombs had recently been discovered. Edith regretted that both the heat in Greece that summer and their lack of reservations—the country was full of tourists—made it impossible to consider a journey to Rhodes or a cruise among the Greek islands.[66]

Once in Athens, Edith met Storer, who had just arrived by airplane, and she found her hotel room filled with flowers from, among others,

Huntington and Florence. She enjoyed the customary routine of a Greek day, with its afternoon rest and dinner at nine in the evening or later, all of which she found "very sensible."[67] The weather in Athens, however, was like that in the rest of Greece—uncomfortably hot, though air-conditioned rooms at her hotel, the Grande-Bretagne, where she and Doris had stayed in 1929, provided some relief. Blanche Yurka recalled that the cast rehearsed outdoors only after sunset, a practice that allowed them to witness the beauty of the Parthenon by moonlight.[68]

Edith faced a constant round of interviews with various members of the press, which she endured with a nagging feeling that the journalists were only interested in her approaching ninetieth birthday.[69] She did, however, welcome a visit from the women writers of Athens on August 2, and she was impressed by their intelligence and their fluency in English. But her hearing impairment made it difficult for her to understand anything spoken with an accent, and Doris had to repeat many of the questions the women asked.[70] Soon after her arrival in Athens, Edith was introduced to cabinet minister Lina Tsaldari. Although the two had to communicate through a translator, Edith found her "a very impressive person."[71] More enjoyable was a surprise meeting with the poet Witter Bynner, with whom she had corresponded about Jean Ingelow's poetry.[72] Most pleasing of all, on August 5, 1957, the mayor of Athens, Pafsanias Katsotas, and the city council officially voted to make Edith an honorary citizen of Athens. "You know I am absurdly pleased" was her comment to her sisters in Hadlyme.[73]

As an event with political implications, the Delphic Festival was the subject of controversy among Karamanlis's political opponents. Political wrangling had evidently caused the dates of the festival, and thus the performance of *Prometheus Bound*, to be altered. Originally to have taken place on July 23, the performance occurred over two weeks later, on August 8, 1957.[74] The question of the festival's cost was raised when it was revealed that the Greek American opera singer Maria Callas had asked for the sum of nine thousand dollars for her appearance on the opening night, August 3.[75] The public outcry was such that Callas was afraid to perform on the night she had originally been scheduled, claiming illness. When she was convinced to sing two nights later, on August 5,

Edith and Doris attended, having been given tickets.[76] This gave Edith an opportunity to see the theater of Herodes Atticus at night with a full audience, conditions that would be repeated just a few nights later when she would give her speech before the performance of *Prometheus Bound*. She was not impressed with Callas but found the crowd's enthusiastic response to the singer thrilling. This eased Edith's fears, as one of the objections to the festival raised by Karamanlis's opponents was that an American company was performing an ancient Greek play.[77]

The political controversy meant that Edith would not meet any members of the Greek royal family. King Paul had succeeded his brother George II ten years before, but the Greek monarchy was still unpopular, having only been restored in 1946.[78] It was necessary, Edith understood, for the royal family to "hold aloof" from any political controversy and avoid showing favor to the Karamanlis government by participating in any of the festival's events.[79] King Paul bestowed the Gold Cross of the Legion of Benefaction upon Edith through an intermediary, Achilles Yerocostopoulos, the minister of national education, at a luncheon on the same day as the performance of *Prometheus Bound*.[80] Storer gave a brief speech introducing Edith before she received the medal and scroll awarded by King Paul. She in turn presented inscribed leather-bound copies of her books to be given to the king and queen.[81]

On the night of the performance, August 8, 1957, Edith and Doris were taken to the theater of Herodes Atticus by U.S. Ambassador George Allen and Mayor Katsotas.[82] The city was festive at night, as many of its ancient monuments, including the Parthenon, were illuminated for the first time. Since the 1930s, the American School of Classical Studies at Athens had been excavating the Athenian agora, the civic center of the ancient city. Though work had been disrupted during the war years, soon after peace had been restored the school had resolved to rebuild the Stoa of Attalos on its original site. The ancient marketplace, dating from the Hellenistic period, had been completely rebuilt and dedicated as a museum the year before the Delphic Festival took place. Those attending the festival could be reminded of Athens's democratic past by seeing the completely excavated agora and other Athenian monuments, including the Stoa of Attalos and the Temple of Zeus, illuminated by night.[83] Upon their arrival, Doris was instructed to take her seat in the front row, where she noted with satisfaction that the theater was nearly full. She was anxious, however, as she waited for Edith to make her appearance. Finally, Edith was led onto the stage on the arm of the ambassador and accompanied by Education Minister Yerocostopoulos and Mayor Katsotas. Doris cried as Edith received a standing ovation, which she acknowledged after Allen whispered to her, "Bow, Miss Hamilton, bow."[84] As Edith acknowledged the audience, Doris felt a sense of satisfaction that Edith had been welcomed with as much enthusiasm as Maria Callas a few nights before. Yerocostopoulos made a brief speech in Greek, and Mayor Katsotas presented her with a scroll, thus making her an honorary citizen of the city, a gesture to which the crowd responded with an enormous round of applause. After receiving the scroll, it was Edith's turn to make a speech.

It was succinct, lasting only three minutes. Edith, as usual, had carefully timed it and provided *Prometheus Bound* with an interpretation that fit the theme of the Delphic Festival and its celebration of Greece as an emerging democracy. She began by exclaiming, "I am a citizen of Athens, of the city I have for so long loved as much as I love my own country. This is the proudest moment of my life." Her statement received a loud roar of approval from the audience. She then went on to address the themes of the Delphic Festival itself. Prometheus was "the great rebel against tyranny." She continued by returning to the ideas of the opening chapters of *The Echo of Greece*: "It is most fitting that he should be presented to the world now, in this period of the world's history, and here, in the city of Athens. For Athens, truly the mother of beauty and of thought, is also the mother of freedom. Freedom was a Greek discovery. The Greeks were the first free nation in the world."[85] Short in duration, it was nevertheless memorable. Storer, describing her speech, wrote that she spoke "slowly, deliberately, and with the simple gestures of an old pro" and "uttered one of the most graceful and pointed brief statements I have ever heard."[86]

Although she felt her legs shaking as she began her address, to those who listened, including Blanche Yurka, it seemed that her "voice carried perfectly in that open-air theatre, as clearly as a violin." Yurka recalled

FIGURE 15. Edith Hamilton on the stage of the Theater of Herodes Atticus in August 1957, when she was made an honorary citizen of Athens. Photograph by James Whitmore for *Life* magazine. Shutterstock.

that Edith looked "marvelous standing there in her pretty evening gown and cloak."[87] Storer thought Edith showed "great dignity looking so very distinguished and really quite beautiful."[88] Elling echoed such sentiments. As late as 1973, he could still remember that night, describing Edith as "a slight elegant figure" speaking on the stage of the Herodes Atticus theater with the "Acropolis humping darkly above."[89] Doris enjoyed recounting to Alice and Margaret how "her speech was superb. It was just stunning. It came from her heart. Her voice was strong and clear. She looked extraordinarily handsome and really noble. She always speaks well but I have never seen her or heard her perform like that."[90] As profuse as Doris's praise was, Anna Antoniades, a former American vice consul in Athens, who had only briefly corresponded with Edith, thought her speech was easily the most memorable part of the evening. She told Edith's friend Mary Crovatt Hambidge, "Edith Hamilton was magnificent. The greatest moment of the evening was when she stood alone, straight as a reed before the microphone, her arms spread out low and said, 'This is the proudest moment of my life.'" Antoniades thought that the "walls of the old theater would crumble with the vibration of the applause."[91]

Brief as it was, Edith's speech proved to be the highlight of the evening. The performance of *Prometheus Bound* itself was a failure. It could not overcome the awkwardness of producer Elliott's decision to stage the play simultaneously in two languages, with Bourlos speaking his lines in Greek and the other cast members in English. Both Edith and Doris claimed that they knew before the performance that such an unusual means of presentation would never be effective. Edith felt the play was "half read and half acted" and "foredoomed to failure."[92] Anna Antoniades was among the many who found the use of two different languages distracting. *New York Times* reporter A. C. Sedgwick, of whom Edith was fond, commented that "sophisticated Athenians sat quietly but later professed to have been bored."[93] Mindful of the criticisms, the cast and crew of *Prometheus Bound* openly praised Edith's performance. At a press conference in Athens the following day, Blanche Yurka said, "If we had known what Miss Hamilton could do we would have put her last. Anyone would have been flat after her. In short, gentlemen, she stole the show."[94]

The speech also brought Edith to the attention of the U.S. Information Agency, which would later call on her to speak on Voice of America. Their Athens office placed an eight-foot-high photograph of Edith in their window, making her recognizable to Athenians as she walked down the street during the remainder of her stay. The day after the speech, Edith had to be extricated by police from a crowd outside the U.S. Information Service that had recognized her from the photograph.[95] The morning after the performance, the U.S. Embassy sent a tape recorder to Edith's hotel to have her make a recording of her speech, to be translated into Greek and played on Greek radio. This permanent record of the speech, though not a completely accurate replication of the one the previous evening, nevertheless made it possible to publish the speech in the *Saturday Review* the following October.[96]

On August 9, Edith's last afternoon in Athens, she had one final encounter with the legacy of Eva Palmer Sikelianos when she received two visitors in her rooms at the Grande-Bretagne. Both Anna Antoniades and Angeliki Hatzimihali had been friends of Eva's. Hatzimihali was a folklorist who had organized the displays of Greek handicrafts that had been exhibited at the two earlier Delphic festivals.[97] The purpose of the women's visit was to ask Edith if she would write an introduction to Eva's unpublished autobiography, the manuscript of which was in Antoniades's possession. To the disappointment of both women, Edith flatly refused.[98]

Edith gave as her reason that she had not known Eva well enough, despite sharing with the women memories of Eva's years at Bryn Mawr College. Edith and Eva, however, had been out of touch from the 1890s, when Eva had left college, until 1935, when their correspondence began. Although Edith's letters to Eva often contained discussions on such matters as translation, they also contained frequent inquiries as to Eva's whereabouts and health, indicating Edith's lack of knowledge of these matters.[99] Edith also stated—truthfully—that she was already planning another book with her publisher and had to concentrate her energies on her new manuscript. Antoniades later told Mary Crovatt Hambidge, however, that that afternoon she had felt that Edith and Eva "were not on the best of terms" though, in fact, other than a disagreement about the translation of Aristophanes in the early 1930s, the two women had not quarreled.[100]

Edith and Eva had, however, grown apart in their visions of postwar Greece. They had not always disagreed on the subject, even if Edith confessed to Eva's friends that she had found the complete fulfillment of Eva's Delphic idea unrealistic. However, she had expressed agreement with Eva's political writings on Greece as it emerged from fascist occupation and civil war. As the Second World War had drawn to a close, Eva had embarked on a series of polemical writings advocating self-determination for Greece, a subject on which she had written to Edith, among many others. In January 1945, Edith had responded warmly to Eva's pamphlet, *In Defence of Greece*, which made such arguments. Edith found Eva's arguments against British and U.S. intervention in Greece compelling, telling her, "If only, if only we give Greece a clean slate. It will be so shameful if we do not."[101] An isolationist herself, Edith shared Eva's wariness of the United States' growing influence in the postwar world. Eva supported the National Liberation Front, a broad coalition of Greek political parties that included communists. She believed that such a coalition should lead Greece after the war, and decisions such as the future of the Greek monarchy should be made by the Greek people. Eva, however, was ultimately blacklisted as a communist by the House Committee on Un-American Activities for her arguments.[102]

By the time of her own trip to Athens, Edith had accepted some U.S. intervention in postwar Greece and would probably have conceded that it had yielded positive benefits by defeating communism and supporting Constantine Karamanlis and the restoration of democracy. It is not clear, however, that she saw Eva as a communist. In fact, Edith saw Eva as someone who valued the individual as much as she did.[103] Both women had been swept up in the postwar revival of Hellenism that connected ancient Greek democracy with its emergence in modern Greece in the Cold War era.[104] Edith also genuinely praised Eva's staging of the two earlier Delphic festivals, giving her full credit for helping to restore interest in Greek drama. Eva's status as a creative genius probably prevented Edith from seeing her as a communist.[105] Antoniades did not fully comprehend Edith's complex attitudes about Eva, and she did not fully understand the relationship between Edith and Doris, describing Doris as Edith's "secretary or companion." She sensed Doris's protectiveness toward Edith, however, and she felt that Doris definitely opposed Edith writing the introduction. Most likely Doris was against it, preferring Edith to work on her own writing and to avoid taking on too much. Eva's autobiography was not published in the United States until 1993.[106]

That night—Edith's last in Athens—she was to attend a party given by Prime Minister Karamanlis.[107] Instead, she joined her friends who had decided to go up to the Acropolis to see it by the full moon, when the monuments were always kept open. Doris decided to go but expressed surprise when Edith announced her intention of joining them. As Doris explained to Alice and Margaret, "It is a terrific walk, very steep and rough. I did everything I could to talk her out of it. I reminded her it took me over fifteen minutes to get from the bottom up to the Parthenon and it [had] taken her nearly twenty-five. I said moonlight was very tricky and she might miss her step, etc. I might as well have whistled to the wind. We started out at nine o'clock and did not get back till after eleven."[108] Thus, three days before her ninetieth birthday, Edith, determined to enjoy the Parthenon under full moonlight, scaled the Acropolis with Doris and others.

Although there were some disappointments on the trip, Edith felt honored by the awards, and she enjoyed the opportunity to appreciate the beauty of Greece once more. The still fragile state of Greek democracy had prevented her from meeting the royal family, and an honorary degree in classical philosophy from Athens College, which seemed to have been a part of the original plan for her recognition, was not awarded.[109] But upon Edith's return from Greece, the scroll that made her a citizen of Athens and the certificate that stated she had been granted the Gold Cross of the Legion of Benefaction by King Paul were placed in simple identical black rectangular frames that hung over the desk where she sometimes wrote.[110] She became a member of the newly founded Hellenic-American Union, which hoped to further foster cultural ties between the two nations, and *The Greek Way* was translated and published in modern Greek.[111]

Edith was also aware of the effect of the enormous publicity she had received upon the sales of her books. This was, in fact, the question that had been uppermost on her mind when Storer had arrived in Athens for the festivities.[112] For Storer, the Greek recognition of Edith's accomplishments was the "high point" of his publishing career. He told Doris, "Our world is better for Edith's valiant performance throughout."[113] He saw the results of Edith's appearance in Athens in the sales figures both immediately and later that year. He informed Doris that 1,300 copies of her books had been purchased in 1956, but that 12,000 copies of her works had been sold by September 1957 alone, including copies of her two latest books, *The Echo of Greece* and *Witness to The Truth*.[114] Moreover, soon upon arriving back in the United States, Edith learned that the Book of the Month Club was releasing a special edition boxed set of *The Greek Way* and *The Echo of Greece*, which subsequently sold well and for which she credited John Mason Brown, a judge for the club.[115]

For Doris, the trip had been one of both delight and responsibility. Anna Antoniades understood Doris's caution that Edith not tire herself too much in the whirlwind of social engagements and press interviews that filled their days in Athens. Antoniades noted that Doris "was constantly hovering over her like a mother hen, and managed to get her out of every party, meeting, gathering as quickly as possible."[116] Yet Doris's delight in the recognition Edith received was apparent. Describing the attention Edith had garnered outside the offices of the U.S. Information Service, Doris told Alice and Margaret, "I knew Edith would be somewhat 'featured' on this trip, but I certainly had not anticipated anything like this."[117] Both Alice, from afar, and Doris, at Edith's side, tried hard to convince Edith to travel back to the United States by boat, believing it would be far more relaxing. Edith, however, was anxious to go home and insisted on flying, hoping for a brief stay at Hadlyme before making the journey to Seawall. Doris enlisted Alice's aid in persuading Edith to at least forgo Hadlyme to avoid any delay in reaching the relaxing environment of Maine.

Edith and Doris flew to New York City, where Edith immediately gave an interview to the *New York Herald Tribune* before they departed for Seawall. There, Edith's ninetieth birthday was celebrated quietly, with Florence Cairns telephoning a message of birthday wishes. Enjoying the peaceful atmosphere that always helped to revive her, Edith told the Cairnses: "My active life has been confined to lying on the rocks and watching the tide. I find that an entrancing occupation." She much preferred the climate of Maine to that of Greece and continued: "Always in the wind is a suggestion that it has passed over a few icebergs not too far away, and I love that."[118] At the age of ninety, she had reached the height of her fame.

Chapter 19

A YEAR WITH PLATO

Edith's status as an honorary citizen of Athens brought her even wider recognition. Soon after her return from Greece, she was elected to the American Academy of Arts and Letters, a more exclusive body than the National Institute of Arts and Letters to which she already belonged.[1] She became a familiar figure to the American public as she appeared in popular magazines and on network television. Two years later, she was invited to the inauguration of President John F. Kennedy. And later in 1961, she sat for fashion photographer Richard Avedon for the pages of *Harper's Bazaar*.[2]

Edith's role as an advocate for the continuing study of the classical world reached its height in the last five years of her life. Her efforts were inspired in part by the Soviet launching of the satellite *Sputnik* on October 4, 1957, shortly after her return from Greece. The event alarmed Americans, who began to feel that their country was lagging behind the Soviet Union technologically, and it sparked numerous calls for greater emphasis on science education, ultimately resulting in the passage of the National Defense Education Act the following year.[3] Edith, however, objected to education as a means of defeating the Soviets, views she expressed in newspaper interviews, a public lecture, and in an essay she wrote for the *Saturday Evening Post*.[4] In the aftermath of *Sputnik*, she spoke and wrote more often on the goals and methods of education. Always a strong individualist, Edith did not believe that the state could effectively compel any individual behavior or create any real consensus in society. Education reforms such as those following *Sputnik* only resulted in a standardization of minds that was superficial and, at its worst, could act to suppress individual thought.

After her return from Greece, Edith's thoughts turned to Plato, the philosopher whose dialogues, particularly those in which Socrates had been the chief speaker, had demonstrated the Greek ability to strive for clarity of thought. By doing so he had educated the Athenians, encouraging them to seek knowledge of the good. The ancient Greeks, she argued, had achieved the proper balance between the individual and the community through their philosophic search for universal laws in nature and society. In this balance, ancient Greeks experienced liberty through service to the community. It was up to the individual to exercise responsibility and self-restraint in political life. In the challenge the United States faced after *Sputnik*, it was essential to maintain individual freedom, not by the state controlling its citizens' behavior but by individuals choosing to participate in their society. By early October 1957 she had told Storer that she planned to write a book on the philosopher that she would title *Plato: An Interpretation*, an idea to which Storer responded with enthusiasm.[5]

As Edith settled into life in Washington that fall, Huntington noted that she was in a lively mood, busily contemplating her proposed book. Soon, however, he was drawing her into a project of his own: the creation of a single volume of translations of all the Platonic dialogues. As a result, 1958 would be what Edith termed her "year with Plato" in which she not only selected the translations to be used in the book but also wrote introductions to each of the dialogues.[6] Her work on the book, however, would stretch into 1960, and the volume would not appear in print until October 1961, when it was published by the Bollingen Foundation as *The Collected Dialogues of Plato*.[7] As Edith continued to experience commercial success as a writer, she came to accept, she told her friend Alan Valentine, that "I am a popularizer, not a scholar."[8] From 1958, however, she was engaged in the most academic work she would ever produce, reaching a far smaller audience than her previous books. *The Collected Dialogues of Plato* was her enduring contribution to classical scholarship. It remains in print and is still the only single volume of Plato translations in English.

Huntington had conceived the idea for the book as Edith had made her journey to Athens. Huntington was still a trustee of Paul Mellon's Bollingen Foundation, and he concluded that the absence of Plato on the Bollingen Foundation's list of publications was a glaring one.[9] Hoping for an academic classicist to edit the work, Huntington first turned to Werner Jaeger at Harvard, who initially agreed to select the translations. Huntington immediately compiled a bibliography of recent translations of Plato. But privately he had already developed reservations about Jaeger. Huntington wanted to produce the volume quickly. When in October 1957 Jaeger agreed to take on the project, he conceded that it would take years for him to complete the work.[10] When, the following month, Jaeger informed Huntington that he did not think he could take on the task, Huntington was almost relieved, and he turned immediately to Edith.[11] One editor at Bollingen later noted that Jaeger at sixty-nine felt too old to take on a task Edith began at the age of ninety.[12]

In fact, Edith was reluctant to take on the project when Huntington first broached the idea. Key to convincing Edith to take on the work, Huntington felt, was to admit that their goal must be attainability, not perfection. Though he had hoped for an academic classicist to take on the work of editor, he was enthusiastic about the prospect of working with Edith, feeling that she would complete her work far more quickly than Jaeger and just as accurately, even without the word-for-word comparison with the ancient Greek text that Jaeger had believed was necessary.[13] Moreover, Huntington felt that her reputation as a translator was well established. He believed that if she was seen as essentially endorsing the translations included in the volume, it would enhance the book's intellectual standing.[14] Once Edith became convinced of the value of a single-volume Plato, she accepted the task and began work immediately.

Early 1958 was devoted largely to the selection of translations to be used in the volume. Huntington gave Edith considerable influence, accepting her choices of translations unless he felt positivism had exercised too great an influence on the translator.[15] Throughout their work on the volume, each of the editors had clearly defined roles, making for a peaceful partnership. While Huntington would write a general introduction to the entire volume and deal with matters such as permission to reprint, Edith's work consisted largely of reading a wide number of translations of the dialogues. She could have read as many as twelve translations of *The Apology* and ten of *The Republic,* working largely from the bibliography of translations that Huntington had compiled, which was thirteen pages long.[16] By February, Edith and Huntington had agreed on translations of eleven of the dialogues.[17]

In reading twentieth-century translations of Plato, Edith was encountering the work of several classical scholars associated with Cambridge University, where, in the late nineteenth century, the study of the later Platonic dialogues from a philosophical, instead of a philological, perspective had produced a wave of translators. The Loeb editions were the other major source of translations of Plato besides the Jowett volumes. As she began work on the selection of the translations, Edith also thumbed through her own copy of Jowett's two-volume *Plato,* with which she had long been familiar and where she had often scribbled marginalia.[18] Ultimately six of his translations were used in Edith and Huntington's volume.

Although Edith had often been seen as ignoring the acceptance of homosexuality among the Greeks, her selection of translations for the Plato volume indicates that she was fully aware of the phenomenon. Indeed, Huntington was warned by his friend James K. Feibleman that Jowett's Victorian moral qualms made some of his work misleading and its inclusion in the Bollingen volume would make the book less useful.[19] Edith would have perceived how homosexuality in ancient Greece was omitted in some of the Plato translations, and she avoided using too many of Jowett's translations in the volume. In the late 1950s, Edith also began to read such authors as Mary Renault and Marguerite Yourcenar, both of whom spent their lives with female partners and used the setting of the ancient world as a safe means of exploring the theme of homosexuality in their fiction. Edith even met Yourcenar when the Belgian-born author and her American partner and translator Grace Frick began paying summer visits to Mount Desert Island during the Second World War. The couple became permanent residents of the island in 1950 when they purchased a white cottage at North East Harbor, which they named Petite Plaisance.[20] Yourcenar became best known for her novel *Memoirs of Hadrian*, an interpretation of the life of the Roman emperor, published in the United States in 1954.[21]

One result of Edith's work with Huntington was an invitation to lecture at the Institute of Contemporary Arts. Founded by the poet Robert Richman, the institute held its lectures at Washington's Museum of Natural History, and its speakers were often scholars whose work was being published by the Bollingen Foundation.[22] Accordingly, Edith gave a lecture titled "Echoes of Greece" at the institute on January 31, 1958. The presentation occurred only a few months after the launch of *Sputnik* and its successor *Sputnik II*, but Edith's lecture boldly objected to "making it the aim of education to defeat the Russians."[23]

Instead, she argued, education was partly for personal pleasure, because it made life more interesting. To her audience, Edith pondered what education had meant to the Greeks and finally concluded that their definition of it was to be drawn into intellectual reflection and debate on a daily basis. The record of Plato's dialogues was of individuals pushed to think abstractly about the good, and to seek truth. The aim of education, Edith exhorted her audience, was not to achieve a comfortable life but to be able to consider what is best for the future good of the state. Edith was not alone in her objections to education as a means of defeating the Soviets, but she stated these more boldly than some of her contemporaries, such as James Conant, a chemist and former president of Harvard University, and Stringfellow Barr, a historian of the classical world and president of St. John's College in Annapolis, where he had established its program in great books.[24]

The audience greeted the end of Edith's lecture with a standing ovation, leaving Doris so overwhelmed by their appreciation that she practically cried. But as members of the audience crowded around Edith, Doris felt some anxiety for her partner, feelings that were noticed by one admiring and perceptive attendee, Mrs. Lorena King Fairbank. She subsequently wrote to Edith, praising her humor and pithy observations. Mrs. Fairbank, however, may have overestimated Doris's anxiety a little. For Edith and Doris, the evening was not over. At home, friends awaited to celebrate the successful lecture.[25]

Doris's retirement, as well as Edith's increasing royalty income, allowed the couple more opportunity for travel, and in April 1958 they journeyed to Spain with Rosamond and Francesca.[26] Edith enjoyed good health and reveled in the natural beauty of coastal Spain, indulging, Doris later reported to Huntington and Florence, in "baskets of wild strawberries, quarts of wine and lobsters."[27] On the voyage home, however, Doris became concerned about Edith's health, as she experienced digestive upset and consequent weight loss. Alarmed, she blamed Edith's diet while in Spain. Once they arrived back in the United States, Doris arranged a flight to Seawall, with her car to be driven up later.[28]

By July, Edith had recovered and begun work on the introductions to the dialogues. That summer she would also be interviewed for an episode of the NBC television series *Wisdom*, which featured half-hour interviews with prominent figures from a variety of fields.[29] It would be Edith's second appearance on television, having been interviewed by the actor Alexander Scourby for a series on mythology, *Arts and Gods*, the previous year. The idea of appearing on one of the *Wisdom* series' episodes had been broached a few months earlier, in January, by its producer, Robert Emmet Ginna.[30] In the months that followed, Edith had arranged for Huntington to interview her at Seawall.

With the two of them seated on the rocky ledge close to the sea, Huntington began the conversation by asking Edith to identify the qualities that had made the Greeks unique. Edith argued that the main quality was their pursuit of knowledge. Their main subject of conversation, however, was Plato. They felt a mutual fascination, and Edith described Plato in the interview as "the greatest mind in the world," an estimation with which Huntington readily concurred.[31] In an effort to assert Plato's relevance for twentieth-century Americans witnessing the civil rights movement, Huntington raised the question of the "darker side of Greece": its acceptance of slavery and its treatment of women. Both were issues that Edith had tried to address in her books, particularly in the chapters on Herodotus and Xenophon that she had later added to *The Greek Way*. To Huntington, Edith asserted that "Plato set exactly the same training for men and women."[32] She again claimed for

FIGURE 16. Edith Hamilton inside her home at Seawall in July 1958. Photograph by Gjon Mili for *Life* magazine. Shutterstock.

the Greeks their place as the first people in world history to question slavery, asserting that Plato had pondered how one man could own another "two thousand years" before the United States had had to confront the question.

That summer, however, Edith also realized the broader implications of the civil rights movement for the United States' international image as the case of Jimmy Wilson became the subject of public debate. Wilson, an African American handyman from Alabama, was convicted in

1958 by an all-white jury and sentenced to death for the alleged robbery of \$1.95. The Alabama Supreme Court subsequently upheld the sentence, causing a public outcry both domestically and internationally.[33] Edith, likely motivated by her sense that the United States had to stand for democracy against communism, was among hundreds who wrote letters to newspaper editors to protest the sentence.[34]

The interview concluded with Edith's interpretation of Plato's importance. *The Dialogues*, she argued, brought ancient Athens to life, in great part because of Plato's extraordinary talent as a writer. He embodied exactly the ideal for which Edith had always strived: the scholar and the artist, the great thinker whose talent allowed him to convey his thought to others.

Edith's main work during 1958, however, was writing introductions to the dialogues of Plato. Though the themes she found in Plato were those she explored many times during these years, her introductions, when read together, reveal the sources of her public arguments as well as her deep reverence for Socrates. The introductions contained the most complete portrait of Socrates that she had written since *Witness to the Truth*. In her introductions, the spiritual Socrates is evident from the beginning as, following the accepted chronology, the Plato volume began with the three dialogues concerning the trial and death of Socrates (*Socrates' Defense*, the *Crito*, and the *Phaedo*). In her introduction to *Socrates' Defense* (also known as the *Apology*), Socrates's words after the sentence of death was pronounced showed the reader that as a "man he was, unlike any other there has ever been." Socrates was "the servant of the divine power, living in complete obedience to God." The key to his unique character was his method of trying to encourage each individual to seek the truth but refraining from criticizing humans for falling short in this task.[35] When, in the *Crito*, Socrates's friends tried to convince him to escape before his execution, Socrates refused to break the laws of Athens and chose to face death since, as he told his friend Crito, "God points out the way."[36]

It was in the *Phaedo*, a long discussion of the immortality of the soul, that Edith found Socrates expressing ideas akin to Christian beliefs, a comparison that had also been made by Edward Caird. As various ideas about immortality were debated during Socrates's final hours, Socrates himself had finally suggested "The soul is immortal because it can perceive, have a share in, truth, goodness, beauty, which are eternal."[37] He then gave a description of the final judgment while urging his listeners to continue to examine the question of the afterlife. To Edith, the clearest indication that he believed in the immortality of the soul was his final words bidding Crito to sacrifice a rooster to Asclepius, the traditional sacrifice of the Greeks upon recovery from sickness; this was an indication that Socrates saw death as the healing of the soul but not the end of its journey. Socrates had urged others to seek the truth and had been firmly convinced of the immortality of the soul.

His teaching method was another aspect of his spiritual nature. The dialogues she enjoyed the most were those in which Socrates's unique character, always questioning others, was most evident. His personality, she felt, was most discernible in the *Symposium*, but *Protagoras*, to Edith, gave the most vivid picture of ancient Athenian life, with Socrates and others vying to listen to the teachings of Protagoras and sometimes to challenge him. The dialogue illustrated the primacy of intellectual life in Athens, but this was balanced by the humor she sometimes saw in Plato's work, making up for the occasionally "tiresome" nature of Socrates as he sometimes indulged in analysis that proved intellectually unsatisfactory.[38] The clearest explication of Socrates's method of teaching was found in *Lysis*, a dialogue concerning the nature of friendship. Socrates's method, Edith believed, set him apart "among all the great teachers of mankind." His goal was not to instruct but to stir others to think critically. As Edith wrote, "It was his conviction that truth cannot be taught, it must be sought."[39] Socrates illustrated the Greek passion for clarity of thought.

By December 1958, as Edith began to write the introductions for the later dialogues, the work proceeded more slowly. Some of these dialogues were, she told Brooks Atkinson, "heavy and dull and un Platonic—at least to me."[40]

Meanwhile, the steady stream of visitors to 2448 continued, with just a few previous guests no longer making their appearances. Gen. Albert Wedemeyer remained among the usual callers, as well as the literary

figures who continued to be brought by Huntington. There were, however, some changes in the regular round of visitors. Ralph Flanders had
decided to give up his Senate seat and did not run for reelection in
1958.[41] And as isolationism spread among Democrats, senators from that
party began to appear at 2448 Massachusetts Avenue. Previously, the
only Democratic member of the Senate that Edith likely knew was
Paul H. Douglas of Illinois, who had been a friend of both Warder Norton and Storer Lunt.[42] In 1959, J. William Fulbright, Democrat of Arkansas and a friend of Huntington's, paid his first visit and immediately
found himself engaged in a discussion of Pericles.[43] In his mid-fifties
when he met Edith, Fulbright had been deeply influenced by *The Echo
of Greece,* particularly its opening chapters on how Athens had lost its
freedom through its pursuit of imperial power, making him one of the
American political figures on whom Edith's intellectual influence was
clear and enduring.

Now in her nineties, Edith still wanted to live according to the Greek
ideal, to remain active and interested in life. She did not stop writing,
socializing, or traveling abroad during what would be the last five years
of her life. At the age of ninety-two, she even joked with visiting poet
Kimon Friar that she was putting off translating another tragedy by Aeschylus until she was older.[44] Doris was largely a full partner in Edith's
embrace of life, though she was occasionally protective of her, wanting
Edith to preserve her energies. As the usual visitors to Massachusetts
Avenue continued, few changes occurred in Edith and Doris's domestic
life. Neither woman saw advancing age as a reason to stop acquiring
pets. For her ninetieth birthday, Mary Reid McKnight had presented
Edith with two kittens, whom Edith named Nip and Tuck. When Edith
wanted a small dog to accompany her on the daily walks she still took
around the neighborhood, Doris responded with a puppy whom Edith
promptly named Dobey Dawson, after a bull terrier once owned by
Agnes's mentor Esther Kelly Bradford. The women made few concessions to age, even as both experienced health problems.

During the compilation of the Plato volume, Edith and Huntington's
respective roles had been clearly defined. Early in their collaboration
they had determined the order in which the dialogues would appear in

the volume. Huntington had been intrigued by Edith's idea that they try to establish a literary order. But in the end neither could create one that seemed logical, and they had resorted to arranging the dialogues in a more standard chronological order.[45] Though he disagreed with some of the links Edith made between Plato and Christianity in some of her introductions, Huntington consciously made the choice not to debate the subject with her or to edit her ideas.[46] He had also readily accepted her choice of translations, feeling strongly only about his preference for A. E. Taylor's translation of the *Laws*, which he felt conveyed its meaning more clearly than the others.[47] Edith reciprocated by not suggesting any changes to the general introduction he wrote for the Plato volume.[48]

In late 1959, Edith suffered an attack of shingles that lasted at least eleven weeks and prevented her from using her right hand. That November she was unable even to indicate her preferences on a ballot she received from the American Academy of Arts and Letters and had to have Doris fill it out for her, Doris having, at this point, assumed power of attorney for her.[49] By January the illness had abated, but it still left her unable to write. Even when she was able to do so, the signs of the debilitating illness were evident in her penmanship. Edith's handwriting, usually neat and clear, became shaky and difficult to read.[50] She continued to experience some paralysis in two fingers of her right hand until the following year, when she received electronic massage therapy from an osteopath and her usual style of handwriting returned.[51] That winter, Edith had a period of enforced inactivity, spending nearly six weeks indoors, rarely venturing out because of heavy snowfall and temperatures in the twenties. Storer took the opportunity to suggest she edit a collection of her essays, a project that he had long hoped she would pursue.[52] Edith, however, remained more interested in writing her book on Plato than editing her old writings.

The year 1960 would bring a number of public appearances for Edith, as she received more recognition from academic classical scholars and from the two institutions that had dominated her life for over thirty years: Bryn Mawr College and the Bryn Mawr School. That April she again addressed the Classical Association of the Atlantic States at their meeting held at George Washington University. Just days before her address, she slipped on a rug at home, hitting a table as she fell and breaking her nose. Despite the injury, she proceeded with her speech and accepted with good humor the comment of Dr. John F. Latimer, dean of the faculty at George Washington University, that her nose appeared more Roman than Greek.[53]

The death of Jessie that May, however, made Edith reflect on her own mortality. Almost three years older than Edith, Jessie was ninety-five and had been in declining health since the previous year. Edith had longed to go to Arizona, where Jessie had gone in hopes of recovery, to see her, but the lingering effects of a protracted bout with shingles prevented her. As she told Agnes, she was also afraid that in her own weakened state she would be more of a hindrance than a help in the face of Jessie's deteriorating health.[54] Soon after the telegram arrived informing her of Jessie's passing, Edith reflected, "I cannot realize Jess. She has been too fundamental in my life too long. It will take time." She was comforted by the knowledge of Jessie's deep Christian faith, remembering to Agnes, "I keep in my mind what she wrote most to me about, her desire to live so in His presence."[55]

Work on *The Collected Dialogues of Plato* was almost complete. By the summer of 1960, Huntington was reading galleys, and he volunteered to see the work through the press.[56] That June, Edith and Doris traveled to France with Francesca Gilder Palmer and Dorna McCollester, now widowed.[57] After a rough crossing, they visited Chartres, followed by several days in the Loire Valley, staying at a chateau at Amboise that faced the river.[58] Edith and Doris then went to the south of France, where they visited Nîmes and Avignon. In spite of the fears expressed by her sisters, Edith was still an able and enthusiastic traveler. "We have perfect weather and I have perfect health," Edith told Alice and Margaret from Avignon, after spending two nights in a thirteenth-century building that had been converted into a hotel. The trip, which concluded in Paris, left Doris feeling "rejuvenated" and Edith in good spirits.[59] It was to be Edith's last trip abroad.

By early 1961, Washington, D.C., was crowded with visitors in anticipation of the inauguration of John F. Kennedy, to be held on January 20.[60]

As a friend of the Lodge family, one of whom, Henry Cabot Lodge Jr., had lost his senate reelection bid to Kennedy in 1952, Edith had long been aware of the Democratic senator from Massachusetts.[61] She had even seen Kennedy spoofed at the Women's National Press Club Stunt Party held at Washington's Statler-Hilton Hotel in May 1959, when she had received the Women's National Press Club Award.[62] Huntington had been appointed chairman of the Presidential Inaugural Concert Committee, a position that gave him the opportunity to secure invitations to the inauguration for people whom the inaugural committee wanted to recognize as outstanding in their fields. Edith was one of the 168 intellectuals invited to the festivities, including the inaugural concert, to be held at Constitution Hall the night before, and to the inauguration itself, as well as to at least one of the balls.[63] She did not attend. The weather kept her at home on inauguration day.

Almost eight inches of snow fell on Washington the night before the inauguration, and the day itself, though clear, was very cold. Consequently, she was not in attendance when the new president delivered the memorable line, "Ask not what your country can do for you, ask what you can do for your country," from his acceptance speech.[64]

Eighteen months later, Edith expressed approval of the sentiment to Jim Birchfield. A longtime editor and photographer for the *Washington Star,* he interviewed her at her home. Edith had expressed similar sentiments in her *Wisdom* interview with Huntington, asserting, "When the individual man had reached that condition in Athens, when he thought not of giving to the state but of what the state could give to him, Athens' freedom was doomed."[65] While acknowledging the similarities, Edith doubted whether her work had provided the inspiration for the famous line in the inaugural address.

However much she might have agreed with Kennedy on certain points, such as his approach to the Soviets, Edith expressed deep reservations about the new president's patronage and his interest in space exploration. In fact, she told Alan Valentine, "I am afraid of Kennedy."[66] Edith noted the new president's seeming preference for youth over experience and expertise with dismay.[67] Nor could Edith share the enthusiasm for lunar exploration. In her introduction to the dialogue the *Ti-*

maeus, Edith had argued that Plato, while curious about scientific discovery, had seen science as part of the constantly changing nature of our world. At best, humans could catch glimpses of truth through scientific observation of the world around them. Science was really meant to serve the human purpose of the search for truth, making goals such as accuracy unimportant. The aim of going to the moon was too literal for Edith, convinced as she was of Plato's view of the purpose of science.[68]

The trips to Spain and France had been so successful that Edith and Doris originally planned to go abroad in the summer of 1961.[69] Ultimately, they planned a trip with Francesca that would take them to the Netherlands, Switzerland, Austria, and Germany. Edith was eager to see Munich again, but that May, just before their departure, Alice became gravely ill with internal bleeding. Ultimately, Edith and Doris gave up their planned European trip but also decided that it would be "bad psychology"—as Doris termed it—to spend the entire summer in Connecticut or New York City since it would appear as if they were waiting for Alice to have a possibly fatal relapse.[70] When Alida decided to use her private plane to fly to her summer home in East Bluehill, Maine, only about thirty miles from Seawall, Edith and Doris gratefully accepted her invitation to join.

In spite of its inauspicious beginnings, the summer passed peacefully. Seven grandchildren visited, as did Sir George Paget Thomson, whose discussion of the possibility of atomic warfare Edith found alarming, if only because Thomson was not given to exaggeration.[71] He had just published, the previous year, a revised edition of his 1955 book *The Foreseeable Future*, which he had dedicated to Doris, feeling that she had helped him.[72] Alice recovered—she would live to the age of 101—but the severity of her illness, coupled with the death of Jessie the previous year, made Edith wonder how Doris would fare after her death.[73] That summer, in a rare disclosure of the depth of the bond between them, Edith told Lucia Valentine, "When I am no longer here your beautiful warmth is what my Doris shall need very greatly."[74] Sadly, Agnes died in late 1961, a little over a year after Jessie, putting a final end to the close-knit circle of cousins whom Edith and her sisters had known all their lives.[75]

Soon, Edith herself was ill, suffering a stroke in the autumn of 1961. Doris recalled being told that Edith would not be able to walk or speak again. But she made a remarkable recovery in the months that followed. By January, Doris was able to tell their friend Vail Motter that Edith was able to walk and her thoughts were lucid.[76] By February she sometimes left the house for rides in Doris's car.[77] Doris's narratives always emphasized Edith's phenomenal strength. But the story of Edith's full recovery is supported by Dorian's daughter, Alice.[78]

That fall, *The Collected Dialogues of Plato* was published. The book received widespread and favorable critical attention, with most reviewers recognizing the two editors' different approaches to Plato. Perhaps this was best appreciated by Rudd Fleming, the University of Maryland literature professor who knew both Huntington and Edith from their years working with Ezra Pound. Calling her introductions to the dialogues "graceful," Fleming recognized the essential role of Socrates for Edith.[79] Only Edith's introduction to the *Parmenides* was criticized by some reviewers, to whom her dislike of the dialogue was obvious.[80]

Edith was now free to turn her full attention to her own book on Plato, which she had tentatively titled *Plato: An Introduction*, and which Storer was eager to publish.[81] During the previous summer at Seawall she had contemplated Plato, as she so often did, telling Agnes, "Plato says we must dwell with what one longs for, keeping it in one's thought, and a spark will leap up into a flame, flooding the soul with light."[82]

The book on Plato was never completed. But she hinted at its main arguments to various journalists. Jesus and St. Paul, she felt, were both inspired by the ancient Greek philosopher.[83] It was a likely subject for Edith, bringing together her love for the ancient Greeks and her belief in Christianity. As she had told Jessie and Agnes when she had first begun her work on Plato in late 1957, Plato "troubled the early Fathers of the church quite a lot because they could not deny that he had utter faith in one God, who was all goodness, and whom men could draw near to, and in whose service alone was happiness." She added: "Plato had a vision of God."[84]

As with many of Edith's ideas, it may have had its roots in her early reading of Edward Caird, who had tried to trace the origins of Christian thought. Caird had pointed out that Plato's belief that it is better to suffer than to do an injustice—the message of *Gorgias*—was an idea familiar to Christians as well. Christianity, according to Caird, had gathered up preexisting philosophical ideas and had given them "a new meaning" and "a new unity."[85]

Through Socrates, Edith argued, Christian ideas had permeated the dialogues. As she had written her introductions, she had referred directly to the Christian ideas she found in some of them. As she had pointed out in her writing, St. Paul had visited Greece and had commented on the Athenians. In her introduction to the *Symposium*, she argued that the speech of the dinner party host Agathon was akin to Corinthians 1:13, and Socrates's words to those of John.[86] The evidence for Jesus having been so influenced was considerably less. But to Brooks Atkinson, Edith argued that "seek and ye shall find" was an essentially Greek idea. In her introduction to the *Theaetetus* she had made the connection she saw between Socrates and Jesus even more explicit than usual, comparing Socrates's pursuit of knowledge of the good to Jesus's saying from John 7:17, "He that willeth to do the will of God shall know the doctrine."[87]

There were few hints that Edith's ability to write was waning. And an interview conducted by Birchfield just months before Edith's death evidences no signs of her losing intellectual or physical vigor. Doris, however, left one clue that by early 1963 Edith's strength, both physical and mental, was waning, writing that in May, a week before she died, "she seemed to have regained some of her keenness" and mentioned again the completion of her own book on Plato.[88] Felix, however, had noticed Edith's decline earlier. When, on the afternoon of April 16, 1963, he and his wife Isabel had had tea at 2448 with Edith, Doris, and Storer, they found Edith "rather withdrawn and silent," though Felix noted that she had been that way in the previous few months. He distinctly remembered, however, that as he and Isabel had prepared to leave, Edith exhibited "sparks of her old self." Clasping Felix's hand, she had, he wrote in his diary, "looked up at me with something of earlier energy and said earnestly 'Oh Felix, do go on writing!'" It was the last time he saw Edith.[89]

Edith died suddenly from a heart attack on Friday evening, May 31, 1963, a little after 9 p.m. Huntington, who had just settled into an armchair with a book, received a phone call from Edith's doctor informing him of her passing and immediately went to 2448 to help Doris.[90] Felix and Isabel Morley learned of Edith's death from the obituary in the Sunday *New York Times*. The news inspired Felix to write, "So passes a remarkable person of whom we have seen much during the past twenty years and who has meant much to both Isabel and me."[91] Upon hearing of Edith's passing, Margaret Shearman, one of only two of Edith's Bryn Mawr College friends to survive her, immediately wrote to Alice, "Loving you all and being with you constantly."[92]

Chapter 20

CONCLUSION

Edith had firmly stated that she did not want a funeral service, but a small one was held at the Hamiltons' house in Hadlyme on June 4, 1963.[1] The minister from the Old Lyme Congregational Church officiated, and Edith was buried next to Gertrude in Cove Cemetery. Besides Doris, Alice, and Margaret, Dorian and Betty, as well as their children Harry and Alice, were present.[2] It was announced beforehand that the service was to be private, which discouraged some Washington friends, including Felix Morley, from attending. But a delegation of Edith's New York social circle, including John and Catherine Brown as well as Dorothy Sands, made the journey to Connecticut for the service. Edith, Dorothy felt, would have wanted them there to comfort Doris.[3]

Doris had never known life without Edith; to her, Edith's death seemed a "sudden" loss and "somehow unreal."[4] After the funeral Doris received an invitation to stay with Felix and Isabel Morley at their summer home on Gibson Island, but she decided that she had to go to Seawall. Elling came to stay with her, recognizing how difficult Doris's first days there without Edith would be for her. During that summer in Maine, Doris made the decision to move back to New York City. She felt unable to return permanently to the house on Massachusetts Avenue. She still had friends in New York, where she had spent much of her youth. By December she had settled into an apartment at 955 Lexington Avenue.[5] With the exception of summers at Seawall, it was to be her home for the rest of her life.

Doris's first task was to finish compiling the book of Edith's essays that she had been editing. It was published as *The Ever-Present Past* the year after Edith's death. Her next task, as she saw it, was to write a biography of Edith, despite having little experience as an author. Only Doris's determination to honor Edith's memory, coupled with a conviction that biographies were often best written by someone who knew their subject personally, could have compelled her to take on such a large task as writing an account of Edith's life.[6] There were entire portions of Edith's life before Doris had been born of which she could have known little. Others stepped in to aid Doris. Alice permitted her to use much of the first chapter of her own autobiography, *Exploring the Dangerous Trades*, to describe Edith's childhood.[7] Dorothy Detzer Denny, whose family had built a house on the Hamilton homestead in Fort Wayne, met with Doris, drew a map of the homestead, and sent her photographs of the White House where Edith had grown up so that Doris could better envision it.[8] Doris also contacted old friends to collect stories for the volume. The biography, *Edith Hamilton: An Intimate Portrait*, published by W. W. Norton in 1967, was essentially the story of a successful author's life.

Slowly, Doris's multiple sclerosis limited her movement. She still went to Seawall each summer but was glad when one of her nieces could accompany her. She still enjoyed the scenery of Mount Desert Island, though she had to admire it from her open convertible. Sir George Paget Thomson sometimes visited, spending July of 1968 with her.[9] In the summer of 1969, Betsey reported that the illness had begun to affect the nerves near her right eye and that few of the prescribed treatments seemed effective.[10] Her brother Francis had died in July 1960, meaning Doris no longer had any immediate family members, but she was generous to old friends and to the surviving Hamilton sisters.[11] She gave financial support to Margaret, who continued to live at Hadlyme with Clara Landsberg until Clara's death in 1966. Margaret died in July 1969 at the age of ninety-eight, but Alice lived until September 22, 1970, dying at the age of 101.[12]

In January 1973, Doris's condition worsened, and Sir George Paget Thomson flew to New York City to be with her. In her final hours, he read to her from the Bible. Others also came to Doris's bedside, including Dorian's daughter Alice.[13] Doris died in her New York apartment on January 15, at the age of seventy-seven.[14]

APPENDIX

FRIENDS OF EDITH HAMILTON

AANNESTAD, ELLING (1904–85). As an assistant editor at W. W. Norton from 1927, he befriended Edith Hamilton at the time of her first visit to the publishing house in 1928. She dedicated her 1948 book, *Witness to the Truth: Christ and His Interpreters*, to him.

ALLINSON, ANNE CROSBY EMERY (1871–1932). A classical scholar and a contemporary of Edith Hamilton at Bryn Mawr College, where she was known as Nan Emery. In 1905 she married Dr. Francis Greenleaf Allinson, professor of Greek literature and history at Brown University, where she subsequently spent the rest of her career.

AMOS, BONTE, see Elgood, Cornelia Bonte Sheldon Amos

ATKINSON, BROOKS (1894–1984). The drama critic began his career at the *New York Times* in 1925 and served in his position until his retirement in 1960. He and his wife, the writer Oriana Atkinson, whom he married in 1926, were Gramercy Park neighbors and longtime friends of Edith Hamilton.

ATKINSON, ORIANA (1895–1989). The author, born Oriana Torrey, was the wife of drama critic Brooks Atkinson. Her autobiography *Manhattan and Me* (1954) earned the praise of Edith Hamilton.

BAILEY, EMMA, see Speer, Emma Bailey

BALDWIN, RAYMOND (1893–1986). The Republican politician from Connecticut befriended Edith Hamilton and Doris Fielding Reid during his brief time as a U.S. senator, from 1946–49. A former Connecticut legislator and three-term governor of the state, he resigned from his Senate seat to become a justice of the Connecticut Supreme Court and eventually became its chief justice.

BATCHELOR, C. D. (1888–1977). The editorial cartoonist, born Clarence Daniel Batchelor, drew a portrait of Edith Hamilton circa 1958.

BEAUX, CECILIA (1855–1942). The artist known for her portraits, she taught Edith Hamilton's cousin Jessie Hamilton in Philadelphia from 1898–1900. The Gilder family, with whom Edith later became friends, were also friends with Beaux, who painted several portraits of the Gilders. Edith Hamilton attended Beaux's memorial service.

BLAISDELL, ELINORE (1904–94). The artist was a friend and correspondent of Edith Hamilton. She illustrated about forty-five books.

BLOGG, ISABEL, see Burger, Isabel Blogg

BROOKS, VAN WYCK (1886–1963). The literary historian discussed his friendships with both Edith and Alice Hamilton in the third volume of his autobiography, *From the Shadow of the Mountain* (1961). He called Edith a scholar and mentioned their meeting at the Connecticut home of set designer Lee Simonson.

BROWN, JOHN MASON (1900–69). The drama critic and writer was an early member of the staff of *Theatre Arts Monthly*, where, as an associate editor and drama critic, he met and befriended Edith Hamilton. Brown later wrote for the *Saturday Review of Literature*, where he published two tributes to Edith Hamilton, in 1948 and after her death in 1963. His wife, Catherine Meredith, whom he married in 1933, was also a good friend of Edith Hamilton.

BROWNELL, LOUISE, see Saunders, Louise Brownell

BRUCE, DOROTHY, see Weske, Dorothy Bruce

BURGER, ISABEL BLOGG (1903–96). The author graduated from the Bryn Mawr School in 1920 and later wrote three textbooks on children's theater.

BYNNER, WITTER (1881–1968). The poet and translator began to correspond with Edith Hamilton after she quoted some lines of the English poet Jean Ingelow in her article "Words, Words, Words," published in the *Saturday Review* in November 1955. Bynner had translated works by Euripides, and Edith Hamilton praised some of his translations from Chinese.

CAIRNS, HUNTINGTON (1904–85). The lawyer, author, and museum executive was friends with Edith Hamilton from the spring of 1946 onward. In 1957, they began work on coediting *The Collected Dialogues of Plato*, which was published by the Bollingen Foundation in 1961. Edith was also friends with Cairns's wife, Florence Faison Butler Cairns (1899–1990).

CLEMENTS, GABRIELLE DE VEAUX (1858–1948). The artist and art teacher taught at the Bryn Mawr School from 1895 until 1908.

CRENA DE IONGH, MARY DOWS DE HERTER NORTON (1892–1985). The violinist assisted her first husband, William Warder Norton, in establishing the publishing firm that would bear his name. She also worked as an editor and translator for the firm. After Warder Norton's death in 1945 she reorganized the company as an employee-owned firm.

DENNY, DOROTHY DETZER (1893–1981). The journalist and peace activist grew up on the Hamilton homestead in Fort Wayne. From 1924 until 1956, she was executive secretary of the Women's International League for Peace and Freedom. She lived in Washington, D.C., where she and her husband, Ludwell Denny, were sometimes guests at Edith Hamilton's house. After Edith's death, Dorothy gave Doris Fielding Reid some assistance in writing her biography of Edith Hamilton, including drawing a map of the Hamilton homestead and providing photographs of Edith's childhood home. She was the younger sister of Karl Detzer.

DERWENT, CLARENCE (1884–1959). The English-born actor and ambassador for theater came to the United States in 1915 and appeared in films and on stage. He was among those who accompanied Edith Hamilton to Athens in 1957 for the ANTA production of *Prometheus Bound*.

DETZER, KARL (1891–1987). The journalist grew up on the Hamilton homestead in Fort Wayne. His autobiography, *Myself When Young* (1968), describes the homestead and contains many anecdotes about the Hamilton family. He was the older brother of Dorothy Detzer Denny.

DIXON, W. MACNEILE (1866–1946). The Regius Professor of English language and literature at the University of Glasgow (1904–35) was a correspondent of Edith Hamilton. She cited his book *Tragedy* in the notes to *The Greek Way*. He praised her translation of *Prometheus Bound* in a letter to her in 1927.

DONNELLY, LUCY MARTIN (1870–1948). Professor of English at Bryn Mawr College, from which she graduated in 1893. During her college and early professional years, she was close to Helen Thomas, later Flexner. Donnelly became a traveling companion to Edith Hamilton and an intellectual and aesthetic influence on her. Their relationship deteriorated as Edith began to withdraw from the Bryn Mawr School. There was no contact between Donnelly and Hamilton from 1923 until a few months before Donnelly's death in 1948.

DOUGLAS, PAUL H. (1892–1976). The economist and Democratic senator from Illinois was a Washington friend of Edith Hamilton. From 1920, he was on the faculty of the University of Chicago and was active in municipal reform campaigns in the city. He was first elected to the Senate in 1948 and ultimately served three terms. His second wife, Emily Taft Douglas, corresponded with Edith Hamilton.

DU PONT, MARCELLA MILLER (1903–85). The poet from Denver married the architect Alfred Victor du Pont, from whom she was divorced in 1948. She then settled in Washington, where she met Edith Hamilton and Doris Fielding Reid, and where, along with Reid, she was active in the Republican Party. She published three volumes of poetry.

DURYEE, LILY (1866–1950). The missionary to China was a friend of Edith Hamilton and Katherine and Jessie Hamilton from their years at Miss Porter's School. She was the younger sister of Susan Rankin Duryee Fahmy. She returned to the United States permanently in 1937.

DURYEE, SUSAN RANKIN, see Fahmy, Susan Rankin Duryee

ELGOOD, CORNELIA BONTE SHELDON AMOS (1874–1960). The medical doctor and hospital administrator earned a medical degree from the University of London in 1900 and subsequently spent her adult life in Egypt. Her brother, Maurice Amos, was a Cambridge friend of Bertrand Russell, and she befriended the philosopher as well, visiting the United States with him and his wife Alys in 1896 and meeting Edith Hamilton.

ELLICOTT, ELIZABETH KING (1858–1914). The women's suffrage and social reform activist was a first cousin of M. Carey Thomas. In 1885, she and Thomas were among the five founders of the Bryn Mawr School. Disagreements among the founders, who formed the school's first board of managers, led to her departure in 1891. She subsequently became active in municipal reform causes and became the first president of the Equal Suffrage League of Baltimore. She married the architect William Ellicott in 1909.

EMERY, NAN, see Allinson, Anne Crosby Emery

EMMET, LYDIA FIELD (1866–1952). The portraitist came from a family of artists. She painted Edith Hamilton's portrait for the Bryn Mawr School in 1925, and the women formed a friendship that endured after the work was finished.

EVERITT, C. RAYMOND (d. 1947). The editor joined the firm of Little, Brown in 1936, eventually becoming vice president of the company in 1940. His interest in publishing an updated version of *Bulfinch's Mythology* led to his meeting with Edith Hamilton and to her writing of *Mythology*. His death from a heart attack at the age of forty-five ended his plans to publish Edith Hamilton's book, which became *Witness to the Truth*.

FAHMY, SUSAN RANKIN DURYEE (1864–1961). The missionary to China was, together with her younger sister Lily Duryee, a friend of Edith Hamilton and Katherine and Jessie Hamilton from their years at Miss Porter's School. From 1900 until 1903, Susan and Edith lived together in Baltimore. From 1903 Susan and her younger sister Alice (1878–1911) served as missionaries in China. In 1905, Susan married the Egyptian-born missionary doctor Ahmed Fahmy and moved inland with him to his hospital at Changchow (Zhang-zhou), where they worked until after the First World War. During her early years in China, Susan knew Lin Yutang, who mentioned her influence in his work *From Pagan to Christian*.

FEIBLEMAN, JAMES K. (1904–87). A philosophy professor, poet, and writer, he was a long-time friend and correspondent of Huntington Cairns and occasionally of Edith Hamilton as well. He was on the faculty of Tulane University from 1943 until 1977.

FITTS, DUDLEY (1903–68). The poet and translator of ancient Greek plays frequently worked with Robert Fitzgerald. Their translations earned the praise of Edith Hamilton, who published positive reviews of his and Fitzgerald's translation of the *Alcestis* of Euripides and of Sophocles's *Oedipus Rex* in the *Saturday Review of Literature* in 1936 and 1950, respectively. Fitts admired Hamilton's translation of the *Prometheus Bound* of Aeschylus, which he included in the volume he edited, *Greek Plays in Modern Translation* (1947).

FITZGERALD, ROBERT (1910–85). The poet and translator of ancient Greek plays frequently worked with Dudley Fitts. In 1948, Hamilton and Fitzgerald were introduced to each other through their mutual friend Huntington Cairns, after which Hamilton encouraged Fitzgerald to continue to translate Sophocles's *Oedipus at Colonus*, a work that he eventually completed.

FITZGERALD, SUSAN WALKER (1871–1943). The politician and women's suffrage activist was the founder of student government at Bryn Mawr College. She attended Bryn Mawr College (1889–93), where, in 1892, she created the first student self-government association in the United States. She recommended Edith Hamilton for the position of dean of Barnard College in 1900, but Hamilton was unable to interview for the post. Walker married Richard Y. FitzGerald in 1901. In 1923, she became one of the first women elected to the Massachusetts State House.

FLANDERS, RALPH E. (1880–1970). The mechanical engineer and Republican senator from Vermont became a close friend of Edith Hamilton during his two terms in the Senate from 1946 until 1958. Fearing the decline of Western civilization in the Cold War era, he looked upon Edith as one of its most articulate proponents. He led the movement in the Senate to censure his fellow Republican Senator Joseph McCarthy, and his criticisms of him likely inspired her chapter on Demosthenes in *The Echo of Greece*. Along with his wife, Helen Hartness Flanders, he was a frequent visitor to Edith's Washington home.

FLEXNER, HELEN THOMAS (1871–1956). The writer was the youngest sibling of M. Carey Thomas and a first cousin of Alys Pearsall Smith Russell. She was a member of the first graduating class of the Bryn Mawr School in 1888. She entered Bryn Mawr College the following year, and in 1890 met fellow student Lucy Martin Donnelly, with whom she was to have a long romantic relationship. She graduated from Bryn Mawr in 1893 and, with Donnelly, became an English instructor at Bryn Mawr College, a position Helen retained until

1902, when she became engaged to Dr. Simon Flexner. The couple married in 1903 and settled in New York City. She published her autobiography, *A Quaker Childhood*, in 1940.

FORSYTH, WILLIAM J. (1854–1935). The artist who would become known as a member of the Hoosier Group taught art in the carriage house on the Hamilton homestead from 1888 until 1889. From 1894, he began to exhibit his work, which began to attract critical acclaim.

FULBRIGHT, J. WILLIAM (1905–95). The Democratic senator from Arkansas was a Washington friend of Edith Hamilton, to whom he was introduced by Huntington Cairns. He served five terms in the Senate, from 1945 until 1974.

GARRETT, MARY ELIZABETH (1854–1915). The philanthropist was born in Baltimore, the only daughter of John Work Garrett, head of the Baltimore and Ohio Railroad. She advocated for women's suffrage and education. In 1885, she was one of the five founders of the Bryn Mawr School, and from 1889 led the campaign for women's admission to the Johns Hopkins Medical School. She later moved to the Deanery at Bryn Mawr College and lived with her partner M. Carey Thomas.

GILDER, FRANCESCA, see Palmer, Francesca Gilder

GILDER, ROSAMOND (1891–1986). The drama critic, editor, and author was the youngest child of *The Century* magazine editor Richard Watson Gilder and the younger sister of Francesca Gilder Palmer. She joined the staff of *Theatre Arts Monthly* in 1924 and encouraged Edith Hamilton to contribute essays to the magazine. Gilder eventually became the editor of *Theatre Arts* and the author of several books on theater. She was also a traveling companion of Edith Hamilton and Doris Fielding Reid.

GILDERSLEEVE, BASIL LANNEAU (1831–1924). The classical scholar was among the scholars who brought German philological study of classical texts to the United States and helped to organize the profession of classical studies. When the Bryn Mawr School was first established in 1885, he evaluated its Latin instruction, a duty later taken on by his former graduate student Gonzalez Lodge. Edith Hamilton knew Gildersleeve during her years in Baltimore and sometimes referred to their acquaintance in later life.

GWINN, MARY, see Hodder, Mary Mackall Gwinn

HAMBIDGE, MARY CROVATT (1885–1973). The weaver who established an art center at Rabun Gap, Georgia, was a friend and correspondent of Edith Hamilton. In 1920–21, she traveled with her husband, the Canadian-born artist Jay Hambidge, to Greece, where she became fascinated with traditional methods of weaving. After her husband's death in 1924, she established a center to revive traditional weaving in America. She corresponded with Edith Hamilton about natural foods and about their mutual friend Eva Palmer Sikelianos.

HARRIS, MARY B. (1874–1957). The prison reformer taught Latin at the Bryn Mawr School from 1906 until 1911, during which time she became friends with Edith Hamilton and Doris Fielding Reid. In 1912, she lived with Doris Fielding Reid in Europe. Harris began her prison reform work upon her return to the United States.

HODDER, MARY MACKALL GWINN (1860–1940). The professor of English at Bryn Mawr College was the longtime companion of M. Carey Thomas. She was one of the five original founders of the Bryn Mawr School, but she resigned from the board of managers and from the faculty of Bryn Mawr College in 1904 upon her marriage to English professor Alfred Hodder.

HOSMER, DR. GEORGE WASHINGTON (1830–1914). The medical doctor and author was the first writer Edith Hamilton ever met. He was the son of a Unitarian minister, also Dr. George Washington Hosmer, who was president of Antioch College in Ohio. The younger Hosmer was the author of several books on the Civil War. His daughter Marion Hosmer attended Miss Porter's School, where she was friends with Edith Hamilton as well as Agnes Hamilton.

HOUGHTON, NORRIS (1909–2001). The set designer, director, and producer was part of Edith Hamilton's Gramercy Park social circle.

HOYT, MARY ELOISE (1864–1947). One of two sisters from Rome, Georgia, who graduated from Bryn Mawr College and subsequently taught at the Bryn Mawr School. Mary Hoyt was teacher of English and head of the department at the Bryn Mawr School from 1895 until 1919. Her younger sister, Florence Hoyt, joined the faculty of the Bryn Mawr School in 1901, a position she maintained until her retirement.

ISAACS, EDITH J. R. (1878–1956). The magazine editor and critic was born in Milwaukee and married the lawyer Lewis Isaacs in 1904. They settled in New York City and had three children, Marian, Lewis Jr., and Hermine. She became editor of the magazine *Theatre Arts Monthly* in 1924. She published the innovative work of aspiring set designers, and she helped many writers, including Edith Hamilton, begin their careers. She was widowed in 1944 and sold her interest in the magazine in 1948.

JAEGER, WERNER (1888–1961). The classical scholar became the chair of classics at Berlin at the relatively young age of thirty-two in 1921. An opponent of the Nazis, Jaeger and his wife, Ruth, who had some Jewish ancestry, came to the United States in 1936. Jaeger joined the faculty of Harvard in 1939, from which he retired in 1960. He met Edith Hamilton in Washington, D.C., in 1960.

KELLY, DR. HOWARD ATWOOD (1858–1944). The medical doctor joined the staff of the Johns Hopkins Hospital in 1889 and became professor of gynecology after the founding of the medical school in 1893. Kelly was an advocate of women's suffrage and education. His daughter Olga Kelly graduated from the Bryn Mawr School in 1909 and from Bryn Mawr College in 1914 with a degree in Greek and English.

KING, ELIZABETH, see Ellicott, Elizabeth King

KING, HORTENSE FLEXNER (1885–1973). The poet was the niece of Dr. Simon Flexner and Abraham Flexner. She attended Bryn Mawr College from 1903 to 1904. She published several volumes of poetry, much of which evoked the beauty of Sutton Island, Maine, where she spent her summers.

KIRK, ABBY (1864–1950). The teacher and headmistress graduated from Bryn Mawr College in 1892 and subsequently taught English and Greek at the college. Later, with one of her sisters, she established the Miss Kirks' School, initially located at Rosemont, near the Bryn Mawr College campus.

LANDSBERG, CLARA (1873–1966). The Latin teacher and social reform advocate was the lifetime partner of Margaret Hamilton, whom she met when both were students at Bryn Mawr College. She taught at Hull House from 1905 until 1920 and at the Bryn Mawr School from 1922 until 1935, when she and Margaret retired to Hadlyme, Connecticut. She is buried next to Margaret in Hadlyme Cove Cemetery.

LEWIS, JOHN L. (1880–1969). The labor union executive was president of the United Mine Workers for forty years, from 1920 until his retirement in 1960. He was an isolationist and a supporter of Senator Robert A. Taft, making him a welcome member of Edith Hamilton and Doris Fielding Reid's Washington, D.C., social circle.

LOCKE, SARAH COOPER, see Richmond, Sarah Cooper Locke

LODGE, ELIZABETH CABOT (1876–1960). The socialite was a native of Washington, D.C. She was the widow of the poet George Cabot Lodge and the mother of senator and ambassador Henry Cabot Lodge Jr. She lived on Massachusetts Avenue NW, eventually becoming a friend and neighbor of Edith Hamilton. She gave Edith the gold lamé cloak Edith wore in Athens in 1957 when she was made an honorary citizen of the city.

LODGE, DR. GONZALEZ (1863–1942). The classical scholar taught at Bryn Mawr College from 1889 until 1900. He acted as mentor to Edith Hamilton from her first term at Bryn Mawr College in the spring of 1891 and eventually helped her to attain the Latin fellowship for 1894–95. He evaluated the Latin instruction at the Bryn Mawr School. He subsequently (1900–29) was on the faculty of Columbia University, where he became known for his study of the Roman playwright Plautus.

LODGE, HENRY CABOT, JR. (1902–85). The Republican senator from Massachusetts, and later ambassador, was the grandson of the first Senator Henry Cabot Lodge and the son of the poet George Cabot Lodge and his wife, Elizabeth, a Washington friend of Edith Hamilton. As a student at Harvard, he befriended John Mason Brown. In 1936, he was elected to the U.S. Senate. He was reelected in 1942 but resigned in 1944 to serve in the Second World War. He was reelected to the Senate in 1946 but lost his reelection bid in 1952. During his years in the Senate, he supported U.S. aid to Greece to defeat the Communists in the Greek Civil War.

LONGWORTH, ALICE ROOSEVELT (1884–1980). The prominent Washington political hostess was the daughter of President Theodore Roosevelt. She was married to the Ohio Congressman Nicholas Longworth from 1906 until his death in 1931. From the 1920s, the couple lived in a house at 2009 Massachusetts Avenue, eventually making her a neighbor of Edith Hamilton and Doris Fielding Reid, whose political views she largely shared.

LUDINGTON, KATHARINE, OR "KITTY" (1869–1953). The women's suffrage advocate and social reformer was a friend of the Hamilton sisters and cousins from their years at Miss Porter's School in Farmington, Connecticut.

LUNT, STORER BOARDMAN (1897–1977). The editor and publishing executive joined the publishing house of W. W. Norton as sales manager in 1929. He eventually became vice president of the firm and succeeded to the presidency upon the death of Warder Norton in 1945. He was also chairman of the company's board from 1958 until his retirement in 1970.

MCCOLLESTER, DORNA (1891–1967). The magazine editor for *Theatre Arts Monthly*, who edited Edith Hamilton's first published essay "Tragedy," written in 1924 and published in 1925. She married attorney Parker McCollester in 1921. After her husband's death in 1954, she became a traveling companion to Edith Hamilton and Doris Fielding Reid.

MCCULLOCH, CHARLES (1840–1921). The banker was the son of Hugh McCulloch. He worked in the banking firm of Allen Hamilton and Company. In 1887, he was chosen over Edith Hamilton's father, Montgomery Hamilton, to become president of what by then was known as the Hamilton National Bank. A competent manager, he led the bank for over thirty years.

MCCULLOCH, HUGH (1808–95). The banker and later U.S. secretary of the Treasury was the business partner of Edith Hamilton's grandfather Allen Hamilton. Born in Maine, McCulloch settled in Fort Wayne in 1833. Twenty years later, he was one of three partners who founded the banking house of Allen Hamilton and Company. McCulloch later served as U.S. Treasury secretary to Presidents Abraham Lincoln, Andrew Johnson, and Chester Arthur. He was the father of Charles McCulloch.

MCINTOSH, MILLICENT CAREY (1898–2001). The college administrator was born in Baltimore, the daughter of M. Carey Thomas's sister, Margaret, and businessman Anthony Morris Carey. After attending the Bryn Mawr School, Bryn Mawr College, and Oxford, she earned a doctorate in English literature at the Johns Hopkins University. She subsequently taught literature at Bryn Mawr College before serving as headmistress of the Brearley School in New York City from 1930 to 1947. She then became dean of Barnard College, and, from 1952, its president.

MANNING, DR. HELEN TAFT (1891–1987). The historian and college administrator was the daughter of President and U.S. Chief Justice William Howard Taft. She was the younger sister of Ohio Senator Robert A. Taft. She graduated from Bryn Mawr College in 1915 and became the dean of the college from 1917–19, during which Edith Hamilton worked with her on matters concerning the Bryn Mawr School.

MILLIKEN, ALIDA LEESE (1879–1975). The patron of the arts and conservative activist was married to the surgeon Dr. Seth Milliken from 1907 until his death in 1957. As a conservative, she supported the John Birch Society and Public Action, a group into which she drew Doris Fielding Reid.

MOFFAT, REV. DAVID W. (1835–1920). The minister of the First Presbyterian Church in Fort Wayne from 1872 until 1905. The Hamilton family socialized with Moffat in both Fort Wayne and on Mackinac Island.

MORLEY, FELIX (1894–1982). The journalist, scholar, and college president was the son of Dr. Frank Morley, professor of mathematics at Johns Hopkins University. In 1936 he won the Pulitzer Prize for his editorial writing while serving as editor of the *Washington Post*. In 1944, he cofounded the journal *Human Events*. From 1948, he and his wife Isabel were frequent visitors to Edith and Doris's Washington home.

MOTTER, VAIL (1901–70). The historian was a friend and correspondent of Edith Hamilton and Doris Fielding Reid. He befriended Edith and Doris when he studied the correspondence of Woodrow Wilson and Edith Gittings Reid. After Edith Hamilton's death, he helped Doris to create the Edith Hamilton Collection at the Firestone Library at Princeton University.

NORTON, MARY, OR "POLLY," see Crena de Iongh, Mary Dows de Herter Norton

NORTON, WILLIAM WARDER (1891–1945). The publisher established the People's Institute Publishing Company in New York City in 1923. Gradually, the firm expanded the number of subjects on which it published and took the name of W. W. Norton in May 1926. He married the musician Mary Dows de Herter, later Crena de Iongh.

OENSLAGER, DONALD (1902–75). The set designer was a member of Yale's drama faculty from 1925. He continued to design sets for the New York theater, ultimately contributing to

250 productions. His wife, Mary Polak, always known as "Zorka," whom he married in 1937, was also a good friend of Edith Hamilton.

PALMER, EVALINA, see Sikelianos, Eva Palmer

PALMER, FRANCESCA GILDER (1888–1984). The daughter of *The Century* magazine editor Richard Watson Gilder, she was also the older sister of Rosamond Gilder. She married Dr. Walter Walker Palmer, a professor of medicine at Columbia University, in 1922. Widowed in 1950, she subsequently became a traveling companion of Edith Hamilton and Doris Fielding Reid.

PEASE, LAURETTE POTTS (1868–1967). The social worker was a friend of Edith Hamilton's at Bryn Mawr College, from which she graduated in 1896.

POPE, THEODATE, see Riddle, Theodate Pope

PORTER, SARAH (1813–1900). The founder and headmistress of Miss Porter's School, which she established in 1842, moved into a former hotel on Farmington's Main Street in 1850.

POTTS, LAURETTE, see Pease, Laurette Potts

POWDERMAKER, DR. FLORENCE (1894–1966). The psychologist earned a doctorate at Johns Hopkins University in 1922 and a medical degree from the University of Chicago in 1926. She practiced largely in New York City over the course of her career and was at Columbia University when she treated Doris Fielding Reid's nephew Ernest Fielding Reid in the winter of 1934–35.

PUTNAM, BERTHA HAVEN (1872–1960). The daughter of the publisher George Haven Putnam, the historian was friends with Edith Hamilton at Bryn Mawr College, from which she graduated in 1893. She taught Latin at the Bryn Mawr School from 1893 until 1895. She earned a doctorate from Columbia University in 1909 and had a long career as a professor of history at Mount Holyoke College. Her stepmother was Emily James Smith Putnam.

PUTNAM, EMILY JAMES SMITH (1865–1944). The classical scholar and author was, from 1894, the first dean of Barnard College. She studied Greek under Paul Shorey at Bryn Mawr College, where she was a member of the college's first graduating class in 1889. Edith Hamilton met Smith as dean of Barnard and was briefly considered as Smith's replacement when Smith resigned after her 1899 marriage to the publisher George Haven Putnam, the father of Bertha Putnam.

RICHMOND, SARAH COOPER LOCKE (1868–1950). The clergyman's wife was a friend and contemporary of Edith Hamilton at Miss Porter's School. In 1891, she married Rev. Charles Alexander Richmond (1862–1940). From 1909 until 1929, she lived in Schenectady, New York, where Richmond was president of Union College.

RIDDLE, THEODATE POPE (1867–1946). The architect entered Miss Porter's School in 1886 to study mathematics. She befriended both Agnes and Alice Hamilton before leaving the school in 1888. In 1927, she opened Avon Old Farms School after designing both the buildings and the school's educational philosophy.

ROGERS, JULIA REBECCA (1854–1944). The philanthropist was active in a variety of women's causes, including education and suffrage. She was one of the five women who established the Bryn Mawr School in Baltimore in 1885. She left the school's board of managers in 1891. Rogers later became active in the women's suffrage movement and in the support of Goucher College, which named its library in her honor.

SANDS, DOROTHY (1893–1980). The actress and drama instructor made her Broadway debut in 1923. She was a friend of John Mason Brown and Edith Hamilton.

SAUNDERS, LOUISE BROWNELL (1870–1961). The professor and headmistress was a Bryn Mawr College friend of Edith Hamilton's. She was the niece of Edith Hamilton's Bryn Mawr School colleague Jane Louise Brownell (1860–1935), a Bryn Mawr College graduate who taught mathematics.

SCHAUMANN, HERBERT (1909–82). The German-born poet fled Nazi Germany and taught literature and writing at the University of Maryland. He met Edith Hamilton during her years in Washington. She wrote an introduction to his translation of part of Homer's *Odyssey*, published as *Odysseus and Calypso* in 1956.

SCHOONMAKER, NANCY MUSSELMAN (1873–1965). The conservationist, politician, and speaker on international affairs coedited, with Doris Fielding Reid, an anthology of isolationist thought, *We Testify*, which was published in the autumn of 1941, shortly before the attack on Pearl Harbor.

SEYMOUR, NATHAN PERKINS (1813–91). The classical scholar was chair of the classics department at Western Reserve College in Ohio from 1840 until 1870. He taught every spring at Miss Porter's School from 1879 until 1891. Edith Hamilton studied Latin under Seymour in the spring of 1886. He later taught Alice and Agnes Hamilton.

SHEARMAN, MARGARET HILLES (1873–1964). The teacher and social reformer was a longtime friend of Edith Hamilton from their years at Bryn Mawr College, from which Shearman graduated in 1894.

SHERWOOD, DR. MARY (1856–1935). The medical doctor at the Bryn Mawr School from 1894 until her death in 1935, she was also Edith Hamilton's colleague in a variety of social and political reform causes, including the women's suffrage movement and efforts to advance women's education. The medical doctor Lilian Welsh settled in Baltimore in 1892 and remained partners until Sherwood's death.

SHOREY, PAUL (1857–1934). The classical scholar was among the founding faculty of both Bryn Mawr College and, from 1892, the University of Chicago. Edith Hamilton studied Greek under Shorey during her first year at Bryn Mawr College and absorbed his method of constructing parallels between ancient and modern authors from him. Shorey's works, *The Unity of Plato's Thought* (1903) and *What Plato Said* (1933), were influential on her friend and coeditor Huntington Cairns. Shorey's translation of *The Republic* appeared in Hamilton and Cairns's work, *The Collected Dialogues of Plato*, published in 1961.

SIKELIANOS, EVA PALMER (1874–1952). The choreographer, theatrical designer, director, and producer was a student at Bryn Mawr College from 1896–98. She became a lifelong friend of her English instructor Lucy Martin Donnelly, through whom she met Edith Hamilton, with whom she eventually corresponded on the staging of Greek tragedies. She married the Greek poet Angelos Sikelianos in 1907. The couple staged two Delphic festivals in 1927 and 1930.

SIMONSON, LEE (1888–1967). The set designer was one of the founding directors of the Theatre Guild in 1919. In 1935, he encouraged Edith Hamilton to translate *The Trojan Women* of Euripides for a possible production by the Theatre Guild, which never performed it.

SMITH, EMILY JAMES, see Putnam, Emily James Smith

SPEER, EMMA BAILEY (1872–1961). The philanthropist studied at Bryn Mawr College, where she was friends with Edith Hamilton. In 1892, she married the prominent Presbyterian layman Robert E. Speer. She served as president of the YWCA from 1915 until 1932.

TAFT, HELEN, see Manning, Helen Taft

TAFT, ROBERT A. (1889–1953). The Republican senator from Ohio was the son of President and U.S. Chief Justice William Howard Taft and the older brother of historian Helen Taft Manning. He was elected to the U.S. Senate in 1938 and served until his death in 1953. After 1946, he became a leader of his party in the body, especially its isolationist wing. Doris Fielding Reid was a strong supporter of Taft, and Edith Hamilton largely agreed with his views as well. Both socialized with Taft and his wife, Martha Bowers Taft, whom he had married in 1914.

THOMAS, HELEN, see Flexner, Helen Thomas

THOMAS, M. CAREY (1857–1935). The college administrator and women's rights advocate was born into a Quaker family in Baltimore. Her youngest sibling was Helen Thomas, later Flexner. She was a first cousin of Elizabeth King Ellicott and Alys Pearsall Smith Russell. In 1885, she was one of the five women who founded the Bryn Mawr School. She was the first dean of faculty of Bryn Mawr College and became president of the college in 1894, a position she held until her retirement in 1922.

THOMSON, SIR GEORGE PAGET (1892–1975). The physicist was the son of Sir Joseph John Thomson, also a physicist. He attended Trinity College, Cambridge, and conducted research in the Cavendish Laboratory before serving with the Royal Flying Corps during the First World War. From 1952, he was Master of Corpus Christi College, Cambridge. He won the Nobel Prize in Physics in 1937 for his work on electron diffraction. He was knighted in 1943. Thomson dedicated his 1955 work, *The Foreseeable Future*, to Doris Fielding Reid.

TSUDA, UME (1864–1929). The women's education advocate was born in Japan and studied biology at Bryn Mawr College from 1889 until 1892. After returning to Japan, Tsuda founded, in 1900, a school for women that taught in the English language. It was renamed Tsuda College after her death.

TURNBULL, GRACE (1880–1976). Sculptor and writer who was born in Baltimore. Her parents founded the Percy Turnbull Lectureship in Poetry, where Edith Hamilton may have met the Reids for the first time. As a sculptor, some of Turnbull's works drew from classical subjects. Her *Naiad* sits on Mount Vernon Place in Baltimore. She was also the author of a work on the third-century neo-Platonic philosopher Plotinus, published as *The Essence of Plotinus* in 1934.

VALENTINE, ALAN (1901–80). College administrator who was sympathetic to efforts to keep the United States from entering the Second World War. He was president of the University of Rochester when it granted Edith Hamilton her first honorary doctorate in 1949. He was later director of the Economic Stabilization Agency under President Truman. His wife, Lucia, was also friends with Edith Hamilton, advising her on what to wear when she was made an honorary citizen of Athens in 1957.

VAN DYKE, HENRY (1852–1932). The clergyman, poet, and diplomat was the uncle of Doris Fielding Reid and the Murray professor of English literature at Princeton University. President Woodrow Wilson appointed him U.S. ambassador to the Netherlands and Luxembourg in 1913, a position he occupied at the time of the outbreak of the First World War.

VAN DYKE, TERTIUS (1886–1958). The theologian was the son of Henry Van Dyke and a first cousin of Doris Fielding Reid. He was headmaster of the Gunnery School in Connecticut before eventually becoming dean of Hartford Theological Seminary from 1943 until 1954.

WALKER, SUSAN, see FitzGerald, Susan Walker

WEDEMEYER, GEN. ALBERT COADY (1897–1989). The U.S. Army general was appointed the U.S. commander in the Southeast Asia Theater in 1943. He befriended Edith Hamilton and Doris Fielding Reid during their years in Washington, D.C., and his controversial 1958 account of his own experiences in the Second World War, titled *Wedemeyer Reports!*, cited both Reid's and Hamilton's work. His wife, born Elizabeth Dade Embick, was also a friend of Edith and Doris.

WELSH, DR. LILIAN (1858–1938). The medical doctor settled in Baltimore in 1892, where she and her lifelong partner Dr. Mary Sherwood established a medical practice. Both were active in a variety of social and political reform causes, including women's suffrage, advancing women's education, and municipal reform. Her autobiography, *Reminiscences of Thirty Years in Baltimore* (1925), mentions Edith Hamilton's role in these causes.

WERGELAND, AGNES MATHILDE (1857–1914). The historian was the first Norwegian woman to obtain a doctorate, earned at the University of Zurich in 1890. She was Bryn Mawr College's fellow in history for 1890–91 and taught art history at the college until 1893.

WESKE, DOROTHY BRUCE (1900–88). Historian and 1920 graduate of the Bryn Mawr School who was a longtime correspondent of Edith Hamilton.

WILDER, ISABEL (1900–95). The novelist was the younger sister of playwright and author Thornton Wilder. She published three novels between 1933 and 1937.

WYATT, EDITH (1873–1958). The writer and social activist became friends with Edith Hamilton when she studied at Bryn Mawr College from 1892 until 1894. She subsequently became a resident of Hull House.

YOURCENAR, MARGUERITE (1903–87). The Belgian-born writer published her novel *Memoirs of Hadrian* in the United States in 1954. She lived with her partner Grace Frick on Mount Desert Island and befriended Edith Hamilton.

YURKA, BLANCHE (1887–1974). The actress played Io in 1957 production of *Prometheus Bound* in Athens and subsequently corresponded with Edith Hamilton.

NOTES

Introduction

1. Edith Hamilton to Jessie Hamilton, March 20 [n.y. but this production of *Electra* was given in 1889], folder 607, reel 28, HFP. For a description of the performance, see "Amusements," *New York Times*, February 13, 1889, p. 4. This production was also described in Foley, *Reimaging Greek Tragedy on the American Stage*, 29, 239, and in Choate, *Electra USA*, 24, 39–45, 93–95, 184, 208–10.

2. Edith Hamilton to Jessie Hamilton, March 20 [n.y.].

3. Willis, "The American Laboratory Theatre," unpublished dissertation, 23.

4. Hartigan, *Greek Tragedy on the American Stage*, 7–10; Choate, *Electra USA*, 46.

5. "Musical and Dramatic Notes," *New York Times*, March 13, 1889, p. 4.

6. Foley, *Reimaging Greek Tragedy on the American Stage*, 3.

7. Edith Hamilton to Jessie Hamilton, March 20 [n.y.].

8. Cleary, *Myths for the Millions*, 257.

9. Edith Hamilton to Alice Hamilton, February 19, 1887, folder 579, reel 27, HFP.

10. Edith Hamilton, *The Echo of Greece*, introduction, chapter 1; 12, 18.

11. Edith Hamilton, *The Greek Way*, chapters 1, 5.

12. Edith Hamilton, *The Greek Way*, chapter 2, 26–27.

13. Edith Hamilton, *The Greek Way*, chapter 2, 40–43; Edith Hamilton, *Witness to the Truth*, chapter 2.

14. Edith Hamilton, *Witness to the Truth*, chapter 1, 19; chapter 9, 218; chapter 10, 222; Edith Hamilton, *Spokesmen for God*, chapter 13, 259.

15. Edith Hamilton, *The Greek Way*, chapter 7, 139; Edith Hamilton, *The Great Age of Greek Literature*, chapter 11, 228; Edith Hamilton, *Witness to the Truth*, new introduction for 1957 edition, not paginated.

16. Edith Hamilton, *Spokesmen for God*. Here the phrase was used as the title for the final, thirteenth chapter, 251.

17. Richard Ellmann, *Oscar Wilde*, 99, 137–38; Edith Hamilton, "Tragedy," 41–46, 41; Edith Hamilton, *The Greek Way*, chapter 7, 140.

18. Goldman, "The Greek Genius"; Hutchison, "The Ancient Greeks."

19. Thornton, *Greek Way*, 2.

20. Lattimore, "Athenian Sunset"; Robinson, "Secrets of Greece's Greatness"; Hadas, "Again Edith Hamilton and the Greeks"; Stockin, "The Classical Association of the Atlantic States," 213–14; Reid, *Edith Hamilton: An Intimate Portrait*, 139–40.

21. Edith Hamilton, "Death Sentence in Theft Case," August 21, 1958, published in *New York Times*, August 28, 1958, p. 26; Dudziak, *Cold War Civil Rights*, 3–6.

22. Johnson, *The Lavender Scare*, 21, 33–36, 85, 125, 166.

23. Johnson, *The Lavender Scare*, 12.

24. Brown, "The Heritage of Edith Hamilton," 16–17, 17; quoted in Johnson, *The Lavender Scare*, 79, 90.

25. Ralph E. Flanders and Helen Flanders to Doris Fielding Reid, June 23, 1963, ABMS.

26. Edith Hamilton, *Mythology*, 92; Hitler, *Mein Kampf*, chapter 11, 290.

27. Edith Hamilton, *The Great Age of Greek Literature*, 215.

28. Reid, *Edith Hamilton: An Intimate Portrait*, 42.

29. White, "The Hamilton Way," 132–57, 137.

30. Undated memo of C. Raymond Everitt, box 39, LBP.

31. Edith Hamilton to Alan Valentine, January 26, postmarked January 28, 1961, box 3.1.1, Collection of Edith Hamilton Letters and Articles from the Valentines, ABMS.

32. Dudley Fitts, *Greek Plays in Modern Translation*, Introduction, vii–xiv, xiv; Edith Hamilton to Eva Palmer Sikelianos, July 12, 1947, folder 67, box 42, AEPS; Edith Hamilton, "Literature of Escape," 30, 35.

33. Brooks, *An Autobiography*, 551; Huntington Cairns to James K. Feibleman, June 11, 1957, folder 7, box 21, JKFP.

34. Lindquist, *The Origins of the Center for Hellenic Studies*, 6–12.

35. Reid, *Edith Hamilton: An Intimate Portrait*, 104–11.

36. Besides Edith Hamilton, they include J. P. Mahaffy, the Anglo-Irish scholar who spent his career at Trinity College, Dublin, who was honored in 1877, and, in the twentieth century, Sir C. M. Bowra, the longtime warden of Wadham College, Oxford. See Stanford and McDowell, *Mahaffy*, 40–42; Mitchell, *Maurice Bowra*, 279.

Chapter 1

1. Helen Bacon, "Edith Hamilton," in Sicherman and Green, eds., *Notable American Women*, 306.

2. Montgomery Hamilton to Andrew Holman Hamilton, July 23, 1866, folder 574, reel 27, HFP.

3. Judith Purver, "Dresden's Literary and Theatrical Traditions," in Clayton and Russell, eds., *Dresden*, 195–222, 197; Turner, *The Greek Heritage in Victorian Britain*, 39–41; Stefano Evangelista and Katherine Harloe, "Pater's 'Winckelmann': Aesthetic Criticism and Classical Reception" in Martindale, Evangelista, and Prettejohn, eds., *Pater the Classicist*, 63–80, 65–66.

4. Edith Hamilton, *The Echo of Greece*, chapter 1, 18.

5. De Forest, *James Colles*, 227.

6. Alice Hamilton, *Exploring the Dangerous Trades*, 25.

7. James Colles Jr. to George W. Colles, July 1, 1863, folder 6, box 6, CFP.

8. Griswold, *The Pictorial History of Fort Wayne, Indiana*, 446.

9. Obituary for Annie Pond Jennings, *New York Times*, November 3, 1876, p. 5.

10. George W. Colles to Harriet Wetmore Colles, January 14, 1852, folder 38, box 6, CFP.

11. Burstein, *The Original Knickerbocker*, 279, 282, 311.

12. Gertrude Pond to George W. Colles, January 24, 1859, folder 27, box 6, CFP.

13. Burstein, *The Original Knickerbocker*, 171–77, 329–30.

14. Alice Hamilton, *Exploring the Dangerous Trades*, 25; Harold Holzer, "Housekeeping on Its Own Terms: Abraham Lincoln in New York," in Harold Holzer, ed., *State of the Union*, 1–16, 4.

15. De Forest, *James Colles*, 226–28; James Colles Jr. to George W. Colles, July 1, 1863, folder 6, box 6, CFP.

16. Lee, *Edith Wharton*, 26, 69.

17. John Soane, "The Renaissance of Dresden after 1985," in Clayton and Russell, eds., *Dresden*, 93–112, 96.

18. Sicherman, *Alice Hamilton*, 15.

19. Poinsatte, *Fort Wayne during the Canal Era*, 8–9; Wetmore, "Allen Hamilton," unpublished dissertation, 55, 49.

20. Blake, *The Holmans of Veraestau*, 5, 15–17; Emerine Holman Hamilton was born near Carrollton, Kentucky, on December 10, 1810, see Dr. Allen Hamilton to Cornelius O'Brien, November 20, 1940, AV.

21. Blake, *The Holmans of Veraestau*, 10–12, 15–17, 27–31, 37–41.

22. Wetmore, "Allen Hamilton," unpublished dissertation, 112; Poinsatte, *Fort Wayne during the Canal Era*, 25–27.

23. Sicherman, *Alice Hamilton*, 15.

24. Poinsatte, *Fort Wayne during the Canal Era*, 215.

25. Alice Hamilton, *Exploring the Dangerous Trades*, 21.

26. "Allen Hamilton Homestead One of Few Landmarks to Survive March of Progress," *Fort Wayne News-Sentinel*, April 17, 1937, p. 5, and rotogravure supplement, p. 3; Karl Detzer, *Myself When Young*, 50–51.

27. Poinsatte, *Fort Wayne during the Canal Era*, 218–19.

28. Marian A. Webb to Alice Hamilton [n.d. but included in a file of letters congratulating Alice on the publication of her autobiography, *Exploring the Dangerous Trades*, so a date of 1943 seems likely], folder 668, reel 31, HFP.

29. Detzer, *Myself When Young*, 53, 142.

30. See, for example, Mary Hamilton to Andrew Holman Hamilton, November 2, 1861, folder 716; Mary Hamilton to Phoebe Taber Hamilton, March 10, 1864, folder 718; Mary Hamilton to Andrew Holman Hamilton, August 18, 1864, folder 716; all reel 32, HFP.

31. Griswold, *The Pictorial History of Fort Wayne, Indiana*, 446.

32. Turner, *The Greek Heritage in Victorian Britain*, 3.

33. Alice Hamilton, *Exploring the Dangerous Trades*, 27.

34. Montgomery Hamilton to Andrew Holman Hamilton, May 20, 1865, folder 574, reel 27, HFP.

35. Griswold, *The Pictorial History of Fort Wayne, Indiana*, 477; Ringenberg, Ringenberg, and Brain, *The Education of Alice Hamilton*, 27.

36. Canceled check dated May 30, 1868, to Huestis and Hamilton, signed by A. H. Hamilton, executor, folder 3; canceled check for $1,000 dated December 14, 1868, signed A. H. Hamilton, executor, folder 8, both box 30, HFPI.

37. Montgomery Hamilton to Andrew Holman Hamilton, July 23, 1866, folder 574, reel 27, HFP.

38. Montgomery Hamilton to Andrew Holman Hamilton, July 23, 1866, folder 574, reel 27, HFP.

39. Mary Hamilton to Andrew Holman Hamilton, July 30 [1866?]; its discussion of Montgomery Hamilton's engagement makes the year 1866 likely; folder 716, reel 32, HFP.

40. Mary Hamilton to Phoebe Taber Hamilton, August 20, 1866, folder 718, reel 32, HFP.

41. Montgomery Hamilton to Andrew Holman Hamilton, August 2, 1866, folder 574, reel 27, HFP.

42. Marriage certificate of Montgomery Hamilton and Gertrude Pond, folder 571, reel 26, HFP.

43. Montgomery Hamilton to Andrew Holman Hamilton, September 21, 1866, folder 574, reel 27, HFP.

44. Edith Hamilton to Eva Noack, November 25, 1957, folder 9, box 1, EHP.

45. Montgomery Hamilton to Andrew Holman Hamilton, June 20, 1870, folder 575, reel 27, HFP.

46. Helen Bacon, "Edith Hamilton," in Sicherman and Green, eds., *Notable American Women*, 306. Edith identified her birthday as August 12 in Edith Hamilton to Jessie Hamilton, August 18, 1885, folder 585. On the time of her birth, see Edith Hamilton to Jessie Hamilton, August 11; the year 1886 has been penciled on to this letter, but internal evidence, including Edith's discussion of her thirteenth birthday, dates it to 1880, see folder 588, reel 27, HFP.

47. Reid, *Edith Hamilton: An Intimate Portrait*, 16; Montgomery Hamilton to Andrew Holman Hamilton, December 2, 1867, Fort Wayne, receipt acknowledging payment of legacy from estate of Allen Hamilton, folder 12, box 29, HFPI.

48. Grant, *Alice Hamilton*, 22.

49. On Margaret's birthday in June see Margaret Hamilton to Jessie Hamilton, June 21 [n.y. but refers to receiving birthday letters on June 13], folder 685, reel 31, HFP; on Norah's birthday see "Pedigree Resource File" database, Family Search, http://familysearch.org/pal:/MM9.2.1 /39KV-MR9, accessed June 18, 2014, entry for Norah Hamilton; Alice Hamilton, *Exploring the Dangerous Trades*, 18; Grant, *Alice Hamilton*, 23.

50. Edith Hamilton to Jessie Hamilton, postmarked June 25, 1899, folder 589, reel 27, HFP.

51. Alice Hamilton, *Exploring the Dangerous Trades*, 18.

52. Bill to Andrew Holman Hamilton from a nursery in Pittsford, New York, April 19, 1869, folder 12, box 30; bill to Andrew Holman Hamilton from Mount Hope Nurseries, Rochester, New York, May 11, 1886, folder 10, box 41; bill to Andrew Holman Hamilton from W. W. Rawson and Company Seed and Horticultural Warehouse, Boston, September 27, 1886, folder 12, box 41, all HFPI.

53. For Jessie's birthday in December see the diary of Agnes Hamilton, December 19, 1883, p. 9, folder 326, reel 15, HFP.

54. Edith Hamilton to Agnes Hamilton, May 10 [n.y. though its discussion of Jessie's death dates it to 1960], folder 6, box 1, EHP; see also Sicherman, *Alice Hamilton*, 411.

55. Alice Hamilton, *Exploring the Dangerous Trades*, 18.

56. For Agnes's birthday, see diary of Agnes Hamilton, December 6, 1883, p. 2, folder 326, reel 15, HFP.

57. Diary of Agnes Hamilton, March 9, 1884, pp. 15–16, folder 326, reel 15, HFP.

58. Diary of Agnes Hamilton, January 7, 1884, p. 13, folder 326, reel 15, HFP.

59. See, for example, the diary of Agnes Hamilton, March 26, 1885, p. 59; diary of Agnes Hamilton, May 4, 1886, p. 68; both folder 326, reel 15, HFP; see also Dorothy Detzer Denny to Doris Fielding Reid [n.d. but after Edith's death in 1963], folder 6, box 1, EHC.

60. Griswold, *The Pictorial History of Fort Wayne, Indiana*, 422, 496, 515; Grant, *Alice Hamilton*, 23.

61. Alice Hamilton, *Exploring the Dangerous Trades*, 22.

62. Edith Hamilton to Jessie Hamilton, December 19, 1918, folder 602, reel 28, HFP.

63. Diary of Agnes Hamilton, December 19, 1883, p. 4, folder 326, reel 15, HFP.

64. Agnes Hamilton to Jessie Hamilton, March 15, 1881, folder 362, reel 18, HFP.

65. Diary of Agnes Hamilton, August 18, pp. 116–21, though this section of the diary is labeled as undated its discussion of Emerine Hamilton's death dates it to 1889, folder 332, reel 16, HFP.

66. Diary of Agnes Hamilton, August 18 [n.y. but its discussion of the last days of Emerine Hamilton's life dates it to 1889], folder 331, reel 16, HFP.

67. Edith Hamilton, *The Great Age of Greek Literature*, chapter 8, 159–62; Edith Hamilton, *The Echo of Greece*, chapter 1, 24; chapter 7, 151; Edith Hamilton, *The Roman Way*, chapter 5, 90; chapter 9, 186–87; chapter 12, 265; Edith Hamilton, *Witness to the Truth*, chapter 7, 170–71.

68. Alice Hamilton, *Exploring the Dangerous Trades*, 24; Ruth Lachenbruch to John Mason Brown, June 19, 1963, folder 4, box 3, EHC.

69. Weatherford, *A History of the American Suffragist Movement*, 42; Barry, *Susan B. Anthony*, 110–13.

70. Griswold, *The Pictorial History of Fort Wayne, Indiana*, 491.

71. Griswold, *The Pictorial History of Fort Wayne, Indiana*, 491.

72. Griswold, *The Pictorial History of Fort Wayne, Indiana*, 446.

73. Edith Hamilton to Jessie Hamilton, August 6, 1952, folder 606, reel 28, HFP.

74. Edith Hamilton to Jessie Hamilton, August 11, later dated 1886 but her discussion of her thirteenth birthday dates this to 1880, folder 588, reel 27, HFP.

75. Edith Hamilton to Jessie Hamilton, July 24, 1884, folder 584; Edith Hamilton to Jessie Hamilton, December 7, 1884, folder 584, reel 27; Edith Hamilton to Jessie Hamilton [n.d. except 1899], folder 599, reel 28, both HFP; Alice Hamilton, *Exploring the Dangerous Trades*, 22.

76. Edith Hamilton, *The Greek Way*, chapter 4, 68.

77. Edith Hamilton, *The Greek Way*, chapter 7, 139; see also introduction to the second edition of Edith Hamilton, *Witness to the Truth*, introduction not paginated; Edith Hamilton to Storer B. Lunt, December 21, 1947, WWNP.

78. Agnes Hamilton to Jessie Hamilton, March 15, 1881, folder 362, reel 18, HFP.

79. Agnes Hamilton to Jessie Hamilton, February 4, 1882, folder 362, reel 18; Jessie Hamilton to Agnes Hamilton, March 30, 1887, folder 191, reel 9; diary of Agnes Hamilton, September 11, 1886, folder 326, reel 15, all HFP.

80. Alice Hamilton, *Exploring the Dangerous Trades*, 33.

81. Alice Hamilton, *Exploring the Dangerous Trades*, 29.

82. Poinsatte, *Fort Wayne during the Canal Era*, 195.

83. Alice Hamilton, *Exploring the Dangerous Trades*, 30.

84. Poinsatte, *Fort Wayne during the Canal Era*, 230.

85. Diary of Agnes Hamilton, November 1, 1891, folder 328, reel 16, HFP.

86. Poinsatte, *Fort Wayne during the Canal Era*, 230.

87. Winterer, *The Culture of Classicism*, 2, 62, 79–84, 96.

88. Edith Hamilton, *The Roman Way*, vii; Frances Willard Kerr, "Author Receives Plaudits," *Christian Science Monitor*, March 13, 1958, p. 6.

89. Whiton, *Six Weeks' Preparation for Reading Caesar*, 38.

90. Whiton, *Six Weeks' Preparation for Reading Caesar*, 111; Winterer, *The Culture of Classicism*, 37–38, 42–43.

91. Whiton, *Six Weeks' Preparation for Reading Caesar*, iii.

92. Winterer, *The Culture of Classicism*, 23.

93. Eileen Summers, "In the Atomic Age, We Can Still Learn from the Greeks," *Washington Post and Times Herald*, March 22, 1959, F3.

94. "Edith Hamilton," in James Nelson, ed., *Wisdom For Our Time*, 15–25, 18–19.

95. Edith Hamilton to Jessie Hamilton, January 6, 1884, folder 584; Edith Hamilton to Jessie Hamilton, August 17; this letter was later dated 1886, but its mention of Edith's twenty-first birthday dates it to 1888, folder 588; both reel 27, HFP.

96. Alice Hamilton, *Exploring the Dangerous Trades*, 28; Edith Hamilton, *The Echo of Greece*, chapter 10, 220.

97. Alice Hamilton, *Exploring the Dangerous Trades*, 27.

98. Alice Hamilton, *Exploring the Dangerous Trades*, 29.

99. Edith Hamilton, *The Greek Way*, chapter 5, 87.

100. Edith Hamilton to Jessie Hamilton [n.d. except "Tuesday evening," but written when Jessie was new to Miss Porter's School, so circa 1880], folder 590, reel 27, HFP; Alice Hamilton, *Exploring the Dangerous Trades*, 30–31.

101. Alice Hamilton, *Exploring the Dangerous Trades*, 29–30.

102. Edith Hamilton to Jessie Hamilton, April 11, 1886, folder 587, reel 27; Jessie Hamilton to Agnes Hamilton, December 26, 1886, folder 189, reel 9, both HFP.

103. Diary of Agnes Hamilton, February 10, 1884, pp. 14–15, folder 326, reel 15, HFP.

104. Diary of Agnes Hamilton, October 4, 1884, p. 44, folder 326, reel 15, HFP.

105. Edith Hamilton to Jessie Hamilton, postmarked October 13, 1883, folder 583; Edith Hamilton to Jessie Hamilton, January 1, 1884, folder 584, both reel 27, HFP.

Chapter 2

1. The school year at Miss Porter's always began in October. See, for example, Edith Hamilton to Jessie Hamilton, January 6, 1884, folder 584; Edith Hamilton to Jessie Hamilton, October 3 [n.y. but clearly describing Edith's first days at Farmington so likely 1883], making it Edith's first letter to Jessie from Miss Porter's School; folder 591, both reel 27, HFP.

2. Edith Hamilton to Jessie Hamilton, July 24, 1884, folder 584; and Edith Hamilton to Jessie Hamilton, February 16, 1885, folder 585, both reel 27, HFP.

3. Edith Hamilton to Jessie Hamilton, March 13 [n.y. but probably 1884, given that Jessie's friend Bessie Lathrop is mentioned as still at Farmington], folder 591, reel 27, HFP.

4. Edith Hamilton to Jessie Hamilton, postmarked October 13, 1883, folder 583, reel 27, HFP.

5. Edith Hamilton to Jessie Hamilton, postmarked October 13, 1883, folder 583, reel 27, HFP. See also Nelson, *Wisdom for Our Time*, 18.

6. Nelson, *Wisdom for Our Time*, 18; Edith Hamilton to Jessie Hamilton, postmarked October 13, 1883.

7. Davis and Donahue, *Miss Porter's School*, 5.

8. Agnes Hamilton to Jessie Hamilton, May 4, 1887, folder 365, reel 18, HFP.

9. Agnes Hamilton to Jessie Hamilton, December 3, 1886, folder 363, reel 18, HFP.

10. Edith Hamilton to Jessie Hamilton, July 24 [1884?], folder 584, reel 27, HFP.

11. Agnes Hamilton to Jessie Hamilton, May 4, 1887, folder 365, reel 18, HFP.

12. Edith Hamilton to Jessie Hamilton, October 2, 1885, folder 585, reel 27, HFP.

13. Sicherman, *Alice Hamilton*, 18.

14. Ringenberg, Ringenberg, and Brain, *The Education of Alice Hamilton*, 27.

15. Edith Hamilton to Jessie Hamilton, February 16, 1885, folder 585, reel 27, HFP.

16. Unidentified correspondent to Jessie Hamilton, August 16 [n.y. but referring to Edith missing a spring term at Miss Porter's], folder 323, reel 15; Edith Hamilton to Jessie Hamilton, July 23 [1885?], folder 585, reel 27, both HFP.

17. Edith Hamilton to Jessie Hamilton, October 25, 1885, folder 585, reel 27, HFP.

18. Obituary for Sarah Locke Richmond, *New York Times*, August 6, 1950, p. 72.

19. Edith Hamilton to Alice Hamilton [n.d.], folder 580, reel 27, HFP; for Sarah Locke's birthdate see "Charles Alexander Richmond," in Somers, *The Encyclopedia of Union College History*, 609–13, 609; and Edith Hamilton to Jessie Hamilton, May 23 [1886?], folder 587; Edith Hamilton to Jessie Hamilton, October 25, 1885, folder 585, both reel 27, HFP.

20. Edith Hamilton to Jessie Hamilton, postmarked May 23 [1886?]; but its mention of Sarah Locke indicates that the year 1886 is correct; folder 588, reel 27, HFP.

21. Edith Hamilton to Jessie Hamilton, December 15, 1885, folder 586, reel 27, HFP.

22. Alice Hamilton, *Exploring the Dangerous Trades*, 36–37; Pedersen, *The Discovery of Language*, 76, 81–83.

23. Diary of Agnes Hamilton, May 25, 1891, pp. 151–54, folder 328; diary of Agnes Hamilton, pp. 100–3, folder 329, both reel 16, HFP. This visit also referred to in Edith Hamilton to Jessie Hamilton, fragments in folders 612 and 613, reel 28, which are probably parts of the letter dated June 8 [1890?], folder 593, reel 27, HFP. All of these discuss a visit to Miss Porter's School and a meeting with the Japanese student Ume Tsuda as well as a day trip to New Haven. See also George St. John to Edith Hamilton, May 20, 1957, folder 9, box 1, EHP.

24. Edith Hamilton to Jessie Hamilton, April 15, 1903, folder 601, reel 28, HFP.

25. Edith Hamilton to Jessie Hamilton, August 13 [1910?], folder 601, reel 18, HFP.

26. Davis and Donahue, *Miss Porter's School*, 25.

27. Herringshaw, *Herringshaw's Library of American Biography*, vol. 3, 220.

28. Edith Hamilton to Jessie Hamilton [n.d. except "Sunday evening"], folder 591, reel 27; Edith Hamilton to Jessie Hamilton, March 20 [n.y. though it describes the *Electra* of Sophocles she saw in New York City in 1889], folder 607, reel 28; both HFP.

29. Edith Hamilton to Jessie Hamilton, August 5, 1881, folder 583, reel 27; Jessie Hamilton to Agnes Hamilton [n.d. except 1921 but written soon after Edith's departure for England in June], folder 237, reel 11, both HFP.

30. Peters, *Jean Ingelow*, 103.

31. Alice Hamilton, *Exploring the Dangerous Trades*, 19.

32. Speech at Vassar College's 100th Commencement, box 3, folder 1, EHC; although labeled as given at Vassar's commencement, it was given at the Centennial of the Vassar Club of Virginia.

33. Diary of Agnes Hamilton, March 31, 1886, p. 63, folder 326, reel 15, HFP.

34. Alice Hamilton, *Exploring the Dangerous Trades*, 18; Edith Hamilton to Alice Hamilton, February 19, 1887, folder 579, reel 27, HFP.

35. Jessie Hamilton to her brother Allen Hamilton, Feb. 1 [n.y. but its discussion of Edith's success on the Bryn Mawr College entrance exam makes a date of February 1891 seem likely], folder 244, reel 11; see also diary of Agnes Hamilton, February 8, 1891, pp. 139–40, folder 328, reel 16, HFP.

36. Diary of Agnes Hamilton, May 1, 1892, p. 28, folder 329, reel 16, HFP.

37. Detzer, *Myself When Young*, 243.

38. Guckenberg, *Hugh McCulloch*, 191.

39. Edith Hamilton to Jessie Hamilton [n.d. except 1889], folder 599, reel 28, HFP.

40. Edith Hamilton to Jessie Hamilton, Aug. 11; this letter has had the year 1886 penciled in on it, however, internal evidence, including Edith's mention of her thirteenth birthday, dates it to 1880; folder 588, reel 27, HFP.

41. Detzer, *Myself When Young*, 36.

42. Stites and Sterling, *Historic Cottages of Mackinac Island*, 10–11, 35.

43. Edith Hamilton to Jessie Hamilton, August 16 [1887]; Edith Hamilton to Jessie Hamilton, August 21 [1887]; Edith Hamilton to Jessie Hamilton, September 14 [1889]; Edith Hamilton to Jessie Hamilton, September 20, 1889, all folder 589, reel 27; Norah Hamilton to Jessie Hamilton, August 11 [1890?], folder 703, reel 32, all HFP.

44. Edith Hamilton to Alice Hamilton, February 19, 1887, folder 579, reel 27, HFP.

45. Prins, *Ladies' Greek*, 5, 7.

46. Edith Hamilton to Jessie Hamilton, March 20 [n.y. but this performance of *Electra* was given in 1889], folder 607, reel 28, HFP; for a description and review of the performance see the *New York Times* "Amusements," February 13, 1889, p. 4; "Notes of the Week," March 10, 1889, p. 3; "Mr. Sargent's Pupils," March 12, 1889, p. 4, and "Musical and Dramatic Notes," March 13, 1889, p. 4. This last article mentions the upcoming performance of March 20, 1889.

47. Edith Hamilton, "The Greek Chorus: Fifteen or Fifty?"; this essay was reprinted in Edith Hamilton, *The Ever-Present Past*, 48–59.

48. Edith Hamilton to Jessie Hamilton, September 14 [1889?], folder 589, reel 27; Edith Hamilton to Jessie Hamilton, summer 1889, folder 599, reel 28, both HFP.

49. Diary of Agnes Hamilton, May 26, 1884, p. 23, folder 326, reel 15; diary of Agnes Hamilton, April 13, 1890, p. 73, folder 328, reel 16, both HFP.

50. Jessie Hamilton to her brother Allen Hamilton, Feb. 1 [n.y. but its discussion of Edith's success on the Bryn Mawr College entrance exam makes a date of February 1891 seem likely], folder 244, reel 11; see also diary of Agnes Hamilton, April 13, 1890, p. 73; February 8, 1891, pp. 139–40; both folder 328. Diary of Agnes Hamilton, September 4, 1895, p. 48, folder 331, all reel 16, HFP. On the Bryn Mawr College entrance exam see Winterer, *The Mirror of Antiquity*, 202.

51. Alice Hamilton, *Exploring the Dangerous Trades*, 38; Edith Hamilton to Jessie Hamilton, July 24, 1892, folder 593, reel 27, HFP. .

52. Agnes Hamilton to Jessie Hamilton, October 10, 1886, folder 363; Agnes Hamilton to Jessie Hamilton, September 13, 1892, folder 369, both reel 18; diary of Agnes Hamilton, October 20, 1895, folder 331, reel 16, all HFP. I am grateful to Mr. Craig Leonard for the reference to Agnes Hamilton working at the firm of Wing and Mahurin.

53. Edith Hamilton to Jessie Hamilton, January 1, 1884, folder 584; Edith Hamilton to Jessie Hamilton, October 11 [1885], folder 585; Edith Hamilton to Jessie Hamilton, October 25 [1885], folder 585; all reel 27, HFP.

54. Jessie Hamilton to Agnes Hamilton, January 23, 1887, folder 190, reel 9, HFP.

55. Perry, *William J. Forsyth*, xv, 28, 30, 88–89, 138; Marian A. Webb to Alice Hamilton [n.d. but written to congratulate Alice on the publication of her autobiography so likely 1943], folder 668, reel 31; diary of Agnes Hamilton, November 23, 1889, pp. 7–8, folder 328, reel 16, both HFP.

56. Edith Hamilton to Jessie Hamilton, April 18, 1898, folder 598, reel 27; Jessie Hamilton to Katherine Hamilton, January 15, 1899, and October 23, 1899, both folder 185, reel 9, all HFP.

57. Gertrude Colles to George W. Colles, January 26, 1885, folder 4, box 6, CFP.

58. Edith Hamilton to Mary E. Garrett, February 28, 1898, frames 396–98, reel 214, MCTP.

59. Jessie Hamilton to Agnes Hamilton, March 26, 1887, folder 191, reel 9, HFP.

60. Edith Hamilton to Agnes Hamilton, August 22 [n.y. but discussion of Edith's hand, experiencing paralysis because of shingles, dates it to 1960 or 1961], folder 6, box 1, EHP.

61. Edith Hamilton to [Jessie or Agnes Hamilton?] Undated letter fragment but describing activities in which Edith participated circa 1889, folder 613, reel 28, HFP.

62. Diary of Agnes Hamilton, November 10, 1889, p. 3; November 23, 1889, p. 7; December 19, 1889, pp. 12–14; March 9, 1889, pp. 63–66; all folder 328, reel 16, HFP. Foley, *Reimagining Greek Tragedy*, 130; Winterer, *The Mirror of Antiquity*, 202.

63. Diary of Agnes Hamilton, January 31, 1890, p. 35, folder 328, reel 16, HFP; Hamilton, *The Greek Way*, chapter 2, 31; Copleston, *Aeschylus*, chapter 1, 19.

64. Edith Hamilton to Jessie Hamilton [n.d. except 1889], folder 599, reel 28, HFP.

65. Diary of Agnes Hamilton, August 13, 1890, p. 89; diary of Agnes Hamilton, September 7, 1890, both folder 328, reel 16, HFP.

66. Jessie Hamilton to her brother Allen Hamilton, September 23, 1890, folder 241, reel 11, HFP.

67. Solomon, *In the Company of Educated Women*, 70.

68. Jessie Hamilton to her brother Allen Hamilton, February 1 [n.y. but since Edith entered Bryn Mawr College in early 1891 that year seems likely], folder 244, reel 11, HFP.

69. Jessie Hamilton to her brother Allen Hamilton [n.d. but its discussion of Edith's success on the Bryn Mawr College entrance exam makes a date of February 1891 seem likely], folder

244, reel 11; diary of Agnes Hamilton, February 8, 1891, and following entry labeled Tuesday, pp. 139–40, folder 328, reel 16, all HFP.

Chapter 3

1. Horowitz, *The Power and Passion of M. Carey Thomas*, 152.

2. Susan Snyder, "Bryn Mawr to Reduce Visibility of Its 2nd President after Reviewing Her History of Racism," *Philadelphia Inquirer*, August 8, 2018; Horowitz, *The Power and Passion of M. Carey Thomas*, 230–32, 341, 364–65, 381, 449.

3. Meigs, *What Makes a College?*, 41; Winterer, *The Mirror of Antiquity*, 202.

4. Edith Hamilton to Jessie Hamilton, July 24, 1892, folder 593, reel 27, HFP.

5. Horowitz, *The Power and Passion of M. Carey Thomas*, 186.

6. Winterer, *The Culture of Classicism*, 6.

7. Horowitz, *The Power and Passion of M. Carey Thomas*, 203.

8. Edith Hamilton to Jessie Hamilton, February 18, 1891, folder 593, reel 27, HFP.

9. Meigs, *What Makes a College?*, 92–93.

10. Edith Hamilton to Jessie Hamilton, February 18, 1891, folder 593, reel 27, HFP.

11. Kopff, "Paul Shorey," 447–48; Putnam, "Paul Shorey," *Atlantic Monthly*, 795–804, 797–98; Horowitz, *The Power and Passion of M. Carey Thomas*, 208.

12. Kopff, "Paul Shorey," 447–53, 448.

13. Putnam, "Paul Shorey," *Atlantic Monthly*, 797; Edith Hamilton to "Dearest Margaret" [Margaret Hamilton], n.d., folder 2, box 1, EHP.

14. Edith Hamilton to Jessie Hamilton, Feb. 18, 1891, folder 593, reel 27, HFP.

15. Edith Hamilton to Alice Hamilton [n.d. but internal evidence, including the discussion of the college's performance of *Iolanthe* and the upcoming wedding of Sarah Locke, date it to the spring of 1891], folder 580, reel 27, HFP; see also Somers, *Encyclopedia of Union College History*, 609.

16. Edith Hamilton, "W. S. Gilbert: A Mid-Victorian Aristophanes," 781–90, 782; this essay was reprinted in Jones, *W. S. Gilbert*, 111–34, 115; slightly edited, it formed the basis for the chapter on Aristophanes in *The Greek Way*.

17. Edith Hamilton to Jessie Hamilton [n.d. though internal evidence, its mention of Edith Child as a member of the 1890 class of Bryn Mawr College as well as the decision of the Duryee family to settle in New Brunswick, New Jersey, date it to Edith's first term at Bryn Mawr in the spring of 1891], folder 604, reel 28, HFP; on the Duryee family's move to New Brunswick, see biography of Lily Duryee published by the Woman's Board of Foreign Missions, n.d., folder 452, reel 22, HFP.

18. Edith Hamilton to Jessie Hamilton, only dated "Tuesday," fragment of a diary letter written from Bryn Mawr College, folder 613, reel 28, HFP; this letter mentions Nan Emery as the European fellow for the previous year so a date of autumn 1892 seems likely since it is written after Shorey's departure.

19. Edith Hamilton, "The Classics," 29–32, 29.

20. George A. Kennedy, "Gildersleeve, the Journal, and Philology in America," in Briggs and Benario, eds., *Basil Lanneau Gildersleeve: An American Classicist*, 42–49, 43–46.

21. Edith Hamilton, "Plato," in Hamilton, *The Ever-Present Past*, 38–47, 40–41.

22. Nancy A. Mavrogenes, "Gonzalez Lodge," in Briggs, ed., *Biographical Dictionary of North American Classicists*, 366–67.

23. Edith Hamilton to Jessie Hamilton [n.d., though internal evidence, its mention of Edith Child as a member of the 1890 class of Bryn Mawr College as well as the decision of the Duryee family to settle in New Brunswick, New Jersey, date it to Edith's first term at Bryn Mawr in the spring of 1891], folder 604, reel 28, HFP.

24. Edith Hamilton to Huntington Cairns, April 7, 1947, box 12, HCP.

25. Edith Hamilton to Alice Hamilton [n.d. but internal evidence, including its discussion of Shorey's classes, dates it to Edith's first year and a half at Bryn Mawr], folder 580, reel 27, HFP.

26. Meigs, *What Makes a College?*, 125; Edith Hamilton to Jessie Hamilton, January 1, 1893, folder 594, reel 27, HFP.

27. Edith Hamilton to Jessie Hamilton, July 24, 1892, folder 593, reel 27, HFP.

28. Edith Hamilton to Alice Hamilton, January 31 [n.y. though Agnes's diary places this in 1892], folder 579, reel 27; see also diary of Agnes Hamilton, January 13, 1892, p. 2, folder 329, reel 16, both HFP.

29. John Clendenin, "My Edith Hamilton," unpublished, p. 7, folder 1, box 2, EHP. Clendenin mistakenly identifies Edith's Bryn Mawr classmate as Mark Twain's wife, also Olivia Clemens.

30. Willis, *Mark and Livy*, 187; on the early tradition of Gilbert and Sullivan at the college, see Meigs, *What Makes a College?*, 233; Edith Hamilton to Alice Hamilton [n.d., although its discussion of the performance of *Iolanthe* dates it to the spring of 1891], folder 580, reel 27, HFP.

31. Clendenin, "My Edith Hamilton," 7.

32. Willis, *Mark and Livy*, 188; Olivia Susan Clemens died in 1896, at the age of twenty-four, from spinal meningitis, see Willis, 237.

33. Piper, *Robert E. Speer*, 84–85, 92–98.

34. Edith Hamilton to Alice Hamilton, Feb. 7 [n.y. though 1892], folder 580, reel 27; this letter to Alice also describes Edith's "high credit" on her English essay, dating it to 1892, see diary of Agnes Hamilton, January 13, 1892, p. 2, folder 329, reel 16, both HFP.

35. Coleman, *Camp Diamond Story*, 18.

36. Piper, *Robert E. Speer*, 78–79, 114.

37. Biography of Lily N. Duryee published by Women's Board of Foreign Missions [n.d.], folder 452, reel 22, HFP.

38. Edith Hamilton to Jessie Hamilton, November 28, 1892, folder 593, reel 27, HFP.

39. Edith Hamilton to Jessie Hamilton, dated February 7, 1897, but more likely 1894 since it describes Lily's impending departure for China and describes Emma Bailey Speer's house in Elizabeth, New Jersey, folder 597, reel 27, HFP; for the Union Street address of the Duryees, see Edith Hamilton to Mary E. Garrett, November 25, 1897, frames 287–88, reel 214, MCTP.

40. Edith Hamilton to Jessie Hamilton, November 28, 1892, folder 593, reel 27, HFP.

41. Piper, *Robert E. Speer*, 83.

42. Edith Hamilton to Jessie Hamilton, erroneously dated June 4, 1896, but more likely June 4, 1892, since it refers to the celebrations for the Bryn Mawr graduating class of that year and to the upcoming marriage of Emma Bailey and Robert Speer, folder 596, reel 27, HFP; Edith Hamilton to Jessie Hamilton February 11, 1932, folder 606, reel 28, HFP.

43. Edith Hamilton to Jessie Hamilton, July 24, 1892, folder 593, reel 27, HFP.

44. Edith Finch, "Lucy Martin Donnelly," in Sicherman and Green, eds., *Notable American Women*, 499–500; Lucy Martin Donnelly to Bertrand Russell, August 1914, box 5.13, BRP; Logan Pearsall Smith to Lucy Martin Donnelly, June 14, 1923, box 1, LPSP.

45. Edith Finch, "Lucy Martin Donnelly," in Sicherman and Green, eds., *Notable American Women*, 499; Morrill, *History of Adelphi Academy*, 16, 18, 62–63, 127.

46. Edith Pettit Borie, "Lucy Martin Donnelly, 1870–1948," *Bryn Mawr Alumnae Bulletin*, November 1948, vol. 24, p. 6–8.

47. Edith Hamilton to Jessie Hamilton [n.d. though its description of Emma Bailey Speer as one of her college friends dates it to Edith's first two years at Bryn Mawr], folder 599, reel 28, HFP.

48. Edith Hamilton to Jessie Hamilton [n.d. though its description of Emma Bailey Speer as one of her college friends dates it to Edith's first two years at Bryn Mawr], folder 599, reel 28, HFP.

49. Lucy Martin Donnelly to M. Carey Thomas, September 23, 1893, frames 483–85, reel 38, MCTP; Edith Hamilton to Jessie Hamilton, July 24, 1892; Edith Hamilton to Jessie Hamilton, August 3, 1892, both folder 593, reel 27, HFP.

50. Faderman, *Surpassing the Love of Men*, 157–78; Leontis, *Eva Palmer Sikelianos*, xxxiv, 10.

51. Edith Hamilton to Jessie Hamilton [n.d., though its description of Emma Bailey Speer as one of her college friends dates this to Edith's first two years at Bryn Mawr], folder 599, reel 28, HFP.

52. Edith Hamilton to Jessie Hamilton, November 28, 1893, reel 27, folder 594, HFP.

53. Edith Hamilton to Jessie Hamilton [n.d. but internal evidence, including reference to Nan Emery as the previous year's European fellow, date it to early 1893], folder 599, reel 28, HFP.

54. Horowitz, *The Power and Passion of M. Carey Thomas*, 299–301.

55. Palmer-Sikelianos, *Upward Panic*, 25.

56. Horowitz, *The Power and Passion of M. Carey Thomas*, 148–51.

57. Edith Hamilton, *Mythology*, 217–18.

58. Edith Hamilton, "Faulkner: Sorcerer or Slave?" 8–10, 39–41; this essay was reprinted in its entirety in Edith Hamilton, *The Ever-Present Past*, 159–74.

59. Edith Hamilton to Jessie Hamilton, August 29, 1897, folder 597, reel 27, HFP; the description of the Roman villa appears in chapter two of the novel; Shelley Hales, "A Search for Home: The Representation of the Domestic in Marius the Epicurean," in Martindale, Evangelista, and Prettejohn, eds., *Pater the Classicist*, 135–48.

60. Pater, *Marius the Epicurean*, chapter 1.

61. James Thomas Flexner, *An American Saga*, 269.

62. Bertha Haven Putnam, "The Music of 'Pallas Athene,'" originally published in the *Bryn Mawr Alumnae Bulletin*, November 1944, reprinted Bruder, *Offerings to Athena*, 54.

63. Helen Thomas Flexner, "Bryn Mawr," 1–7; Livingstone, *The Greek Genius*, 30.

64. Louise Sheffield Brownell, "Day," and Lucy Martin Donnelly, "Night," in the *Lantern I*, 1891, p. 59. The poems are signed "L.S.B." and "L.M.D."

65. Jenkyns, *The Victorians and Ancient Greece*, 302.

66. Alice Hamilton, *Exploring the Dangerous Trades*, 41.

67. Edith Hamilton to "Dear Children" [Katherine, Jessie, and Agnes Hamilton], January 6, 1899, folder 598, reel 27, HFP; Abse, *John Ruskin*, 108, 120, 197.

68. Edith Pettit Borie, "Lucy Martin Donnelly, 1870–1948," *Bryn Mawr Alumnae Bulletin*, November 1948, p. 6; Horowitz, *The Power and Passion of M. Carey Thomas*, 94–95; Eva Palmer Sikelianos to Mary Crovatt Hambidge, December 16 [1931], frames 880–93, reel 3179, JMCHP.

69. Honan, *Matthew Arnold*, 290–91, 338, 396–400, 407, 421.

70. Edith Hamilton to Jessie Hamilton, spring 1895, folder 595, reel 27, HFP; Edith Hamilton to "Dearest Peggy" [Margaret Hamilton], n.d. but mentions this essay so likely also spring 1895, folder 2, box 1, EHP.

71. Arnold, "Culture and Anarchy," 87–229, chapter 4, 164–65, 171–74.

72. Turner, *The Greek Heritage in Victorian Britain*, 19.

73. Turner, *The Greek Heritage in Victorian Britain*, 27; Stray, *The Living Word*, 1.

74. Honan, *Matthew Arnold*, 346; Edith Hamilton, *The Greek Way*, chapter 2, 27.

75. Arnold, "Culture and Anarchy," 113; Edith Hamilton, *The Greek Way*, chapter 1, 4–5.

76. Arnold, "Literature and Dogma."

77. Edith Hamilton to Clara Landsberg [n.d. but the letter concerns some drafts of chapters of *Witness to the Truth*, so likely circa 1945]; she implies fifty years of familiarity with Caird's work, indicating that she first encountered it while at Bryn Mawr College, folder 2, box 3, EHC.

78. Jones and Muirhead, *The Life and Philosophy of Edward Caird*, 245–51.

79. Jones and Muirhead, 126–28.

80. Brittain, *The Women at Oxford*, 101.

81. Helen Thomas Flexner, "Bryn Mawr," 13; Jones and Muirhead, 28, 47, 93–101, 126, 128, 136, 144, 155.

82. Boucher and Vincent, *British Idealism and Political Theory*, 2–3, 9–11.

83. Caird, *The Evolution of Religion*, vol. 1, 7–8; Brittain, *The Women at Oxford*, 38, 95.

84. Caird, *The Evolution of Religion*, vol. 1, 64, 234, 271.

85. Caird, *The Evolution of Religion*, vol. 1, 264–66.

86. Caird, *The Evolution of Religion*, vol. 1, 23.

87. Caird, *The Evolution of Religion*, vol. 1, 372–76.

88. Caird, *The Evolution of Religion*, vol. 2, 316–17, 322.

89. Edith Hamilton, *The Greek Way*, chapter 3, 48–60; Edith Hamilton, *Mythology*, 8–9; Edith Hamilton, *The Great Age of Greek Literature*, chapter 15, 289–90.

90. Edith Hamilton, *Witness to the Truth*, chapter 8, 199–206.

91. Caird, *The Evolution of Religion*, vol. 1, 16, 20–21, 25, 73.

92. Edith Hamilton, *The Greek Way*, chapter 1, 5.

93. Jones and Muirhead, *The Life and Philosophy of Edward Caird*, 34–35; Caird, *The Evolution of Religion*, volume 1, 15–16, 19, 21, 24–25, 29–31, 37–38, 53–62, 65–67, 73, 77, 84, 139–40, 164–66, 191, 206–7, 235–37; volume 2, 14–18.

94. Caird, *The Evolution of Religion*, vol. 1, 234.

95. Edith Hamilton, *Witness to the Truth*, chapter 8, 215–16.

96. Edith Hamilton to Jessie Hamilton October 29 [n.y., though its address of 517 Cathedral Street indicates a likely date of 1897], folder 599, reel 28, HFP.

97. Patricia A. Palmieri, "Here Was Fellowship: A Social Portrait of Academic Women at Wellesley College, 1895–1920," in Prentice and Theobold, eds., *Women Who Taught*, 233–57, 240.

98. Edith Hamilton to [Jessie Hamilton?]. This letter fragment is not dated, but its discussion of Lady Henry Somerset's speech on the Bryn Mawr campus dates it to 1890–1891, folder 612, reel 28, HFP.

99. Niessen, *Aristocracy, Temperance, and Social Reform*, 83–89.

100. Edith Hamilton to Jessie Hamilton [n.d., though internal evidence, including her discussion of the marriage between a fellow Bryn Mawr student Evangeline Walker and the historian Charles McLean Andrews, dates this to the spring of 1895], folder 607, reel 28, HFP.

101. Edith Hamilton, "Cruel Slaughtering Protested," letter to the editor of the *New York Times*, April 30, 1958, p. 32.

102. Edith Hamilton to Jessie Hamilton, February 6, 1893, reel 27, folder 594, HFP.

103. Edith Hamilton to Jessie Hamilton [n.d. though its discussion of student government having formed the previous year and its mention of Nan Emery as the previous year's European fellow, as well as references the upcoming election in February, dates it to January 1893], folder 607, reel 28, HFP.

104. Edith Hamilton to Jessie Hamilton [January 1893?], folder 607, reel 28, HFP.

105. Edith Hamilton to Jessie Hamilton [January 1893?], folder 607, reel 28, HFP.

106. Helen Thomas Flexner, "Bryn Mawr," 6.

107. Jessie Hamilton to Agnes Hamilton, April 26, 1922, folder 214, reel 10, HFP.

108. *The Lantern*, 1893, 99.

109. Edith Hamilton to Jessie Hamilton, November 28 [1893], folder 594, reel 27, HFP.

110. Edith Hamilton to Jessie Hamilton, February 7 [1894?]. This letter has been dated as 1897, but its contents, including its discussion of her work with Laurette Potts in student government, dates it to early 1894, folder 597, reel 27, HFP.

111. Edith Hamilton to Jessie Hamilton, November 28 [1893], folder 594, reel 27, HFP.

112. Edith Hamilton to Jessie Hamilton, February 7 [1894?]. This letter has been dated as 1897 but its contents, including its discussion of her work with Laurette Potts in student government, dates it to early 1894, folder 597, reel 27, HFP.

113. Edith Hamilton to Jessie Hamilton, November 28 [1893], folder 594, reel 27, HFP. For Rhoads as a Christian ethics lecturer at the college, see Meigs, *What Makes a College?*, 50.

114. Edith Hamilton to Jessie Hamilton [n.d. except "Tuesday evening"]; Edith Hamilton to Jessie Hamilton, January 3 [n.y. but its reference to her high credit in English dates it to 1892], both folder 592, reel 27, HFP; Somers, *The Encyclopedia of Union College History*, 609–13.

115. Edith Hamilton to Alice Hamilton [n.d. but internal evidence dates it to Edith's first year at Bryn Mawr], folder 580, reel 27, HFP.

116. Somers, *The Encyclopedia of Union College History*, 609.

117. Edith Hamilton to Jessie Hamilton, June–July 1890, folder 593, reel 27, HFP.

118. Edith Hamilton to Rosamond Gilder, August 9 [1925?], box 11, GM.

119. Edith Hamilton to Alice Hamilton [n.d.], folder 580, reel 27, HFP.

120. Edith Hamilton to Jessie Hamilton, summer 1893, folder 594, reel 27, HFP.

121. Edith Hamilton to Jessie Hamilton, January 1, 1893, reel 27, folder 594, HFP.

122. Edith Hamilton to Jessie Hamilton, February 7 [1893?]. This letter is dated 1897, but internal evidence, including Edith's participation in student government at Bryn Mawr College, makes it more likely 1893, folder 597, reel 28, HFP.

123. Bryn Mawr College, *Bryn Mawr College Calendar, Vol. 1, Part 1: Register of Alumnae and Former Students* (Bryn Mawr: Bryn Mawr College, March 1908), 5, 29. On Edith's interest in Edith Child and lack of interest in Helen Bartlett, see Edith Hamilton to Jessie Hamilton [n.d. but internal evidence, including the decision of Dr. William Rankin Duryee to settle in New Brunswick, New Jersey, and Edith Child's graduation, date it to the spring of 1891], folder 604, reel 28, HFP. On the Duryee family's move to New Brunswick, see printed biography of Lily Duryee published by the Woman's Board of Foreign Missions [n.d.], folder 452, reel 22, HFP.

124. Ibid.

125. Edith Hamilton to Jessie Hamilton, July 24, 1892, folder 593, reel 27, HFP.

126. Edith Hamilton to Jessie Hamilton, June 4 [n.y. but internal evidence, including the celebrations of the graduation of the class of 1892, date this to that year], folder 596, reel 27, HFP.

127. Edith Hamilton to Jessie Hamilton, July 24, 1892, folder 593, reel 27, HFP.

128. Kopff, "Paul Shorey," 447.

Chapter 4

1. Solomon, *In the Company of Educated Women*, 72–74; Edith Hamilton to Jessie Hamilton, July 24, 1892, folder 593, reel 27, HFP.

2. Edith Hamilton to Jessie Hamilton [n.d. but clearly written during Edith's years at Bryn Mawr College], folder 607, reel 28, HFP; M. Carey Thomas to Edith Hamilton, March 22, 1897, frame 1198, reel 213, MCTP.

3. Edith Hamilton to Jessie Hamilton, January 1, 1893, folder 594, reel 27, HFP.

4. Margaret Hamilton to Agnes Hamilton, October 15 [1893], folder 686, reel 31, HFP.

5. Margaret Hamilton to Agnes Hamilton, November 8, 1893; Margaret Hamilton to Agnes Hamilton, postmarked February 1894; both folder 686, reel 31, HFP.

6. Margaret Hamilton to Agnes Hamilton, postmarked February 1894, folder 686, reel 31, HFP.

7. Edith Hamilton to Jessie Hamilton, May 8, 1894, folder 594, reel 27, HFP.

8. Edith Hamilton to Jessie Hamilton, November 28 [1893], folder 594, reel 27, HFP.

9. Edith Hamilton to Jessie Hamilton, March 6 [1894], folder 594, reel 27, HFP.

10. Edith Hamilton to Jessie Hamilton, spring [1895], though a date of 1894 seems more likely, folder 595, reel 27, HFP.

11. Edith Hamilton to Margaret Hamilton [n.d. though during her year as fellow in Latin], folder 2, box 1, EHP.

12. Edith Hamilton to Jessie Hamilton, February 18, 1891, folder 593, reel 27, HFP.

13. Edith Hamilton to [Jessie Hamilton?] This letter fragment is undated except for "Sunday" but refers to Nan Emery as the European fellow from the previous year, folder 613, reel 28, HFP.

14. Edith Hamilton to Peggy [Margaret] Hamilton [n.d. but Edith described similar conditions, including working on a paper on the opinion of ancient authors on Thucydides and interaction with Evangeline Walker and Charles McLean Andrews in her letter to Jessie Hamilton dated spring 1895], folder 595, reel 27, EHP.

15. Ibid. Edith Hamilton to Peggy [Margaret] Hamilton.

16. Griffin, *Seneca*, 35–36, 67, 367.

17. Edith Hamilton to Jessie Hamilton [n.d. but most likely during her year as fellow in Latin], folder 599, reel 28, HFP.

18. Emery, *The Historical Present in Early Latin*.

19. Griffin, *Seneca*, 367.

20. Caird, *The Evolution of Religion*, vol. 1, 372–76.

21. Edith Hamilton, *The Roman Way*, chapter 12, 245; Edith Hamilton, *Witness to the Truth*, chapter 7, 170–71; Edith Hamilton, *The Echo of Greece*, chapter 8, 164–65.

22. See alumna file of Edith Hamilton, ABMC.

23. Edith Hamilton to Jessie Hamilton [Spring 1895], folder 595, reel 27, HFP.

24. Diary of Agnes Hamilton, May 17, 1895, p. 14–16, folder 331, reel 16; Margaret Hamilton to Agnes Hamilton, May 11, 1895, folder 686, reel 31. Edith Hamilton to [Jessie Hamilton?], this letter fragment is not dated but internal evidence dates it to Edith's last year at Bryn Mawr College, folder 613, reel 28, all HFP; Mamie Gwinn to Mary E. Garrett, September 25, 1895, frames 25–27, reel 213, MCTP.

25. Mamie Gwinn to Mary E. Garrett, September 25, 1895, frames 25–27, reel 213, MCTP.

26. Margaret Hamilton to Agnes Hamilton, March 28, 1898, folder 686, reel 31, HFP.

27. James Thomas Flexner, *An American Saga*, 282.

28. Sicherman, *Alice Hamilton*, 56.

29. Robertson, *An Experience of Women*, 390.

30. Laetitia Boehm, "The University at Its Final Home: Munich, 1826–1918," in *University of Munich*, 48–91, 90.

31. Singer, *Adventures Abroad*, 5.

32. Alice Hamilton, "Edith and Alice Hamilton: Students in Germany," *Atlantic Monthly* 215 (March 1965), 129–32, 129.

33. Edith Hamilton to Jessie Hamilton, spring 1895, folder 595, reel 27, HFP.

34. Edith Hamilton to Jessie Hamilton, spring 1895, folder 595, reel 27, HFP. Edith also mentioned this paper in Edith Hamilton to Peggy [Margaret] Hamilton [n.d. but clearly dating from the spring of 1895], folder 2, box 1, EHP.

35. Mamie Gwinn to Mary E. Garrett, September 25, 1895, frames 25–27, reel 213, MCTP.

36. Diary of Agnes Hamilton, June 15, 1895, pp. 23–24, folder 331, reel 16, HFP.

37. Diary of Agnes Hamilton, June 25, 1895, pp. 24–25; diary of Agnes Hamilton, September 22, 1895, p. 59, both folder 331, reel 16; Edith Hamilton to Jessie Hamilton, spring 1895, folder 595, reel 27; Edith Hamilton to Jessie Hamilton, September 2, 1896, folder 596, reel 27, all HFP.

38. Edith Hamilton to Jessie Hamilton [n.d. but internal evidence dates this to her months in Leipzig], folder 608, reel 28, HFP.

39. Edith Hamilton to Jessie Hamilton, December 23, 1895, folder 595, reel 27, HFP.

40. Singer, *Adventures Abroad*, 8, 10.

41. Edith Hamilton to Jessie Hamilton, December 23, 1895, folder 596, reel 27, HFP.

42. Edith Hamilton to Margaret Hamilton, January 18 [n.y. but internal evidence, including Edith's descriptions of her activities in Germany, date this to 1896], folder 581, reel 27, HFP.

43. Edith Hamilton to Jessie Hamilton, January 26, 1896, folder 596, reel 27, HFP.

44. Edith Hamilton to Jessie Hamilton, May 4, 1896, folder 596, reel 27, HFP.

45. Edith Hamilton to Jessie Hamilton, May 4, 1896, folder 596, reel 27, HFP; Edith Hamilton to Jessie Hamilton, June 2, 1896, folder 596, reel 27, HFP.

46. Michelet, *Glimpses of the Life of Agnes Mathilde Wergeland*, 47–50.

47. M. Carey Thomas to Edith Hamilton, July 3, 1896, frames 677–78, reel 213, MCTP.

48. Singer, *Adventures Abroad*, 75, 82. For Winifred Warren as the winner of the Mary E. Garrett European Fellowship, see Bryn Mawr College, *Bryn Mawr College Calendar, Vol. 1, Part 1: Register of Alumnae and Former Students* (Bryn Mawr: Bryn Mawr College, 1908), 10.

49. Singer, *Adventures Abroad*, 5–6.

50. Edith Hamilton to Jessie Hamilton, June 2, 1896, folder 596, reel 27, HFP; Alice Hamilton, *Exploring the Dangerous Trades*, 131; Helen Thomas Flexner, "Bryn Mawr," 13; originally published in the *Bryn Mawr Alumnae Quarterly*, 1905; the essay does not mention Edith by name but does refer to Professor Eduard von Wolfflin.

51. Boehm, 54; Van der Kiste, *Kings of the Hellenes*, 14–15.

52. Alice Hamilton, *Exploring the Dangerous Trades*, 131.

53. Boehm, 80.

54. Boehm, 60.

55. Edith Hamilton to Jessie Hamilton, January 26, 1896, folder 596, reel 27.

56. Alice Hamilton, *Exploring the Dangerous Trades*, 131.

57. Boehm, 83.

58. Margaret Hamilton to "Dear People" (Edith, Alice, Quint, and Gertrude), July 12 [1914], folder 679, reel 31, HFP.

59. Margaret Hamilton to "Dear People" (Edith, Alice, Quint, and Gertrude), July 12 [1914], folder 679, reel 31, HFP.

60. Singer, *Adventures Abroad*, 65, 68.

61. Mamie Gwinn to Mary E. Garrett, January 10, 1895, frames 791–94, reel 212, MCTP.

62. Mamie Gwinn to Mary E. Garrett, January 10, 1895, frame 793, reel 212, MCTP; Edith Hamilton to M. Carey Thomas, July 18, 1896, frames 695–702, reel 213, MCTP.

63. Edith Hamilton to M. Carey Thomas, June 5, 1896, frames 560–63, reel 213, MCTP.

64. Mamie Gwinn to Mary E. Garrett, April 4, 1895, frames 1097–1103, reel 212, MCTP.

65. Edith Hamilton to Alice Hamilton [n.d. but discussing the offer to become headmistress of the Bryn Mawr School, so likely early 1895], folder 580, reel 27, HFP.

66. Edith Hamilton to M. Carey Thomas, July 18, 1896, frames 695–702, reel 213, MCTP.

67. Edith Hamilton to Jessie Hamilton, July 24, 1892, folder 593, reel 27, HFP.

68. Edith Hamilton to Alice Hamilton [n.d. but early 1895], folder 580, reel 27, HFP.

69. M. Carey Thomas to Edith Hamilton, March 2, 1896, frames 344–46, reel 213, MCTP.

70. Edith Hamilton to M. Carey Thomas, March 26, 1896, frames 426–31, reel 213, MCTP.

71. Edith Hamilton to M. Carey Thomas, March 26, 1896, frames 426–31, reel 213, MCTP.

72. Edith Hamilton to Jessie Hamilton, June 2, 1896, folder 596, reel 27, HFP.

73. Edith Hamilton to Jessie Hamilton, June 2, 1896, folder 596, reel 27, HFP.

74. Edith Hamilton to M. Carey Thomas, May 3, 1896, frames 599–602; Edith Hamilton to M. Carey Thomas, June 30, 1896, frames 591–94, both reel 213, MCTP; Nickerson, *A Long Way Forward*, 106.

75. Edith Hamilton to M. Carey Thomas, July 18, 1896, frames 695–700, reel 213, MCTP.

76. M. Carey Thomas to Laurette Potts, June 24, 1896, frames 41–45, reel 146, MCTP.

77. Laurette Eustis Potts to M. Carey Thomas [n.d. except 1896, but obviously discussing the events of June and July 1896], frames 1018–20, reel 213, MCTP.

78. Edith Hamilton to Jessie Hamilton, July 24, 1892, folder 593, reel 27, HFP.

79. Edith Hamilton to M. Carey Thomas, June 30, 1896, frames 591–94, reel 213, MCTP.

80. M. Carey Thomas to Edith Hamilton, March 2, 1896, frames 344–46, reel 213, MCTP.

81. Edith Hamilton to M. Carey Thomas, August 1, 1896, frames 710–11, reel 213, MCTP.

82. Edith Hamilton to Jessie Hamilton, June 30, 1897, folder 597; Edith Hamilton to Jessie Hamilton, postmarked June 25, 1899, folder 589, both reel 27, HFP.

Chapter 5

1. Beirne, *Let's Pick the Daisies*, 8; Andrea Hamilton, *A Vision for Girls*, 37–38; Sander, *Mary Elizabeth Garrett*, 143.

2. Di Cataldo, *Ex Solo Ad Solem*, 8–9; Beirne, *Let's Pick the Daisies*, 8.

3. Beirne, *Let's Pick the Daisies*, 10, 14–15, 18, 112; Sander, *Mary Elizabeth Garrett*, 63–64, 90.

4. Edith Hamilton to Mary E. Garrett, November 10, 1896, frame 966, reel 213; Edith Hamilton to M. Carey Thomas, February 17, 1901, frames 951–56; and Edith Hamilton to M. Carey Thomas, February 26, 1901, frames 961–63, both reel 214, MCTP.

5. Beirne, *Let's Pick the Daisies*, 5.

6. Lilian Welsh, *Reminiscences of Thirty Years in Baltimore*, 74.

7. Edith Hamilton to Mary E. Garrett, October 20, 1896, frame 929, reel 213, MCTP.

8. Edith Hamilton to M. Carey Thomas, October 14, 1897, frames 214–16; and M. Carey Thomas to Edith Hamilton, October 13, 1897, frame 220, both reel 214, MCTP.

9. Beirne, *Let's Pick the Daisies*, 6.

10. Sander, *Mary Elizabeth Garrett*, 125; Andrea Hamilton, *A Vision for Girls*, 52.

11. Andrea Hamilton, *A Vision for Girls*, 48.

12. Sander, *Mary Elizabeth Garrett*, 81–82, 174–75.

13. Andrea Hamilton, *A Vision for Girls*, 37; Di Cataldo, *Ex Solo Ad Solem*, 12–13; Horowitz, *The Power and Passion of M. Carey Thomas*, 233.

14. Mary E. Garrett to Edith Hamilton, April 19, 1897, frames 1272–73, reel 213, MCTP.

15. Di Cataldo, *Ex Solo Ad Solem*, 189.

16. Andrea Hamilton, *A Vision for Girls*, 50–51.

17. Edith Hamilton to Mary E. Garrett, September 24, 1896, frames 860–66, reel 213, MCTP.

18. Edith Hamilton to Jessie Hamilton January 26, 1897, folder 597, reel 27, HFP.

19. Sicherman, *Alice Hamilton*, 105; Edith Hamilton to Jessie Hamilton, fall 1896, folder 596, reel 27, HFP; Edith Hamilton to Mary E. Garrett, September 17, 1897, frames 166–68, reel 214, MCTP.

20. Sander, *Mary Elizabeth Garrett*, 129.

21. Edith Hamilton to Mary E. Garrett, September 16, 1896, frames 798–805, reel 213, MCTP.

22. Mary E. Garrett to Edith Hamilton, September 23, 1896, frames 854–56, reel 213, MCTP.

23. Edith Hamilton to Mary E. Garrett, September 25, 1896, frame 868, reel 213, MCTP.

24. Edith Hamilton to Mary E. Garrett, September 23, 1896, frames 857–59, reel 213, MCTP.

25. Edith Hamilton to Mary E. Garrett, September 22, 1896, frames 836–41, reel 213, MCTP.

26. Edith Hamilton to Mary E. Garrett, January 9, 1897, frames 1035–40, reel 213, MCTP.

27. Edith Hamilton to Mary E. Garrett, January 12, 1898, frames 352–55, reel 214, MCTP.

28. Edith Hamilton to Mary E. Garrett, March 16, 1897, frames 1179–85, reel 213, MCTP.

29. Edith Hamilton to M. Carey Thomas, September 30, 1897, frames 193–96, reel 214, MCTP.

30. Sander, *Mary Elizabeth Garrett*, 130–31; Horowitz, *The Power and Passion of M. Carey Thomas*, 231–32.

31. Edith Hamilton to M. Carey Thomas, May 3, 1897, frame 6; M. Carey Thomas to Edith Hamilton, May 5, 1897, frame 13; Edith Hamilton to Mary E. Garrett, May 13, 1897, frames 36–37; Edith Hamilton to Mary E. Garrett, April 18, 1899, frames 794–98; Mary E. Garrett, April 24, 1899; Edith Hamilton to Mary E. Garrett, October 31, 1901, frame 1027; M. Carey Thomas to Mary E. Garrett, November 1, 1901, frame 1028; all reel 214, MCTP.

32. Edward Caird, *The Evolution of Religion*, vol. 1, 20–21, 23–25.

33. Edith Hamilton to Edith J. R. Isaacs, April 7, 1948, folder 3, box 1, EJRIP.

34. Edith Hamilton to Mary E. Garrett, March 15, 1897, frames 1176–77, reel 213, MCTP.

35. Edith Hamilton to Mary E. Garrett, February 28, 1898, frames 396–98, reel 214, MCTP.

36. Edith Hamilton to Mary E. Garrett, April 19, 1898, frames 510–14, reel 214, MCTP.

37. Edith Hamilton to Mary E. Garrett, April 26, 1899, frames 807–10, reel 214, MCTP.

38. Andrea Hamilton, *A Vision for Girls*, 35.

39. Edith Hamilton to M. Carey Thomas, May 31, 1897, frames 111–12, reel 214, MCTP.

40. Horowitz, *The Power and Passion of M. Carey Thomas*, 325–32; Edith Hamilton to M. Carey Thomas, June 9, 1902, frames 1130–32, reel 214, MCTP.

41. Edith Hamilton to Mary E. Garrett, September 18, 1897, frames 169–71; Mary E. Garrett to Edith Hamilton, November 9, 1897, frame 254, both reel 214, MCTP.

42. Edith Hamilton to Mary E. Garrett, February 28, 1898, frame 399, reel 214, MCTP.

43. Edith Hamilton to Mary E. Garrett, May 10, 1897, frame 28 and Edith Hamilton to Mary E. Garrett, April 20, 1904, frames 1348–49, both reel 214, MCTP.

44. Edith Hamilton to Mary E. Garrett, December 7, 1896, frame 999, reel 213, MCTP.

45. M. Carey Thomas to Edith Hamilton, December 11, 1896, frame 1004, reel 213, MCTP.

46. Edith Hamilton to Jessie Hamilton, January 26, 1897, folder 597, reel 27, HFP.

47. Edith Hamilton to Jessie Hamilton, fall 1896, folder 596, reel 27, HFP.

48. Edith Hamilton to Jessie Hamilton, December 18, 1896, folder 596, reel 27, HFP.

49. M. Carey Thomas to Nan Emery, February 5, 1897, frame 1082, reel 213, MCTP.

50. Board of managers to Sylvia Church Scudder, February 6, 1902, frame 1095, reel 214, MCTP.

51. Edith Hamilton to Jessie Hamilton, fall 1896, folder 596, reel 27, HFP.

52. Edith Hamilton to Jessie Hamilton, June 30, 1897, folder 597, reel 27, HFP.

53. Edith Hamilton to Jessie Hamilton, August 17, 1897, folder 597, reel 27, HFP.

54. Edith Hamilton to Jessie Hamilton, June 30, 1897, folder 597, reel 27, HFP.

55. Edith Hamilton to Mary E. Garrett, July 14, 1897, frames 141–44; Edith Hamilton to Mary E. Garrett, July 26, 1897, frames 150–51, both reel 214, MCTP.

56. M. Carey Thomas to Edith Hamilton, February 14, 1900, frames 891–94, reel 214, MCTP.

57. Memorandum of agreement between the board of managers of the Bryn Mawr School and Miss Edith Hamilton, October 30, 1899, frames 1475–77; and Memorandum of Agreement between the board of managers of the Bryn Mawr School and Miss Edith Hamilton, January 28, 1902, frames 1542–43, both reel 215, MCTP.

58. Norah Hamilton to Agnes Hamilton [n.d.], folder 706, reel 32, HFP.

59. Sicherman, *Alice Hamilton*, 108–11; Ringenberg, Ringenberg, and Brain, *The Education of Alice Hamilton*, 31–33.

60. Edith Hamilton to Jessie Hamilton, August 29, 1897, folder 597, reel 27, HFP.

61. Edith Hamilton to Mary E. Garrett, September 17, 1897, frames 166–68, reel 213, MCTP.

62. Edith Hamilton to Jessie Hamilton, June 30, 1897, folder 597, reel 27, HFP.

63. Edith Hamilton to Jessie Hamilton, March 6, 1898, folder 598, reel 27, HFP.

64. Tanner, *Dewey's Laboratory School*, 15–16.

65. Tanner, *Dewey's Laboratory School*, 9, 51; Mayhew and Edwards, *The Dewey School*, 3, 39.

66. Edith Hamilton to "Dear Children," January 6, 1899, folder 598, reel 27, HFP.

67. Mary E. Garrett to "Dear Girls" [M. Carey Thomas and Mamie Gwinn], January 17, 1899, frame 735, reel 214, MCTP.

68. Tanner, *Dewey's Laboratory School*, 35.

69. Roth, *John Dewey and Self-Realization*, 9.

70. Jones and Muirhead, *The Life and Philosophy of Edward Caird*, 207–8, 356–57.

71. Edith Hamilton, *The Greek Way*, chapter 12, 231.

72. Roth, *John Dewey and Self-Realization*, 16.

73. Edith Hamilton to M. Carey Thomas, October 28, 1901, frames 1022–25, reel 214, MCTP.

74. Winterer, *The Culture of Classicism*, 2.

75. Edith Hamilton, speech at the Bryn Mawr School's 75th anniversary, p. 3, PJT.

76. Edith Hamilton, *The Greek Way*, chapter 12, 234.

77. Edith Hamilton to Mary E. Garrett, December 17, 1898, frames 724–26, reel 214, MCTP.

78. Memorandum of Agreement between the board of managers of the Bryn Mawr School and Miss Edith Hamilton, September 4, 1896, frames 1411–12, reel 215, MCTP.

79. Gonzalez Lodge to Ida Wood, March 14, 1895, frame 976, reel 212, MCTP.

80. Edith Hamilton to Jessie Hamilton [1897? 1901?], folder 599, reel 27; Margaret's presence in Munich and Norah's in Florence makes the earlier suggested year more likely.

81. Hamilton, *The Roman Way*, chapter 11, 213.

82. Molly Weinburgh, "Ethel Nicholson Browne Harvey (1885–1965)," in Shearer and Shearer, eds., *Notable Women in the Life Sciences*, 156–59, 156; Ethel Browne Harvey to Edith Hamilton, February 16, 1958, folder 9, box 1, EHP.

83. Beirne, *Let's Pick the Daisies*, 49.

84. Beirne, *Let's Pick the Daisies*, 37; Emilie Packard Harrison to Edith Hamilton, October 7 [n.y.], folder 9, box 1, EHP.

85. Edith Hamilton to Mary E. Garrett [January 24, 1899], frames 736–38, reel 214, MCTP.

86. M. Carey Thomas to Edith Hamilton, February 14, 1900, frames 891–94, reel 214, MCTP.

87. Edith Hamilton to M. Carey Thomas [n.d. except 1900 written on the top], frames 943–45, reel 214, MCTP.

88. Edith Hamilton to Margaret Hamilton [n.d. though its reference to a Greek play at Vassar the previous year (the *Antigone* performed in 1893) suggests a date of 1894], folder 2, box 1, EHP; Horowitz, *Alma Mater*, 249.

89. Reid, *Edith Hamilton: An Intimate Portrait*, 41.

Chapter 6

1. Kelly Hensley, "Cornelia Bonte Sheldon Amos Elgood," in Shearer and Shearer, eds., *Notable Women in the Life Sciences*, 111–13; Clark, *The Life of Bertrand Russell*, 42–43.

2. Strachey, *Remarkable Relations*, 145.

3. Edith Hamilton to Jessie Hamilton, January 26, 1897, folder 597, reel 27, HFP.

4. Allison, *Mildred Minturn*, 62; Strachey, *Remarkable Relations*, 153; Clark, *The Life of Bertrand Russell*, 46, 58; Horowitz, *The Power and Passion of M. Carey Thomas*, 303–4.

5. Edith Hamilton to Jessie Hamilton, December 18, 1896, folder 596, reel 27, HFP.

6. Edith Hamilton to [Jessie Hamilton?]. This letter fragment has no date but discusses a visit to the Duryees soon after the sisters had acquired a stepmother, folder 612, reel 28, HFP.

7. Edith Hamilton to Jessie Hamilton, April 24, 1897, folder 597, reel 27, HFP.

8. Edward Caird, *The Evolution of Religion*, vol. 2, 116, 140, 156, 160; see, for example, Lumsden, *Inez*, 37, 63.

9. Margaret Hamilton to Agnes Hamilton, May 11, 1895, folder 686, reel 31, HFP.

10. Edith Hamilton to Jessie Hamilton, fall 1896, folder 596, reel 27, HFP.

11. Edith Hamilton to Jessie Hamilton, April 18, 1898, folder 598, reel 27.

12. Susan Duryee to Jessie and Agnes Hamilton [n.d.], folder 316, reel 15; Jessie Hamilton to Katherine Hamilton, January 15, 1899, and January 30, 1899, both folder 185; Jessie Hamilton to Katherine Hamilton, October 23, 1899, folder 186, all reel 9, all HFP.

13. Mina J. Carson, "Agnes Hamilton of Fort Wayne: The Education of a Christian Settlement Worker," *Indiana Magazine of History* 80 (March 1984): 1–34, 32; Jessie Hamilton to Katherine Hamilton, January 15, 1899, and January 30, 1899, both folder 185; Jessie Hamilton to Katherine Hamilton, October 23, 1899, folder 186, both reel 9, HFP.

14. Sicherman, *Alice Hamilton*, 147–48.

15. Sicherman, *Alice Hamilton*, 100.

16. Elizabeth Sprigge, "Journal in Search of Gertrude Stein," December 15 [1954], p. 121, folder 307, box 18, GSABTP; Wineapple, *Sister Brother*, 114.

17. Sprigge, *Gertrude Stein*, 95; Edith Hamilton to Jessie Hamilton, March 16, 1903, folder 600, reel 28, HFP.

18. Elizabeth Sprigge, "Journal in Search of Gertrude Stein," December 15 [1954], p. 121, folder 307, box 18, GSABTP.

19. Wineapple, *Sister Brother*, 78–81.

20. Edith Hamilton, "Private Idiom," 156, 206–7, 218. This essay was reprinted in Edith Hamilton, *The Ever-Present Past*, 142–50, 146.

21. Elizabeth Sprigge, "Journal in Search of Gertrude Stein," December 15 [1954], p. 121, folder 307, box 18, GSABTP; Wineapple, *Sister Brother*, 124–25.

22. Wineapple, *Sister Brother*, 146.

23. Wineapple, *Sister Brother*, 143.

24. Elizabeth Sprigge, "Journal in Search of Gertrude Stein," December 15 [1954], p. 120, folder 307, box 18, GSABTP; Edith Hamilton to Jessie Hamilton July 16 [1910], folder 601, reel 28, HFP.

25. Sprigge, *Gertrude Stein*, 265.

26. Edith Hamilton, "Echoes of Greece," 1958 [recording].

27. Bryn Mawr College, *Program: Bryn Mawr College 1905–1906* (Philadelphia: John C. Winston, 1905), 172.

28. See her alumna file, ABMC.

29. Sicherman, *Alice Hamilton*, 87.

30. M. Carey Thomas to Edith Hamilton, March 22, 1897, frame 1198, reel 213, MCTP; for Margaret's letter on winning the European fellowship, see Margaret Hamilton to Edith and Alice Hamilton [n.d. but speaks of her joy on receiving the award, so clearly written in the spring of 1897], folder 680, reel 31, HFP; see also Margaret Hamilton to Agnes Hamilton, March 28, 1898, folder 686, reel 31, HFP.

31. Edith Hamilton to Jessie Hamilton [1899–1900?], folder 600, reel 28, HFP.

32. Jessie Hamilton to Allen Hamilton, February 7, 1898, folder 243, reel 11, HFP.

33. Margaret Hamilton to Jessie Hamilton, March 18, 1898, folder 683, reel 31, HFP.

34. Norah Hamilton to Jessie Hamilton, October 29, 1893, folder 697; Norah Hamilton to Margaret Hamilton, April 12, 1895, folder 695, both reel 32, HFP.

35. The Académie Carmen was only open from the autumn of 1898 until April 1901; Fleming, *James Abbott McNeil Whistler*, 3, 78, 312–16, 325.

36. Norah Hamilton to Jessie Hamilton, postmarked March 14, 1900, folder 698, reel 32, HFP.

37. Edith Hamilton to Jessie Hamilton [n.d., likely 1899], folder 599, reel 28, HFP.

38. M. Carey Thomas to Edith Hamilton, February 14, 1900, frames 891–94, reel 214, MCTP.

39. Sicherman, *Alice Hamilton*, 137.

40. Edith Hamilton to Jessie Hamilton, January 14, 1897, folder 597, reel 27, HFP.

41. Margaret Hamilton to Jessie Hamilton, postmarked December 21, 1899, folder 683, reel 31, HFP.

42. Agnes Hamilton to Katherine Hamilton, March 28, 1900, folder 358, reel 18, HFP.

43. Edith Hamilton to Jessie Hamilton, summer 1900, folder 600, reel 28, HFP.

44. Edith Hamilton to Norah Hamilton [n.d. except September 1920?], though its mention of Doris helping Edith with Bryn Mawr School correspondence makes this date seem likely, folder 581, reel 27, HFP.

45. Edith Hamilton to Rosamond Gilder [n.d. but its reference to Edith's article on tragedy for *Theatre Arts Monthly* dates it to early summer 1925], box 11, GM.

46. Mary Sherwood to Mary E. Garrett, November 26, 1899, frame 875, reel 214, MCTP.

47. Edith Hamilton to Mary E. Garrett [n.d. but written at 517 Cathedral Street so likely late 1899], frames 446–48, reel 215, MCTP.

48. M. Carey Thomas to Edith Hamilton, February 14, 1900, frames 891–94, reel 214, MCTP.

49. Mary E. Garrett to Mamie Gwinn and M. Carey Thomas, May 7, 1903, frame 1240, reel 214, MCTP.

50. Edith Hamilton to Jessie Hamilton, October 29 [n.y. but Edith's address of 517 Cathedral Street dates it to the end of 1898], folder 599, reel 28; Susan Duryee Fahmy to Jessie Hamilton, letter fragment [n.d.], folder 317, reel 15, both HFP.

51. Steiner et al., *Men of Mark in Maryland*, 354–56; Shepherd, *Great Preachers as Seen by a Journalist*, 44.

52. Margaret Hamilton to Mary E. Garrett, March 19 [1901], frame 982, reel 214, MCTP.

53. Edith Hamilton to M. Carey Thomas, July 26, 1902, frame 1145, reel 214, MCTP; Susan Duryee to Agnes Hamilton [n.d. but describes Edith's recovery in Chicago so a date of 1902 seems likely], folder 453, reel 22, HFP.

54. Ibid.

55. Edith Hamilton to Jessie Hamilton, March 25, 1903, folder 600, reel 28, HFP.

56. Edith Hamilton to Jessie Hamilton, April 15, 1903, folder 601, reel 28, HFP.

57. Susan Duryee to Agnes Hamilton, April 18 [n.y. but mentions sailing for China a year from the following September, so a date of 1902 seems likely], folder 453, reel 22; Edith Hamilton to Jessie Hamilton, November 20, 1903, folder 601, reel 28, both HFP; De Jong, *The Reformed Church in China*, 348.

58. Edith Hamilton to "Dear People" [Jessie and Agnes], February 14, 1955, folder 4, box 1, EHP.

59. Margaret Hamilton to Jessie Hamilton, September 12 [n.y. but its description of Edith's trip with the Shearmans and Edith and Alice's plans to return to the United States on the *Noordam* dates it to 1903], folder 685, reel 31, HFP.

60. See, for example, Edith Hamilton to M. Carey Thomas, May 17, 1898, frames 594–96, reel 214, MCTP; Helen Thomas to Edith Hamilton, March 5 [1899], frames 764–66, reel 214, MCTP.

61. Board of managers to Sylvia Church Scudder, February 6, 1902, frame 1095, reel 214, MCTP.

62. See, for example, Edith Hamilton to M. Carey Thomas, October 25, 1899, frames 862–864, reel 214, MCTP.

63. Edith Hamilton to Jessie Hamilton, December 20, 1900, folder 600, reel 28, HFP.

64. James Thomas Flexner, *Maverick's Progress*, 9.

65. James Thomas Flexner, *An American Saga*, 394, 396, 407.

66. Edith Hamilton to Jessie Hamilton, January 1, 1893, folder 594, reel 27, HFP.

67. Edith Hamilton to Jessie Hamilton, January 14, 1897, folder 597, reel 27, HFP.

68. Horowitz, *The Power and Passion of M. Carey Thomas*, 292, 353, 367.

69. Horowitz, *The Power and Passion of M. Carey Thomas*, 355, 367–68, 370, 373.

70. Edith Hamilton to Jessie Hamilton, postmarked December 29, 1903, folder 601, reel 28, HFP.

71. Edith Hamilton to Jessie Hamilton, postmarked June 25, 1899, folder 589; Edith Hamilton to Jessie Hamilton, October 29 [n.y. but its address of 517 Cathedral Street places it between 1897 and 1899], folder 599, both reel 27, HFP.

72. Reid, *Woodrow Wilson*, 236; Berg, *Wilson*, 259.

73. McAdoo with Gaffey, *The Woodrow Wilsons*, 50.

74. Quoted in Reid, *Woodrow Wilson*, 85. The quote does not mention Edith Hamilton specifically. Edith Reid wrote: "As was said of a brilliant woman by an irate admirer when she was

offered the head-mistressship of a girls' school, 'It was like using a razor to sharpen a lead pencil.'"

75. Edith Hamilton to Grace Turnbull, January 25 [n.y. though written at 2448 Massachusetts Avenue NW, probably during or soon after the publication of *Witness to the Truth*], GHTP.

76. Sorley, *Lewis of Warner Hall*, 257–58.

77. Bertrand Russell to Lucy Martin Donnelly, December 23, 1904, quoted in Forte, "Bertrand Russell's Letters to Helen Thomas Flexner and Lucy Martin Donnelly," unpublished dissertation.

78. Ibid.

79. Bertrand Russell to Lucy Martin Donnelly, November 10, 1905, quoted in Forte, "Bertrand Russell's Letters to Helen Thomas Flexner and Lucy Martin Donnelly," unpublished dissertation.

80. Ibid.

81. Edith Hamilton to Jessie Hamilton, June 23, 1905, folder 601, reel 28, HFP.

82. Edith Hamilton to Jessie Hamilton, July 30 [n.y. but internal evidence dates this to 1905], folder 605, reel 27, HFP.

Chapter 7

1. *Proceedings of the Thirty-Eighth Annual Convention of the National-American Woman Suffrage Association*. The National American Woman Suffrage Association was created by the merger of Susan B. Anthony's National Woman Suffrage Association and Lucy Stone Blackwell's American Woman Suffrage Association in 1890, see Barry, *Susan B. Anthony*, 296.

2. Harper, *History of Woman Suffrage*, 263.

3. Scott and Scott, *One Half the People*, 29–30; Lumsden, *Inez*, 88; White, "The Hamilton Way," 132–57, 137.

4. See, for example, Jessie Hamilton to Agnes Hamilton, June 9, 1922, folder 214, reel 10; Agnes Hamilton to Katherine Hamilton, November 2, 1920, folder 359, reel 18, both HFP; Griswold, *The Pictorial History of Fort Wayne, Indiana*, 491.

5. "Miss Hamilton Makes Address," *Maryland Suffrage News*, November 9, 1912, p. 125; Barry, *Susan B. Anthony*, 314–16.

6. Barry, *Susan B. Anthony*, 316.

7. Thomas, *Why Equal Suffrage Has Been a Success*, 3; Kelly, *A Plea for Equal Suffrage*, 1–2 [author's pagination].

8. Sara Hunter Graham, "Woman Suffrage in Virginia: The Equal Suffrage League and Pressure-Group Politics, 1909–1920," *The Virginia Magazine of History and Biography* 101 (April 1993): 227–50, 233–34.

9. Thomas, *Why Equal Suffrage Has Been a Success*, 2; Kelly, *A Plea for Equal Suffrage*, 2; Harrison, *Equal Suffrage as a Reform Factor*, 1 [author's pagination].

10. Kelly, *A Plea for Equal Suffrage*, 2–3 [author's pagination]; Harrison, *Equal Suffrage as a Reform Factor*, 1 [author's pagination].

11. Thomas, *Why Equal Suffrage Has Been a Success*, 2.

12. Welsh, *Reminiscences of Thirty Years in Baltimore*, 108; "Miss Hamilton on Suffrage," *Baltimore Sun*, February 16, 1912.

13. Jones and Muirhead, *The Life and Philosophy of Edward Caird*, 34.

14. Edith Hamilton to "Dear Children" [Katherine, Jessie, and Agnes Hamilton], January 6, 1899, folder 598, reel 27, HFP.

15. Welsh, *Reminiscences of Thirty Years in Baltimore*, 63, 67.

16. "Laws for Child Labor," *Baltimore Sun*, December 20, 1901, p. 6.

17. Welsh, *Reminiscences of Thirty Years in Baltimore*, 68; "Arundell Club Active," *Baltimore Sun*, October 24, 1907, p. 9.

18. Weatherford, *A History of the American Suffragist Movement*, 157.

19. Logan Pearsall Smith to Lucy Martin Donnelly, October 24, 1903, box 1, LPSP.

20. Forte, "Bertrand Russell's Letters to Helen Thomas Flexner and Lucy Martin Donnelly," unpublished dissertation, 20.

21. Forte, "Bertrand Russell's Letters to Helen Thomas Flexner and Lucy Martin Donnelly," unpublished dissertation, 20–21, 37.

22. Logan Pearsall Smith to Lucy Martin Donnelly, June 23, 1904, and December 23, 1904, box 1, LPSP.

23. Logan Pearsall Smith to Lucy Martin Donnelly, December 23, 1904, box 1, LPSP.

24. Lucy Martin Donnelly to Bertrand Russell, May 26, 1911, box 5.13, BRP; James Thomas Flexner, *Maverick's Progress*, 30.

25. Lucy Martin Donnelly to Bertrand Russell, June 22, 1913, box 5.13, BRP.

26. Lucy Martin Donnelly to Bertrand Russell, June 10 [1910] and July 14, 1912, both box 5.13, BRP; Sicherman, *Alice Hamilton*, 182.

27. Lucy Martin Donnelly to M. Carey Thomas, September 16, 1923, frames 639–47, reel 38, MCTP.

28. Margaret Hamilton to Norah Hamilton [n.d. but reference to Clara Landsberg in Europe and accepting a position at the Bryn Mawr School for the following year makes a date of 1921 seem likely], folder 681, reel 31, HFP.

29. Edith Hamilton to Jessie Hamilton, July 16 [1910], folder 601, reel 28, HFP.

30. Edith Hamilton to Jessie Hamilton, July 16 [1910], folder 601, reel 28, HFP.

31. Wilson, *Gilbert Murray OM*, 124; Murray visited Bryn Mawr College May 18–21, 1907, see M. Carey Thomas to Alys Russell, May 1, 1907, frames 473–75, reel 112; and journal of M. Carey Thomas, May 18–21, 1907, frames 863–64, reel 6, both MCTP.

32. Bertrand Russell to Lucy Martin Donnelly, August 15, 1904; Bertrand Russell to Helen Thomas Flexner, June 9, 1907; see Forte, "Bertrand Russell's Letters to Helen Thomas Flexner and Lucy Martin Donnelly," unpublished dissertation, 42, 67–68; journal of M. Carey Thomas, May 20, 1907, frame 864, reel 6, MCTP.

33. William Bruneau, "Gilbert Murray, Bertrand Russell, and the Theory and Practice of Politics," in Stray, ed., *Gilbert Murray Reassessed: Hellenism, Theatre, and International Politics*, 201–16; Strachey, *Remarkable Relations*, 216–25.

34. Wilson, *Gilbert Murray OM*, 35, 57, 64, 121.

35. Wilson, *Gilbert Murray OM*, 105–8.

36. Wilson, *Gilbert Murray OM*, 108–9.

37. Huntington Cairns to James K. Feibleman, June 11, 1957, folder 7, box 21, JKFP.

38. Wilson, *Gilbert Murray OM*, 44, 156.

39. Murray, *The Rise of the Greek Epic*, 16, 19; Edith Hamilton, *The Great Age of Greek Literature*, chapter 8, 159–62; chapter 10, 208–9.

40. Wilson, *Gilbert Murray OM*, 70–77, 91.

41. Journal of M. Carey Thomas, May 18–20, 1907, frames 863–64, reel 6, MCTP.

42. Foley, *Reimagining Greek Tragedy*, 34.

43. Diary of Helen Evans Lewis, February 11, 1909, ABMS.

44. Mary E. Garrett to Dodd, Mead, January 16, 1895, frame 804, reel 212, MCTP.

45. Ackerman, "The Cambridge Group: Origins and Composition."

46. Edith Hamilton to Alice Hamilton [n.d. though the mention of the Museum of Fine Arts Boston in a new building dates this to after the museum opened in November 1909], folder 579, reel 27, HFP; on the opening of the new building to the public see Walter Muir Whitehill, *Museum of Fine Arts Boston: A Centennial History* (Cambridge: The Belknap Press, 1970), 233.

47. Edith Hamilton to Alice Hamilton [n.d. though the mention of the Museum of Fine Arts Boston in a new building dates this to after the museum opened in November 1909], folder 579, reel 27, HFP.

48. Diary of Helen Evans Lewis, January 28, 1909, ABMS.

49. Ibid.

50. Sutherland, *Mrs. Humphry Ward*, 299.

51. Wachter, "Surname: Arnold, Occupation: Spinster, Avocation: New Victorian Woman," unpublished dissertation, 150; see also Harrison, *Connecting Links*, 91.

52. Wachter, "Surname: Arnold, Occupation: Spinster, Avocation: New Victorian Woman," unpublished dissertation, 150.

53. Diary of Helen Evans Lewis, January 28, 1909, ABMS.

54. *Maryland Suffrage News*, vol. 1, November 9, 1912, p. 125.

55. "To Plan Suffrage Fight," *Baltimore Sun*, January 7, 1910, p. 14.

56. Ibid.

57. "Miss Hamilton on Suffrage," *Baltimore Sun*, January 12, 1910, p. 9.

58. Logan Pearsall Smith to Lucy Martin Donnelly, April 25, 1910, box 1, LPSP.

59. Lucy Martin Donnelly to Bertrand Russell, June 10 [1910], box 5.13, BRP.

60. Lucy Martin Donnelly to Bertrand Russell, June 26, 1910, box 5.13, BRP.

61. Edith Hamilton to Jessie Hamilton, July 16 [1910], folder 601, reel 28, HFP.

62. Lucy Martin Donnelly to Bertrand Russell, June 26, 1910, box 5.13, BRP.

63. Allison, *Mildred Minturn*, 103.

64. Edith Hamilton to Jessie Hamilton, July 16 [1910], folder 601, reel 28, HFP.

65. Colby, *Vernon Lee*, 174–77; Lee sometimes rented cottages on the Il Palmerino estate and it may have been one of these, rather than the villa itself, in which the Bories were staying; see Colby, 317–318.

66. Edith Hamilton to Jessie Hamilton, July 16 [1910], folder 601, reel 28, HFP.

67. Edith Hamilton to Jessie Hamilton, July 16 [1910], folder 601, reel 28, HFP; Benjamin, *A Castle in Tuscany*, 99–100, 113–14.

68. Edith Hamilton to Jessie Hamilton, July 16 [1910], folder 601, reel 28, HFP; Allison, *Mildred Minturn*, 105–6.

69. Elizabeth Sprigge, "Journal in Search of Gertrude Stein," December 15 [1954], p. 121, folder 307, box 18, GSABTC.

70. Edith Hamilton to Jessie Hamilton, August 13 [1910], folder 601, reel 28, HFP; Lucy Martin Donnelly to Bertrand Russell, August 3, 1910, box 5.13, BRP; Edith Hamilton, "Femininity in the Bible."

71. Lucy Martin Donnelly to Bertrand Russell, April 3, 1910, and Lucy Martin Donnelly to Alys Pearsall Smith Russell, August 1, 1910, both box 5.13, BRP; Edith Hamilton to Jessie Hamilton, August 13 [1910], folder 601, reel 28, HFP.

72. Grant, *Alice Hamilton*, 74–80; Alice Hamilton, *Exploring the Dangerous Trades*, 3, 119; Ringenberg, Ringenberg, and Brain, *The Education of Alice Hamilton*, 56, 60, 78.

73. Edith Hamilton to Jessie Hamilton, September 19 [1910], folder 601, reel 28, HFP.

74. Lucy Martin Donnelly to Bertrand Russell, September 21, 1910, box 5.13, BRP.

75. Edith Hamilton to Jessie Hamilton, September 19 [1910], folder 601, reel 28, HFP.

76. Ibid.

77. Lucy Martin Donnelly to Bertrand Russell, September 21, 1910, box 5.13, BRP.

78. Edith Hamilton to Jessie Hamilton [1899?], folder 599; on the school's financial difficulties see Edith Hamilton to Jessie Hamilton, April 15, 1901, folder 600, both reel 28, HFP; the school apparently survived, see obituary for Abby Kirk, *New York Times*, January 2, 1951, p. 23.

79. Lucy Martin Donnelly to Bertrand Russell, September 21, 1910, box 5.13, BRP; Bertrand Russell to Lucy Martin Donnelly, October 7, 1910, quoted in Forte, "Bertrand Russell's Letters to Helen Thomas Flexner and Lucy Martin Donnelly," unpublished dissertation, 161.

80. Di Cataldo, *Ex Solo Ad Solem*, 23.

81. "The Suffragists' Great Day," *Baltimore Sun*, February 4, 1912, p. 12.

82. Ibid.

83. "Women Ask Justice," *Baltimore Sun*, February 14, 1912, p. 1 and 11.

84. "Miss Hamilton to Speak," *Baltimore Sun*, February 15, 1912, p. 8; "Miss Hamilton on Suffrage," *Baltimore Sun*, February 16, 1912, p. 8.

85. "Suffragists Meet Today," *Baltimore Sun*, March 29, 1912, p. 10.

86. "Miss Hamilton Makes Address," *Maryland Suffrage News*, November 9, 1912, p. 125.

87. File labeled "Speech at Vassar College's 100th Commencement," folder 1, box 3, EHC; Weatherford, *A History of the American Suffragist Movement*, 196; Berg, *Wilson*, 273; Lumsden, *Inez*, 212.

88. "Washington Parade—500 Marylanders Practice for May 31," *Maryland Suffrage News*, March 8, 1913, p. 195.

89. Lumsden, *Inez*, 84.

90. Weatherford, *A History of the American Suffragist Movement*, 196.

91. File labeled "Speech at Vassar College's 100th Commencement," folder 1, box 3, EHC.

92. M. Carey Thomas to LeBaron Russell Briggs, May 30, 1914, frames 86–88, reel 130, MCTP.

93. White, "The Hamilton Way," 137.

94. Ruth Lachenbruch to John Mason Brown, June 19, 1963, folder 4, box 3, EHC.

95. Lumsden, *Inez*, 87.

96. Norah Hamilton to Jessie Hamilton, postmarked December 21, 1914, folder 699, reel 32, HFP; Harper, *History of Woman Suffrage*, 263–64.

97. Weatherford, *A History of the American Suffragist Movement*, 208.

98. Degen, *The History of the Woman's Peace Party*, 11, 43.

99. "League of Women to Work for Place," *Baltimore Sun*, April 4, 1922, p. 8.

Chapter 8

1. "The Reply," 46–47; on Bourne as the author of this editorial, see Clayton, *Forgotten Prophet*, 160.

2. Sicherman, *Alice Hamilton*, 153–54; Crenson, *Baltimore*, 342.

3. Anderson, *The Origins and Resolution of an Urban Crisis*, 15–16, 30.

4. Susan Duryee to Agnes Hamilton, but letter fragment contained in Jessie Hamilton's correspondence [n.d. but written during Susan's years of residency in Baltimore], folder 324, reel 15, HFP; Crenson, *Baltimore*, 343.

5. Sander, *Mary Elizabeth Garrett*, 256.

6. Margaret Hamilton to Gertrude Pond Hamilton, August 27, 1914, folder 679, reel 31, HFP.

7. Edith Hamilton to Jessie Hamilton [April 25, 1912], folder 602, reel 28, HFP; Lucy Martin Donnelly to Bertrand Russell, May 7, 1912, box 5.13, BRP.

8. Edith Hamilton to Lucia Valentine, August 16 [1960], box 3.1.1, collection of Edith Hamilton letters from the Valentines, ABMS.

9. Edith Hamilton to Agnes Hamilton, May 19, 1936, folder 609, reel 28; Doris Fielding Reid to Alice Hamilton, June 17 [n.y. but postmarked June 18, 1960], folder 672, reel 31, both HFP.

10. Edith Hamilton, "Private Idiom," 156, 206–7, 218; this essay was reprinted in Hamilton, *The Ever-Present Past*, 142–150, 147.

11. Cooper, *The Cubist Epoch*, 100–2, 113; the other cubist exhibition was known as La Section D'Or.

12. Edith Hamilton, "Private Idiom," 206.

13. Kamm, *How Different from Us*, 30, 51, 160, 256.

14. "Uniform at Bryn Mawr," *Baltimore Sun*, June 15, 1913, p. 12; Di Cataldo, *Ex Solo Ad Solem*, 24.

15. Kamm, *How Different from Us*, 30.

16. Quoted by artist Mary Meigs to Hortense Flexner King, May 12, 1967, box 2, HFKP.

17. Di Cataldo, *Ex Solo Ad Solem*, 23.

18. "Y.W.C.A. Holds Exercises," *Baltimore Sun*, March 3, 1919, p. 4.

19. Diary of Helen Evans Lewis, January 28, 1909, ABMS.

20. *The Bryn Mawrtyr* yearbook, 1911, 46.

21. Ibid.

22. Harper, *History of Woman Suffrage*, 264.

23. Jones, *Elisabeth Gilman*, 59, 69–70, 75–76.

24. Anne Kirk Cooke, "Memories of My Days at the Bryn Mawr School," solicited by the Bryn Mawr School as an alumnae centennial letter, p. 2, PJT.

25. Diary of Helen Evans Lewis, January 15, 1909, ABMS.

26. Millicent Carey McIntosh, "An Extraordinary Headmistress," originally published in *Parade* magazine, May 1959, copy ABMS, not paginated.

27. Ruth T. Shafer to John Mason Brown, July 13, 1963, folder 4, box 3, EHC. I am grateful to the Bryn Mawr School librarian Gail Batts for help in identifying Ruth T. Shafer.

28. Mabel Snibbe Bennett to Edith Hamilton, September 13, 1957, folder 4, box 2, EHP.

29. Diary of Helen Evans Lewis, February 12, 1909, ABMS.

30. Diary of Helen Evans Lewis, February 26, 1909, ABMS.

31. Lucy Martin Donnelly to Bertrand Russell, February 6, 1914, box 5.13, BRP.

32. Lucy Martin Donnelly to Bertrand Russell, February 6, 1914, box 5.13, BRP.

33. "Will Curb Young," *Baltimore Sun*, March 31, 1914, p. 14.

34. M. Carey Thomas to Edith Hamilton, April 29, 1914, frame 426, reel 129, MCTP.

35. Hamilton, *A Vision for Girls*, 28–29.

36. Edith Hamilton, Speech at the 75th Anniversary of the Bryn Mawr School, November 4, 1960, p. 1–3, PJT.

37. Andrea Hamilton, *A Vision for Girls*, 52.

38. Edith Hamilton, "Interesting Schools," 45–46.

39. Anne Kirk Cooke, "Memories of My Days at the Bryn Mawr School," solicited by the Bryn Mawr School as an alumnae centennial letter, p. 4, PJT.

40. M. Carey Thomas to Margaret Thomas Carey, May 23, 1914, frames 53–54, reel 130, MCTP; on Margaret Thomas Carey serving on the Bryn Mawr School's board of managers, see Horowitz, *The Power and Passion of M. Carey Thomas*, 429.

41. Edith Hamilton, Speech at the 75th Anniversary of the Bryn Mawr School, November 4, 1960, p. 2, PJT.

42. M. Carey Thomas to Edith Hamilton, September 8, 1914, reel 130, MCTP.

43. M. Carey Thomas to Lucy Martin Donnelly, March 11, 1914, frame 93; March 12, 1914, frame 106; and March 12, 1914, frame 121, all reel 129, MCTP.

44. Strachey, *Remarkable Relations*, 262; see also note in Russell's hand appended to Lucy Martin Donnelly to Bertrand Russell, April 15, 1914, box 5.13, BRP.

45. Lucy Martin Donnelly to Bertrand Russell, April 15, 1914, box 5.13 BRP.

46. Clark, *The Life of Bertrand Russell*, 45–46.

47. Lucy Martin Donnelly to Bertrand Russell, April 26, 1914, box 5.13, BRP.

48. Lucy Martin Donnelly to Bertrand Russell, July 8, 1914, box 5.13, BRP; Lucy Martin Donnelly to M. Carey Thomas [n.d. except circa 1914–15, but its references to Mary Garrett still struggling with illness suggest the earlier year], frames 491–93, reel 38, MCTP.

49. Margaret Hamilton to Gertrude Pond Hamilton, July 22, 1914, folder 679, reel 31, HFP.

50. Margaret Hamilton to Gertrude Pond Hamilton, August 1, 1914, folder 679, reel 31, HFP.

51. Margaret Hamilton to "Dear People," August 4, 1914, folder 679, reel 31, HFP.

52. Margaret Hamilton to Gertrude Pond Hamilton, August 7, 1914, folder 679, reel 31, HFP.

53. Margaret Hamilton to "Dear People," August 20, 1914, folder 679, reel 31, HFP.

54. Determined by examination of the Bryn Mawr School class lists. I am grateful to Elizabeth Nye Di Cataldo, archivist of the Bryn Mawr School, for this information.

55. Reid, *Edith Hamilton: An Intimate Portrait*, 42–44.

56. Felix Morley, "A Memoir of Edith Hamilton," review of *Edith Hamilton: An Intimate Portrait*, by Doris Fielding Reid, April 30, 1967, copy in box 84, HCP.

57. *The Bryn Mawrtyr* yearbook, 1909, 26–28.

58. Reid, *Edith Hamilton: An Intimate Portrait*, 42.

59. Doris Fielding Reid to Francesca Gilder Palmer and Rosamond Gilder, postmarked July 23, 1933, box 14, GM.

60. Reid, *Edith Hamilton: An Intimate Portrait*, 42.

61. Doris Fielding Reid, unpublished autobiography, folder 28, box 2, p. 1, EHP.

62. Doris Fielding Reid to Rosamond Gilder [n.d. but its discussion of moving into a hotel—the Hotel Irving on Gramercy Park—dates it to the summer of 1924], box 14, GM; on moving into the Hotel Irving, see Edith Hamilton to Dorothy Bruce, November 30, 1924, A/H217.1a, EHL.

63. Doris Fielding Reid to John Mason and Catherine Brown, April 10, 1954, JMBP.

64. Doris Fielding Reid, unpublished autobiography, folder 28, box 2, p. 1, EHP.

65. "Biographical Sketch" in Harris, *Thirty Years as President of Bucknell*, xi–xlii, xxi–xxii; Claudine Schweber, "Mary Belle Harris," in Sicherman and Green, eds., *Notable American Women*, 315–17; Doris Fielding Reid, "Publisher's Note," in Harris, *I Knew Them in Prison*, vii–x, ixi.

66. Doris Fielding Reid, "Publisher's Note," in Harris, *I Knew Them in Prison*, vii–x, ix; see also Doris Fielding Reid to Harry Fielding Reid, March 11, 1914, folder 27, box 2, EHP.

67. Doris Fielding Reid, "Publisher's Note," in Harris, *I Knew Them in Prison*, ix.

68. Edith Hamilton to Dorothy Bruce, August 24, 1922, A/H217.1a, EHL.

69. Van Dyke, *Henry van Dyke*, 313–14.

70. Margaret Hamilton to Gertrude Pond Hamilton, August 1, 1914; Margaret Hamilton to Gertrude Pond Hamilton, August 2, 1914; both folder 679, reel 31, HFP.

71. Jessie Hamilton to Agnes Hamilton, April 16, 1920, folder 211, reel 10, HFP.

72. Margaret Hamilton to Gertrude Hamilton, August 18, 1914, folder 679, reel 31, HFP.

73. Margaret Hamilton to Gertrude Pond Hamilton, August 27, 1914, folder 679, reel 31, HFP.

74. Edith Hamilton to Rosamond Gilder, July 16 [n.y. but internal evidence, including Rosamond's new work at *Theatre Arts Monthly*, dates this to 1924], box 11, GM.

75. Reid, *Edith Hamilton: An Intimate Portrait*, 76–77.

76. Alice Hamilton, *Exploring the Dangerous Trades*, 163.

77. Edith Hamilton, "Germany Take the Lead in the Education of Children—Maryland Needs a Compulsory Education Law," *Baltimore Sun*, February 4, 1912, p. 6.

78. Alice Hamilton, "Edith and Alice Hamilton: Students in Germany," 129–32, 131.

79. Isabel Blogg Bürger, "Roots from the Past Bring Forth Fruit," essay written for the centennial of the Bryn Mawr School, PJT.

80. Edith Hamilton to Jessie Hamilton [n.d. except Wednesday morning, but early 1900s], folder 604, reel 28, HFP.

81. Edith Hamilton to Jessie Hamilton, September 9, 1906, folder 601, reel 28, HFP.

82. See material in the Bryn Mawr School League file, box 3.1.1, ABMS.

83. Sander, *Mary Elizabeth Garrett*, 258.

84. Sander, *Mary Elizabeth Garrett*, 260; Beirne, *Let's Pick the Daisies*, 30.

85. Beirne, *Let's Pick the Daisies*, 31–32.

86. Edith Hamilton to Dr. David Eugene Smith, January 19, 1920, DESP.

87. Horowitz, *The Power and Passion of M. Carey Thomas*, 424; "Garrett Millions to Miss Thomas," *New York Times*, April 9, 1915, p. 6; M. Carey Thomas to Edith Hamilton, September 8, 1919, reel 154, MCTP.

88. Sicherman, *Alice Hamilton*, 184.

89. Katz, *Dearest of Geniuses*, 107–20.

90. Edith Hamilton to Jessie Hamilton [May 9, 1915], folder 602, reel 28, HFP; Sicherman, *Alice Hamilton*, 193.

91. Beirne, *Let's Pick the Daisies*, 4.

92. "Taft Glad We Have No Jingo President," *New York Times*, June 4, 1915, p. 1. This article is a report on Taft's speech at the Bryn Mawr College commencement. For his daughter Helen Taft, later Manning, as a member of the Bryn Mawr College class of 1915, see her obituary in the *New York Times*, February 23, 1987, p. 17.

93. Cooper, *Breaking the Heart of the World*, 13.

94. Edith Hamilton to "Dear Children" [Katherine, Jessie, and Agnes Hamilton], January 6, 1899, folder 598, reel 27, HFP; Degen, *The History of the Woman's Peace Party*, 11.

95. "League of Women to Work for Place [sic]," *Baltimore Sun*, April 4, 1922, p. 8.

96. Nelson, *Wisdom for Our Time*, 18.

97. "Argument for Peace to Be Seen Here," *Baltimore Sun*, May 4, 1915, p. 6; Degen, *The History of the Woman's Peace Party*, 50, 60.

98. Hartigan, *Greek Tragedy on the American Stage*, 15–19; Foley, *Reimagining Greek Tragedy*, 62.

99. Edith Hamilton to Jessie Hamilton, May 21 [1917], folder 602, reel 28, HFP.

100. Edith Hamilton, "W. S. Gilbert: A Mid-Victorian Aristophanes"; this essay was reprinted in its original form in Jones, *W.S. Gilbert*, 111–34.

101. Edith Hamilton, "W. S. Gilbert: A Mid-Victorian Aristophanes," 782.

102. Hamilton, *The Greek Way*, chapter 2, 34.

103. Benjamin, *A Castle in Tuscany*, 11.

Chapter 9

1. Sicherman, *Alice Hamilton*, 194; Hamilton, *Exploring the Dangerous Trades*, 179; minutes of the meeting of the board of managers of the Bryn Mawr School, March 12, 1915, ABMS.

2. Lucy Martin Donnelly, "The Sage of Shantung"; Nimura, *Daughters of the Samurai*, 74–75.

3. Edith Hamilton to the board of managers, September 24, 1921, written when discussing her prolonged stay in England; minutes of the board of managers, November 12, 1921, ABMS.

4. Lucy Martin Donnelly to Bertrand Russell, August 12, 1915, box 5.13, BRP; Agnes Hamilton to Jessie Hamilton, February 25, 1916, folder 375, reel 18, HFP.

5. Lucy Martin Donnelly to M. Carey Thomas, September 28, 1915, frame 490, reel 38, MCTP.

6. Edith Hamilton, *The Echo of Greece*, chapter 6, 117.

7. Edith Hamilton to the board of managers, September 24, 1921, written when discussing her prolonged stay in England; minutes of the board of managers, November 12, 1921, ABMS.

8. Ewald and Clute, *San Francisco Invites the World*, 16–17, 40, 72, 117; Weatherford, *A History of the American Suffragist Movement*, 185–86.

9. Edith Hamilton to Jessie Hamilton, October 28 [1915], folder 602, reel 28, HFP.

10. Edith Hamilton to Jessie Hamilton, November 21 [1915], folder 602, reel 28, HFP; on Honolulu see Edith Hamilton to "Dear People" [Jessie and Agnes Hamilton] April 30 [n.y. but written during her 1958 trip through Spain], folder 4, box 1, EHP.

11. Edith Hamilton to Jessie Hamilton, November 21 [1915], folder 602, reel 28, HFP.

12. Edith Hamilton to Agnes Hamilton, February 11 [1916], folder 609, reel 28, HFP.

13. Edith Hamilton to Agnes Hamilton, December 24 [1915], folder 609, reel 28, HFP.

14. Lucy Martin Donnelly to Bertrand Russell, December 26, 1915, box 5.13, BRP.

15. Edith Hamilton to Jessie Hamilton, December 17 [1915], folder 602, reel 28, HFP.

16. Ibid.

17. Edith Hamilton to Agnes Hamilton, December 24 [1915], folder 609, reel 28, HFP.

18. Edith Hamilton to Jessie Hamilton, January 15 [1916], folder 602, reel 28, HFP.

19. Ibid.

20. Dougill, *Kyoto*, 81; Edith spelled this Kenka-Ku-ji, see Edith Hamilton to Jessie Hamilton January 15 [1916], folder 602, reel 28, HFP.

21. Edith Hamilton to Jessie Hamilton, January 15 [1916], folder 602, reel 28, HFP.

22. Ibid.

23. Edith Hamilton, *The Greek Way*, chapter 3, 46.

24. Edith Hamilton to Agnes Hamilton, December 24 [1915], folder 609, reel 28, HFP.

25. Ibid.

26. Edith Hamilton to Agnes Hamilton, February 11 [1916], folder 609, reel 28, HFP.

27. Ibid.

28. Ibid.; Dougill, *Kyoto*, 199.

29. Edith Hamilton to Jessie Hamilton, April 30, 1929, folder 603, reel 28, HFP.

30. Edith Hamilton to Jessie Hamilton, December 17 [1915], folder 602; Edith Hamilton to Agnes Hamilton, December 24 [1915], folder 609, both reel 28, HFP.

31. Lucy Martin Donnelly to Bertrand Russell, April 14, 1916, box 5.13, BRP.

32. Edith Hamilton to Jessie Hamilton, March 30 [1916], folder 602, reel 28, HFP; Lily Duryee to Jessie and Agnes Hamilton, March 6, 1916, folder 298, reel 15, HFP.

33. Edith Hamilton to Jessie Hamilton, March 30 [1916], folder 602, reel 28, HFP.

34. Edith Hamilton to Jessie Hamilton, March 30 [1916], folder 602, reel 28, HFP. Edith spelled the name of this island as "Kolugan."

35. De Jong, *The Reformed Church in China*, 129–30.

36. De Jong, *The Reformed Church in China*, 20, 347.

37. Hunter, *The Gospel of Gentility*, 64.

38. Edith Hamilton to Jessie Hamilton, March 30 [1916], folder 602, reel 28, HFP.

39. Biography of Lily Duryee published by the Woman's Board of Foreign Missions [n.d. but included in Agnes Hamilton's correspondence], folder 452, reel 22, HFP; De Jong, *The Reformed Church in China*, 131, 120.

40. De Jong, *The Reformed Church in China*, 205.

41. Hunter, *The Gospel of Gentility*, 22–24.

42. Edith Hamilton to Norah Hamilton, May 15 [1916], folder 581, reel 27, HFP.

43. Edith Hamilton to Jessie Hamilton, April 8 [1916], folder 602, reel 28, HFP.

44. Hunter, *The Gospel of Gentility*, 178.

45. Marriage announcement, *New York Times*, May 8, 1905, p. 9.

46. Obituary for George Van Wagenen Duryee, *New York Times*, June 29, 1912, p. 11.

47. I am grateful to Dr. Heather Sharkey for this reference, drawn from her research at the School of Oriental and African Studies, University of London; SOAS, CWM South Chine—Fukien-Incoming Correspondence, box 10, folder 2, 1911; Alice Duryee's obituary in the *New York Times* does not refer to cause of death, see *New York Times*, February 2, 1911, p. 11; Lily Duryee to Agnes Hamilton [n.d. but written on black bordered paper and referring to Alice's death, so likely early 1911], folder 452, reel 22, HFP.

48. Elizabeth R. Lathrop to Jessie Hamilton, September 15, 1916, folder 298, reel 15; Edith Hamilton to Jessie Hamilton, April 30, 1929, folder 603; Edith Hamilton to Jessie Hamilton, December 17 [1915], folder 602, both reel 28, HFP. See also Sharkey, "An Egyptian in China," 325.

49. Susan Duryee Fahmy to Jessie Hamilton, written on photograph enclosed in letter of November 10, 1918, folder 299, reel 15, HFP.

50. Edith Hamilton to Jessie Hamilton, November 29, 1897, folder 597, reel 27, HFP.

51. Lin Yutang, *From Pagan to Christian*, 19–24, 27–29, 34, 234; Susan Duryee Fahmy to Jessie Hamilton, postmarked December 9, 1936, folder 311, reel 15, HFP; Edith Hamilton to John Mason Brown, October 4, 1943, JMBP.

52. Susan Duryee Fahmy to Jessie Hamilton, March 5 [n.y. but just after Edith's visit in 1916], folder 315, reel 15, HFP.

53. Edith Hamilton to Jessie Hamilton, April 8 [1916], folder 602, reel 28, HFP.

54. Edith Hamilton to Agnes Hamilton [n.d. but written after receiving the news of Dr. Fahmy's death in 1933], folder 610, reel 28, HFP; on Dr. Fahmy's death see Sharkey, "An Egyptian in China," 309.

55. Elizabeth R. Lathrop to Jessie Hamilton, September 15, 1916, folder 298; Susan Duryee Fahmy to Jessie Hamilton, March 5 [n.y. but just after Edith's visit in 1916], folder 315, both reel 15, HFP.

56. De Jong, *The Reformed Church in China*, 241.

57. Donnelly, "The Sage of Shantung," 260–63, 261.

58. Lucy Martin Donnelly, "China and Bryn Mawr," *Bryn Mawr Alumnae Bulletin* 1 (March 1921): 6–7.

59. Ibid.

60. Edith Hamilton, "Private Idiom," 218; reprinted in Hamilton, *The Ever-Present Past*, 142–50, 150.

61. Donnelly, "The Sage of Shantung," 262.

62. Donnelly, "The Sage of Shantung," 262.

63. Edith Hamilton to Gertrude Pond Hamilton, June 1 [1916], folder 578, reel 27, HFP.

64. Edith Hamilton to Gertrude Pond Hamilton, June 30 [1916], folder 578, reel 27, HFP.

65. Ibid.

66. Lucy Martin Donnelly to Bertrand Russell, December 26, 1915, and April 14, 1916, both box 5.13, BRP.

67. Edith Hamilton to Gertrude Pond Hamilton, June 30 [1916], folder 578, reel 27, HFP.

68. On Edith's carved Chinese table tops, see Doris Fielding Reid to Francesca Gilder Palmer [n.d. but during their early days at Seawall circa 1923–24], box 14, GM; on her matching Chinese vases, Alice Reid Abbott to author, August 18, 2009.

69. Edith Hamilton to Jessie Hamilton, October 21, 1932, folder 606, reel 28, HFP; Margaret Hamilton to Phoebe Taber Hamilton, October 7 [1915], folder 682, reel 31, HFP.

70. Sicherman, *Alice Hamilton*, 195–96; also Hamilton, *Exploring the Dangerous Trades*, 405–9; on its eleven rooms, see Edith Hamilton to Jessie Hamilton, July 30, 1919, folder 602, reel 28, HFP.

71. Norah Hamilton to Jessie Hamilton, July 3 [n.y.], folder 704, reel 32, HFP.

72. Margaret Hamilton to Katherine Hamilton, April 4 [n.y. but its description of their first visit to the house at Hadlyme dates it to 1917], folder 682, reel 31, HFP.

73. Sicherman, *Alice Hamilton*, 245.

74. Margaret Hamilton to Jessie Hamilton, November 6, 1932, folder 684, reel 31, HFP.

75. Fran Myers, "UI's Foreign Students Find a Friend in Dean-Professor 'Quint' Hamilton," *Champaigne-Urbana News-Gazette*, April 8, 1954, preserved in his biographical file, AUI; Edith Hamilton to Jessie Hamilton [May 9, 1915], folder 602, reel 28, HFP; also obituary for Dr. Arthur Hamilton, *Champaigne-Urbana News-Gazette*, May 31, 1967, preserved in his biographical file, AUI.

76. Arthur Hamilton to Phoebe Taber Hamilton, April 5, 1915, folder 715, reel 32, HFP.

77. Beirne, *Let's Pick the Daisies*, 33.

78. Edith Hamilton to M. Carey Thomas, December 16, 1918, ABMS; *The Bryn Mawrtyr* yearbook, 1920, 87; Di Cataldo, *Ex Solo Ad Solem*, 192.

79. Isabel Blogg Burger, "Roots from the Past Bring Forth Fruit," essay to celebrate the centennial of the Bryn Mawr School, p. 1, PJT.

80. West, *Value of the Classics*, 3.

81. James Thomas Flexner, *Maverick's Progress*, 30.

82. Abraham Flexner, *A Modern School*, 6.

83. Abraham Flexner, *A Modern School*, 5, 15–16, 18.

84. Abraham Flexner, *A Modern School*, 16.

85. Edith Hamilton, "Interesting Schools," 45–46, 45.

86. Edith Hamilton, "Interesting Schools," 46.

87. Edith Hamilton, *The Echo of Greece*, chapter 4, 68.

88. Edith Hamilton, "Interesting Schools," 46.

89. "The Reply," 46–47; on Bourne as the author of this, see Clayton, *Forgotten Prophet*, 160.

90. Edith Hamilton to "Dear Children" [Katherine, Jessie, and Agnes Hamilton], January 6, 1899, folder 598, reel 27, HFP.

91. Bourne, *Education and Living*, 161, 163.

92. Gress, *From Plato to NATO*, 34–35; Clayton, *Forgotten Prophet*, 147–51, 161–62.

93. Bourne, *Education and Living*, 164–67.

94. West, *Value of the Classics*, 20–21, 24–27, 29, 31–32, 301.

95. Davies, *The Humanism of Paul Elmer More*, 12–14.

96. Shorey, "The Bigotry of the New Education," 253–56, 254. His *Atlantic Monthly* essay, titled "The Assault on Humanism," was published in two parts in June and July 1917, see Shorey, "The Assault on Humanism," 793–801, and Shorey, "The Assault on Humanism, II," 94–105.

97. Norah Hamilton to Jessie Hamilton, May 6, 1917, folder 699, reel 32, HFP.

98. Norah Hamilton to Jessie Hamilton, September 19, 1917, folder 699, reel 32, HFP.

99. Ibid.; Edith Hamilton to Jessie Hamilton [n.d. but internal evidence, including the discussion of U.S. participation in the war, dates this to late 1917], folder 604, reel 28, HFP.

100. Edith Hamilton to Jessie Hamilton, August 18, 1929, folder 603, reel 28, HFP.

101. Reid, *Edith Hamilton: An Intimate Portrait*, 56; December 10, 1917, is the date carved on Gertrude Pond Hamilton's tombstone in Cove Cemetery, Hadlyme.

102. Susan Duryee Fahmy to Jessie Hamilton, February 7, 1918, folder 299, reel 15, HFP.

103. Norah Hamilton to Jessie Hamilton, postmarked February 7, 1918, folder 699, reel 32, HFP.

104. Reid, *Edith Hamilton: An Intimate Portrait*, 56.

105. Edith Hamilton to Jessie Hamilton, May 21 [1917], folder 602, reel 28, HFP.

106. Gilder, *Letters of Richard Watson Gilder*, 466, 483–84, 490; Edith Hamilton to Jessie Hamilton, February 11, 1932, folder 606, reel 28, HFP.

107. Sorley, *Lewis of Warner Hall*, 257–58.

108. Thomson, *J. J. Thomson and the Cavendish Laboratory in His Day*, 137.

109. Turnbull, *Chips from My Chisel*, 64.

110. Edith Hamilton to Jessie Hamilton, May 21 [1917], folder 602, reel 28, HFP.

111. Edith Hamilton to Jessie Hamilton July 4 [n.y. but its description of World's End Cottage dates it to the summer of 1918], folder 605, reel 28, HFP.

112. Ibid.

113. Edith Hamilton to Dorothy Bruce, June 27, 1920, A/H217.1a, EHL.

114. Edith Hamilton to Jessie Hamilton, June 21, 1918 and [August 16, 1918], both folder 602, reel 28, HFP.

115. Edith Hamilton to Jessie Hamilton [n.d. except Monday but the reference to Norah's summer at the art colony of Cornish dates it to summer 1918], folder 605, reel 28, HFP.

Chapter 10

1. Edith Hamilton to Jessie Hamilton, November 6 [1933?], folder 606, reel 28, HFP.

2. Edith Hamilton to Jessie Hamilton, July 30, 1919, folder 602, reel 28, HFP.

3. Susan Duryee Fahmy to Jessie and Agnes Hamilton, August 10, 1919, folder 299, reel 15, HFP.

4. Edith Hamilton to Jessie Hamilton, July 30, 1919, folder 602, reel 28; Edith Hamilton to Alice Hamilton [n.d. except 1918? More likely 1919 since Lily Duryee is mentioned as being in the United States, also mention is made of Quint taking his position at the University of Illinois, which he did in 1919], folder 579, reel 27; both HFP.

5. Dr. Simon Flexner to M. Carey Thomas, February 15, 1924, SFP.

6. Lucy Martin Donnelly, "The Sage of Shantung," 260–63.

7. Donnelly, "The Sage of Shantung," 262–63; Lucy Martin Donnelly to Mildred Minturn Scott, June 15, 1916, box 5.13, BRP.

8. Hamilton, *A Vision for Girls*, 77.

9. Jessie Hamilton to Agnes Hamilton, February 16, 1920, folder 211, reel 10, HFP.

10. Katharine Van Bibber, "Edith Hamilton," in *The Bryn Mawr School Faculty: A Centennial Tribute* (Baltimore: The Bryn Mawr School, 1985), 13.

11. Jessie Hamilton to Agnes Hamilton, February 16, 1920, folder 211, reel 10, HFP.

12. Ibid.

13. Susan Duryee Fahmy to Jessie Hamilton, February 10 [n.y. but the address 833 Park and the Fahmys' residency at the house dates this to 1920], folder 315, reel 15, HFP; Jessie repeated some of Susan's comments in a letter to Agnes, see Jessie Hamilton to Agnes Hamilton, February 16, 1920, folder 211, reel 10, HFP.

14. Susan Duryee Fahmy to Jessie Hamilton, February 10 [n.y. but the address 833 Park and the Fahmys' residency at the house dates this to 1920], folder 315, reel 15, HFP.

15. Susan Duryee Fahmy to Jessie Hamilton, February 26 [n.y. but its use of the address 833 Park and the Fahmys' residence there dates it to 1920], folder 316, reel 15, HFP.

16. Susan Duryee Fahmy to Agnes Hamilton March 5 [n.y. but the address of 833 Park Avenue dates this to the spring of 1920]; Susan Duryee Fahmy's emphasis, folder 452, reel 22, HFP.

17. Susan Duryee Fahmy to Jessie Hamilton, February 10 [n.y. but its use of the address 833 Park and the Fahmys' residence there dates it to 1920], folder 315, reel 15, HFP.

18. Jessie Hamilton to Agnes Hamilton, April 16, 1920, folder 211, reel 10, HFP.

19. Jessie Hamilton to Agnes Hamilton, April 24, 1920, folder 211, reel 10, HFP.

20. "Mary Garrett Mansion Is Robbed of Furniture," *Baltimore Sun*, December 17, 1920, p. 20; M. Carey Thomas to Edith Hamilton, February 10, 1921, frames 278–79, reel 142, MCTP.

21. Reid, *Woodrow Wilson*, 46.

22. Jessie Hamilton to Agnes Hamilton, May 15, 1919, folder 210, reel 10, HFP.

23. D. W. "The Fourth Class Debate," *Bryn Mawrter*, 1909, 28–29.

24. M. Carey Thomas to Simon Flexner, June 13, 1920, SFP.

25. Edith Hamilton to Jessie Hamilton, September 19 [1920], folder 603, reel 28, HFP.

26. Bok, "Just Because I Want to Play," 369–74.

27. Edith Hamilton to Jessie Hamilton, September 19 [1920], folder 603, reel 28, HFP.

28. Minutes of the Bryn Mawr School board of managers, October 30, 1920, ABMS.

29. Edith Hamilton to Jessie Hamilton, September 19 [1920], folder 603, reel 28, HFP.

30. On Edith not at the Bryn Mawr School during the mornings, see "Head of Bryn Mawr Replies to Charges," unidentified newspaper article covering Edith's resignation in early 1922, contained in PJT; on Doris helping to answer Bryn Mawr School letters, see Edith Hamilton to Norah Hamilton [n.d. except September 1920? but given its description of Doris's activity this date seems likely], folder 581, reel 27, HFP; on consulting Dr. Walter Walker Palmer, see Doris Fielding Reid to Margaret Hamilton [n.d. but written on the stationery of Tors Hotel, Lynmouth, North Devon, and clearly dating from late August 1921, since it details plans for September and recounts the long stay at Colwyn Bay, which had included Edith's birthday], folder 3, box 1, EHP; on the marriage of Francesca Gilder to Dr. Walter Walker Palmer, see "Miss Gilder Weds Dr. Walter Palmer," *New York Times*, October 13, 1922, p. 16.

31. Harry Fielding Reid to Henry van Dyke, June 17, 1921, folder 16, box 123, HVDFP; see also "Society," *Baltimore Sun*, June 16, 1921, p. 7.

32. M. Carey Thomas to Lucy Martin Donnelly, January 25, 1921, frame 221, reel 142, MCTP.

33. Lucy Martin Donnelly to M. Carey Thomas, June 11, 1921, frames 543–544, reel 38, MCTP.

34. Susan Duryee Fahmy to Jessie Hamilton [n.d. but clearly written during Edith's 1921 trip to Britain with Edith and Doris Reid and included with Agnes Hamilton's correspondence], folder 453, reel 22, HFP.

35. Edith Hamilton to Norah Hamilton, August 13 [n.y. but written on stationery of the Pwllycrochan Hotel, Colwyn Bay, so 1921], folder 3, box 1, EHP.

36. F.C.B., "Baltimore Visited by Half a Dozen Notables," *Musical America*, April 23, 1921, p. 39; the concert was held on April 12, 1921.

37. Doris Fielding Reid to Margaret Hamilton [n.d. but written on the stationery of Tors Hotel, Lynmouth, North Devon, and clearly dating from late August 1921, since it details plans for September and recounts the long stay at Colwyn Bay, which had included Edith's birthday], folder 3, box 1, EHP.

38. Margaret Hamilton to Norah Hamilton [n.d. but internal evidence, including Edith's departure for England and her initial plans to return when the school year began dates this to 1921], folder 681, reel 31, HFP.

39. Doris Fielding Reid to Margaret Hamilton [n.d. but written on the stationery of Tors Hotel, Lynmouth, North Devon, and clearly dating from late August 1921, since it details plans for September and recounts the long stay at Colwyn Bay, which had included Edith's birthday], folder 3, box 1, EHP. See also Doris Fielding Reid to Rosamond Gilder [October 1921?], box 14, GM.

40. Doris Fielding Reid to Rosamond Gilder, October 1921, box 14, GM.

41. Edith Hamilton to Dorothy Bruce, November 1921, A/H217.1a, EHL.

42. Doris Fielding Reid to Rosamond Gilder, October 1921, box 14, GM.

43. Edith Hamilton to board of managers, September 24, 1921, read into minutes of the meeting of the board of managers of the Bryn Mawr School, November 12, 1921, ABMS.

44. Edith Hamilton to Jessie Hamilton, January 4, 1922, folder 603, reel 28, HFP.

45. M. Carey Thomas to Edith Hamilton, February 10, 1921, frames 278–79, reel 142, MCTP.

46. Janet Brock Koudelka, "Mary Sherwood," in Sicherman and Green, eds., *Notable American Women*, 283–84, 284.

47. Minutes of the board of managers meeting, November 12, 1921, ABMS.

48. Minutes of the board of managers meeting, January 27, 1922, ABMS.

49. Minutes of the board of managers of the Bryn Mawr School, February 21, 1922, ABMS.

50. "Bryn Mawr Principal to Quit," *Baltimore Sun*, March 9, 1922, p. 3.

51. Petition of the school faculty to the board of managers, PJT; text also included in the minutes of the board of managers meeting, March 20, 1922, ABMS.

52. Horowitz, *The Power and Passion of M. Carey Thomas*, 438.

53. Minutes of the meeting of the board of managers, February 21, 1921, ABMS.

54. Minutes of the meeting of the board of managers, March 20, 1922, ABMS.

55. Edith Hamilton to board of managers, March 23, 1922, box 3.1.1; Edith Hamilton's Resignation, ABMS.

56. John H. Latane to Bishop John Gardner Murray, May 8, 1922, box 3.1.1: Edith Hamilton's resignation, ABMS; "Grave Charges Made in Fight on Bryn Mawr," *Baltimore Sun*, March 21, 1922.

57. Margaret Hamilton to the board of managers of the Bryn Mawr School, March 23, 1922, box 3.1.1; Edith Hamilton's resignation, ABMS; "Breach Widens in Bryn Mawr School Fight," *Baltimore Sun*, March 25, 1922, p. 22.

58. Minutes of the meeting of the board of managers, March 25, 1922, ABMS; Edith Hamilton to Agnes Hamilton [n.d. but clearly concerning her final resignation from the Bryn Mawr School], folder 610, reel 28, HFP.

59. Minutes of the meeting of the board of managers, March 25, 1922, ABMS; Edith Hamilton to Agnes Hamilton [n.d. but clearly concerning her final resignation from the Bryn Mawr School], folder 610, reel 28, HFP.

60. Di Cataldo, *Ex Solo Ad Solem*, 35.

61. Edith Hamilton to Margaret Hamilton [n.d. except "in the train" but clearly dating from the period of Edith's resignation], folder 3, box 1, EHP.

62. Lucy Martin Donnelly to M. Carey Thomas [n.d. except "Tuesday"], frame 895, reel 38, MCTP.

63. Lucy Martin Donnelly to M. Carey Thomas, April 8, 1922, frames 553–57, reel 38, MCTP.

64. "Wills for Probate," *New York Times*, June 10, 1923, p. 57; this gives Henry Donnelly's date of death as May 28, 1923.

65. Edith Hamilton to Eva Palmer Sikelianos, October 25, 1948, folder 54, box 43, AEPS.

66. Edith Hamilton to Jessie Hamilton, April 23, 1922, folder 603, reel 28, HFP.

67. "Parents Advance Bryn Mawr Peace," *Baltimore Sun*, March 31, 1922, p. 9.

68. I am grateful to Elizabeth Nye Di Cataldo, former archivist of the Bryn Mawr School, for this reference to Edith giving a photograph of herself to Dr. Kelly. The photograph is reproduced in Di Cataldo's *Ex Solo Ad Solem*, 164.

69. Edith Hamilton to Margaret Hamilton, January 23, 1924, folder 581, reel 27, HFP.

70. Reid, *Edith Hamilton: An Intimate Portrait*, 57–58.

71. Doris Fielding Reid to Bill and Francesca Gilder Palmer [n.d. except "Monday" but its discussion of the Palmers' recent marriage dates it to October 1922], box 14, GM.

72. Sorley, *Lewis of Warner Hall*, 258.

73. Sorley, *Lewis of Warner Hall*, 257–58.

74. Francis Fielding Reid to Henry van Dyke, March 3, 1920, folder 15, box 123, HVDFP.

75. Sorley, *Lewis of Warner Hall*, 258; Dorian Fielding Reid to Walter Walker Palmer [September 19? 1925], box 14 GM.

76. Sorley, *Lewis of Warner Hall*, 258.

77. Edith Hamilton to Rosamond Gilder, July 16 [n.y. though 1924 since it mentions Rosamond's first article in *Theatre Arts Monthly*], box 11, GM.

78. Margaret Hamilton to Gertrude Pond Hamilton, August 27, 1914, folder 679, reel 31, HFP.

79. Ibid.

80. Alice Reid Abbott to author, August 18, 2009.

81. Judith P. Hallett, "The Anglicizing Way: Edith Hamilton (1867–1963) and the Twentieth-Century Transformation of Classics in the U.S.A." in Hallett and Stray, eds., *British Classics Outside England*, 149–65, 151.

82. Edith Hamilton to Agnes Hamilton, August 19 [n.y. though if Dorian was five it would have been the summer of 1923, since the letter was written from Seawall], folder 610, reel 28, HFP.

83. Edith Hamilton to Jessie Hamilton, July 25, 1925; Edith Hamilton to Jessie Hamilton, August 19, 1926, both folder 603, reel 28, HFP.

84. Edith Hamilton to Rosamond Gilder, August 1 [1925], box 11, GM; Doris Fielding Reid to Rosamond Gilder, September 19, 1925, box 14, GM; Edith Hamilton to Florence Butler Cairns, August 19, 1956, box 12, HCP.

85. Melosh, *Strangers and Kin*, 3; for other examples of Progressive Era reformers and adoption, see Shaw, *The Story of a Pioneer*, 144–45; Schwarz, *Radical Feminists of Heterodoxy*, 1, 17, 21.

86. Edith Hamilton to Jessie Hamilton, February 11, 1932, folder 606, reel 28, HFP.

87. Edith Hamilton to Rosamond Gilder [March 23, 1924], box 11, GM.

88. Doris Fielding Reid to Rosamond Gilder and Francesca Gilder Palmer [n.d. but likely summer 1925 since written from Seawall and mentioning Edith's first article for *Theatre Arts Monthly*], box 14, GM.

89. Edith Hamilton to Dorothy Bruce, November 30 [1924], A/H217.1a, EHL.

90. Edith Hamilton to Rosamond Gilder, postmarked March 23, 1924, box 11, GM.

91. Edith Hamilton to Rosamond Gilder, postmarked August 9, 1925, box 11, GM.

92. Edith Hamilton to Jessie Hamilton, August 18 [1923? given the unfinished state of the house at Seawall, the year 1923 seems likely for this letter], folder 603, reel 28, HFP; Edith described this very similarly to Rosamond Gilder, see Edith Hamilton to Rosamond Gilder, August 1 [n.y. but very likely 1923 since it is similar to her letter to Jessie and also discusses plans for the winter of 1923], box 11, GM.

93. Edith Hamilton to Rosamond Gilder, August 1 [n.y. but internal evidence, including its discussion of living in Europe, dates it to the summer of 1923], box 11, GM.

94. Reid, *Edith Hamilton: An Intimate Portrait*, 61.

95. Edith Hamilton to Rosamond Gilder [n.d. but internal evidence dates this letter to the winter spent at Seawall], box 11, GM.

96. Doris Fielding Reid to Rosamond Gilder, January 6, 1924, box 14, GM.

97. Edith Hamilton to Jessie Hamilton, August 17, 1925, folder 603, reel 28, HFP.

98. Edith Hamilton to Jessie Hamilton, November 23, 1932, and Edith Hamilton to Jessie Hamilton, January 25, 1933, both folder 606, reel 28, HFP.

99. Doris Fielding Reid to Rosamond Gilder, postmarked [August 13? 1923], box 14, GM.

100. Reid, *Edith Hamilton: An Intimate Portrait*, 61; Doris Fielding Reid to Francesca Gilder Palmer [n.d. but circa 1923], box 14, GM.

101. Dorian Fielding Reid to Rosamond Gilder [n.d.], box 14, GM.

102. Doris Fielding Reid to Rosamond Gilder, postmarked [August 13? 1923], box 14, GM.

103. Doris Fielding Reid to Rosamond Gilder, February 17, 1924, box 14, GM.

104. Edith Hamilton to Margaret Hamilton, January 23, 1924, folder 581, reel 27, HFP.

105. Margaret Hamilton to Alice Hamilton, January 14 [1924?], folder 680, reel 31, HFP; the discussion of the property settlement makes the suggested year of 1924 likely.

106. Doris Fielding Reid to Rosamond Gilder, May 3, 1924, box 14, GM.

107. Doris Fielding Reid to Rosamond Gilder, postmarked July 26, 1924, box 14, GM.

108. Susan Duryee Fahmy to Jessie Hamilton, October 6, 1929, folder 308, reel 15, HFP.

109. Edith Hamilton to Dorothy Bruce, November 30, 1924, A/H217.1a, EHL; Reid, 65.

110. Ibid.

111. Klein, *Gramercy Park*, 115.

112. Philip S. Cook, "Edith Hamilton, at 90, Flies in From Greece," *New York Herald Tribune*, August 13, 1957, p. 1.

113. Edith Hamilton to Rosamond Gilder, December 21 [1923], box 11, GM.

114. Edith Hamilton to Rosamond Gilder, July 16 [n.y. but internal evidence, including Rosamond's new work at *Theatre Arts Monthly*, dates this to 1924], box 11, GM; Faderman, *Odd Girls and Twilight Lovers*, 62–65.

115. Edith Hamilton, "Private Idiom," 141, 156, 206–7, 218.

116. Edith Hamilton to Lucia Norton Valentine, postmarked August 15, 1961, box 3.1.1, collection of Edith Hamilton letters from the Valentines, ABMS.

117. Edith Hamilton to Jessie Hamilton, April 11, 1937, folder 606, reel 28, HFP.

118. Doris Fielding Reid to Rosamond Gilder, postmarked June 22, 1924, box 14, GM; Rosamond Gilder, "The Season in Print," *Theatre Arts Monthly* 8 (July 1924): 499–500; Thomas W. Ennis, "Rosamond Gilder, an Author Influential in World Theater," *New York Times*, September 9, 1986, p. B6.

119. Edith Hamilton to Rosamond Gilder, July 29 [n.y. but discussion of Rosamond's first article in *Theatre Arts Monthly* dates this to 1924], box 11, GM.

Chapter 11

1. Beirne, *Let's Pick the Daisies*, 77; Hoppen, *The Emmets*, 9–10.

2. Lydia Field Emmet to Jane Emmet De Glehn, April 30, 1925, frames 805–14, reel 4760, EFP.

3. Parker and Bronough, "Edith Hamilton at 94," 183–84, 184; Katter, "'Theatre Arts' under the Editorship of Edith J. R. Isaacs," unpublished dissertation, 89, 97, 101.

4. Foley, *Reimaging Greek Tragedy on the American Stage*, 3.

5. Katter, "'Theatre Arts' under the Editorship of Edith J. R. Isaacs," unpublished dissertation, 340; Houghton, *Entrances and Exits*, 201.

6. Katter, "'Theatre Arts' under the Editorship of Edith J. R. Isaacs," unpublished dissertation, 11–12.

7. Katter, "'Theatre Arts' under the Editorship of Edith J. R. Isaacs," unpublished dissertation, 19–23; obituary for Edith J. R. Isaacs, *New York Times*, January 11, 1956, p. 31.

8. Niven, *Thornton Wilder*, 240; Katter, "'Theatre Arts' under the Editorship of Edith J. R. Isaacs," unpublished dissertation, 155–70.

9. Lewis Mumford to Edith J. R. Isaacs, August 31, 1927, folder 1, box 1, EJRIP.

10. Katter, "'Theatre Arts' under the Editorship of Edith J. R. Isaacs," unpublished dissertation, 48–52, 330–31.

11. Edith Hamilton to Edith J. R. Isaacs, May 23, 1940, folder 3, box 1, EJRIP.

12. Reid, *Edith Hamilton: An Intimate Portrait*, 66–67; Edith Hamilton to Rosamond Gilder, May 29 [n.y. but its discussion of the arrival of the Reid family dates it to 1925], box 11, GM.

13. Edith Hamilton to Rosamond Gilder, May 29 [n.y. but internal evidence dates this to 1925], box 11, GM.

14. Edith Hamilton, *Three Greek Plays*, chapter 1, 12–14.

15. Edith Hamilton, *Three Greek Plays*, chapter 2, 17.

16. Edith Hamilton, *Three Greek Plays*, chapter 1, 10.

17. Cowling, *On Classic Ground*, 1–2; McAuliffe, *When Paris Sizzled*, 21, 126, 133, 138, 183.

18. W. Macneile Dixon to Edith Hamilton, July 11, 1927, folder 16, box 1, EHP.

19. Dixon, *Hellas Revisited*, 167–69; Hamilton, *The Greek Way*, chapter 2, 22.

20. Palmer-Sikelianos, *Upward Panic*, 117, 129; Leontis, *Eva Palmer Sikelianos*, xl, xli, 137, 172; Scott, 127, 277.

21. Gregory, *H. D. and Hellenism*, 4, 13, 16; Dixon, *Hellas Revisited*, 8, 16, 70–71, 94, 108, 155.

22. Hamilton, *The Greek Way*, chapter 1, 8.

23. Hamilton, *The Greek Way*, chapter 1, 5.

24. Hamilton, *The Greek Way*, chapter 1, 12–19.

25. T. S. Eliot, "Euripides and Professor Murray," reprinted in T.S. Eliot, *The Sacred Wood*, 71–77, 73–76; Hamilton, *The Greek Way*, chapter 1, 6–7; Ackerman, "The Cambridge Group: Origins and Composition," 1–19.

26. Doris Fielding Reid to Rosamond Gilder and Francesca Gilder Palmer [n.d. except Monday but written from Seawall and discussing *Theatre Arts Monthly*'s acceptance of Edith's article and the presence of the Reid children, so likely summer 1925], box 14, GM.

27. Doris Fielding Reid to Rosamond Gilder [n.d. but its clear description of the writing of the essay "Tragedy" dates it to the summer of 1925], box 14, GM.

28. Edith Hamilton to Rosamond Gilder [n.d. but concerning "Tragedy" and written from Seawall, likely dating it to the summer of 1925], box 11, GM.

29. Edith Hamilton, "Tragedy," 41–46, 41–42.

30. Edith Hamilton, "Tragedy," 45.

31. Dixon, *Tragedy*, 5, 23–26.

32. Dixon, *Tragedy*, 31, 100, 183.

33. Doris Fielding Reid to Rosamond Gilder and Francesca Gilder Palmer [n.d. except Monday but written from Seawall and discussing *Theatre Arts Monthly*'s acceptance of Edith's article and the presence of the Reid children, so likely summer 1925], box 14, GM.

34. Doris Fielding Reid to Rosamond Gilder, September 19, 1925, box 14, GM.

35. Edith Hamilton to Rosamond Gilder, August 1 [1925], box 11, GM.

36. Edith Hamilton to Rosamond Gilder, August 9 [1925? Given its discussion of her inability to adopt Ernest Reid a date of 1925 seems likely], box 11, GM.

37. Willis, "The American Laboratory Theatre," unpublished dissertation, 11–17, 20–22, 78–79.

38. Willis, "The American Laboratory Theatre," unpublished dissertation, 1, 20.

39. Niven, *Thornton Wilder*, 175.

40. Edith Hamilton to Isabel Wilder, May 11, 1943, folder 960, box 37, TWP.

41. Edith Hamilton to John Mason Brown, November 7, 1936, folder 3, box 3, EHC.

42. Stevens, *Speak for Yourself, John*, 83.

43. Stevens, *Speak for Yourself, John*, 96.

44. Hamilton, *The Greek Way*, viii; see also "Miss Mary Polak Wed to Donald Oenslager in Roof Garden by the Rev. H.W.B. Donegan," *New York Times*, March 18, 1937, p. 29.

45. Katter, "'Theatre Arts' under the Editorship of Edith J. R. Isaacs," unpublished dissertation, 149.

46. Edith Hamilton to Margaret Hamilton [n.d. but its reference to the death of Ellen Reid Van Dyke makes a date of 1935 likely], folder 581, reel 27, HFP.

47. Kinne, *George Pierce Baker and the American Theatre*, 231; Edith Hamilton to John Mason Brown, December 28, 1931, folder 3, box 3, EHC.

48. Katter, "'Theatre Arts' under the Editorship of Edith J. R. Isaacs," unpublished dissertation, 95.

49. Edith Hamilton to Dorothy Bruce, April 21, 1926, A/H217.1a, EHL.

50. Ibid.

51. Edith Hamilton, "The Prometheus Bound of Aeschylus," 545–62, illustrations appear on pages 557 and 558.

52. Leontis, *Eva Palmer Sikelianos*, 137, 150, 163, 172.

53. Reid, *Edith Hamilton: An Intimate Portrait*, 77–79; Edith Hamilton, "The Greek Chorus: Fifteen or Fifty?" 459–67, 461; this essay was reprinted posthumously in Hamilton, *The Ever-Present Past*, 48–59.

54. Doris Fielding Reid to Rosamond Gilder, postmarked July 24, 1927, box 14, GM.

55. W. Macneile Dixon to Edith Hamilton, July 11, 1927, folder 16, box 1, EHP.

56. Edith Hamilton, "Comedy," 503–12; this essay was reprinted posthumously in Hamilton, *The Ever-Present Past*, 60–72.

57. Edith Hamilton to Dorothy Bruce, July 21, 1927, A/H217.1a, EHL.

58. Edith Hamilton to Jessie Hamilton, August 10, 1930, folder 606, reel 28, HFP; Hamilton, *The Greek Way*, chapter 8, 152–53, 158–64.

59. Gregory, *H. D. and Hellenism*, 23–24.

60. Edith Hamilton to Jessie Hamilton, December 12, 1927, folder 603, reel 28, HFP.

61. Edith Hamilton to Jessie Hamilton, November 10, 1932, folder 606, reel 28, HFP.

62. Edith Hamilton, "W. S. Gilbert: A Mid-Victorian Aristophanes"; Edith Hamilton to Rosamond Gilder [n.d. but mentions sending "Tragedy" to Dorna McCollester at *Theatre Arts Monthly* so a date of 1925 likely], box 11, GM.

63. Edith Hamilton to Jessie Hamilton [n.d. except "Sunday evening" but referring to her vacations with the Pond family], folder 590, reel 27, HFP.

64. Edith Hamilton, "W. S. Gilbert: A Mid-Victorian Aristophanes," 783.

65. Edith Hamilton, *The Greek Way*, chapter 6, 136.

66. Shorey, *Greek Life and Thought at Its Culmination*, 8.

67. Hamilton, *The Greek Way*, chapter 5, 85.

68. Christopher Stray, "Richard Winn Livingstone," in Todd, ed., *The Dictionary of British Classicists*, vol. 2, 585–87.

69. Edith Hamilton, *The Greek Way*, preface, viii; Edith Hamilton, "The Classics," 29–32, 31.

70. Livingstone, *The Greek Genius*, 37, 40–42.

71. Storer B. Lunt to Edith Hamilton, April 9, 1958, folder 9, box 1, EHP.

72. Office memorandum, December 14, 1953, box 118, series II, WWNP.

73. Wilson, "Norton's Ingredients for Success," 3–15, 4, WWNP; Howard P. Wilson, "An Account of the Early Days of W. W. Norton & Company," unpublished, series II, box 336, p. 4–5; Clark, *The Life of Bertrand Russell*, 455.

74. Howard P. Wilson, "An Account of the Early Days of W. W. Norton & Company," unpublished, series II, box 336, p. 9, WWNP.

75. Howard P. Wilson, "An Account of the Early Days of W. W. Norton & Company," unpublished, series II, box 336, p. 12, WWNP.

76. Storer B. Lunt to Edith Hamilton, April 9, 1958, folder 9, box 1, EHP.

77. Margaret Hamilton to Jessie Hamilton, February 12, 1928, folder 684, reel 31, HFP.

78. Edith Hamilton, "Greek and the English Genius," 333–38; this is the chapter "The Greek Way of Writing" in *The Greek Way*.

79. Edith Hamilton to John Mason Brown, November 7, 1936, folder 3, box 3, EHC.

80. John Mason Brown to Elling Aannestad, July 11, 1963, folder 4, box 3, EHC.

81. Elling Aannestad, "Memoir of Maine Seasons" [unpublished autobiography], p. 92, folder 6 and p. 243, folder 7, both box 2, EAP; Wilson, "Norton's Ingredients for Success," 4.

82. Elling Aannestad, "Memoir of Maine Seasons," unpublished autobiography, p. 42, folder 6, box 2, EAP.

83. Elling Aannestad, journal, undated except January, folder 31, box 1; "Memoir of Maine Seasons," unpublished autobiography, p. 70, p. 130, folder 6, box 2; "Memoir of Maine Seasons," unpublished autobiography, p. 164, p. 391, folder 7, box 2, all EAP.

84. Stevens, *Speak for Yourself, John*, 7; Certificate of confirmation for Elling Aannestad, folder 2, box 1, EAP.

85. Edith Hamilton, *The Greek Way*, chapter 8, 151, 154.

86. Edith Hamilton, *The Greek Way*, chapter 8, 156.

87. Edith Hamilton, *The Greek Way*, chapter 8, 153.

88. Edith Hamilton, *The Greek Way*, chapter 8, 167.

89. Edith Hamilton, *The Greek Way*, chapter 8, 169.

90. Edith Hamilton, *The Greek Way*, chapter 8, 168–71.

91. Edith Hamilton, *The Greek Way*, chapter 9, 176, 180–83; Jenkyns, *The Victorians and Ancient*, 105.

92. Edith Hamilton, *The Greek Way*, chapter 10, 187–88, 192–94.

93. Edith Hamilton to Agnes Hamilton [n.d. but written at 24 Gramercy Park during the writing of *The Greek Way*], folder 610, reel 28, HFP.

94. Edith Hamilton, "Greek and the English Genius," 333; Edith Hamilton, *The Greek Way*, chapter 1, 3–4.

95. Edith Hamilton, *The Greek Way*, chapter 1, 12–13.

96. Lily Duryee to Jessie and Agnes Hamilton, February 8, 1927, folder 306, reel 15, HFP; "Mission Leader, 84, Is Here from China," *New York Times*, November 8, 1937, p. 5.

97. Edith Hamilton, *The Greek Way*, chapter 3, 46.

98. Edith Hamilton, *The Greek Way*, chapter 3, 55; Henry, *The Life and Art of Luca Signorelli*, 1, 12, 17; Weaver, *A Legacy of Excellence*, 60, 123; Hamilton, *The Greek Way*, chapter 4, 64, 162.

99. Edith Hamilton, *The Greek Way*, chapter 2, 23.

100. Arnold, "Culture and Anarchy," vol. 5, 87–229, 95.

101. Edward Caird, *The Evolution of Religion*, vol. 1, 234.

102. Edith Hamilton to Agnes Hamilton [n.d. except "Tuesday" but its reference to Edith publishing an article in *Atlantic Monthly* dates it to early 1929], folder 610, reel 28, HFP.

Chapter 12

1. Edith Hamilton to Jessie Hamilton, December 12, 1927, folder 603, reel 27, HFP.

2. Doris Fielding Reid to Rosamond Gilder, [September 28?] 1930, box 14, GM; Agnes Hamilton to Katherine Hamilton, May 27, 1931, folder 360, reel 18, HFP; both these letters contain descriptions of the apartment at 24 Gramercy Park.

3. Ibid. Doris Fielding Reid to Rosamond Gilder.

4. Edith Hamilton, "A Mystic Looks at Shakespeare," 717–18; Edith Hamilton, "Brass Tacks," 449–50.

5. Pickard-Cambridge, *Dithyramb, Tragedy, and Comedy*, v, 1–3, 5.

6. Ackerman, "The Cambridge Group: Origins and Composition," 1–19, 1, 6–7.

7. Edith Hamilton, "Brass Tacks," 449–50.

8. Edith Hamilton, "Born under a Rhyming Planet," 11–12.

9. Edith Hamilton, "Gaudeamus Igitur," 6.

10. Edith Hamilton to Agnes Hamilton [n.d. except "Tuesday" but its discussion of their upcoming departure on the *Adriatic* on February 28 dates it to early 1929], folder 610, reel 28, HFP.

11. Murray, *Aldous Huxley*, 12, 50–52, 150–51, 169.

12. Edith Hamilton, "These Sad Young Men," 656–62, 658; this essay was reprinted in its entirety in Edith Hamilton, *The Ever-Present Past*, 127–41.

13. Edith Hamilton to Jessie Hamilton, April 30, 1929, folder 603, reel 28, HFP.

14. Doris Fielding Reid to Rosamond Gilder, March 20 [1929], box 14, GM.

15. Edith Hamilton to Agnes Hamilton [n.d. except "Tuesday" but describes their upcoming trip to Greece and the upcoming publication of "These Sad Young Men" in the *Atlantic Monthly*, so a date of early 1929 is likely], folder 610, reel 28, HFP; Norah Hamilton to Jessie Hamilton, postmarked March 29, 1929, folder 701, reel 32, HFP; Dixon, *Hellas Revisited*, 33–34; Miller, *Greek Horizons*, 80.

16. Doris Fielding Reid to Rosamond Gilder, March 20 [1929], box 14, GM.

17. Van der Kiste, *Kings of the Hellenes*, 144, 152; Mazower, *Greece and the Inter-War Economic Crisis*, 136.

18. Doris Fielding Reid to Rosamond Gilder, March 20 [1929], box 14, GM.

19. Edith Hamilton to Jessie Hamilton, April 30, 1929, folder 603, reel 28, HFP.

20. Edith Hamilton, *The Greek Way*, chapter 3, 60.

21. Doris Fielding Reid to Rosamond Gilder [n.d. but written on a postcard of a Greek marble relief and describing Dorian's recovery and their schedule], box 14, GM.

22. Edith Hamilton to Jessie Hamilton, April 30, 1929, folder 603, reel 28, HFP; Miller, *Greek Horizons*, 121.

23. Edith Hamilton, "The Greek Chorus: Fifteen or Fifty?" 459–67, 461; Miller, *Greek Horizons*, 93.

24. Reid, *Edith Hamilton: An Intimate Portrait*, 79; photograph album in the possession of Alice Reid Abbott; Alice Reid Abbott to author, August 18, 2009.

25. Edith Hamilton to Jessie Hamilton, April 30, 1929, folder 603, reel 28, HFP.

26. Doris Fielding Reid to Rosamond Gilder, April 15 [1929]; the context of this letter, written on board the *S.S. Adriatic*, suggests that the year 1929 is correct; box 14, GM; Edith Hamilton, *The Roman Way*, chapter 4, 75.

27. Susan Duryee Fahmy to Jessie Hamilton, October 6, 1929, folder 308, reel 15, HFP.

28. Doris Fielding Reid to Mrs. Matthew Josephson, April 1 [n.y. but responding to a letter written in February 1955]; AAAL.

29. Goldman, "The Greek Genius," 35–36.

30. Hutchison, "The Ancient Greeks."

31. Jessie Hamilton to Agnes Hamilton [n.d. but its mention that the publisher has requested a second book places it after the publication of *The Greek Way* and before the writing of *The Roman Way*], folder 238, reel 11, HFP.

32. Doris Fielding Reid to Rosamond Gilder, postmarked September 11, 1930, box 14, GM.

33. Edith Hamilton to Vail Motter, December 3, 1952, box 6, VMP.

34. Dennison, *Behind the Mask*, 30, 215, 223–28, 239; Sackville-West's novel was *The Edwardians*.

35. Edith Hamilton to Vail Motter, December 3, 1952, box 6, VMP.

36. Review of *The Greek Way*, *Times Literary Supplement*, September 18, 1930, p. 736; Review of *The Greek Way*, *The New Statesman*, September 20, 1930, p. 744; Mitchison, "Athens Re-Explored," 985–86.

37. John Hadfield to C. Raymond Everitt, December 13, 1938, box 39, LBP.

38. Edith Hamilton to Jessie Hamilton, November 10 1932, folder 606, reel 28, HFP.

39. Edith Hamilton to Jessie Hamilton, November 30 [n.y.], folder 605, reel 28, HFP.

40. Edith Hamilton to Warder Norton, August 27, 1936, WWNP.

41. Edith Hamilton to [Jessie or Agnes Hamilton?]. Undated letter fragment, folder 613, reel 28, HFP.

42. Agnes Hamilton to Katherine Hamilton, May 27, 1931, folder 360, reel 18, HFP.

43. Brown, "The Fruit of Enlightenment," 28–30; Brown repeated this remark in a tribute to Edith that he published after her death, see Brown, "The Heritage of Edith Hamilton: 1867–1963," 16–17.

44. Edith Hamilton, *The Roman Way*, chapter 13, 272.

45. Edith Hamilton, *The Roman Way*, chapter 10, 199.

46. Edith Hamilton, *The Greek Way*, chapter 1, 8–9; chapter 2, 22–23.

47. Edith Hamilton, *The Roman Way*, chapter 11, 228.

48. Edith Hamilton, *The Roman Way*, chapter 9, 181.

49. Edith Hamilton, *The Roman Way*, chapter 12, 262.

50. Edith Hamilton, *The Roman Way*, chapter 1, 4; chapter 10, 202.

51. Edith Hamilton, *The Roman Way*, chapter 11, 212.

52. Notebook labeled "Romans," p. 39 [author's pagination], box 2, EHC; Sabine Grebe, "Henry Nettleship," in Todd, ed., *The Dictionary of British Classicists*, vol. 2, 706–7.

53. Edith Hamilton, *The Roman Way*, chapter 5, 93–94.

54. Edith Hamilton, *The Roman Way*, chapter 2, 29, 31.

55. Edith Hamilton, *The Roman Way*, chapter 2, 36–37, 41.

56. Edith Hamilton, *The Roman Way*, chapter 12, 264.

57. Edith Hamilton, *The Roman Way*, chapter 10, 192.

58. Edith Hamilton, *The Roman Way*, chapter 10, 193–94.

59. Edith Hamilton, *The Roman Way*, chapter 10, 194; chapter 12, 264.

60. Notebook labeled "Roman Comedy," p. 4 [author's pagination], box 2, EHC.

61. Edith Hamilton to Jessie Hamilton, January 25, 1933, folder 606, reel 28, HFP.

62. Edith Hamilton, *The Greek Way*, chapter 12, 232.

63. Edith Hamilton, *The Roman Way*, chapter 12, 264.

64. N. Hopkinson, "Edward Vernon Arnold," in Todd, ed., *The Dictionary of British Classicists*, vol. 1, 19–20.

65. Arnold, *Roman Stoicism*, 1, 19–20.

66. Edith Hamilton, *The Roman Way*, chapter 12, 260–62.

67. Caird, *The Evolution of the Religion*, vol. 1, 372–76.

68. Notebook labeled "Rome," box 2, EHC.

69. Caird, *The Evolution of the Religion*, vol. 1, 372–76.

70. Notebook labeled "Rome," box 2, EHC.

71. Edith Hamilton, *The Roman Way*, chapter 12, 259.

72. Edith Hamilton, *The Roman Way*, chapter 12, 260.

73. Edith Hamilton, *The Roman Way*, chapter 12, 263.

74. Edith Hamilton, *The Roman Way*, chapter 12, 265.

75. Edith Hamilton, *Witness to the Truth*, chapter 7, 170.

76. Edith Hamilton, *The Roman Way*, chapter 1, 16.

77. Detzer, *Appointment on the Hill*, 2–3, 7–8, 86–89, 101, 108.

78. Edith Hamilton, *The Roman Way*, chapter 10, 197.

79. "Edith Hamilton," in James Nelson, ed., *Wisdom For Our Time*, 15–25, 23; this book contains a complete transcript of Edith Hamilton's 1958 *Wisdom* interview.

80. Edith Hamilton, *The Roman Way*, chapter 10, 199.

81. Davis, "What the Romans Were," 303.

82. Edith Hamilton, *The Roman Way*, chapter 13, 270.

83. Edith Hamilton to Jessie Hamilton, November 18, 1925, folder 603, reel 28; Margaret Hamilton to Katherine Hamilton, November 23 [1925?], given its discussion of Katherine's illness, this year seems likely, folder 682, reel 31, HFP.

84. Edith Hamilton to Jessie Hamilton, November 18, 1925, folder 603, reel 28; Margaret Hamilton to Katherine Hamilton, November 23 [1925?] folder 682, reel 31, given its discussion of Katherine's illness, this year seems likely, both HFP.

85. Edith Hamilton to Jessie Hamilton, January 10, 1932, folder 606 reel 28; Lily Duryee to Jessie and Agnes Hamilton, March 30, 1932, folder 309, reel 15, both HFP; Sicherman, *Alice Hamilton*, 317.

86. Edith Hamilton to Agnes Hamilton, November 25 [n.y. but written shortly after Jessie's death in 1960], folder 5, box 1, EHP.

87. Edith Hamilton to Jessie Hamilton, November 10, 1932, folder 606, reel 28, HFP.

88. Norah Hamilton to Jessie Hamilton, postmarked December 1, 1932, folder 702, reel 32, HFP.

89. Davis, "What the Romans Were," 303.

90. "Life among the Romans," 8.

91. Becker, "The Reader's Guide," 320.

92. Doris Fielding Reid to Rosamond Gilder, postmarked September 11, 1930, box 14, GM; Edith Hamilton to Storer B. Lunt, May 23, 1933, WWNP.

93. Reid, *Edith Hamilton: An Intimate Portrait*, 76.

94. Doris Fielding Reid to Rosamond Gilder [n.d. but describes Edith and Doris working on the unfinished Seawall house in 1923], box 14, GM; Doris Fielding Reid, unpublished autobiography, p. 1, folder 28, box 2, EHP.

95. Doris Fielding Reid to Rosamond Gilder, postmarked June 17, 1928, box 14, GM.

96. Reid, unpublished autobiography, p. 2, folder 28, box 2, EHP; Loomis-Sayles Mutual Fund Prospectus, p. 3, enclosed with Doris Fielding Reid to John Mason Brown, February 10, 1954, JMBP.

97. Schwarz, *Radical Feminists of Heterodoxy*, 51–52; Fraser, "Wall Street Women," 40–41, 180–85.

98. Reid, unpublished autobiography, p. 3, folder 28, box 2, EHP.

99. Reid, unpublished autobiography, p. 4, folder 28, box 2, EHP.

100. Reid, *Edith Hamilton: An Intimate Portrait*, 77.

101. Edith Hamilton to Agnes Hamilton [n.d. except Wednesday, but written at 24 Gramercy Park in the early 1930s], folder 610, reel 28, HFP.

102. Obituary for Dorian F. Reid, *The Avonian* (Spring/Summer 2008): 65.

103. Edith Hamilton to Jessie Hamilton, February 11, 1932, folder 606, reel 28, HFP; Wilson, *Francis Wilson's Life of Himself*, 76, 118, 122, 130; obituary for Francis Wilson, *New York Times*, October 8, 1935, p. 23; obituary for Jules Guerin, *New York Times*, June 15, 1946, p. 21; both of these identify the men's address as 24 Gramercy Park.

104. Edith Hamilton to Jessie Hamilton, February 4 [n.y. but written at 24 Gramercy Park], folder 605, reel 28, HFP.

Chapter 13

1. Edith Hamilton to Agnes Hamilton, January 4, 1933, folder 609, reel 28, HFP; on Hitler assuming the chancellorship, see Guido Enderis, "Group Formed by Papen: Nationalists to Dominate in Government Led by National Socialist," *New York Times*, January 31, 1933, p. 1.

2. Ankenbruck, *Fort Wayne in the Years of the Bank Panic*, 75; Susan Duryee Fahmy to Jessie and Agnes Hamilton, April 25, 1933, folder 311, reel 15, HFP.

3. Susan Duryee Fahmy to Jessie Hamilton, March 26, 1933, folder 311, reel 15, HFP.

4. Margaret E. Hodge to Agnes Hamilton, March 30, 1936, folder 446, reel 22, HFP; Sicherman, *Alice Hamilton*, 336.

5. Edith Hamilton to Agnes Hamilton [n.d. but internal evidence, including the closure of Rurode's, New York Dry Goods Store, dates this to the spring of 1933], folder 610, reel 28, HFP.

6. Ibid.

7. Edith Hamilton to Jessie Hamilton [n.d. but its discussion of the courtship of John Mason Brown and Catherine Meredith dates it to likely late 1932 since the couple married on February 11, 1933], folder 605, reel 28, HFP.

8. Edith Hamilton to Agnes Hamilton [n.d. but the mention of the closure of Rurode's New York Dry Goods Store dates it to 1933], folder 610, reel 28, HFP.

9. Ibid.

10. Edith Hamilton to Agnes Hamilton [n.d. but internal evidence dates this to the summer of 1930, which was spent at Seawall, during which time Edith Reid tore a ligament in her ankle], folder 610, reel 28, HFP. For Edith Reid's injury see Edith Hamilton to Jessie Hamilton, August 10, 1930, folder 606, reel 28, HFP.

11. Clark, *The Oxford Group*, 17–18, 25, 79; Sack, *Moral Re-Armament*, 60, 68–69.

12. Harris, *The Breeze of the Spirit*, 55; Sack, *Moral Re-Armament*, 84.

13. Clark, *The Oxford Group*, 30.

14. Shoemaker, *I Stand By the Door*, 24; Lean, *Frank Buchman*, 76; Sack, *Moral Re-Armament*, 42–43.

15. Edith Hamilton to Agnes Hamilton [n.d. but internal evidence dates this to 1930], folder 610, reel 28, HFP.

16. Clark, *The Oxford Group*, 27–31; Sack, *Moral Re-Armament*, 29, 36–37.

17. Clark, *The Oxford Group*, 67–74; Sack, *Moral Re-Armament*, 49–50.

18. Clark, *The Oxford Group*, 53, 75, 24; Lean, *Frank Buchman*, 106, 176–79; Helen Smith Shoemaker, *I Stand By the Door*, 79.

19. Edith Hamilton to Agnes Hamilton [n.d. but internal evidence dates this to the summer of 1930, which was spent at Seawall during which time Edith Reid tore a ligament in her ankle], folder 610, reel 28, HFP. For Edith Reid's injury see Edith Hamilton to Jessie Hamilton, August 10, 1930, folder 606, reel 28, HFP.

20. Edith Hamilton to Jessie Hamilton, December 13, 1933, folder 606, reel 28, HFP.

21. Ibid.; Edith Hamilton to Agnes Hamilton, October 16, 1934, folder 609, reel 28, HFP.

22. Williamson, *Inside Buchmanism*, 210; obituary for Rev. Dr. Samuel Shoemaker, *New York Times*, November 2, 1963, p. 2; Harris, *The Breeze of the Spirit*, 40–41; Sack, *Moral Re-Armament*, 53, 61, 78.

23. Edith Hamilton to Agnes Hamilton, January 4, 1933, folder 609, reel 28, HFP; on attending the services at Calvary, Edith Hamilton to Agnes Hamilton [n.d. but its inquiry concerning the health of Phoebe Taber Hamilton, who died in the summer of 1932, probably dates it to early that year], folder 610, reel 28, HFP; see also Russell, *For Sinners Only*, 172–83.

24. Samuel M. Shoemaker, *Calvary Church*, 236, 256.

25. Harris, *The Breeze of the Spirit*, 23, 41; Helen Smith Shoemaker, *I Stand By the Door*, 54; Samuel M. Shoemaker, *Calvary Church*, 243, 259–60, 276.

26. Edith Hamilton to Jessie Hamilton, February 11, 1932, folder 606, reel 28, HFP; Piper, *Robert E. Speer*, 86.

27. Margaret Shearman to Agnes Hamilton, May 1936, folder 446, reel 22, HFP.

28. Edith Hamilton to Jessie Hamilton, August 16, postmarked August 15, 1936, folder 3, box 1, EHP; Susan Duryee Fahmy to Jessie and Agnes Hamilton, December 2, 1936; Susan Duryee Fahmy to Jessie Hamilton, postmarked December 9, 1936, both folder 311, reel 15, HFP; for the death of Dr. Ahmed Fahmy in 1933, see Sharkey, "An Egyptian in China," 309–326, 309.

29. Susan Duryee Fahmy to Jessie and Agnes Hamilton, December 2, 1936, and Susan Duryee Fahmy to Jessie Hamilton, December 9, 1936, both folder 311, reel 15, HFP.

30. Russell, *For Sinners Only*, 21–22.

31. Edith Hamilton to Jessie Hamilton, November 1933, folder 606, reel 28, HFP.

32. Clark, *The Oxford Group*, 32.

33. Lean, *Frank Buchman*, 122.

34. Edith Hamilton to Agnes Hamilton, August 31, 1937, folder 609, reel 28, HFP.

35. Edith Hamilton to Agnes Hamilton, August 22 [n.y. although written at 24 Gramercy Park, where Edith lived between 1929 and 1936], folder 610, reel 28, HFP.

36. Edith Hamilton to Agnes Hamilton, January 19, 1934, folder 609, reel 28, HFP.

37. Van Dusen, "'Apostle to the Twentieth Century,'" 1, 7.

38. Sack, *Moral Re-Armament*, 72.

39. Edith Hamilton to Agnes Hamilton, January 4, 1933, folder 609, reel 28, HFP.

40. Edith Hamilton to Jessie Hamilton, December 13, 1933, folder 606, reel 28, HFP.

41. Edith Hamilton, *The Prophets of Israel*, 24.

42. Edith Hamilton to Jessie Hamilton, December 13, 1933, folder 606, reel 28, HFP.

43. Akin, *Technocracy and the American Dream*, 64, 81; Parrish, "What is Technocracy?" 8–10, 9–10.

44. Edith Hamilton to Jessie Hamilton, January 25, 1933, folder 606, reel 28, HFP.

45. Edith Hamilton, *The Prophets of Israel*, chapter 1, 32; chapter 3, 57.

46. Obituary for Alida Milliken, *New York Times*, February 14, 1975, p. 40; Alice Reid Abbott to author, August 18, 2009.

47. Journal of Felix M. Morley, August 14, 1958, p. 197, vol. 12, box 55, FMMP.

48. *Bryn Mawr School Alumnae Bulletin* (May 1932), not paginated, ABMS.

49. Doris Fielding Reid to Francesca Gilder Palmer and Rosamond Gilder, July 23, 1933, box 14, GM.

50. *Bryn Mawr School Alumnae Bulletin* (1934), not paginated, ABMS.

51. Doris Fielding Reid to John Mason Brown, July 10 [n.y. but likely 1933 since it mentions Edith Gittings Reid writing her book on President Woodrow Wilson, which was published in 1934], JMBP.

52. Edith Hamilton to Jessie Hamilton, January 25, 1933, folder 606, reel 28, HFP. In her autobiography, Doris identified Ralph T. Sayles as vice president of Loomis-Sayles from 1930; see Doris Fielding Reid, unpublished autobiography, p. 4, box 3, EHP.

53. Ibid. Edith Hamilton to Jessie Hamilton.

54. Clark, *The Oxford Group*, 25.

55. Russell, *For Sinners Only*, 69.

56. Edith Hamilton, *The Prophets of Israel*, foreword, 21.

57. Harris, *The Breeze of the Spirit*, 59.

58. Bradshaw et. al., *Kagawa in Lincoln's Land*, 21; Axling, *Kagawa*, 4, 17, 30, 62, 87–88, 91; Mowat, *Report on Moral Re-Armament*, 39.

59. Edith Hamilton to Agnes Hamilton, February 11 [1916], folder 609, reel 28, HFP; Edith Hamilton to Agnes Hamilton, January 4, 1933, folder 609, reel 28, HFP.

60. Kagawa, *Meditations on the Cross*, 183; Edith Hamilton, *Witness to the Truth*, 23–40.

61. Kagawa, *Meditations on the Cross*, 182.

62. Edith Hamilton, *The Prophets of Israel*, chapter 1, 25.

63. Robinson, *The Life and Work of Jane Ellen Harrison*, 164, 184; see also Ackerman, "The Cambridge Group: Origins and Composition," 1–19; Notebook labeled "Hebrews," pp. 65–69 [author's pagination], box 2, EHC.

64. Wilson, *Gilbert Murray OM*, 158.

65. Robert L. Fowler, "Gilbert Murray: Four (Five) Stages of Greek Religion," in William M. Calder III, ed., *The Cambridge Ritualists Reconsidered*, 79–95, 84–85.

66. Edith Hamilton, *The Prophets of Israel*, chapter 1, 29.

67. Edith Hamilton, *The Prophets of Israel*, chapter 1, 34.

68. Edith Hamilton, *The Prophets of Israel*, chapter 1, 38–39.

69. Edith Hamilton, *The Prophets of Israel*, chapter 2, 45.

70. Notebook labeled "Hebrews," p. 3 [author's pagination], box 2, EHC.

71. Edith Hamilton, *The Prophets of Israel*, foreword, 21.

72. Edith Hamilton to Jessie Hamilton [n.d. but internal evidence, including the mention of the courtship of John Mason Brown and the actress Catherine Meredith, likely dates this to late 1932], folder 605, reel 28, HFP; see also Stevens, *Speak for Yourself, John*, 96.

73. Edith Hamilton to Jessie Hamilton [n.d. but internal evidence, including the mention of the courtship of John Mason Brown and the actress Catherine Meredith, likely dates this to late 1932], folder 605, reel 28, HFP.

74. Edith Hamilton, *The Prophets of Israel*, chapter 5, 98.

75. Edith Hamilton, *The Prophets of Israel*, chapter 5, 97.

76. Ibid.

77. Edith Hamilton, *The Prophets of Israel*, chapter 2, 44.

78. Edith Hamilton to Margaret Hamilton [n.d. but its mention of the death of Ellen Reid Van Dyke, which had occurred on March 6, 1935, dates it to shortly after], folder 581, reel 27, HFP; see obituary for Mrs. Henry Van Dyke, *New York Times*, March 7, 1935, p. 23; on Francis's behavior, Edith Hamilton to Agnes Hamilton, January 19, 1934, folder 609, reel 28, HFP.

79. Obituary for Dorian F. Reid, January 29, 2008; Alice Reid Abbott to author, August 18, 2009.

80. Edith Hamilton to Margaret Hamilton [n.d. but its mention of the death of Ellen Reid Van Dyke, which had occurred on March 6, 1935, dates it to shortly after], folder 581, reel 27, HFP.

81. Ibid.

82. Edith Hamilton to Agnes Hamilton, April 7, 1937, but written at 24 Gramercy Park and describing Ernest's age as 15, so a date of 1935 seems likely, folder 609, reel 28, HFP.

83. Edith Hamilton to Margaret Hamilton [n.d. but its mention of the death of Ellen Reid Van Dyke, which had occurred on March 6, 1935, dates it to shortly after], folder 581, reel 27, HFP.

84. Edith Hamilton to [Jessie Hamilton?] This letter fragment is undated but refers to events around 1935, when the Theatre Guild considered producing *The Trojan Women*, folder 612, reel 28, HFP.

85. Edith Hamilton to Margaret Hamilton [n.d. but its mention of the death of Ellen Reid Van Dyke, which had occurred on March 6, 1935, dates it to shortly after], folder 581, reel 27, HFP.

86. Murray, *Euripides and His Age*, 128, 130.

87. Edith Hamilton, *The Greek Way*, 192.

88. Edith Hamilton, *Three Greek Plays*, 19.

89. Wilson, *Gilbert Murray OM*, 218–20, 254, 284, 291, 324, 387.

90. Edith Hamilton, "Born under a Rhyming Planet," 11–12; review reprinted in Edith Hamilton, *The Ever-Present Past*, 111–15.

91. Dame Sybil Thorndike was in the United States from August 31, 1934, until March 27, 1935; see "Sybil Thorndike Arrives for Play," *New York Times*, September 1, 1934, p. 16; "Sybil Thorndike Departs," *New York Times*, March 28, 1935, p. 25.

92. Edith Hamilton to Margaret Hamilton [n.d. but its mention of the death of Ellen Reid Van Dyke, which had occurred on March 6, 1935, dates it to shortly after], folder 581, reel 27, HFP; Croall, *Sybil Thorndike*, 72, 129, 317, 358.

93. Edith Hamilton to Warder Norton, May 27 [1935] WWNP.

94. Edith Hamilton to Storer B. Lunt, August 5, 1935, WWNP.

95. Margaret Hamilton to Agnes Hamilton, May 11 [1936], folder 686, reel 31, HFP.

96. Margaret Hamilton to Agnes Hamilton, May 27 [1936], folder 686, reel 31, HFP.

97. Edith Hamilton to Agnes Hamilton, May 19, 1936, folder 609, reel 28, HFP.

98. Margaret Hamilton to Agnes Hamilton, May 27 [1936], folder 686, reel 31, HFP.

99. Margaret Hamilton to Agnes Hamilton, May 11 [1936], folder 686, reel 31, HFP.

100. Ibid.

101. A. L. Sachar, "The Hebrew Conscience." Review of *The Prophets of Israel* in the *New York Herald Tribune*, May 31, 1936, VII, p. 14.

102. Edith Hamilton to "Dear People" [Jessie and Agnes], postmarked August 15, 1936, folder 3, box 1, EHP.

103. Notebook labeled "Hebrews," p. 50 [author's pagination], box 2, EHC.

104. Edith Hamilton to Agnes Hamilton, March 28, 1937, folder 609, reel 28, HFP.

105. Edith Hamilton to John Mason Brown, February 21 [n.y. but its mention of the performance of her translation of *The Trojan Women* dates it to 1938], folder 3, box 3, EHC; Edith Hamilton to Jessie Hamilton, postmarked June 19, 1938, folder 3, box 1, EHP.

106. Alice Reid Abbott to author, August 18, 2009.

107. Burleigh, *A Very Private Woman*, 80.

108. Edith Hamilton to Dorothy Bruce April 21, 1926, and May 11, 1926, both A/H217.1a, EHL; Storer B. Lunt to Edith Hamilton, April 9, 1958, box 2, EHP.

109. Edith Hamilton to Warder Norton, April 27, 1937, WWNP.

110. Gilder, "Greek Plays," 156–57; Brooks Atkinson, "The Play: Review of The Trojan Women," *New York Times*, January 25, 1938, p. 24; Hartigan, *Greek Tragedy on the American Stage*, 44–45.

111. Brooks Atkinson, "The Play: Experimental Theatre Begins Career with Modernized Version of Euripides's 'The Trojan Women,'" *New York Times*, April 9, 1941, p. 32.

112. Lean, *Frank Buchman*, 261–63; Sack, *Moral Re-Armament*, 107.

113. Margaret Hamilton to Agnes Hamilton, February 19 [1938?]. Although the year is uncertain, given Edith's comments on Buchman written from Bermuda, a date of 1938 seems likely, folder 687, reel 31, HFP; see also Edith Hamilton to Jessie Hamilton, February 1 [n.y.], folder 599, reel 28, HFP.

114. Helen Smith Shoemaker, *I Stand By the Door*, 90–92.

115. Edith Hamilton to Agnes Hamilton, August 31, 1937, folder 609, reel 28, HFP.

116. Edith Hamilton to Agnes Hamilton [n.y. though its reference to the death of Frank N. D. Buchman means a date of 1961 likely], folder 6, box 1, EHP; on Buchman's death in 1961, see Lean, *Frank Buchman*, 528.

117. Edith Hamilton to C. Raymond Everitt [n.d. but written from 3023 P Street, so likely early 1944], box 67, LBP; Edith Hamilton lived at 3023 P Street for the first nine months of 1944, see, for example, Edith Hamilton to John Mason Brown, January 26, 1944, and Edith Hamilton to John Mason Brown July 16, 1944, both folder 4, box 3, EHC.

Chapter 14

1. Edith Hamilton to Warder Norton, April 27, 1937, WWNP.

2. C. Raymond Everitt to Edith Hamilton, September 19, 1938, box 39, LBP.

3. Undated memo of C. Raymond Everitt, box 39, LBP.

4. C. Raymond Everitt to Edith Hamilton, October 19, 1938, box 39, LBP.

5. C. Raymond Everitt to Edith Hamilton, November 17, 1938, box 39, LBP.

6. C. Raymond Everitt to Edith Hamilton, December 1, 1938; C. Raymond Everitt to John Hadfield, December 1, 1938; and C. Raymond Everitt to Edith Hamilton, November 23, 1938, all box 39, LBP.

7. Cleary, *Myths for the Millions*, 60, 67, 71–72, 90, 196, 202, 292, 315, 319, 320.

8. C. Raymond Everitt to Edith Hamilton, November 17, 1938, box 39, LBP.

9. Quotation from Edith Hamilton included in C. Raymond Everitt to John Hadfield, December 1, 1938, box 39, LBP; C. Raymond Everitt to Edith Hamilton, November 23, 1938; C. Raymond Everitt to Edith Hamilton, October 19, 1938, both box 39, LBP; Edith Hamilton to Storer B. Lunt, June 19, 1955, WWNP.

10. Cleary, *Myths for the Millions*, 289, 293–94.

11. C. Raymond Everitt to Edith Hamilton, November 17, 1938, box 29, LBP.

12. Edith Hamilton, *The Roman Way*, chapter 1, 34; Edith Hamilton, *Mythology*, 227–29; C. Raymond Everitt to John Hadfield, December 1, 1938, box 39, LBP.

13. Quoted in C. Raymond Everitt to John Hadfield, December 1, 1938, box 39, LBP.

14. C. Raymond Everitt to Edith Hamilton, November 17, 1938, box 39, LBP.

15. Judith P. Hallett, "Edith Hamilton and Greco-Roman Mythology," in Staley, ed., *American Women and Classical Myths*, 105–30.

16. Kurtz, *Charles Mills Gayley*, 92–95, 129–31, 259, 262–63.

17. "Estimate," included in box 39, LBP.

18. Colloms, *Charles Kingsley*, 205.

19. *Bulletin of the Bryn Mawr School*, Twelfth Year [1896–97], not paginated, frames 350–51, reel 216, MCTP.

20. Kingsley, *The Heroes*, viii–ix; Colloms, *Charles Kingsley*, 206.

21. Colloms, *Charles Kingsley*, 205.

22. Kingsley, *The Heroes*, xv–xvii.

23. Edith Hamilton, *Mythology*, 13–15.

24. Brown notebook with *Mythology* notes, pp. 1–2 [author's pagination], box 2, EHC.

25. Brown notebook with *Mythology* notes, pp. 20–21 [author's pagination], box 2, EHC.

26. Brown notebook with *Mythology* notes, p. 20 [author's pagination], box 2, EHC.

27. Brown notebook with *Mythology* notes, p. 21 [author's pagination], box 2, EHC; Edith Hamilton, *Mythology*, 411–13, 425, 429.

28. Brown notebook with *Mythology* notes, pp. 20–21 [author's pagination], box 2, EHC; Edith Hamilton, *Mythology*, 135–50.

29. Brown notebook with *Mythology* notes, p. 24 [author's pagination], box 2, EHC.

30. "Edith Hamilton—quotations from letters," enclosed in C. Raymond Everitt to John Hadfield, December 1, 1938, box 39, LBP.

31. Brown notebook with *Mythology* notes, pp. 1–3 [author's pagination], box 2, EHC.

32. C. Raymond Everitt to Edith Hamilton, November 17, 1938, box 39, LBP.

33. Edith Hamilton, *Mythology*, 447; Lindow, *Norse Mythology*, 33–34.

34. Lindow, *Norse Mythology*, 38.

35. Brown notebook with *Mythology* notes, p. 33 [author's pagination], box 2, EHC.

36. Brown notebook with *Mythology* notes, p. 43, 60 [author's pagination], box 2, EHC.

37. Brown notebook with *Mythology* notes, p. 35 [author's pagination], box 2, EHC.

38. Colum, "Back to Theseus and Asgard," 14.

39. Edith Hamilton, *Mythology*, 9.

40. Caird, *The Evolution of Religion*, vol. 1, 230, 264–69; Livingstone, *The Greek Genius*, 111; Judith P. Hallett, "The Anglicizing Way: Edith Hamilton (1867–1963) and the Twentieth-Century Transformation of Classics in the U.S.A." in Hallett and Stray, eds., *British Classics Outside England*, 149–65, 157.

41. Edith Hamilton, *Mythology*, 155–56.

42. Edith Hamilton, *Mythology*, 7.

43. Homer W. Davis, "Greek War Relief and the Greek Spirit," in Davis, ed., *Greece Fights*, 27–36, 27; Lincoln MacVeagh, "The Greek Miracle," in Davis, ed., 7–13.

44. Membership of the Greek War Relief Association's National Citizen Committee as of January 1, 1941, enclosed in George Moore, president of Greek War Relief Association, to Mary Crovatt Hambidge, March 18, 1941, frames 815–17, reel 3179, JMCHP.

45. Edith Hamilton to John Mason Brown, October 4, 1943, JMBP.

46. Caird, *The Evolution of Religion*, vol. 2, 8.

47. Edith Hamilton, "Goethe and Faust," 451–61, 451–52; this essay was reprinted in Edith Hamilton, *The Ever-Present Past*, 89–106.

48. Edith Hamilton, "Goethe and Faust," 451–52.

49. Quoted in C. Raymond Everitt to John Hadfield, December 1, 1938, box 39, LBP.

50. Edith Hamilton, "Who Is This Dionysus?" 430–40; Edith Hamilton, "The Family of Oedipus," 889–96; Edith Hamilton to Warder Norton, July 1, 1941, WWNP.

51. Review of *The Greek Way*, *Times Literary Supplement*, September 18, 1930, p. 736.

52. Edith Hamilton, *Mythology*, 17.

53. Edith Hamilton, *Mythology*, 159, 184, 224; Edith Hamilton, *The Great Age of Greek Literature*, chapter 5, 86.

54. Edith Hamilton to Warder Norton, July 1, 1941, WWNP.

55. Warder Norton to Edith Hamilton, December 11, 1941, WWNP.

56. Ibid.

57. Edith Hamilton, *The Great Age of Greek Literature*, preface, 7.

58. Storer B. Lunt to Edith Hamilton, August 28, 1947, WWNP; Storer B. Lunt to Edith Hamilton, February 9, 1953, WWNP.

59. Edith Hamilton, *The Great Age of Greek Literature*, chapter 8, 159–62, 165.

60. Edith Hamilton, *The Great Age of Greek Literature*, chapter 9, 183.

61. Edith Hamilton, *The Great Age of Greek Literature*, chapter 9, 184.

62. Nancy Schoonmaker, "Foreword," in Nancy Schoonmaker and Doris Fielding Reid, eds., *We Testify*, ix–xiv, xii.

63. Hirsch, *The Friendship of the Barbarians*, 2.

64. Pomeroy et. al., *Ancient Greece*, 334.

65. Edith Hamilton, *The Great Age of Greek Literature*, chapter 10, 212.

66. Edith Hamilton to Eva Palmer Sikelianos, March 9, 1943, folder 98, box 39, AEPS; Edith Hamilton, *The Great Age of Greek Literature*, chapter 10, 214.

67. Hirsch, *The Friendship of the Barbarians*, 14–15.

68. Edith Hamilton, *The Great Age of Greek Literature*, chapter 10, 215.

69. Edith Hamilton, *The Great Age of Greek Literature*, chapter 10, 211.

70. Edith Hamilton, *The Great Age of Greek Literature*, chapter 10, 212.

71. Edith Hamilton, *The Great Age of Greek Literature*, chapter 10, 214.

72. Edith Hamilton, *Mythology*, 394.

73. Edith Hamilton, *The Great Age of Greek Literature*, chapter 10, 208.

74. Edith Hamilton, *The Great Age of Greek Literature*, chapter 10, 209.

75. Edith Hamilton, *The Great Age of Greek Literature*, chapter 10, 209–10.

76. Edith Hamilton, *The Great Age of Greek Literature*, chapter 10, 207.

77. Brown notebook with *Mythology* notes, p. 32 [author's pagination], box 2, EHC; this is the case with, for example, her rendering of the story of Biton and Cleobis, which appears in outline in her notebook and in more finished detail in *Mythology*, 429.

78. John Cournos, review of *Mythology*, *New York Times*, May 24, 1942, p. 4.

79. Review of *Mythology*, *New Yorker* 18 (May 9, 1942): 79.

80. Colum, "Back to Theseus and Asgard," 14.

81. Sternlicht, *Padraic Colum*, 131–33.

82. Brown notebook with *Mythology* notes, p. 54 [author's pagination], box 2, EHC.

83. Colum, "Back to Theseus and Asgard," 14.

84. Kingsley, *The Heroes*, xvii.

85. Colum, "Back to Theseus and Asgard," 14.

86. Brown notebook with *Mythology* notes, p. 21 [author's pagination], box 2, EHC; Edith Hamilton, *Mythology*, 434.

87. Edith Hamilton, *Mythology*, 394–97; Colum, "Back to Theseus and Asgard," 14.

88. Edith Hamilton, *Mythology*, 85–86, 91–92.

89. Hitler, *Mein Kampf*, chapter 11, 290.

90. Edith Hamilton, *Mythology*, 93.

91. Edith Hamilton, "The True Light," 47.

92. Stenehjem, *An American First*, 51.

93. Cole, *America First*, 10–11, 71; Olson, *Those Angry Days*, 220–26.

94. Cole, *America First*, 37.

95. Doris Fielding Reid to John Mason Brown, January 12, 1955, JMBP.

96. Cole, *America First*, 89.

97. Olson, *Those Angry Days*, 319–25.

98. Stenehjem, *An American First*, 60.

99. Ibid.

100. Stenehjem, *An American First*, 35–136; Cole, *Charles A. Lindbergh*, 160–63, 171; Olson, *Those Angry Days*, 386–90.

101. Cole, *Charles A. Lindbergh*, 177–180; Stenehjem, *An American First*, 136–37; Olson, *Those Angry Days*, 388.

102. Stenehjem, *An American First*, 47, 51, 99, 117.

103. Olson, *Those Angry Days*, 170, 174.

104. Wedemeyer, *Wedemeyer Reports!*, 484.

105. Stenehjem, *An American First*, 183.

106. Edith Hamilton to John Mason Brown, February 2, 1943, folder 3, box 3, EHC.

107. Doris Fielding Reid to John Mason Brown, March 23 [n.y. but its discussion of Edith's lectures at Alida Milliken's dates it to the spring of 1943], JMBP.

108. Edith Hamilton to John Mason Brown, March 13, 1943, folder 3, box 3, EHC.

109. Storer B. Lunt to Edith Hamilton, January 3, 1946, WWNP.

110. Alice Reid Abbott to author, August 18, 2009.

111. Obituary for Dorian Fielding Reid, *The Avonian*, spring–summer 2008, p. 65; "News of Alumnae in College," *Bryn Mawr School Bulletin*, 1940, not paginated, ABMS.

112. Edith Hamilton to Alice Hamilton, April 6, 1943, folder 666, reel 31, HFP; Edith Hamilton to John Mason Brown, February 2, 1943, folder 3, box 3, EHC; Mary Fielding Reid to John Mason and Catherine Brown, June 8, 1948; see also undated form letter from Mary Fielding Reid to John Mason and Catherine Brown, which identifies her as a special sales representative for Theatre World, both JMBP.

113. Edith Hamilton to Isabel Wilder, May 11, 1943, folder 960, box 37, TWP.

114. Ibid.

115. Edith Hamilton to John Mason Brown, May 21, 1943, folder 3; John Mason Brown to Doris Fielding Reid, May 6, 1947, folder 4; Edith Hamilton to John Mason Brown, May 29, 1943, folder 3, all box 3, EHC.

116. Reid, *Edith Hamilton: An Intimate Portrait*, 88.

117. Edith Hamilton to John Mason Brown, May 29, 1943, folder 3, box 3, EHC.

Chapter 15

1. Reid, *Edith Hamilton: An Intimate Portrait*, 88; for the 2101 Connecticut Avenue address, see, for example, Edith Hamilton to Catherine Meredith Brown, August 26, 1943, JMBP; Brinkley, *Washington Goes to War*, 107, 231–41.

2. Edith Hamilton to John Mason Brown, March 13, 1943, folder 3, box 3, EHC.

3. Brown, *To All Hands*, 83.

4. Brown, *To All Hands*, 92.

5. Parker, *Monte Cassino*, 149, 174.

6. Edith Hamilton to Eva Palmer Sikelianos, April 21, 1944, folder 63, box 40, AEPS.

7. Edith Hamilton to John Mason Brown, January 26, 1944, folder 3, box 3, EHC.

8. Edith Hamilton to John Mason Brown, April 17, 1944, folder 3, box 3, EHC.

9. Edith Hamilton to Eva Palmer Sikelianos, April 21, 1944, folder 63, box 40, AEPS.

10. Obituary for Dr. Harry Reid, *New York Times*, June 19, 1944, p. 19; Reid, *Edith Hamilton: An Intimate Portrait*, 89.

11. Edith Hamilton to John Mason and Catherine Meredith Brown, June 26, 1944, folder 3, box 3, EHC.

12. Brinkley, *Washington Goes to War*, 33.

13. Edith Hamilton to John Mason Brown, October 29, 1944, folder 3, box 3, EHC.

14. This description of the house is based on several sources as well as the author's own visit to the address. Journalists and writers who published descriptions of the house include Muriel Dobbin, "Woman, 90, Still Writing," *Baltimore Sun*, February 23, 1958, p. A5; Eileen Summers, "In the Atomic Age We Can Still Learn from the Ancient Greeks," *The Washington Post and Times-Herald*, March 22, 1959, F2–F3; Reck, *Ezra Pound*, 89; Fruhauf, *Making Faces*, 223; also Alice Reid Abbott to author, August 18, 2009; Edith Hamilton to Jessie and Agnes Hamilton, July 17, 1947, folder 611, reel 28, HFP.

15. Edith Hamilton's list of important dates, ABMS.

16. For Norah's address, see, for example, Roger L. Scaife to Norah Hamilton, September 11, 1943, box 67, LBP.

17. Glenn, *The Washingtons*, vol. 6, part 1, 180.

18. Edith Hamilton's list of important dates, ABMS.

19. Edith Hamilton to Jessie Hamilton, December 10, 1948, folder 606, reel 28, HFP; Doris Fielding Reid to John Mason Brown, September 28 [n.y. but its reference to Brown's correspondence with Frederick A. Earle on Edith's writing dates this to 1948], both JMBP; see also Frederick A. Earle to Edith Hamilton, September 21, 1948, and Frederick A. Earle to John Mason Brown, September 7, 1948, both folder 16, box 1, EHP.

20. Edith Hamilton's list of important dates, ABMS; see also "Miss Mary Reid Engaged to Wed," *Washington Post*, April 26, 1949, p. B4; "Mary Reid Fiancee of Boyd M'Knight," *New York Times*, April 26, 1949, p. 31; "Marriage Announcement," *Washington Post*, June 27, 1949, p. B3; Edith Hamilton to "Dear People" [Jessie and Agnes Hamilton], May 28, 1949, folder 611, reel 28, HFP.

21. Storer B. Lunt to Edith Hamilton, February 9, 1953, WWNP.

22. Edith Hamilton to John Mason Brown, October 29, 1944, folder 3, box 3, EHC.

23. Cousins, "Modern Man Is Obsolete," 5–9.

24. Axling, *Kagawa*, 133, 143, 147–48.

25. Edith Hamilton to Storer B. Lunt, August 13, 1945, WWNP.

26. Edith Hamilton, *Witness to the Truth*, chapter 6, 158.

27. Edith Hamilton to John Mason Brown, September 22, 1945; Edith Hamilton to John Mason Brown, October 22, 1945; Edith Hamilton to John Mason Brown, November 19, 1945; Edith Hamilton to Catherine Meredith Brown, December 5, 1945, all folder 3, box 3; John Mason Brown to Edith Hamilton, November 14, 1945; John Mason Brown to Edith Hamilton, December 10, 1945, folder 4, box 3, all EHC.

28. John Mason Brown to Edith Hamilton, November 14, 1945, folder 4; Edith Hamilton to John Mason Brown, November 19, 1945, folder 3; Edith Hamilton to John Mason Brown, July 30, 1947, folder 3, all box 3, EHC.

29. Doris Fielding Reid to John Mason Brown, November 6 [n.y. but its reference to the death of Warder Norton dates it to 1945], JMBP.

30. Doris Fielding Reid to John Mason Brown, November 6 [n.y. but its discussion of Everitt's response to the two chapters makes a year of 1945 likely], JMBP.

31. Reid, *Edith Hamilton: An Intimate Portrait*, 90; Edith Hamilton to Clara Landsberg [n.d. except "Saturday" but discusses Elling and Doris's criticisms of drafts of *Witness to the Truth*], folder 2, box 3, EHC.

32. Edith Hamilton, *Witness to the Truth*, chapter 9, 216, dedication not paginated; Reid, *Edith Hamilton: An Intimate Portrait*, 90.

33. Obituary for Warder W. Norton, *New York Times*, Nov. 9, 1945, p. 19.

34. Edith Hamilton to Storer B. Lunt, November 14, 1945, WWNP.

35. Obituary for Mary Norton Crena de Iongh, *New York Times*, April 20, 1985, p. 28.

36. Edith Hamilton to Storer B. Lunt, December 3, 1945, private collection of the author.

37. Obituary for Storer Boardman Lunt, *New York Times*, September 12, 1977, p. 36; Howard P. Wilson, "An Account of the Early Days of W.W. Norton & Company," 13, unpublished, series II, box 336, WWNP.

38. Edith Hamilton to Storer B. Lunt, May 23, 1933, WWNP.

39. Katharine Barnard to Paul Quinn, May 10, 1954, series II, box 118, WWNP.

40. Storer B. Lunt to Edith Hamilton, January 3, 1946; Edith Hamilton to Storer B. Lunt, January 10, 1946; Edith Hamilton to Storer B. Lunt, February 6, 1946, all WWNP.

41. Edith Hamilton to John Mason Brown, May 1, 1946, folder 3, box 3, EHC; Edith Hamilton, *Witness to the Truth*, chapter 1, 19; chapter 9, 218; chapter 10, 222; Edith Hamilton, *Spokesmen for God*, chapter 13, 259.

42. Obituary for C. Raymond Everitt, *New York Times*, May 24, 1947, p. 15; Storer B. Lunt to Edith Hamilton, August 4, 1947, WWNP.

43. Edith Hamilton to Catherine Meredith Brown, November 18, 1946, folder 3, box 3, EHC; Edith Hamilton to Jessie Hamilton, March 30, 1948, folder 606, reel 28, HFP; Edith Hamilton's list of important dates, ABMS.

44. Edith Hamilton to Jessie and Agnes Hamilton, July 17, 1947 and August 26, 1947, both folder 611, reel 28, HFP; Edith Hamilton to Eva Palmer Sikelianos, July 12, 1947, folder 67, box 42, AEPS.

45. Edith Hamilton to Jessie and Agnes Hamilton, August 26, 1947, folder 611, reel 28, HFP.

46. Storer B. Lunt to Edith Hamilton, August 11, 1947, WWNP.

47. Edith Hamilton, *Witness to the Truth*, chapter 1, 14.

48. Edith Hamilton, *Witness to the Truth*, chapter 7, 164.

49. Edith Hamilton, *Witness to the Truth*, chapter 1, 14.

50. Edith Hamilton, *The Great Age of Greek Literature*, chapter 15, 287.

51. Edith Hamilton, *Witness to the Truth*, chapter 1, 18; see also Jaeger, *Paideia*, 13.

52. Jenkyns, *The Victorians and Ancient Greece*, 229–30, 367; Turner, *The Greek Heritage in Victorian Britain*, 265; Kagawa, *Meditations on the Cross*, 183.

53. Edith Hamilton, *Witness to the Truth*, chapter 2, 25–26.

54. Edith Hamilton, *Mythology*, 14–15; *Witness to the Truth*, chapter 2, 27–28.

55. Edith Hamilton, *Witness to the Truth*, chapter 2, 27.

56. Edith Hamilton to Storer B. Lunt, October 12, 1947, WWNP.

57. Edith Hamilton, *Witness to the Truth*, chapter 3, 55.

58. Edith Hamilton, *Witness to the Truth*, chapter 3, 60–61.

59. Grant, *Saint Paul*, 230; Edith Hamilton, *Witness to the Truth*, chapter 4, 69–70.

60. Hall, *Papias and His Contemporaries*, 3, 5, 103.

61. Jessie Hamilton to Agnes Hamilton, April 23, 1923, folder 215, reel 10, HFP.

62. Edith Hamilton, *Witness to the Truth*, chapter 8, 200–2.

63. Edith Hamilton, *Witness to the Truth*, chapter 6, 133–34.

64. Edith Hamilton, *Witness to the Truth*, chapter 6, 143, 147–48.

65. Edith Hamilton, *Witness to the Truth*, chapter 5, 84; Grant, *Alice Hamilton*, 30–31.

66. Edith Hamilton, *Witness to the Truth*, chapter 7, 173.

67. Ibid.

68. Edith Hamilton, *Witness to the Truth*, chapter 7, 164–65.

69. Edith Hamilton, *Witness to the Truth*, chapter 7, 183.

70. Edith Hamilton, *Witness to the Truth*, chapter 8, 199–202.

71. Edith Hamilton, *Witness to the Truth*, chapter 8, 205; see also Caird, *The Evolution of Religion*, vol. 1, 282–88.

72. Edith Hamilton to Storer B. Lunt, August 22, 1947; Edith Hamilton to Storer B. Lunt, August 31, 1947, both WWNP.

73. Storer B. Lunt to Edith Hamilton, September 22, 1947; Storer B. Lunt to Edith Hamilton, October 3, 1947, both WWNP.

74. Edith Hamilton to Storer B. Lunt, March 16, 1948, WWNP.

75. John Mason Brown to Edith Hamilton, November 9, 1944, folder 4, box 3, EHC.

76. Brown, "The Fruit of Enlightenment," 28–30; Edith Hamilton to Alan Valentine, January 26, 1960, box 3.1.1 collection of Edith Hamilton letters and articles from the Valentines, ABMS.

77. Edith Hamilton to Storer B. Lunt, March 16, 1948, WWNP.

78. George R. Stephenson, "The Work of Jesus," review of *Witness to the Truth, New York Times,* May 2, 1948, p. 23.

79. Storer B. Lunt to Edith Hamilton, May 28, 1948, WWNP; Doris Fielding Reid to John Mason Brown, June 9 [n.y. but its discussion of publicity for *Witness to the Truth* dates it to 1948], folder 3, box 3, EHC.

80. Felix Morley, Review of *Witness to the Truth, Human Events* 5, May 26, 1948, not paginated, copy in folder 8, box 1, EHP; Storer B. Lunt to Edith Hamilton, December 30, 1947, WWNP.

81. Doris Fielding Reid to John Mason Brown, June 9 [n.y. but its discussion of publicity for *Witness to the Truth* dates it to 1948], folder 3, box 3, EHC; advertisement for *Witness to the Truth, New York Times Book Review,* August 1, 1948, p. 14.

82. Edith Hamilton to Storer B. Lunt, July 13, 1948, WWNP.

83. "Teacher Turned Writer, at 80, Still Proving Aeschylus Right," *Washington Post,* March 13, 1948, p. 2B.

84. Edith Hamilton to Storer B. Lunt, April 4, 1949, WWNP.

85. Edith Hamilton to Storer B. Lunt, April 4, 1949, WWNP.

86. Edith Hamilton, *Spokesmen for God,* chapter 12, 239.

87. Edith Hamilton, *Spokesmen for God,* chapter 12, 246.

88. Edith Hamilton, *Spokesmen for God,* chapter 13, 258–59.

89. Ralph E. Flanders to Edith Hamilton, March 7, 1957, folder 9, box 1, EHP; Brooks Atkinson to Storer B. Lunt, February 22, 1955, folder 22, box 2, EHP.

Chapter 16

1. Edith Hamilton to John Mason and Catherine Meredith Brown, October 22, 1945, folder 3, box 3, EHC.

2. Herken, *The Georgetown Set,* 19, 86, 165.

3. Cordery, *Alice,* 328.

4. Reid, *Edith Hamilton: An Intimate Portrait,* 129; Adams, *The Life of George Cabot Lodge,* 98, 153, 173–180, 206; Lodge, *The Storm Has Many Eyes,* 22–23, 25; Joseph R. Sizoo to Edith Hamilton, October 25, 1958, folder 9, box 1, EHP; Storer B. Lunt to Howard P. Wilson, August 10 [n.y. but written on Hotel Grand-Bretagne stationery from Athens and describing events in Athens in 1957], private collection of the author.

5. Huntington Cairns to James K. Feibleman, March 6, 1946, folder 9, box 15, JKFP; Reid, *Edith Hamilton: An Intimate Portrait,* 94.

6. Huntington Cairns to James K. Feibleman, May 2, 1944; Huntington Cairns to James K. Feibleman, May 15, 1944; Huntington Cairns to James K. Feibleman, June 7, 1944, all folder 1, box 15, JKFP.

7. Cairns, *The Limits of Art,* 143.

8. Edith Hamilton to Huntington Cairns, March 12, 1946, box 12, HCP.

9. John D. Barrett to Edith Hamilton, November 27, 1957, folder 9, box 1, EHP; Huntington Cairns to James K. Feibleman, November 18, 1957, folder 12, box 21, JKFP.

10. McGuire, *Bollingen*, 150–58; Huntington Cairns to James K. Feibleman, October 9, 1956, folder 2; Huntington Cairns to James K. Feibleman, January 24, 1957, folder 4, both box 21, JKFP.

11. Edith Hamilton to Huntington Cairns, April 28, 1950; Edith Hamilton to Huntington Cairns, June 28, 1951, both box 12, HCP; McGuire, 170–71.

12. For the date of their marriage, see the brief biography of Huntington Cairns in the HCP, Manuscript Division, the Library of Congress.

13. Edith Hamilton to Florence Cairns, November 18, 1948, box 12, HCP.

14. Huntington Cairns to James K. Feibleman, November 1, 1939, folder 2, box 14; Huntington Cairns to James K. Feibleman, January 27, 1947, folder 13, box 15, both JKFP; Glendon, *A World Made New*, 125–27.

15. Huntington Cairns to James K. Feibleman, February 13, 1939, folder 1, box 14, JKFP.

16. Huntington Cairns to James K. Feibleman, September 23, 1957, folder 10, box 21, JKFP; Myron Simon, "Foreword," in Emerson, *Representative Men*, vii–xiv, viii; Emerson, *Representative Men*, 25.

17. Kopff, "Paul Shorey," 447–53, 447.

18. Huntington Cairns to Edith Hamilton, April 7, 1947, box 12, HCP.

19. Huntington Cairns to James K. Feibleman, February 20, 1943, folder 11, box 14, JKFP; Edith Hamilton to Huntington Cairns, January 13, 1953, box 12, HCP.

20. Huntington Cairns to James K. Feibleman, April 25, 1939, folder 2, box 14, JKFP.

21. Bode, *Mencken*, 171, 180.

22. Reid, *Edith Hamilton: An Intimate Portrait*, 94; Huntington Cairns to James K. Feibleman, June 11, 1957, folder 7, box 21, JKFP.

23. Huntington Cairns to Robert Fitzgerald, April 19, 1948, folder 219, box 6, RFP; Huntington Cairns to Edith Hamilton, April 7, 1947, box 12, HCP.

24. Huntington Cairns to James K. Feibleman, October 4, 1941, folder 6, box 14, JKFP; Huntington Cairns to Edith Hamilton, August 1, 1946, box 12, HCP.

25. Edith Hamilton to Huntington Cairns, July 31, 1946, box 12, HCP; Edith Hamilton to John Mason Brown, August 3, 1949, folder 4, box 3, EHC.

26. Edith Hamilton to Florence Cairns, June 11, 1948, box 12, HCP.

27. Huntington Cairns to James K. Feibleman, May 29, 1946, folder 9, Huntington Cairns to James K. Feibleman, May 31, 1946, folder 9; Huntington Cairns to James K. Feibleman, October 11, 1946, folder 11, all box 15, JKFP; program for Plato's Annual Birthday Dinner, folder 1, box 163, HCP; Shorey, *What Plato Said*, 1.

28. Journal of Felix M. Morley, May 14, 1948, vol. 10, p. 161, FMMP; Felix Morley, Review of *Witness to the Truth*, *Human Events* 5 (May 26, 1948), not paginated, copy in folder 8, box 1, EHP.

29. Morley, *For the Record*, 7, 11, 279; Lucy Martin Donnelly to Bertrand Russell, April 15, 1914, box 5.13, BRP; Edith Hamilton to Jessie Hamilton [n.d. except "Wednesday morning" but written in Baltimore in the early 1900s], folder 604, reel 28, HFP.

30. Obituary for Felix Morley, *Washington Post*, March 15, 1982, p. B4.

31. Felsenthal, *Power, Privilege, and the Post*, 102.

32. Morley, *The Power in the People*, 175–76, 276.

33. Morley, *The Power in the People*, 276.

34. Edith Hamilton, "When Liberty Departs," 19–20.

35. Morley, *The Power in the People*, 23–25, 41–42, 93–94, 96–98, 102–3, 107, 145, 149–50, 192; Edith Hamilton, *The Great Age of Greek Literature*, chapter 10, 214–15; Edith Hamilton to Catherine Meredith Brown, October 2, 1943, JMBP.

36. Journal of Felix M. Morley, December 1, 1958, vol. 13, p. 6, box 55, FMMP.

37. Journal of Felix M. Morley, August 14, 1958, vol. 12, p. 197, box 55, FMMP.

38. Journal of Felix M. Morley, June 3, 1963, vol. 15, p. 12, box 55, FMMP.

39. Felix Morley, "A Memoir of Edith Hamilton," review of Doris Fielding Reid, *Edith Hamilton: An Intimate Portrait*, April 30, 1967, copy in box 84, HCP.

40. Wedemeyer, *Wedemeyer Reports!*, 267, 270; Steuck, *The Wedemeyer Mission*, 11, 13.

41. Wedemeyer, *Wedemeyer Reports!*, 95–96.

42. Steuck, *The Wedemeyer Mission*, 12, 14, 40–51, 74, 78, 95, 114.

43. Steuck, *The Wedemeyer Mission*, 17, 87–88, 93, 104.

44. Wedemeyer, *Wedemeyer Reports!*, 25.

45. Doris Fielding Reid to Dade Embick Wedemeyer, November 27, 1972, folder 24, box 57, ACWP.

46. Cordery, *Alice*, 431; on Alice Roosevelt Longworth visiting Edith and Doris at 2448 Massachusetts Avenue NW, see Elling Aannestad, "Memoir of Maine Seasons," unpublished autobiography, p. 40, folder 6, box 2, EAP.

47. Cordery, *Alice*, 401, 404–12, 425, 437, 442.

48. Elling Aannestad, "Memoir of Maine Seasons," unpublished autobiography, p. 40, folder 6, box 2, EAP.

49. Edith Hamilton to Florence Butler Cairns, January 29, 1951, and [February 8?] 1951, box 12, HCP.

50. Reid, *Edith Hamilton: An Intimate Portrait*, 93; Morley, *For the Record*, 151; Cordery, *Alice*, 431, 435–36.

51. Dubofsky and Van Tine, *John L. Lewis*, 18, 39, 54, 65–66, 213, 245, 293–301, 447.

52. Dubofsky and Van Tine, 197, 289, 317, 320–21, 330–40, 343–46, 389, 446, 476.

53. John Clendenin to Edith Hamilton, November 10, 1949; John Clendenin, "My Edith Hamilton," unpublished memoir, p. 2, both folder 8, box 1, EHP.

54. Edith Hamilton to Marcella Miller du Pont, April 25, 1950, and Marcella Miller du Pont to Edith Hamilton and Doris Fielding Reid, April 1954, both folder 15, box 11, MMDP.

55. Schoonmaker and Reid, *We Testify*, 295; Cordery, *Alice*, 404–12; Wedemeyer, *Wedemeyer Reports!*, 25.

56. Doenecke, *Storm on the Horizon*, 333; Klotz, "Freda Utley," unpublished dissertation, 191, 206.

57. Felix Morley to Robert Taft, March 18, 1948, box 2, FMMP.

58. Marie McNair, "Fireside Rallies Will Listen as Election Returns Roll In," *Washington Post*, October 31, 1948, p. S1; "Statler 'Hq' of GOP Tops Lively Spots," *Washington Post*, November 3, 1948, p. 8.

59. Reid, *Edith Hamilton: An Intimate Portrait*, 91; Edith Hamilton to Florence Butler Cairns, December 27 [1949?], box 12, HCP.

60. Bachrack, *The Committee of One Million*, 3–4.

61. Cordery, *Alice*, 115–37.

62. Bachrack, *The Committee of One Million*, 16–17.

63. Hill, *Lord Acton*, 415–16; Gooch, "Lord Acton: Apostle of Liberty," 629–42.

64. Huntington Cairns to Felix Morley, January 6, 1947, folder 7, box 105, HCP; Felix Morley, *For the Record*, 130; Hill, *Lord Acton*, 285–86.

65. Hill, *Lord Acton*, 64–65, 87.

66. Morley, *The Power in the People*, 3, 132, 268.

67. Edith Hamilton to Huntington Cairns [1950?], box 12, HCP.

68. Edith Hamilton, "Introduction," in Plutarch, *Selected Lives and Essays*, vii–xxiv, xxiii; this essay became the ninth chapter of *The Echo of Greece*.

69. Hill, *Lord Acton*, 300, 478; Edith Hamilton, *The Echo of Greece*, chapter 4, 78; chapter 10, 217; see also Edith Hamilton, "The Way of the Church," in Edith Hamilton, *The Ever-Present Past*, 174–82, 177.

70. Huntington Cairns to Ezra Pound [December 28?] 1948, PM.

71. Torrey, *The Roots of Treason*, 167, 176–77, 237.

72. Hillyer, "Treason's Strange Fruit," 9–11, 28; Cousins and Smith, "Ezra Pound and the Bollingen Award," 20–21.

73. Storer B. Lunt to Edith Hamilton, August 8, 1945; Storer B. Lunt to Edith Hamilton, August 28, 1945; Edith Hamilton to Storer B. Lunt, April 10, 1946; Storer B. Lunt to Edith Hamilton, April 12, 1946, all WWNP.

74. Vincent Sheean to Edith Hamilton, April 30 [n.y. but its congratulations on her National Achievement Award and its discussion of the performance of the *Agamemnon* date it to 1951], folder 4, box 2, EHP; Henry B. Williams to Edith Hamilton, February 5, 1951, folder 16, box 1, both EHP; Edith Hamilton to Henry B. Williams, February 19, 1951, folder 45, box 5, HBWP.

75. Tytell, *Ezra Pound*, 302; Reck, *Ezra Pound*, 154; Rudd Fleming to Ezra Pound, June 6, 1949, PM.

76. Tytell, *Ezra Pound*, 95, 136; Dougill, *Kyoto*, 97–104; Edith Hamilton to Dorothy Pound, January 5, 1950, PM; Foley, *Reimagining Greek Tragedy*, 97, 217–18.

77. Reck, *Ezra Pound*, 154.

78. Edith Hamilton to Ezra Pound, June 17, 1949, PM.

79. Edith Hamilton to Ezra Pound, April 19, 1950, PM.

80. Edith Hamilton to Ezra Pound, February 6, 1955; Edith Hamilton to Ezra Pound, March 24, 1955; Edith Hamilton to Ezra Pound, March 20, 1958, all folder 903, box 20, EPP.

81. Ezra Pound to Edith Hamilton, December 13 [1954]; Ezra Pound to Edith Hamilton, March 25, 1955, both folder 22, box 2, EHP.

82. Edith Hamilton to Ezra Pound, December 9, 1954, folder 903, box 20, EPP.

83. Edith Hamilton to Ezra Pound, December 14 [1956?], the suggested year is correct since she stated in the letter that she would turn ninety the following summer, folder 903, box 20, EPP.

84. Reck, *Ezra Pound*, 141; Tytell, *Ezra Pound*, 316–17, 332, 337; Hartigan, *Greek Tragedy on the American Stage*, 131, 138; Foley, *Reimaging Greek Tragedy on the American Stage*, 133; Brooks Atkinson, "Theatre: 2 One-Acters: 'Marrying Maiden' and 'Women of Trachis,'" *New York Times*, June 23, 1960, p. 18.

85. Reid, *Edith Hamilton: An Intimate Portrait*, 93–94.

86. Ezra Pound to Edith Hamilton, June 23, 1959, folder 22, box 2, EHP.

87. Tytell, *Ezra Pound*, 10, 23, 50, 57, 325–27.

88. Edith Hamilton to Storer B. Lunt, June 10, 1951, WWNP.

89. Edith Hamilton to "Dear People" [Jessie and Agnes Hamilton], dated March 22, 1920, but the year is clearly incorrect as it was written from 2448 Massachusetts Avenue; its reference to her Wellesley lecture dates it to 1950, folder 611, reel 28, HFP; *Wellesley College News*, March 30, 1950; I am grateful to Laura Reiner, Wellesley College archivist, for this citation.

90. Edith Hamilton, "Introduction," xiii.

91. Edith Hamilton, "Introduction," xix–xx.

92. Edith Hamilton, "The German Question," letter to the editor of the *New York Times*, dated November 21, 1949, published November 28, 1949, p. 26.

93. Klotz, "Freda Utley," unpublished dissertation, 4–5, 92, 96, 100–1, 106, 159–62, 171–72, 188–89, 208, 225, 241.

94. Utley, *The High Cost of Vengeance*, 182; Alan Russell, "Dresden and the Dresden Trust," in Clayton and Russell, eds., *Dresden*, 1–8.

95. Utley, *The High Cost of Vengeance*, 19, 25–26, 28–29, 31, 48, 50, 129, 147.

96. Delbert Clark, "Western Rule in Germany," review of *The High Cost of Vengeance*, *New York Times*, July 10, 1949, p. 13; W. L. White, "Allied Failure in Germany," review of *The High Cost of Vengeance*, *Saturday Review of Literature* 32 (August 13, 1949): 11; for the response of readers see Letters to the Editor, *Saturday Review of Literature* 32 (August 27, 1949): 21–23; "What to do with Germany," *New York Times*, November 20, 1949, p. E8; Edith Hamilton, "The German Question," letter to the editor of the *New York Times*, dated November 21, 1949, published November 28, 1949, p. 26.

97. Edith Hamilton, "Introduction," xxii.

98. I am grateful to Laura Reiner, Wellesley College archivist, for the information on the Horton Lectureship.

Chapter 17

1. "Edith Hamilton, Nearing 90, Feted by Friends," *The Evening Star*, April 17, 1957, p. B22.

2. Topolski, "In Washington," 57–59.

3. Doenecke, *Not to the Swift*, 75.

4. Edith Hamilton, fragments of mss., folder 2, box 3, EHC.

5. Storer B. Lunt to Edith Hamilton, January 2, 1951, WWNP.

6. Storer B. Lunt to Edith Hamilton, November 20, 1951; Storer B. Lunt to Edith Hamilton, February 24, 1955, WWNP.

7. Patterson, *Mr. Republican*, 205, 228, 288, 332, 375–76, 382, 394, 413, 415, 426, 435–37, 476, 499, 506; Doenecke, *Not to the Swift*, 25.

8. Darrah to Doris Fielding Reid, January 3, 1958, folder 9, box 1, EHP; this letter is merely signed "Darrah," but Darrah Dunham Wunder was a longtime friend of Robert and Martha Taft, and the letter is written on stationery from the Tafts' home Sky Farm, near Cincinnati.

9. Patterson, *Mr. Republican*, 232–33; Robert A. Taft to Felix Morley, August 12, 1947; Felix Morley to Robert A. Taft, March 18, 1948; Felix Morley to Robert A. Taft, December 19, 1951;

Felix Morley to Robert A. Taft, January 25, 1952; Felix Morley to Robert A. Taft, October 9, 1952, all box 2, FMMP.

10. Ralph E. and Helen Flanders to Doris Fielding Reid, June 23, 1963, ABMS; for Flanders's address as 2701 O Street, see Ralph E. Flanders to Edith Hamilton, October 1, 1958, box 105, REFP; Edith Hamilton to Helen Taft, October 15, 1919, frames 186–88, reel 162, MCTP; Gen. Albert C. Wedemeyer to Edith Hamilton, August 8, 1953, folder 5, box 40, ACWP.

11. Edith Hamilton to Agnes Hamilton, September 8, 1951, folder 609, reel 28, HFP.

12. Storer B. Lunt to Edith Hamilton, March 18, 1952, WWNP.

13. Caird, *The Evolution of Religion*, vol. 1, 234.

14. Edith Hamilton, "Private Idiom," 156, 206–7, 218; this essay was reprinted in its entirety in Edith Hamilton, *The Ever-Present Past*, 142–150; Elizabeth Sprigge, "Journal in Search of Gertrude Stein," December 15 [1954], 120–21, folder 307, box 18, GSABTP.

15. Edith Hamilton, "Faulkner: Sorcerer or Slave?" 8–10, 39–41, 8–9; Edith Hamilton, "Words, Words, Words," 15–16, 52–53, 15.

16. Edith Hamilton, *The Greek Way* chapter 12, 236–37.

17. Edith Hamilton, *The Greek Way*, chapter 12, 236.

18. Edith Hamilton, "Private Idiom," 206.

19. Edith Hamilton, "Faulkner: Sorcerer or Slave?" 8; also reprinted in Edith Hamilton, *The Ever-Present Past*, 159–73.

20. FitzGibbon, *The Life of Dylan Thomas*, 334–37, 345.

21. Edith Hamilton, "Words, Words, Words," 16.

22. Hamilton, *The Echo of Greece*, chapter 1, 18.

23. Hamilton, *The Echo of Greece*, chapter 1, 19.

24. Edith Hamilton, fragments of mss., folder 2, box 3, EHC.

25. Edith Hamilton, *The Echo of Greece*, chapter 2, 40–42.

26. Stanford and McDowell, *Mahaffy*, 42, 177, 187, 240.

27. Turner, *The Greek Heritage in Victorian Britain*, 10; Notebook labeled "History after Alexander" p. 7 [author's pagination], box 2, EHC.

28. Edith Hamilton, *The Echo of Greece*, chapter 1, 23; chapter 4, 68–70.

29. Edith Hamilton, *The Echo of Greece*, chapter 1, 22–23.

30. Hamilton, *The Echo of Greece*, chapter 1, 25.

31. Gutzman, *James Madison and the Making of America*, 1–2.

32. Obituary for Mrs. Edith Gittings Reid, *Baltimore Sun*, April 6, 1954, p. 23.

33. Edith Hamilton to John Mason Brown, May 19, 1954, folder 3, box 3, EHC.

34. Doris Fielding Reid to Marcella Miller du Pont, April 17, 1954, folder 15, box 11, MMDP; "Doctor, Wife Cleared in Death of Drinking-Bout Companion," *The Washington Post and Times-Herald*, April 23, 1954, p. 3.

35. Edith Hamilton to John Mason Brown, May 19, 1954, folder 3, box 3, EHC.

36. Edith Hamilton to Storer B. Lunt, August 24, 1954, WWNP.

37. Edith Hamilton to Storer B. Lunt, June 19, 1955, WWNP.

38. Edith Hamilton, "The World of Plato"; reprinted in Edith Hamilton, *The Ever-Present Past*, 107–11.

39. Edith Hamilton to Eva Palmer Sikelianos, April 21, 1944, folder 63, box 40, AEPS.

40. Notebook labeled "Hist. after Alexander", p. 1 [author's pagination], box 2, EHC.

41. Flanders, *Senator from Vermont*, 209.

42. Ralph E. and Helen Flanders to Doris Fielding Reid, June 23, 1963, ABMS; on the friendship with Flanders, see Reid, *Edith Hamilton: An Intimate Portrait*, 99.

43. Flanders, *Senator from Vermont*, 165.

44. Flanders, *Letter to a Generation*, 9.

45. Flanders, *Letter to a Generation*, 23.

46. Her full comment was: "Unswerving principle, wisdom, breadth of view are written large on every page, and the trained and cultivated mind which knows the past and can grasp the essentials of the present. I wish it could be required reading in the colleges."

47. Flanders, *Senator from Vermont*, 220–21.

48. Griffith, *The Politics of Fear*, 15–17.

49. Johnson, *Raymond E. Baldwin*, 186–94, 198–99, 206, 243, 254; Raymond Baldwin to Edith Hamilton, January 25, 1960, folder 10, box 1, EHP; Reid, *Edith Hamilton: An Intimate Portrait*, Acknowledgments.

50. Johnson, *Raymond E. Baldwin*, 251; Griffith, *The Politics of Fear*, 22–26.

51. Quoted in Flanders, *Senator from Vermont*, 257; Griffith, *The Politics of Fear*, 273.

52. Flanders, *Senator from Vermont*, 255.

53. Flanders, *Senator from Vermont*, 260; Griffith, *The Politics of Fear*, 270–74, 285.

54. Flanders, *Senator from Vermont*, 267; Griffith, *The Politics of Fear*, 314–15.

55. Jeffords, *An Independent Man*, 1, 185, 193, 197, 202, 244, 254, 273, 277, 303–4; Jeffords, *My Declaration of Independence*, 19–21, 23, 25, 32, 83, 95, 103, 113–17; a transcript of Jefford's speech in which he mentioned Flanders was printed in the *New York Times*, see Senator James M. Jeffords, "A Struggle for Our Leaders to Deal with Me and for Me to Deal with Them," *New York Times*, May 25, 2001, p. A18.

56. Edith Hamilton, *The Echo of Greece*, chapter 5, 107–8.

57. Edith Hamilton, *The Echo of Greece*, chapter 5, 107.

58. Edith Hamilton, *The Echo of Greece*, chapter 5, 110.

59. Edith Hamilton, *The Echo of Greece*, chapter 5, 113; Pomeroy, Burstein, Donlan, and Roberts, *Ancient Greece*, 387–88.

60. Edith Hamilton, *The Echo of Greece*, chapter 5, 114; Jenkyns, *The Victorians and Ancient Greece*, 74.

61. Edith Hamilton, fragments of mss., folder 2, box 3, EHC.

62. "Introduction to Swedish Edition," folder 1, box 3, EHC; Edith Hamilton, "The Lessons of the Past," 25, 114–17, 117; reprinted as "The Ever-Present Past" in Edith Hamilton, *The Ever-Present Past*, 25–37.

63. Edith Hamilton, *The Echo of Greece*, chapter 6, 117, 121.

64. Edith Hamilton, *The Echo of Greece*, chapter 6, 121.

65. Edith Hamilton to Margaret Hamilton, February 5 [n.y. though its discussion of the Hungarian Revolution suggests a date of 1957, a few months after the revolution had concluded], folder 4, box 1, EHP; Detzer, *Appointment on the Hill*, 7, 63.

66. Sack, *Moral Re-Armament*, 143; Williamson, *Inside Buchmanism*, 157.

67. Sack, *Moral Re-Armament*, 131; Williamson, *Inside Buchmanism*, 3, 24, 68, 86, 89,151, 157, 210.

68. Edith Hamilton to Jessie Hamilton, December 10, 1948, folder 606, reel 28, HFP.

69. Edith Hamilton to Jessie and Agnes Hamilton, May 28, 1949; Edith Hamilton to Jessie and Agnes Hamilton, March 22, 1920, though Edith clearly misidentified the year, since it was written from 2448 Massachusetts Avenue; Edith Hamilton to Jessie and Agnes Hamilton, December 17, 1952, all folder 611, reel 28, HFP; on *New World News* as a Moral Re-Armament publication, see Williamson, *Inside Buchmanism*, 187.

70. Edith Hamilton to Jessie and Agnes Hamilton, May 16 [n.y. but its reference to Yale granting her an honorary doctorate dates this to 1959], folder 5, box 1, EHP; for the honorary doctorate from Yale, see Reid, *Edith Hamilton: An Intimate Portrait*, 175.

71. Doenecke, *Not to the Swift*, 10, 171–75.

72. Frances Willard Kerr, "Author Receives Plaudits", *Christian Science Monitor*, March 13, 1958, p. 6.

73. Edith Hamilton, *The Echo of Greece*, chapter 7, 145.

74. Edith Hamilton, *The Echo of Greece*, chapter 7, 153.

75. Marcella Miller du Pont to Doris Fielding Reid, May 18, 1955, folder 15, box 11, MMDP.

76. Marie Smith, "10 GOP Speakers Graduate," *The Washington Post and Times Herald*, December 9, 1955, p. 67; Hemmer, *Messengers of the Right*, 141.

77. Edith Hamilton to "Dear People," dated January 22, 1955, but most likely January 22, 1956, since it discusses Doris's intended retirement from Loomis-Sayles and their upcoming trip to Italy, folder 4, box 1, EHP.

78. Ibid.

79. Edith Hamilton to "Dearest People" [Jessie and Agnes Hamilton], February 14, 1955, folder 4, box 1, EHP.

80. Obituary for Dr. Walter Walker Palmer, *New York Times*, October 29, 1950, p. 92; see also Rosamond Gilder to John Mason Brown, December 8, 1950, JMBP.

81. Edith Hamilton to "Dearest People" [Jessie and Agnes Hamilton], March 8, 1956, folder 4, box 1, EHP.

82. Edith Hamilton to "Dearest People" [Jessie and Agnes Hamilton], March 15 [1956], folder 4, box 1, EHP.

83. Edith Hamilton to "Dearest People" [Jessie and Agnes Hamilton], April 3, 1956, folder 4, box 1, EHP.

84. Doris Fielding Reid to John Mason Brown, June 8 [1956], JMBP.

85. Storer B. Lunt to Edith Hamilton, July 5, 1956; Storer B. Lunt to Edith Hamilton and Doris Fielding Reid, August 22, 1956, both WWNP.

86. Edith Hamilton, *The Roman Way*, chapter 12, 245.

87. Edith Hamilton, *The Echo of Greece*, chapter 8, 166.

88. Edith Hamilton, *The Echo of Greece*, chapter 8, 165.

89. Edith Hamilton, *The Echo of Greece*, chapter 8, 166.

90. Edith Hamilton, *The Echo of Greece*, chapter 10, 215.

91. Caird, *The Evolution of Religion*, vol. 1, 372–76.

92. Edith Hamilton to Agnes Hamilton, April 18, 1953, folder 4, box 1, EHP.

93. Vallon, *An Apostle of Freedom*, 42, 119, 139, 145.

94. Berdyaev, *The Realm of Spirit and the Realm of Caesar*, 156.

95. Berdyaev, *The Realm of Spirit and the Realm of Caesar*, 91–92.

96. Edith Hamilton to Mrs. Matthew Josephson, April 10, 1955, AAAL.

97. Storer B. Lunt to Edith Hamilton, July 13, 1956, WWNP.

98. Storer B. Lunt to Edith Hamilton, January 31, 1957 and March 26, 1957, both folder 5, box 3, EHC.

Chapter 18

1. Storer B. Lunt to Edith Hamilton, December 17, 1956, WWNP; see also Edith Hamilton, "The Greek Freedom: Truth, Discipline, and Reality," 9–10, 58.

2. Edith Hamilton to Huntington Cairns, January 25, 1957, box 12, HCP.

3. Stockin, "The Classical Association of the Atlantic States," 213–14.

4. Edith Hamilton to Elinore Blaisdell, January 4 [n.y. but its description of her broken pelvis dates this to 1957], private collection of the author.

5. John Mason Brown to Edith Hamilton, December 27, 1956, folder 4, box 3, EHC.

6. Edith Hamilton to Vail Motter, January 30 [n.y. but postmarked January 31, 1957], box 6, VMP.

7. Huntington Cairns to James K. Feibleman, January 8, 1957; Huntington Cairns to James K. Feibleman, January 24, 1957, both folder 4; Huntington Cairns to James K. Feibleman, March 29, 1957, folder 6, all box 21, JKFP.

8. "Edith Hamilton, Nearing 90, Feted by Friends," *Washington Star*, April 17, 1957, p. B22.

9. Storer B. Lunt to Edith Hamilton, February 20, 1957, folder 5, box 3, EHC.

10. Lattimore, "Athenian Sunset"; "Hamilton Talks on Plutarch's Age and Greek Spirit," *Wellesley College News*, March 30, 1950; I am grateful to Wellesley archivist Laura Reiner for this reference.

11. Robinson, "Secrets of Greece's Greatness," 19.

12. Edith Hamilton to Hortense Flexner King, April 6, 1957, box 1, HFKP.

13. Hadas, "Again Edith Hamilton and the Greeks," review of *The Echo of Greece, New York Herald Tribune Book Review*, January 13, 1957, p. 3.

14. W. R. Connor, "The New Classical Humanities and the Old," in Culham and Edmunds, eds., *Classics*, 25–38, 27.

15. Werner Jaeger to Edith Hamilton, January 5, 1957, folder 9, box 1, EHP.

16. Stockin, "The Classical Association of the Atlantic States," 213.

17. "Edith Hamilton, Nearing 90, Feted by Friends," *Washington Star*, April 17, 1957, p. B22; Doris Fielding Reid to Storer B. Lunt, April 15 [1957], folder 5, box 3, EHC.

18. "Nineteen and a Half Minutes," 36–37.

19. Edith Hamilton, "The Classics," 29–32.

20. Edith Hamilton, "The Lessons of the Past," 15, 114–17.

21. Stockin, "The Classical Association of the Atlantic States," 213.

22. Edith Hamilton to Huntington Cairns, January 25, 1957, box 12, HCP.

23. Edith Hamilton, *The Echo of Greece*, chapter 4, 91.

24. Edith Hamilton, *The Echo of Greece*, chapter 4, 91; Edith Hamilton to Huntington Cairns, January 25, 1957.

25. Werner Jaeger to Edith Hamilton, January 5, 1957, folder 9, box 1, EHP.

26. Huntington Cairns to James K. Feibleman, November 18, 1957, folder 12, box 21, JKFP.

27. Brooks Atkinson to Edith Hamilton, January 4, 1957, folder 22, box 2, EHP.

28. Marcella Miller du Pont to Edith Hamilton, February 8, 1957, folder 15, box 11, MMDP.

29. See her biography in the Marguerite Yourcenar Papers, Houghton Library, and her biography in the HFKP, archives of the University of Louisville.

30. Edith Hamilton to Hortense Flexner King, April 6, 1957, box 1, HFKP.

31. Edith Hamilton to Vail Motter, April 6, 1957, box 6, VMP.

32. Herman Schaden, "Miss Hamilton to Aid 'Prometheus' in Athens," *Washington Star*, June 23, 1957; George J. Bourlos to Edith Hamilton [n.d. but it describes the Delphic Festival to be held in Athens in 1957, the thirtieth anniversary of the previous festival in 1927], folder 8, box 1, EHP.

33. Woodhouse, *Karamanlis*, 53–54.

34. Clogg, *A Short History of Modern Greece*, 164.

35. Miller, *Henry Cabot Lodge*, 190.

36. Clogg, *A Short History of Modern Greece*, 168.

37. Woodhouse, *Karamanlis*, 42–43, 56–57, 103.

38. Herman Schaden, "Miss Hamilton to Aid 'Prometheus' in Athens," *Washington Star*, June 23, 1957.

39. Louis Calta, "ANTA to Present Classic in Athens," *New York Times*, June 15, 1957, p. 11; Maurice Dolbier, "Books and Authors," *New York Herald Tribune*, July 21, 1957.

40. Herman Schaden, "Miss Hamilton to Aid 'Prometheus' in Athens," *Washington Star*, June 23, 1957.

41. Edith Hamilton to Huntington Cairns, June 24 [1957], box 12, HCP.

42. Storer B. Lunt to Howard P. Wilson, August 10 [n.y. but written on Hotel Grande-Bretagne stationery from Athens and describing events in 1957], private collection of author.

43. Edith Hamilton to Lucia Valentine, July 4, 1957, box 3.1.1, Collection of Edith Hamilton letters and articles from the Valentines, ABMS.

44. Alice Reid Abbott to author, August 18, 2009.

45. Reid, *Edith Hamilton: An Intimate Portrait*, 109.

46. Derwent, *The Derwent Story*, 19.

47. Johnson, "The Greek Productions of Margaret Anglin," unpublished dissertation, 133, 247, 291; Derwent, *The Derwent Story*, 161.

48. Derwent, *The Derwent Story*, 302–3; "ANTA Officers Elected," *New York Times*, February 2, 1957, p. 13; Louis Calta, "Play by Ginsbury Opening Tonight," *New York Times*, April 25, 1957, p. 34; Milton Bracker, "Federal Support for Arts Urged," *New York Times*, May 24, 1957, p. 22.

49. Derwent, *The Derwent Story*, 214.

50. Yurka, *Bohemian Girl*, 3, 86–93, 137–39, 296–98; see also her obituary in the *New York Times*, June 7, 1974, p. 38.

51. Yurka, *Bohemian Girl*, 153–63.

52. Choate, *Electra USA*, 56–63, 107–12; Yurka, *Bohemian Girl*, 155.

53. Yurka, *Bohemian Girl*, 256.

54. Yurka, *Bohemian Girl*, 84, 195, 273, 281; Blanche Yurka to Edith Hamilton, September 20, 1958, folder 9, box 1, EHP; Edith Hamilton, *Mythology*, 95.

55. Reid, *Edith Hamilton: An Intimate Portrait*, 108–9.

56. Yurka, *Bohemian Girl*, 165–66; John P. Anton, "Introduction" in Palmer-Sikelianos, *Upward Panic*, xi–xxv, xxi; Leontis, *Eva Palmer Sikelianos*, 222; Anna Antoniades to Eleni Sikelianos, June 16, 1952, frames 1153–54, reel 3180, JMCHP.

57. Edith Hamilton to Mary Crovatt Hambidge, July 31, 1952, frames 936–38; Edith Hamilton to Mary Crovatt Hambidge, January 14, 1953, frames 939–41, both reel 3179, JMCHP.

58. Anna Antoniades to Mary Crovatt Hambidge, September 21, 1957, frames 476–77, reel 3178, JMCHP.

59. George J. Bourlos to Edith Hamilton [n.d. though its invitation to Edith to attend the Delphic Festival in Athens suggests a date of early 1957], folder 8, box 1, EHP; see also "Books News," W. W. Norton press release, June 25, 1957, copy in folder 5, box 3, EHC.

60. Yurka, *Bohemian Girl*, 166.

61. Louis Calta, "ANTA to Present Classic in Athens," *New York Times*, June 15, 1957, p. 11; Palmer-Sikelianos, *Upward Panic*, 93–101, 107–8, 115–16.

62. Anna Antoniades to Mary Crovatt Hambidge, September 21, 1957, frames 476–77, reel 3178, JMCHP.

63. Reid, *Edith Hamilton: An Intimate Portrait*, 110.

64. Edith Hamilton, probably to Alice and Margaret Hamilton, although no correspondent is identified this is included among a series of postcards she sent to her sisters from Greece in 1957, July 29 [n.y.], folder 1, box 1, EHP.

65. Edith Hamilton, probably to Alice and Margaret Hamilton, although no correspondent is identified it is included among a series of postcards Edith sent to her sisters from Greece in 1957, August 5 [n.y.], folder 1, box 1, EHP.

66. Edith Hamilton to either Alice or Margaret Hamilton, although no correspondent is identified it is contained among a series of postcards Edith wrote her sisters from Greece in 1957, August 2 [n.y.], folder 1, box 1, EHP.

67. Edith Hamilton to Huntington and Florence Cairns, August 2, 1957, box 12, HCP.

68. Yurka, *Bohemian Girl*, 281–82.

69. Edith Hamilton to Huntington and Florence Cairns, August 2, 1957, box 12, HCP.

70. Edith Hamilton to "Dearest People," August 3 [n.y. but clearly describing the visit to Athens in 1957], folder 5, box 1, EHP.

71. Woodhouse, *Karamanlis*, 57; Reid, *Edith Hamilton: An Intimate Portrait*, 112; Edith Hamilton, probably to Alice and Margaret Hamilton, although no correspondent is identified it is among the series of postcards Edith sent to her sisters from Athens in 1957, dated only July 24, folder 1, box 1, EHP.

72. Storer B. Lunt to Edith Hamilton, March 28, 1958, WWNP; Edith Hamilton to "Dearest People," August 3 [n.y.], though clearly describing events in Athens in 1957, folder 5, box 1, EHP.

73. Edith Hamilton probably to Alice and Margaret Hamilton, although no correspondent is identified it is among the series of postcards Edith sent to her sisters from Athens in 1957, August 6 [n.y.], folder 1, box 1, EHP.

74. Herman Schaden, "Miss Hamilton to Aid 'Prometheus' in Athens," *Washington Star*, June 23, 1957; A. C. Sedgwick, "Aeschylus Play Is Seen in Athens," *New York Times*, August 9, 1957, p. 11.

75. Edith Hamilton to "Dearest People," August 3 [n.y. but clearly describing the Athens visit of 1957], folder 5, box 1, EHP.

76. Edith Hamilton to Miss Hamilton [either Alice or Margaret], August 6 [n.y. but a postcard of the Parthenon frieze and describing Callas's performance], box 1, folder 1, EHP.

77. Edith Hamilton to "Dearest People," August 3 [n.y. but describing events in Athens in 1957], folder 5, box 1, EHP.

78. Woodhouse, *Karamanlis*, 27, 29.

79. Edith Hamilton to "Dearest People," August 3 [n.y. but describing events in Athens in 1957], folder 5, box 1, EHP.

80. Doris Fielding Reid to Alice and Margaret Hamilton, August 7 [n.y. but describing the events in Athens in 1957], folder 5, box 1, EHP.

81. Storer B. Lunt to Howard P. Wilson, August 10 [n.y. but written on Hotel Grande-Bretagne stationery from Athens and describing events there in 1957], private collection of the author.

82. A. C. Sedgwick, "Aeschylus Play Is Seen in Athens," *New York Times*, August 9, 1957, p. 11; see also Doris Fielding Reid to Margaret and Alice Hamilton, August 9, 1957, folder 5, box 1, EHP.

83. Reid, *Edith Hamilton: An Intimate Portrait*, 115; Meritt, *History of the American School of Classical*, 175–78, 182, 184–88, 191; see also Storer B. Lunt to Howard P. Wilson, August 10 [n.y. but written on Hotel Grand-Bretagne stationery from Athens and describing events in Athens in 1957], private collection of the author.

84. Doris Fielding Reid to Margaret and Alice Hamilton, August 9, 1957, folder 5, box 1, EHP.

85. Edith Hamilton, "The True Light," 188–89.

86. Storer B. Lunt to Howard P. Wilson, August 10 [n.y. but written on Hotel Grand-Bretagne stationery from Athens and describing events in Athens in 1957], private collection of the author.

87. Yurka, *Bohemian Girl*, 282.

88. Storer B. Lunt to Howard P. Wilson, August 10 [n.y. but written on Hotel Grande-Bretagne stationery from Athens and describing events in 1957], private collection of the author.

89. Elling Aannestad, "Memoir of Maine Seasons," unpublished autobiography, p. 43, folder 6, box 2, EAP.

90. Doris Fielding Reid to Margaret and Alice Hamilton, August 9, 1957, folder 5, box 1, EHP.

91. Anna Antoniades to Mary Crovatt Hambidge, September 21, 1957, frames 476–77, reel 3178, JMCHP.

92. Edith Hamilton to Brooks Atkinson, August 17, 1957, BAP.

93. A. C. Sedgwick, "Aeschylus Play Is Seen in Athens," *New York Times*, August 9, 1957, p. 11; for Edith's comments on Sedgwick, see Edith Hamilton to Brooks Atkinson, August 17, 1957, BAP.

94. Quoted in Doris Fielding Reid to Margaret and Alice Hamilton, August 9, 1957, folder 5, box 1, EHP.

95. Doris Fielding Reid to Margaret and Alice Hamilton, August 9, 1957, folder 5, box 1, EHP.

96. Ibid.; Edith Hamilton, "The True Light."

97. See catalogue of the Hellenic-American Union's 1967 exhibit "Eva Palmer Sikelianou and the Delphic Festivals," frames 1179–80, reel 3180, JMCHP.

98. Anna Antoniades to Mary Crovatt Hambidge, September 21, 1957, frames 476–77, reel 3178, JMCHP.

99. Edith Hamilton to Eva Palmer Sikelianos, March 9, 1943, folder 98, box 39; Edith Hamilton to Eva Palmer Sikelianos, April 21, 1944, folder 63; Edith Hamilton to Eva Palmer Sikelianos, October 20, 1944, folder 146, both box 40, all AEPS.

100. Anna Antoniades to Mary Crovatt Hambidge, February 20 [n.y. though its discussion of the preservation of Palmer Sikelianos's house at Delphi dates this to circa 1965], frames 515–16, reel 3178, JMCHP.

101. Edith Hamilton to Eva Palmer Sikelianos, January 4, 1945, folder 2, box 41, AEPS.

102. Leontis, *Eva Palmer Sikelianos*, 201–2, 215–16, 218–19.

103. Edith Hamilton to Eva Palmer Sikelianos, March 9, 1943, folder 98, box 39; Edith Hamilton to Eva Palmer Sikelianos, April 21, 1944, folder 63, box 40; Edith Hamilton to Eva Palmer Sikelianos, January 4, 1945, folder 2, box 41, all AEPS; Leontis, *Eva Palmer Sikelianos*, 229.

104. Leontis, *Eva Palmer Sikelianos*, 226–27.

105. Anna Antoniades to Mary Crovatt Hambidge, September 21, 1957, frames 476–477, reel 3178, JMCHP.

106. John P. Anton, "Introduction" in Palmer-Sikelianos, *Upward Panic*, xxii; Leontis, *Eva Palmer Sikelianos*, 226, 228.

107. Storer B. Lunt to Howard P. Wilson, August 10 [n.y. but written on Hotel Grande-Bretagne stationery from Athens and describing events in 1957], private collection of the author.

108. Doris Fielding Reid to Margaret and Alice Hamilton, August 9, 1957, folder 5, box 1, EHP.

109. Herman Schaden, "Miss Hamilton to Aid 'Prometheus' in Athens," *Washington Star*, June 23, 1957.

110. Muriel Dobbin, "Woman, 90, Still Writing," *Baltimore Sun*, February 23, 1958, A5.

111. Storer B. Lunt to Edith Hamilton, May 20, 1958, WWNP.

112. Edith Hamilton to Dearest People, July 30 [n.y. but written from Athens and describing the trip of 1957], folder 5, box 1, EHP.

113. Storer B. Lunt to Doris Fielding Reid, August 13, 1957, folder 5, box 3, EHC.

114. Storer B. Lunt to Doris Fielding Reid, October 3, 1957, folder 5, box 3, EHC.

115. Edith Hamilton to John Mason Brown, August 29 [1957], JMBP; Storer B. Lunt to Edith Hamilton, November 20, 1958, WWNP; Stevens, *Speak for Yourself, John*, 237.

116. Anna Antoniades to Mary Crovatt Hambidge, September 21, 1957, frames 476–77, reel 3178, JMCHP.

117. Doris Fielding Reid to Alice and Margaret Hamilton, August 9, 1957, folder 5, box 1, EHP.

118. Edith Hamilton to Huntington and Florence Cairns, August 29, 1957, box 12, HCP.

Chapter 19

1. Allan Nevins to Edith Hamilton, November 26, 1957; Louis Kronenberger to Edith Hamilton, January 17, 1955, both AAAAL; *New York Herald Tribune*, December 20, 1957, clippings file on Edith Hamilton, AAAAL. The Academy was limited to fifty members—the Institute to 250—and Edith was one of only four women in the more elite body.

2. John P. Shanley, "Edith Hamilton Talks," *New York Times*, February 9, 1959, p. 51; Reid, *Edith Hamilton: An Intimate Portrait*, 137; Avedon, "Avedon: Observations on Women in the Affairs of Man," 83–87, 84–85.

3. Divine, *The* Sputnik *Challenge*, xiii, 8–10, 164.

4. Edith Hamilton, "Echoes of Greece," lecture given at the Institute for Contemporary Arts, Washington, D.C. A transcript of this recording is in Edith Hamilton's alumna file, ABMC; Edith Hamilton, "The Lessons of the Past," 25, 114–17; this essay was reprinted in its entirety as "The Ever-Present Past" in Edith Hamilton, *The Ever-Present Past*; Eileen Summers, "In the Atomic Age, We Can Still Learn from Ancient Greeks Says Classicist," *Washington Post and Times-Herald*, March 22, 1959, p. F2–F3.

5. Storer B. Lunt to Edith Hamilton, October 7, 1957, folder 5, box 3, EHC.

6. Huntington Cairns to James K. Feibleman, September 30, 1957, folder 8; Huntington Cairns to James K. Feibleman, November 18, 1957, folder 12, both box 21, JKFP; John D. Barrett to Edith Hamilton, November 27, 1957, folder 9, box 1, EHP; Edith Hamilton to Huntington Cairns, July 13 [1959], box 12, HCP.

7. McGuire, *Bollingen*, 222; Reid, *Edith Hamilton: An Intimate Portrait*, 126.

8. Edith Hamilton to Alan Valentine, January 26, addenda to a letter begun January 10, 1960, box 3.1.1, Collection of Edith Hamilton's correspondence with Alan and Lucia Valentine, ABMS.

9. Huntington Cairns to James K. Feibleman, September 23, 1957, folder 10, box 21, JKFP.

10. Huntington Cairns to James K. Feibleman, October 15, 1957, folder 11, box 21, JKFP.

11. Huntington Cairns to James K. Feibleman, November 12, 1957, folder 12, box 21, JKFP.

12. McGuire, *Bollingen*, 222.

13. Huntington Cairns to James K. Feibleman, November 18, 1957, folder 12, box 21, JKFP.

14. Huntington Cairns to James K. Feibleman, December 3, 1957, folder 12, box 21, JKFP.

15. Ibid.

16. Bibliography of Plato Translations, folder 5, box 62, HCP.

17. Huntington Cairns to James K. Feibleman, February 25, 1958, folder 13, box 21, JKFP.

18. Last will and testament of Elling Aannestad, box 1, folder 15, EAP; Edith's two-volume Plato was given to Elling after Edith's death; he in turn willed it to Mary Reid McKnight upon his death in 1984.

19. Brown, "The Heritage of Edith Hamilton," 16–17; James K. Feibleman to Huntington Cairns, January 22, 1959, folder 1, box 22, JKFP.

20. Beekman W. Cottrell to Edith Hamilton, May 21, 1959, folder 10, box 1, EHP; Savigneau, *Marguerite Yourcenar*, 15, 133–34, 141, 145, 192, 217; Howard, *"We Met in Paris,"* xxv, 118, 162, 240.

21. Howard, *"We Met in Paris,"* 199.

22. McGuire, *Bollingen*, 234.

23. Phil Casey, "Learning to Top Russia Is Ridiculed by Writer," *Washington Post*, February 2, 1958; Divine, *The Sputnik Challenge*, xiii, 10, 43; Edith Hamilton, "Echoes of Greece."

24. Divine, *The Sputnik Challenge*, 91–92.

25. Lorena King [Mrs. Arthur Boyce] Fairbank to Edith Hamilton, February 14, 1958, folder 9, box 1, EHP; Doris Fielding Reid to John Mason Brown, February 2, 1958, JMBP; Reid, *Edith Hamilton: An Intimate Portrait*, 123.

26. Reid, *Edith Hamilton: An Intimate Portrait*, 127; Edith Hamilton to "Dear People" [Jessie and Agnes Hamilton], April 21 [n.y. but its discussion of their upcoming trip to Spain dates it to 1958], folder 4, box 1, EHP.

27. Doris Fielding Reid to Florence Cairns, June 26 [1958], box 12 HCP.

28. Ibid.

29. Edith Hamilton to Vail Motter, July 7, 1958, box 6, VMP.

30. Robert Emmet Ginna to Edith Hamilton, March 10, 1958, folder 9, box 1, EHP; Raymond H. Wittcoff, "Educational Television as a Civilizing Force," *St. Louis Post-Dispatch*, January 19, 1958, 15–16; Program for "Arts and Gods," 1957, folder 2, box 2, EHP; Reid, *Edith Hamilton: An Intimate Portrait*, 120–21.

31. Nelson, ed., "Edith Hamilton," in *Wisdom for Our Time*, 15–25, 21; this book contains a complete transcript of the *Wisdom* episode on which she appeared.

32. Nelson, ed., "Edith Hamilton," in *Wisdom for Our Time*, 21.

33. Dudziak, *Cold War Civil Rights: Race and the Image of American Democracy*, 3–6.

34. Edith Hamilton, "Death Sentence in Theft Case," August 21, 1958, *New York Times*, August 28, 1958, p. 26.

35. Edith Hamilton and Cairns, eds., *The Collected Dialogues of Plato*, 3.

36. Edith Hamilton and Cairns, eds., *The Collected Dialogues of Plato*, 27.

37. Edith Hamilton and Cairns, eds., *The Collected Dialogues of Plato*, 40.

38. Edith Hamilton and Cairns, eds., *The Collected Dialogues of Plato*, 308, 526–27.

39. Edith Hamilton and Cairns, eds., *The Collected Dialogues of Plato*, 145.

40. Edith Hamilton to Brooks Atkinson, December 15 [1958], BAP.

41. Flanders, *Senator from Vermont*, 290.

42. Douglas, *In the Fullness of Time*, 83; Storer B. Lunt to Edith Hamilton, March 16, 1951, WWNP; Biles, *Crusading Liberal*, 100, 129.

43. White, "The Hamilton Way," 132–57; Huntington Cairns to James K. Feibleman, March 19, 1958, folder 14, box 21, JKFP; Coffin, *Senator Fulbright*, 9–13, 16–17, 23, 26, 35, 46, 55, 67–68, 71, 106, 129–38, 211; Doenecke, *Not to the Swift*, 245.

44. Reid, *Edith Hamilton: An Intimate Portrait*, 135–36.

45. Huntington Cairns to James K. Feibleman, November 18, 1957; Huntington Cairns to James K. Feibleman, November 26, 1957, both folder 12, box 21, JKFP.

46. Huntington Cairns to James K. Feibleman, December 17, 1958, folder 21, box 21, JKFP.

47. Huntington Cairns to James K. Feibleman, November 5, 1956, folder 3, box 21, JKFP.

48. Huntington Cairns to James K. Feibleman, October 6, 1958, and October 13, 1958, both folder 20, box 21, JKFP.

49. Edith Hamilton to Florence Cairns, December 30, 1959, box 12, HCP; Doris Fielding Reid to "Gentlemen" [the American Academy of Arts and Letters], November 3, 1959, AAAL.

50. Doris Fielding Reid to Felicia Geffen, January 30 [n.y. but its discussion of Edith's American Academy of Arts and Letters medal continues an exchange begun earlier in January 1960], AAAL.

51. Edith Hamilton to Agnes Hamilton, March 3 [n.y. but Edith described the paralysis in her fingers as lasting for sixteen months, so a date of 1961 seems likely], folder 6, box 1, EHP.

52. Storer B. Lunt to Edith Hamilton, January 22, 1960, EHP; Edith Hamilton to Alan Valentine, January 26, 1960, box 3.1.1, Collection of Edith Hamilton Letters from the Valentines, ABMS.

53. Jean M. White, "Noted Greek Scholar at 92 Shows She's a Real Spartan," *Washington Post and Times Herald*, April 30, 1960, p. B16; Reid, *Edith Hamilton: An Intimate Portrait*, 139–40.

54. Edith Hamilton to Agnes Hamilton [n.d. except "Sunday," but its discussion of Jessie's health and Edith's shingles dates it to spring 1960], folder 6, box 1, EHP.

55. Edith Hamilton to Agnes Hamilton, May 10 [n.y. but its discussion of Jessie's death dates it to 1960], folder 6, box 1, EHP.

56. Huntington Cairns to Felix M. Morley, December 20, 1960, folder 8, box 105, HCP.

57. Obituary for Parker McCollester, *New York Times*, January 13, 1954, p. 31.

58. Doris Fielding Reid to Alice Hamilton, postmarked June 8, 1960, folder 672, reel 31, HFP.

59. Doris Fielding Reid to Huntington and Florence Cairns, June 16 [1960], box 12, HCP; Doris described this trip in Reid, *Edith Hamilton: An Intimate Portrait*, 136–37.

60. Clarke, *Ask Not*, 5, 7, 114, 117–18.

61. Lodge, *The Storm Has Many Eyes*, 125, 127.

62. "Press Club Twits Nation's Leaders," *New York Times*, May 10, 1959, p. 51; "WNPC Stunt Dinner to Honor Scholar," *Washington Star*, May 6, 1959.

63. Clarke, *Ask Not*, 115; Miller, *Henry Cabot Lodge*, 255; see Huntington Cairns's biography in the HCP, Manuscript Division, Library of Congress; Cairns secured an invitation for his friend James K. Feibleman, preserved in folder 20; see also Huntington Cairns to James K. Feibleman, December 20, 1960, folder 19, both box 22, JKFP.

64. John F. Kennedy, "Inaugural Address," in David, ed., *The Kennedy Reader*, 7–11.

65. Nelson, ed., "Edith Hamilton," in *Wisdom for Our Time*, 23; Edith Hamilton, *The Echo of Greece*, 29–32; Jim Birchfield, "Edith Hamilton Is Still at Work," *The Star Magazine* [Washington], July 29, 1962, p. 11.

66. Edith Hamilton to Alan Valentine, dated January 10 and January 26, 1960, by Edith but postmarked January 28, 1961, and clearly written after Kennedy became president, box 3.1.1, Collection of Edith Hamilton letters from the Valentines, ABMS.

67. Ibid.; Edith Hamilton, *The Echo of Greece*, chapter 7, 154.

68. Edith Hamilton and Cairns, eds., *The Collected Dialogues of Plato*, 151–52.

69. Edith Hamilton to Agnes Hamilton [n.d. except "Sunday" but written from Seawall and referring to the death of the Moral Re-Armament founder Dr. Frank N. D. Buchman, making a date of August 1961 likely], folder 6, box 1, EHP; Frank N. D. Buchman died August 6, 1961, see Lean, *Frank Buchman*, 528; Brooks Atkinson, "Critic at Large," *New York Times*, March 17, 1961, p. 28; Reid, *Edith Hamilton: An Intimate Portrait*, 140–41.

70. Doris Fielding Reid to Huntington and Florence Cairns, June 13, 1961, box 12, HCP.

71. Ibid.; Edith Hamilton to Agnes Hamilton [n.d. except "Sunday" but referring to the death of Frank N. D. Buchman], folder 6, box 1, EHP.

72. Thomson, *The Foreseeable Future*, the dedication (not paginated) reads, "To D.F.R. for helping me."

73. Sicherman, *Alice Hamilton*, 416.

74. Edith Hamilton to Lucia Valentine, postmarked August 15, 1961, Collection of Edith Hamilton Letters and Articles from the Valentines, box 3.1.1, ABMS.

75. Sicherman, *Alice Hamilton*, 411.

76. Doris Fielding Reid to Vail Motter, January 9, 1962, box 6, VMP; see also Reid, *Edith Hamilton: An Intimate Portrait*, 141.

77. Elling Aannestad to Edith Hamilton and Doris Fielding Reid [n.d. except Sunday but included with editorial material from the *New York Times* dated February 11, 1962], folder 12, box 1, EHP.

78. Alice Reid Abbott to author, August 18, 2009.

79. Rudd Fleming, "Why Plato Now?" *Washington Post and Times-Herald*, October 15, 1961, p. E6.

80. L. E. Girard, Review of *The Collected Dialogues of Plato*, *Main Currents in Modern Thought* (November-December 1961), copy in HCP.

81. Storer B. Lunt to Edith Hamilton, April 9, 1958, box 2, EHP; Eileen Summers, "In the Atomic Age, We Can Still Learn from Ancient Greeks Says Classicist," *Washington Post and Times-Herald*, March 22, 1959, p. F2–F3.

82. Edith Hamilton to Agnes Hamilton [n.d. except "Sunday" but its discussion of the death of Frank N. D. Buchman dates it to August 1961].

83. Jim Birchfield, "Edith Hamilton Is Still at Work," *The Star Magazine* [Washington], July 29, 1962, p. 11; Brooks Atkinson, "Critic at Large," *New York Times*, March 17, 1961, p. 28.

84. Edith Hamilton to "Dear People" [Jessie and Agnes Hamilton] December 20 [n.y. though its context of beginning work on the Plato volume with Huntington Cairns suggests a year of 1957], folder 5, box 1, EHP.

85. Caird, *The Evolution of Religion*, vol. 2, 89.

86. Edith Hamilton and Cairns, eds., *The Collected Dialogues of Plato*, 526.

87. Brooks Atkinson, "Critic at Large," *New York Times*, March 17, 1961, p. 28; Edith Hamilton, *The Echo of Greece*, chapter 10, 216; Edith Hamilton and Cairns, eds., *The Collected Dialogues of Plato*, 845.

88. Reid, *Edith Hamilton: An Intimate Portrait*, 142.

89. Journal of Felix M. Morley, June 3, 1963, p. 12, box 55, FMMP.

90. Huntington Cairns to James K. Feibleman, June 3, 1963, folder 6, box 24, JKFP.

91. Journal of Felix M. Morley, June 3, 1963, p. 12, box 55, FMMP; Edith had died, as Morley noted, on a Friday evening.

92. Margaret Shearman to Alice Hamilton, June 1, 1963, ABMS; the other college friend to survive Edith was Laurette Potts Pease, who died in 1967.

Chapter 20

1. Huntington Cairns to James K. Feibleman, June 3, 1963, folder 6, box 24, JKFP; "Edith Hamilton Dies, Was Classical Scholar," *Hartford Courant*, June 3, 1963, p. 4.

2. Alice Reid Abbott to author, August 18, 2009.

3. Journal of Felix Morley, July 24, 1960, p. 68, FMMP; Dorothy Sands to John Mason Brown June 28, 1963, folder 4, box 3, EHC.

4. Doris Fielding Reid, "Prologue," in Edith Hamilton, *The Ever-Present Past*, 9–19, 9; Reid, *Edith Hamilton: An Intimate Portrait*, 15.

5. Isabel Morley to Doris Fielding Reid, June 5 [1963], ABMS; Elling Aannestad to John Mason Brown, June 24, 1963, folder 4, box 3, EHC; Grace Drake to Doris Fielding Reid, postmarked December 18, 1963, ABMS.

6. Reid, *Edith Hamilton: An Intimate Portrait*, 15–16.

7. Edith Hamilton to Alice Hamilton, April 6, 1943, folder 666, reel 31, HFP; Reid, *Edith Hamilton: An Intimate Portrait*, 16.

8. Dorothy Detzer Denny to Doris Fielding Reid [n.d. but clearly written after Edith's death], folder 6, box 1, EHC.

9. Doris Fielding Reid to Vail Motter, July 30, 1968, box 6, VMP.

10. Betsey Reid Pfeiffer to Vail Motter, August 30, 1969, box 6, VMP.

11. Obituary for Dr. Francis Fielding Reid, *Washington Post*, July 23, 1960, p. C4.

12. Alice Reid Abbott to author, August 18, 2009, for the date of Clara Landsberg's death, see her alumna file, ABMC; obituary for Margaret Hamilton, *Washington Post and Times Herald*, July 9, 1969, p. B6; Sicherman, *Alice Hamilton*, 416.

13. Alice Reid Abbott to author, August 18, 2009.

14. Obituary for Doris Fielding Reid, *New York Times*, January 17, 1973, p. 42.

BIBLIOGRAPHY

Interviews

Ms. Alice Reid Abbott, granddaughter of Edith Hamilton, August 18, 2009
Dr. Christina Marsden Gillis, authority on history of Gott's Island, Maine, July 2009

Manuscript Collections

Elling Aannestad Papers (EAP), Rauner Special Collections Library, Dartmouth College
Archives of the American Academy of Arts and Letters (AAAAL), New York City
Brooks Atkinson Papers (BAP), New York Public Library for the Performing Arts, Lincoln Center
John Mason Brown Papers (JMBP), Houghton Library, Harvard University
Archives of Bryn Mawr College (ABMC), Canaday Library, Bryn Mawr College
Archives of the Bryn Mawr School (ABMS), Baltimore, Maryland
Witter Bynner Papers (WBP), Houghton Library, Harvard University
Huntington Cairns Papers (HCP), Manuscript Division of the Library of Congress
Colles Family Papers (CFP), Special Collections, New York Public Library
Marcella Miller du Pont Papers (MMDP), Manuscript Division of the Library of Congress
Emmet Family Papers (EFP), Archives of American Art, Smithsonian Institution
James K. Feibleman Papers (JKFP), Morris Library, University of Southern Illinois
Robert Fitzgerald Papers (RFP), Beinecke Library, Yale University
Ralph E. Flanders Papers (REFP), Ernest S. Bird Library, Syracuse University
Simon Flexner Papers (SFP), American Philosophical Society
The Gilder Manuscripts (GM), Lilly Library, Indiana University
Jay and Mary Crovatt Hambidge Papers (JMCHP), Archives of American Art, Smithsonian Institution
Edith Hamilton Collection (EHC), Special Collections, Princeton University Library
Edith Hamilton Letters (EHL), Schlesinger Library, Radcliffe Institute
Edith Hamilton Papers (EHP), Schlesinger Library, Radcliffe Institute

Hamilton Family Papers (HFP), Schlesinger Library, Radcliffe Institute

Hamilton Family Papers (HFPI), Indiana State Library, Indianapolis

Alfred and Mary Gwinn Hodder Papers (AMGHP), Special Collections, Princeton University Library

Archives of the University of Illinois (AUI)

Edith J. R. Isaacs Papers (EJRIP), Wisconsin Historical Society, Madison

Hortense Flexner King Papers (HFKP), Archives of the University of Louisville

Little, Brown Papers (LBP), Houghton Library, Harvard University

Miss Porter's School Archives (MPSA), Farmington, Connecticut

Felix Morley Collection (FMC), Special Collections, Magill Library, Haverford College

Felix M. Morley Papers (FMMP), Herbert Hoover Presidential Library, West Branch, Iowa

Vail Motter Papers (VMP), Special Collections, Princeton University Library

The W. W. Norton Papers (WWNP), Butler Library, Columbia University

Pound Manuscripts (PM), Lilly Library, Indiana University

Ezra Pound Papers (EPP), Beinecke Library, Yale University

Bertrand Russell Archive (BRP), Bertrand Russell Archive and Research Center, McMaster University

Archive of Eva Palmer Sikelianos (AEPS), Benaki Museum Historical Archives, Kifissia, Athens

Dr. David Eugene Smith Papers (DESP), Butler Library, Columbia University

Logan Pearsall Smith Papers (LPSP), Lilly Library, Indiana University

Society of Women Geographers (SWG), Manuscript Division of the Library of Congress

Gertrude Stein and Alice B. Toklas Papers (GSABTP), Beinecke Library, Yale University

M. Carey Thomas Papers (MCTP), Canaday Library, Bryn Mawr College

Papers of Juliette Tomlinson (PJT), Archives of the Bryn Mawr School, Baltimore

Grace Hill Turnbull Papers (GHTP), Maryland Historical Society, Baltimore

Van Dyke Family Papers (VDFP), Special Collections, Princeton University Library

Archives of Veraestau (AV), Aurora, Indiana

Albert Coady Wedemeyer Papers (ACMP), Hoover Institution, Stanford University

Thornton Wilder Papers (TWP), Beinecke Library, Yale University

Henry B. Williams Papers (HBWP), Rauner Special Collections Library, Dartmouth College

Marguerite Yourcenar Papers (MYP), Houghton Library, Harvard University

Dissertations

Forte, Maria. "Bertrand Russell's Letters to Helen Thomas Flexner and Lucy Martin Donnelly." Unpublished dissertation, McMaster University, 1988.

Johnson, Gordon Arnold. "The Greek Productions of Margaret Anglin." Unpublished dissertation, Case Western Reserve University, 1971.

Katter, Nafe Edmund. "'Theatre Arts' under the Editorship of Edith J. R. Isaacs." Unpublished dissertation, University of Michigan, 1963.

Klotz, Daniel James. "Freda Utley: From Communist to Anti-Communist." Unpublished dissertation, Yale University, 1987.

Wachter, Phyllis E. "Surname: Arnold, Occupation: Spinster, Avocation: New Victorian Woman." Unpublished dissertation, Temple University, April 1984.

Wardrip, Mark Allen. "A Western Portal of Culture: The Hearst Greek Theatre of the University of California, 1903–1984." Unpublished dissertation, University of California, Berkeley, 1984.

Wetmore, Allyn C. "Allen Hamilton: The Evolution of a Frontier Capitalist." Unpublished dissertation, Ball State University, 1974.

Willis, Ronald Arthur. "The American Laboratory Theatre, 1923–1930." Unpublished dissertation, University of Iowa, 1968.

Recording

Hamilton, Edith. "Echoes of Greece." New Rochelle: Spoken Arts, 1966.

Articles

"Aged Lover of the Ancients." *Life* 45 (September 15, 1958): 76, 79–80.

Avedon, Richard. "Avedon: Observations on Women in the Affairs of Man." *Harper's Bazaar* (December 1961): 83–87.

Becker, May Lamberton. "The Reader's Guide." *Saturday Review of Literature* 9 (December 10, 1932): 320.

Bok, Edward. "Just Because I Want to Play." *Atlantic Monthly* 126 (September 1920): 369–74.

Brown, John Mason. "The Fruit of Enlightenment." *Saturday Review of Literature* 31 (March 27, 1948): 28–30.

———. "The Heritage of Edith Hamilton: 1867–1963." *Saturday Review* 46 (June 22, 1963): 16–17.

Carson, Mina J. "Agnes Hamilton of Fort Wayne: The Education of a Christian Settlement Worker." *Indiana Magazine of History* 80 (March 1984): 1–34.

Casazza, Joseph. "'Taming the Savageness of Man': Robert Kennedy, Edith Hamilton, and Their Sources." *The Classical World* 96 (Winter 2003): 197–99.

Colum, Padraic. "Back to Theseus and Asgard." *Saturday Review of Literature* 25 (August 1, 1942).

Cousins, Norman. "Modern Man Is Obsolete: An Editorial." *Saturday Review of Literature* 28 (August 18, 1945): 5–9.

Cousins, Norman, and Harrison Smith. "Ezra Pound and the Bollingen Award." *Saturday Review of Literature* 32 (June 11, 1949): 20–21.

Davis, Elmer. "What the Romans Were." Review of *The Roman Way*, by Edith Hamilton. *Saturday Review of Literature* 9 (December 10, 1932): 303.

Donnelly, Lucy Martin. "The Celebrated Mrs. Macaulay." *The William and Mary Quarterly* 6 (April 1949): 173–207.

———. "The Heart of a Bluestocking." *Atlantic Monthly* 102 (October 1908): 536–39.

———. "Poet and Feminist." *New Republic* 6 (April 29, 1916): 337–39.

———. "The Sage of Shantung." *New Republic* 20 (October 1, 1919): 260–63.

Frazer, Elizabeth. "Wall Street Women." *Good Housekeeping* 93 (August 1931): 41.

Gilder, Rosamond. "Greek Plays." Review of *Three Greek Plays*, by Edith Hamilton. *Theatre Arts Monthly* 22 (February 1938): 156–57.

———. "The Season in Print." *Theatre Arts Monthly* 8 (July 1924): 499–500.

Girson, Rochelle. "Gentle Nonagenarian." *Saturday Review* 25 (August 1, 1957): 29.

Goldman, Hetty. "The Greek Genius." Review of *The Greek Way*, by Edith Hamilton. *Saturday Review of Literature* 7 (August 9, 1930): 35–36.

Gooch, G. P. "Lord Acton: Apostle of Liberty." *Foreign Affairs* 25 (July 1947): 629–42.

Graham, Sara Hunter. "Woman Suffrage in Virginia: The Equal Suffrage League and Pressure-Group Politics, 1909–1920." *Virginia Magazine of History and Biography* 101 (April 1993): 227–50.

"Groupers in Stockbridge." *Time* 27 (June 15, 1936): 35–38.

Hadas, Moses. "Again Edith Hamilton and the Greeks." Review of *The Echo of Greece*, by Edith Hamilton. *New York Herald Tribune Book Review* (January 13, 1957).

Hamilton, Alice. "Edith and Alice Hamilton: Students in Germany." *Atlantic Monthly* 215 (March 1965): 129–32.

Hamilton, Edith. "Born under a Rhyming Planet." Review of *The Seven against Thebes*, by Aeschylus, translated by Gilbert Murray. *Saturday Review of Literature* 12 (June 29, 1935): 11–12.

———. "Brass Tacks." Review of *Dithyramb, Tragedy, and Comedy*, by A. W. Pickard-Cambridge. *Theatre Arts Monthly* 12 (June 1928): 449–50.

———. "The Classics." *The Classical World* 51 (November 1957): 29–32.

———. "Comedy." *Theatre Arts Monthly* 11 (July 1927): 503–12.

———. "The Family of Oedipus." *Theatre Arts Monthly* 24 (December 1940): 889–96.

———. "Faulkner: Sorcerer or Slave?" *Saturday Review* 35 (July 12, 1952): 8–10, 39–41.

———. "Femininity in the Bible." Review of *Women in the Old Testament*, by Norah Lofts. *Saturday Review of Literature* 33 (February 18, 1950): 42.

———. "Gaudeamus Igitur." Review of *Gaudy Night*, by Dorothy L. Sayers. *Saturday Review of Literature* 13 (February 22, 1936): 6.

———. "Goethe and Faust." *Theatre Arts Monthly* 25 (June 1941): 451–61.

———. "Greece and the Good Life." Review of *The Story of Instruction: The Beginnings*, by Ernest Carroll Moore. *Saturday Review of Literature* 14 (July 4, 1936): 17.

———. "Greek and the English Genius." *Theatre Arts Monthly* 12 (May 1928): 333–38.

———. "The Greek Chorus: Fifteen or Fifty?" *Theatre Arts Monthly* 17 (June 1933): 459–67.

———. "The Greek Freedom: Truth, Discipline, and Reality." *Saturday Review of Literature* 40 (January 12, 1957): 9–10, 58.

———. "Introduction," in Plutarch's *Selected Lives and Essays*. Translated from the Greek by Louise Ropes Loomis. Roslyn, NY: Walter J. Black for the Classics Club, 1951.

———. "Interesting Schools." *New Republic* X (February 10, 1917): 45–46.

———. "The Lessons of the Past." *Saturday Evening Post* 231 (September 27, 1958): 25, 114–17.

———. "Literature of Escape." *Saturday Review of Literature* 15 (December 5, 1936): 30, 35.

———. "A Mystic Looks at Shakespeare." Review of *Keats and Shakespeare*, by John M. Murry. *Theatre Arts Monthly* 10 (October 1926): 717–18.

———. "Private Idiom." *Vogue* 141 (September 15, 1951): 156, 206–7, 218.

———. "The Prometheus Bound of Aeschylus: Translated with an Introduction." *Theatre Arts Monthly* 11 (July 1927): 545–62.

————. "These Sad Young Men." *Atlantic Monthly* 143 (May 1929): 656–62.

————. "Tragedy." *Theatre Arts Monthly* 10 (January 1926): 41–46.

————. "Triumph in Tragedy." Review of *Sophocles' Oedipus Rex: An English Version. Saturday Review of Literature* 33 (February 11, 1950): 30.

————. "The True Light." [Address to the Athenians]. *Saturday Review* 40 (October 19, 1957).

————. "When Liberty Departs." Review of *The Power in the People*, by Felix Morley. *Saturday Review of Literature* 32 (September 3, 1949): 19–20.

————. "Who Is This Dionysus?" *Theatre Arts Monthly* 24 (June 1940): 430–40.

————. "Words, Words, Words." *Saturday Review* 38 (November 19, 1955), 15–16, 52–53.

————. "The World of Plato." Review of *Paideia: The Ideals of Greek Culture*, by Werner Jaeger. *New York Times* (January 2, 1944): 6.

Hillyer, Robert. "Treason's Strange Fruit: The Case of Ezra Pound and the Bollingen Award." *Saturday Review of Literature* 32 (June 11, 1949): 9–11, 28.

Hutchison, Percy. "The Ancient Greeks." Review of *The Greek Way*, by Edith Hamilton. *New York Times* (June 15, 1930): 2.

Lattimore, Richmond. "Athenian Sunset." Review of *The Echo of Greece*, by Edith Hamilton. *New York Times* (January 27, 1957).

"Life among the Romans." Review of *The Roman Way*, by Edith Hamilton. *New York Herald Tribune Book Review* (December 18, 1932): 8.

Mitchison, Naomi. "Athens Re-Explored." Review of *The Greek Way*, by Edith Hamilton. *Theatre Arts Monthly* 14 (November 1930): 985–86.

"Nineteen and a Half Minutes." *New Yorker* 33 (May 11, 1957): 36–37.

Parker, Franklin, and Joyce Bronough. "Edith Hamilton at 94: A Partial Bibliography." *Bulletin of Bibliography* 23 (May 1962): 183–84.

Parrish, Wayne W. "What Is Technocracy?" *Readers Digest* 11 (January 1933): 8–10.

Putnam, Emily James. "Paul Shorey." *Atlantic Monthly* 161 (June 1938): 795–804.

Reid, Doris Fielding. "Edith Hamilton." *Greek Heritage* 1 (1963): 44–48.

"The Reply." *New Republic* X (February 10, 1917): 46–47.

Robinson, C. A., Jr. "Secrets of Greece's Greatness." Review of *The Echo of Greece*, by Edith Hamilton. *Saturday Review of Literature* 40 (March 9, 1957): 19.

Schmidt, David. "The Main Line's Classical Inspiration." *Main Line Life* (November 21–27, 2001): 14–16.

Sharkey, Heather. "An Egyptian in China: Ahmed Fahmy and the Making of 'World Christianities.'" *Church History* 78 (June 2009): 309–26.

Shorey, Paul. "The Assault on Humanism." *Atlantic Monthly* 119 (June 1917): 793–801.

————. "The Assault on Humanism II." *Atlantic Monthly* 120 (July 1917): 94–105.

————. "The Bigotry of the New Education." *The Nation* 105 (September 6, 1917): 253–56.

Stockin, F. Gordon. "The Classical Association of the Atlantic States: Report of Secretary-Treasurer 1956–1957." *The Classical Weekly* 50 (May 20, 1957): 213–14.

Topolski, Feliks. "In Washington." *Vogue* (August 1, 1950): 57–59.

Van Dusen, Henry P. "'Apostle to the Twentieth Century': Frank N. D. Buchman, Founder of the Oxford Group Movement." *Atlantic Monthly* 154 (July 1934): 1–16.

Westbrook, Theodoric. "A New Language for Greek Drama." Review of *Three Greek Plays*, by Edith Hamilton. *Saturday Review of Literature* 17 (December 4, 1937): 38.

White, John. "The Hamilton Way." *Georgia Review* 24 (Summer 1970): 132–57.

White, W. L. "Allied Failure in Germany." Review of *The High Cost of Vengeance*, by Freda Utley. *Saturday Review of Literature* 32 (August 13, 1949): 11.

Wilson, Howard P. "Norton's Ingredients for Success." *Columbia Library Columns* 18 (February 1969): 3–15.

Books

Abse, Joan. *John Ruskin: The Passionate Moralist*. New York: Alfred A. Knopf, 1981.

Ackerman, Robert. "The Cambridge Group: Origins and Composition," in *The Cambridge Ritualists Reconsidered: Proceedings of the First Oldfather Conference, Held on the Campus of the University of Illinois at Urbana-Champaign April 27–30, 1989*. Edited by William M. Calder III. Atlanta, GA: Scholars Press, 1991.

Ackroyd, Peter. *T. S. Eliot: A Life*. New York: Simon and Schuster, 1984.

Adams, Henry. *The Life of George Cabot Lodge*. Delmar, NY: Scholars' Facsimiles and Reprints, 1978 [1911].

Akin, William E. *Technocracy and the American Dream: The Technocracy Movement, 1900–1941*. Berkeley: University of California Press, 1988.

Albisetti, James A. *Schooling German Girls and Women: Secondary and Higher Education in the Nineteenth Century*. Princeton, NJ: Princeton University Press, 1988.

Allinson, Anne C. E. *Selected Essays*. New York: Harcourt Brace, 1933.

Allison, Leslie Minturn. *Mildred Minturn: A Biography*. Sainte Anne-de-Bellevue, Quebec: Shoreline, 1995.

Anderson, Alan D. *The Origin and Resolution of an Urban Crisis: Baltimore, 1890–1930*. Baltimore, MD: The Johns Hopkins Press, 1977.

Ankenbruck, John. *Fort Wayne in the Years of the Bank Panic*. Privately printed, 1979.

Arnold, Edward Vernon. *Roman Stoicism: Being Lectures on the History of the Stoic Philosophy with Special Reference to its Development within the Roman Empire*. New York: Books for Libraries Press, 1971 [1911].

Arnold, Matthew. *The Complete Prose Works of Matthew Arnold*. Edited by R. H. Super. Ann Arbor: University of Michigan Press, 1960–77. Eleven volumes.

———. "Culture and Anarchy," in *The Complete Prose Works of Matthew Arnold*. Edited by R. H. Super. Ann Arbor: University of Michigan Press, 1960–77. Eleven volumes.

———. "Literature and Dogma," in *The Complete Prose Works of Matthew Arnold*. Edited by R. H. Super. Ann Arbor: University of Michigan Press, 1960–77. Eleven volumes.

Axling, William. *Kagawa*. New York: Harper, 1932, rev. 1946.

Bachrack, Stanley D. *The Committee of One Million: "China Lobby" Politics, 1953–1971*. New York: Columbia University Press, 1976.

Barolini, Helen. *Their Other Side: Six American Women and the Lure of Italy*. New York: Fordham University Press, 2006.

Barry, Kathleen. *Susan B. Anthony: A Biography of a Singular Feminist*. New York: New York University Press, 1988.

Beaux, Cecilia. *Background with Figures: The Autobiography of Cecilia Beaux.* New York: Houghton Mifflin, 1930.

Beirne, Francis F. *Amiable Baltimoreans.* New York: E. P. Dutton, 1951.

Beirne, Rosamond Randall. *Let's Pick the Daisies: The History of the Bryn Mawr School, 1884–1967.* Baltimore, MD: The Bryn Mawr School, 1970.

Bell, Millicent. *Marquand: An American Life.* Boston: Little, Brown, 1979.

Benjamin, Sarah. *A Castle in Tuscany: The Remarkable Life of Janet Ross.* Millers Point, Australia: Pier 9, 2006.

Benson, Sally. *Stories of the Gods and Heroes.* New York: The Dial Press, 1940.

Berdyaev, Nicolas. *The Realm of Spirit and the Realm of Caesar.* Westport, CT: Greenwood Press, 1975 [1953].

Berg, A. Scott. *Wilson.* New York: G. P. Putnam's Sons, 2013.

Biles, Roger. *Crusading Liberal: Paul H. Douglas of Illinois.* DeKalb: Northern Illinois University Press, 2002.

Blake, Israel George. *The Holmans of Veraestau.* Oxford, OH: The Mississippi Valley Press, 1943.

Bode, Carl. *Mencken.* Carbondale: Southern Illinois University Press, 1969.

Bosher, Kathryn, Fiona Macintosh, Justine McConnell, and Patrice Rankine, eds. *The Oxford Handbook of Greek Drama in the Americas.* Oxford, UK: Oxford University Press, 2015.

Boucher, David, and Andrew Vincent. *British Idealism and Political Theory.* Edinburgh, Scotland: Edinburgh University Press, 2000.

Bourne, Randolph. *Education and Living.* New York: The Century Company, 1917.

Bowra, C. M. *Memories: 1898–1939.* Cambridge, MA: Harvard University Press, 1967.

Bradshaw, Emerson, O., et al., eds. *Kagawa in Lincoln's Land.* New York: National Kagawa Co-ordinating Committee, 1936.

Briggs, Ward W., Jr., ed. *Biographical Dictionary of North American Classicists.* Westport, CT: Greenwood Press, 1994.

Briggs, Ward W., Jr., and Herbert W. Benario, eds. *Basil Lanneau Gildersleeve: An American Classicist.* Baltimore, MD: The Johns Hopkins University Press, 1986.

Briggs, Ward W., Jr., and William M. Calder III, eds. *Classical Scholarship: A Biographical Encyclopedia.* New York: Garland Publishing, 1990.

Brinkley, David. *Washington Goes to War.* New York: Alfred A. Knopf, 1988.

Brittain, Vera. *The Women at Oxford: A Fragment of History.* London: George G. Harrap, 1960.

Brooks, Van Wyck. *An Autobiography.* New York: E. P. Dutton, 1965.

Brown, John Mason. *Many a Watchful Night.* New York: McGraw-Hill, 1944.

———. *Through These Men: Some Aspects of Our Passing History.* New York: Harper's, 1956.

———. *To All Hands: An Amphibious Adventure.* New York: McGraw-Hill, 1943.

Bruder, Anne L., ed. *Offerings to Athena: 125 Years at Bryn Mawr College.* Bryn Mawr, PA: Friends of the Bryn Mawr College Library, 2010.

Burleigh, Nina. *A Very Private Woman: The Life and Unsolved Murder of Presidential Mistress Mary Meyer.* New York: Bantam Books, 1998.

Burstein, Andrew. *The Original Knickerbocker: The Life of Washington Irving.* New York: Basic Books, 2007.

Caird, Edward. *The Evolution of Religion: The Gifford Lectures Delivered Before the University of St. Andrews in Sessions 1890–91 and 1891–92*. Glasgow, Scotland: James Maclehose and Sons, 1893. Two volumes.

Cairns, Huntington. *The Bollingen Adventure: A Toast to J.D.B. and V. G.* Princeton, NJ: Princeton University Press, 1969.

Cairns, Huntington, ed. *The Limits of Art: Poetry and Prose Chosen by Ancient and Modern Critics*. New York: Bollingen Foundation/Pantheon Books, 1948.

Calder, William M., III, ed. *The Cambridge Ritualists Reconsidered: Proceedings of the First Oldfather Conference, Held on the Campus of the University of Illinois at Urbana-Champaign, April 27–30, 1989*. Atlanta, GA: Scholars Press, 1991.

Choate, E. Teresa. *Electra USA: American Stagings of Sophocles' Tragedy*. Madison, WI: Fairleigh Dickinson University Press, 2009.

Clark, Ronald W. *The Life of Bertrand Russell*. New York: Alfred A. Knopf, 1976.

Clark, Walter Houston. *The Oxford Group: Its History and Significance*. New York: Bookman Associates, 1951.

Clarke, M. L. *George Grote: A Biography*. London: University of London/The Athlone Press, 1962.

Clarke, Thurston. *Ask Not: The Inauguration of John F. Kennedy and the Speech That Changed America*. New York: Henry Holt, 2004.

Clayton, Anthony, and Alan Russell, eds. *Dresden: A City Reborn*. New York: Berg, 1999.

Clayton, Bruce. *Forgotten Prophet: The Life of Randolph Bourne*. Baton Rouge: Louisiana State University Press, 1984.

Cleary, Marie Sally. *Myths for the Millions: Thomas Bulfinch, His America, and His Mythology Book*. New York: Peter Lang, 2007.

Clogg, Richard. *A Short History of Modern Greece*. Cambridge, UK: Cambridge University Press, 1979.

Coffin, Tristram. *Senator Fulbright: Portrait of a Public Philosopher*. New York: E. P. Dutton, 1966.

Colby, Vineta. *Vernon Lee: A Literary Biography*. Charlottesville: University of Virginia Press, 2003.

Cole, Wayne S. *America First: The Battle against Intervention 1940–1941*. Madison: University of Wisconsin Press, 1953.

———. *Charles A. Lindbergh and the Battle against American Intervention in World War II*. New York: Harcourt Brace Jovanovich, 1974.

Coleman, Helen Turnbull Waite. *Camp Diamond Story*. Privately printed, circa 1941.

Colloms, Brenda. *Charles Kingsley: The Lion of Eversley*. New York: Barnes and Noble, 1975.

Cooper, Douglas. *The Cubist Epoch*. London: Phaidon, 1970.

Cooper, John Milton, Jr. *Breaking the Heart of the World: Woodrow Wilson and the Fight for the League of Nations*. Cambridge, UK: Cambridge University Press, 2001.

Copleston, Reginald S. *Aeschylus*. Philadelphia, PA: J. B. Lippincott, 1872.

Cordery, Stacy A. *Alice: Alice Roosevelt Longworth, from White House Princess to Washington Power Broker*. New York: Viking, 2007.

Coser, Lewis A. *Refugee Scholars in America: Their Impact and Their Experiences*. New Haven, CT: Yale University Press, 1984.

Cowling, Elizabeth. *On Classic Ground: Picasso, Leger, de Chirico and the New Classicism 1910–1930*. London: The Tate Gallery, 1990.

Crenson, Matthew. *Baltimore: A Political History*. Baltimore: The Johns Hopkins University Press, 2017.

Croall, Jonathan. *Sybil Thorndike: A Star of Life*. London: Haus Books, 2008.

Croghan, Moira. *Timeless: Inside Mackinac Island's Historic Cottages*. Mackinac Island, ME: Mackinac Jane's Publishing, 2020.

Culham, Phyllis, and Lowell Edmunds, eds. *Classics: A Discipline and Profession in Crisis?* Lanham, MD: University Press of America, 1989. `

Curti, Carlo. *Skouras: King of Fox Studios*. Los Angeles: Holloway House, 1967.

Davey, Cyril J. *Kagawa of Japan*. London: The Epworth Press, 1960.

David, Jay, ed. *The Kennedy Reader*. Indianapolis: The Bobbs-Merrill Company, 1967.

Davies, Robert M. *The Humanism of Paul Elmer More*. New York: Bookman, 1958.

Davis, Homer W., ed. *Greece Fights: The People behind the Front*. New York: American Friends of Greece, 1942.

Davis, Nancy, and Barbara Donahue. *Miss Porter's School: A History*. Farmington, CT: Miss Porter's School, 1992.

De Forest, Emily Johnston. *James Colles 1788–1883: Life and Letters*. New York: Privately printed, 1926.

Degen, Marie Louise. *The History of the Woman's Peace Party*. Baltimore, MD: The Johns Hopkins University Press, 1939.

De Jong, Gerald Francis. *The Reformed Church in China, 1842–1951*. Grand Rapids, MI: Eerdmans, 1992.

Dennison, Matthew. *Behind the Mask: The Life of Vita Sackville-West*. New York: St. Martin's Press, 2014.

Derwent, Clarence. *The Derwent Story: My First Fifty Years in the Theatre in England and America*. New York: Henry Schuman, 1953.

Detzer, Dorothy. *Appointment on the Hill*. New York: Henry Holt, 1948.

Detzer, Karl. *Myself When Young*. New York: Funk and Wagnalls, 1968.

Di Cataldo, Elizabeth Nye. *Ex Solo Ad Solem: A History of the Bryn Mawr School*. Baltimore, MD: The Bryn Mawr School, 2011.

Dickinson, Frederick R. *War and National Reinvention: Japan and the Great War, 1914–1919*. Cambridge, MA: Harvard University Asia Center, 1999.

Divine, Robert A. *The* Sputnik *Challenge*. New York: Oxford University Press, 1993.

Dixon, W. Macneile. *Hellas Revisited*. London: Edward Arnold, 1929.

———. *Tragedy*. London: Edward Arnold, 1924.

Doenecke, Justus D. *Not to the Swift: The Old Isolationists in the Cold War Era*. Lewisburg, PA: Bucknell University Press, 1979.

———. *Storm on the Horizon: The Challenge to American Intervention, 1939–1941*. Lanham, MD: Rowman and Littlefield, 2000.

Dougill, John. *Kyoto: A Cultural History*. Oxford, UK: Oxford University Press, 2006.

Douglas, Paul H. *In the Fullness of Time: The Memoirs of Paul H. Douglas*. New York: Harcourt, Brace, Jovanovich, 1971.

Dubofsky, Melvyn, and Warren Van Tine. *John L. Lewis: A Biography*. New York: Quadrangle/ The New York Times Book Company, 1977.

Dudziak, Mary L. *Cold War Civil Rights: Race and the Image of American Democracy*. Princeton, NJ: Princeton University Press, 2000.

Easterling, P. E., ed. *The Cambridge Companion to Greek Tragedy*. Cambridge, UK: Cambridge University Press, 1997.

Eliot, T. S. *The Sacred Wood: Essays on Poetry and Criticism*. London: Methuen, 1920.

Ellmann, Richard. *Oscar Wilde*. New York: Alfred A. Knopf, 1988.

Emery, Anne Crosby. *The Historical Present in Early Latin*. Ellsworth, ME: Hancock County Publishing, 1897.

Emerson, Ralph Waldo. *Representative Men*. Joseph Simon: 1980 [1850].

Ewald, Donna, and Peter Clute. *San Francisco Invites the World: The Panama-Pacific International Exposition of 1915*. San Francisco: Chronicle Books, 1991.

Faber, Geoffrey. *Jowett: A Portrait with Background*. Cambridge, MA: Harvard University Press, 1957.

Faderman, Lillian. *Odd Girls and Twilight Lovers: A History of Lesbian Life in Twentieth Century America*. New York: Columbia University Press, 1991.

——. *Surpassing the Love of Men: Romantic Friendship and Love between Women from the Renaissance to the Present*. New York: Morrow, 1981.

Felsenthal, Carol. *Power, Privilege, and the Post: The Katharine Graham Story*. New York: G. P. Putnam's Sons, 1993.

Finley, David Edward. *A Standard of Excellence: Andrew W. Mellon Founds the National Gallery of Art*. Washington: Smithsonian Institution Press, 1973.

Fitts, Dudley, ed. *Greek Plays in Modern Translation*. New York: Dial Press, 1947.

FitzGibbon, Constantine. *The Life of Dylan Thomas*. Boston: Little, Brown, 1965.

Flanders, Ralph E. *Letter to a Generation*. Boston: The Beacon Press, 1956.

——. *Senator from Vermont*. Boston: Little, Brown, 1961.

Fleming, G. H. *James Abbott McNeill Whistler: A Life*. Moreton-in-Marsh, UK: Windrush Press, 1991.

Flexner, Abraham. *Daniel Coit Gilman: Creator of the American Type of University*. New York: Harcourt Brace, 1946.

——. *A Modern School*. New York: The General Education Board, 1919.

Flexner, Helen Thomas. "Bryn Mawr: A Characterisation (Bryn Mawr: Bryn Mawr College, 1908)," in *Offerings to Athena: 125 Years at Bryn Mawr College*, edited by Anne L. Bruder. Bryn Mawr, PA: Friends of the Bryn Mawr College Library, 2010.

Flexner, James Thomas. *An American Saga: The Story of Helen Thomas and Simon Flexner*. Boston: Little, Brown, 1984.

——. *Maverick's Progress: An Autobiography*. New York: Fordham University Press, 1996.

Foley, Helene P. *Reimagining Greek Tragedy on the American Stage*. Berkeley: University of California Press, 2012.

Franklin, Fabian. *The Life of Daniel Coit Gilman*. New York: Dodd, Mead, 1910.

Fruhauf, Aline. *Making Faces: Memoirs of a Caricaturist*. Cabin John, MD: Seven Locks Press, 1987.

Furuki, Yoshiko. *The White Plum: A Biography of Ume Tsuda, Pioneer in the Higher Education of Japanese Women.* New York: Weatherhill, 1991.

Gathorne-Hardy, Robert. *Recollections of Logan Pearsall Smith: The Story of a Friendship.* New York: The Macmillan Company, 1950.

Gilbert, W. S. *The Complete Operas of W. S. Gilbert.* New York: Random House, 1932.

Gilder, Richard Watson. *Letters of Richard Watson Gilder Edited by His Daughter Rosamond Gilder.* New York: Houghton Mifflin, 1916.

Gillis, Christina Marsden. *Writing on Stone: Scenes from a Maine Island Life.* Hanover: University Press of New England, 2008.

Glendon, Mary Anne. *A World Made New: Eleanor Roosevelt and the Universal Declaration of Human Rights.* New York: Random House, 2001.

Glenn, Justin. *The Washingtons: A Family History.* El Dorado Hills: Savas Publishing, 2016. Seven Volumes.

Grant, Madeleine P. *Alice Hamilton: Pioneer Doctor in Industrial Medicine.* New York: Abelard-Schuman, 1967.

Grant, Michael. *Saint Paul.* London: Weidenfield and Nicolson, 1976.

Gregory, Eileen. *H. D. and Hellenism: Classic Lines.* Cambridge: Cambridge University Press, 1997.

Gress, David. *From Plato to NATO: The Idea of the West and Its Opponents.* New York: The Free Press, 1998.

Griffin, Miriam T. *Seneca: A Philosopher in Politics.* Oxford: Clarendon Press, 1976.

Griffith, Robert. *The Politics of Fear: Joseph R. McCarthy and the Senate, 2nd ed.* Amherst: The University of Massachusetts Press, 1987.

Griswold, B. J. *The Pictorial History of Fort Wayne, Indiana: A Review of Two Centuries of Occupation of the Region about the Head of the Maumee River.* Chicago: Robert O. Law Company, 1917.

Guckenberg, Susan Lee. *Hugh McCulloch: Father of Modern Banking.* Fort Wayne: Allen County-Fort Wayne Historical Society, 2004.

Guest, Barbara. *Herself Defined: The Poet H. D. and Her World.* New York: Quill, 1984.

Guinness, Joy. *Mrs. Howard Taylor: Her Web of Time.* London: China Inland Mission, 1949.

Gutzman, Kevin R.C. *James Madison and The Making of America.* New York: St. Martin's Press, 2012.

Hall, Edward H. *Papias and His Contemporaries.* Boston: Houghton Mifflin, 1899.

Hallett, Judith P., and Christopher Stray, eds. *British Classics Outside England: The Academy and Beyond.* Waco, TX: Baylor University Press, 2009.

Hamilton, Alice. *Exploring the Dangerous Trades.* Boston: Little, Brown, 1943.

Hamilton, Andrea. *A Vision for Girls: Gender, Education, and The Bryn Mawr School.* Baltimore, MD: The Johns Hopkins University Press, 2004.

Hamilton, Edith. *The Echo of Greece.* New York: W. W. Norton, 1957.

———. *The Ever-Present Past.* New York: W. W. Norton, 1964.

———. *The Great Age of Greek Literature.* New York: W. W. Norton, 1942.

———. *The Greek Way.* New York: W. W. Norton, 1930.

———. *Mythology.* Boston: Little, Brown, and Company, 1942.

Hamilton, Edith. *The Prophets of Israel*. New York: W. W. Norton, 1936.

———. *The Roman Way*. New York: W. W. Norton, 1932.

———. *Spokesmen for God: The Great Teachers of the Old Testament*. New York: W. W. Norton, 1949.

———. *Three Greek Plays*. New York: W. W. Norton, 1937.

———. *A Treasury of Edith Hamilton*. Selected by Doris Fielding Reid. New York: W. W. Norton, 1969.

———. *Witness to the Truth: Christ and His Interpreters*. New York: W. W. Norton, 1948.

Hamilton, Edith, and Huntington Cairns, eds. *The Collected Dialogues of Plato*. New York: Bollingen/Pantheon Books, 1961.

Harper, Ida Husted. *History of Woman Suffrage, Volume Six: 1900–1920*. New York: Arno and New York Times, 1969.

Harris, Irving. *The Breeze of the Spirit: Sam Shoemaker and the Story of Faith at Work*. New York: Seabury Press, 1978.

Harris, John Howard. *Thirty Years as President of Bucknell: With Baccalaureate and Other Addresses*. Compiled and edited by Mary B. Harris. Privately printed, 1926.

Harris, Mary B. *I Knew Them in Prison*. New York: The Viking Press, 1942.

Harrison, Donald Frederic. *Equal Suffrage as a Reform Factor*. The University of Illinois, n.d.

Harrison, Patricia Greenwood. *Connecting Links: The British and American Suffrage Movements, 1900–1914*. Westport, CT: Greenwood Press, 2000.

Hartigan, Karelisa V. *Greek Tragedy on the American Stage: Ancient Drama in the Commercial Theater, 1882–1994*. Westport, CT: Greenwood Press, 1995.

Hemmer, Nicole. *Messengers of the Right: Conservative Media and the Transformation of American Politics*. Philadelphia: University of Pennsylvania Press, 2016.

Henry, Tom. *The Life and Art of Luca Signorelli*. New Haven, CT: Yale University Press, 2012.

Herken, Gregg. *The Georgetown Set: Friends and Rivals in Cold War Washington*. New York: Alfred A. Knopf, 2014.

Herndon, Sarah, J. Russell Reaver, Robert F. Davidson, William Ruff, and Nathan Comfort Starr, eds. *The Humanistic Tradition*. New York: Holt, Rinehart, and Winston, 1964.

Herringshaw, Thomas William, ed. *Herringshaw's Library of American Biography*. Chicago: American Publishers' Association, 1914. Five volumes.

Hill, Roland. *Lord Acton*. New Haven, CT: Yale University Press, 2000.

Hirsch, Steven W. *The Friendship of the Barbarians*. Hanover: University Press of New England, 1985.

Hitler, Adolf. *Mein Kampf*. Translated by Ralph Manheim. Boston: Houghton Mifflin, 1943.

Holzer, Harold, ed. *State of the Union: New York and the Civil War*. New York: Fordham University Press, 2002.

Honan, Park. *Matthew Arnold: A Life*. Cambridge: Harvard University Press, 1983.

Hoopes, James. *Van Wyck Brooks: In Search of American Culture*. Amherst: The University of Massachusetts Press, 1977.

Hoppen, Martha J. *The Emmets: A Family of Woman Painters*. Pittsfield, MA: The Berkshire Museum, 1982.

Horowitz, Helen Lefkowitz. *Alma Mater: Design and Experience in the Women's Colleges from Their Nineteenth-Century Beginnings to the 1930s*. New York: Alfred A. Knopf, 1984.

————. *The Power and Passion of M. Carey Thomas*. New York: Alfred A. Knopf, 1994.

Houghton, Norris. *Entrances and Exits: A Life In and Out of the Theatre*. New York: Limelight Editions, 1991.

Howard, Joan E. *"We Met in Paris": Grace Frick and Her Life with Marguerite Yourcenar*. Columbia: University of Missouri Press, 2018.

Hunter, Jane. *The Gospel of Gentility: American Women Missionaries in Turn-of-the-Century China*. New Haven, CT: Yale University Press, 1984.

Jaeger, Werner. *Demosthenes: The Origin and Growth of His Policy*. Berkeley: University of California Press, 1938.

————. *Paideia: The Ideals of Greek Culture. Volume II: In Search of the Divine Centre*. New York: Oxford University Press, 1943.

Jeffords, James M. *An Independent Man: Adventures of a Public Servant*. New York: Simon and Schuster, 2003.

————. *My Declaration of Independence*. New York: Simon and Schuster, 2001.

Jenkyns, Richard. *The Victorians and Ancient Greece*. Cambridge, MA: Harvard University Press, 1984.

Johnson, Curtiss S. *Raymond E. Baldwin: Connecticut Statesman*. Chester, CT: Pequot Press, 1972.

Johnson, David K. *The Lavender Scare: The Cold War Persecution of Gays and Lesbians by the Federal Government*. Chicago: The University of Chicago Press, 2004.

Jones, Sir Henry, and John Henry Muirhead. *The Life and Philosophy of Edward Caird: Professor of Moral Philosophy in the University of Glasgow and Master of Balliol College, Oxford*. Glasgow, Scotland: Maclehose and Jackson, 1921.

Jones, John Bush, ed. *W. S. Gilbert: A Century of Scholarship and Commentary*. New York: New York University Press, 1970.

Jones, Mervyn. *The Amazing Victorian: A Life of George Meredith*. London: Constable, 1999.

Jones, Ross. *Elisabeth Gilman: Crusader for Justice*. Salisbury, MD: Secant Publishing, 2018.

Kagawa, Toyohiko. *Meditations on the Cross*. New York: Willett, Clark, 1935.

Kamm, Josephine. *How Different from Us: A Biography of Miss Buss and Miss Beale*. London: The Bodley Head, 1958.

Katz, Sandra L. *Dearest of Geniuses: A Life of Theodate Pope Riddle*. Windsor, CT: Tide-Mark, 2003.

Kelly, Glenn D. *A Plea for Equal Suffrage*. Eureka, CA: Eureka College, n.d.

Kenway, Rita Johnson. *Gott's Island Maine: Its People 1880–1992*. Penobscot, ME: Penobscot Press, 1993.

Kingsley, Charles. *The Heroes: Or, Greek Fairy Tales for My Children*. London: Macmillan, 1868 [1855].

Kinne, Wisner Payne. *George Pierce Baker and the American Theatre*. Cambridge, MA: Harvard University Press, 1954.

Kirk, Russell, and James McClellan. *The Political Principles of Robert A. Taft*. New York: Fleet Press, 1967.

Klein, Carole. *Gramercy Park: An American Bloomsbury*. Boston: Houghton Mifflin, 1987.

Kopff, E. Christian. "Paul Shorey," in *Classical Scholarship: A Biographical Encyclopedia*. Edited by Ward W. Briggs Jr. and William M. Calder III. New York: Garland Publishing, 1990.

Kurtz, Benjamin P. *Charles Mills Gayley: The Glory of a Lighted Mind*. Berkeley: University of California Press, 1943.

Lawson, Andrew C., and Perry Byerly. *Biographical Memoir of Harry Fielding Reid 1859–1944*. Washington: National Academy of Sciences, 1949.

Lean, Garth. *Frank Buchman: A Life*. London: Constable, 1985.

Lee, Hermione. *Edith Wharton*. New York: Alfred A. Knopf, 2007.

Leontis, Artemis. *Eva Palmer Sikelianos: A Life in Ruins*. Princeton, NJ: Princeton University Press, 2019.

Lin Yutang. *From Pagan to Christian*. New York: World Publishing, 1959.

Lindow, John. *Norse Mythology: A Guide to Gods, Heroes, Rituals, and Beliefs*. Oxford, UK: Oxford University Press, 2002.

Lindquist, Eric N. *The Origins of the Center for Hellenic Studies*. Princeton, NJ: Princeton University Press, 1990.

Livingstone, R. W. *The Greek Genius and Its Meaning to Us*. Oxford, UK: Clarendon Press, 1912.

Lodge, Henry Cabot, Jr. *The Storm Has Many Eyes: A Personal Narrative*. New York: W. W. Norton, 1973.

Longfield, Bradley J. *The Presbyterian Controversy: Fundamentalists, Modernists, and Moderates*. New York: Oxford University Press, 1991.

Lumsden, Linda J. *Inez: The Life and Times of Inez Milholland*. Bloomington: Indiana University Press, 2004.

Martindale, Charles, and Richard F. Thomas, eds. *Classics and the Uses of Reception*. Oxford, UK: Blackwell Publishing, 2006.

Martindale, Charles, Stefano Evangelista, and Elizabeth Prettejohn, eds. *Pater the Classicist: Classical Scholarship, Reception, and Aestheticism*. Oxford, UK: Oxford University Press, 2017.

May, Arthur J. *A History of the University of Rochester, 1850–1962*. Rochester, NY: The University of Rochester, 1977.

Mayhew, Katherine Camp, and Anna Camp Edwards. *The Dewey School: The Laboratory School of the University of Chicago 1896–1903*. New York: Atherton Press, 1966.

Mazower, Mark. *Greece and the Inter-War Economic Crisis*. Oxford, UK: Clarendon Press, 1991.

McAdoo, Eleanor Wilson, with Margaret Y. Gaffey. *The Woodrow Wilsons*. New York: Macmillan, 1937.

McAuliffe, Mary. *When Paris Sizzled: The 1920s Paris of Hemingway, Chanel, Cocteau, Cole Porter, Josephine Baker, and Their Friends*. Lanham, MD: Rowman and Littlefield, 2016.

McGuire, William. *Bollingen: An Adventure in Collecting the Past*. Princeton, NJ: Princeton University Press, 1982.

Meigs, Cornelia. *What Makes a College? A History of Bryn Mawr*. New York: Macmillan, 1956.

Melosh, Barbara. *Strangers and Kin: The American Way of Adoption*. Cambridge, MA: Harvard University Press, 2002.

Meritt, Lucy Shoe. *History of the American School of Classical Studies at Athens, 1939–1980*. Princeton, NJ: American School of Classical Studies at Athens, 1984.

Michelet, Maren. *Glimpses from Agnes Mathilde Wergeland's Life*. Privately printed, 1916.

Miller, Helen Hill. *Greek Horizons*. New York: Charles Scribner's Sons, 1961.

Miller, Henry. *Farewell from France: A Letter to Huntington Cairns, April 30, 1939*. Ann Arbor, MI: Roger Jackson, 1995.

Miller, William J. *Henry Cabot Lodge: A Biography*. New York: James H. Heineman, 1967.

Mitchell, Leslie. *Maurice Bowra: A Life*. Oxford, UK: Oxford University Press, 2009.

Morley, Felix. *For the Record*. South Bend, IN: Regnery/Gateway, 1979.

———. *Freedom and Federalism*. Chicago: Henry Regnery, 1959.

———. *Gumption Island*. Caldwell, ID: The Caxton Press, 1956.

———. *Our Far Eastern Assignment*. New York: Doubleday, Page, 1926.

———. *The Power in the People*. New York: D. Van Nostrand, 1949.

Morrill, Charlotte. *History of Adelphi Academy*. New York: Associate Alumnae of Adelphi Academy, 1916.

Mosley, Leonard. *Blood Relations: The Rise and Fall of the du Ponts of Delaware*. New York: Atheneum, 1980.

Mowat, R. C., ed. *Report on Moral Re-Armament*. London: Blandford Press, 1955.

Murray, Gilbert. *Euripides and His Age*. London: Williams and Norgate, 1913.

———. *The Rise of the Greek Epic*. New York: Oxford University Press, 1960 [1907].

Murray, Nicholas. *Aldous Huxley: An English Intellectual*. London: Little, Brown, 2002.

Nadel, Ira B., ed. *The Cambridge Companion to Ezra Pound*. Cambridge, UK: Cambridge University Press, 1999.

Navarro, Jaume. *A History of the Electron: J. J. and G. P. Thomson*. Cambridge: Cambridge University Press, 2012.

Nelson, James, ed. *Wisdom for Our Time*. New York: W. W. Norton, 1961.

Niessen, Owen Claire. *Aristocracy, Temperance, and Social Reform: The Life of Lady Henry Somerset*. New York: Tauris Academic Studies, 2007.

Nickerson, Marjorie L. *A Long Way Forward: The First Hundred Years of the Packer Collegiate Institute*. Brooklyn, NY: The Packer Collegiate Institute, 1945.

Nimura, Janice P. *Daughters of the Samurai: A Journey from East to West and Back*. New York: W. W. Norton, 2015.

Niven, Penelope. *Thornton Wilder: A Life*. New York: Harper Collins, 2012.

Olson, Lynne. *Those Angry Days: Roosevelt, Lindbergh, and America's Fight over World War II, 1939–1941*. New York: Random House, 2013.

Palmer-Sikelianos, Eva. *Upward Panic: The Autobiography of Eva Palmer-Sikelianos*. Edited by John P. Anton. Philadelphia, PA: Harwood Academic Publishers, 1993.

Parker, Matthew. *Monte Cassino: The Hardest Fought Battle of World War II*. New York: Doubleday, 2004.

Pater, Walter. *Marius the Epicurean*. London: Penguin, 1985 [1885].

Patterson, James T. *Mr. Republican: A Biography of Robert A. Taft*. Boston: Houghton Mifflin, 1972.

Pedersen, Holger. *The Discovery of Language: Linguistic Science in the Nineteenth Century*. Translated by John Webster Spargo. Bloomington: Indiana University Press, 1931.

Perry, Rachel Berenson. *William J. Forsyth: The Life and Work of an Indiana Artist*. Bloomington: Indiana University Press, 2014.

Peters, Maureen. *Jean Ingelow: Victorian Poetess*. Ipswich, UK: The Boydell Press, 1972.

Pickard-Cambridge, Arthur. *Dithyramb, Tragedy, and Comedy*. 2nd edition revised by T.B.L. Webster. Oxford: Clarendon Press, 1962.

Piper, John F. *Robert E. Speer: Prophet of the American Church*. Louisville: Geneva Press, 2000.

Plutarch. *Selected Lives and Essays*. Translated from the Greek by Louise Ropes Loomis. Roslyn, NY: Walter J. Black for the Classics Club, 1951.

Poinsatte, Charles R. *Fort Wayne during the Canal Era, 1828–1855: A Study of a Western Community in the Middle Period of American History*. Indianapolis: Indiana Historical Bureau, 1969.

Pomeroy, Sarah, B., Stanley M. Burstein, Walter Donlan, and Jennifer Tolbert Roberts. *Ancient Greece: A Political, Social, and Cultural History*. New York: Oxford University Press, 1999.

Prentice, Alison, and Marjorie R. Theobold, eds. *Women Who Taught: Perspectives on the History of Women and Teaching*. Toronto, Canada: University of Toronto Press, 1991.

Prins, Yopie. *Ladies' Greek: Victorian Translations of Tragedy*. Princeton, NJ: Princeton University Press, 2017.

Proceedings of the Thirty-Eighth Annual Convention of the National-American Woman Suffrage Association Held at Baltimore, Maryland, February 7th to 13th inclusive, 1906. Warren, OH: The National-American Suffrage Association, 1906.

Purvis, June. *Emmeline Pankhurst: A Biography*. London: Routledge, 2002.

Reck, Michael. *Ezra Pound: A Close-Up*. New York: McGraw-Hill, 1973.

Reid, Doris Fielding. *Edith Hamilton: An Intimate Portrait*. New York: W. W. Norton, 1967.

Reid, Edith Gittings. *The Great Physician: A Short Life of Sir William Osler*. London: Oxford University Press, 1931.

———. *The Life and Convictions of William Sydney Thayer, Physician*. New York: Oxford University Press, 1936.

———. *Woodrow Wilson: The Caricature, the Myth, and the Man*. New York: Oxford University Press, 1934.

Ringenberg, Matthew C., William C. Ringenberg, and Joseph D. Brain. *The Education of Alice Hamilton: From Fort Wayne to Harvard*. Bloomington: Indiana University Press, 2019.

Robertson, Priscilla. *An Experience of Women: Continuity and Change in Nineteenth Century Europe*. Philadelphia, PA: Temple University Press, 1982.

Robinson, Annabel. *The Life and Work of Jane Ellen Harrison*. Oxford: Oxford University Press, 2002.

Roth, Robert J. *John Dewey and Self-Realization*. Englewood Cliffs, NJ: Prentice-Hall, 1962.

Russell, Arthur J. *For Sinners Only*. New York: Harper, 1932.

Sachar, Abram Leon. *A History of the Jews*. New York: Alfred A. Knopf, 1930.

Sack, Daniel. *Moral Re-Armament: The Reinventions of an American Religious Movement*. New York: Palgrave Macmillan, 2009.

Sander, Kathleen Waters. *Mary Elizabeth Garrett: Society and Philanthropy in the Gilded Age*. Baltimore, MD: The Johns Hopkins University Press, 2008.

Sarles, Ruth. *A Story of America First: The Men and Women Who Opposed U.S. Intervention in World War II*. Westport, CT: Praeger, 2003.

Saunders, Frances Wright. *Ellen Axson Wilson: First Lady between Two Worlds*. Chapel Hill: University of North Carolina Press, 1985.

Savigneau, Josyane. *Marguerite Yourcenar: Inventing a Life*. Chicago: University of Chicago Press, 1993.

Schaumann, Herbert. *Odysseus and Calypso*. Orange, NJ: Omnibus Studio Enterprises, 1956.

Schoonmaker, Nancy Musselman, and Doris Fielding Reid, eds. *We Testify*. New York: Smith and Durrell, 1941.

Schwarz, Judith. *Radical Feminists of Heterodoxy: Greenwich Village, 1912–1940*. Lebanon, NH: New Victoria Publishers, 1982.

Scott, Anne F., and Andrew M. Scott. *One Half the People: The Fight for Woman Suffrage*. Philadelphia, PA: J. B. Lippincott, 1975.

Scott, Michael. *Delphi: A History of the Center of the Ancient World*. Princeton, NJ: Princeton University Press, 2014.

Scotti, R. A. *Sudden Sea: The Great Hurricane of 1938*. Boston: Little, Brown, 2003.

Secrest, Meryle. *Being Bernard Berenson: A Biography*. New York: Penguin Books, 1980.

Shaw, Anna Howard, with Elizabeth Jordan. *The Story of a Pioneer*. New York: Harper Brothers, 1915.

Shearer, Benjamin F., and Barbara S. Shearer, eds. *Notable Women in the Life Sciences: A Biographical Dictionary*. Westport, CT: Greenwood Press, 1996.

Shepherd, William G. *Great Preachers as Seen by a Journalist*. New York: Fleming H. Revell, 1924.

Shoemaker, Helen Smith. *I Stand by the Door: The Life of Sam Shoemaker*. New York: Harper and Row, 1967.

Shoemaker, Samuel M. *Calvary Church: Yesterday and Today: A Centennial History*. New York: Fleming H. Revell, 1936.

Shorey, Paul. *Greek Life and Thought at Its Culmination: The Age of Pericles: Syllabus of a course of Six Lecture Studies*. Chicago: University of Chicago Press, 1897.

———. *Syllabus of a Course of Six Lectures on Studies in English Poetry of the Nineteenth Century*. Philadelphia, PA: The American Society for the Extension of University Teaching, 1891.

———. *What Plato Said*. Chicago: University of Chicago Press, 1933.

Sicherman, Barbara. *Alice Hamilton: A Life in Letters*. Cambridge, MA: Harvard University Press, 1984.

Sicherman, Barbara, and Carol Hurd Green, eds. *Notable American Women: The Modern Period*. Cambridge, MA: The Belknap Press, 1980.

Simonson, Lee. *The Stage Is Set*. New York: Harcourt Brace, 1932.

Singer, Sandra L. *Adventures Abroad: North American Women at German-Speaking Universities, 1868–1915*. Westport, CT: Praeger, 2003.

Smith, Logan Pearsall. *A Portrait of Logan Pearsall Smith: Drawn from His Letters and Diaries and Introduced by John Russell*. London: Dropmore, 1950.

Solomon, Barbara Miller. *In the Company of Educated Women: A History of Women and Higher Education in America*. New Haven, CT: Yale University Press, 1985.

Somers, Wayne, ed. *The Encyclopedia of Union College History*. Schenectady, NY: Union College Press, 2003.

Sorley, Merrow Egerton. *Lewis of Warner Hall: The History of a Family*. Privately printed, 1935.

Sprigge, Elizabeth. *Gertrude Stein: Her Life and Work*. New York: Harper and Brothers, 1957.

Staley, Gregory, ed. *American Women and Classical Myths*. Waco, TX: Baylor University Press, 2009.

Stanford, W. B., and R. B. McDowell. *Mahaffy: A Biography of an Anglo-Irishman*. London: Routledge and Kegan Paul, 1971.

Stein, Gertrude. *The Autobiography of Alice B. Toklas*. New York: Harcourt Brace, 1933.

Steiner, Bernard Christian, et al. *Men of Mark in Maryland: Biographies of Leading Men of the State, Vol. I*. Washington, D.C.: Johnson-Wynne, 1907.

Stenehjem, Michele Flynn. *An American First: John T. Flynn and the America First Committee*. New Rochelle, NY: Arlington House, 1976.

Sternlicht, Sanford. *Padraic Colum*. Boston: Twayne Publishers, 1985.

Steuck, William. *The Wedemeyer Mission: American Politics and Foreign Policy during the Cold War*. Athens: University of Georgia Press, 1984.

Stevens, George. *Speak for Yourself, John: The Life of John Mason Brown*. New York: Viking Press, 1974.

Stimpson, Catherine R., and Harriet Chessman, eds. *Gertrude Stein: Writings 1903–1932*. New York: The Library of America, 1998.

Stites, Susan, and Lea Ann Sterling. *Historic Cottages of Mackinac Island*. Mayfield, MI: Arbutus Press, 2001.

Strachey, Barbara. *Remarkable Relations: The Story of the Pearsall Smith Women*. New York: Universe Books, 1980.

Stray, Christopher, ed. *Gilbert Murray Reassessed: Hellenism, Theatre, and International Politics*. Oxford, UK: Oxford University Press, 2007.

Stray, Christopher. *The Living Word: W.H.D. Rouse and the Crisis of Classics in Edwardian England*. London: Bristol Classical Press, 1992.

Sutherland, John. *Mrs. Humphry Ward: Eminent Victorian, Pre-Eminent Edwardian*. Oxford, UK: Clarendon Press, 1980.

Swann, Thomas Burnett. *The Classical World of H. D.* Lincoln: University of Nebraska Press, 1962.

Sweetman, David. *Mary Renault: A Biography*. New York: Harcourt Brace, 1993.

Tanner, Laurel N. *Dewey's Laboratory School: Lessons for Today*. New York: Teachers College Press, 1997.

Thomas, Thaddeus P. *Why Equal Suffrage Has Been a Success*. Harrisburg: Pennsylvania Woman Suffrage Association, n.d.

Thomson, George Paget. *The Foreseeable Future*. Cambridge, UK: Cambridge University Press, 1960.

———. *J. J. Thomson and the Cavendish Laboratory in His Day*. New York: Doubleday, 1965.

Thornton, Bruce. *Greek Ways: How the Greeks Created Western Civilization*. New York: MJF Books, 2000.

Todd, Robert B., ed. *The Dictionary of British Classicists*. Bristol, UK: Thoemmes Continuum, 2004. Three volumes.

Tofel, Richard J. *Sounding the Trumpet: The Making of John F. Kennedy's Inaugural Address*. Chicago: Ivan R. Dee, 2005.

Torrey, E. Fuller. *Roots of Treason: Ezra Pound and the Secret of St. Elizabeth's*. New York: McGraw-Hill, 1984.

Trout, Jessie. *Kagawa, Japanese Prophet: His Witness in Life and Word*. New York: Association Press, 1959.

Turnbull, Grace H. *Chips from My Chisel: An Autobiography*. Rindge, NH: Richard R. Smith, 1953.

Turner, Frank M. *The Greek Heritage in Victorian Britain*. New Haven, CT: Yale University Press, 1981.

Tytell, John. *Ezra Pound: The Solitary Volcano*. New York: Doubleday, 1987.

United States Department of the Army. *Fort Belvoir: Host to History*. 1996.

University of Munich, ed. *Ludwig-Maximilians-Universitat Munchen*. Munich, Germany: Verlag Lutz Garnies, Neukeferloh, 1995.

Utley, Freda. *The High Cost of Vengeance*. Chicago: Henry Regnery, 1949.

Valentine, Alan. *Trial Balance: The Education of an American*. New York: Pantheon, 1956.

Vallon, Michael Alexander. *An Apostle of Freedom: Life and Teachings of Nicolas Berdyaev*. New York: Philosophical Library, 1960.

Van der Kiste, John. *Kings of the Hellenes: The Greek Kings 1863–1974*. Dover, NH: Alan Sutton, 1994.

Van Dyke, Tertius. *Henry van Dyke: A Biography*. New York: Harper Brothers, 1935.

Wagner-Martin, Linda. *"Favored Strangers": Gertrude Stein and Her Family*. New Brunswick, NJ: Rutgers University Press, 1995.

Weatherford, Doris. *A History of the American Suffragist Movement*. Santa Barbara, CA: ABC-Clio, 1998.

Weaver, William. *A Legacy of Excellence: The Story of Villa I Tatti*. New York: Harry N. Abrams, 1997.

Wedemeyer, Gen. Albert C. *Wedemeyer Reports!* New York: Holt, 1958.

Welsh, Lilian. *Reminiscences of Thirty Years in Baltimore*. Baltimore, MD: The Norman, Remington Company, 1925.

West, Andrew Fleming, ed. *Value of the Classics*. Princeton, NJ: Princeton University Press, 1917.

Whiton, James Morris. *Six Weeks' Preparation for Reading Caesar: With Reference to Allen & Greenough's, Gildersleeve's, and Harkness's Grammars*. Boston: Ginn and Heath, 1877.

Whyte, Kenneth. *Hoover: An Extraordinary Life in Extraordinary Times*. New York: Alfred A. Knopf, 2017.

Wilamowitz-Moellendoerff, Ulrich von. *Greek Historical Writing and Apollo: Two Lectures Delivered before the University of Oxford June 3 and 4 1908*. Oxford, UK: The Clarendon Press, 1908.

———. *My Recollections: 1848–1914*. London: Chatto and Windus, 1930.

———. *The Prussian and the Poet: The Letters of Ulrich von Wilamowitz-Moellendoerff to Gilbert Murray (1894–1930)*. Edited by Anton Bierl, William M. Calder III, and Robert L. Fowler. Hildesheim, Germany: Weidmann, 1991.

Williamson, Geoffrey. *Inside Buchmanism: An Independent Inquiry into the Oxford Group Movement and Moral Re-Armament*. New York: The Philosophical Library, 1954.

Willis, Resa. *Mark and Livy: The Love Story of Mark Twain and the Woman Who Almost Tamed Him*. New York: Atheneum, 1992.

Wilson, Duncan. *Gilbert Murray, OM 1866–1957*. Oxford, UK: Clarendon Press, 1987.

Wilson, Francis. *Francis Wilson's Life of Himself*. Cambridge, MA: The Riverside Press, 1924.

Wineapple, Brenda. *Sister Brother: Gertrude and Leo Stein*. New York: G. P. Putnam, 1996.

Winkler, Martin M., ed. *Classical Myth and Culture in the Cinema*. Oxford: Oxford University Press, 2001.

Winterer, Caroline. *The Culture of Classicism: Ancient Greece and Rome in American Intellectual Life 1780–1910*. Baltimore, MD: The Johns Hopkins University Press, 2002.

———. *The Mirror of Antiquity: American Women and the Classical Tradition, 1750–1900*. Ithaca, NY: Cornell University Press, 2007.

Wofford, Harris. *Of Kennedys and Kings: Making Sense of the Sixties*. New York: Farrar, Straus, and Giroux, 1980.

Wyles, Rosie, and Edith Hall, eds. *Women Classical Scholars: Unsealing the Fountain from the Renaissance to Jacqueline de Romilly*. Oxford: Oxford University Press, 2016.

Yonge, Charlotte Mary. *The Dove in the Eagle's Nest*. New York: A. L. Burt, 1909 [1866].

Yurka, Blanche. *Bohemian Girl: Blanche Yurka's Theatrical Life*. Athens: Ohio University Press, 1970.

Zilboorg, Caroline. *The Masks of Mary Renault: A Literary Biography*. Columbia: University of Missouri Press, 2001.

INDEX

Page numbers in *italics* refer to illustrations.